SOCIAL SECURITY LEGISL
SUPPLEMENT 2008/(

General Editor
David Bonner, LL.B., LL.M.

Commentary by
David Bonner, LL.B., LL.M.
Professor of Law, University of Leicester
Formerly Member, Social Security Appeal Tribunals

Ian Hooker, LL.B.
Lecturer in Law, University of Nottingham
Formerly Member, Social Security Appeal Tribunals

Richard Poynter B.C.L., M.A. (Oxon)
District Tribunal Judge,
Deputy Judge of the Upper Tribunal

Mark Rowland, LL.B.
Judge of the Upper Tribunal

Robin White, M.A., LL.M.
Professor of Law, University of Leicester,
Deputy Judge of the Upper Tribunal

Nick Wikeley, M.A.
Emeritus Professor of Law, University of Southampton,
Judge of the Upper Tribunal

David Williams, LL.M., Ph.D., C.T.A.
Judge of the Upper Tribunal, Deputy Special Commissioner of Income Tax and part-time Chairman of VAT and Duties Tribunal

Penny Wood, LL.B., M.Sc.
District Tribunal Judge

Consultant to Vol. II
John Mesher, B.A., B.C.L., LL.M.
Professor Associate of Law, University of Sheffield,
Judge of the Upper Tribunal

Consultant Editor
Child Poverty Action Group

SWEET & MAXWELL

THOMSON REUTERS

Published in 2009 by
Thomson Reuters (Legal) Limited (Registered in England & Wales,
Company No 1679046. Registered office and address for service:
100 Avenue Road, Swiss Cottage,
London NW3 3PF, trading as Sweet and Maxwell)
(http://www.sweetandmaxwell.co.uk)
Typeset by Interactive Sciences Ltd, Gloucester
Printed in Great Britain by
Ashford Colour Press, Gosport, Hants

No natural forests were destroyed to make this product.
Only farmed timber was used and re-planted.

A catalogue record for this book is
available from the British Library

ISBN–9781847038067

PREFACE

This is a rather larger Supplement to the 2008/09 edition of the four-volume work, *Social Security Legislation*, which was published in September 2008. It is larger principally because of the introduction of the new Employment and Support Allowance (ESA) from October 27, 2008, which is expected to form a significant part of the case load of both the First-tier Tribunal and Upper Tribunal in 2009 and subsequent years. It is also larger in consequence of the publication of new rules governing those Tribunals.

Part I contains new legislation (Acts and Regulations) presented in the same format as the main volumes. This will enable readers to note very quickly new sets of legislation. Section A deals with ESA; Section B with Tribunal Rules; and Section C with other matters.

Parts II, III, IV and V contain the updating material—a separate Part for each volume of the main work—which amended the legislative text and key aspects of the commentary so as to be up to date as at November 5, 2008. Part VI gives some notice of changes forthcoming between that date and the date to which the main work (2009/10 edition) will be up to date (mid-April) and some indication of the April 2008 benefit rates, and takes account of changes known to us as at mid-January 2009.

As always we welcome comments from those who use this Supplement. Please address these to the General Editor, David Bonner, at the Faculty of Law, The University, Leicester LE1 7RH.

David Bonner
Ian Hooker
John Mesher
Richard Poynter
Mark Rowland
Robin White
Nick Wikeley
David Williams
Penny Wood
January 27, 2009

CONTENTS

PAGES OF MAIN VOLUMES AFFECTED BY MATERIAL IN THIS SUPPLEMENT

VOLUME II

Main volume page affected	Relevant paragraph in supplement
252	3.20
260	3.21
261–262	3.22
263	3.23
284	3.24
285	3.25
306	3.26
309	3.27
316	3.28
338	3.29–3.30
347–349	3.31
349	3.32
352	3.3
378–379	3.34
381	3.35
382	3.36
383	3.37
404	3.38
408	3.39
445	3.40
445–447	3.41
447	3.42
448	3.43
449	3.44–3.45
451	3.46
452	3.47
452	3.48
453	3.49
454	3.50
445–460	3.51
476	3.52
484	3.53
500	3.54
501	3.55
503	3.56
504–505	3.57
515–517	3.58
518	3.59–3.60
545	3.61–3.62
548	3.63
550–551	3.64
552	3.65
555–558	3.66
561	3.67
574–575	3.68
577–578	3.69
610	3.70

Pages of Main Volumes Affected by Material in this Supplement

TABLE OF ABBREVIATIONS USED IN THIS SERIES

2002 Act	Tax Credits Act 2002
AA	Attendance Allowance
A.C.	Appeal Cases
A.C.D.	Administrative Court Digest
ADHD	Attention Deficit Hyperactivity Disorder
Adjudication Regulations	Social Security (Adjudication) Regulations 1986
Admin. L.R.	Administrative Law Reports
All E.R.	All England Law Reports (Butterworths)
All E.R. (EC)	All England Law Reports European Cases
AMA	Adjudicating Medical Authority
AO	Adjudication Officer
AOG	*Adjudication Officers' Guide*
ASPP	Additional Statutory Paternity Pay
Attendance Allowance Regulations	Social Security (Attendance Allowance) Regulations 1991
BAMS	Benefits Agency Medical Service
B.H.R.C.	Butterworths Human Rights Cases
B.L.G.R.	Butterworths Local Government Reports
Blue Books	*The Law Relating to Social Security*, Vols 1–11
B.M.L.R.	Butterworths Medico-Legal Reports
B.P.I.R.	Bankruptcy and Personal Insolvency Reports
B.T.C.	British Tax Cases
CAA 2001	Capital Allowance Act 2001
CAB	Citizens Advice Bureau
CAO	Chief Adjudication Officer
CBA	Child Benefit Act 1975
CBJSA	Contribution-based Jobseeker's Allowance
C.C.L. Rep.	Community Care Law Reports
CCM	Claimant Compliance Manual
CCN	New Tax Credits Claimant Compliance Manual
C.E.C.	European Community Cases
CERA	Cortical Evoked Response Audiogram
CESA	Contributory Employment and Support Allowance

Table of Abbreviations used in this Series

Ch.	Chancery Law Reports
Child Benefit Regulations	Child Benefit (General) Regulations 2006
Claims and Payments Regulations 1979	Social Security (Claims and Payments) Regulations 1979
Claims and Payments Regulations 1987	Social Security (Claims and Payments) Regulations 1987
C.M.L.R.	Common Market Law Reports
C.O.D.	Crown Office Digest
Commissioners Procedure Regulations	Social Security Commissioners (Procedure) Regulations 1999
Computation of Earnings Regulations 1978	Social Security Benefit (Computation of 1978 Earnings) Regulations 1978
Computation of Earnings Regulations 1996	Social Security Benefit (Computation of 1996 Earnings) Regulations 1996
Const.L.J.	Construction Law Journal
Council Tax Benefit Regulations	Council Tax Benefit (General) Regulations 1992 (SI 1992/1814)
CP	Carer Premium
CPAG	Child Poverty Action Group
C.P.L.R.	Civil Practice Law Reports
CPR	Civil Procedure Rules
C.P.Rep.	Civil Procedure Reports
Cr.App.R.	Criminal Appeal Reports
Cr.App.R.(S)	Criminal Appeal Reports (Sentencing)
CRCA	Commissioners for Revenue and Customs Act 2005
Crim.L.R.	Criminal Law Review
Crim.L.R.	Criminal Law Review
CRU	Compensation Recovery Unit
CSA 1995	Child Support Act 1995
CS(NI)O	Child Support (Northern Ireland) Order 1995
CSO	Child Support Officer
CSPSSA	Child Support, Pensions and Social Security Act 2000
CTC	Child Tax Credit
DAT	Disability Appeal Tribunal
DCP	Disabled Child Premium
Decisions and Appeals Regulations 1999	Social Security and Child Support (Decisions and Appeals) Regulations 1999
Dependency Regulations	Social Security Benefit (Dependency) Regulations 1977
Disability Working Allowance Regulations	Disability Working Allowance (General) Regulations 1991

DLA	Disability Living Allowance
DLADAA 1991	Disability Living Allowance and Disability Allowance Act 1991
DM	Decision Maker
DMA	Decision-making and Appeals
DMG	*Decision-Makers Guide*
DMP	Delegated Medical Practitioner
DPTC	Disabled Person's Tax Credit
DSDNI	Department for Social Development, Northern Ireland
DSS	Department of Social Security
DTI	Department of Trade and Industry
DWA	Disability Working Allowance
DWP	Department for Work and Pensions
EAA	Extrinsic Allergic Alveolitis
ECHR	European Court of Human Rights
E.C.R.	European Court Reports
ECSMA Agreement	European Convention on Social and Medical Assistance
EEA	European Economic Area
E.G.	Estates Gazette
E.H.R.R.	European Human Rights Reports
E.L.R.	Education Law Reports
EMA	Education Maintenance Allowance
EMO	Examining Medical Officer
EMP	Examining Medical Practitioner
EP (Recoupment of JSA and IS) Regulations 1996	Employment Protection (Recoupment of Jobseeker's Allowance and Income Support) Regulations
ERA	Evoked Response Audiometry
ERA 1996	Employment Rights Act 1996
ER(NI)O	Employers Rights (Northern Ireland) Order 1996
ESA	Employment and Support Allowance
ESA Regulations	Employment and Support Allowance Regulations 2008
Eur. L. Rev.	European Law Review
FA	Finance Act
Fam.Law	Family Law
Family Credit Regulations	Family Credit (General) Regulations 1987
FAS	Financial Assistance Scheme
FIS	Family Income Supplement

Fixing and Adjustment of Rates (Amendment) Regulations 1998	Child Benefit and Social Security (Fixing and Adjustment of Rates) (Amendment) Regulations 1998
Fixing and Adjustment of Rates Regulations 1976	Child Benefit and Social Security (Fixing and Adjustment of Rates) Regulations 1976
F.L.R.	Family Law Reports
GA Regulations	Social Security (Guardian's Allowance) Regulations 1975
General Benefit Regulations	Social Security (General Benefit) Regulations 1982
General Regulations	Statutory Maternity Pay (General) Regulations 1986
G.P.	General Practitioner
Graduated Retirement Benefit Regulations 2005	Social Security (Graduated Retirement Benefit) Regulations 2005
GRP	Graduated Retirement Pension
G.W.D.	Green's Weekly Digest
HASSASSA	Health and Social Services and Social Security Adjudication Act 1983
HCD	House of Commons Debates
HCWA	House of Commons Written Answers
H.L.R.	Housing Law Reports
HMRC	Her Majesty's Revenue and Customs
HNCIP	(Housewives') Non-Contributory Invalidity Pension
Hospital In-Patients Regulations	Social Security (Hospital In-Patients) Regulations 1975
Housing Benefit Regulations	Housing Benefit (General) Regulations 1987 (SI 1987/1971)
HPP	Higher Pensioner Premium
HRA 1998	Human Rights Act 1998
H.R.L.R.	Human Rights Law Reports
HSE	Health and Safety Executive
IB	Incapacity Benefit
IB Regulations	Social Security (Incapacity Benefit) Regulations 1994
IBS	Irritable Bowel Syndrome
ICA	Invalid Care Allowance
I.C.R.	Industrial Cases Reports
ICTA	Income and Corporation Taxes Act 1988
IIAC	Industrial Injuries Advisory Council
I.L.J.	Industrial Law Journal
Imm.A.R.	Immigration Appeals Reports

Incapacity for Work Regulations	Social Security (Incapacity for Work) (General) Regulations 1995
Income Support Regulations	Income Support (General) Regulations 1987
Increases for Dependents Regulations	Social Security Benefit (Dependency) Regulations 1977
IND	Immigration and Nationality Directorate of the Home Office
I.N.L.R.	Immigration and Nationality Law Reports
Invalid Care Allowance Regulations	Social Security (Invalid Care Allowance) Regulations 1976
IPPR	Institute of Public Policy Research
IRESA	Income Related Employment and Support Allowance
I.R.L.R.	Industrial Relations Law Reports
IS	Income Support
ISAs	Individual Savings Accounts
IS Regs	Income Support (General) Regulations 1987
ITA	Income Tax Act 2007
ITEPA	Income Tax (Earnings and Pensions) Act 2003
ITTOIA	Income Tax (Trading and Other Income Act 2005)
ITS	Independent Tribunal Service
IWA	Social Security (Incapacity for Work) Act 1994
IW (Dependants) Regs	Social Security (Incapacity for Work) (Dependants) Regulations
IW (General) Regulations	Social Security (Incapacity for Work) (General) Regulations 1995
IW (Transitional) Regulations	Social Security (Incapacity for Work) (Transitional) Regulations 1995
IVB	Invalidity Benefit
J.P.	Justice of the Peace
JSA	Jobseeker's Allowance
JSA 1995	Jobseekers Act 1995
JSA Regulations	Jobseeker's Allowance Regulations 1996
JSA (Transitional) Regulations	Jobseeker's Allowance (Transitional) Regulations 1996
JS(NI)O	Jobseekers (Northern Ireland) Act 1995
J.S.W.F.L.	Journal of Social Welfare and Family Law
J.S.W.L.	Journal of Social Welfare Law
J.S.S.L.	Journal of Social Security Law

Table of Abbreviations used in this Series

K.I.R.	Knights Industrial Reports
LEL	Lower Earnings Limit
Ll.L.Report	Lloyds' Law Report
Lloyd's Rep.	Lloyd's Law Reports
L.S.G.	Law Society Gazette
LTAHAW	Living Together As Husband And Wife
L.&T.R.	Landlord and Tenant Reports
LCWA	Limited Capability for Work Assessment
MA	Maternity Allowance
MAF	Medical Assessment Framework
MAT	Medical Appeal Tribunal
Maternity Benefit Regulations	Social Security (Maternity Benefit) Regulations 1975
Medical Evidence Regulations	Social Security (Medical Evidence) Regulations 1976
NCIP	Non-Contributory Invalidity Pension
NDPD	Notes on the Diagnosis of Prescribed Diseases
NI	National Insurance
N.I.	Northern Ireland Law Reports
NIC	National Insurance Contribution
N.L.J.	New Law Journal
N.P.C.	New Property Cases
Ogus, Barendt and Wikeley	A. Ogus, E. Barendt and N. Wikeley, *The Law of Social Security* (4th ed., Butterworths, 1995)
OPA	Overseas Pensions Act 1973
OPB	One Parent Benefit
OPPSSAT	Office of the President of the Social Security Appeals Tribunal
Overlapping Benefits Regulations	Social Security (Overlapping Benefits) Regulations 1979
Overpayments Regulations	Social Security (Payments on account, Overpayments and Recovery) Regulations
P.	Probate, Divorce and Admiralty
PAYE	Pay as You Earn
PCA	Personal Capability Assessment
P.&C.R.	Property, Planning & Compensation Reports
P.D.	Practice Direction
PD	Prescribed Disease
PPF	Pension Protection Fund

Pens.L.R.	Pensions Law Reports
Persons Abroad Regulations	Social Security Benefit (Persons Abroad) Regulations 1975
Persons Residing Together Regulations	Social Security Benefit (Persons Residing Together) Regulations 1977
PIE	Period of Interruption of Employment
PILON	Pay in Lieu of Notice
PIW	Period of Incapacity for Work
P.L.R.	Planning Law Reports
Polygamous Marriage Regulations	Social Security and Family Allowances (Polygamous Marriages) Regulations 1975 (SI 1975/561)
PPF	Pension Protection Fund
Prescribed Diseases Regulations	Social Security (Industrial Injuries) (Prescribed Diseases) Regulations 1985
PTA	Pure Tone Audiometry
PVS	Private or Voluntary Sectors
Q.B.	Queen's Bench
Recoupment Regulations	Social Security (Recoupment) Regulations 1990
REA	Reduced Earnings Allowance
RIPA	Regulation of Investigatory Powers Act 2000
RMO	Regional Medical Officer
RSI	Repetitive Strain Injury
R.T.R.	Road Traffic Reports
SAP	Statutory Adoption Pay
SAYE	Save As You Earn
S.C.	Session Cases
S.C.(H.L.)	Session Cases (House of Lords)
S.C.(P.C.)	Session Cases (Privy Council)
S.C.C.R.	Scottish Criminal Case Reports
S.C.L.R.	Scottish Civil Law Reports
SDA	Severe Disablement Allowance
SDP	Severe Disability Premium
SERPS	State Earnings-Related Pension Scheme
Severe Disablement Allowance	Social Security (Severe Disablement Regulations Allowance) Regulations 1984
S.J.	Solicitors' Journal
S.J.L.B.	Solicitors' Journal Law Brief
S.L.T.	Scots Law Times
SMP	Statutory Maternity Pay
SPC	State Pension Credit

SPCA	State Pension Credit Act 2002
SPCA(NI)	State Pension Credit Act (Northern Ireland) 2002
SPP	Statutory Paternity Pay
SPP and SAP (Administration) Regulations 2002	Statutory Paternity Pay and Statutory Adoption Pay (Administration) Regulations 2002
SPP and SAP (General) Regulations 2002	Statutory Paternity Pay and Statutory Adoption Pay (General) Regulations 2002
SPP and SAP (National Health Service Employees) Regulations 2002	Statutory Paternity Pay and Statutory Adoption Pay (National Health Service Employees) Regulations 2002
SPP and SAP (Weekly Rates) Regulations 2002	Statutory Paternity Pay and Statutory Adoption Pay (Weekly Rates) Regulations 2002
SSA	Social Security Act
SSAA	Social Security Administration Act 1992*
SSAC	Social Security Advisory Committee
SSAT	Social Security Appeal Tribunal
SSCBA	Social Security Contributions and Benefits Act 1992*
SSCB(NI)	Social Security Contributions and Benefits (Northern Ireland) Act 1992
SS(CP)A	Social Security (Consequential Provisions) Act 1992
SSHBA	Social Security and Housing Benefits Act 1982
SS(MP)A	Social Security (Miscellaneous Provisions) Act 1977
SSP	Statutory Sick Pay
SSPA	Social Security Pensions Act 1975
S.T.C.	Simon's Tax Cases
S.T.C. (S.C.D.)	Simon's Tax Cases: Special Commissioners Decisions
STIB	Short-term Incapacity Benefit
S.T.I.	Simon's Tax Intelligence
TC	Tax Cases
TCA	Tax Credits Act
TC (Claims and Notifications) Regs	Tax Credit (Claims and Notifications) Regulations 2002
TCGA	Taxation of Chargeable Gains Act 1992
TCTM	Tax Credits Technical Manual
TMA	Taxes Management Act 1970
U.K.H.R.R.	United Kingdom Human Rights Reports

Unemployment, Sickness and Invalidity Benefit Regs	Social Security (Unemployment, Sickness and Invalidity Benefit) Regulations 1983
USI Regulations	Social Security (Unemployment, Sickness and Invalidity Benefit) Regulations 1983
VERA 1992	Vehicle Excise and Registration Act 1992
WCA	Work Capability Assessment
WCAt	Limited Capability for Work Assessment
WFHRAt	Work-focused Health Related Assessment
WFTC	Working Family Tax Credit
White Paper	Jobseeker's Allowance, Cm.2687 (October 1994)
Widow's Benefit and Retirement Pensions Regulations	Social Security (Widow's Benefit and Retirement Pensions) Regulations 1979
Wikeley, Annotations	N. Wikeley, "Annotations to Jobseekers Act 1995 (c. 18)" in *Current Law Statutes Annotated* (1995)
Wikeley, Ogus and Barendt	Wikeley, Ogus and Barendt, *The Law of Social Security* (5th ed., Butterworths, 2002)
W.L.R.	Weekly Law Reports
Workmen's Compensation Acts	Workmen's Compensation Acts 1925 to 1945
WRA 2007	Welfare Reform Act 2007
WRAAt	Work-related Activity Assessment
WRPA	Welfare Reform and Pensions Act 1999
WRP(NI)O	Welfare Reform and Pensions (Northern Ireland) Order 1999
WTC	Working Tax Credit
WTC (Entitlement and Maximum Rate) Regulations 2002	Working Tax Credit (Entitlement and Maximum Rate) Regulations 2002
W.T.L.R.	Wills & Trusts Law Reports

* Where the context makes it seem more appropriate, these could also be referred to as Contributions and Benefits Act 1992, Administration Act 1992 (AA 1992).

TABLE OF CASES

Table of Cases

TABLE OF SOCIAL SECURITY COMMISSIONER'S DECISIONS

TABLE OF EUROPEAN MATERIALS

TABLE OF STATUTES

TABLE OF STATUTORY INSTRUMENTS

PART I

NEW LEGISLATION

[A] Employment and support allowance

[B] Tribunal Reform

[C] Other legislation

PART I

SECTION A

EMPLOYMENT AND SUPPORT ALLOWANCE

Commentary by

David Bonner

Richard Poynter

Penny Wood

Welfare Reform Act 2007

(2007 c.5)

An Act to make provision about social security; to amend the Vaccine Damage Payments Act 1979; and for connected purposes.

[3rd May 2007]

PART 1

EMPLOYMENT AND SUPPORT ALLOWANCE

Entitlement

Employment and support allowance

1.—(1) An allowance, to be known as an employment and support allowance, shall be payable in accordance with the provisions of this Part. **1A.3**

(2) Subject to the provisions of this Part, a claimant is entitled to an employment and support allowance if he satisfies the basic conditions and either—

(a) the first and the second conditions set out in Part 1 of Schedule 1 (conditions relating to national insurance) or the third condition set out in that Part of that Schedule (condition relating to youth), or

(b) the conditions set out in Part 2 of that Schedule (conditions relating to financial position).

(3) The basic conditions are that the claimant—

(a) has limited capability for work,

(b) is at least 16 years old,

(c) has not reached pensionable age,

(d) is in Great Britain,

(e) is not entitled to income support, and

(f) is not entitled to a jobseeker's allowance (and is not a member of a couple who are entitled to a joint-claim jobseeker's allowance).

(4) For the purposes of this Part, a person has limited capability for work if—

(a) his capability for work is limited by his physical or mental condition, and

(b) the limitation is such that it is not reasonable to require him to work.

(5) An employment and support allowance is payable in respect of a week.

(6) In subsection (3)—

"joint-claim jobseeker's allowance" means a jobseeker's allowance entitlement to which arises by virtue of section 1(2B) of the Jobseekers Act 1995 (c. 18);

"pensionable age" has the meaning given by the rules in paragraph 1 of Schedule 4 to the Pensions Act 1995 (c. 26).

(7) In this Part—

"contributory allowance" means an employment and support allowance entitlement to which is based on subsection (2)(a);

"income-related allowance" means an employment and support allowance entitlement to which is based on subsection (2)(b).

DEFINITIONS

"contributory allowance"—see subs.(7).
"income-related allowance"—see subs.(7).
"joint-claim jobseeker's allowance"—see subs.(6).
"pensionable age"—see subs.(6).

GENERAL NOTE

Subs. (1)

1A.4   This establishes the new Employment and Support Allowance (ESA), which is payable in accordance with the terms set out in the remainder of Part I of the Act, a framework clothed with the detail afforded by several sets of regulations:

- *Employment and Support Allowance Regulations 2008 (SI 2008/794) (ESA Regulations) (as amended)*
  Like the JSA and IS Regs which in many respects they emulate, these set out the key detailed rules on ESA and are set out with commentary later in this section of the Supplement.

- *Employment and Support Allowance (Transitional Provisions) Regulations 2008 (SI 2008/795) (as amended)*
  These deal with the transition to ESA (key rules for "existing customers" of the IB/IS/SDA incapacity benefits' regime). They are set out with commentary later in this section of the Supplement.

- *Employment and Support Allowance (Consequential Provisions) Regulations 2008 (SI 2008/1082)*
  These effect amendments to Housing and Council Tax benefits and are not reproduced in this Supplement.

- *Employment and Support Allowance (Consequential Provisions) (No. 2) Regulations 2008 (SI 2008/1554)*
  These effect a variety of changes to legislation covered in *Social Security Legislation*. Their impact is noted in the appropriate updating sections of this Supplement.

- *Employment and Support Allowance (Consequential Provisions) (No. 3) Regulations 2008 (SI 2008/1879)*
  These effect a variety of changes to tax credits and child benefit. Their impact is noted in the appropriate updating sections of this Supplement.

A brief overview of ESA and its purpose may be useful to place the detailed rules and commentary in context.

State support towards the income replacement needs of those incapable of work has been the province of incapacity benefit (IB), income support (IS), or a mixture of both, since the non-contributory incapacity benefit, Severe Disablement Allowance (SDA), was closed to new claimants from April 6, 2001. From October 27, 2008 (the "appointed day", "commencement") both will be closed to new claimants who claim benefit on the basis of a health condition or disability which so affects their ability to work that it is not reasonable to expect them to do so. From then, any such claim will instead be treated as one for a new benefit: Employment and Support Allowance (ESA), claimed to be less complex and easier to claim. "Existing customers" (those already in receipt of those benefits, or whose claim for a new spell of incapacity links back to a period of incapacity for work prior to commencement, or whose claim is backdated to a day pre-

8

commencement) will be able to retain entitlement to them after the appointed day, but will lose it once the relevant period of incapacity for work comes to an end without linking to another which started prior to commencement. All new claimants (and those "existing customers" unable to link in that way) will instead have to look for income replacement to the new ESA. Thus yet another client group has been removed from IS, leaving it very much as a residual benefit, probably one ultimately to be abolished. Over time, all existing incapacity regime claimants will be migrated to ESA.

Like JSA, ESA is a single benefit with two forms: contributory ESA (CESA) and income related ESA (IRESA). A claimant may be entitled to one or the other or, in some cases, both. ESA, payable in respect of a week, is a benefit to provide support to those clearly unable to work, through a "support component" paid in addition to their basic allowance, and to require those capable of work-related activity to engage in it in return for a "work-related activity component" on top of their basic allowance, the hope being that they will eventually return to the labour force. ESA is a benefit with similarities to JSA (even CESA can be reduced on account of certain other income), but no time limit on either its contributory or income related forms, save that entitlement ceases on reaching pensionable age (s.1(3)(c)).

ESA is accessible by persons with an employer (after SSP is exhausted) (s.20(1)), the self-employed, and those without employment.

Eligibility for CESA depends, like that for IB, on fulfillment of contribution conditions showing a recent connection with the world of work. But, as with IB after the abolition of SDA for new claimants, persons incapacitated in youth (before 20 or in some cases 25) can have access to this ostensibly contributory form without meeting the contribution conditions. Otherwise, claimants who do not meet those conditions will have to seek IRESA. Depending on their precise financial circumstances, and the intricacies of the income related "balance sheet", in terms of capital and income (including income from capital), those entitled to the CESA may also receive IRESA as a top-up.

The conditions of entitlement common to the basic allowance aspect of both forms of ESA are that the claimant is at least 16; has not reached pensionable age; is in Great Britain; is not entitled to IS; is not entitled to JSA in his own right or as part of a joint-claim couple; and has limited capability for work (see subs.(3)). The matter of capacity is either assessed by a work-related capability assessment (a functional test similar to the IB personal capability assessment or all work test), involving a medical examination, or, is deemed to exist for a much reduced set of "exempt" groups. Generally, three "waiting days" of non-entitlement have to be served (s.22, Sch.2, para.4; ESA Regs, reg.144). During the (generally 13-week) assessment period, only basic allowance ESA is payable. Additional components (support or work-related activity) depend on the claimant being assessed or treated as having limited capability for work/work-related activity respectively. The personal allowance aspect of ESA basic allowance (a lower rate for those under 25) is based on the personal allowances in JSA (single person, lone parent or couple), but those able to qualify for IRESA can also access applicable premiums. After the assessment period ends (when the claimant has been assessed or treated as having limited capacity for work), claimants become eligible for one (but not both) of two additional components: the *support* component; or the *work-related activity* component. To be eligible for the *support* component, claimants must have limited capability for work-related activity (capacity for that must be limited by their physical or mental condition to such an extent that it is not reasonable to require them to undertake such activity). If they do not have limited capacity for work-related activity (i.e. capability for work-related activity is not limited by physical or mental condition or, if it is, the limitations are not such as to render it unreasonable to undertake such activity), they will be eligible for the work-related activity component on top of the basic allowance, provided they meet prescribed conditions on work-related activity. Should they not do so, they can be sanctioned by progressive reduction (ultimately removal) of the amount of that component to which they would otherwise be entitled.

As with IB/IS, claimants entitled to ESA can be disqualified from it where their conduct conduces to their incapacity (e.g. because of misconduct in bringing it about or in refusing treatment which would alleviate it) or their failure to adhere to prescribed rules of behaviour (s.18; ESA Regs, regs 157, 159). "Persons in hardship" cannot be disqualified but receive a reduced rate of personal allowance (ESA Regs, reg.158, Sch.5, para.14). Absences from Great Britain (other than certain temporary absences) preclude entitlement to ESA (s.18(4), Sch.2, paras 5, 6, 8; ESA Regs, regs 151–155). Imprisonment or detention in legal custody each disqualify from CESA and, if longer than six weeks, results in the person being treated as not having limited capability for work, thus impacting on ability to link spells of limited capability for work (s.18(4); ESA Regs, reg.159 and Sch.5, para.3).

ESA is part of a broader governmental strategy to assist people with a health condition or disability. Government is convinced that benefit dependency, particularly strong in respect of benefits for incapacity, is a major element in hardship and deprivation, and that work is the route out of poverty. The measures set out in its 2006 Green Paper (Cm 6730) were intended to increase the numbers who are able to remain in work when they fall sick or become disabled; to raise the numbers moving from benefits into employment; and better to meet the needs of those requiring extra help and support because of a health condition. Unlike IB (rather caricatured by a Government determined like its predecessors to reduce the cost to the public purpose of supporting the once favourably-treated group—those incapable of work), ESA does not automatically assume incapacity for work merely because someone has a significant health condition or disability. It is built on experience with the pilots of the Pathways to Work project which was rolled out nationally in April 2008. It is claimed that this initiative has significantly increased the IB claimants being helped into work, and that "these pilots have demonstrated that, with the right help and support, many people on incapacity benefits can move back into work, reinforcing the view that labelling people on incapacity benefits as 'incapable of work' is wrong and damaging". Government considered that no lesser approach than ESA would provide the necessary cultural shift, from a benefits package based on "incapacity for work" to one founded firmly on what a person can do.

Government expects that ESA will have a significant and wide-ranging positive impact on disabled people and people with health conditions who are out of work. ESA is a benefit designed to help these people overcome barriers, and where appropriate move into work and improve their lives. The Work Capability Assessment (WCA) seeks to relate more accurately to modern context than the 12-year-old IB/IS system, and to focus more on what people can do, rather on what they are unable to do. The conditionality regime for the work-related activity component seeks to engage customers placed in the work-related activity group. It affords them access to the employment and condition management programmes of Pathways to Work. But ESA recognises the needs of those in the Support Group; their entitlement to the support component is not conditional on work-related activity but they can engage, if they wish, with those programmes. ESA seeks better to reflect the aspirations of disabled people, and improve the "customer experience" of individuals on the benefit.

ESA in outline was broadly welcomed as to its purpose of, and potential for, helping disabled people fulfil their aspiration to work, by spokespersons across all parties, and as a potential route out of poverty by groups representing the disabled. But concerns (becoming stronger as more detail emerged) were none-theless expressed about a range of aspects: conditionality (sanctions welcomed and seen as vital by some to "persuade" the reluctant to engage with help and knowledge, seen as problematic or unnecessary by others); the impact on persons with a variety of conditions (mental health problems, cancer sufferers, Asperger's syndrome), particularly fluctuating ones, and on the terminally ill; which groups would be exempt from the WCA; what would be the categories of permitted work so vital to building confidence that someone could return to work; the nature of the law-making process leaving too much to secondary legislation or ministerial fiat; adding to the complexity of the benefits system with a supposed single benefit involving six rates; the nature and interrelationship of two capability assessments with different criteria; and, crucially, the other side of the coin—the provisions deal with the attitude of the disabled to work but leave untouched the attitude of employers to the disabled would-be worker.

The introduction of ESA will generate more appeals, in part because there are more appealable issues challenging the bona fides of claimants than with IB/IS support for the sick and disabled (membership of the work-related activity group rather than the support group; sanctions for not engaging in work-related activity) and because the WCA is expected to "fail" more people than the PCA. DWP estimates put the extra appeals load in a full year at 26,500 with 21,000 going to a hearing. This obviously has expenditure implications, but, since more people are expected to move off benefit and into the labour market or into employment, Government estimates expenditure savings of £50 million in the first full year of operation of ESA (2009/10), rising progressively to £155 million in 2013/14 and £215 million in 2017/18.

Subss. (2), (7)

As with JSA, read together these envisage two ways of gaining title to ESA: the **1A.5** "contributory route" to the "contributory allowance" (CESA); and the "income-related" route to "income-related allowance" (IRESA). They provide that entitlement to CESA is grounded on satisfaction of the "basic conditions" in subs.(3) plus *either* (a) satisfaction of the national insurance contribution conditions (Sch.1, Pt 1) *or* (b) that the claimant is someone incapacitated in youth (Sch.1, Pt 1). It provides that entitlement to IRESA is grounded on satisfaction of the basic conditions in subs.(3) plus those relating to financial position (Sch.1, Pt 2).

Subs. (3)

This stipulates the "basic conditions" which must be satisfied whether the **1A.6** claimant claims CESA, IRESA or both. The claimant must

- *be at least 16*
  this is the current school-leaving age and so this lower limit is apt for a benefit that is an earnings replacement one;

- *under pensionable age*
  "pensionable age" is here defined according to the rules in Pensions Act 2004, Sch.4, para.1 (see subs.(6)). It thus links to the sliding scale of pensionable ages found there as the pensions system moves steadily towards equal pension ages for men and women;

- *in Great Britain*
  absences from Great Britain (other than certain temporary absences) preclude entitlement to ESA. See further s.18(4), Sch.2, paras 5, 6, 8; ESA Regs, regs 151–155. Essentially this is a presence rather than a residence test. However, note that ESA Regs, regs 69–70 and Sch.5, apply to IRESA much the same rules on residence as apply in IS and IBJSA;

- *not be entitled to IS under SSCBA 1992, s.124*
  this establishes the mutual exclusivity of ESA and IS;

- *not be entitled to JSA whether in his/her own right or as part of a joint-claim couple*
  this establishes the mutual exclusivity of ESA and JSA. Entitlement to JSA as a joint-claim couple arises under Jobseekers Act 1995, s.1(2B);

- *have limited capability for work*
  the basic test for this is set out in subs.(4): claimants will have limited capability for work where their capability for work is limited by their physical or mental condition and that limitation is such that it is not reasonable to require them to work. ESA Regs 2008, reg.19(1) elaborates that this is to be determined on the basis of a limited capability for work assessment (hereinafter WCAt), one element in the three-element Work Capability Assessment which has been developed out of a review of the Personal Capability Assessment (PCA) in the IB/IS/SDA incapacity benefits' regime. The WCAt is

  > "an assessment of the extent to which a claimant who has some specific disease or bodily or mental disablement is capable of performing the activities prescribed in Schedule 2 [to the ESA Regs] or is incapable by reason of such disease or bodily or mental disablement of performing those activities" (ESA Regs, reg.19(2)).

  This is familiar stuff to anyone who has worked with the PCA or its predecessor, the "all work" test. The claimant is to be matched, in the light of all the evidence, by the decision-maker or tribunal against a reformulated range of activities and descriptors, and an appropriate "score" awarded. The threshold "score" for entitlement remains 15 points, but as regards its computation, there are both "old" and "new" elements". See further the commentary to s.8 and to ESA Regs, Pt 5 (regs 19–33) and Sch.2.

Subs. (4)

1A.7   This sets out the basic definition of "limited capability for work". See commentary to subs.(3), s.8 and to ESA Regs, Pt 5 (regs 19–33) and Sch.2.

Subs. (5)

1A.8   Emulating JSA, ESA is a weekly benefit, one paid in respect of a week. For cases of part-week entitlement see s.22, Sch.2, para.3 and ESA Regs, Pt 14 (regs 165–169).

Subs. (6)

1A.9   This defines, by reference to other legislation, "joint-claim jobseeker's allowance" and "pensionable age".

Subs. (7)

1A.10   Another definition provision. See commentary to subss.(2), (7), above.

Amount of contributory allowance

1A.11   **2.**—(1) In the case of a contributory allowance, the amount payable in respect of a claimant shall be calculated by—
  (a) taking such amount as may be prescribed;
  (b) if in his case the conditions of entitlement to the support component or the work-related activity component are satisfied, adding the amount of that component; and

(c) making prescribed deductions in respect of any payments to which section 3 applies.

(2) The conditions of entitlement to the support component are—

(a) that the assessment phase has ended;

(b) that the claimant has limited capability for work-related activity; and

(c) that such other conditions as may be prescribed are satisfied.

(3) The conditions of entitlement to the work-related activity component are—

(a) that the assessment phase has ended;

(b) that the claimant does not have limited capability for work-related activity; and

(c) that such other conditions as may be prescribed are satisfied.

(4) Regulations may—

(a) prescribe circumstances in which paragraph (a) of subsection (2) or (3) is not to apply;

(b) prescribe circumstances in which entitlement under subsection (2) or (3) is to be backdated;

(c) make provision about the amount of the component under subsection (2) or (3).

(5) For the purposes of this Part, a person has limited capability for work-related activity if—

(a) his capability for work-related activity is limited by his physical or mental condition; and

(b) the limitation is such that it is not reasonable to require him to undertake such activity.

DEFINITIONS

"assessment phase"—see s.24(2), (3).
"claimant"—see s.24(1).
"contributory allowance"—see s.1(6).
"limited capability for work-related activity"—see subs.(5).
"prescribed"—see s.24(1).
"regulations"—see s.24(1).
"work-related activity"—see ss.24(1), 13(7), below.

GENERAL NOTE

This section deals with the calculation of amount of contributory allowance (CESA) (see s.1(6)) to which a particular claimant can be entitled, both during the "assessment phase" and after it has ended (subss.(1)–(3)). It provides rule-making powers to modify some of the conditions, to set amounts and to enable backdating of entitlement (subs.(4)). Finally it defines when someone has "limited capability for work-related activity" (subs.(5)).   **1A.12**

Subs.(1)

This sets out the elements making up CESA and the basic arithmetic for determining the amount of CESA to which the claimant is entitled. The basic arithmetic during the "assessment phase" is prescribed amount (age-related) minus any s.3 deductions. After the "assessment phase", it changes to single prescribed amount plus appropriate component (support or work related activity) minus any s.3 deductions. Since entitlement varies as between the period of   **1A.13** the "assessment phase" and after it has ended, it is useful to begin with analysis of that concept.

The "assessment phase" starts on the first day of the period for which the claimant is entitled to ESA (the day after service of the three waiting days of non-entitlement (see s.22, Sch.2, para.2, and ESA Regs, reg.144)). It ends on whichever is the later of either 13 weeks from that first day of entitlement or the date of determination of limited capability for work (either of actual limited capability or of "deemed" limited capability (treated as having limited capability) (see s.24(2), ESA Regs, reg.4). The ESA scheme deals with intermittent incapacity through "linking" rules. These impact on identification of the end of the "assessment phase". Under ESA Regs, reg.145, periods of limited capability for work "link" and are treated as one single period (to which further ones may be added if the linking rules are met). Typically periods not separated by more than 12 weeks' "link" in this way (see ESA Regs, reg.145(1)), but for "work or training beneficiaries" (see ESA Regs, reg.148), the separation period rises to a maximum 104 weeks (see ESA Regs, reg.145(2)). Where the assessment phase had not ended in the first such period, it ends at the appropriate point (the later of 13 weeks or the date of the limited capability of work determination) in the linked period(s). There can only be one assessment period in any single period of limited capability for work. So where another spell of such limited capability arises and is forged into one with an earlier period by the appropriate linking rules (12 or 104 weeks), and the "assessment phase" had ended in the earlier period, the claimant's entitlement in this second (or subsequent "spell") will be to prescribed amount plus appropriate component minus any s.3 deductions (s.2(4)(a); ESA Regs, reg.7(1)(b)). If the linking rules do not operate so as to forge the two spells into one, the second "spell" constitutes a new period of incapacity, in respect of which the three "waiting days" will again have to be served and a new "assessment phase" will begin again on the first day of entitlement after service of those waiting days and end according to the rules considered above.

Note finally that appealing against a determination that the claimant does not have limited capability for work extends the "assessment phase" until the appeal is determined by an appeal tribunal (s.24(2)(b); ESA Regs, regs 6, 7(2)).

The first element of CESA is the prescribed amount of "basic allowance". Although this is not a term used in the Act or the Regulations, its use is standard in the literature, policy and explanatory documents on ESA, and accordingly is also deployed here. It is normally the only element of CESA to which a claimant (other than one terminally ill) can be entitled during the "assessment phase". During that phase, the amount of CESA (subject to any s.3 deductions) to which the claimant can be entitled varies according to age. If under 25, a lower weekly rate is prescribed: £47.95 (see ESA Regs, reg.67(2), Sch.4, para.1(1)(c)). If 25 or over the weekly amount during the assessment phase is £60.50 (see ESA Regs, reg.67(2), Sch.4, para.1(1)(b)). The rates are thus equivalent to those in CBJSA.

During the assessment phase (whether ending after 13 weeks or a later date of determination of limited capability for work), it will have been determined whether the claimant has limited capability for work (actual limited capability) or should be treated as having it (deemed limited capability). It will also have been determined whether the claimant has limited capability for work related activity or should be treated as having it. If the claimant does have (or is treated as having) such limited capacity, this grounds entitlement to "support component", subject to other conditions set out in regulations, but generally only once the assessment phase has ended (subs.(2)) (see below for an exception in respect of the terminally ill). If the claimant does not have (or is treated as not having) such limited capacity, entitlement (subject to conditionality (see commentary to ss.11–16)) can only be to the work-related activity component (see subs.(3)). So the basic picture after the assessment period is prescribed amount plus appropriate component minus any s.3 deductions.

Once the assessment phase has ended there is a single prescribed weekly amount (£60.50), regardless of age (see ESA Regs, reg.67(2), Sch.4, para.1(1)(b)). If the claimant is then entitled to support component, the weekly amount to be added to the prescribed amount is £29.00 (see para.(b); ESA Regs, reg.67(3), Sch.4, Pt 4, para.13). If entitlement is to work-related activity component, the weekly amount to be added to the prescribed amount is £24.00 (see para.(b); ESA Regs, reg.67(3), Sch.4, Pt 4, para.12). The amount of CESA actually payable, however, is subject to reduction in accordance with s.3.

For those who are "terminally ill" (subs.(4)(a); ESA Regs, regs 2(1), 7(1)(a)), entitlement to the components (support or work-related activity) is not conditioned on the assessment phase having ended. So throughout their period of limited capability for work, entitlement will be to CESA composed of basic allowance plus appropriate component minus any s.3 deductions.

Subs.(2)
This sets out the conditions of entitlement to the support component in ESA. **1A.14** Entitlement can generally only arise after the assessment phase has ended. An exception to this is in the case of the terminally ill (subs.(4)(a); ESA Regs, reg.7(1)(a)). The claimant must be assessed as having, or be treated by regulations as having, limited capability for work-related activity. Entitlement also depends on other prescribed conditions (i.e. ones set out in regulations).

Subs.(3)
This stipulates the conditions of entitlement to the work-related activity com- **1A.15** ponent of ESA. Entitlement can generally only arise after the assessment phase has ended. An exception to this is in the case of the terminally ill (subs.(4)(a); ESA Regs, reg.7(1)(a)). The claimant must be assessed as not having, or be treated by regulations as not having, limited capability for work-related activity. Entitlement also depends on other prescribed conditions (i.e. ones set out in regulations).

Subs.(5)
This defines "limited capability for work-related activity". Whether the claim- **1A.16** ant has it or not is crucial for identifying which component of ESA (support or work related activity) is applicable in the case. A claimant has it where his capability for work-related activity is limited by his physical or mental condition such that it is not reasonable to require him to undertake such activity. "Work-related activity" is defined as activity which makes it more likely that the person whose capability is being tested will obtain or remain in work or be able to do so (ss.24(1), 13(7)).

Deductions from contributory allowance: supplementary

3.—(1) This section applies to payments of the following kinds which **1A.17** are payable to the claimant—
  (a) pension payments,
  (b) PPF periodic payments, and
  (c) payments of a prescribed description made to a person who is a member of, or has been appointed to, a prescribed body carrying out public or local functions.
  (2) Regulations may—

(a) disapply section 2(1)(c), so far as relating to pension payments or PPF periodic payments, in relation to persons of a prescribed description;

(b) provide for pension payments or PPF periodic payments of a prescribed description to be treated for the purposes of that provision as not being payments to which this section applies;

(c) provide for sums of a prescribed description to be treated for the purposes of this section as payable to persons as pension payments or PPF periodic payments (including, in particular, sums in relation to which there is a deferred right of receipt);

(d) make provision for the method of determining how payments to which this section applies are, for the purposes of section 2, to be related to periods for which a person is entitled to a contributory allowance.

(3) In this section—

"pension payment" means—

(a) a periodical payment made in relation to a person under a personal pension scheme or, in connection with the coming to an end of an employment of his, under an occupational pension scheme or a public service pension scheme,

(b) a payment of a prescribed description made under an insurance policy providing benefits in connection with physical or mental illness or disability, and

(c) such other payments as may be prescribed;

"PPF periodic payment" means—

(a) any periodic compensation payment made in relation to a person, payable under the pension compensation provisions as specified in section 162(2) of the Pensions Act 2004 (c.35) or Article 146(2) of the Pensions (Northern Ireland) Order 2005 (S.I. 2005/255) (NI 1) (the pension compensation provisions), and

(b) any periodic payment made in relation to a person, payable under section 166 of the Pensions Act 2004 or Article 150 of the Pensions (Northern Ireland) Order 2005 (duty to pay scheme benefits unpaid at assessment date etc.).

(4) For the purposes of subsection (3), "occupational pension scheme", "personal pension scheme" and "public service pension scheme" each have the meaning given by section 1 of the Pension Schemes Act 1993 (c.48), except that "personal pension scheme" includes—

(a) an annuity contract or trust scheme approved under section 620 or 621 of the Income and Corporation Taxes Act 1988 (c. 1), and

(b) a substituted contract within the meaning of section 622(3) of that Act,

which is treated as having become a registered pension scheme by virtue of paragraph 1(1)(f) of Schedule 36 to the Finance Act 2004 (c.12).

DEFINITIONS

"claimant"—see s.24(1), below.
"occupational pension scheme"—see subs.(4).
"pension payment"—see subs.(3).
"personal pension scheme"—see subs.(4).
"PPF periodic payment"—see subs.(3).
"prescribed"—see s.24(1), below.
"public service pension scheme"—see subs.(4).
"regulations"—see s.24(1), below.

GENERAL NOTE

Under s.2, the amount of CESA to which the claimant is otherwise entitled **1A.18** will normally (see subs.(2)(a) of this section) be reduced as set out in regulations (ESA Regs, regs 72–79) by the payments set out in this section which are payable to the claimant. This section and ESA Regs, regs 72–79 thus bring into ESA the concept of abatement of contributory benefit familiar from unemployment benefit (see SSCBA 1992, s.30 and USI Regs, 23–28 in the 1995 edition of Bonner, Hooker and White, *Non-Means Tested Benefits: the Legislation*), jobseeker's allowance (see JSA 1995, s.21, Sch.1, para.7; JSA Regs, regs 80, 81 in Vol.II) and incapacity benefit (see SSCBA 1992, ss.30DD [pension and PPF periodic payments] and 30E [councillor's allowance]; IB Regs, regs 20–26 in Vol.I). While not making them fully income-related benefits along the lines of income support, income-related jobseeker's allowance or tax credits, such abatement of ESA nonetheless continues the practice of bringing into a contributory benefit an element of means testing. In interpreting this section and its associated regulations, cross-reference to case law under those JSA and IB schemes will be appropriate insofar as the definitions are identical or analogous.

Subs.(1)
This stipulates that this section covers pension payments (para.(a)—defined in **1A.19** subss.(3), (4)), PPF periodic payments (para.(b)—defined in subs.(3)) and "payments of a prescribed description made to a person who is a member of, or has been appointed to, a prescribed body carrying out public or local functions" (para.(c)). For the rules on taking pension payments and PPF payments into account, see ESA Regs, reg.74. Currently, under para.(c), ESA Regs, reg.73 prescribes only "councillor's allowance" in respect of those councils referred to in the definition of "councillor in ESA Regs, reg.2(1). For the rules on taking "councillor's allowance" into account, see ESA Regs, reg.76.
On "payable to", see *R(IB)1/04* and *R(IB)1/05*.

Subs.(2)
Under para.(b), see ESA Regs, reg.75. **1A.20**
Under para.(d), see ESA regs 77–79.

Subs.(3)
Under para.(b) of the definition of pension payment, see ESA regs, reg.72 **1A.21** whereby "pension payment" includes a "permanent health insurance payment" as defined in that reg.

Amount of income-related allowance

4.—(1) In the case of an income-related allowance, the amount paya- **1A.22** ble in respect of a claimant shall be—
(a) if he has no income, the applicable amount;

(b) if he has an income, the amount by which the applicable amount exceeds his income.

(2) Subject to subsection (3), the applicable amount for the purposes of subsection (1) shall be calculated by—

(a) taking such amount, or the aggregate of such amounts, as may be prescribed, and

(b) if in the claimant's case the conditions of entitlement to the support component or the work-related activity component are satisfied, adding the amount of that component.

(3) Regulations may provide that, in prescribed cases, the applicable amount for the purposes of subsection (1) shall be nil.

(4) The conditions of entitlement to the support component are—

(a) that the assessment phase has ended,

(b) that the claimant has limited capability for work-related activity, and

(c) that such other conditions as may be prescribed are satisfied.

(5) The conditions of entitlement to the work-related activity component are—

(a) that the assessment phase has ended,

(b) that the claimant does not have limited capability for work-related activity, and

(c) that such other conditions as may be prescribed are satisfied.

(6) Regulations may—

(a) prescribe circumstances in which paragraph (a) of subsection (4) or (5) is not to apply;

(b) prescribe circumstances in which entitlement under subsection (4) or (5) is to be backdated;

(c) make provision about the amount of the component under subsection (4) or (5).

DEFINITIONS

"assessment phase"—s.24(2)
"income-related allowance"—ss.24(1) and 1(7).
"limited capability for work-related activity"—ss.24(1) and 2(5).
"prescribed"—s.24(1).
"regulations"—*ibid.*

GENERAL NOTE

1A.23   This section is similar in effect to ss.124(4) and 135(1)–(2) of the Contributions and Benefits Act and ss.3(1)(a) and (4) of the Jobseekers Act. Applicable amounts (including the work-related activity component and the support component) are prescribed by regs 67–70 of, and Schs 4 and 5 to, the ESA Regulations. Income (including tariff income from capital) is governed by s.17 and Pt 10 of, and Schs 7, 8 and 9 to, the ESA Regs.

Advance award of income-related allowance

1A.24   **5.**—(1) This section applies to claims for an employment and support allowance by a person who—

(a) would be entitled to an income-related allowance, but for the fact that he does not satisfy the condition in paragraph 6(1)(a) of Schedule 1,

(b) would satisfy that condition if he were entitled to the component mentioned in section 4(4) or (5), and

(c) is not entitled to a contributory allowance.

(2) In relation to claims to which this section applies, section 5(1) of the Administration Act (regulations about claims for benefit) shall have effect as if—

(a) in paragraph (d) (power to permit an award on a claim for benefit for a future period to be made subject to the condition that the claimant satisfies the requirements for entitlement when the benefit becomes payable under the award), there were inserted at the end "and to such other conditions as may be prescribed", and

(b) in paragraph (e) (power to provide for such an award to be revised or superseded under the Social Security Act 1998 (c. 14) if any of those requirements are found not to have been satisfied), for "any of those requirements" there were substituted "any of the conditions to which the award is made subject".

(3) Regulations may, in relation to claims to which this section applies, make provision enabling an award to be made on terms such that the time at which benefit becomes payable under the award is later than the start of the period for which the award is made.

DEFINITIONS

"Administration Act"—s.65.
"contributory allowance"—ss.24(1) and 1(7).
"income-related allowance"—*ibid.*

GENERAL NOTE

The support component and work-related activity component (see s.4(4) and (5) above) are normally only paid after the end of the assessment phase. During that phase, there will be some claimants who are not entitled to income-related ESA because their income exceeds their applicable amount, who would be so entitled if their applicable amount included the support component or work-related activity component. This section allows an advance award to be made where such a person makes a claim during the assessment phase. See also reg.146 of the ESA Regulations.

1A.25

Amount payable where claimant entitled to both forms of allowance

6.—(1) This section applies where a claimant is entitled to both a contributory allowance and an income-related allowance.

1A.26

(2) If the claimant has no income, the amount payable by way of an employment and support allowance shall be the greater of—

(a) his personal rate, and

(b) the applicable amount.

(3) If the claimant has an income, the amount payable by way of an employment and support allowance shall be the greater of—

(a) his personal rate, and

(b) the amount by which the applicable amount exceeds his income.

(4) Where the amount payable to the claimant by way of an employment and support allowance does not exceed his personal rate, the allowance shall be treated as attributable to the claimant's entitlement to a contributory allowance.

(5) Where the amount payable to the claimant by way of an employment and support allowance exceeds his personal rate, the allowance shall be taken to consist of two elements, namely—

(a) an amount equal to his personal rate, and

(b) an amount equal to the excess.

(6) The element mentioned in subsection (5)(a) shall be treated as attributable to the claimant's entitlement to a contributory allowance.

(7) The element mentioned in subsection (5)(b) shall be treated as attributable to the claimant's entitlement to an income-related allowance.

(8) In this section—

"applicable amount" means the amount which, in the claimant's case, is the applicable amount for the purposes of section 4(1);

"personal rate" means the amount calculated in accordance with section 2(1).

DEFINITIONS

"applicable amount"—see subs.(8), s.4(1).
"claimant"—see s.24(1).
"contributory allowance"—see s.1(7).
"income-related allowance"—see s.1(7).
"personal rate"—see subs.(8), s.2(1).

GENERAL NOTE

1A.27   This is similar to Jobseekers Act 1995, s.4(6)–(12), where, as with ESA, JSA has both a contributory element and an income related element. Like those provisions, this section deals with situations where a claimant is entitled to both a contributory allowance (CESA) and an income-related allowance (IRESA). Here, the amount calculated under s.2(1) (amount of CESA) is referred to as the "personal rate". The applicable amount for IRESA is made up of an amount in respect of the claimant and any partner, plus applicable premiums plus eligible housing costs (see s.4(1); ESA Regs, reg.67(1)). If the claimant has no income and the personal rate is higher than the applicable amount (the amount for the purposes of IRESA), the claimant receives the personal rate (the CESA amount). If the claimant has no income and the applicable amount exceeds the personal rate, he will receive the personal rate, topped up with an additional amount of IRESA equal to the excess. If the person has an income, the amount payable will be the greater of the personal allowance and the amount by which his applicable amount exceeds his income.

Exclusion of payments below prescribed minimum

1A.28   7.—Except in such circumstances as regulations may provide, an employment and support allowance shall not be payable where the amount otherwise payable would be less than a prescribed minimum.

DEFINITIONS

"prescribed"—see s.24(1).
"regulations"—see s.24(1).

GENERAL NOTE

ESA is not payable where it falls below the minimum amount prescribed in regulations. This amount is set at 10p in the Claims and Payments Regs 1987, reg.26C(6), inserted with effect from October 27, 2008 by reg.21 of the ESA (Consequential Provisions)(No. 2) Regs 2008 (SI 2008/1554). Compare JSA Regs, reg.87A.   **1A.29**

Assessments relating to entitlement

Limited capability for work

8.—(1) For the purposes of this Part, whether a person's capability for work is limited by his physical or mental condition and, if it is, whether the limitation is such that it is not reasonable to require him to work shall be determined in accordance with regulations.   **1A.30**

(2) Regulations under subsection (1) shall—

(a) provide for determination on the basis of an assessment of the person concerned;

(b) define the assessment by reference to the extent to which a person who has some specific disease or bodily or mental disablement is capable or incapable of performing such activities as may be prescribed;

(c) make provision as to the manner of carrying out the assessment.

(3) Regulations under subsection (1) may, in particular, make provision—

(a) as to the information or evidence required for the purpose of determining the matters mentioned in that subsection;

(b) as to the manner in which that information or evidence is to be provided;

(c) for a person in relation to whom it falls to be determined whether he has limited capability for work to be called to attend for such medical examination as the regulations may require.

(4) Regulations under subsection (1) may include provision—

(a) for a person to be treated as not having limited capability for work if he fails without good cause—

　　(i) to provide information or evidence which he is required under such regulations to provide,

　　(ii) to provide information or evidence in the manner in which he is required under such regulations to provide it, or

　　(iii) to attend for, or submit himself to, a medical examination for which he is called under such regulations to attend;

(b) as to matters which are, or are not, to be taken into account in determining for the purposes of any provision made by virtue of paragraph (a) whether a person has good cause for any act or omission;

(c) as to circumstances in which a person is, or is not, to be regarded for the purposes of any such provision as having good cause for any act or omission.

(5) Regulations may provide that, in prescribed circumstances, a person in relation to whom it falls to be determined whether he has limited capability for work, shall, if prescribed conditions are met, be treated as having limited capability for work until such time as—

(a) it has been determined whether he has limited capability for work, or

(b) he falls in accordance with regulations under this section to be treated as not having limited capability for work.

(6) The prescribed conditions referred to in subsection (5) may include the condition that it has not previously been determined, within such period as may be prescribed, that the person in question does not have, or is to be treated as not having, limited capability for work.

DEFINITIONS

"limited capability for work"—see s.1(4).
"medical examination"—
"prescribed"—see s.24(1).
"regulations"—see s.24(1).

GENERAL NOTE

Subss. (1), (2)

1A.31   A key condition of entitlement to ESA is that the claimant has limited capability for work, namely that his capability for work is limited by his physical or mental condition such that it is not reasonable to require him to work (s.1(3)(c), (4)). This section provides that whether this is so is to be determined in accordance with regulations made under subss.(2)–(6) of this section. The regulations are Pt 5 of the ESA Regs, regs 19–33. These embody the first element in the new three-part Work Capability Assessment, governing entitlement to ESA, an analogue of the Personal Capability Assessment (PCA) in the previous incapacity benefits' regime (Incapacity Benefit/Income Support/Severe Disablement Allowance). But while there are many similarities with the PCA there are some significant differences as regards activities/descriptors, those exempt from the test and the system of scoring. The approach taken here, however, is that where terminology and basic issues are the same as with the PCA, the extensive case law interpreting and applying the PCA will carry over into the interpretation and application of comparable provisions and the resolution of comparable issues with this first element of the WCA, referred to for convenience as the WCAt to distinguish it from the other two elements of the WCA which only come into play if, applying the WCAt, the claimant is found not to have limited capability for work. These other two elements are the work-related activity assessment (WRAAt) (more stringent than the WCAt) (see s.9) and the work-focused health related assessment (WFHRAt) (see s.11). The former determines whether or not a claimant has limited capability for work-related activity. If he does, he will be placed in the support group as eligible for the support component and will not have to undergo the WFHRAt. If he does not have limited capability for work-related activity, he will be placed in the work-related activity group, eligible for work-related activity component, subject to the conditionality regime (see ss.11–16), including having normally to undergo the WFHRAt (see s.11), participate in work-related interviews (see s.12) and (eventually) work-related activity (see s.13).

Subss.(3), (4)

Note that whether the claimant has good cause for failure to comply with the information-gathering and examination aspects of that assessment is to some extent structured by regulations in that ESA Regs, reg.24 provides an non-exhaustive list of matters to be taken into account in determining that good cause issue. No regulations have yet been made under para.(4)(c) to determine what does, or does not, rank as good cause. 　1A.32

Limited capability for work-related activity

9.—(1) For the purposes of this Part, whether a person's capability for work-related activity is limited by his physical or mental condition and, if it is, whether the limitation is such that it is not reasonable to require him to undertake such activity shall be determined in accordance with regulations. 　1A.33

(2) Regulations under subsection (1) shall—

(a) provide for determination on the basis of an assessment of the person concerned;

(b) define the assessment by reference to such matters as the regulations may provide;

(c) make provision as to the manner of carrying out the assessment.

(3) Regulations under subsection (1) may, in particular, make provision—

(a) as to the information or evidence required for the purpose of determining the matters mentioned in that subsection;

(b) as to the manner in which that information or evidence is to be provided;

(c) for a person in relation to whom it falls to be determined whether he has limited capability for work-related activity to be called to attend for such medical examination as the regulations may require.

(4) Regulations under subsection (1) may include provision—

(a) for a person to be treated as not having limited capability for work-related activity if he fails without good cause—

   (i) to provide information or evidence which he is required under such regulations to provide,

   (ii) to provide information or evidence in the manner in which he is required under such regulations to provide it, or

   (iii) to attend for, or submit himself to, a medical examination for which he is called under such regulations to attend;

(b) as to matters which are, or are not, to be taken into account in determining for the purposes of any provision made by virtue of paragraph (a) whether a person has good cause for any act or omission;

(c) as to circumstances in which a person is, or is not, to be regarded for the purposes of any such provision as having good cause for any act or omission.

DEFINITIONS

"regulations"—see s.24(1).
"work-related activity"—see ss.24(1), 13(7).

GENERAL NOTE

Subss. (1), (2)

1A.34 Whether an ESA claimant is entitled to the more generous support component (£29 per week) or the less generous work-related activity component (£24 per week) in addition to his basic allowance turns on whether he does (support component)) or does not (work-related activity component) have limited capability for work-related activity (s.2(2), (3)). He has "limited capability for work-related activity" where his capability for such activity is limited by his physical or mental condition such that it is not reasonable to require him to undertake it (s.2(5)). "Work-related activity" is activity which makes it more likely that he will obtain or remain in work or be able to do so (ss.24(1), 13(7)). This section provides that whether or not he has such limited capability is to be determined in accordance with regulations under subss.(2), (4) of this section. The regulations in question are ESA Regs, Pt 6, regs 34–39. These flesh out the second element in the new three element Work Capability Assessment: the work related activity assessment (WRAAt).

Subss. (3), (4)

1A.35 Note that whether the claimant has good cause for failure to comply with the information-gathering and examination aspects of that assessment is to some extent structured by regulations in that ESA Regs, reg.39 provides an non-exhaustive list of matters to be taken into account in determining that good cause issue. No regulations have yet been made under para.(4)(c) to determine what does, or does not, rank as good cause.

Report

1A.36 **10.**—The Secretary of State shall lay before Parliament an independent report on the operation of the assessments under sections 8 and 9 annually for the first five years after those sections come into force.

GENERAL NOTE

1A.37 The new capability assessments in respect of work and work related activity were controversial. So this section provides—but only for the first five years after commencement—for independent annual review of their operation, a report on which must be laid before Parliament by the Secretary of State.

Conditionality

Work-focused health-related assessments

1A.38 **11.**—(1) Regulations may make provision for or in connection with imposing on a person who is—

24

(a) entitled to an employment and support allowance, and

(b) not a member of the support group,

a requirement to take part in one or more work-focused health-related assessments as a condition of continuing to be entitled to the full amount payable to him in respect of the allowance apart from the regulations.

(2) Regulations under this section may, in particular, make provision—

(a) prescribing circumstances in which such a person is subject to a requirement to take part in one or more work-focused health-related assessments;

(b) for notifying such a person of any such requirement;

(c) prescribing the work-focused health-related assessments in which a person who is subject to such a requirement is required to take part;

(d) for the determination, and notification, of the time and place of any such assessment;

(e) prescribing circumstances in which a person attending such an assessment is to be regarded as having, or not having, taken part in it;

(f) for securing that the appropriate consequence follows if a person who is required under the regulations to take part in a work-focused health-related assessment—

(i) fails to take part in the assessment, and

(ii) does not, within a prescribed period, show that he had good cause for that failure;

(g) prescribing matters which are, or are not, to be taken into account in determining whether a person had good cause for any failure to comply with the regulations;

(h) prescribing circumstances in which a person is, or is not, to be regarded as having good cause for any such failure.

(3) For the purposes of subsection (2)(f), the appropriate consequence of a failure falling within that provision is that the amount payable to the person in question in respect of an employment and support allowance is reduced in accordance with regulations.

(4) Regulations under subsection (3) may, in particular, make provision for determining—

(a) the amount by which an allowance is to be reduced,

(b) when the reduction is to start, and

(c) how long it is to continue,

and may include provision prescribing circumstances in which the amount of the reduction is to be nil.

(5) Regulations under this section shall include provision for a requirement to take part in one or more work-focused health-related assessments to cease to have effect if the person subject to the requirement becomes a member of the support group.

(6) Regulations under this section may include provision—

(a) that in such circumstances as the regulations may prescribe a requirement to take part in a work-focused health-related assessment that would otherwise apply to a person by virtue of such regulations is not to apply, or is to be treated as not having applied;

(b) that in such circumstances as the regulations may prescribe such a requirement is not to apply until a prescribed time;

(c) that in such circumstances as the regulations may prescribe the time and place of a work-focused health-related assessment in which a person is required by regulations under this section to take part may be redetermined.

(7) In this section, "work-focused health-related assessment" means an assessment by a health care professional approved by the Secretary of State which is carried out for the purpose of assessing—

(a) the extent to which a person still has capability for work,

(b) the extent to which his capability for work may be improved by the taking of steps in relation to his physical or mental condition, and

(c) such other matters relating to his physical or mental condition and the likelihood of his obtaining or remaining in work or being able to do so, as may be prescribed.

(8) In subsection (7), "health care professional" means—

(a) a registered medical practitioner,

(b) a registered nurse,

(c) an occupational therapist or physiotherapist registered with a regulatory body established by an Order in Council under section 60 of the Health Act 1999, or

(d) a member of such other profession regulated by a body mentioned in section 25(3) of the National Health Service Reform and Health Care Professions Act 2002 as may be prescribed.

DEFINITIONS

"appropriate consequence"—see subs.(3).
"entitled"—see s.24(1).
"health care professional" (in subs.(7))—see subs.(8).
"prescribed"—see s.24(1).
"regulations"—see s.24(1).
"support group"—see s.24(4).
"work-focused health-related assessment"—see subs.(7)

GENERAL NOTE

1A.39   This section covers those claimants who do not have limited capability for work-related activity and who are thus entitled not to the support component but instead to the work-related activity component (they are not part of the "support group" (see s.24(4))). Those entitled to the work-related activity component must comply with certain conditions—the regime is one of "conditionality" (stipulating required behaviour and using sanctions to regulate and change behaviour). One of these conditions is participation in work-focused health-related assessments. These assessments are defined in subs.(7). They are carried out by an approved "health care professional" as defined in subs.(8), covering a wider range of personnel than a doctor or nurse (so as to embrace, for example, a registered occupational therapist or physiotherapist), as indeed is appropriate given the aim of such assessments. They are carried out for the purpose of assessing the extent to which the claimant still has capability for work; the extent to which that might be improved by taking steps in relation to his physical or mental condition; and other matters (to be set out in regulations) relating to that condition and the likelihood of obtaining work, remaining in work or being able to do so (subs.(7)).

This section enables the making of regulations to impose that requirement of participation in such an assessment and to exempt persons from it (subss.(1), (5), (6)); to deal with the process of carrying out such an assessment, and with the consequences of not participating in one without good cause (subs.(2)). Subsection (3) stipulates that a reduction in the amount of ESA otherwise payable is the appropriate consequence, and that subsection and subs.(4) enable the making of regulations determining the amount and period of the reduction and the circumstances in which the reduction is to be nil. Subsection (5) enables regulations to provide that the requirement shall cease to have effect if the person becomes a member of the support group, that is, if it is determined that he has, or is to be treated as having, limited capability for work-related activity.

The relevant regulations are the ESA Regs, Pt 8 (Conditionality) Ch.1 (work-focused health related assessment), regs 47–53. Despite the width of the rule-making power (which would appear to authorise reduction in the amount of ESA payable) the sanction operates only by reduction of the work-related activity component of ESA, rather than on the whole allowance. It would appear that this has always been the policy intention, but, if so, it would have been better so to confine the rule-making power (see JHRC, *Second Report of Session 2006–07*, HL 34/HC 263 (2006–07), para.3.18).

Note that whether the claimant has good cause for failure to participate in a work-focused health-related assessment is to some extent structured by regulations in that ESA Regs, reg.53(3) provides an non-exhaustive list of matters to be taken into account in determining that good cause issue. No regulations have yet been made under para.(2)(h) to determine what does, or does not, rank as good cause.

Work-focused interviews

12.—(1) Regulations may make provision for or in connection with 1A.40 imposing on a person who is—

    (a) entitled to an employment and support allowance, and

    (b) not a member of the support group,

a requirement to take part in one or more work-focused interviews as a condition of continuing to be entitled to the full amount payable to him in respect of the allowance apart from the regulations.

(2) Regulations under this section may, in particular, make provision—

    (a) prescribing circumstances in which such a person is subject to a requirement to take part in one or more work-focused interviews;

    (b) for notifying such a person of any such requirement;

    (c) prescribing the work-focused interviews in which a person who is subject to such a requirement is required to take part;

    (d) for determining, in relation to work-focused interviews under the regulations, when and how the interview is to be conducted and, if it is to be conducted face to face, where it is to take place;

    (e) for notifying persons who are required under the regulations to take part in a work-focused interview of what is determined in respect of the matters mentioned in paragraph (d);

(f) prescribing circumstances in which a person who is a party to a work-focused interview under the regulations is to be regarded as having, or not having, taken part in it;

(g) for securing that the appropriate consequence follows if a person who is required under the regulations to take part in a work-focused interview—

(i) fails to take part in the interview, and

(ii) does not, within a prescribed period, show that he had good cause for that failure;

(h) prescribing matters which are, or are not, to be taken into account in determining whether a person had good cause for any failure to comply with the regulations;

(i) prescribing circumstances in which a person is, or is not, to be regarded as having good cause for any such failure.

(3) For the purposes of subsection (2)(g), the appropriate consequence of a failure falling within that provision is that the amount payable to the person in question in respect of an employment and support allowance is reduced in accordance with regulations.

(4) Regulations under subsection (3) may, in particular, make provision for determining—

(a) the amount by which an allowance is to be reduced,

(b) when the reduction is to start, and

(c) how long it is to continue,

and may include provision prescribing circumstances in which the amount of the reduction is to be nil.

(5) Regulations under this section shall include provision for a requirement to take part in one or more work-focused interviews to cease to have effect if the person subject to the requirement becomes a member of the support group.

(6) Regulations under this section may include provision—

(a) that in such circumstances as the regulations may prescribe a requirement to take part in a work-focused interview that would otherwise apply to a person by virtue of such regulations is not to apply, or is to be treated as not having applied;

(b) that in such circumstances as the regulations may prescribe such a requirement is not to apply until a prescribed time;

(c) that in such circumstances as the regulations may prescribe matters mentioned in subsection (2)(d) may be redetermined.

(7) In this section, "work-focused interview" means an interview by the Secretary of State conducted for such purposes connected with getting the person interviewed into work, or keeping him in work, as may be prescribed.

DEFINITIONS

"appropriate consequence"—see subs.(3).
"entitled"—see s.24(1).
"prescribed"—see s.24(1).
"regulations"—see s.24(1).
"support group"—see s.24(4).
"work-focused interview"—see subs.(7).

GENERAL NOTE

This section covers those claimants, entitled to ESA, who do not have limited capability for work-related activity and who are thus entitled not to the support component but instead to the work-related activity component (they are not part of the "support group" (see s.24(4)). Those entitled to the work-related activity component must comply with certain conditions—the regime is one of "conditionality" (stipulating required behaviour and using sanctions to regulate and change behaviour). One of these conditions is participation in one or more work-focused interviews conducted either by Jobcentre Plus or (as envisaged by s.16) one of the contractors in the private or voluntary sectors (PVS).

1A.41

A "work-focused interview" is one conducted for such purposes connected with keeping the interviewee in work or getting him into work, as may be set out in regulations (subs.(7)).

This section enables the making of regulations to impose the requirement of participation in such an interview and to exempt persons from it, whether totally or delaying its application for a particular period (subss.(1), (5), (6)); to deal with the process of carrying out such an interview, and with the consequences of not participating in one without good cause (subs.(2)). Subsection (3) stipulates that a reduction in the amount of ESA otherwise payable is the appropriate consequence, and that subsection and subs.(4) enable the making of regulations determining the amount and period of the reduction and the circumstances in which the reduction is to be nil. Subsection (5) enables regulations to provide that the requirement shall cease to have effect if the person becomes a member of the support group, that is, if it is determined that he has, or is to be treated as having, limited capability for work-related activity.

The relevant regulations are the ESA Regs, Pt 8 (Conditionality) Ch.2 (work-focused interviews), regs 54–62. Despite the width of the rule-making power (which would appear to authorise reduction in the amount of ESA payable) the sanction operates only by reduction of the work-related activity component of ESA, rather than on the whole allowance. It would appear that this has always been the policy intention, but, if so, it would have been better in terms of compliance with Convention Rights so to confine the rule-making power (see JHRC, *Second Report of Session 2006–07*, HL 34/HC 263 (2006–07), para.3.18).

Note that whether the claimant has good cause for failure to participate in a work-focused health-related interview is to some extent structured by regulations in that ESA Regs, reg.61(3) provides a non-exhaustive list of matters which may be taken into account by decision-maker or appeal tribunal in determining that good cause issue. No regulations have yet been made under para.(2)(i) to determine what does, or does not, rank as good cause.

Work-related activity

13.—(1) Regulations may make provision for or in connection with imposing on a person who is subject to a requirement imposed under section 12(1) a requirement to undertake work-related activity in accordance with regulations as a condition of continuing to be entitled to the full amount payable to him in respect of an employment and support allowance apart from the regulations.

1A.42

(2) Regulations under this section may, in particular, make provision—

(a) prescribing circumstances in which such a person is subject to a requirement to undertake work-related activity in accordance with regulations;

(b) for notifying such a person of any such requirement;

(c) prescribing the time or times at which a person who is subject to such a requirement is required to undertake work-related activity and the amount of work-related activity he is required at any time to undertake;

(d) prescribing circumstances in which a person who is subject to such a requirement is, or is not, to be regarded as undertaking work-related activity;

(e) for securing that the appropriate consequence follows if a person who is subject to such a requirement—
  (i) fails to comply with the regulations, and
  (ii) does not, within a prescribed period, show that he had good cause for that failure;

(f) prescribing the evidence which a person who is subject to such a requirement needs to provide in order to show that he has complied with the regulations;

(g) prescribing matters which are, or are not, to be taken into account in determining whether a person has complied with the regulations;

(h) prescribing matters which are, or are not, to be taken into account in determining whether a person had good cause for any failure to comply with the regulations;

(i) prescribing circumstances in which a person is, or is not, to be regarded as having good cause for any such failure.

(3) For the purposes of subsection (2)(e), the appropriate consequence of a failure falling within that provision is that the amount payable to the person in question in respect of an employment and support allowance is to be reduced in accordance with regulations.

(4) Regulations under subsection (3) may, in particular, make provision for determining—

(a) the amount by which an allowance is to be reduced,

(b) when the reduction is to start, and

(c) how long it is to continue,

and may include provision prescribing circumstances in which the amount of the reduction is to be nil.

(5) Regulations under this section shall include provision for a requirement to undertake work-related activity in accordance with regulations to cease to have effect if the person subject to the requirement becomes a member of the support group.

(6) Regulations under this section may include provision that in such circumstances as the regulations may provide a person's obligation under the regulations to undertake work-related activity at a particular time is not to apply, or is to be treated as not having applied.

(7) In this Part, "work-related activity", in relation to a person, means activity which makes it more likely that the person will obtain or remain in work or be able to do so.

DEFINITIONS

"appropriate consequence"—see subs.(3).
"regulations"—see s.24(1).

"support group"—see s.24(4).
"work-related activity"—see subs.(7).

GENERAL NOTE

This section applies only to those subject to a requirement to participate in a work-focused interview ("a requirement imposed under s.12(1)"). It thus covers those claimants, entitled to ESA, who do not have limited capability for work-related activity and who are thus entitled not to the support component but instead to the work-related activity component (they are not part of the "support group" (see s.24(4)), who have not been exempted from the requirement or had it delayed. Those entitled to the work-related activity component must comply with certain conditions in order to retain entitlement—the regime is one of "conditionality" (stipulating required behaviour and using sanctions to regulate and change behaviour). The first envisaged condition is participation in a work-focused health related assessment" (s.11). The second is participation in a work-focused interview (s.12). This section enables the imposition on those subject to the second of a third condition: a requirement to undertake work-related activity. That is to undertake activity which makes it more likely that the person to be subjected to the condition will obtain or remain in work or be able to do so (ss.24(1), 13(7)).

This section enables the making of regulations to impose the requirement to undertake such activity and to exempt persons from it, whether totally or delaying its application for a particular period (subss.(1), (5), (6)); to deal with the process of imposition of the requirement, and with the consequences of not undertaking it without good cause (subs.(2)). Subsection (3) stipulates that a reduction in the amount of ESA otherwise payable is the appropriate consequence, and that subsection and subs.(4) enable the making of regulations determining the amount and period of the reduction and the circumstances in which the reduction is to be nil. Subsection (5) enables regulations to provide that the requirement shall cease to have effect if the person becomes a member of the support group, that is, if it is determined that he has, or is to be treated as having, limited capability for work-related activity.

As yet, no regulations have been made. It is envisaged that this aspect of "conditionality" will only come in when resources permit, probably not before 2011 (Pathways to Work contracts will be recontracted in 2010–2011). Activities envisaged are work tasters; programmes to manage health in work; job search assistance; and programmes to assist in stabilising the individual's life (*Explanatory Notes to the Welfare Reform Act 2007*, paras 86–91). Information presented to the Commons by the DWP when the Welfare Reform Bill was being considered there indicated that claimants would be asked to participate in a minimum amount of work-related activity (e.g. one activity) in a given time period (e.g. four weeks), and in between each period they would in their work-focused interview review what they had done and discuss what they would like to do in the next period (DWP, *Welfare Reform Bill: Draft Regulations and Supporting Material*, January 2007). That same material stressed that no-one would be forced to undertake a particular activity; the requirement is to participate in some work-related activity. Perhaps an appropriate analogy may be with the proper approach to the question in JSA of whether a claimant is actively seeking work (see commentary to Jobseekers Act 1995, ss.7, 9; and to JSA Regs, regs 18. Note also the power to direct that specific activity will not count a work-related activity for a particular person (s.15).

Despite the width of the rule-making power (which would appear to authorise reduction in the amount of ESA payable) it is envisaged that, as with that

1A.43

applicable to the other elements in respect of work-related activity "condition-ality' (see ss.11, 12, above), the sanction will operate only by reduction of the work-related activity component of ESA, rather than on the whole allowance. It would appear that this has always been the policy intention, but, if so, it would have been better so to confine the rule-making power (see JHRC, *Second Report of Session 2006–07*, HL 34/HC 263 (2006–07), para.3.18).

Action plans in connection with work-focused interviews

1A.44   **14.**—(1) The Secretary of State shall in prescribed circumstances provide a person subject to a requirement imposed under section 12(1) with a document prepared for such purposes as may be prescribed (in this section referred to as an action plan).

(2) Regulations may make provision about—

(a) the form of action plans;

(b) the content of action plans;

(c) the review and updating of action plans.

(3) Regulations under this section may, in particular, make provision for action plans which are provided to a person who is subject under section 13 to a requirement to undertake work-related activity to contain particulars of activity which, if undertaken, would enable the requirement to be met.

(4) Regulations may make provision for reconsideration of an action plan at the request of the person to whom the plan is provided and may, in particular, make provision about—

(a) the circumstances in which reconsideration may be requested;

(b) the period within which any reconsideration must take place;

(c) the matters to which regard must be had when deciding on reconsideration whether the plan should be changed;

(d) notification of the decision on reconsideration;

(e) the giving of directions for the purpose of giving effect to the decision on reconsideration.

DEFINITIONS

"action plan"—see subs.(1).
"prescribed"—see s.24(1).
"regulations"—see s.24(1).
"work-related activity"—see ss.24(1), 13(7).

GENERAL NOTE

1A.45   Part of the "work-related activity" process requires the drawing up of written "action plans" as part of the work-related interview process, envisaging that these will be reviewed and amended as conditions change. This section imposes that requirement and authorises regulations to give it effect. The regulation is the ESA Regs, reg.58. An action plan records the interview; any work-related activity the claimant is willing to undertake; and any other information considered appropriate by the Secretary of State. The plan will doubtless influence the shape of future interviews and be relevant to the question of whether the claimant is undertaking work-related activity and whether he should be sanctioned by reduction or eventually removal of work-related activity component in accordance with ESA Regs, regs 63, 64. It may be tempting to draw analogies with the jobseeker's agreement in JSA, but the plan is just that: a plan drawn up by

32

officialdom and agreement to it is not directly a condition of entitlement to ESA.

Directions about work-related activity

15.—(1) In prescribed circumstances, the Secretary of State may by direction given to a person subject to a requirement imposed under section 13(1) provide that the undertaking of activity specified in the direction is, in his case, to be treated as not being the undertaking of work-related activity.   **1A.46**

(2) The power under subsection (1) to give directions—

(a) is exercisable by instrument in writing, and

(b) includes power to vary or revoke a direction given in previous exercise of the power.

(3) Where a direction under subsection (1) varies or revokes a previous direction, it may provide for the variation or revocation to have effect from a time before the giving of the direction.

DEFINITIONS

"prescribed"—see s.24(1).
"work-related activity"—see ss.24(1), 13(7).

GENERAL NOTE

Engagement in work-related activity is a condition of entitlement to work-related activity component for most of the claimants who are not in the support group. Failure to engage in such activity can be sanctioned by reduction or removal of work-related activity component, leaving such a claimant reliant solely on basic allowance ESA. This section enables a written direction to be given to a claimant with the effect that the activity specified in the direction will in his case be treated as not being work-related activity. The DWP envisages that this power will only be used in limited circumstances "where a given activity was wholly inappropriate for the claimant" (DWP, *Welfare Reform Bill: Draft Regulations and Supporting Material*, January 2007). Since engagement in work-related activity will not be an operative part of "conditionality" until resources permit (probably not before 2011 (see commentary to s.13), the regulations envisaged by subs.(1), setting out the circumstances, in which a direction can be given, have not yet been made.   **1A.47**

Contracting out

16.—(1) The following functions of the Secretary of State may be exercised by, or by employees of, such person (if any) as the Secretary of State may authorise for the purpose, namely—   **1A.48**

(a) conducting interviews under section 12;

(b) providing documents under section 14;

(c) giving, varying or revoking directions under section 15.

(2) Regulations may provide for any of the following functions of the Secretary of State to be exercisable by, or by employees of, such person (if any) as the Secretary of State may authorise for the purpose—

(a) any function under regulations under any of sections 11 to 15, except the making of a decision to which subsection (3) applies (an "excluded decision");

(b) the function under section 9(1) of the Social Security Act 1998 (c. 14) (revision of decisions), so far as relating to decisions, except excluded decisions, that relate to any matter arising under such regulations;

(c) the function under section 10(1) of that Act (superseding of decisions), so far as relating to decisions, except excluded decisions, of the Secretary of State that relate to any matter arising under such regulations;

(d) any function under Chapter 2 of Part 1 of that Act (social security decisions), except section 25(2) and (3) (decisions involving issues that arise on appeal in other cases), which relates to the exercise of any of the functions falling within paragraphs (a) to (c).

(3) This subsection applies to the following decisions—

(a) a decision about whether a person has failed to comply with a requirement imposed by regulations under section 11, 12 or 13;

(b) a decision about whether a person had good cause for failure to comply with such a requirement;

(c) a decision about reduction of an employment and support allowance in consequence of failure to comply with such a requirement.

(4) Regulations under subsection (2) may provide that a function to which that subsection applies may be exercised—

(a) either wholly or to such extent as the regulations may provide,

(b) either generally or in such cases or areas as the regulations may provide, and

(c) either unconditionally or subject to the fulfilment of such conditions as the regulations may provide.

(5) An authorisation given by virtue of subsection (1), or by virtue of regulations under subsection (2), may authorise the exercise of the function concerned—

(a) either wholly or to such extent as may be specified in the authorisation,

(b) either generally or in such cases or areas as may be so specified, and

(c) either unconditionally or subject to the fulfilment of such conditions as may be so specified.

(6) In the case of an authorisation given by virtue of regulations under subsection (2), subsection (5) is subject to the provisions of the regulations.

(7) An authorisation given by virtue of subsection (1), or by virtue of regulations under subsection (2)—

(a) may specify its duration,

(b) may be revoked at any time by the Secretary of State, and

(c) shall not prevent the Secretary of State or any other person from exercising the function to which the authorisation relates.

(8) Where a person is authorised to exercise any function by virtue of subsection (1), or by virtue of regulations under subsection (2), anything done or omitted to be done by or in relation to him (or an employee of his) in, or in connection with, the exercise or purported exercise of the function shall be treated for all purposes as done or omitted to be done by or in relation to the Secretary of State.

(9) Subsection (8) shall not apply—

(a) for the purposes of so much of any contract made between the authorised person and the Secretary of State as relates to the exercise of the function, or

(b) for the purposes of any criminal proceedings brought in respect of anything done or omitted to be done by the authorised person (or an employee of his).

(10) Any decision which a person authorised to exercise any function by virtue of subsection (1), or by virtue of regulations under subsection (2), makes in exercise of the function shall have effect as a decision of the Secretary of State under section 8 of the Social Security Act1998.

(11) Where—

(a) a person is authorised to exercise any function by virtue of subsection (1), or by virtue of regulations under subsection (2), and

(b) the authorisation is revoked at a time when a relevant contract is subsisting,

the authorised person shall be entitled to treat the relevant contract as repudiated by the Secretary of State (and not as frustrated by reason of the revocation).

(12) In subsection (11), the reference to a relevant contract is to so much of any contract made between the authorised person and the Secretary of State as relates to the exercise of the function.

(13) In this section, references to functions of the Secretary of State under—

(a) an enactment contained in, or in regulations under, this Part, or

(b) an enactment contained in Chapter 2 of Part 1 of the Social Security Act 1998,

include a reference to any function which the Secretary of State has by virtue of the application in relation to that enactment of section 8(1)(c) of that Act (decisions under certain enactments to be made by the Secretary of State).

DEFINITIONS

"regulations"—see s.24(1).

GENERAL NOTE

This section authorises, to such a degree as is specified in regulations and/or   **1A.49** an authorisation (subss.(5), (6)), the contracting out of certain functions vested in the Secretary of State (DWP/JobCentre Plus decision-makers and Personal Advisers) in respect of the conditionality aspect of entitlement to the work-related activity component, and of a wide (but not unlimited) range of decisions related to the exercise of those functions.

Those functions are conducting work-focused interviews under s.12; providing documents under s.14 (action plans in connection with work-focused interviews); and giving, varying or revoking directions under s.15 (subs.(1)). The functions can be exercised by the contractor ("such person as the Secretary of State may authorise for the purpose") or by employees of the contractor (subs.(1)). Anything done (or omitted to be done) by them must be treated as if done (or omitted to be done) by the Secretary of State (subss.(8), (9)). Their decisions in respect of the authorised functions are to be given effect as ones of the Secretary of State under s.8 SSA 1998 (subs.(10). Revocation of the authorisation may be treated as a repudiation of the contract by the Secretary of State and not as a matter of frustration of the contract (subss.(11, (12)).

In addition, subs.(2) enables the making of regulations authorising a number of other functions to be so exercisable by the contractor or the contractor's employees. The regulations can authorise the exercise of any functions under ss.11–15, above (subs.(2)(a)), other than "excluded decisions" which are enumerated in subs.(3). Put shortly, this prevents authorising contractors or their employees to make decisions in respect of the sanctioning aspect of "conditionality" as regards entitlement to the work-related activity component, although information and material from them will perforce feed into and inform decisions on these matters made by DWP/JobCentre Plus decision-makers. Thus subs.(3) provides that regulations cannot enable the making by contractors or their employees of decisions on whether the claimant has failed to comply with requirements, set out in regulations, on work-focused health-related assessments (s.11), work-focused interviews (s.12) or work-related activity (s.13) (para.(a)). Regulations cannot authorise them to make decisions on whether the claimant had good cause for any failure to comply with such a requirement (para.(b)), or on whether failure to comply must be sanctioned by reduction or removal of the amount of work-related activity component to which the claimant would otherwise be entitled (para.(c)). But, save so far as they relate to excluded decisions, regulations can authorise contractors or their employees to exercise powers of revision and supersession under ss.9 and 10, respectively, of the Social Security Act 1998, in respect of any functions under ss.11–15 (subs.(2)(b), (c)). Subsection (2)(d) enables regulations to authorise them also to exercise, in respect of those functions, any function under Ch.2 of Pt I of that 1998 Act, other than ones under ss.25(2) and (3) of it (decisions involving issues that arise on appeal in other cases).

The ESA regime envisages that helping claimants return to work or to the labour market need not solely be the task of the DWP or Jobcentre Plus, important as their role is. Contractors in the private and voluntary sector (PVS) have specialist knowledge and innovative approaches which, properly harnessed and deployed, may well ensure the best possible support for claimants in the work-related activity group. As with the Provider Led Pathways aspect of the Pathways to Work project on which the ESA approach is built, JobCentre Plus will conduct the first work-focused interview. It will be recalled that a "work-focused interview" is one conducted for such purposes connected with keeping the interviewee in work or getting him into work, as may be set out in regulations (s.12(7)). A secondary purpose will be to provide information on benefit and service entitlement. This renders it appropriate that it be done by JobCentre Plus. But a principal reason for its staff doing so is that at that stage, very early in a claim, eligibility for ESA will not have been determined by the medical test. Although interviews after the claimant's first work-focused interview may well be carried out by PVS providers, JobCentre Plus will during the lifetime of the claim exercise functions relating to entitlement to benefit, sanctioning decisions and processing of benefit payments.

Miscellaneous

Income and capital: general

17.—(1) In relation to a claim for an employment and support allow-   1A.50
ance, the income and capital of a person shall be calculated or estimated
in such manner as may be prescribed.

(2) A person's income in respect of a week shall be calculated in
accordance with prescribed rules, which may provide for the calculation
to be made by reference to an average over a period (which need not
include the week concerned).

(3) Circumstances may be prescribed in which—

(a) a person is to be treated as possessing capital or income which he
    does not possess;
(b) capital or income which a person does possess is to be disre-
    garded;
(c) income is to be treated as capital;
(d) capital is to be treated as income.

(4) Regulations may provide that a person's capital shall be deemed
for the purposes of this Part to yield him an income at a prescribed
rate.

DEFINITIONS

"prescribed"—s.24(1).
"regulations"—*ibid.*
"week"—*ibid.*

GENERAL NOTE

This section is very similar to s.136(3)–(5) of the Contributions and Benefits
Act and s.12 of the Jobseekers Act.

It enables the Secretary of State to introduce detailed regulations governing
the treatment of income and capital for the purposes of employment and support
allowance. See Pt 10 of and Schs 7, 8 and 9 to the ESA Regs.

See also para.6(2) of Sch.1 which contains the "aggregation rule" for the
purposes of income-related JSA, i.e., that where the claimant is a member of a
couple, his partner's income and capital counts as that of the claimant (except in
prescribed circumstances).

Disqualification

18.—(1) Regulations may provide for a person to be disqualified for   1A.51
receiving an employment and support allowance, or treated for such
purposes as the regulations may provide as not having limited capability
for work, if—

(a) he has become someone who has limited capability for work
    through his own misconduct,
(b) he remains someone who has limited capability for work through
    his failure without good cause to follow medical advice, or
(c) he fails without good cause to observe any prescribed rules of
    behaviour.

(2) Regulations under subsection (1) shall provide for any such disqualification, or treatment, to be for such period not exceeding 6 weeks as may be determined in accordance with Chapter 2 of Part 1 of the Social Security Act 1998 (c. 14).

(3) Regulations may prescribe for the purposes of subsection (1)—

(a) matters which are, or are not, to be taken into account in determining whether a person has good cause for any act or omission;

(b) circumstances in which a person is, or is not, to be regarded as having good cause for any act or omission.

(4) Except where regulations otherwise provide, a person shall be disqualified for receiving a contributory allowance for any period during which he is—

(a) absent from Great Britain, or

(b) undergoing imprisonment or detention in legal custody.

DEFINITIONS

"contributory allowance"—see s.1(7).
"limited capability for work"—see s.1(4).
"prescribed"—see s.24(1).
"regulations"—see s.24(1).
"week"—see s.24(1).

GENERAL NOTE

Subss. (1)–(3)

1A.52   Like previous incapacity benefits' regimes (compare SSCBA 1992, s.171E and IW (General) Regs, reg.18), ESA embodies disqualification from benefit, or treating someone as not having limited capability for work, for a period not exceeding six weeks as sanctions in respect of conduct which conduces to a person's limited capability for work either by bringing it about through misconduct (subs.(1)(a)) or by remaining someone with limited capacity by failing without good cause to follow medical advice (subs.(1)(b)) or by failing without good cause to adhere to prescribed rules of behaviour (subs.(1)(c)). These subsections provide rule-making power for the regime of disqualification. The relevant regulations are the ESA Regs, regs 157–158. Note the protection from disqualification for a "person in hardship" (regs 157(3)(a), 158) and someone disqualified from receiving ESA because of regulations made pursuant to s.7 of the Social Security Fraud Act 2001 (reg.157(3)(b); for that section and the consequent Social Security (Loss of Benefit) Regs 2001, see Vol.III).

Although subs.(3) enables regs to be made dealing with aspects of the "good cause" issue (matters to take into or leave out of account; things which do or do not rank as "good cause"), no such regs have yet been made. "Good cause" thus remains a matter for the decision-maker or tribunal, circumscribed by case law on analogous provisions.

Subs. (4)

1A.53   This mandates for the ESA regime disqualification from CESA in respect of periods of absence from GB or of imprisonment or detention in legal custody. Exceptions from disqualification can be afforded by regs : see ESA Regs, regs 151–155 (temporary absence from GB), 160, 161 (imprisonment or detention in legal custody). Compare, with respect to incapacity benefit, SSCBA 1992, s.113.

Pilot schemes

19.—(1) Any regulations to which this subsection applies may be made so as to have effect for a specified period not exceeding 24 months.   1A.54

(2) Subject to subsection (3), subsection (1) applies to—

(a) regulations which are made under any provision of this Part, other than sections 3, 8 and 9;

(b) regulations which are made under the Administration Act, so far as they relate to an employment and support allowance.

(3) Subsection (1) only applies to regulations if they are made with a view to ascertaining whether their provisions will or will be likely to—

(a) encourage persons to obtain or remain in work, or

(b) make it more likely that persons will obtain or remain in work or be able to do so.

(4) Regulations which, by virtue of subsection (1), are to have effect for a limited period are referred to in this section as a "pilot scheme".

(5) A pilot scheme may provide that its provisions are to apply only in relation to—

(a) one or more specified areas;

(b) one or more specified classes of person;

(c) persons selected—

(i) by reference to prescribed criteria, or

(ii) on a sampling basis.

(6) A pilot scheme may make consequential or transitional provision with respect to the cessation of the scheme on the expiry of the specified period.

(7) A pilot scheme may be replaced by a further pilot scheme making the same or similar provision.

DEFINITIONS

"Administration Act"—s.65.
"prescribed"—s.24(1).
"regulations"—*ibid.*

GENERAL NOTE

This is modelled on s.29 of the Jobseekers Act, except that under subs.(1) pilot schemes are limited to 24, rather than 12, months; as in the case of JSA pilot schemes, they may be repeated (see subs.(7)). Any regulations under Pt 1 of the Act or associated rules under the Social Security Administration Act 1992 may be piloted, other than regulations concerning deductions from contributory ESA (s.3), limited capability for work (s.8) and limited capability for work-related activity (s.9). Regulations made under this section are subject to the affirmative resolution procedure (s.26(1)(c)).   1A.55

The power under s.29 of the Jobseekers Act has been used on a fairly regular basis to test in particular changes to "conditionality" and it seems likely that this will also be the case for ESA.

Relationship with statutory payments

1A.56   **20.**—(1) A person is not entitled to an employment and support allowance in respect of a day if, for the purposes of statutory sick pay, that day—

(a) is a day of incapacity for work in relation to a contract of service, and

(b) falls within a period of entitlement (whether or not it is a qualifying day).

(2) Except as regulations may provide, a woman who is entitled to statutory maternity pay is not entitled to a contributory allowance in respect of a day that falls within the maternity pay period.

(3) Regulations may provide that—

(a) an amount equal to a woman's statutory maternity pay for a period shall be deducted from a contributory allowance in respect of the same period,

(b) a woman shall only be entitled to a contributory allowance if there is a balance after the deduction, and

(c) if there is such a balance, a woman shall be entitled to a contributory allowance at a weekly rate equal to it.

(4) Except as regulations may provide, a person who is entitled to statutory adoption pay is not entitled to a contributory allowance in respect of a day that falls within the adoption pay period.

(5) Regulations may provide that—

(a) an amount equal to a person's statutory adoption pay for a period shall be deducted from a contributory allowance in respect of the same period,

(b) a person shall only be entitled to a contributory allowance if there is a balance after the deduction, and

(c) if there is such a balance, a person shall be entitled to a contributory allowance at a weekly rate equal to it.

(6) Except as regulations may provide, a person who is entitled to additional statutory paternity pay is not entitled to a contributory allowance in respect of a day that falls within the additional paternity pay period.

(7) Regulations may provide that—

(a) an amount equal to a person's additional statutory paternity pay for a period shall be deducted from a contributory allowance in respect of the same period,

(b) a person shall only be entitled to a contributory allowance if there is a balance after the deduction, and

(c) if there is such a balance, a person shall be entitled to a contributory allowance at a weekly rate equal to it.

(8) In this section—

"the additional paternity pay period" has the meaning given in section 171ZEE(2) of the Contributions and Benefits Act;

"the adoption pay period" has the meaning given in section 171ZN(2) of that Act;

"the maternity pay period" has the meaning given in section 165(1) of that Act.

"the additional paternity pay period"—see subs.(8).
"the adoption pay period"—see subs.(8).
"Contributions and Benefits Act"—see s.65.
"contributory allowance"—see s.1(7).
"entitled"—see s.24(1).
"the maternity pay period"—see subs.(8).

GENERAL NOTE

This deals with the relationship between ESA and certain other "employer paid" statutory payments, the overall responsibility for them lying with HMRC. The payments covered by this section are statutory sick pay (SSP), statutory maternity pay (SMP), statutory adoption pay (SAP) and additional statutory paternity pay (ASPP). They are dealt with in Vol.IV. The relationships are not all of a piece. ESA cannot be paid in respect of days for which there is SSP entitlement (subs.(1)). As regards SMP, SAP and ASPP, the interrelationship only concerns CESA. The general rule is that CESA cannot be payable at the same time as any of these other payments, but exceptions can be made by regulations (subss.(2)–(7)). The relevant regs are the ESA Regs, regs 80 (SMP), 81 (SAP) and 82 (ASPP). Where they operate to enable ESA to be paid, however, the amount of CESA payable is reduced by the amount of the relevant statutory payment, and only any balance of CESA remaining is payable.

1A.57

Deemed entitlement for other purposes

21.—Regulations may provide for a person who would be entitled to an employment and support allowance but for the operation of any provision of, or made under, this Part, the Administration Act or Chapter 2 of Part 1 of the Social Security Act 1998 (c. 14) (social security decisions and appeals) to be treated as if entitled to the allowance for the purposes of any rights or obligations (whether his own or another's) which depend on his entitlement, other than the right to payment of it.

1A.58

DEFINITIONS

"Administration Act"—see s.65.
"regulations"—see s.24(1).

GENERAL NOTE

This section is identical to SSCBA 1992, s.113(3). It enables regs to be made enabling someone to be treated as still entitled to ESA, though not to payment of it, even though provisions of or made under this Part of the WRA, the AA 1992 or SSA 1998, Pt I Ch.2 operate to disentitle him. The person will only be treated as entitled in this way to enable him or someone else to retain rights and obligations under social security law more generally.

1A.59

Supplementary provisions

22.—Schedule 2 (which contains further provisions in relation to an employment and support allowance) has effect.

1A.60

1A.61   This provides the basis for giving effect to the detailed provisions on ESA set out in Sch.2. These concern rule making in respect of: treating someone as having or not having limited capability for work/work-related activity (as the case may be), waiting days, linking periods, payments of benefit for less than a week, presence in GB, entitlement to CESA by persons not in GB, retained entitlement to IRESA after someone has left GB, modifying entitlement to CESA in respect of employment on ships, vessels, aircraft or hovercraft, the effect of work, treating ESA as "benefit", attribution of reductions where someone is entitled both to CESA and IRESA, ESA information to be treated as social security information, the making of advance claims, and modifying provisions in respect of ESA as regards Members of Her majesty's forces.

1A.62   **Recovery of sums in respect of maintenance**

23.—(1) Regulations may make provision for the court to have power to make a recovery order against any person where an award of income-related allowance has been made to that person's spouse or civil partner.

(2) The reference in subsection (1) to a recovery order is to an order requiring the person against whom it is made to make payments to the Secretary of State or to such other person or persons as the court may determine.

(3) Regulations under subsection (1) may include—

(a) provision as to the matters to which the court is, or is not, to have regard in determining any application under the regulations;

(b) provision as to the enforcement of orders under the regulations;

(c) provision for the transfer by the Secretary of State of the right to receive payments under, and to exercise rights in relation to, orders under the regulations.

(4) In this section, "the court" means—

(a) in relation to England and Wales, a magistrates' court;

(b) in relation to Scotland, the sheriff.

DEFINITIONS

"income-related allowance"—s.1(7).
"regulations"—s.24(1).

GENERAL NOTE

1A.63   This is similar to s.23 of the Jobseekers Act in relation to income-based JSA. For the powers in relation to income support see s.106 of the Administration Act.

General

Interpretation of Part 1

1A.64   **24.**—(1) In this Part—

"claimant" means a person who has claimed an employment and support allowance;

"contributory allowance" has the meaning given by section 1(7);

"employment" and "employed" have the meanings prescribed for the purposes of this Part;

"entitled", in relation to an employment and support allowance, is to be construed in accordance with—

  (a) the provisions of this Act,
  (b) section 1 of the Administration Act (entitlement dependent on making of claim), and
  (c) section 27 of the Social Security Act 1998 (c. 14) (restrictions on entitlement in certain cases of error);

"income-related allowance" has the meaning given by section 1(7);

"income support" means income support under section 124 of the Contributions and Benefits Act;

"limited capability for work" shall be construed in accordance with section 1(4);

"limited capability for work-related activity" shall be construed in accordance with section 2(5);

"period of limited capability for work" has the meaning prescribed for the purposes of this Part;

"prescribed" means specified in, or determined in accordance with, regulations;

"regulations" means regulations made by the Secretary of State;

"week" means a period of 7 days beginning with a Sunday or such other period of 7 days as may be prescribed;

"work-related activity" has the meaning given by section 13(7).

(2) For the purposes of this Part, the assessment phase, in relation to a claimant, is the period—

  (a) beginning, subject to subsection (3), with the first day of the period for which he is entitled to an employment and support allowance, and
  (b) ending with such day as may be prescribed.

(3) Regulations may prescribe circumstances in which the assessment phase is to begin with such day as may be prescribed.

(4) For the purposes of this Part, a person is a member of the support group if he is a person in respect of whom it is determined that he has, or is to be treated as having, limited capability for work-related activity.

DEFINITIONS

  "Administration Act"—see s.65.
  "Contributions and Benefits Act"—see s.65.

GENERAL NOTE

This defines, sometimes by referring the reader to other provisions or leaving **1A.65** the meaning to be set out in regulations, a number of key terms in respect of ESA. Note in particular that the "assessment phase", during which there can generally only be entitlement to basic allowance ESA, is generally to begin on the first such day of entitlement and to end in accordance with regulations (subss.(2), (3)). See on this ESA Regs, regs (4)–(7). Note also that membership of the support group, and thus eligibility for the more generous "support component" in addition to basic allowance ESA, is dependent on a determination that the person has, or is to be treated as having, limited capability for work-related activity (subs.(4)).

General

Regulations

1A.66   **25.**—(1) Any power under this Part to make regulations shall be exercisable by statutory instrument.

(2) Any such power may be exercised—

(a) in relation to all cases to which it extends,

(b) in relation to those cases subject to specified exceptions, or

(c) in relation to any specified cases or classes of case.

(3) Any such power may be exercised so as to make, as respects the cases in relation to which it is exercised—

(a) the full provision to which the power extends or any less provision (whether by way of exception or otherwise);

(b) the same provision for all cases in relation to which it is exercised, or different provision for different cases or different classes of case or different provision as respects the same case or class of case for different purposes of this Part;

(c) any such provision either unconditionally or subject to any specified condition.

(4) Where any such power is expressed to be exercisable for alternative purposes, it may be exercised in relation to the same case for all or any of those purposes.

(5) Any such power includes power—

(a) to make such incidental, supplementary, consequential or transitional provision or savings as appear to the Secretary of State to be expedient;

(b) to provide for a person to exercise a discretion in dealing with any matter.

(6) Without prejudice to the generality of the provisions of this section, regulations under any of sections 11 to 15 may make provision which applies only in relation to an area or areas specified in the regulations.

(7) The fact that a power to make regulations is conferred by this Part is not to be taken to prejudice the extent of any other power to make regulations so conferred.

GENERAL NOTE

1A.67   This section is similar to s.175 of the Contributions and Benefits Act and s.36 of the Jobseekers Act.

Parliamentary control

1A.68   **26.**—(1) None of the following regulations shall be made unless a draft of the statutory instrument containing them has been laid before, and approved by a resolution of, each House of Parliament—

44

(a) regulations under section 2(2)(c) or (3)(c) or 4(4)(c) or (5)(c);

(b) the first regulations under section 13;

(c) regulations which by virtue of section 19(1) are to have effect for a limited period.

(2) A statutory instrument that—

(a) contains regulations made under this Part, and

(b) is not subject to a requirement that a draft of the instrument be laid before, and approved by a resolution of, each House of Parliament, shall be subject to annulment in pursuance of a resolution of either House of Parliament.

GENERAL NOTE

This section is similar to s.176 of the Contributions and Benefits Act and s.37 **1A.68** of the Jobseekers Act.

Financial provisions relating to Part 1

27.—(1) There shall be paid out of the National Insurance Fund so **1A.69** much of any sums payable by way of employment and support allowance as is attributable to entitlement to a contributory allowance.

(2) There shall be paid out of money provided by Parliament—

(a) so much of any sums payable by way of employment and support allowance as is attributable to entitlement to an income-related allowance, and

(b) any administrative expenses of the Secretary of State or the Commissioners for Her Majesty's Revenue and Customs in carrying this Part into effect.

(3) The Secretary of State shall pay into the National Insurance Fund sums estimated by him to be equivalent in amount to sums recovered by him in connection with payments of contributory allowance.

(4) The Secretary of State shall pay into the Consolidated Fund sums estimated by him to be equivalent in amount to sums recovered by him in connection with payments made by way of income-related allowance.

DEFINITIONS

"contributory allowance"—ss.24(1) and 1(7).
"income-related allowance"—*ibid.*

GENERAL NOTE

This section is similar to s.163 of the Administration Act, s.38 of the Job- **1A.70** seekers Act and s.20 of the State Pension Credit Act.

Consequential amendments relating to Part 1

28.—(1) Schedule 3 (which makes amendments consequential on this **1A.71** Part) has effect.

(2) Regulations may make provision consequential on this Part amending, repealing or revoking any provision of—

(a) an Act passed on or before the last day of the Session in which this Act is passed, or

(b) an instrument made under an Act before the passing of this Act.

(3) In subsection (2), "Act" includes an Act of the Scottish Parliament.

DEFINITIONS

"Act"—see subs.(3).
"regulations"—see s.24(1).

GENERAL NOTE

Subs. (1)
1A.72   This gives effect to a range of consequential amendments of other Acts of Parliament set out in Sch.3. Where the provisions to be amended are contained in the main volumes of *Social Security Legislation 2008/09*, the amendments are noted at the appropriate point(s) in the updating Parts of this Supplement.

Subs. (2)
1A.73   This enables the making of consequential regulations amending Acts (including ones of the Scottish Parliament) passed on or before the last day of the 2006–07 Westminster parliamentary session (the one in which the WRA 2007 was passed) (para.(a), subs.(3)). It also enables consequential regulations to amend subordinate legislation, already made before the passing of the WRA 2007, under Acts (including those of the Scottish Parliament) (para.(b), subs.(3)).

Transition relating to Part 1

1A.74   **29.**—Schedule 4 (which makes provision with respect to transition in relation to this Part) has effect.

GENERAL NOTE

1A.75   This gives effect to Sch.4, reproduced in full with provisions not yet in force set out in italics. That Schedule embodies rule-making powers for pre- and post-commencement claims, awarding ESA in respect of a pre-commencement period , converting existing awards of IB/IS/SDA to ESA, the post-commencement up-rating of IB/SDA, and a general power to provide for transitional matters with respect to ESA. The regulations so made are the Employment and Support Allowance (Transitional Provisions) Regulations 2008 (SI 2008/795).

SECTIONS 30–64 OMITTED

PART 5

GENERAL

Northern Ireland

1A.76   **64.**—(1) This section applies to an Order in Council under paragraph 1(1) of the Schedule to the Northern Ireland Act 2000 (c. 1) (legislation for Northern Ireland during suspension of devolved government) which contains a statement that it is made only for purposes corresponding to those of this Act.

(2) Such an Order—

(a) is not subject to paragraph 2 of that Schedule (affirmative resolution of both Houses of Parliament), but

(b) is subject to annulment in pursuance of a resolution of either House of Parliament.

GENERAL NOTE

Part I of the WRA 2007 dealing with ESA applies only to Great Britain 1A.77 (England, Wales and Scotland). This is true of the social security system generally. But comparable provision in respect of social security for Northern Ireland is always made by Order in Council under its devolution Act. This section deals with parliamentary scrutiny and control over such an Order. It provides that any such Order, stated to be made only for purposes corresponding to those of the WRA 2007, is to be subject to annulment by either House of Parliament rather than to the affirmative resolution procedure that would otherwise be applicable.

General interpretation

65.—In this Act— 1A.78
"Administration Act" means the Social Security Administration Act 1992 (c. 5);
"Contributions and Benefits Act" means the Social Security Contributions and Benefits Act 1992 (c. 4).

Financial provisions: general

66.—(1) There shall be paid out of money provided by Parlia- 1A.79 ment—

(a) any expenditure incurred by the Secretary of State in consequence of Parts 2 to 4 of this Act, and

(b) any increase attributable to this Act in the sums payable out of money so provided under any other enactment.

(2) There shall be paid into the Consolidated Fund any increase attributable to this Act in the sums payable into that Fund under any other enactment.

Repeals

67.—The enactments specified in Schedule 8 are hereby repealed to 1A.80 the extent specified.

GENERAL NOTE

Insofar as this affects legislation in the main volumes, the changes are noted in 1A.81 the relevant updating Parts of this Supplement (II–V, as appropriate).

Section 68 omitted

Extent

69.—(1) Subject to the following provisions, this Act extends to Eng- 1A.82 land and Wales and Scotland only.

(2) The following provisions extend to England and Wales only—

(a) sections 42(1) to (10) and 43, and

(b) paragraphs 6, 11(2) and 16 of Schedule 3.

(3) Paragraphs 1, 2, 4, 11(3), 14 and 22 of Schedule 3 extend to Scotland only.

(4) The following provisions also extend to Northern Ireland—

(a) sections 33(7), 49, 56, 57, 61, 64, 65, 68, this section and sections 70 and 71,

(b) paragraph 15 of Schedule 2, and sections 22 and 24 to 26 so far as relating thereto,

(c) paragraphs 5, 10(1) and (28), 17(1) and (2), 19, 23(1) to (3) and (6) to (8) and 24 of Schedule 3, and section 28 so far as relating thereto,

(d) paragraph 1 of Schedule 7, and section 63 so far as relating thereto, and

(e) Schedule 8, so far as relating to the Vaccine Damage Payments Act 1979 (c. 17), the Income and Corporation Taxes Act 1988 (c. 1), the Disability (Grants) Act 1993 (c. 14), section 2 of the Social Security Act 1998 (c. 14) and the Income Tax (Earnings and Pensions) Act 2003 (c. 1), and section 67 so far as relating thereto.

(5) The following provisions extend to Northern Ireland only—

(a) section 45, and

(b) Schedule 8, so far as relating to the Social Security Administration (Northern Ireland) Act 1992 (c. 8), and section 67 so far as relating thereto.

(6) The following provisions also extend to the Isle of Man—

(a) sections 56 and 57, section 68, this section and sections 70 and 71,

(b) paragraph 1 of Schedule 7, and section 63 so far as relating thereto, and

(c) Schedule 8, so far as relating to the Vaccine Damage Payments Act 1979, and section 67 so far as relating thereto.

GENERAL NOTE

1A.83   Only subs.(1) concerns ESA. It means that the ESA scheme under Pt I of the Act applies only to England, Wales and Scotland. Comparable provision can be made for Northern Ireland through Order in Council under the devolution legislation (s.64). The devolution arrangements and the complicated political background in Northern Ireland may, however, mean that relevant legislation may have to be enacted by the Northern Ireland Assembly.

Commencement

1A.84   **70.**—(1) The following provisions shall come into force at the end of the period of 2 months beginning with the day on which this Act is passed—

(a) sections 41(2) and (3), 44, 45, 54, 55, 59, 61(1)(b) and (2) to (6) and 62,

(b) paragraphs 1 to 4, 10, 11 and 14 of Schedule 5, and section 40 so far as relating thereto,

(c) paragraphs 2(1) and (3), 3 and 4 of Schedule 7, and section 63 so far as relating thereto, and

(d) Schedule 8, so far as relating to—

   (i) section 3(5) of the Pneumoconiosis etc. (Workers' Compensation) Act 1979 (c. 41),

   (ii) section 140(1A) of the Contributions and Benefits Act,

   (iii) sections 71(5), 71ZA(2), 134(8)(a) and 168(3)(d) of the Administration Act,

   (iv) section 69(5) of the Social Security Administration (Northern Ireland) Act 1992,

   (v) Schedule 13 to the Local Government etc. (Scotland) Act 1994 (c. 39), (vi) section 38(7)(a) of, and paragraph 81(2) of Schedule 7 to, the Social Security Act 1998 (c. 14), and

   (vii) paragraph 65 of Schedule 24 to the Civil Partnership Act 2004 (c. 33), and section 67 so far as relating thereto.

(2) The remaining provisions of this Act, except—

(a) this section,

(b) sections 64, 65, 66, 68, 69 and 71, and

(c) paragraph 8 of Schedule 5, and section 40 so far as relating thereto,

shall come into force on such day as the Secretary of State may by order made by statutory instrument appoint, and different days may be so appointed for different purposes.

GENERAL NOTE

The key operative date for the ESA regime is October 27, 2008.   **1A.85**

Short title

71.—This Act may be cited as the Welfare Reform Act 2007.   **1A.86**

SCHEDULES

SCHEDULE 1   **Section 1**

EMPLOYMENT AND SUPPORT ALLOWANCE: ADDITIONAL CONDITIONS

PART 1 CONTRIBUTORY ALLOWANCE

Conditions relating to national insurance

1.—(1) The first condition is that—   **1A.87**

(a) the claimant has actually paid Class 1 or Class 2 contributions in respect of one of the last three complete tax years ("the base tax year") before the beginning of the relevant benefit year,

(b) those contributions must have been paid before the relevant benefit week, and

(c) the earnings factor derived as mentioned in sub-paragraph (2) must be not less than the base tax year's lower earnings limit multiplied by 25.

(2) The earnings factor referred to in sub-paragraph (1)(c) is the aggregate of the claimant's earnings factors derived—

(a) from so much of his earnings as did not exceed the base tax year's upper earnings limit and upon which primary Class 1 contributions have been paid or treated as paid, and

(b) from Class 2 contributions.

(3) Where primary Class 1 contributions have been paid or treated as paid on any part of a person's earnings, sub-paragraph (2)(a) shall have effect as if such contributions had been paid or treated as paid on so much of the earnings as did not exceed the base tax year's upper earnings limit.

(4) Regulations may—

(a) provide for the condition set out in sub-paragraph (1) to be taken to be satisfied in the case of persons who have been entitled to any prescribed description of benefit during any prescribed period or at any prescribed time;

(b) with a view to securing any relaxation of the requirements of that condition in relation to persons who have been so entitled, provide for that condition to apply in relation to them subject to prescribed modifications.

(5) In sub-paragraph (4), "benefit" means—

(a) any benefit within the meaning of section 122(1) of the Contributions and Benefits Act,

(b) any benefit under Parts 7 to 12 of that Act,

(c) credits under regulations under section 22(5) of that Act,

(d) a contributory allowance, and

(e) working tax credit.

1A.87   2.—(1) The second condition is that—

(a) the claimant has in respect of the last two complete tax years before the beginning of the relevant benefit year either paid or been credited with Class 1 or Class 2 contributions or been credited with earnings, and

(b) the earnings factor derived as mentioned in sub-paragraph (2) must be not less in each of those years than the year's lower earnings limit multiplied by 50.

(2) The earnings factor referred to in sub-paragraph (1)(b) is the aggregate of the claimant's earnings factors derived—

(a) from so much of his earnings as did not exceed the upper earnings limit for the year and upon which primary Class 1 contributions have been paid or treated as paid or from earnings credited, and

(b) from Class 2 contributions.

(3) Where primary Class 1 contributions have been paid or treated as paid on any part of a person's earnings, sub-paragraph (2)(a) shall have effect as if such contributions had been paid or treated as paid on so much of the earnings as did not exceed the upper earnings limit for the year.

1A.88   3.—(1) For the purposes of paragraphs 1 and 2—

(a) "benefit year" means a period which is a benefit year for the purposes of Part 2 of the Contributions and Benefits Act or such other period as may be prescribed for the purposes of this Part of this Schedule;

(b) "Class 1 contributions", "Class 2 contributions" and "primary Class 1 contributions" have the same meaning as in the Contributions and Benefits Act (see section 1 of that Act);

(c) "earnings" shall be construed in accordance with sections 3, 4 and 112 of that Act;

(d) "earnings factor" shall be construed in accordance with sections 22 and 23 of that Act;

(e) "lower earnings limit" and "upper earnings limit" shall be construed in accordance with section 5 of that Act and references to the lower or upper earnings limit of a tax year are to whatever is (or was) the limit in force for that year under that section;

(f) "relevant benefit year" is the benefit year which includes the beginning of the period of limited capability for work which includes the relevant benefit week;

(g) "tax year" means the 12 months beginning with 6th April in any year.

(2) Regulations may provide for sub-paragraph (1)(f) to have effect in prescribed circumstances with prescribed modifications in the case of—

(a) a person who has previously ceased to be entitled to a contributory allowance;

(b) a person who has made a claim for an employment and support allowance in connection with which he failed to satisfy one or both of the conditions in paragraphs 1 and 2.

Condition relating to youth

4.—(1) The third condition is that— 1A.89
(a) the claimant was under 20 or, in prescribed cases, 25 when the relevant period of limited capability for work began,
(b) he is not receiving full-time education,
(c) he satisfies such conditions as may be prescribed with respect to residence or presence in Great Britain (or both), and
(d) there has been a day in the relevant period of limited capability for work—
    (i) which was a day on which he was aged at least 16, and
    (ii) which was preceded by a period of 196 consecutive days throughout which he had limited capability for work.

(2) In sub-paragraph (1), "relevant period of limited capability for work" means the period of limited capability for work which includes the relevant benefit week.

(3) Regulations may prescribe circumstances in which sub-paragraph (1)(a) does not apply in the case of a person who has previously ceased to be entitled to an employment and support allowance to which he was entitled by virtue of satisfying the condition set out in sub-paragraph (1).

(4) Regulations may make provision about when, for the purposes of sub-paragraph (1)(b), a person is, or is not, to be treated as receiving full-time education.

"Relevant benefit week"

5.—In this Part of this Schedule, "relevant benefit week" means the week in relation to 1A.90
which the question of entitlement to an employment and support allowance is being considered.

DEFINITIONS

"the base tax year"—see para.1(1)(a).
"benefit"—see para.1(5).
"benefit year"—see para.3(1)(a).
"Class 1 contributions"—see para.3(1)(b).
"Class 2 contributions"—see para.3(1)(b).
"Contributions and Benefits Act"—see s.65.
"earnings"—see para.3(1)(c).
"earnings factor"—see para.3(1)(d).
"entitled"—see s.24(1).
"limited capability for work"—see s.1(4).
"lower earnings limit"—see para.3(1)(e).
"primary Class 1 contributions"—see para.3(1)(b).
"regulations"—see s.24(1).
"relevant benefit week"—see para.5.
"relevant benefit year"—see para.3(1)(f).
"relevant period of limited capability for work"—see para.4(2).
"tax year"—see para.3(1)(g).
"upper earnings limit"—see para.3(1)(e).
"week"—see s.24(1).

GENERAL NOTE

Paras (1)–(3)
CESA is principally a contributory or national insurance benefit. Entitlement 1A.91
to it generally requires the claimant to have an adequate contribution record. He must satisfy the first and second conditions set out in paras 1 and 2 (s.1(2)(a)), with respect to which paras 3 and 5 provide key definitions. Paragraph 3 also enables modifications to be effected by regs The contribution conditions, their application and modification essentially emulate those applicable to IB after April 2001. Compare SSCBA 1992, Sch.3, para.3. This annotation should be read in the light of those parts of the commentary to SSCBA 1992, Sch.3 dealing

with "Contributions matters: a division of responsibility" and "an outline of the contributory system: payments, credits and the earnings factor (the amount added to the contribution record)".

The national insurance conditions: Unless he is a person incapacitated in youth (before 20 or sometimes 25) (see s.30A(1)(b), (2A)) a claimant must satisfy both of the contribution conditions elaborated in paras 1 and 2. The first (para.1) can be met only by *paid* contributions of the relevant class (primary Class 1 or Class 2) reaching the requisite level in a specific tax year. The second can be satisfied by *paid and/or credited* contributions in both of two specific tax years. Like those applicable to IB since April 2001, the conditions thus require a more recent connection with the world of work in terms of paid contributions than had previously been the case, whether with incapacity benefit or its predecessors, sickness and invalidity benefits. However, the rigour of the first condition is relaxed in certain situations (paras 1(4), 3(2), ESA Regs, Pt IA, reg.8).

In order to appreciate the requirements of paras 1 and 2, and the terms and operation of the contribution conditions, take first, as an illustrative example, the position of someone claiming CESA for the very first time in November 2008 (that is, with no link back to any previous period of incapacity for work) and never having claimed or received any other benefit. He must meet *both of the two contribution conditions* set out in paras 1 and 2. The first step is to identify the relevant benefit year, the one which includes the first day of the period of limited capability for work of which his claim is part (para.3(1(f))). This identification of the relevant benefit year is the real substantive matter for the Secretary of State or the tribunal to focus on, since that determines the tax years in which the requisite record must be fulfilled. His first day of claim in the relevant benefit week (para.5, in November 2008 falls in benefit year 2008–2009 (the relevant benefit year: defined to refer to SSCBA 1992, s.21(6) and any modifying regulations made for the purposes of this Part of this Schedule (see para.3(1)(a))). The tax years in *one of which* the first contribution condition (sub-para.(2)) must be fulfilled are the last three tax years (April 6–April 5)(para.3(1)(g)) complete before the start of the relevant benefit year (early January 2008). The tax years to which to have regard are thus 2004/2005, 2005/2006, and 2006/2007. The contribution record in tax year 2007/2008 cannot be taken into account because it was not complete at the start of the relevant benefit year (early January 2008). The first contribution condition (para.1(1)) can only be met with paid contributions of the relevant class—Class 1 (employed earners) or Class 2 (self-employed earners)—reaching the requisite level (an earnings factor of 25 times the lower earnings limit (LEL) for Class 1 contributions purposes for the tax year in question—remember that each Class 2 contribution generates an earnings factor equal to the LEL pertinent to the tax/contribution year in question, while the amount of earnings on which Class 1 contributions are paid generates the earnings factor for an employed earner claimant. See further, the "outline of the contributory system" in the commentary to SSCBA 1992, Sch.3.

The second contribution condition (para.1(2)) requires examination of the last two tax years complete before the start of the relevant benefit year (early January 2008), that is 2005/2006 and 2006/2007. The claimant's contribution record in each of those tax/contribution years must attain 50 times the lower earnings limit for the year. But the condition can be met through paid and/or credited contributions (a Class 1 credit can be received, for example, for each week of unemployment; see further Social Security (Credits) Regulations 1975).

Note that para.1(4) enables regulations to provide for the first condition to be taken to be satisfied by certain benefit recipients and provide for it to apply in modified form. The relevant "relaxation" reg is ESA Regs, reg.8 and is the subject of commentary there. Note also that para.3(2) enables regulations to relax the rules on relevant benefit year. The product is ESA Regs, reg.13.

Various groups will have difficulty meeting the contribution conditions:

(a) *those who have never been employed:* The requirement in the first contribution condition for payment of contributions effectively excludes those who, whether through unemployment, incapacity or disability, have been unable to build a contribution record in terms of paid contributions.

(b) *some of the long-term unemployed:* (last employed in a tax year earlier than the first of the three on which the first contribution condition focuses).

(c) *very low-paid, probably part-time, employees:* those whose weekly or monthly earnings fall below the lower earnings limit for the whole or main part of the relevant tax years will not satisfy the contribution conditions since there is no liability or ability to pay Class 1 contributions where earnings fall below that limit, and, because they are in work, no Class 1 credits are generated from unemployment.

(d) *certain married women and widows paying reduced rate contributions*: these do not generate any earnings factor (and so do not count) for ESA purposes (para.3(d); SSCBA 1992, s.22(4)).

Para.4

Severe Disablement Allowance (SDA) was introduced in 1984 to cater for **1A.92** those who were incapacitated below the age of 20, or, if incapacitated later, were also assessed as 80 per cent disabled (see SSCBA 1992, ss.68, 69). SDA was abolished on April 6, 2001 for new claims, but non-contributory access was afforded to IB for persons incapacitated in youth (before 20 or sometimes 25). This paragraph affords the same facility in respect of CESA. Those incapacitated, even through severe disability, later in life, will have to look to IRESA, with its disability premiums, to underwrite their incapacity for work. They may well also be eligible for various components of disability living allowance. That is not an income replacement benefit, but is rather one designed to provide for the extra costs that disability, as opposed to incapacity for work, brings with it.

Non-contributory access to CESA: Condition relating to youth: This is the third condition referred to in s.1(2)(a). The provisions are similar to those brought into IB (SSCBA 1992, 30A(1)(b), (2A); IB Regulations 14–19) when the non-contributory incapacity benefit SDA was closed to new claimants from April 6, 2001. There is an immediate key difference, however, in that under the IB scheme the "person incapacitated in youth" route only opened if the person did not satisfy the contribution conditions (SSCBA 1992, s.30A(1)(b)), whereas with CESA there is no such pre-condition (WRA 2007, s.1(2)(a)).

To succeed by this "youth" route, all of a number of conditions must be fulfilled: (1) the claimant must be under 20 (or in some cases defined in regs, under 25) when the period of limited capability for work began (sub-para.(1)(a)); (2) he must not be receiving full-time education (sub-para.(1)(b)); (3) he must meet prescribed conditions with respect to residence and/or presence in GB (sub-para.(1)(c); ESA Regs, reg.11); and (4) in his period of limited capacity for work there must be a day on which he was at least 16 which was preceded by a period of 196 days throughout which he had limited capability for work (sub-para.(1)(d)).

The age condition in sub-para.(1)(a) is disapplied by ESA Regs, reg.10 in respect of certain claimants previously entitled to ESA as a person incapacitated in youth whose previous entitlement ended solely with a view to him taking up employment or training.

Note that regs can specify when someone is or is not to be treated as receiving full-time education (sub-para.(4)). The regulation in question is ESA Regs, reg.12.

PART 2

INCOME RELATED ALLOWANCE

1A.93   6.—(1) The conditions are that the claimant–
(a) has an income which does not exceed the applicable amount or has no income;
(b) does not have capital which, or a prescribed part of which, exceeds the prescribed amount;
(c) is not entitled to state pension credit;
(d) is not a member of a couple the other member of which is entitled to an income-related allowance, state pension credit, income support or an income-based job-seeker's allowance;
(e) is not engaged in remunerative work;
(f) is not a member of a couple the other member of which is engaged in remunerative work;
(g) is not receiving education.

(2) Where the claimant is a member of a couple, the income and capital of the other member of the couple shall, except in prescribed circumstances, be treated for the purpose of this paragraph as income and capital of the claimant.

(3) Regulations may prescribe circumstances in which, for the purposes of sub-paragraph (1)(e) and (f)—
(a) a person who is not engaged in remunerative work is to be treated as engaged in remunerative work; or
(b) a person who is engaged in remunerative work is to be treated as not engaged in remunerative work

(4) Regulations may—
(a) make provision about when, for the purposes of sub-paragraph (1)(g), a person is, or is not, to be treated as receiving education;
(b) prescribe circumstances in which sub-paragraph (1)(g) does not apply.

(5) In this paragraph—
"applicable amount" means the amount which, in the claimant's case, is the applicable amount for the purposes of section 4(1);
"couple" means—
  (a) a man and woman who are married to each other and are members of the same household;
  (b) a man and woman who are not married to each other, but are living together as husband and wife otherwise than in prescribed circumstances;
  (c) two people of the same sex who are civil partners of each other and are members of the same household; or
  (d) two people of the same sex who are not civil partners of each other, but are living together as if they were civil partners otherwise than in prescribed circumstances;
"education" has such meaning as may be prescribed;
"income-based jobseeker's allowance has the same meaning as in the Jobseekers Act 1995(c.18);
"remunerative work" has such meaning as may be prescribed.

(6) For the purposes of this paragraph, two people of the same sex are to be regarded as living together as if they were civil partners if, but only if, they would be regarded as living together as husband and wife were they instead two people of the opposite sex.

(7) Regulations may make provision for the preceding provisions of this paragraph to have effect with prescribed modifications in a case where—
(a) the claimant is a husband or wife by virtue of a marriage entered into under a law which permits polygamy,
(b) either party to the marriage has for the time being any spouse additional to the other party, and
(c) the claimant, the other party to the marriage and the additional spouse are members of the same household.

(8) Regulations may make provision for the purposes of this paragraph as to circumstances in which people are to be treated as being or not being members of the same household.

SCHEDULE 2

EMPLOYMENT AND SUPPORT ALLOWANCE: SUPPLEMENTARY PROVISIONS

Limited capability for work

1.—Regulations may make provision—   1A.94
(a) for a person to be treated in prescribed circumstances as having, or as not having, limited capability for work;
(b) for the question of whether a person has limited capability for work to be determined notwithstanding that he is for the time being treated by virtue of regulations under sub-paragraph (a) as having limited capability for work;
(c) for the question of whether a person has limited capability for work to be determined afresh in prescribed circumstances.

Waiting days

2.—Except in prescribed circumstances, a person is not entitled to an employment and   1A.95
support allowance in respect of a prescribed number of days at the beginning of a period of limited capability for work.

Periods of less than a week

3.—Regulations may make provision in relation to—   1A.96
(a) entitlement to an employment and support allowance, or
(b) the amount payable by way of such an allowance,
in respect of any period of less than a week.

Linking periods

4.—(1) Regulations may provide for circumstances in which a period of limited capa-   1A.97
bility for work which is separated from another period of limited capability for work by not more than a prescribed length of time is to be treated for the purposes of this Part as a continuation of the earlier period.

(2) Regulations may provide, in relation to periods which are linked by virtue of regulations under sub-paragraph (1), that a condition which was satisfied in relation to the earlier period is to be treated for the purposes of this Part as satisfied in relation to the later period.

Presence in Great Britain

5.—Regulations may make provision for the purposes of this Part as to the circumstances   1A.98
in which a person is to be treated as being, or not being, in Great Britain.

Contributory allowance: entitlement in case of absence from Great Britain

6.—Regulations may provide that in prescribed circumstances a claimant who is not in   1A.99
Great Britain may nevertheless be entitled to a contributory allowance.

Contributory allowance: modification in relation to employment on ships etc.

7.—(1) Regulations may modify any provision of this Part, so far as relating to a   1A.100
contributory allowance, in its application to any person who is, has been, or is to be—
(a) employed on board any ship, vessel, hovercraft or aircraft,
(b) outside Great Britain at any prescribed time or in any prescribed circumstances, or
(c) in prescribed employment in connection with continental shelf operations.
(2) Regulations under this paragraph may, in particular, provide—
(a) for any provision of this Part to apply even though it would not otherwise apply;
(b) for any such provision not to apply even though it would otherwise apply;
(c) for the taking of evidence, in a country or territory outside Great Britain, by a consular official or other prescribed person;
(d) for enabling the whole, or any part, of a contributory allowance to be paid to such of the claimant's dependants as may be prescribed.
(3) In this paragraph, "continental shelf operations" has the same meaning as in section 120 of the Contributions and Benefits Act.

Income-related allowance: entitlement in case of absence from Great Britain

1A.101   8.—(1) Regulations may provide that in prescribed circumstances a claimant who is entitled to an income-related allowance immediately before ceasing to be in Great Britain continues to be entitled to such an allowance after ceasing to be in Great Britain.

(2) Regulations may modify any provision of this Part, so far as relating to an income-related allowance, in its application to a person who is entitled to such an allowance by virtue of regulations under sub-paragraph (1).

(3) Regulations under sub-paragraph (2) may, in particular, provide—

(a) for any provision of this Part to apply even though it would not otherwise apply;

(b) for any such provision not to apply even though it would otherwise apply.

Limited capability for work-related activity

1A.102   9.—Regulations may make provision—

(a) for a person to be treated in prescribed circumstances as having, or as not having, limited capability for work-related activity;

(b) for the question of whether a person has limited capability for work-related activity to be determined notwithstanding that he is for the time being treated by virtue of regulations under sub-paragraph (a) as having limited capability for work-related activity;

(c) for the question of whether a person has limited capability for work-related activity to be determined afresh in prescribed circumstances.

Effect of work

1A.103   10.—Regulations may prescribe circumstances in which a person is to be treated as not entitled to an employment and support allowance because of his doing work.

Treatment of allowance as "benefit"

1A.104   11.—Regulations may provide for—

(a) an employment and support allowance,

(b) a contributory allowance, or

(c) an income-related allowance,

to be treated, for prescribed purposes of the Contributions and Benefits Act, as a benefit, or a benefit of a prescribed description.

Attribution of reductions in cases where allowance taken to consist of two elements

1A.105   12.—Where an employment and support allowance is taken by virtue of section 6(5) to consist of two elements, any reduction in the amount payable in respect of the allowance which falls to be made by virtue of—

(a) section 11,

(b) section 12,

(c) section 13, or

(d) section 2AA of the Administration Act (full entitlement to certain benefits conditional on work-focused interview for partner),

shall be treated as reducing such of those elements by such amount as may be prescribed.

Treatment of information supplied as information relating to social security

1A.106   13.—Information supplied in pursuance of regulations under any of sections 8, 9 and 11 to 13 shall be taken for all purposes to be information relating to social security.

Advance claims

1A.107   14.—This Part shall have effect with prescribed modifications in relation to cases where a claim to an employment and support allowance is by virtue of regulations under section 5(1)(c) of the Administration Act (advance claims) made, or treated as if made, for a period wholly or partly after the date on which it is made.

Members of the forces

1A.108   15.—(1) Regulations may modify—

(a) any provision of this Part, or

(b) any corresponding provision made for Northern Ireland,
in its application to persons who are or have been members of Her Majesty's forces.

(2) For the purposes of this paragraph, Her Majesty's forces shall be taken to consist of prescribed establishments and organisations in which persons serve under the control of the Defence Council.

DEFINITIONS   1A.109

"Administration Act"—see s.65.
"continental shelf operations"—see para.7(3).
"Contributions and Benefits Act"—see s.65.
"contributory allowance"—see s.1(7).
"employed"—see s.24(1).
"employment"—see s.24(1).
"entitled"—see s.24(1).
"Her Majesty's forces"—see para.15(2).
"income-related allowance"—see s.1(7).
"limited capability for work-related activity"—see s.2(5).
"period of limited capability for work"—see s.24(1).
"prescribed"—see s.24(1).
"regulations"—see s.24(1).
"week"—see s.24(1).
"work-related activity"—see ss.24(1), 13(7).

GENERAL NOTE

Para.2 (waiting days)
See ESA Regs, reg.144. The general rule, as with previous contributory   1A.110
incapacity benefit regimes, is that there is no entitlement to ESA in respect of the
first three "waiting days" at the beginning of a period of limited capability for
work. The general rule has a number of exceptions set out in reg.144(2):
terminally ill claimants; discharge from Her Majesty's forces where three or more
days of recorded sickness absence from duty preceded it; and where entitlement
to ESA begins within 12 weeks of entitlement to IS, SPC, JSA, carer's allowance
or SSP coming to an end. In addition, the general rule is, of course, affected by
the "linking rules" (on which see reg.145) in a case of intermittent incapacity
where those rules fuse into one ostensibly separate spells of limited capability for
work: the "waiting days" only have to be served once in a period of limited
capability for work.

Para.3 (periods of less than a week)
Like JSA, ESA is a weekly benefit, paid in respect of a week of limited   1A.111
capability for work. It is paid fortnightly in arrears, and the day of the week on
which payment is to be made is determined by reference to the last two digits of
the claimant's national insurance number (Claims and Payments Regs, reg.26C
(see updating material with respect to Vol.III). This para of Sch.2 enables regs to
make provision for payment in respect of periods of less than a week: see ESA
Regs, regs 165–169.

Para.4 (linking periods)
See ESA Regs, reg.145. The linking rules are crucial for those suffering from   1A.112
intermittent incapacity. They impact, to the claimant's benefit, as regards "waiting days"; those days of non-entitlement (see para.(2) and ESA Regs, reg.144)
only have to be served once in any period of limited capability for work. They are
also relevant to determining the relevant benefit year and hence the appropriate
tax years to which to have regard with respect to the application of the national

insurance contribution conditions (see further the commentary to Sch.1, Pt 1, paras 1–3).

Generally, the linking rule works on the basis that two ostensibly separate spells of limited capability for work will be fused into one where the separation period between the spells is not more than 12 weeks. This fusing does not, however, mean that days in the separation period thereby become ones of limited capability for work (*Chief Adjudication Officer v Astle* (Court of Appeal, judgment of March 17, 1999, available on LEXIS and noted in [1999] 6 J.S.S.L. 203). See further for more detail the commentary to SSCBA 1992, s.30C(1)(c) (the "linking" rule)). A period of limited capability for work can only be formed of days of actual limited capability for work and/or ones which the legislative scheme treats as ones of limited capability for work.

However, where a claimant is a "work or training beneficiary", the "linking period" is 104 weeks (See ESA Regs, reg.145(2)). It is also 104 weeks between spells of limited capability for work where a claimant, entitled to ESA, then went into qualifying remunerative work supported or (but for income) supportable by tax credits ("satisfies the relevant tax credit conditions"), and the period of limited capability for work in respect of which the claimant is now seeking ESA began on the day after he ceased that work (see ESA Regs, reg.145(3), (4)).

Para. 5 (presence in Great Britain)

1A.113   Entitlement to ESA generally requires presence in Great Britain (s.1(3)(d)). This paragraph enables regulations to treat someone, whatever the actual reality in terms of presence or absence, as being or not being in Great Britain. See ESA Regs, reg.11 (condition relating to youth—residence or presence).

Para. 6 (entitlement to CESA when absent from Great Britain)

1A.114   Entitlement to CESA generally requires presence in Great Britain (s.1(3)(d)). This para. enables regulations to give entitlement where the claimant is not in Great Britain. See ESA Regs, regs 151–155, dealing with periods of temporary absence. Note also that CESA is an exportable benefit for purposes of EC law.

Para. 7 (Modification of CESA for those employed on ships etc)

1A.115   This enables regulations to modify the rules on entitlement to CESA as regards those who are, have been or are to be, employed on any ship, vessel, hovercraft or aircraft; outside Great Britain; or in prescribed employment in connection with continental shelf operations. See the various amendments made with effect from October 27, 2008 by the Employment and Support Allowance (Consequential Provisions) (No.2) Regulations 2008 (SI 2008/1554), regs 65 and 67, respectively to the Social Security (Airmen's Benefits) Regulations 1975 (SI 1975/494), Social Security (Mariners' Benefits) Regulations 1975 (SI 1975/529).

Para. (8) (retaining entitlement to IRESA when absent from Great Britain)

1A.116   See ESA Regs, regs 151–155.

Para. 10 (effect of work)

1A.117   Unsurprisingly, in a benefits regime founded on limited capability for work, the general rule in respect of ESA is that the doing of any work negatives limited capability: see ESA Regs, reg.40, precluding entitlement to ESA in any week in which a claimant does work. But like the previous incapacity benefit regime, the general preclusive rule is modified to permit engagement in a range of work without loss of benefit. This recognizes that work can assist recovery or help the claimant into thinking about work and a possibility to return to work, or merely not wanting to exclude the sick and disabled from participation in civic office or a range of voluntary or charitable work. Under ESA, unlike its predecessor regime, the rules more fully protect through more generous earnings disregards those only in receipt of the income related form of the benefit as well as those receiving its contributory form. See ESA Regs, regs 41–46.

Para.12 (attribution of deductions from ESA)
A claimant may be entitled to CESA to IRESA or to both. Where someone is   **1A.118**
entitled to both IRESA and CESA, this para enables the making of regulations to provide for which component or components is or are to be reduced because of provisions enabling reduction set out in the specified provisions dealing with ESA conditionality (ss.11–13) or where, under SSAA 1992, s.2AA, entitlement depends on the claimant's partner complying with conditions in respect of work-focused interviews. See ESA Regs, reg.63. See also, in Vol.III, with respect to SSAA 1992, s.2AA, the Social Security (Jobcentre Plus Interviews for Partners) Regs 2003 (SI 2003/1886), reg.11, as amended with effect from October 27, 2008, by reg.71 of the Employment and Support Allowance (Consequential Provisions) (No.2) Regs 2008 (SI 2008/1554).

Para.14 (Advance claims)
See ESA Regs, reg.66.   **1A.119**

Para.15 (members of Her Majesty's forces)
This enables regulations to modify the rules on entitlement to ESA in respect   **1A.120**
of persons who are or have been members of those forces. See ESA Regs, regs 155 and Sch.1. See also the Social Security (Benefit) (Members of the Forces) Regs 1975 (S I 1975/493) as amended with effect from October 27, 2008 by reg.66 of the Employment and Support Allowance (Consequential Provisions) (No.2) Regs 2008 (SI 2008/1554).

SCHEDULE 3   **Section 28**

CONSEQUENTIAL AMENDMENTS RELATING TO PART 1

Insofar as the provisions in this Schedule amend legislation contained in the main   **1A.121**
volumes, these amendments are incorporated in the Updating Sections to the relevant volume (Parts II–V) of this Supplement

SCHEDULE 4   **Section 29**

TRANSITION RELATING TO PART 1

General power to provide for transition relating to Part 1

1.—(1) Regulations may make such provision as the Secretary of State considers neces-   **1A.121.1**
sary or expedient—
(a) in connection with the coming into force of any provision of, or repeal relating to, this Part, or
(b) otherwise for the purposes of, or in connection with, the transition to employment and support allowance.
(2) The following provisions of this Schedule are not to be taken as prejudicing the generality of sub-paragraph (1).

Pre-commencement claims

2.—Regulations may—   **1A.122**
(a) make provision for a claim for incapacity benefit, income support or severe disablement allowance which is made before the appointed day to be treated wholly or partly as a claim for an employment and support allowance;

(b) make provision for the purpose of enabling claims for an employment and support allowance to be made before the appointed day for a period beginning on or after that day.

Post-commencement claims

1A.123   **3.**—Regulations may—

(a) *make provision excluding the making of a claim for incapacity benefit or severe disablement allowance on or after the appointed day;*

(b) make provision for a claim for incapacity benefit, income support or severe disablement allowance which is made on or after the appointed day to be treated in prescribed circumstances as a claim for an employment and support allowance;

(c) make provision for a claim for an employment and support allowance to be treated wholly or partly as a claim for incapacity benefit, income support or severe disablement allowance;

(d) make provision excluding the making of a claim for an employment and support allowance by a person who is entitled to an existing award.

Award of employment and support allowance for pre-commencement period

1A.124   **4.**—*Regulations may—*

(a) *make provision for an employment and support allowance of such a kind as the regulations may provide to be awarded in prescribed circumstances for a period before the appointed day;*

(b) *make provision with respect to conditions of entitlement in relation to an award under sub-paragraph (a) and the amount payable by way of an allowance under such an award.*

Matching of awards of employment and support allowance

1A.125   **5.**—*(1) For the purposes of this paragraph, an award of an employment and support allowance is one that falls to be made on matching terms if—*

(a) *it is made in pursuance of a claim by a person who was previously entitled to an existing award, and*

(b) *had it continued to be possible to make an award of incapacity benefit, income support on grounds of incapacity for work, or severe disablement allowance, the award which would have been made to him ("the hypothetical award") would have been made on the basis of the linking of periods of incapacity for work.*

(2) Regulations may—

(a) *make provision for the purpose of securing that an award of an employment and support allowance that falls to be made on matching terms is made on terms which match in whole or part the hypothetical award;*

(b) *make provision for the modification of matched awards for the purpose of securing that the person with the award is put in the position he would have been had he been made the hypothetical award which was then the subject of conversion under paragraph 7.*

(3) In sub-paragraph (2)(b), the reference to matched awards is to awards of an employment and support allowance that have been the subject of matching in pursuance of regulations under sub-paragraph (2)(a).

1A.126   **6.**—*(1) For the purposes of this paragraph an award of an employment and support allowance is one which falls to be made on matching terms if—*

(a) *it is made in pursuance of a claim by a person who was previously entitled to an existing award,*

(b) *had he continued to be entitled to that award, it would have been the subject of conversion under paragraph 7 before the date of his claim for an employment and support allowance, and*

(c) *had it continued to be possible to make an award of incapacity benefit, income support on grounds of incapacity for work, or severe disablement allowance, the award which would have been made to him would have been made on the basis of the linking of periods of incapacity for work.*

(2) Regulations may make provision for the purpose of securing that an award of an employment and support allowance that falls to be made on matching terms is made on terms which match

in whole or part the award that would have resulted from conversion under paragraph 7 had entitlement to the existing award continued.

Treatment of existing awards

7.—*(1) Regulations may—*   **1A.127**
(a) make provision for converting existing awards into awards of an employment and support allowance, and with respect to the terms of conversion;
(b) make provision for the termination of existing awards in prescribed circumstances.
(2) Regulations under sub-paragraph (1)(a) may, in particular—
(a) make provision for conversion of an existing award—
  (i) on application, in accordance with the regulations, by the person entitled to the award, or
  (ii) without application;
(b) make provision about the conditions to be satisfied in relation to an application for conversion;
  I make provision about the timing of conversion;
(d) provide for an existing award to have effect after conversion as an award of an employment and support allowance—
  (i) of such a kind,
  (ii) for such period,
  (iii) of such an amount, and
  (iv) subject to such conditions,
  as the regulations may provide;
(e) make provision for determining in connection with conversion of an existing award whether a person has limited capability for work-related activity.
(3) Regulations under sub-paragraph (1)(a) may, in relation to existing awards which have been the subject of conversion under this paragraph, include provision about revision under section 9 of the Social Security Act 1998 (c. 14), or supersession under section 10 of that Act in respect of the period before conversion.

Transitional allowances

8.—*(1) Regulations may—*   **1A.128**
(a) make provision for a person's continuing entitlement to an employment and support allowance awarded by virtue of regulations under paragraph 7 (a "transitional allowance") to be determined by reference to such provision as may be made by the regulations;
(b) make provision for the review of an award of a transitional allowance;
(c) make provision for the termination of an award of a transitional allowance;
(d) make provision for this Part, or any other enactment relating to social security, to have effect with prescribed modifications in relation to a person with a transitional allowance;
(e) make provision for the purpose of enabling a transitional allowance to be revised under section 9 of the Social Security Act 1998 (c. 14) or superseded under section 10 of that Act.
(2) In this paragraph "enactment" includes an enactment contained in subordinate legislation (within the meaning of the Interpretation Act 1978 (c. 30)).

9.—*(1) Regulations may prescribe circumstances in which a person who is entitled to a*   **1A.129**
transitional allowance immediately before reaching pensionable age is to be treated as having satisfied the condition in paragraph 5(2) of Schedule 3 to the Contributions and Benefits Act (first contribution condition for entitlement to state pension).
(2) In this paragraph, "pensionable age" has the meaning given by the rules in paragraph 1 of Schedule 4 to the Pensions Act 1995 (c. 26).

Post-commencement up-rating of incapacity benefit and severe disablement allowance

10.—Regulations may provide for section 150 of the Administration Act (annual up-rat-   **1A.130**
ing of benefits), so far as relating to—
(a) incapacity benefit under section 30A of the Contributions and Benefits Act, or
(b) severe disablement allowance,
to have effect with prescribed modifications in relation to tax years beginning on or after the appointed day.

61

Interpretation

1A.131   **11.**—In this Schedule—

"appointed day" means the day appointed for the coming into force of section 1;

"existing award" means—

  (a) an award of incapacity benefit,

  (b) an award of severe disablement allowance, and

  (c) an award of income support made to a person to whom regulation 6(4)(a) or 13(2)(b) or (bb) of, or paragraph 7(a) or (b), 10, 12 or 13 of Schedule 1B to, the Income Support (General) Regulations 1987 (S.I. 1987/1967) (persons incapable of work or disabled) applies;

"incapacity benefit" (except in paragraph 10(a)) means—

  (a) incapacity benefit under section 30A, 40 or 41 of the Contributions and Benefits Act,

  (b) long-term incapacity benefit under regulation 11(4) of the Social Security (Incapacity Benefit) (Transitional) Regulations 1995 (S.I. 1995/310) (former sickness benefit), and

  (c) invalidity benefit which has effect by virtue of regulation 17(1) of those regulations as if it were long-term incapacity benefit;

"severe disablement allowance" means severe disablement allowance under section 68 of that Act (as it has effect by virtue of article 4 of the Welfare Reform and Pensions Act 1999 (Commencement No. 9, and Transitional and Savings Provisions) Order 2000 (S.I. 2000/2958) (C. 89));

"transitional allowance" has the meaning given by paragraph 8(1)(a).

DEFINITIONS

"Administration Act"—see s.65.

"appointed day"—see para.11.

"Contributions and Benefits Act"—see s.65.

"enactment"—see para.8(2).

"existing award"—see para.11.

"the hypothetical award"—see para.5(1)(b).

"incapacity benefit" (except in paragraph 10(a))—see para.11.

"income support"—see s.24(1).

"limited capability for work-related activity"—see s.2(5).

"pensionable age"—see para.9(2).

"prescribed"—see s.24(1).

"regulations"—see s.24(1).

"severe disablement allowance"—see para.11.

"transitional allowance"—see paras 11, 8(1)(a).

"work-related activity"—see ss.24(1), 13(7).

GENERAL NOTE

Provisions in italics were not yet in force as at January 23, 2009.

Paras 1–3

1A.132   See further the Employment and Support Allowance (Transitional Provisions) Regs 2008, regs 1–4 of which entered into force on July 27, 2008.

The Employment and Support Allowance Regulations 2008

(SI 2008/794) *(as amended)*

PART 1

GENERAL

1A.133

PART 2

THE ASSESSMENT PHASE

PART 3

CONDITIONS OF ENTITLEMENT—CONTRIBUTORY ALLOWANCE

PART 4

CONDITIONS OF ENTITLEMENT—INCOME-RELATED ALLOWANCE

PART 5

LIMITED CAPABILITY FOR WORK

PART 6

LIMITED CAPABILITY FOR WORK-RELATED ACTIVITY

PART 7

EFFECT OF WORK ON ENTITLEMENT TO AN EMPLOYMENT AND SUPPORT ALLOWANCE

PART 8

CONDITIONALITY

CHAPTER 1

WORK-FOCUSED HEALTH-RELATED ASSESSMENT

CHAPTER 2

WORK-FOCUSED INTERVIEWS

CHAPTER 3

REDUCTION OF EMPLOYMENT AND SUPPORT ALLOWANCE

CHAPTER 4

NOTIFICATION

CHAPTER 5

MODIFICATION OF THE ACT IN RELATION TO CLAIMS TO WHICH SECTION 5(1)(C) OF THE ADMINISTRATION ACT APPLIES

PART 9

AMOUNTS OF ALLOWANCE

CHAPTER 1

PRESCRIBED AMOUNTS

CHAPTER 2

DEDUCTIONS FROM THE CONTRIBUTORY ALLOWANCE

CHAPTER 3

STATUTORY PAYMENTS

PART 10

INCOME AND CAPITAL

CHAPTER 1

GENERAL

CHAPTER 2

INCOME

CHAPTER 7

CAPITAL

CHAPTER 8

LIABLE RELATIVES

CHAPTER 9

CHILD SUPPORT

CHAPTER 10

STUDENTS

PART 11

SUPPLEMENTARY PROVISIONS

CHAPTER 1

MISCELLANEOUS

CHAPTER 2

WORK OR TRAINING BENEFICIARIES

CHAPTER 3

TEMPORARY ABSENCE FROM GREAT BRITAIN

Chapter 4

Membership of household

Part 12

Disqualification

Part 13

Urgent Cases

Part 14

Periods of Less than a Week

SCHEDULE 1   1A.134

Her Majesty's Forces

Part 1

Prescribed Establishments and Organisations

SCHEDULE 9

CAPITAL TO BE DISREGARDED

The Secretary of State for Work and Pensions, in exercise of the powers conferred by sections 2(1)(a) and (c), (4)(a) and (c), 3(1)(c), (2)(b) and (d) and (3)(1), 4(2)(a), (3), (6)(a) and (c), 5(2) and (3), 8(1) to (3), (4)(a) and (b), (5) and (6), 9(1) to (3) and (4)(a) and (b), 11(1), (2)(a) to (g), (3) to (5), (6)(a) and (7)(c), 12(1), (2)(a) to (h), (3) to (7), 14(1) and (2)(a) and (b), 16(2)(a) and (4), 17, 18(1), (2) and (4), 20(2) to (7), 22(2), 23(1) and (3), 24(1)(3), (2)(b) and (3), 25(1) to (5) and 26(2) of, and paragraphs 1(4), 3(2), 4(1)(a) and (c), (3) and (4) and 6(1)(b), (2) to (5)(4), (7) and (8) of Schedule 1 to, and paragraphs 1 to 7, 8(1), 9, 10, 12 and 14 of Schedule 2 to, the Welfare Reform Act 2007, section 5(1) of the Social Security Administration Act 1992 and section 21(1)(a) of the Social Security Act 1998(7) makes the following Regulations, which are made by virtue of, or consequential on, the provisions of the Welfare Reform Act 2007 and which are made before the end of a period of 6 months beginning with the coming into force of those provisions:

PART 1

GENERAL

Citation and commencement

1. These Regulations may be cited as the Employment and Support Allowance Regulations 2008 and shall come into force—   1A.135

(a) subject to paragraphs (b) and (c), on 27th October 2008;

(b) in relation to regulation 128(6)(a) and paragraph 15(2) of Schedule 6, so far as it applies to a maintenance calculation, in relation to a particular case, on the day on which paragraph 11(20)(d) of Schedule 3 to the 2000 Act comes into force for the purposes of that type of case;

(c) in relation to regulation 82 and paragraph 4 of Schedule 8, so far as it applies to additional statutory paternity pay, on the day on which regulations made under or by virtue of sections 171ZEA to 171ZEE of the Contributions and Benefits Act come into force.

Interpretation

2.—(1) In these Regulations—   1A.136

"Abbeyfield Home" means an establishment run by the Abbeyfield Society including any body corporate or incorporate which is affiliated to that Society;

"the Act" means the Welfare Reform Act 2007;

"action plan" has the meaning given by regulation 58;

"adoption leave" means a period of absence from work on ordinary or additional adoption leave under section 75A or 75B of the Employment Rights Act 1996;

"aircraft worker" means a person who is, or has been, employed under a contract of service either as a pilot, commander, navigator or other member of the crew of any aircraft, or in any other capacity on board any aircraft where—

    (a) the employment in that other capacity is for the purposes of the aircraft or its crew or of any passengers or cargo or mail carried on that aircraft; and

    (b) the contract is entered into in the United Kingdom with a view to its performance (in whole or in part) while the aircraft is in flight, but does not include a person who is in employment as a member of Her Majesty's forces;

"Armed Forces and Reserve Forces Compensation Scheme" means the scheme established under section 1(2) of the Armed Forces (Pensions and Compensation) Act 2004;

"attendance allowance" means—

    (a) an attendance allowance under section 64 of the Contributions and Benefits Act;

    (b) an increase of disablement pension under section 104 or 105 of that Act;

    (c) a payment under regulations made under section 111 of, and paragraph 7(2)(b) of Schedule 8 to, that Act;

    (d) an increase in allowance which is payable in respect of constant attendance under section 111 of, and paragraph 4 of Schedule 8 to, that Act;

    (e) a payment by virtue of article 14, 15, 16, 43 or 44 of the Personal Injuries (Civilians) Scheme 1983 or any analogous payment;

    (f) any payment based on the need for attendance which is paid as an addition to a war disablement pension;

[¹ "basic rate" has the same meaning as in the Income Tax Act 2007 (see section 989 of that Act);]

"benefit Acts" means the Contributions and Benefits Act, Jobseekers Act and Part 1 of the Act;

"benefit week" means a period of 7 days ending on such day as the Secretary of State may direct but for the purposes of calculating any payment of income "benefit week" means the period of 7 days ending on the day before the first day of the first benefit week following the date of claim or the last day on which an employment and support allowance is paid if it is in payment for less than a week;

"board and lodging" means—

    (a) accommodation provided to a person or, if the person is a member of a family, to that person or any other member of that person's family, for a charge which is inclusive of the provision of that accommodation and at least some cooked or prepared meals which both are cooked or prepared (by a person other than the person to whom the accommodation is provided or a member of that person's family) and are consumed in that accommodation or associated premises; or

    (b) accommodation provided to a person in a hotel, guest house, lodging house or some similar establishment, except accommodation provided by a close relative of the person or any other member of the person's family, or other than on a commercial basis;

"care home" in England and Wales has the meaning assigned to it by section 3 of the Care Standards Act 2000, and in Scotland means a care home service within the meaning assigned to it by section 2(3) of the Regulation of Care (Scotland) Act 2001;

"carer's allowance" means an allowance under section 70 of the Contributions and Benefits Act;

"child" means a person under the age of 16;

"child tax credit" means a child tax credit under section 8 of the Tax Credits Act;

"close relative" means a parent, parent-in-law, son, son-in-law, daughter, daughter-in-law, step-parent, step-son, step-daughter, brother, sister, or if any of the preceding persons is one member of a couple, the other member of that couple;

"college of further education" means a college of further education within the meaning of Part 1 of the Further and Higher Education (Scotland) Act 1992;

"concessionary payment" means a payment made under arrangements made by the Secretary of State with the consent of the Treasury which is charged either to the National Insurance Fund or to a Departmental Expenditure Vote to which payments of benefit or tax credits under the benefit Acts or the Tax Credits Act are charged;

"confinement" has the meaning given to it by section 171(1) of the Contributions and Benefits Act;

"co-ownership scheme" means a scheme under which a dwelling is let by a housing association and the tenant, or the tenant's personal representative, will, under the terms of the tenancy agreement or of the agreement under which the tenant became a member of the association, be entitled, on that tenant ceasing to be a member and subject to any condition stated in either agreement, to a sum calculated by reference directly or indirectly to the value of the dwelling and "co-ownership agreement" will be construed accordingly;

"councillor" means—

(a) in relation to England and Wales, a member of a London borough council, a county council, a district council, a parish or community council, the Common Council of the City of London or the Council of the Isles of Scilly; and

(b) in relation to Scotland, a member of a council constituted under section 2 of the Local Government etc. (Scotland) Act 1994;

"councillor's allowance" means—

(a) in England or Wales, an allowance under or by virtue of—

(i) section 173 or 177 of the Local Government Act 1972; or

(ii) a scheme made by virtue of section 18 of the Local Government and Housing Act 1989, other than such an allowance as is mentioned in section 173(4) of the Local Government Act 1972; or

(b) in Scotland, an allowance or remuneration under or by virtue of—

    (i) a scheme made by virtue of section 18 of the Local Government and Housing Act 1989; or

    (ii) sections 11 and 16 of the Local Governance (Scotland) Act 2004;

"couple" means—

(a) a man and woman who are married to each other and are members of the same household;

(b) a man and woman who are not married to each other but are living together as husband and wife;

(c) two people of the same sex who are civil partners of each other and are members of the same household; or

(d) two people of the same sex who are not civil partners of each other but are living together as if they were civil partners, and for the purposes of paragraph (d), two people of the same sex are to be regarded as living together as if they were civil partners if, but only if, they would be regarded as living together as husband and wife were they instead two people of the opposite sex;

"Crown tenant" means a person who occupies a dwelling under a tenancy or licence where the interest of the landlord belongs to Her Majesty in right of the Crown or to a government department or is held in trust for Her Majesty for the purposes of a government department, except (in the case of an interest belonging to Her Majesty in right of the Crown) where the interest is under the management of the Crown Estate Commissioners;

"dependent child" means any child or qualifying young person who is treated as the responsibility of the claimant or the claimant's partner, where that child or young person is a member of the claimant's household;

"descriptor" means, in relation to an activity specified in column (1) of Schedule 2, a descriptor in column (2) of that Schedule which describes a person's ability to perform that activity;

"disability living allowance" means a disability living allowance under section 71 of the Contributions and Benefits Act;

"doctor" means a registered medical practitioner, or in the case of a medical practitioner practising outside the United Kingdom of whom the Secretary of State may request a medical opinion, a person registered or recognised as such in the country in which the person undertakes medical practice;

"dwelling" means any residential accommodation, whether or not consisting of the whole or part of a building and whether or not comprising separate and self-contained premises;

"dwelling occupied as the home" means the dwelling together with any garage, garden and outbuildings, normally occupied by the claimant as the claimant's home including any premises not so occupied which it is impracticable or unreasonable to sell separately, in particular, in Scotland, any croft land on which the dwelling is situated;

"Eileen Trust" means the charitable trust of that name established on 29th March 1993 out of funds provided by the Secretary of State for the benefit of persons eligible for payment in accordance with its provisions;

"employed earner" is to be construed in accordance with section 2(1)(a) of the Contributions and Benefits Act;

"employment" includes any trade, business, profession, office or vocation and "employed" has a corresponding meaning;

"employment zone" means an area within Great Britain designated for the purposes of section 60 of the Welfare Reform and Pensions Act 1999 and an "employment zone programme" means a programme established for such an area or areas designed to assist claimants for a jobseeker's allowance to obtain sustainable employment;

"enactment" includes an enactment comprised in, or in an instrument made under—

(a) an Act; or

(b) an Act of the Scottish Parliament;

"failure determination" has the meaning given by regulation 63(1);

"family" means—

(a) a couple;

(b) a couple and a member of the same household for whom one of them is or both are responsible and who is a child or a young person;

(c) a person who is not a member of a couple and a member of the same household for whom that person is responsible and who is a child or a young person;

"first contribution condition" means the condition set out in paragraph 1(1) of Schedule 1 to the Act;

"full-time student" has the meaning prescribed in regulation 131 (students: interpretation);

"the Fund" means monies made available from time to time by the Secretary of State for the benefit of persons eligible for payment in accordance with the provisions of a scheme established by the Secretary of State on 24th April 1992 or, in Scotland, on 10th April 1992;

"guaranteed income payment" means a payment made under article 14(1)(b) or 21(1)(a) of the Armed Forces and Reserve Forces (Compensation Scheme) Order 2005;

"health care professional" means—

(a) a registered medical practitioner;

(b) a registered nurse; or

(c) an occupational therapist or physiotherapist registered with a regulatory body established by an Order in Council under section 60 of the Health Act 1999;

"Health Service Act" means the National Health Service Act 2006;

"Health Service (Wales) Act" means the National Health Service (Wales) Act 2006;

"housing association" has the meaning given to it by section 1(1) of the Housing Associations Act 1985;

"housing benefit expenditure" means expenditure in respect of which housing benefit is payable as specified in regulation 12(1) of the Housing Benefit Regulations 2006 but does not include any such expenditure in respect of which an additional amount is applicable under regulation 67(1)(c) or 68(1)(d)(housing costs);

"Immigration and Asylum Act" means the Immigration and Asylum Act 1999;

"income-related benefits" means the benefits listed in section 123(1) of the Contributions and Benefits Act;

"Income Support Regulations" means the Income Support (General) Regulations 1987;

"independent hospital" in England and Wales has the meaning assigned to it by section 2 of the Care Standards Act 2000, and in Scotland means an independent healthcare service as defined in section 2(5)(a) and (b) of the Regulation of Care (Scotland) Act 2001;

[¹ . . .]

"the Independent Living Fund (2006)" means the Trust of that name established by a deed dated 10th April 2006 and made between the Secretary of State for Work and Pensions of the one part and Margaret Rosemary Cooper, Michael Beresford Boyall and Marie Theresa Martin of the other part;

[¹ . . .]

"Jobseekers Act" means the Jobseekers Act 1995;

"Jobseeker's Allowance Regulations" means the Jobseeker's Allowance Regulations 1996;

"last day of the course" means the last day of the final academic term of the course in which the student is enrolled;

"limited capability for work assessment" means the assessment of whether a person has limited capability for work as set out in regulation 19(2) and in Schedule 2;

"London Bombings Relief Charitable Fund" means the company limited by guarantee (number 5505072) and registered charity of that name established on 11th July 2005 for the purpose of (amongst other things) relieving sickness, disability or financial need of victims (including families or dependants of victims) of the terrorist attacks carried out in London on 7th July 2005;

"lone parent" means a person who has no partner and who is responsible for, and a member of the same household as, a child or young person;

"long tenancy" means a tenancy granted for a term of years certain exceeding twenty one years, whether or not the tenancy is, or may become, terminable before the end of that term by notice given by or to the tenant or by re-entry, forfeiture (or, in Scotland, irritancy) or otherwise and includes a lease for a term fixed by law under a grant with a covenant or obligation for perpetual renewal

unless it is a lease by sub-demise from one which is not a long
tenancy;

"Macfarlane (Special Payments) Trust" means the trust of that name,
established on 29th January 1990 partly out of funds provided by
the Secretary of State, for the benefit of certain persons suffering
from haemophilia;

"Macfarlane (Special Payments) (No. 2) Trust" means the trust of
that name, established on 3rd May 1991 partly out of funds
provided by the Secretary of State, for the benefit of certain
persons suffering from haemophilia and other beneficiaries;

"Macfarlane Trust" means the charitable trust, established partly out
of funds provided by the Secretary of State to the Haemophilia
Society, for the relief of poverty or distress among those suffering
from haemophilia;

"main phase employment and support allowance" means an employment and support allowance where the calculation of the amount
payable in respect of the claimant includes a component under
section 2(1)(b) or 4(2)(b) of the Act;

"mariner" means a person who is or has been in employment under a
contract of service either as a master or member of the crew of any
ship or vessel, or in any other capacity on board any ship or vessel
where—

   (a) the employment in that other capacity is for the purposes of
that ship or vessel or her crew or any passengers or cargo or
mails carried by the ship or vessel; and

   (b) the contract is entered into in the United Kingdom with a
view to its performance (in whole or in part) while the ship
or vessel is on her voyage; but does not include a person
who is in employment as a member of Her Majesty's
forces;

"maternity allowance period" has the meaning it has in section 35(2)
of the Contributions and Benefits Act;

"medical evidence" means—

   (a) evidence from a health care professional approved by the
Secretary of State; and

   (b) evidence (if any) from any health care professional or a
hospital or similar institution, or such part of such evidence
as constitutes the most reliable evidence available in the
circumstances;

"Medical Evidence Regulations" means the Social Security (Medical
Evidence) Regulations 1976;

"medical examination centre" means premises which are equipped
and suitable for conducting a medical examination;

"medical treatment" means medical, surgical or rehabilitative treatment (including any course or diet or other regimen), and references to a person receiving or submitting to medical treatment are
to be construed accordingly;

"member of Her Majesty's forces" means a person, other than one
mentioned in Part 2 of Schedule 1 who is—

   (a) over 16 years of age; and

(b) a member of an establishment or organisation specified in Part 1 of that Schedule who gives full pay service, but does not include any such person while absent on desertion;

"mobility supplement" means any supplement under article 20 of the Naval, Military and Air Forces Etc. (Disablement and Death) Service Pensions Order 2006 including such a supplement by virtue of any other scheme or order or under article 25A of the Personal Injuries (Civilians) Scheme 1983;

"net earnings" means such earnings as are calculated in accordance with regulation 96;

"net profit" means such profit as is calculated in accordance with regulation 98;

"New Deal options" means the employment programmes specified in regulation 75(1)(a)(ii) of the Jobseeker's Allowance Regulations and the training scheme specified in regulation 75(1)(b)(ii) of those Regulations;

"non-dependant" has the meaning prescribed in regulation 71;

"non-dependant deduction" means a deduction that is to be made under regulation 67(1)(c) (prescribed amounts) and paragraph 19 of Schedule 6 (housing costs);

"occupational pension" means any pension or other periodical payment under an occupational pension scheme but does not include any discretionary payment out of a fund established for relieving hardship in particular cases;

"occupational pension scheme" has the meaning given by section 1 of the Pension Schemes Act 1993;

"ordinary clothing or footwear" means clothing or footwear for normal daily use, but does not include school uniforms, or clothing or footwear used solely for sporting activities;

"partner" means where a claimant—

(a) is a member of a couple, the other member of that couple;

(b) is a husband or wife by virtue of a polygamous marriage, the other party to the marriage or any spouse additional to either party to the marriage;

"passenger" means any person carried on a ship except—

(a) a person employed or engaged in any capacity on board the ship on the business of the ship; or

(b) a person on board the ship either in pursuance of the obligation to carry shipwrecked, distressed or other persons, or by reason of any circumstance that neither the master nor the owner nor the charterer (if any) could have prevented or forestalled;

"payment" includes a part of a payment;

"pay period" means the period in respect of which a claimant is, or expects to be, normally paid by the claimant's employer, being a week, a fortnight, four weeks, a month or other shorter or longer period as the case may be;

"pension fund holder" means in relation to a personal pension scheme or an occupational pension scheme, the trustees, managers or scheme administrators, as the case may be, of the scheme concerned;

"pensionable age" has the meaning given by the rules in paragraph 1 of Schedule 4 to the Pensions Act 1995;

"period of limited capability for work" means a period throughout which a person has, or is treated as having, limited capability for work;

"period of study" means the period beginning with the date on which a person starts attending or undertaking a course of study and ending with the last day of the course or such earlier date (if any) as that person finally abandons it or is dismissed from it;

"personal pension scheme" means—

(a) a personal pension scheme as defined by section 1 of the Pension Schemes Act 1993;

(b) an annuity contract or trust scheme approved under section 620 or 621 of the Income and Corporation Taxes Act 1988 or a substituted contract within the meaning of section 622(3) of that Act which is treated as having become a registered pension scheme by virtue of paragraph 1(1)(f) of Schedule 36 to the Finance Act 2004;

(c) a personal pension scheme approved under Chapter 4 of Part 14 of the Income and Corporation Taxes Act 1988 which is treated as having become a registered pension scheme by virtue of paragraph 1(1)(g) of Schedule 36 to the Finance Act 2004;

"policy of life insurance" means any instrument by which the payment of money is assured on death (except death by accident only) or the happening of any contingency dependent on human life, or any instrument evidencing a contract which is subject to payment of premiums for a term dependent on human life;

"polygamous marriage" means any marriage entered into under a law which permits polygamy where—

(a) either party has for the time being any spouse additional to the other party; and

(b) the claimant, the other party to the marriage and the additional spouse are members of the same household;

"qualifying person" means a person in respect of whom payment has been made from the Fund, the Eileen Trust, the Skipton Fund or the London Bombings Relief Charitable Fund;

"qualifying remunerative work" has the meaning given by Part 1 of the Tax Credits Act;

"qualifying young person" has the meaning given by section 142 of the Contributions and Benefits Act (child and qualifying young person);

"relative" means close relative, grand-parent, grand-child, uncle, aunt, nephew or niece;

"relevant disease" means—

(a) in England and Wales, any disease, food poisoning, infection, infectious disease or notifiable disease—

(i) to which section 20(1) of the Public Health (Control of Disease) Act 1984 (stopping of work to prevent spread of disease) applies;

(ii) to which—

  (aa) regulation 3 (public health enactments applied to certain diseases) of, and Schedule 1 to,

  (bb) regulation 9(1) (provisions for preventing the spread of typhus and relapsing fever) of, and Schedule 3 to, or

  (cc) regulation 9(2) (provisions for preventing the spread of food poisoning and food borne infections) of, and Schedule 4 to, the Public Health (Infectious Diseases) Regulations 1988 apply;

(iii) to which regulation 9 (powers in respect of persons leaving aircraft) of the Public Health (Aircraft) Regulations 1979 applies; or

(iv) to which regulation 10 (powers in respect of certain persons on ships) of the Public Health (Ships) Regulations 1979 applies; and

(b) in Scotland, any food poisoning or infectious disease—

(i) to which section 71(1) of the Health Services and Public Health Act 1968 (compensation for stopping employment to prevent spread of disease in Scotland) applies; or

(ii) to which—

  (aa) regulations 8 and 9 (examination, etc. of persons on aircraft and powers in respect of persons leaving aircraft) of the Public Health (Aircraft) (Scotland) Regulations 1971; or

  (bb) regulations 9 and 10 (examination, etc. of persons on ships and powers in respect of certain persons on ships) of the Public Health (Ships) (Scotland) Regulations 1971, apply;

"relevant enactment" means the Army Act 1955, the Air Force Act 1955, the Naval Discipline Act 1957, the Matrimonial Proceedings Children Act 1958, the Social Work (Scotland) Act 1968, the Family Law Reform Act 1969, the Children and Young Persons Act 1969, the Matrimonial Causes Act 1973, the Domestic Proceedings and Magistrates' Courts Act 1978, the Adoption (Scotland) Act 1978, the Family Law Act 1986, the Children Act 1989 and the Adoption and Children Act 2002;

"remunerative work" has the meaning prescribed in regulations 41 and 42 except in relation to Schedules 6 and 7;

"second contribution condition" means the condition set out in paragraph 2(1) of Schedule 1 to the Act;

"self-employed earner" is to be construed in accordance with section 2(1)(b) of the Contributions and Benefits Act;

"self-employment route" means assistance in pursuing self-employed earner's employment whilst participating in—

(a) an employment zone programme; or

    (b) a programme provided or other arrangements made under section 2 of the Employment and Training Act 1973 (functions of the Secretary of State) or section 2 of the Enterprise and New Towns (Scotland) Act 1990 (functions in relation to training for employment etc.);

"single claimant" means a claimant who neither has a partner nor is a lone parent;

"Skipton Fund" means the ex-gratia payment scheme administered by the Skipton Fund Limited, incorporated on 25th March 2004, for the benefit of certain persons suffering from hepatitis C and other persons eligible for payment in accordance with the scheme's provisions;

"sports award" means an award made by one of the Sports Councils named in section 23(2) of the National Lottery etc. Act 1993 out of sums allocated to it for distribution under that section;

[¹ . . .]

[¹ "state pension credit" means a state pension credit under the State Pension Credit Act 2002;]

"subsistence allowance" means an allowance which an employment zone contractor has agreed to pay to a person who is participating in an employment zone programme;

"the Tax Credits Act" means the Tax Credits Act 2002;

"terminally ill", in relation to a claimant, means the claimant is suffering from a progressive disease and death in consequence of that disease can reasonably be expected within 6 months;

"training" means—

    (a) training in pursuance of arrangements made under section 2(1) of the Employment and Training Act 1973 or section 2(3) of the Enterprise and New Towns (Scotland) Act 1990; or

    (b) any training received on a course which a person attends for 16 hours or more a week, the primary purpose of which is the teaching of occupational or vocational skills;

"training allowance" means an allowance (whether by way of periodical grants or otherwise) payable—

    (a) out of public funds by a Government department or by or on behalf of the Secretary of State for Work and Pensions, Scottish Enterprise or Highlands and Islands Enterprise, the Learning and Skills Council for England or the Welsh Ministers;

    (b) to a person for that person's maintenance or in respect of a member of that person's family; and

    (c) for the period, or part of the period, during which the person is following a course of training or instruction provided by, or in pursuance of arrangements made with, that department or approved by that department in relation to that person or so provided or approved by or on behalf of the Secretary of State for Work and Pensions, Scottish Enterprise or Highlands and Islands Enterprise, or the Welsh Ministers, but does not include an allowance paid by any Government department to or in respect of a person by reason of the fact that that person is following a course of full-time education, other than under arrangements made under section 2 of the Employment and Training Act 1973 or section 2 of the Enterprise and New Towns (Scotland) Act 1990, or is training as a teacher;

"voluntary organisation" means a body, other than a public or local authority, the activities of which are carried on otherwise than for profit;

"war disablement pension" means any retirement pay, pension or allowance granted in respect of disablement under an instrument specified in section 639(2) of the Income Tax (Earnings and Pensions) Act 2003;

"war widow's pension" means a pension payable to a woman as a widow under an instrument specified in section 639(2) of the Income Tax (Earnings and Pensions) Act 2003 in respect of the death or disablement of any person;

"war widower's pension" means a pension payable to a man as a widower or to a surviving civil partner under an instrument specified in section 639(2) of the Income Tax (Earnings and Pensions) Act 2003 in respect of the death or disablement of any person;

"water charges" means—

(a) as respects England and Wales, any water and sewerage charges under Chapter 1 of Part 5 of the Water Industry Act 1991;

(b) as respects Scotland, any water and sewerage charges under Part 2 of the Local Government etc. (Scotland) Act 1994, in so far as such charges are in respect of the dwelling which a person occupies as the home;

"week" means a period of 7 days except in relation to regulation 26;

"work or training beneficiary" has the meaning prescribed in regulation 148;

"working day" means any day except for a Saturday, Sunday, Christmas Day, Good Friday or bank holiday under the Banking and Financial Dealings Act 1971 in England, Wales or Scotland;

"working tax credit" means a working tax credit under section 10 of the Tax Credits Act;

"young person" is a person who, except where section 6 of the Children (Leaving Care) Act 2000 (exclusion from benefits) applies, falls within the definition of qualifying young person in section 142 of the Contributions and Benefits Act (child and qualifying young person).

(2) In [² . . .] paragraph 15(2) of Schedule 6 (housing costs—linking rule)—

"child support maintenance" means such periodical payments as are referred to in section 3(6) of the Child Support Act 1991 and includes any payments made by the Secretary of State in lieu of such payments;

"the 1991 Act" means the Child Support Act 1991;

"the 2000 Act" means the Child Support, Pensions and Social Security Act 2000;

"maintenance assessment" has the same meaning as in the 1991 Act by virtue of section 54 of that Act as it has effect apart from the 2000 Act;

"maintenance calculation" has the same meaning as in the 1991 Act by virtue of section 54 of that Act as amended by the 2000 Act.

(3) Any reference to the claimant's family is to be construed as if it included in relation to a polygamous marriage a reference to any partner and any child or young person who is a member of the claimant's household.

(4) For the purposes of paragraph 5 of Schedule 1 to the Act, "week" means a period of 7 days.

AMENDMENT

1. Employment and Support Allowance (Miscellaneous Amendments) Regulations 2008 (SI 2008/2428), reg.3 (October 27, 2008).
2. Employment and Support Allowance (Miscellaneous Amendments) Regulations 2008 (SI 2008/2428), reg.20(1) (October 27, 2008).

GENERAL NOTE

Most of these definitions are either self-explanatory, or references to definitions in other regulations or are similar to those in reg.2(1) of the IS Regs and reg.1(2) of the JSA Regs. The following merit comment   **1A.137**

"aircraft worker": The definition is used in reg.11 (Condition relating to youth—residence or presence). By para.4 of Sch.1 to the Welfare Reform Act, those under 20 (or in prescribed cases 25) may, if they satisfy certain conditions (set out in reg.11), be entitled to contributory ESA even though they do not satisfy the second contribution condition. For the purposes of reg.11, the claimant is treated as being resident and present in Great Britain while absent "abroad in the capacity of being an aircraft worker or mariner". The definition covers all those employed on an aircraft while in flight under a contract that was entered into in the UK, other than members of the armed forces.

"confinement": The definition in s.171 of the Contributions and Benefits Act reads as follows:

"confinement" means—

(a) labour resulting in the issue of a living child, or
(b) labour after 24 weeks of pregnancy resulting in the issue of a child whether alive or dead,

and "confined" shall be construed accordingly; and where a woman's labour begun on one day results in the issue of a child on another day she shall be taken to be confined on the day of the issue of the child or, if labour results in the issue of twins or a greater number of children, she shall be taken to be confined on the day of the issue of the last of them;"

"dependent child": This definition (which does not appear in the IS Regulations or the JSA Regs) refers to any child or qualifying young person who a member of the claimant's household and is treated as the responsibility of the claimant or the claimant's partner (i.e., under reg.156(10)).

"mariner": See the commentary on "aircraft worker" above. The definition is similar except that the reference to "aircraft" is to "ship or vessel".

"member of Her Majesty's forces": Members of the armed forces and their families are, in certain circumstances, treated as being in Great Britain while abroad. The definition is supplemented by Sch.1 below.

Rounding of fractions

1A.138   **3.** For the purposes of these Regulations—
  (a) where any calculation under these Regulations results in a fraction of a penny that fraction is, if it would be to the claimant's advantage, to be treated as a penny, otherwise it must be disregarded;
  (b) where an employment and support allowance is awarded for a period which is not a complete benefit week and the applicable amount in respect of the period results in an amount which includes a fraction of a penny that fraction is to be treated as a penny.

GENERAL NOTE

Fractions are always rounded in the claimant's favour.

PART 2

THE ASSESSMENT PHASE

The end of the assessment phase

1A.140   **4.**—(1) Subject to paragraph (2) and regulations 5 and 6, the assessment phase in relation to a claimant ends on the last day of a period of 13 weeks beginning on the first day of the assessment phase as determined under section 24(2)(a) of the Act.

(2) If at the end of the period of 13 weeks referred to in paragraph (1), it has not yet been determined whether the claimant has limited capability for work—
  (a) the claimant having been assessed in accordance with a limited capability for work assessment; or
  (b) as a result of the claimant being treated as having limited capability for work in accordance with regulation 20, 25, 26, 29 or regulation 33(2) (persons to be treated as having limited capability for work),
the assessment phase will end when the limited capability for work determination is made.

DEFINITIONS

  "the assessment phase"—see WRA 2007, s.24(2).
  "claimant"—see WRA 2007, s.24(1).
  "limited capability for work"—see WRA 2007, s.1(4).
  "limited capability for work assessment"—see reg.2(1).
  "week"—see reg.2(1).

General Note

During an initial "assessment phase", generally (reg.7, below, affords excep- **1A.141**
tions) a claimant can only be entitled to "basic allowance" ESA; entitlement to
the appropriate additional component (support or work-related) only arises after
the end of that phase (WRA 2007, s.2(2), (3)). Section 24(2)(a) of the WRA
2007 stipulates that the "assessment phase" begins on the first day of entitlement
to ESA, i.e. the first day of limited capability for work after service of the "waiting
days" (these are days of non-entitlement: see WRA 2007, Sch.2, para.2 and
reg.144). This regulation in contrast sets out when the "assessment phase" ends.
It ends after 13 weeks, unless at that time it still has not been determined
whether the claimant has, or is to be treated under the regulations enumerated
in para.(2) as having, limited capability for work. In that case the "assessment
phase" lasts longer than the 13-week period and ends when the limited capability
for work determination is made, that is, when it is decided whether or not the
person has, or is to be treated as having, limited capability for work.

In short, the assessment phase ends after the later of 13 weeks or the decision
on whether the claimant has (or is to be treated as having) limited capability for
work. Where, however, the claimant appeals a decision embodying an adverse
determination on limited capability for work, the assessment phase ends only
when the appeal is determined by an appeal tribunal (see reg.6).

The assessment phase—previous claimants

5.—(1) Where the circumstances in paragraph (2) apply in relation to **1A.142**
a claimant the assessment phase —

(a) begins on the first day of the period for which the claimant was
previously entitled to an employment and support allowance;
and

(b) subject to paragraph (3) and regulation 6, ends on the day when
the sum of the period for which the claimant was previously
entitled to an employment and support allowance and the period
for which the claimant is currently entitled to such an allowance is
13 weeks.

(2) The circumstances are that—

(a) (i) the claimant's current period of limited capability for work is
to be treated as a continuation of an earlier period of limited
capability for work under regulation 145(1) or (2);

(ii) the claimant was entitled to an employment and support
allowance in the earlier period of limited capability for work;
and

(iii) the assessment phase had not ended in the previous period
for which the claimant was entitled to an employment and
support allowance; or

(b) (i) paragraph (3) or (5) of regulation 145 applies to the claimant;
and

(ii) the assessment phase had not ended in the previous period
for which the claimant was entitled to an employment and
support allowance.

(3) If, on the day referred to in paragraph (1)(b), it has not yet been
determined whether the claimant has limited capability for work—

(a) the claimant having been assessed in accordance with a limited
capability for work assessment; or

(b) as a result of the claimant being treated as having limited capability for work in accordance with regulation 20, 25, 26, 29 or regulation 33(2) (persons to be treated as having limited capability for work),

the assessment phase will end when the limited capability for work determination is made.

DEFINITIONS

"the assessment phase"—see WRA 2007, s.24(2).
"claimant"—see WRA 2007, s.24(1).
"entitled"—see WRA 2007, s.24(1).
"limited capability for work"—see WRA 2007, s.1(4).
"limited capability for work assessment"—see reg.2(1).
"week"—see reg.2(1).

GENERAL NOTE

1A.143   This regulation deals with determining the end of the "assessment phase" in cases of intermittent limited capability for work (where spells of limited capability for work are interspersed with spells in which capability for work is not limited), where the ostensibly separate spells of limited capability are fused into one by the operation of the "linking rule" in reg.145. As noted in the commentary to that regulation, this will happen generally where the two spells are not separated by more than 12 weeks, but in some cases the permissible separation period can be as long as 104 weeks. The effect of reg.5 is that the weeks of entitlement to ESA in each period thus linked are added together and the assessment phase ends when their sum reaches 13, unless no limited capability for work determination (see commentary to reg.4) has by then been made, in which case, as with continuous periods of limited capability for work under reg.4, it ends when that determination has been made. In short, the assessment phase ends after the later of 13 weeks (in two or more linked spells of limited capability) or the decision on whether the claimant has (or is to be treated as having) limited capability for work. Where, however, the claimant appeals a decision embodying an adverse determination on limited capability for work, the assessment phase ends only when the appeal is determined by an appeal tribunal (see reg.6).

The assessment phase—claimants appealing against a decision

1A.144   **6.** Where the period for which the claimant is entitled to an employment and support allowance commences and the claimant has made and is pursuing an appeal against a decision which embodies a determination that that claimant does not have limited capability for work, the assessment phase in relation to that claimant ends when the appeal is determined by an appeal tribunal constituted under Chapter 1 of Part 1 of the Social Security Act 1998.

DEFINITIONS

"the assessment phase"—see WRA 2007, s.24(2).
"claimant"—see WRA 2007, s.24(1).
"limited capability for work"—see reg.2(1).

88

GENERAL NOTE

Where the claimant appeals a decision embodying an adverse determination 1A.145
on limited capability for work, the assessment phase ends only when the appeal
is determined by an appeal tribunal under the SSA 1998.

Circumstances where the condition that the assessment phase has ended before entitlement to the support component or the work-related activity component arises does not apply

7.—(1) Subject to paragraph (2), sections 2(2)(a), 2(3)(a), 4(4)(a) 1A.146
and 4(5)(a) of the Act do not apply where—
  (a) a claimant is terminally ill and has either—
      (i) made a claim expressly on the ground of being terminally ill;
          or
      (ii) made an application for supersession or revision in accor-
           dance with the Social Security and Child Support (Decisions
           and Appeals) Regulations 1999 which contains an express
           statement that the claimant is terminally ill; or
  (b) (i) a period of limited capability for work is to be treated as a
          continuation of an earlier period of limited capability for work
          under regulation 145(1) or (2);
      (ii) the claimant was entitled to an employment and support
           allowance in the earlier period of limited capability for work;
           and
      (iii) the assessment phase had ended in the previous period for
            which the claimant was entitled to an employment and sup-
            port allowance.
  (2) Paragraph (1)(b) does not apply where the claimant is appealing a
decision which embodies a determination that the claimant does not
have limited capability for work.

DEFINITIONS

  "claimant"—see WRA 2007, s.24(1).
  "entitled"—see WRA 2007, s.24(1).
  "limited capability for work"—see WRA 2007, s.1(4).
  "period of limited capability for work"—see reg.2(1).
  "terminally ill"—see reg.2(1).
  "the assessment phase"—see WRA 2007, s.24(2).

GENERAL NOTE

  WRA 2007, s.2 stipulates that generally until the "assessment phase" ends 1A.147
there can be no entitlement other than to basic allowance ESA; entitlement to
the appropriate additional component (support or work related) normally cannot arise until the assessment phase has ended (on which see WRA 2007, s.24(2)
and ESA Regs, regs 4–6). This reg provides that the general rule precluding
entitlement does not apply in two situations. First of all it does not apply to
someone terminally ill who has claimed ESA expressly on that basis or has
sought supersession or revision expressly stating that he is terminally ill
(para.(1)(a)). Note that someone is terminally ill where he is suffering from a
progressive disease and death as a consequence of it can reasonably be expected
within six months (reg.2(1)). The second situation where the general preclusive
rule is disapplied is where the assessment phase had ended in an earlier spell of

limited capability for work which is forged into one ("linked") by the operation of the linking rule in reg.145(1) (the 12 week rule) or that in reg.145(2) (the 104 week rule in respect of a work or training beneficiary under reg.148). Note that the preclusion is *not* disapplied where the two spells "link" because of the other 104 week rule which is afforded by reg.145(3), (4) (person who has immediately before claiming ESA again ceased qualifying remunerative work supported or (but for income) supportable by tax credits).

PART 3

CONDITIONS OF ENTITLEMENT—CONTRIBUTORY ALLOWANCE

Relaxation of the first contribution condition

1A.148   **8.**—(1) A claimant who satisfies any of the conditions in paragraph (2) is to be taken to satisfy the first contribution condition if—
   (a) the claimant paid Class 1 or Class 2 contributions before the relevant benefit week in respect of any one tax year; and
   (b) the earnings factor is derived—
      (i) from earnings, on which primary Class 1 contributions have been paid or treated as paid, which are not less than that year's lower earnings limit multiplied by 25; or
      (ii) from Class 2 contributions multiplied by 25.
   (2) The conditions referred to in paragraph (1) are that the claimant—
   (a) was entitled to a carer's allowance in the last complete tax year immediately preceding the relevant benefit year;
   (b) had been engaged in qualifying remunerative work for a period of more than 2 years immediately before the first day of the period of limited capability for work and who was entitled to working tax credit where the disability element or the severe disability element of working tax credit specified in regulation 20(1) (b) or (f) of the Working Tax Credit (Entitlement and Maximum Rate) Regulations 2002 was included in the award;
   (c) in respect of any week in any tax year preceding the relevant benefit year—
      (i) is entitled to be credited with earnings or contributions in accordance with regulation 9D of the Social Security (Credits) Regulations 1975 (credits for certain periods of imprisonment or detention in legal custody); or
      (ii) would have been so entitled had an application to the Secretary of State been made for the purpose of that regulation; or
   (d) on the first day of the period of limited capability for work, had received a contributory allowance in the last complete tax year immediately preceding the relevant benefit year in which entitlement to a contributory allowance is now being decided.

DEFINITIONS

"benefit week"—see reg.2(1).
"carer's allowance"—see reg.2(1).
"claimant"—see WRA 2007, s.24(1).
"Class 1 contributions"—see WRA 2007, s.1, Sch.1, Pt 1, para.3(1)(b).
"Class 2 contributions—see WRA 2007, s.1, Sch.1, Pt 1, para.3(1)(b).
"contributory allowance"—see WRA 2007, s.1(7).
"earnings"—see WRA 2007, s.1, Sch.1, Pt 1, para.3(1)(c).
"earnings factor"—see WRA 2007, s.1, Sch.1, Pt 1, para.3(1)(d).
"first contribution condition"—see reg.2(1); WRA 2007, Sch.1, para.1(1).
"lower earnings limit"—see WRA 2007, s.1, Sch.1, Pt 1, para.3(1)(e).
"period of limited capability for work,"—see reg.2(1).
"primary Class 1 contributions"—see WRA 2007, s.1, Sch.1, Pt 1, para.3(1)(b).
"qualifying remunerative work"—see reg.2(1).
"relevant benefit year"—see WRA 2007, s.1, Sch.1, Pt 1, para.3(1)(f).
"tax year"—see WRA 2007, s.1, Sch.1, Pt 1, para.3(1)(g).
"week"—see reg.2(1).

GENERAL NOTE

The national insurance contribution conditions, affording the sole route into **1A.149**
CESA for anyone not incapacitated in youth, are found in WRA 2007, s.1(2)(a)
and Sch.1, Pt 1, paras 1–3. They are the same as those governing access to IB
from April 6, 2001 (SSCBA 1992, s.30A and Sch.3, para.2). The conditions
were tightened from then so as to require a recent connection with the world of
paid employment. Prior to that date the first contribution condition (then, as
now, only able to be met by paid contributions) governing access to IB could be
met by a sufficient record of paid contributions in any tax year prior to the claim.
As now, IB contribution condition one had from April 6 2001 to be met in one
of the last three tax years (April 6–April 5) complete before the start of the
benefit year (early January–early January) in which falls the first day of the period
of incapacity for work (now limited capability for work) of which the claim is
part. This reg. affords some relief for some of the people disadvantaged by that
rule. It is comparable to (but not wholly coterminous with) the relaxation in IB
Regs, Pt 1A, reg.2B.

The rules are relaxed in the sense that if one of the conditions in reg.8(2) is
met, such a claimant is treated as satisfying the first contribution condition if he
has paid, in respect of any one tax/contribution year (complete or not) before the
day of claim, Class 1 contributions to a level of 25 times that year's lower
earnings limit or 25 Class 2 contributions (para.2B(1)). In short, such claimants
are in effect subject to the first contribution condition as it stood before the April
6, 2001 changes. The rules are "relaxed" in the following situations:

(a) where the claimant was, in the last complete tax year immediately preceding the relevant benefit year in which occurred the first day of limited
capability for work, entitled to carer's allowance (para.2(a))(in express
terms (but not effect) this is narrower than IB reg.2B(2)(a) which also
explicitly covered someone who would have been entitled to one but for
the provisions of reg.4 of the Overlapping Benefit Regs (he was receiving
another higher value benefit), but this is because that regulation merely
precluding benefit being payable, rather than affecting entitlement, the
explicit reference was in law otiose);

(b) where the claimant was engaged in qualifying remunerative work for a
period of more than two years immediately before the first day of limited
capability for work and throughout that period was in receipt of working

91

tax credit which included in the award the disability or severe disability element (para.(2)(b));

(c) certain convicted prisoners whose conviction is overturned whose contribution record is credited in respect of their period of imprisonment under Social Security (Credits) Regulations 1975, reg.9D or would be if they applied to the Secretary of State (para.(2)(c));

(d) where the claimant is on the first day of his limited capability for work someone who had received CESA in the last complete tax year before the relevant benefit year in which he again becomes entitled to it (para. (2)(d)).

Condition relating to youth—claimants aged 20 or over but under 25

1A.150   **9.**—(1) For the purposes of paragraph 4(1)(a) of Schedule 1 to the Act, a claimant who satisfies the conditions specified in paragraph (2) falls within a prescribed case.

(2) The conditions are that the claimant—

(a) registered on a course of—

   (i) full-time advanced or secondary education; or

   (ii) training,

at least 3 months before attaining the age of 20; and

(b) not more than one academic term immediately after registration attended one or more such courses in respect of a period referred to in paragraph (3).

(3) The period mentioned in sub-paragraph (2)(b) is a period which—

(a) began on or before a day at least 3 months before the day the claimant attained the age of 20; and

(b) ended no earlier than the beginning of the last two complete tax years before the relevant benefit year which would have applied if the claimant was entitled to an employment and support allowance having satisfied the first contribution condition and the second contribution condition.

(4) For the purposes of this regulation a claimant is to be treated as attending a course on any day on which the course is interrupted by an illness or domestic emergency.

(5) In this regulation—

"advanced education" means education for the purposes of—

(a) a course in preparation for a degree, a diploma of higher education, a higher national diploma, a higher national diploma of the Business and Technician Education Council or the Scottish Qualifications Authority, or a teaching qualification; or

(b) any other course which is of a standard above ordinary national diploma, a diploma of the Business and Technical Education Council or a higher or advanced higher national certificate of the Scottish Qualifications Authority or a general certificate of education (advanced level);

"full-time" includes part-time where the person's disability prevents attendance at a full-time course;

"secondary education" means a course of education below a course of advanced education—

    (a) by attendance at an establishment recognised by the Secretary of State as being, or as comparable to, a university, college or school; or

    (b) elsewhere where the Secretary of State is satisfied that the education is equivalent to that given in an establishment recognised as being, or as comparable to, a university, college or school.

[[1](6) A claimant is to be treated as not having limited capability for work on a day which is not, for the purposes of paragraph 4(1)(d)(ii) of Schedule 1 to the Act (period of 196 consecutive days preceding the relevant period of limited capability for work), part of any consecutive days of limited capability for work.]

AMENDMENTS

1. Employment and Support Allowance (Miscellaneous Amendments) Regulations 2008 (SI 2008/2428), reg.4 (October 27, 2008).

DEFINITIONS

"advanced education"—see para.(5).
"claimant"—see WRA 2007, s.24(1).
"first contribution condition"—see reg.2(1); WRA 2007, Sch.1, para.1(1).
"full-time"—see para.(5).
"relevant benefit year"—see WRA 2007, s.1, Sch.1, Pt 1, para.3(1)(f).
"secondary education"—see para.(5).
"second contribution condition"—see reg.2(1); WRA 2007, Sch.1, para.2(1).
"tax year"—see WRA 2007, s.1, Sch.1, Pt 1, para.3(1)(g).
"training"—see reg.2(1).

GENERAL NOTE

Meeting the national insurance contributions conditions affords only one route to CESA (WRA 2007, s.1(2)(a) and Sch.1, Pt 1, paras 1–3; reg.8). The second route (condition relating to youth) is covered by WRA 2007, s.1(2)(a), Sch.1, Pt 1, para.4 (the key provision), this regulation and regs 10–12. This regulation stipulates when there can be access to CESA through the "youth" route for those 20 or over but under 25; it sets out the conditions in which their case is a "prescribed" one for purposes of WRA 2007, Sch.1, Pt 1, para.4(1)(a) (para.(1)). The comparable IB provision is IB Regs, reg.15. It is here assumed that case law on that almost identically worded provision will carry over into interpretation of this ESA provision.

1A.151

Someone over 20 but under 25 can qualify for the "youth" route where, at least three months before reaching 20, he registered on a course of full time education or of training (see below), provided that not more than one academic term immediately after his registration, he attended one or more such courses in respect of a specified period (para.(2)). Note that he is treated as attending on any day on which the course or training is interrupted by an illness or domestic emergency (para.4). The specified period is set out in para.(3): a period beginning on or before a day three months before his twentieth birthday (para.(3)(a)) and ending on a day not earlier than the beginning of the last two complete tax years before the benefit year which would have governed a claim for CESA by the national insurance route. The terms "advanced education" and "secondary education" are defined in para.(5) in an interlocking way, so that "secondary education" is a level below that of "advanced education" and it requires attendance at a educational establishment recognised by the Secretary of State as, or as comparable, to a university, college or school, or elsewhere so long as the Secretary of State is satisfied that the education afforded there is equivalent to that in such an establishment. Note that while both "advanced education" and "secondary education" require a "full-time" course, para.(5) stipulates that "full-time" covers also "part-time" where the claimant's disability is such as to preclude him attending a full-time course.

The reference in the IB provision was to "vocational or work-based training". This regulation refers to "training", defined in reg.2(1) as (a) training in pursuance of arrangements made under s.2(1) of the Employment and Training Act 1973 or s.2(3) of the Enterprise and New Towns (Scotland) Act 1990; or (b) any training received on a course which a person attends for 16 hours or more a week, the primary purpose of which is the teaching of occupational or vocational skills. In respect of the IB provision, whether the claimant was registered on a "full-time" course or on a course of "vocational or work-based training" was considered by Commissioner Jacobs in *CIB/1410/2005*. Her course was described as part-time by the College in question (not conclusive in itself) and she was required to attend College one day a week and undertake eight to ten hours of private study. She had also to arrange and undertake 60 hours of work experience over the period of the course. Commissioner Jacobs held that the tribunal was entitled to disregard the work experience, since it was essential to, but not part of, the course, and to regard the course as part-time. Moreover, she could not in such circumstances be regarded as registered on a course of vocational or work-based training.

Condition relating to youth—previous claimants

1A.152   **10.**—(1) Paragraph 4(1)(a) of Schedule 1 to the Act does not apply to a claimant—

(a) who has previously ceased to be entitled to an employment and support allowance, entitlement for which was as a result of satisfying the condition set out in sub-paragraph (1) of that paragraph;

(b) whose previous entitlement had not been ended by a decision which embodied a determination (other than a determination in the circumstances applicable to a claimant under paragraph (2)(a)) that the claimant did not have limited capability for work;

(c) in relation to whom regulation 145 (linking rules) does not apply;

(d) aged 20 or over, or, where regulation 9 would otherwise apply to the person, aged 25 or over; and

(e) to whom paragraph (2) applies.

(2) This paragraph applies to a claimant—

(a) whose previous entitlement to an employment and support allowance ended solely with a view to that person taking up employment or training;

(b) whose earnings factor from an employment or series of employments pursued in the period from the end of the previous entitlement to the beginning of the period of limited capability for work, was below the lower earnings limit multiplied by 25 in any of the last three complete tax years before the beginning of the relevant benefit year; and

(c) who—

    (i) in respect of the last two complete tax years before the beginning of the relevant benefit year has either paid or been credited with earnings equivalent in each of those years to the year's lower earnings limit multiplied by 50, of which at least one, in the last tax year, was in respect of the disability element or severe disability element of working tax credit; or

    (ii) makes a claim for an employment and support allowance within a period of 12 weeks after the day on which the last such employment pursued in accordance with sub-paragraph (b) ceased.

DEFINITIONS

"claimant"—see WRA 2007, s.24(1).
"earnings factor"—see WRA 2007, s.1, Sch.1, Pt 1, para.3(1)(d).
"employment"—see reg.2(1).
"limited capability for work"—see WRA 2007, s.1(4).
"lower earnings limit"—see WRA 2007, s.1, Sch.1, Pt 1, para.3(1)(e).
"period of limited capability for work"—see reg.2(1).
"relevant benefit year"—see WRA 2007, s.1, Sch.1, Pt 1, para.3(1)(f).
"tax year"—see WRA 2007, s.1, Sch.1, Pt 1, para.3(1)(g).
"training"—see reg.2(1).
"week"—see reg.2(1).
"working tax credit"—see reg.2(1).

GENERAL NOTE

Made pursuant to WRA 2007, Sch.1, Pt 1, para.4(3), this regulation, comparable to IB Regulations, reg.18, prescribes circumstances in which someone previously entitled to CESA under the youth route, can again be entitled even though the age condition in WRA 2007, Sch.1, Pt 1, para.4(1)(a) is not met. It deals with the situation where someone has been entitled to incapacity benefit as a person incapacitated in youth, ceases to be entitled to it other than on the basis of being found not to have limited capability for work, and claims again in a new period of limited capability for work (not being helped by the variety of linking rules in the ESA scheme (reg.145), but is over age (20 or 25 as the case may be) when he makes that new claim. He can again become entitled in in certain cases where his previous entitlement was terminated solely with a view to him taking up employment or training which proved to be very low paid or very intermittent. The rule will not operate where entitlement ended because of a determination that he did not have limited capability for work (para.(1)(c)). The regulation covers the person whose entitlement terminated solely with a view to him taking up an employment or training (see definition of "training" in reg.2(1)) (para.(2)(a)). He can qualify by way of the "youth" route (albeit over-age) if his earnings factor from the employment or series of employments pursued since the termination of his previous entitlement was below a specified level in *any* of the three complete tax years relevant for qualification by way of the national insurance contributions route (see WRA 2007, s.1(2)(a), Sch.1, paras (1)–(3)). The specified level is less than 25 times the lower earnings level set for

1A.153

Class 1 contributions purposes in the tax year in question. However, he can only be eligible if in addition, he is either: (a) claiming by way of the youth route within 12 weeks of his last such employment (para.(2)(c)(ii)); or (b) in each of the last two complete tax years (identified as above) he has paid or been credited with earnings to the level of 50 times the year's lower earnings limit for Class 1 contributions purposes, and at least one of those contributions or creditings was, in the last such year, in respect of the disability or severe disability element of working tax credit (para.(2)(c)(i)).

Condition relating to youth—residence or presence

1A.154   **11.**—(1) The prescribed conditions for the purposes of paragraph 4(1)(c) of Schedule 1 to the Act as to residence or presence in Great Britain are that the claimant—

(a) is ordinarily resident in Great Britain;

(b) is not a person subject to immigration control within the meaning of section 115(9) of the Immigration and Asylum Act or is a person to whom paragraph (3) applies;

(c) is present in Great Britain; and

(d) has been present in Great Britain for a period of, or for periods amounting in aggregate to, not less than 26 weeks in the 52 weeks immediately preceding the relevant benefit week.

(2) For the purposes of paragraph (1), a claimant is to be treated as being resident and present in Great Britain where the claimant is absent from Great Britain by reason only of being—

(a) the spouse, civil partner, son, daughter, father, father-in-law, mother or mother-in-law of, and living with, a member of Her Majesty's forces who is abroad in that capacity;

(b) in employment prescribed for the purposes of paragraph 7(1)(c) of Schedule 2 to the Act in connection with continental shelf operations; or

(c) abroad in the capacity of being an aircraft worker or mariner.

(3) This paragraph applies where a person is—

(a) a member of a family of a national of an European Economic Area state;

(b) a person who is lawfully working in Great Britain and is a national of a State with which the Community has concluded an agreement under Article 310 of the Treaty of Amsterdam amending the Treaty on European Union, the Treaties establishing the European Communities and certain related Acts providing, in the field of social security, for the equal treatment of workers who are nationals of the signatory State and their families;

(c) a person who is a member of a family of, and living with, a person specified in sub-paragraph (b); or

(d) a person who has been given leave to enter, or remain in, the United Kingdom by the Secretary of State upon an undertaking by another person or persons pursuant to the immigration rules within the meaning of the Immigration Act 1971 to be responsible for that person's maintenance and accommodation.

(4) A person is to be treated as having satisfied the residence or presence conditions in paragraph (1) throughout a period of limited

capability for work where those conditions are satisfied on the first day of that period of limited capability for work.

<small>DEFINITIONS</small>

"aircraft worker"—see reg.2(1).
"benefit week"—see reg.2(1).
"claimant"—see WRA 2007, s.24(1).
"continental shelf operations"—see WRA 2007, s.22, Sch.2, para.7(3).
"employment"—see reg.2(1).
"family"—see reg.2(1).
"Immigration and Asylum Act"—see reg.2(1).
"member of Her Majesty's forces"—see reg.2(1).
"mariner"—see reg.2(1).
"period of limited capability for work"—see reg.2(1).
"prescribed"—see WRA 2007, s.24(1).
"week"—see reg.2(1).

<small>GENERAL NOTE</small>

WRA 2007, Sch.1, para.4(1)(c) requires that to gain non-contributory access **1A.155** to incapacity benefit as a person incapacitated in youth, a claimant must on the relevant day satisfy the prescribed conditions as to residence or presence in Great Britain. This regulation sets out those prescribed conditions. They are such as to require both residence and presence. Residence is "ordinary residence" rather than simple residence (para.(1)(a)). There is no requirement of "habitual residence". "Presence" (para.(1)(c)) means "physically present". The requirements are that the claimant must on the first day of claim in the period of incapacity for work (see para.(4)) be both ordinarily resident and present in Great Britain. (On "ordinarily resident", see further the commentary to Persons Abroad Regs, reg.5.) He must also have been present in Great Britain for a period or aggregate periods of at least 26 weeks in the immediately preceding 52 weeks (para.(1)(d)). In addition he must not be subject to immigration control within the meaning of Immigration and Asylum Act 1999, s.115(9) (set out in *Vol.II: Income Support, Jobseeker's Allowance, Tax Credits and the Social Fund* and see the provisions noted in the commentary thereto) or (if prima facie he is) he must be someone protected by para.(3). That paragraph protects the same groups as are covered in Pt II of the Schedule to the Social Security (Immigration and Asylum) Consequential Amendments Regulations 2000, set out in *Vol.II: Income Support, Jobseeker's Allowance, Tax Credits and the Social Fund.*

Absence from Great Britain would negate presence. Paragraph (2) enables certain actual absences to be treated, legally speaking, as if the person was present or resident in Great Britain. It protects aircraft workers and mariners within the meaning of reg.2(1). It protects also those in employment prescribed for the purposes of SSCBA 1992, s.120 in connection with continental shelf operations. It also protects someone abroad as the spouse, son, daughter, father, mother, father-in-law, mother-in-law of and living with a member of the forces abroad.

Condition relating to youth—full-time education

12.—(1) For the purposes of paragraph 4(4) of Schedule 1 to the Act, **1A.156** a claimant is to be treated as receiving full-time education for any period during which the claimant—

(a) is at least 16 years old but under the age of 19; and
(b) attends a course of education for 21 hours or more a week.

(2) For the purposes of paragraph (1)(b), in calculating the number of hours a week during which a claimant attends a course, no account is to be taken of any instruction or tuition which is not suitable for persons of the same age who do not have a disability.

(3) In determining the duration of a period of full-time education under paragraph (1) any temporary interruption of that education may be disregarded.

(4) A claimant who is 19 years of age or over is not to be treated for the purposes of paragraph 4(1)(b) of Schedule 1 to the Act as receiving full-time education.

DEFINITIONS

"claimant"—see WRA 2007, s.24(1).
"week"—see reg.2(1).

GENERAL NOTE

1A.157   WRA 2007, Sch.1, para.4(41)(b) precludes someone from ranking as a person incapacitated in youth (thus denying non-contributory access to incapacity benefit) where on the day of claimed incapacity he is receiving full-time education. This regulation, pursuant to para.4(4) of that Schedule, sets out what is, and what is not, to be regarded as full-time education. Someone who is 19 or over cannot be so precluded even though he is in fact undergoing a full-time education (para.(4)). Preclusive "full-time education" covers a person aged 16–18 inclusive for any period in which he attends a course of education for 21 or more hours a week (para.(1)). In determining the length of any such preclusive period, a decision-maker may disregard any temporary interruption of that education (para.(3)). This, it is submitted, is ambiguous, leaving it unclear whether such periods are to be counted as part of the preclusive period or ones that are to be left out. The DMG offers no assistance in resolving the ambiguity. As regards the 21 hours aspect, no account is to be taken in calculating those hours of any instruction or tuition unsuitable for a person of the same age as the claimant but who is not suffering from a physical or mental disability (para.(2)). In other words, one ignores special classes for the disabled.

Modification of the relevant benefit year

1A.158   **13.**—(1) Where paragraph (2) applies, sub-paragraph (1)(f) of paragraph 3 of Schedule 1 to the Act has effect as if "relevant benefit year" is the benefit year which includes the day which would be the beginning of the period of limited capability for work if regulation 145 did not apply.

(2) This paragraph applies where a claimant does not satisfy—

(a) the first contribution condition;

(b) the second contribution condition; or

(c) both contribution conditions,

but would satisfy those conditions if the modified definition of "relevant benefit year" provided in paragraph (1) applied.

DEFINITIONS

"claimant"—see WRA 2007, s.24(1).
"first contribution condition"—see reg.2(1); WRA 2007, s.1, Sch.1, para.1(1).

"period of limited capability for work"—see reg.2(1).
"relevant benefit year"—see para.(1).
"second contribution condition"—see reg.2(1); WRA 2007, s.1, Sch.1, para.2(1).

GENERAL NOTE

This operates where a claimant fails to satisfy one or both of the standard contribution conditions for ESA. As noted in the commentary to WRA 2007, Sch.1, paras 1–3, the key to determining the tax years to which to have regard is determined by identifying the benefit year in which there falls the first day of the period of limited capability for work. The effect of the linking rules (where one period is fused with an earlier one) may mean that the benefit year in question is not the current one in which the most recent claim falls. If, ignoring the effect of the linking rules in reg.145 (so that period of limited capability for work is not joined to an earlier one) would mean that the relevant benefit year would be later so that the relevant tax years to which to have regard would change to ones in which the contribution condition(s) in question was (were) met, then the relevant benefit year for the purposes of the contribution conditions is to be the later one determined by ignoring the linking rules.

1A.159

PART 4

CONDITIONS OF ENTITLEMENT—INCOME-RELATED ALLOWANCE

Meaning of education

14.—(1) Subject to regulations 15 and 16, for the purposes of paragraph 6 of Schedule 1 to the Act, "education" means a course of study to which paragraph (2) applies which is being undertaken at an educational establishment.

1A.160

(2) This paragraph applies to a course of study which is—

(a) a full-time course which is not funded in whole or in part by—
  (i) the Learning and Skills Council for England;
  (ii) the Welsh Ministers; or
  (iii) the Scottish Ministers at a college of further education;

(b) a full-time course of higher education which is funded in whole or in part by the Scottish Ministers;

(c) funded in whole or in part by the Learning and Skills Council for England or by the Welsh Ministers if it involves more than 16 guided learning hours per week for the student in question, according to the number of guided learning hours per week for that student set out—
  (i) in the case of a course funded by the Learning and Skills Council for England, in the student's learning agreement signed on behalf of the establishment which is funded by that Council for the delivery of that course; or
  (ii) in the case of a course funded by the Welsh Ministers, in a document signed on behalf of the establishment which is funded by those Ministers for the delivery of that course;

(d) not a course of higher education and which is funded in whole or in part by the Scottish Ministers at a college of further education and involves—

    (i) more than 16 hours per week of classroom-based or workshop-based programmed learning under the direct guidance of teaching staff according to the number of hours set out in a document signed on behalf of the college; or

    (ii) 16 hours or less per week of classroom-based or workshop-based programmed learning under the direct guidance of teaching staff and it involves additional hours using structured learning packages supported by the teaching staff where the combined total of hours exceeds 21 per week according to the number of hours set out in a document signed on behalf of the college; or

(e) a sandwich course within the meaning prescribed in regulation 2(9) of the Education (Student Support) Regulations 2007, regulation 4(2) of the Education (Student Loans) (Scotland) Regulations 2007 or regulation 2(8) of the Education (Student Support) Regulations (Northern Ireland) 2007.

(3) In this regulation "higher education" means higher education within the meaning of Part 2 of the Further and Higher Education (Scotland) Act 1992.

GENERAL NOTE

1A.161   It is a condition of entitlement to income-related ESA that a claimant is not receiving education (see para.6(1)(g) of Sch.1 to the Welfare Reform Act 2007). But see reg.18 below which exempts claimants who are entitled to disability living allowance from this requirement.

"Education" for these purposes means a course of study that comes within para.(2) that is being undertaken at an educational establishment. Paragraph (2) is in the same terms as the definitions of "full-time course of study" and "sandwich course" in reg.131(1) (which in turn reproduces the definitions of these terms in reg.61(1) of the Income Support Regs; see also the definitions of "full-time student" and "sandwich course" in reg.1(3) of the JSA Regs). Regulation 17 provides when a person will count as undertaking a course of study. It is in the same terms as reg.131(2)–(4) (which in turn reproduces the provisions in reg.61(2)–(4) of the Income Support Regulations and reg.1(3A)–(3C) of the JSA Regulations). The combined effect of regs 14 and 17 is to exclude full-time students from income-related ESA (except those who are entitled to disability living allowance: see reg.18 and the note to that regulation). But note that in the case of a person aged under 19 this will only apply if he is attending a course of advanced education (reg.16).

In addition, a "qualifying young person", unless he is entitled to disability living allowance, is to be treated as receiving education (see reg.15).

Claimants to be treated as receiving education

1A.162   **15.** Subject to regulation 18, a qualifying young person is to be treated as receiving education for the purposes of paragraph 6(1)(g) of Schedule 1 to the Act.

DEFINITION

"qualifying young person"—reg.2(1), s.142 SSCBA.

GENERAL NOTE

A qualifying young person (other than one who is entitled to disability living 1A.163
allowance: see reg.18) is to be treated as receiving education and so is excluded
from income-related ESA. A "qualifying young person" (as defined in s.142 of
the Contributions and Benefits Act) is a person who is 16 or over but who has not
attained a prescribed age and who satisfies prescribed conditions.

The substance of the definition of "qualifying young person" is in reg.3 of the
Child Benefit Regulations 2006 (see Vol.1 in this series). It applies to a person
who is (i) under 20; *and* (ii) undertaking a course of full-time, non-advanced
education, which is not provided by virtue of his employment or any office held
by him, but which is provided at a school or college, or elsewhere as approved by
the Revenue (in the latter case he must have been receiving the approved
education before he was 16); *or* (iii) undertaking approved training that is not
provided by means of a contract of employment. "Approved training" covers
various training programmes under "arrangements made by the Government"
(see the definition of both these terms in reg.1(2) of the 2006 Regulations).
"Full-time education" (also defined in reg.1(2)) requires contact hours of at least
12 a week during term-time. Note that a person aged 19 can only be a qualifying
young person if he began, or was enrolled on, or had been accepted to undertake,
the full-time, non-advanced education or approved training before he was 19
(although a person who was on such a course/training and has been accepted or
enrolled to undertake another such course/training is also included).

Claimants not to be treated as receiving education

16. Where a claimant is under 19 but not a qualifying young person, 1A.164
that claimant is not to be treated as receiving education where the course
of study is not—

(a) a course leading to a postgraduate degree or comparable qualification, a first degree or comparable qualification, a diploma of
higher education or a higher national diploma; or

(b) any other course which is of a standard above advanced GNVQ or
equivalent, including a course which is of a standard above a
general certificate of education (advanced level) or above a Scottish national qualification (higher or advanced higher).

DEFINITION

"qualifying young person"—see reg.2(1), s.142 SSCBA.

GENERAL NOTE

The effect of this regulation is that if the claimant is aged less than 19 and is 1A.165
not a qualifying young person (see the note to reg.15), he will not count as
receiving education unless he is undertaking a course of advanced education (see
the definition of "course of advanced education" in reg.131(1) which is in the
same terms as paras (a) and (b), and which in turn reproduces the definition of
"course of advanced education" in reg.61(1) of the Income Support Regs and
reg.1(3) of the JSA Regs). See further the note to reg.14.

Courses of study

1A.166   **17.**—(1) For the purposes of the definition of "education" in regulation 14, a person is to be regarded as undertaking a course of study—

(a) subject to paragraph (2), in the case of a person undertaking a part of a modular course that would be a course of study for the purposes of these Regulations, for the period beginning on the day on which that part of the course starts and ending—

  (i) on the last day on which the person is registered with the educational establishment as attending or undertaking that part as a full-time course of study; or

  (ii) on such earlier date (if any) as the person finally abandons the course or is dismissed from it;

(b) in any other case, throughout the period beginning on the date on which the person starts undertaking the course and ending on the last day of the course or on such earlier date (if any) as the person finally abandons it or is dismissed from it.

(2) For the purpose of sub-paragraph (a) of paragraph (1), the period referred to in that sub-paragraph includes—

(a) where a person has failed examinations or has failed to successfully complete a module relating to a period when the person was attending or undertaking a part of the course as a course of study, any period in respect of which the person attends or undertakes the course for the purpose of retaking those examinations or that module;

(b) any period of vacation within the period specified in that paragraph or immediately following that period except where the person has registered with the educational establishment to attend or undertake the final module in the course and the vacation immediately follows the last day on which the person is required to attend or undertake the course.

(3) In paragraph (1), "modular course" means a course of study which consists of two or more modules, the successful completion of a specified number of which is required before a person is considered by the educational establishment to have completed the course.

GENERAL NOTE

1A.167   See the note to reg.14.

Circumstances in which the condition that the claimant is not receiving education does not apply

1A.168   **18.** Paragraph 6(1)(g) of Schedule 1 to the Act does not apply where the claimant is entitled to a disability living allowance.

GENERAL NOTE

1A.169   Paragraph 6(1)(g) of Sch.1 to the Welfare Reform Act 2007 provides that it is a condition of entitlement to income-related ESA that the claimant is not receiving education—this effectively excludes full-time students and qualifying young persons from income-related ESA: see regs 14–17. However the effect of reg.18 is that such claimants will not be excluded if they are entitled to disability living allowance (either component at any rate). Note that this exemption only applies if the claimant is entitled to disability living allowance. Previously a full-time student could claim income support if he had been incapable of work for at least 28 weeks, qualified for the disability or severe disability premium, or was receiving a disabled student's allowance on the grounds of deafness (see paras 10 and 12 of Sch.1B to the Income Support Regs in Vol.II of this series). Similarly, a qualifying young person who had been incapable of work for at least 28 weeks or met the conditions for the disability premium or severe disability premium was eligible for income support (see reg.13(2)(b) and (bb) of, para.15 of Sch.1B to, the Income Support Regs). However from October 27, 2008 *new* claims for income support on these grounds are no longer possible as they are treated as claims for ESA (see reg.2(1) of the Employment and Support Allowance (Transitional Provisions) Regs 2008 (SI 2008/795)), unless they link with (i.e. are made not more than eight weeks after) a previous income support entitlement for at least four days on the grounds of disability: see reg.2(2)(c) of the Transitional Provisions Regulations, or the claimant is entitled to incapacity benefit or severe disablement allowance: see reg.2(2)(d) of those Regulations, as amended by the Employment and Support Allowance (Transitional Provisions) (Amendment) Regs 2008 (SI 2008/2783), or they are in respect of a period before October 27, 2008. Income support on the grounds of disability means "income support awarded to a person to whom regulation 13(2)(b) or (bb) of, or paragraph 7(a) or (b), 10, 12 or 13 of Schedule 1B to, the Income Support (General) Regulations 1987 (prescribed categories of person) applies" (reg.1(4) of the Transitional Provisions Regs, as amended by reg.42 of the Employment and Support Allowance (Miscellaneous Amendments) Regs 2008 (SI 2008/2428)).

Thus from October 27, 2008 disabled full-time students or qualifying young persons making a new claim have to claim ESA but the basic rule is that such a person will not qualify for income-related ESA unless he is entitled to disability living allowance. Note also that such claimants, if they were eligible for income support on grounds other than incapacity for work, would previously have been subject to the income support remunerative work (i.e. 16 hours a week) rule, whereas the "incapacity" remunerative work rules will now apply to them (see regs 41, 44 and 45).

See also reg.33(2) which treats a claimant who is receiving education but who is entitled to disability living allowance as having limited capability for work for the purposes of income-related ESA. But this does not apply in the case of a qualifying young person (reg.33(2)(a)). A qualifying young person who is entitled to disability living allowance and who claims income-related ESA will have to satisfy the limited capability for work test (as will any claimant who counts as receiving education who claims contributory ESA, even though he is entitled to disability living allowance).

PART 5

LIMITED CAPABILITY FOR WORK

Determination of limited capability for work

19.—(1) For the purposes of Part 1 of the Act, whether a claimant's capability for work is limited by the claimant's physical or mental condition and, if it is, whether the limitation is such that it is not reasonable to

1A.170

require the claimant to work is to be determined on the basis of a limited capability for work assessment of the claimant in accordance with this Part.

(2) The limited capability for work assessment is an assessment of the extent to which a claimant who has some specific disease or bodily or mental disablement is capable of performing the activities prescribed in Schedule 2 or is incapable by reason of such disease or bodily or mental disablement of performing those activities.

(3) Subject to paragraph (6), for the purposes of Part 1 of the Act a claimant has limited capability for work if, by adding the points listed in column (3) of Schedule 2 against any descriptor listed in that Schedule, the claimant obtains a total score of at least—

  (a) 15 points whether singly or by a combination of descriptors speci-
      fied in Part 1 of that Schedule;
  (b) 15 points whether singly or by a combination of descriptors speci-
      fied in Part 2 of that Schedule; or
  (c) 15 points by a combination of descriptors specified in Parts 1 and
      2 of that Schedule.

(4) In assessing the extent of a claimant's capability to perform any activity listed in Part 1 of Schedule 2, the claimant is to be assessed as if wearing any prosthesis with which the claimant is fitted or, as the case may be, wearing or using any aid or appliance which is normally worn or used.

(5) In assessing the extent of a claimant's capability to perform any activity listed in Schedule 2, it is a condition that the claimant's incapability to perform the activity arises from—

  (a) a specific bodily disease or disablement;
  (b) a specific mental illness or disablement; or
  (c) as a direct result of treatment provided by a registered medical
      practitioner, for such a disease, illness or disablement.

(6) Where more than one descriptor specified for an activity apply to a claimant, only the descriptor with the highest score in respect of each activity which applies is to be counted.

(7) Where a claimant—

  (a) has been determined to have limited capability for work; or
  (b) is to be treated as having limited capability for work under regula-
      tions 20, 25, 26, 29 or 33(2),

the Secretary of State may, if paragraph (8) applies, determine afresh whether the claimant has or is to be treated as having limited capability for work.

(8) This paragraph applies where—

  (a) the Secretary of State wishes to determine whether there has been
      a relevant change of circumstances in relation to the claimant's
      physical or mental condition;
  (b) the Secretary of State wishes to determine whether the previous
      determination of limited capability for work or that the claimant is
      to be treated as having limited capability for work, was made in
      ignorance of , or was based on a mistake as to, some material fact;
      or

(c) at least 3 months have passed since the date on which the claimant
was determined to have limited capability for work or to be treated
as having limited capability for work.

DEFINITIONS

"claimant"—see WRA 2007, s.24(1).
"descriptor"—see reg.2(1).
"limited capability for work"—see WRA 2007, s.1(4).
"limited capability for work assessment"—see para.(2).

GENERAL NOTE

Entitlement to ESA requires that the claimant has limited capability for work   1A.171
(WRA 2007, s.1(3)(a)). Whether his capability for work is limited by his physical
or mental condition such that it is not reasonable to require him to work is to be
determined in accordance with regulations (WRA 2007, s.8(1)). This regulation,
setting out how "actual" limited capability to work is to be determined through
the limited capability for work assessment is the product. The remainder of this
Part (regs 20–33), deal with situations in which someone, whatever the reality, is
to be treated as having limited capability for work, and also with aspects of the
decision-making process.

Para. (1)
ESA is a benefit designed to help people with a limiting health condition   1A.172
overcome barriers, and where appropriate move into work and improve their
lives. The Work Capability Assessment (WCA) seeks more accurately to relate to
modern context than the 12-year-old IB/IS system, and to focus more on what
people can do, rather on what they are unable to do. The matter of whether the
claimant's capability for work is limited by his physical or mental condition, and,
if so, whether the limitation is to such an extent that it is not reasonable to
require him to work, is to be decided on the basis of the "limited capability for
work assessment" (WCAt or LCWA). This is the first element in a new three-
part "work capability assessment" (WCA), developed out of the review of the IB
"personal capability assessment" (PCA), which governs entitlement to the basic
allowance and the additional components of ESA. The new WCA underpinning
ESA was devised by the DWP's Health Work and Wellbeing Directorate with
input from two technical working groups, one focusing on mental health and
learning difficulties, the other on physical function and conditions (hereinafter
"review group"). The review group consisted of medical and other relevant
experts. It examined how the IB Personal Capability Assessment (PCA) (characterized by them as "the best assessment of its type in the world" could nonetheless be improved and updated so as to reflect the many changes since its
inception:

"in the prevalence of disabling conditions; in advances in medical science
resulting in the availability of new and more effective medical interventions;
and in the workplace environment. The Disability Discrimination Act, introduced after the PCA had been developed, has influenced the ability of employers to make reasonable adjustments to accommodate people with long term
disabilities. It has also raised the expectations of disabled people that adjustments should be made to enable them to work."

Government anticipates that the WCA will "fail" some 60,000 claimants a
year who would have "passed" the PCA. (DWP, *Impact Assessment of the Employment and Support Allowance Regulations 2008—Public sector Impact Only* in *Explanatory Memorandum to Employment and Support Allowance Regulations 2008 (SI*

2008/794) and the Employment and Support Allowance (Transitional Provisions) Regulations 2008 (SI 2008/795), p.9). But the three-element WCA is not merely an incapacity-based tool for determining entitlement to ESA. That remains true of its first element the subject of this regulation. However, its second element is rather a more positive assessment considering ability to benefit from work-related activity with a view to promoting capacity for work. The assessment has two aspects: an assessment of limited capability to work (WCAt) and an assessment of limited capacity to engage in work-related activity (WRAAt). Both assessments will generally be conducted at the same time. The WCAt is a more rigorous test than the PCA and far fewer groups are exempted from it. Those found not to have limited capacity for work (expected to be some 90% of new claimants) will in addition have to undergo the third element of the WCA: a work-focused health related assessment (WFHRAt).

Paras (2) and (5)

1A.173   This defines the "limited capability for work assessment" (WCAt). Like the IB "personal capability assessment" (PCA) and its predecessor, the "all work" test, the ESA WCAt is an assessment of the extent to which someone with a specific disease or bodily or mental disablement is (despite that) capable of performing the activities set out in Sch.2 or is because of it incapable of performing them. Since the test is thus so similar to that in IB (see Incapacity for Work Regs, reg.24 and Sch.), the position taken here is that case authorities (whether Commissioner or court) on the PCA will also apply to the WCAt. As with the IB PCA, the tasks involved in applying the WCAt are twofold:

1.   ascertaining from all the evidence in the case which descriptors apply (paras (2), (5) and Sch.2);
2.   computing the scores (paras (3), (6)).

The terms of para.(2) require the incapacity to perform the Sch.2 activities to arise by reason of "some specific disease or bodily or mental disablement". This is further stressed in paras (5)(a) and (b), the latter of which specifically also brings in "mental illness", while para.(5)(c) in effect adds that the rubric will also cover incapability as a direct result of treatment provided by a registered medical practitioner for such a disease, illness or disablement: This "specific disease or bodily or mental disablement" phraseology was found in the sickness/invalidity benefits statutory test and in both the "own occupation" test and the IB PCA, so decisions on this phraseology from those regimes will still be authoritative here.

"Specific" means "of a kind identified by medical science" (*CS/57/82*, noted in [1983] J.S.W.L. 306). "Disease" has been described as "a departure from health capable of identification by its signs and symptoms, an abnormality of some sort", and sickness falls within the definition (*CS/221/49*, para.3; *CS/7/82*, noted in [1983] J.S.W.L. 306). "Disablement"—which may be bodily or mental—constitutes a state of deprivation or incapacitation of ability measured against the abilities of a normal person (*CS/7/82*, *ibid.*). "Illness" is surely comparable to concepts of "disease" or "sickness".

In most cases there will be little problem, given the medical evidence, as to whether the claimant's condition amounts to disease or disablement; disagreement will generally centre on whether it prevents him carrying out the activities in Sch.2. However, a number of areas can be identified where difficult lines may have to be drawn on whether or not the condition comes within the rubric "disease or ... disablement" at all. Pregnancy alone does not, but a disease or disablement associated with, but going beyond the normal incidents of, pregnancy does, as in *CS/221/49* where the certified incapacity, "sickness of pregnancy", was suffered throughout the day. See also *R(S) 4/93*. But note now that certain pregnant women are to be treated as incapable of work (see reg.20(e)).

Alcoholism can come within the rubric, but in some circumstances might bring about a period of disqualification from benefit (see reg.157). Whether certain conditions constitute a disease of the mind or a mental disablement can be problematical in that the line between a recognisable mental illness or disablement, on the one hand, and states of malingering or being workshy on the other, can be fine and uncertain. The difficulty is to decide from the available evidence whether the claimant is genuinely ill or disabled and thereby incapacitated for work in the sense understood above, or whether his is a voluntary attitude of workshyness where he could but will not work. The problem will be compounded where the outward symptoms of these alternative states are the same. What will be crucial will be the terms in which the medical (psychiatric) evidence is cast, and the inevitable value judgments about whether a particular claimant's attitudes to doing work are voluntary or involuntary. Perhaps here the appellate authorities' jurisdiction to seek further medical (in this case psychiatric) reports at public expense could prove valuable. In *R(S) 6/59*, the Commissioner considered a particular case of Munchausen's syndrome, under which condition a person repeatedly presents himself for treatment to a hospital or series of hospitals recounting symptoms of a particular disease or disability from which he is not in fact suffering, which the Commissioner there described as a strange condition in the nature of malingering. The Commissioner in that case was not satisfied on the evidence that the claimant believed the symptoms actually to exist, and felt unable to regard the condition as a psychosis, which would have come within the statutory rubric. The claim for benefit failed, the Commissioner stating as an additional ground for the decision his view that the syndrome in any event did not affect that particular claimant's capacity to work since he had driven from hospital to hospital in his lorry. In effect, the condition was treated as a defect of character. In *CS/1/81* (noted in [1982] J.S.W.L. 48), the dispute initially centred on whether the claimant, suffering from what the RMO (now a DWP MS doctor) and his own doctor described as an anxiety state, was as a result incapable of work. The consultant psychiatrist to whom the claimant was referred considered him an inadequate personality by reason of his total self-indulgence and extreme degree of sheltering behind psychiatric symptoms to avoid responsibility. His condition resulted from a dismal personality structure rather than illness. Accordingly the Commissioner held that he was incapable of work but not by reason of disease or disablement, so the claim failed. Mesher (now Commissioner Mesher) suggests in [1982] J.S.W.L. 48 that the Commissioner there gave inadequate consideration to whether the defect (clearly on the evidence not an illness) could nevertheless be a mental disablement. In contrast, *CS 7/82* (noted in [1983] J.S.W.L. 306) dealt with a situation in which the claimant was said to have a severe personality disorder but not to be mentally ill. "Personality disorder" is a term sometimes used as a euphemism for workshy. The Commissioner held that its use in the particular case conveyed a notion of disability of mind sufficient to bring the claimant within the statutory rubric. It is submitted that one should avoid using euphemisms which may confuse; the loser in the case is entitled to know why he has lost. If he is thought workshy, that should be stated and reasons given for that conclusion. Sheltering behind euphemisms may also cloud the steps in reasoning which go towards good adjudication and decision-making.

What has to be established, to what standard of proof, and by what evidence, is analysed well by Commissioner Jacobs in *CIB/26/2004*. There must be established, on the civil standard of balance of probabilities, that the claimant has a recognised medical condition (paras 18, 25, citing *R2/99 (IB)*, para.8; *CSDLA/552/2001*, para.27; and *CDLA/944/2001*, paras 9 and 10). A medical diagnosis is useful evidence, but is not decisive in that an appeal tribunal, giving appropriate reasons, can refuse to accept it. The cogency of a diagnosis varies according to a number of factors: the nature of the condition (some being easier to diagnose than others); how well qualified in the relevant area of medicine the doctor is who makes the diagnosis; the range of information and material on which the diagnosis is based; and the degree of certainty with which it is made (e.g. is the diagnosis "firm", or qualified as "working", "presumptive" or "provisional") (para.22). If there is general consensus among medical authorities as to the existence of a particular condition, a tribunal (even one containing a medical member) will normally err in law if, being sceptical, it denies its existence (para.21, citing a Northern Ireland Tribunal of Commissioners in *C38/03–04 (DLA)*, para.20(3)). If a medical diagnosis is not necessarily decisive, nor is the lack of one necessarily fatal; in appropriate circumstances a tribunal can make a diagnosis without medical evidence (para.19). While agreeing to some extent with Commissioner Brown's view (*R 2/99 (IB)*, para.11) that a tribunal should be cautious of making a diagnosis of mental disease or disablement in the absence of supportive medical evidence, Commissioner Jacobs qualified that by noting that at the time of that decision there was no medical member on the tribunal—it merely then had advice from an assessor—that change in composition rendering it easier now for a tribunal to make a diagnosis on the evidence available (para.20).

Paras (3) and (6)

1A.174   *Computing the scores:* Like the IB PCA, and its predecessor "all work" test (see Incapacity for Work Regs, reg.25), achievement of a particular score is required before the claimant can be found to have limited capability for work. Under ESA, the scoring system is simpler. The score attained must be at least 15 points whether from Sch.2, Pt 1 alone (physical disabilities), Pt 2 alone (mental, cognitive and intellectual function assessment), or from a combination of the descriptors in both parts. In each case, where more than one descriptor for an activity applies, only the highest scoring one counts (para.(6)). Following the approach to the IB PCA (see commentary to Incapacity for Work Regs, reg.25), it is submitted that there are no implied limits on simply adding together the highest scores from each activity (*R(IB) 3/98*).

Paras (7), (8)

1A.175   These make clear that the matters of whether someone actually has limited capability for work, or whether he is to be treated as having it under regs 20, 25, 26, 29 or 33(2), are ones that can be revisited where one or more of the situations in para.(8) arise:

- a desire to determine whether there has been a relevant change of circumstances in relation to the claimants health condition (is he getting better or worse?) (sub-para.(a);
- a wish to determine whether the prior determination of actual or deemed limited capability was made in ignorance of, or was based on a mistake as to, a material fact (sub-para.(b);
- at least three months have elapsed since the previous decision on actual or deemed limited capability (sub-para.(c)).

Certain claimants to be treated as having limited capability for work

1A.176   **20.** A claimant is to be treated as having limited capability for work if—

  (a) the claimant is terminally ill;
  (b) the claimant is—

      (i) receiving treatment by way of intravenous, intraperitoneal or intrathecal chemotherapy; or

      (ii) recovering from that treatment and the Secretary of State is satisfied the claimant should be treated as having limited capability for work;

(c) the claimant is—

      (i) excluded or abstains from work, or from work of such a kind, pursuant to a request or notice in writing lawfully made under an enactment; or

      (ii) otherwise prevented from working pursuant to an enactment,

by reason of the claimant being a carrier, or having been in contact with a case, of a relevant disease;

(d) in the case of a pregnant woman, there is a serious risk of damage to her health or to the health of her unborn child if she does not refrain from work;

(e) in the case of a pregnant woman, she—

      (i) is within the maternity allowance period; and

      (ii) is entitled to a maternity allowance under section 35(1) of the Contributions and Benefits Act;

(f) in the case of a pregnant woman whose expected or actual date of confinement has been certified in accordance with the Medical Evidence Regulations, on any day in the period—

      (i) beginning with the first date of the 6th week before the expected week of her confinement or the actual date of her confinement, whichever is earlier; and

      (ii) ending on the 14th day after the actual date of her confinement,

if she would have no entitlement to a maternity allowance or statutory maternity pay were she to make a claim in respect of that period.

DEFINITIONS

"claimant"—see WRA 2007, s.24(1).
"confinement"—see reg.2(1).
"Contributions and Benefits Act"—see WRA 2007, s.65.
"limited capability for work"—see WRA 2007, s.1(4).
"maternity allowance period"—see reg.2(1).
"Medical Evidence Regulations"—see reg.2(1).
"terminally ill"—see reg.2(1).
"week"—see reg.2(1).

GENERAL NOTE

This regulation—the parent power for which is WRA 2007, s.22 and Sch.2, **1A.177** para.9—sets out the situations in which a claimant is to be treated as having limited capability for work. This is important because such claimants will be exempt from the WCA and its information gathering processes (see reg.21). In conception, its IB comparator is Incapacity for Work Regs, reg.10. But in terms of detail the provisions are rather different. The IB reg. exempted a much longer group of claimants. In contrast the list in reg.20 is much more curtailed. This is because the ESA tests are designed to assess which claimants can benefit from the help towards work afforded by work-related activity, to "write off" from the chance of work as few people as possible. Those exempt are:

- the terminally ill (para.(a))—"suffering from a progressive disease and death in consequence of that disease can reasonably be expected within 6 months" (reg.2(1));
- those receiving treatment by way of intravenous, intraperitoneal or intra-thecal chemotherapy (para.(b)(i)); such of those recovering from such treatment as the Secretary of State is satisfied (note the discretion) should be treated as having limited capability for work (para.(b)(ii));
- those excluded or prevented from working as a carrier, or having been in contact with a case of relevant disease (food poisoning, infectious or notifi-able diseases covered by a variety of public health enactments) (para.(c));
- pregnant women where there is a serious risk of damage to their or their unborn child's health if they do not refrain from work (para.(d));
- pregnant women at a certain stage in pregnancy (paras (e), (f)). Paragraph (e) covers the pregnant woman during the maternity allowance period (see reg.2(1) and SSCBA 1992, s.35(2)) entitled to a maternity allowance under SSCBA 1992, s.35. Para.(f) in contrast deals with the pregnant woman whose expected or actual date of confinement has been duly certified in accordance with the Medical Evidence Regulations. It covers her during a period beginning with the earlier of the actual date of confinement or the first day of the sixth week before the expected week of confinement and ending on the 14th day after the actual date of confinement. But it does so only where she would not be entitled to maternity allowance or SMP if she were to claim in respect of that period.

Information required for determining capability for work

1A.178   **21.**—(1) Subject to paragraphs (2) and (3), the information or evi-dence required to determine whether a claimant has limited capability for work is—

(a) evidence of limited capability for work in accordance with the Medical Evidence Regulations (which prescribe the form of doc-tor's statement or other evidence required in each case);

(b) any information relating to a claimant's capability to perform the activities referred to in Schedule 2 as may be requested in the form of a questionnaire; and

(c) any such additional information as may be requested.

(2) Where the Secretary of State is satisfied that there is sufficient information to determine whether a claimant has limited capability for work without the information specified in paragraph (1)(b), that infor-mation will not be required for the purposes of making the determina-tion.

(3) Paragraph (1) does not apply in relation to a determination whether a claimant is to be treated as having limited capability for work under any of regulations 20 (certain claimants to be treated as having limited capability for work), 25 (hospital in-patients), 26 (claimants receiving certain regular treatment) and 33(2) (additional circumstances in which a claimant is to be treated as having limited capability for work).

DEFINITIONS

"claimant"—see WRA 2007, s.24(1).
"doctor"—see reg.2(1).
"limited capability for work"—see WRA 2007, s.1(4).
"Medical Evidence Regulations"—see reg.2(1).

GENERAL NOTE

This regulation deals with the information required for determining whether   **1A.179**
someone has limited capability for work. It is designed to give the decision-maker
sufficient information to decide that matter for himself (the minority of cases), or
whether to seek advice from a health care professional on the basis of the papers
in respect of that decision, or to refer the claimant for a face to face WCAt,
including a medical examination (see reg.23).
Unless para.(3) operates, the claimant will have to supply: (i) evidence of his
incapacity for work in accordance with the Medical Evidence Regs (para.(1)(a));
and (ii) such additional information relating to the relevant test as the Secretary
of State asks for (para.(1)(c)). Furthermore, he must generally complete and
return the appropriate questionnaire (para.(1)(b)), unless para.(3) operates or
the Secretary of State decides that completion of the questionnaire is not necessary because without it he has sufficient information to determine whether the
claimant does or does not have limited capability for work (para.(2)). Note that
where the claimant is requested by the Secretary of State to complete and return
the questionnaire, failure to do so can result in his being treated as capable of
work (and thus not entitled to ESA) (reg.22).

Failure to provide information in relation to limited capability for work

22.—(1) Where a claimant fails without good cause to comply with the   **1A.180**
request referred to in regulation 21(1)(b), that claimant is, subject to
paragraph (2), to be treated as not having limited capability for work.
(2) Paragraph (1) does not apply unless—
(a) at least 6 weeks have passed since the claimant was sent the first
request for the information; and
(b) the claimant was sent a further request at least 4 weeks after the
date of the first request, and at least 2 weeks have passed since the
further request was sent.

DEFINITIONS

"claimant"—see WRA 2007, s.24(1).
"limited capability for work"—see WRA 2007, s.1(4).
"week"—see reg.2(1)

GENERAL NOTE

If a claimant fails without good cause (on which more, below) to comply with   **1A.181**
the requirement to complete and return a limited capability for work questionnaire, he must be treated as not having limited capability for work, that is, as
having no entitlement to ESA. This can only happen, however, if at least six
weeks have passed since the claimant was first sent the request for information,
a further request for information was sent at least four weeks after the first and
at least two weeks have gone by since the second request was sent. The compara-
bly worded IB provision is Incapacity for Work Regs, reg.7. Commissioners'
decisions on that establish that as regards calculating a period before the end of

111

which something cannot be done (e.g. "at least six weeks have passed"—
para.(2)(a)), one must ignore the day from which the period runs as well as the
day on which it expires (per Commissioner Jacobs in *R(IB) 1/00*). "Week" here
means any period of seven days (reg.2(1)). But note that the para refers, like the
IB provision, to a request being "sent" rather than "received" (as stressed by
Commissioner Rowland in *CIB/3512/1998*). Non-receipt has, however, an
important bearing on "good cause". "Good cause" is not exhaustively defined in
legislation, although reg.24 non-exhaustively prescribes certain matters which
must be taken into account in determining the issue. Some guidance may be
found in authorities on the corresponding area in unemployment benefit (see
USI Regs, regs 7(1)(i), (j)—see pp.720–21 of Bonner, Hooker and White, *Non
Means Tested Benefits: The Legislation* (1996)), the matter of relief from disqualification from sickness and invalidity benefit under the now revoked USI
Regs, reg.17 (see pp.737–740 of the 1994 edition of *Non- Means Tested Benefits,
The Legislation*), and that from disqualification/being treated as incapable under
Incapacity for Work Regs, reg.18 or, in time, reg.157 of these ESA Regs. Some
assistance may be derived from disqualification from unemployment benefit
under the now repealed SSCBA 1992, s.28, but caution must be exercised
because both that section itself and the now revoked USI Regs 12E set statutory
limits to the concept applicable only for the purposes of that section, since use
was made there of a power to circumscribe and define good cause (see
pp.133–34, 143–44, 150, and 752–56 of *Non Means Tested Benefits: The Legislation* 1996). A similar power exists in this context (WRA 2007, s.8(4)) but has not
yet been exercised other than as set out in reg.24.

Claimant may be called for a medical examination to determine whether the claimant has limited capability for work

1A.182   **23.**—(1) Where it falls to be determined whether a claimant has
limited capability for work, that claimant may be called by or on behalf
of a health care professional approved by the Secretary of State to attend
for a medical examination.

(2) Subject to paragraph (3), where a claimant fails without good
cause to attend for or to submit to an examination listed in paragraph
(1), the claimant is to be treated as not having limited capability for
work.

(3) Paragraph (2) does not apply unless written notice of the time and
place for the examination was sent to the claimant at least 7 days in
advance, or unless that claimant agreed to accept a shorter period of
notice whether given in writing or otherwise.

DEFINITIONS

"claimant"—see WRA 2007, s.24(1).
"health care professional"—see reg.2(1).
"limited capability for work"—see WRA 2007, s.1(4).

GENERAL NOTE

1A.183   This regulation enables the DWP to have a claimant medically examined by a
DWP Medical Service (DWPMS) health service professional (technically any
health service professional approved by the Secretary of State) when a question
arises as to the claimant's capability for work. Failure without good cause to
attend for or submit to such an examination, of which he was given proper

written notice (see para.(3)), will result in the claimant being treated as not having limited capability for work and not entitled to ESA.

This reg. is directly comparable to Incapacity for Work Regs, reg.8 and the approach taken here is that authorities on that and analogous regulations are applicable here.

Note that proper written notice means written notice of the time and place of the examination, sent to him at least seven days beforehand, unless the person agreed to accept a shorter period of notice, whether given in writing or otherwise. Interpreted by analogy with the approach to another time period issue in *R(IB)2/00*, para.(3) requires at least seven days' clear notice so that neither the day of sending nor that of receipt count in determining that period (*CIB/2576/2007*, para.6). The notice may be given by or on behalf of the approved (generally DWPMS) health care professional concerned (para.(1)). The notice must, however, be written. So, where an appointment had been made over the telephone by leaving a message with the claimant's sister, which the claimant asserted was not passed on, he could not properly be treated as capable of work for not having attended without good cause, since the regulation's clear requisite of written notice had not been satisfied (see *CIB/969/97*). In *R(IB) 1/01*, Commissioner Rowland considered that where, when a claimant stated that he would not be able to attend a medical examination, the Department in consequence said they would cancel it, the claimant cannot be held not to have attended it. If, however, a claimant makes it clear that he or she will not be medically examined, then that arguably constitutes failure to "submit to" an examination. Going to the medical examination but refusing to be examined, constitutes attendance but also a failure to submit. In *CIB/849/2001*, Commissioner Turnbull stated:

> "The purpose of the medical examination was of course to enable the adjudication officer, with the benefit of the doctor's report, to determine whether the Claimant passed the all work test. The condition which the Claimant wished to impose on his submitting to an examination—i.e. that the doctor's report should not be passed to any layman, including an adjudication officer—rendered an examination useless for the purpose for which it was required. I have no doubt that, by imposing such a condition, the Claimant was failing to submit himself to a medical examination within the meaning of reg.8(2) [by analogy ESA Regs, reg.23(2)]. A person 'fails' to submit himself to an examination not only if he absolutely refuses to be examined, but also if he seeks to impose as a condition of being examined a term which would render the examination useless for the purpose for which it is required" (para.11).

The nature and extent of the medical examination to which the claimant must submit is a matter for the examining health care professional rather than the claimant, tribunal or Commissioner, "fundamentally a medical matter and for the judgment of the clinician in each individual case" (*C1/07–08(IB)*, para.12). The health care professional's demands of the claimant must, however, fall within the bounds of a "medical examination" and there remains the issue of whether a claimant has good cause for refusing to submit to the examination (*C1/07–08(IB)*, para.15).

A health care professional can insist on the presence of a suitable chaperone (e.g. a DWP employee bound by confidentiality not to broadcast details to the world at large), and unreasonable refusal to allow such a chaperone to be present constitutes refusing to submit to the examination (*CIB/2645/99*; *CIB/2011/2001*, para.15). Claimants cannot expect their medical details to be kept from those who must determine their claims; those who insist on strict medical confidentiality can do so, but only at the cost of foregoing their rights to benefit or credits (*CIB/2011/2001*, para.15). In *CIB/1381/2003*, Deputy Commissioner Wikeley declined, after reviewing a range of authority on analogous provisions in child support and jobseeker's allowance, to determine whether "sent" meant "despatched" or "delivered", since a failure to attend because of not receiving the notice could in any event constitute "good cause" as the tribunal had held. In *CSIB/721/2004*, however, Commissioner Parker was of the view that where the claimant proved that the notification duly despatched (a matter for the Secretary of State to establish) had not in fact been received by him, in the ordinary course of post or at all, then it had not been "sent" within the meaning of para.(3), thus precluding treating the claimant as capable of work for "failure to attend or submit to examination" so that the issue of "good cause" never arose. She there took account of a Secretary of State concession on the point noted in *CIB/4512/2002* (not on the Commissioners' website), to which the Secretary of State's representative referred her. But in contrast note that Commissioner Rowland in *CIB/3512/1998*, dealing with an analogous Incapacity for Work Reg., stressed that it said "sent" rather than "received", albeit that non-receipt would be a matter as regards "good cause".

The Northern Ireland decision *C11/03–04(IB)* is a useful reminder of the need to ascertain the precise facts and be careful in applying to them the concept of "good cause". The case concerned a common "defence", where the claimant alleged he had never received a particular letter sent by the Department, a typical case of conflict of evidence. Deputy Commissioner Powell thought that sometimes it is right to reject such allegations in a robust manner, for example, where the excuse extends to a number of letters, or is coupled with suspicious circumstances, or if the non-receipt of mail is selective so that only certain letters are not received. The case before him, however, concerned a rather different situation—the uncontradicted evidence of the claimant, who did not attend the appeal hearing, of the non-receipt of a single letter in plausible circumstances, namely, a communal delivery of mail to particular premises and the possibility that another went through it before the claimant had a chance to do so. The Commissioner could not see how an effective challenge could be mounted to the claim and that, in these circumstances, the claimant had established good cause. The Secretary of State bears the burden of proof in establishing that the requirements of para.(3) have been met, a precondition for being able to find the claimant capable of work for non-attendance etc. In *CIB/4012/2004*, deputy Commissioner Mark, considering the cases noted above, found that the burden had not been discharged. Computer records showing that a letter had been issued were not sufficient evidence of it being "sent". He said helpfully:

"I can see no reason why, in establishing whether the requirements of regulation 8(3) have been met, the secretary of state cannot provide a simple short written statement from the appropriate person giving the date on which the written notice was posted, the time at least to an extent sufficient to show whether or not it would have been collected that day by Royal Mail from the post box, and the address to which it was posted, and also stating whether it was sent by first or second class post. The statement should also confirm that the letter has not been returned undelivered. It appears to me that in future there should be evidence available from the secretary of state dealing with those issues before a decision-maker comes to a decision. If it is not stated whether first or second class post was used, the decision-maker should either seek further evidence or assume that second class post was used. If there is a further issue as to whether it was posted to the correct address, as in this case where there has been a change of address, the secretary of state will normally need better evidence of the address to which it was posted than a later computer generated print out showing the address on the file at that later date" (paras 21–22).

The effect of a finding of lack of good cause precludes benefit until a new claim is submitted and a new period of incapacity for work begins (para.6 of the decision). It may also prevent the claimant being treated under reg.30 as incapable of work pending a limited capability for work assessment. However, if the claimant is found to have limited capability for work in that assessment, benefit can be backdated to the beginning of the period covered by the new claim or application. See also on this aspect *R(IB)2/01* and para.8 of *CIB/3512/1998*. On "good cause", see the commentary to reg.22 and note the non-exhaustive prescription in reg.24 of matters which must be taken into account in determining good cause. If it was unreasonable of the Secretary of State to arrange a medical examination, the claimant can argue that he had good cause for refusing to submit to it (*CIB/2645/99*; *CIB/2011/2001*, para.16). But since, as Commissioner Rowland stressed, "the integrity of the system depends upon their being appropriate tests in place" (*CIB/2011/2001*, para.16), establishing unreasonableness is unlikely to be easy.

Matters to be taken into account in determining good cause in relation to regulations 22 or 23

24. The matters to be taken into account in determining whether a claimant has good cause under regulations 22 (failure to provide information in relation to limited capability for work) or 23 (failure to attend a medical examination to determine limited capability for work) include—   **1A.184**

(a) whether the claimant was outside Great Britain at the relevant time;

(b) the claimant's state of health at the relevant time; and

(c) the nature of any disability the claimant has.

DEFINITION

"claimant"—see WRA 2007, s.24(1).

GENERAL NOTE

This regulation, made pursuant to WRA 2007, s.8(4), stipulates that in determining whether someone had good cause for failing to provide information (under reg.22) or for failing to attend for or submit to a medical examination (under reg.23) decision-makers and appellate bodies must take into account (i) whether the person was outside Great Britain at the relevant time, (ii) his state of health at the relevant time, and (iii) the nature of his disability. This list is not, however, exhaustive (the regulation says "shall include"). On "good cause", see further the commentary to regs 22 and 23.   **1A.185**

Hospital in-patients

25.—(1) A claimant is to be treated as having limited capability for work on any day on which that claimant is undergoing medical or other treatment as an in-patient in a hospital or similar institution, or which is a day of recovery from that treatment.   **1A.186**

(2) For the purposes of this regulation, "day of recovery" means a day on which a claimant is recovering from treatment as an in-patient in a hospital or equivalent under paragraph (1) and the Secretary of State is satisfied that the claimant should be treated as having limited capability for work on that day.

DEFINITIONS

"claimant"—see WRA 2007, s.24(1).
"day of recovery"—see para.(2).
"limited capability for work"—see WRA 2007, s.1(4).
"medical treatment"—see reg.2(1).

GENERAL NOTE

1A.187   This regulation is comparable to, but goes a little further than, Incapacity for Work Regs, reg.12. Like that regulation, it stipulates that those undergoing medical or other treatment as an in-patient of a hospital or other institution, must be treated as having limited capability for work on any day on which they are undergoing that treatment. The notion of "undergoing ... treatment" is not defined. Note, however, that a prolonged stay in hospital (more than 52 weeks) results in benefit being reduced: see Hospital In-patients Regulations. Where this regulation goes further is that it also treats the person as having limited capability for work on any day of recovery from that treatment. "Day of recovery" is defined in para.(2). Note the discretion given to the Secretary of State—the day on which the former in-patient is recovering from that treatment will only count if the Secretary of State is satisfied that it the claimant should on that day be treated as having limited capability for work.

Regulation 21(1) (information gathering requirements) does not apply to a determination under this regulation (see reg.21(3)).

Claimants receiving certain regular treatment

1A.188   **26.**—(1) Subject to paragraph (2), a claimant receiving—
(a) regular weekly treatment by way of haemodialysis for chronic renal failure;
(b) treatment by way of plasmapheresis or by way of radiotherapy; or
(c) regular weekly treatment by way of total parenteral nutrition for gross impairment of enteric function,

is to be treated as having limited capability for work during any week in which that claimant is engaged in that treatment or has a day of recovery from that treatment.

[1(2) A claimant who receives the treatment referred to in paragraph (1) is only to be treated as having limited capability for work from the first week of treatment in which the claimant undergoes no fewer than—
(a) two days of treatment;
(b) two days of recovery from any of the forms of treatment listed in paragraph 1(a) to (c); or
(c) one day of treatment and one day of recovery from that treatment,

but the days of treatment or recovery from that treatment or both need not be consecutive.]

(3) For the purpose of this regulation "day of recovery" means a day on which a claimant is recovering from any of the forms of treatment listed in paragraph (1)(a) to (c) and the Secretary of State is satisfied that the claimant should be treated as having limited capability for work on that day.

116

AMENDMENTS

1. Employment and Support Allowance (Miscellaneous Amendments) Regulations 2008 (SI 2008/2428), reg.5(1) (October 27, 2008).

DEFINITIONS

"claimant"—see WRA 2007, s.24(1).
"day of recovery"—see para.(3).
"limited capability for work"—see WRA 2007, s.1(4).
"week"—see WRA 2007, s.24(1); reg.2(1).

GENERAL NOTE

This regulation has similarities with Incapacity for Work Regs, reg.13, but is **1A.189** narrower in the range of treatments covered and its wording reflects that ESA is a weekly rather than, as with IB, a daily benefit.

Someone undergoing certain treatments is treated as having limited capability for work on during any week in which he is engaged in that treatment or has a day of recovery from that treatment (para.(1)). The treatments concerned are: regular weekly treatment by way of haemodialysis for chronic renal failure (para.(1)(a)); treatment by way of plasmapheresis or by way of radiotherapy (para.(1)(b)); or regular weekly treatment by way of total parenteral nutrition for gross impairment of enteric function (para.(1)(c)). "Day of recovery" is defined in para.(3) as one on which the claimant is recovering from any of the forms of treatment so long as the Secretary of State (note the discretion) is satisfied that the claimant should be treated as having limited capability for work on that day. Paragraph (2) deals with the first week of any such treatment. During that week, the claimant can only be treated as having limited capability for work if in that week he undergoes no fewer than two days of treatment, or two days of recovery from such treatment or one day of treatment and one day of recovery. The days of treatment or recovery from it need not be consecutive.

Regulation 21(1) (information gathering requirements) does not apply to a determination under this regulation (see reg.21(3)).

Claimant to be treated as having limited capability for work throughout a day

27. A claimant who at the commencement of any day has, or thereafter **1A.190** develops, limited capability for work as determined in accordance with the limited capability for work assessment is to be treated as having limited capability for work throughout that day.

DEFINITIONS

"claimant"—see WRA 2007, s.24(1).
"limited capability for work"—see WRA 2007, s.1(4).
"limited capability for work assessment"—see reg.2(1).

GENERAL NOTE

The situation encompassed here in which someone is to be treated as having **1A.191** limited capability for work, confers no exemption from the information gathering processes for the limited capability for work assessment (reg.21(3)).

This regulation is analogous to Incapacity for Work Regs, reg.15 and its predecessor (USI Regs, reg.3(2); see pp.688, 690 of Bonner, Hooker and White, *Non Means Tested Benefits: The Legislation* 1994). It is submitted that authorities on those provisions are also applicable to its interpretation and application.

The effect of this regulation is that those with limited capability for work at the start of a day or who thereafter develop it on that day are to be treated as having limited capability for work throughout that day. In *CIB/6244/1997*, Commissioner Jacobs considered the application of the IB regulation to intermittent and variable conditions. He considered that the provision must be read in the light that, under the all work test/PCA and its descriptors, one cannot confine consideration merely to a particular time on a particular day—otherwise a claimant could always satisfy the "cannot" descriptors and the "sometimes" ones (not in any event in the ESA limited capability for work assessment activities and descriptors) would never apply. The "cannot" and "sometimes" descriptors inevitably require a focus over a period and not at a specific moment in time. Thus he thought that Incapacity for Work Regs, reg.15 "does not operate to ensure that a claimant with a variable condition that incapacitates him for a part of each day must be considered as incapable throughout the whole of every day" (para.23).However, it will "apply where there is a sudden onset of or recovery from an incapacitating condition, including an intermittent incapacitating condition or the incapacitating intermittent features of a condition" (*ibid.* and see also *CIB/15482/1996*, paras 7–9). In *CIB/243/1998*. Deputy Commissioner Mark considered that a claimant who suffered an asthma attack for part of a day had to be treated as incapable of work throughout that day under this regulation, provided that the effect of the attack when ongoing was such that he would score at least 15 points for more than a minimal period on that day. In *CIB/399/2003*, Commissioner Mesher very firmly rejected that approach of Deputy Commissioner Mark in *CIB/243/1998* and preferred the approach taken by Commissioner Jacobs in *CIB/6244/1997* and by Deputy Commissioner Ramsay in *CIB/15482/1996*, thus establishing a strong line of authority against Deputy Commissioner Mark's view of the application of Incapacity for Work Regs, reg.15. Commissioner Mesher thought the rejected approach to be inconsistent with the concept of "reasonable regularity" applicable to the "cannot" descriptors and out of tune with the tenor of *R(IB)2/99(T)* (on which see further the commentary to Sch.2).

Night workers

1A.192 **28.**—(1) Where a claimant works for a continuous period which extends over midnight into the following day, that claimant is to be treated as having limited capability for work on the day on which the lesser part of that period falls if that claimant had limited capability for work for the remainder of that day.

(2) Where, in relation to a period referred to in paragraph (1), the number of hours worked before and after midnight is equal—

(a) if the days in question fall at the beginning of a period of limited capability for work, the claimant is to be treated as having limited capability on the second day; and

(b) if the days in question fall at the end of a period of limited capability for work, the claimant is to be treated as having limited capability for work on the first day.

DEFINITIONS

"claimant"—see WRA 2007, s.24(1).
"limited capability for work"—see WRA 2007, s.1(4).
"period of limited capability for work"—see reg.2(1).

GENERAL NOTE

This is analogous to IB Regulations, reg.5 and its predecessors in the sickness and invalidity benefits regime. Although unlike IB and those benefits, ESA is a weekly rather than a daily benefit, there is still need to be able to attribute limited capability for work to a particular day, where the person doing nightwork has a shift spanning midnight and thus covering two days. The ESA scheme in some circumstances permits awards for periods of less than a week (the amount payable being determined under regs 165–169) (e.g. the period at the start or end of a claim; persons receiving certain regular treatments). Although the ESA scheme neither in Act or Regs defines "day", the general rule for benefit purposes has been that a day is the period midnight to midnight, and performance of work on a day will generally preclude the week in which it is done ranking as one of entitlement to ESA (see reg.40(1)). But there are exceptions to that preclusive rule (regs 40(4), 46) where the preclusion is only to affect the day(s) actually worked. There is thus a need to attribute a nightshift spanning two days to one day or the other. Otherwise, the application of the rules to nightworkers whose shifts span midnight could cause hardship since they would, without this regulation, be regarded as working on two days and thus be treated less favourably than their day worker counterparts whose shift of exactly the same length (period of work) would be attributed to one day. Equally, even though the nightworker suffered the same degree of limited capability for work on one of those days, the day could not count as one of limited capability for work This regulation attempts some easing of the position of nightworkers in this regard.

Paragraph (1) provides that where someone works for a continuous period beginning one day and spanning midnight into the following day, the day on which there falls the lesser part of the period worked will be treated as one of limited capability for work if the claimant has limited capability for work for the rest of that day. To put it another way, the day with the longer period worked is to be treated for the purpose of the exceptions to the preclusive rules noted above as the day of work. Paragraph (2) deals with the situation in which the hours worked each side of midnight are equal. If the two days in question fall at the beginning of a period of limited capability for work, the second day is to be treated as one of incapacity and the first as the one of work. If the two days fall at the end of a period of incapacity for work, the first day is the one to be regarded as a day of limited capability for work and the second as the one of work.

Exceptional circumstances

29.—(1) A claimant who does not have limited capability for work as determined in accordance with the limited capability for work assessment is to be treated as having limited capability for work if paragraph (2) applies to the claimant.

(2) This paragraph applies if—

(a) the claimant is suffering from a life threatening disease in relation to which—

(i) there is medical evidence that the disease is uncontrollable, or uncontrolled, by a recognised therapeutic procedure; and

(ii) in the case of a disease that is uncontrolled, there is a reasonable cause for it not to be controlled by a recognised therapeutic procedure; or

1A.193

1A.194

(b) the claimant suffers from some specific disease or bodily or mental disablement and, by reasons of such disease or disablement, there would be a substantial risk to the mental or physical health of any person if the claimant were found not to have limited capability for work.

DEFINITIONS

"claimant"—see WRA 2007, s.24(1).
"limited capability for work"—see WRA 2007, s.1(4).
"limited capability for work assessment"—see reg.2(1).
"medical evidence"—see reg.2(1).

GENERAL NOTE

1A.195   This has affinities with Incapacity for Work Regs, reg.27, and insofar as that is so, case authorities on equivalent terms in that reg. are applicable to the interpretation and application of this one. Of no relevance at all, however, to those questions are the authorities on the matter of whether changes sought to be made in 1997 to reg.27 were invalid as procedurally ultra vires. The precise terms of reg.27 have, of course, caused problems of interpretation and application since its inception, and issues about some of its provisions are still before the Court of Appeal and will be relevant to the interpretation and application of the comparable terms in this ESA regulation.

Like reg.27 in the IB scheme, this regulation reflects the fact that functional assessment systems like the IB PCA or the ESA WCAt would not properly measure the incapacitating effect of certain conditions, and so would "fail" some people who properly ought to be regarded as being incapable of work (IB) or having limited capability for work (ESA). Headed "exceptional circumstances", the regulation envisages two classes of case in which someone not assessed as having limited capability for work can nonetheless be treated as having it.

The first situation is where the claimant suffers from a life threatening disease (the IB requirement that it be "severe" is not continued into ESA) which medical evidence establishes is uncontrollable by a recognized therapeutic procedure or (but only with reasonable cause) is uncontrolled by such a procedure (para. (2)(a)). Dealing with the substantially similarly worded IB provision in *CIB/4506/01*, Commissioner Howell stated that here:

"the question is only whether the nature of [the claimant's] condition is such that it is capable of being controlled by medical science, or not. Consequently the tribunal were right in taking account not only of the inhalers and adrenaline injector she is able to use for herself, but also the hospital treatment which unhappily she finds also has to be used on occasions as a means of bringing the condition under control. On the tribunal's findings the claimant's condition is thus controllable in the relevant sense, and their reasons are clearly and adequately given" (para.10).

The tribunal had not erred in law.

In *CIB/155/2004*, Commissioner Jacobs thought it inappropriate to deploy as a test whether the level of control would suffice to allow the claimant to work; since that test would always be satisfied. Rather, he thought that IB reg.27 [ESA reg.29] comes into play where a claimant is capable of work but has a condition that makes it inappropriate that he be expected to work. Since, as regards para.(2)(a) what makes that inappropriate is the fact that the condition is a threat to the claimant's life, the threshold for control should be whether the control is sufficient to remove the threat to the claimant's life. In the case at hand, while the

120

evidence disclosed that the claimant's diabetes was poorly controlled, it was nonetheless sufficiently controlled that para.(2)(a) was inapplicable. While there were longer-term complications to which the Consultant referred, they were not yet present, and not currently threatening the claimant's life.

The term "medical evidence" embraces (i) evidence from a health care professional approved by the Secretary of State, (ii) evidence (if any) from any other health care professional, hospital or similar institution, or such part of evidence in (i) or (ii) as constitutes the most reliable evidence available in the circumstances (reg.2(1)). "Health care professional" covers a registered medical practitioner, a registered nurse or an occupational therapist or physiotherapist registered with a regulatory body established by an Order in Council under section 60 of the Health Act 1999 (reg.2(1). In a Northern Ireland decision *C5/00–01(IB)* Commissioner Brown stressed that the evidence "must relate to the claimant himself, it is not constituted by extracts from medical textbooks unless the doctor relates them to the claimant" (para.16).

The second class of case in which someone not assessed as having limited capability for work can nonetheless be treated as having it, concerns a claimant, suffering from some specific disease or bodily or mental disablement, and by reason of such there would be substantial risk to the mental or physical health of any person if the claimant were found not to have limited capability for work (para.(2)(b)). The scheme thus carries into ESA something the Department had tried unsuccessfully to remove as regards IB in 1997.

On "specific disease or bodily or mental disablement", see the commentary to reg.19.

The meaning of "substantial risk to the mental or physical health of any person if the claimant were found not to have limited capability for work" has produced a number of Commissioners' decisions, some of which conflict. "Substantial" does not only refer to the likelihood of the risk occurring: "a risk may be 'substantial' if the harm would be serious, even though it was unlikely to occur and, conversely, may not be 'substantial' if the harm would be insignificant, even though the likelihood of some such harm is great. Paragraph (b) must be viewed in the light of the other paragraphs of regulation 27 and the general scheme of the Regulations" (para.7).

Commissioner Fellner accepted this as "probably right" in *CIB/2767/2004*, but added that:

> "his invocation of the other paragraphs of regulation 27 as guides to interpretation suggests that the interpretation should be rather narrow. Under the original as well as the amended form, the other paragraphs refer to more or less factual medical questions—presence of life-threatening or severe uncontrolled or uncontrollable disease, need for an identified major medical procedure within a short time" (para.6).

The real division of opinion concerns whether "substantial risk to health" has to be evaluated against specific employments or in the abstract. That question is now before the Court of Appeal in *Charlton v Secretary of State for Work & Pensions*. That appeal is floated for hearing in December 2008. Pending that decision one is left with the conflicting Commissioners decisions, with the bulk of the authorities supporting the "specific employments" approach and Commissioner May strongly maintaining the "in the abstract" approach.

There are a number of decisions by a variety of Commissioners, supporting the "specific employments" approach. In *CIB 26/2004* Commissioner Jacobs held that the rubric is not limited to the rare case in which a decision in favour of capacity for work would itself cause the risk to the claimant's health (para.33). Instead one looks to the consequences of such a decision, namely that the claimant will become a jobseeker, and be available for work, the type determined taking account of the claimant's health, qualifications, skills and experience. On that view "the risk must be assessed in relation to the type of work for which the claimant would otherwise be required to be available. That retains the emphasis on the effect of the claimant being found capable of work. It confines within a sensible scope the range of work that must be taken into account when assessing the risk to the claimant's health. And it makes a sensible relationship between the conditions governing entitlement to benefit for those incapable for work and for those seeking work. It prevents claimants relying on reg.27(b) when there is work that they could do without risk to their health. But it allows claimants to rely on the provision when the work they would otherwise be required to seek would put their health, or someone else's, at substantial risk. This does not mean a return to the previous law on invalidity benefit, under which capacity for work was determined by reference to specific job descriptions suggested by the adjudication officer. It involves a wider consideration than that. It involves a consideration of the risk to health involved in the general type of work that the claimant is otherwise qualified, experienced or skilled to undertake" (paras 35, 36). In *CSIB/33/2004*, Commissioner Parker expressly approved Commissioner Jacob's analysis as making sense of a difficult regulation. She also gave some helpful approaches to resolving some of the problems created as a result of that analysis:

"A claimant whose IB is refused may have claimed jobseeker's allowance (JSA) pending the IB appeal; alternatively, he or she may have claimed income support (IS), (despite a 'benefit penalty' unless certain circumstances are applicable), or have claimed no other benefit. If a claim for JSA has been made, a claimant must have suggested some employment which there is a reasonable prospect of securing having regard to his or her skills, qualifications and experience. A JSA claimant may, however, place restrictions, if these are reasonable in the light of the claimant's physical or mental condition, irrespective of the effect these restrictions have on the reasonable prospect of obtaining work, provided there are none which cannot be so justified. It is a complex process. In this kind of case, the task of the IB tribunal is to elicit the kind of work which the Jobcentre has accepted as that for which the claimant must be both available and actively seeking, as set out in the 'Jobseeker's Agreement'. The claimant then has to satisfy the IB tribunal that even such work nevertheless raises the necessary 'substantial risk'. It is important to keep in mind that the question only arises following a determination that a claimant is not incapable of work in accordance with the PCA, nor does he or she fall under regulation 10 where their condition is expressly acknowledged as sufficiently severe. So far as those who have not made a JSA claim are concerned, the tribunal (which through its chairman possesses the necessary expertise in the conditions of entitlement to JSA) will have to consider all the evidence and relevant law to determine the likely content of a jobseeker's agreement to which a claimant would be subject had a successful JSA claim been made and then ask if the type of job set out in the hypothetical agreement raises the specified risk. The problems are not insuperable but it does illustrate the difficult interface between the IB and JSA rules when applying regulation 27(b)" (paras 36–40).

In *CIB/360/2007*, deputy Commissioner Paines thought it clear that the provision is not confined to cases in which merely learning of the finding of capacity for work would cause damage to health but also the health consequences of the claimant returning to the workplace. This perforce involves some consideration of the work the claimant would be required to do, something on which a tribunal with its knowledge of work and of the claimant's background and condition, can readily form a view on to enable it to decide whether, within that range of work, there is work he could do without the risk to health contemplated by the provision. So, in the case of a claimant with a depressive condition, determining any effect on his mental health in response to the demands of a return to work, a tribunal would need to decide whether, as his consultant had suggested, "the demands of any form of work that the claimant would have the physical or intellectual ability to perform would be too much for him given his susceptibility to stress" (para.19).

In an earlier decision, *CIB/1695/2005*, the deputy Commissioner had considered the case of a claimant with epilepsy. There he thought the requirements of the provision were not met:

"because—while one could readily imagine types of work that the claimant could not safely perform, such as work involving driving or the operation of heavy machinery—there was an adequate range of work that the claimant could do in which there would not be a substantial risk to health from his suffering a seizure in the workplace."

In that case, the deputy Commissioner endorsed Commissioner Jacobs' approach in *CIB/26/2004*, so that where someone suffers from a specific disease or disablement (in that case, epilepsy), the issue of whether there would be a substantial risk to his own or someone else's health ensuing from the finding that he was not incapable of work falls to be decided by reference, among other things, to the type of work that he would be likely to be required to be available for.

The range of work to consider is not limited to the claimant's own occupation but must be considered against a broader range of alternative employments, limited as suggested in the cases considered above (*CSIB/164/2008*, paras 13–16).

In *CIB/1064/2006*, Deputy Commissioner Ovey, having considered the authorities noted above, encapsulated her task thus:

"I must consider whether there is evidence that a job of the kind which it is likely the claimant would be required to be available for would result in consequences for his health which, although not necessarily life-threatening, would be substantial having regard to both likelihood of occurrence and degree of harm" (para.20).

Here the claimant had been a chauffeur, a job he had lost because of his dermatitis. The Deputy Commissioner concluded that the evidence before the tribunal was capable of putting the provision in issue. The claimant, to a degree supported by his doctor, stated that his removal from that working environment, in which friction and repeated activities would cause his dermatitis to flare up, had improved matters. Where the Deputy Commissioner parted company with the tribunal was in its failure adequately to explain its confinement of the work the claimant should be measured against to driving (his previous job) and why it thought the risk to the claimant to be "substantial". The tribunal in this way had erred in law and the Deputy Commissioner remitted to matter to another tribunal.

As Commissioner Parker stated in *CSIB/33/2004* (para.40) and reiterated in *CSIB/719/2006* (para.11):

"the risk must arise from the broad results of a claimant being found capable of work and is not confined to the risks arising directly from the tasks within a claimant's job description. Thus, for example, if a claimant sustains the relevant risk because she has to get up quickly in the morning to go to work, rather than pace herself as would be the situation if no such necessity arose, this is a pertinent factor for consideration. Likewise, [the Secretary of State's representative] accepted that any apprehension sustained by a claimant with mental disablement at the prospect of having to look for work, is pertinent. But there must be a causal link between being 'found capable of work' and an ensuing 'substantial risk to the mental or physical health of any person if [the claimant] were found capable of work".

In contrast, Commissioner May has firmly and consistently (see *CSIB/179/2006* and *CSIB/656/2006*) rejected this approach as flawed and propounded an "in the abstract" approach. In *CSIB/0223/2005*, Commissioner May rejected the broader approach to the phrase applied by Commissioner Jacobs in *CIB/26/2004*. Instead he found attractive the approach suggested by the claimant's representative; while recognising that Commissioner Jacob's broader approach would be beneficial to some claimants, he considered that s.27(b) [ESA Regs, reg.29(2)(b)]should be applied according to its terms, and referred to the difficulties on the broader approach in a tribunal deciding what work might be taken into account, especially as in this case, when the claimant had claimed JSA, the disability adviser thought a jobseeker's agreement problematic given his health problems and the occupational psychologist regarded him as incapable of work (para.7). Commissioner May elaborated:

"The question as to whether, if the tribunal find that there was a risk to the claimant's health it was substantial, is a jury question for them on which they must make a reasonable judgement. I have made the direction I have for the following reasons. It is quite clear to me that Parliament intended regulation 27(b) to be applied in the restrictive way that the language of the paragraph provides. Unlike Mr Commissioner Jacobs in paragraph 33 of his decision, I can see the sense of the limitation and I am prepared to accept that Parliament meant what it said. The regulation is headed 'Exceptional circumstances' and the other circumstances contained in (a), (c) and (d) demonstrate severe and exceptional conditions. I consider that Mr Commissioner Jacobs has sought to broaden the scope of the regulation beyond what it says. It is quite clear from evidence which exists in this case that it is possible to apply the regulation on the basis that it means what it says and that it is not in the terms in which it is written without content or meaning. Further, it is also clear that in cases where a person has not passed the personal capability assessment and does not fall within the statutory exceptions contained in regulation 27 that, in respect of a jobseeker's agreement, health can be a material factor in the framing and constitution of such an agreement. The circumstances in this case following the claimant's application for jobseeker's allowance following his unsuccessful appeal to the tribunal, as outlined to me by Miss Docherty, demonstrate that claimants who neither satisfy the personal capability assessment and do not fall within the exceptions of regulation 27 can have such disabilities they have taken into account when a jobseeker's agreement is sought to be framed and constituted. I am at a loss to see how tribunals can properly apply the legislation in the context set out by Mr Commissioner Jacobs and by Mr Bartos in his submission. How a tribunal is to determine what range of work that must be taken into account when assessing the risk to the claimant's health is beyond me in the absence as in this case of an evidential basis to do so. I do not consider the questions that Mr Bartos posed were particularly helpful as in most cases the reply from the claimant would be likely to be 'I am unfit for work'. It further appears to me that if the interpretative gloss set out by Mr Commissioner Jacobs was to be applied, then the question posed to the examining medical practitioner would be incomplete as it makes no reference to the broader interpretation set out by him. It is these considerations which cause me to frame the direction I have given to the fresh tribunal in the manner I have" (para.14).

Endorsing what he called the Jacobs/Parker/Paines approach—the "specific employments" approach—Commissioner Williams in *CIB/143/2007* nonetheless built on Deputy Commissioner Paines' epilepsy example to suggest that identifying the two risks reduced the practical effect of the differences in approach:

"regulation 27(b) [ESA regs, reg.29(2)(b)]can be seen to be asking officials and tribunals to make two separate assessments of risk: that to the claimant and that to other people in a work situation with the claimant. Those risks may or may not be parallel. For example, on the facts in CIB 1695 2005, an epileptic may put both herself and work colleagues at risk if she collapses without warning, perhaps dropping hot food or liquid or falling downstairs. By contrast, risks caused by some systemic disabilities may pose a major risk to the individual with the weakness but little risk to others ... Take the example of heart disease ... Approved doctors are asked to consider the position of someone found capable of work with uncontrolled heart disease, particularly if also suffering from other problems such as lung disease. In such cases there may be a substantial risk to the individual whatever he or she is asked to do, notwithstanding that he or she does not score 15 points in the personal capability assessment on the day of examination. Any work may occasion that risk, and the nature of the work may be irrelevant. It is not evident that there will also be a high risk to others arising from the heart disease of a workmate or colleague. Another example is the risk of violence or psychological harm by the claimant to others ... This may pose little risk to the claimant. The nature of the risk to others will depend to some extent on the kind of work that the claimant may be asked to do. That requires going beyond the non-specific idea that the risk is to be assessed without any focus on the kind of work the claimant may do. Consider this example further. If it were known that a person whose presence in the workplace might, because of a specific mental disablement, lead to a risk of violence that may on occasion be severe, it could be relevant to know the context of that individual's work before the risk could be assessed. Commissioner May's approach appears to assume that this could be dealt with by assumptions about the jobseeker's agreement that the individual would be asked to agree. But that is a question of evidence not of assumption. What has the claimant done in the past? What was the claimant doing at the time of the decision? What are the claimant's qualifications? Take the case of a qualified person who now suffers from unpredictable violent behaviour following an accident or illness. Different views might be taken of someone whose background suggested that the person might work with children or old or defenceless adults—in other words, in one of the millions of jobs in health, education, welfare, caring and similar activities, as compared with someone whose background suggested that the sort of work to be expected is manual work in a disciplined context" (paras 41–43).

Here, however, the evidence about the effect of the claimant's specific disease or disablement (alcohol dependency disorder aggravated by drug misuse) did not suggest a risk to the claimant's health; that came from his lifestyle and work might in fact assist his situation.

Conditions for treating a claimant as having limited capability for work until a determination about limited capability for work has been made

30.—(1) A claimant is, if the conditions set out in paragraph (2) are met, to be treated as having limited capability for work until such time as it is determined—

    (a) whether or not the claimant has limited capability for work;

1A.196

(b) whether or not the claimant is to be treated as having limited capability for work otherwise than in accordance with this regulation; or

(c) whether the claimant falls to be treated as not having limited capability for work in accordance with regulation 22 (failure to provide information in relation to limited capability for work) or 23 (failure to attend a medical examination to determine limited capability for work).

(2) The conditions are—

(a) that the claimant provides evidence of limited capability for work in accordance with the Medical Evidence Regulations; and

(b) that it has not, within the 6 months preceding the date of claim, been determined, in relation to the claimant's entitlement to any benefit, allowance or advantage which is dependent on the claimant having limited capability for work, that the claimant does not have limited capability for work or is to be treated as not having limited capability for work under regulation 22 or 23 unless—

  (i) the claimant is suffering from some specific disease or bodily or mental disablement from which the claimant was not suffering at the time of that determination;

  (ii) a disease or bodily or mental disablement from which the claimant was suffering at the time of that determination has significantly worsened; or

  (iii) in the case of a claimant who was treated as not having limited capability for work under regulation 22 (failure to provide information), the claimant has since provided the information requested under that regulation.

(3) Paragraph (2)(b) does not apply where a claimant has made and is pursuing an appeal against a decision that embodies a determination that the claimant does not have limited capability for work and that appeal has not yet been determined by an appeal tribunal constituted under Chapter 1 of Part 1 of the Social Security Act 1998.

DEFINITIONS

"claimant"—see WRA 2007, s.24(1).
"limited capability for work"—see WRA 2007, s.1(4).
"Medical Evidence Regulations"—see reg.2(1).

GENERAL NOTE

1A.197   This has affinities with Incapacity for Work Regs, reg.28, and it is submitted that case authorities on that are applicable to the interpretation and application of this regulation.

Like that IB provision, this regulation, in the circumstances set out in para.(2), treats the claimant as having limited capability for work (thus grounding eligibility for ESA) until: (a) the matter of actual capability is determined in accordance with the work capability assessment (WCAt) under reg.19 and Sch.2); (b) it is decided whether some other "treated as having limited capability for work" regulation applies (e.g. person receiving certain regular treatment); or (c) a decision is made that, as a sanction for non-compliance with information gathering or medical examination aspects of the assessment process under regs 22 and

23, he is to be treated as not having limited capability for work and thus disentitled to ESA.

In short, if, but only if, para.(2) applies will the claimant be treated as having limited capability for work. So it will be treated as satisfied only while the person continues to provide a doctor's statement in accordance with the Medical Evidence Regs (see further those regulations and the commentary to them), and, save in appeal cases covered by para.(3), only if there has been no determination in the last six months that he is capable of work or that he is to be treated as capable of work for such failures to comply with those aspects of the process. Determination here covers one in relation to any benefit, allowance or advantage (e.g. contributions credits) dependent on the claimant having limited capability for work. If there has been such a determination, however, benefit can still be paid pending assessment if the specific disease or bodily or mental disablement from which he suffered at the time of that earlier determination has significantly worsened or the one(s) he is now suffering from is (are) different; or, if treated as capable because of failure to supply claims information (reg.22), he has since complied with the Secretary of State's requests. The supply of medical certificates will thus continue to be required to support a claim.

Useful clarification of the operation of the comparable IB regulation has been given by Commissioner Rowland in *CIB/3106/2003* and by Commissioner Howells in *R(IB) 8/04*. Where the six-month period mentioned has expired, there is no need to make a new claim to take advantage of the protection of the regulation. It should be considered by the decision-maker as a change of circumstances (*CIB/3106/2003*, para.5). Moroever, where, on a claim for limited capability for work, the decision-maker decides that the claimant cannot be treated as having limited capability under the regulation pending assessment, the decision-maker must still arrange a limited capability for work assessment (WCAt) to determine the *actual* capability. If the result of that assessment was limited capability for work arrears of benefit will be payable from the date of claim. As explained in *R(IB) 1/01* and *R(IB) 2/01*, the purpose of the regulation is simply to enable payment of benefit pending assessment and irrespective of the results of that assessment (*ibid.*, para.6). In contrast, where the period of six months since a previous determination has not expired, the regulation can only come into play where one of the conditions in para.(2)(b)(i)–(iii) are met, for example, that the claimant is suffering from some fresh disease or disablement, or a significant worsening of an existing disease or disablement, since the date of that determination (the determination by the Secretary of State, not the date of a tribunal decision confirming it on appeal) (*R(IB) 8/04*).

Since the regulation only applies until the claimant has been "assessed", it cannot apply where the claimant is immediately assessed (*CIB/1959/1997 and CIB/2198/1997*, paras 28, 29).

The words "significantly worsened", as regards the claimant's condition, must be related to the limited capability for work assessment (WCAt), so that it will only have significantly worsened if it has done so to an extent that the claimant would satisfy that test of limited capability for work if he were subjected to it. If there is actual evidence that he would fail to satisfy that test, the Secretary of State can proceed on the basis that the condition has not significantly worsened (*CIB/1959/1977 and CIB/2198/1997*, para.30).

On "specific disease or bodily or mental disablement", see commentary to reg.19.

Paragraph (3) deals with the situation where a claimant is appealing a determination that he does not have limited capability for work. In this situation, supplying medical certificates evidencing limited capability for work will preserve the claimant's position. He is to be treated under para.(1) as having limited capability for work until the appeal has been determined—the "last six months" provisions in para.(2)(b) do not apply (para.(3)).

Claimant who claims jobseeker's allowance to be treated as not having limited capability for work

1A.198   **31.**—(1) A claimant who—

(a) claims a jobseeker's allowance; and

(b) is able to show a reasonable prospect of obtaining employment,

is, throughout the period of that claim, to be treated as not having limited capability for work.

(2) Paragraph (1) applies even though it has been determined that the claimant—

(a) has limited capability for work; or

(b) is to be treated as having limited capability for work under any of regulations 20 (certain claimants to be treated as having limited capability for work), 25 (hospital in-patients), 26 (claimants undergoing certain regular treatment) or 29 (exceptional circumstances).

DEFINITIONS

"claimant"—see WRA 2007, s.24(1).
"employment"—see reg.2(1).
"limited capability for work"—see WRA 2007, s.1(4).

GENERAL NOTE

1A.199   This maintains a boundary between ESA and JSA; one can have one or the other but not both (WRA 2007, s.1(1)(f)). This regulation makes clear that days when one claims JSA and has a reasonable prospect of employment do not rank as ones of limited capability for work (para.(1)). The preclusion applies even where someone has been found to have limited capability for work in accordance with the limited capability for work assessment (WCAt)) (para.(2)(a)), or is treated as having limited capability for work under the regulations specified in para.(2)(b).

Certain claimants to be treated as not having limited capability for work

1A.200   **32.** [¹(1)] A claimant [²who is or has been a member of Her Majesty's Forces] is to be treated as not having limited capability for work on any day which is recorded by the Secretary of State for Defence as a day of sickness absence from duty.

[³(2) A claimant is to be treated as not having limited capability for work on any day on which the claimant attends a training course in respect of which the claimant is paid a training allowance or premium pursuant to arrangements made under section 2 of the Employment and Training Act 1973 or section 2(3) of the Enterprise and New Towns (Scotland) Act 1990.

(3) Paragraph (2) is not to apply—

(a) for the purposes of any claim to employment and support allowance for a period commencing after the claimant ceased attending the training course in question; or

(b) where any training allowance or premium paid to the claimant is paid for the sole purpose of travelling or meal expenses incurred or to be incurred under the arrangement made under section 2 of the Employment and Training Act 1973 or section 2(3) of the Enterprise and New Towns (Scotland) Act 1990.]

AMENDMENTS

1. Employment and Support Allowance (Miscellaneous Amendments) Regulations 2008 (SI 2008/2428), reg.5(2)(a) (October 27, 2008).
2. Employment and Support Allowance (Miscellaneous Amendments) Regulations 2008 (SI 2008/2428), reg.5(2)(b) (October 27, 2008).
3. Employment and Support Allowance (Miscellaneous Amendments) Regulations 2008 (SI 2008/2428), reg.5(2)(c) (October 27, 2008).

DEFINITIONS

"claimant"—see WRA 2007, s.24(1).
"limited capability for work"—see WRA 2007, s.1(4).

GENERAL NOTE

Para. (1)

This draws a boundary between ESA and the sickness payment scheme operated by the Ministry of Defence. Days recorded by the Secretary of State for Defence as ones of sickness absence from duty are to be treated for ESA purposes as ones on which the person concerned does not have limited capability for work.

1A.201

Additional circumstances where claimants are to be treated as having limited capability for work

33.—(1) For the purposes of paragraph 4(1)(d)(ii) of Schedule 1 to the Act, a claimant is to be treated as having limited capability for work on any day in respect of which that claimant is entitled to statutory sick pay.

1A.202

(2) For the purposes of an income-related allowance, a claimant is to be treated as having limited capability for work where—
(a) that claimant is not a qualifying young person;
(b) that claimant is receiving education; and
(c) paragraph 6(1)(g) of Schedule 1 to the Act does not apply in accordance with regulation 18.

DEFINITIONS

"claimant"—see WRA 2007, s.24(1).
"income-related allowance"—see WRA 2007, s.1(7).
"limited capability for work"—see WRA 2007, s.1(4).
"qualifying young person"—see reg.2(1).

GENERAL NOTE

Para. (1)

Like WRA 2007, s.20(1), this regulation deals with the relationship between ESA and employer paid statutory sick pay (SSP). Days of entitlement to SSP

1A.203

cannot rank as ones of entitlement to ESA. However, para.(1) of this regulation stipulates that such days are to be treated as ones of limited capability for work for the purposes of computing the 196 consecutive days of limited capability for work essential if someone is to qualify through the "condition relating to youth route" to CESA (WRA 2007, Sch.1, para.4(1)(d)(ii)). Being so treated confers no exemption from the information gathering requirements in reg.21 (see para.(3) of that regulation).

Para. (2)

1A.204   This deals only with IRESA. It treats certain disabled students as having limited capability for work. It covers someone receiving education (sub-para.(b)) but not debarred from IRESA on account of that because he is receiving DLA (sub-para.(c) [WRA 2007, Sch.1, para.6(1)(g) disapplied by reg.18]). If this person is not a qualifying young person, he is to be treated as having limited capability for work. A qualifying young person bears the same meaning as in SSCBA 1992, s.142 (see reg.2(1)): someone aged 16–19 inclusive undergoing a full-time course of non-advanced education or approved training which commenced before he attained 19 (see Child Benefit Regs, reg.3).

Being treated as having limited capability for work in this way confers exemption from the information gathering requirements in reg.21 (see para.(3) of that regulation).

PART 6

LIMITED CAPABILITY FOR WORK-RELATED ACTIVITY

Determination of limited capability for work-related activity

1A.205   **34.**—(1) For the purposes of Part 1 of the Act, where, by reason of a claimant's physical or mental condition, at least one of the descriptors set out in Schedule 3 applies to the claimant, the claimant's capability for work-related activity will be limited and the limitation will be such that it is not reasonable to require that claimant to undertake such activity.

(2) A descriptor applies to a claimant if that descriptor applies to the claimant for the majority of the time or, as the case may be, on the majority of the occasions on which the claimant undertakes or attempts to undertake the activity described by that descriptor.

(3) In determining whether a descriptor applies to a claimant, the claimant is to be assessed as if the claimant were wearing any prosthesis with which the claimant is fitted or, as the case may be, wearing or using any aid or appliance which the claimant normally wears or uses.

(4) Where a determination has been made about whether a claimant—

(a) has limited capability for work-related activity;

(b) is to be treated as having limited capability for work-related activity; or

(c) is to be treated as not having limited capability for work-related activity,

130

the Secretary of State may, if paragraph (5) applies, determine afresh whether the claimant has or is to be treated as having limited capability for work-related activity.

(5) This paragraph applies where—

(a) the Secretary of State wishes to determine whether there has been a relevant change of circumstances in relation to the claimant's physical or mental condition;

(b) the Secretary of State wishes to determine whether the previous determination about limited capability for work-related activity or about treating the claimant as having or as not having limited capability for work-related activity, was made in ignorance of, or was based on a mistake as to, some material fact; or

(c) at least 3 months have passed since the date of the previous determination about limited capability for work-related activity or about treating the claimant as having or as not having limited capability for work-related activity.

DEFINITIONS

"the Act"—see reg.2(1).
"claimant"—see WRA 2007, s.24(1).
"descriptor"—see reg.2(1).
"limited capability for work-related activity"—see WRA 2007, s.2(5).
"work-related activity"—see WRA 2007, ss.24(1), 13(7).

GENERAL NOTE

Establishing limited capability for work is the central condition governing entitlement to ESA. Establishing limited capacity for work related activity is, in contrast, the core condition of entitlement to support component, the more generous of the two components (support or work-related activity) only one of which can be added to ESA basic allowance. This regulation, read with WRA 2007, s.9 and Sch.3 to these Regs, sets out how limited capacity for work related activity is assessed and determined.   **1A.206**

The assumption behind ESA is that the vast majority of claimants, if given the right support, are in fact capable of some work. Government anticipates that only some 10% of claimants (those with more severe health conditions) will be entitled to the support allowance and so not be subject to work-related activity conditionality requirements (DWP, *Employment and Support Allowance Regulations 2008: Equality Impact Assessment* in *Explanatory Memorandum to Employment and Support Allowance Regulations 2008 (SI 2008/794)* and the *Employment and Support Allowance (Transitional Provisions) Regulations 2008 (SI 2008/795)*, p.19) Entry to this protected support group depends on it being established—generally through a work-related activity assessment (WRAAt) of a more stringent nature than the WCAt—that the claimant has limited capacity for work related activity. The WRAAt is the second element in the new Work Capability Assessment (WCA) which will eventually replace the IB PCA. Establishing limited capability for work related activity is based on someone demonstrating that they have a severe level of functional limitation. This is established when by reason of the claimant's physical or mental condition, at least one of the range of descriptors in Sch.3 applies to the claimant (WRA 2007, s.9; para.(1)).

There is no scoring system (it is a matter of the descriptor being applicable that counts) and the criteria are deliberately more stringent than in the WCAt:

"The levels of functional limitation used in the descriptors for determining limited capability for work-related activity are greater because we intend to place in the support group only the minority of customers who are so severely impaired that it would not be reasonable to require them to undertake work-related activity . . . People with less severe functional limitations across a range of descriptors might score highly and be inappropriately included in the support group when they might benefit from work-related activity. . . . A number of case studies were provided in the background information, which hon. Members will find helpful [see DWP, *Welfare Reform Bill: Draft Regulations and Supporting Material* (January 2007), pp.13–17]. Under the revised PCA, someone with a moderate learning disability would score 50 points. They would be significantly above the 15-point threshold, but we clearly would not wish to put even someone with 50 points into the support group automatically, because we are determined to ensure that the new system does not write off people with learning disabilities. The technical groups considered all the options. A crude points-based system would have unintended consequences." (*Hansard*, Standing Committee A, October 19, 2006 (afternoon), col.120 (Mr Jim Murphy MP, Minister for Employment and Welfare Reform)).

Paragraph (2) makes clear (as indeed does the expected transposition to the WRAAt of central elements in existing case law on approaching the PCA) that a descriptor applies to a claimant if it applies to him for the majority of the time or, as the case may be, on the majority of the occasions on which he undertakes or attempts to undertake the relevant activity. Moreover, as is the case with the IB PCA and the ESA WCAt, in matching claimant to descriptor, the claimant is to be assessed as if the claimant were wearing any prosthesis with which the claimant is fitted or, as the case may be, wearing or using any aid or appliance which the claimant normally wears or uses (para.(3) and see commentary to reg.19(4)).

There are only 11 activities in Sch.3: walking or moving on level ground; rising from sitting and transferring from one seated position to another; picking up and moving or transferring by means of the upper body and arms; reaching; manual dexterity; continence; maintaining personal hygiene; eating and drinking (conveying food or drink to the mouth and chewing or swallowing it); learning or comprehension in the completion of tasks; personal action (planning, organisation, problem solving, prioritising or switching tasks); and communication. The terms of the descriptors are also more stringent than in the WCAt, to avoid removing too many people from the group which affords incentive to engage in work-related activity and thus denying them the opportunity to take steps to make real their fundamental right to work. Thus, as regards walking, the single descriptor can only be met where a claimant cannot "walk" more than 30 metres without repeatedly stopping, experiencing breathlessness or severe discomfort. Here "walk" covers walking with a walking stick, other aid or crunches, each if normally used; and embraces the claimant moving by manually propelling a wheelchair (Sch.3, para.1). That on rising from sitting etc, requires in effect that the claimant fulfil two of the 15 point descriptors in the WCAt. Most, with counterparts in the WCAt, are couched in terms equivalent to the more difficult of their 15 point descriptors.

Those meeting the WRAAt test will be placed in the support group and receive support component without having to satisfy work-related activity conditions, although they can voluntarily participate in those programmes. Their position can be reviewed periodically or where there has been a change of circumstances in the claimant's physical or mental condition or it is thought that a previous determination was made in ignorance of or a mistake as to some material fact (paras (4), (5)) The threshold for membership of the support group is high; CPAG consider that "many claimants in receipt of the middle and higher rates of Disability Living Allowance (DLA) may not meet the eligibility criteria". Those who fail to establish limited capability for work-related activity will instead receive the work-related activity component, receipt of which has stringent conditions attached in terms of appropriate behaviour (participation in work focussed health related assessments, work focused interviews and, eventually, specified work-related activity (see regs.47–60), involving the private and voluntary sector as well as JobCentre Plus).

Certain claimants to be treated as having limited capability for work-related activity

35.—(1) A claimant is to be treated as having limited capability for work-related activity if—   1A.207
  (a) the claimant is terminally ill;
  (b) the claimant is—
    (i) receiving treatment by way of intravenous, intraperitoneal or intrathecal chemotherapy; or
    (ii) recovering from that treatment and the Secretary of State is satisfied that the claimant should be treated as having limited capability for work-related activity; or
  (c) in the case of a woman, she is pregnant and there is a serious risk of damage to her health or to the health of her unborn child if she does not refrain from work-related activity.

(2) A claimant who does not have limited capability for work-related activity as determined in accordance with regulation 34(1) is to be treated as having limited capability for work-related activity if—
  (a) the claimant suffers from some specific disease or bodily or mental disablement; and
  (b) by reasons of such disease or disablement, there would be a substantial risk to the mental or physical health of any person if the claimant were found not to have limited capability for work-related activity.

DEFINITIONS

  "claimant"—see WRA 2007, s.24(1).
  "limited capability for work-related activity"—see WRA 2007, s.2(5).
  "terminally ill"—see reg.2(1).
  "work-related activity"—see WRA 2007, ss.24(1), 13(7).

GENERAL NOTE

This has affinities with reg.20 (treating someone as having limited capability   1A.208
for work). Regulation 35 treats someone as having limited capability for work-related activity but the range of groups so treated is much narrower. The terminally ill (para.(1)(a)) and those undergoing or recovering from chemotherapy (para.(1)(b)) are so treated, as is a pregnant woman where there is a serious risk of damage to her health or that of her unborn child if she does not refrain from work-related activity (para.(1)(c). Unlike reg.20 there is no protection for other pregnant women or for those receiving hospital treatment or certain regular treatments such as dialysis. However, in para.(2) there is a partial equivalent of the "exceptional circumstances" provision (reg.29) applicable to the limited

capacity for work question, considered above. A claimant who does not pass the WRAAt can nonetheless be treated as having the requisite limited capability for work-related activity grounding membership of the support group where, by reason of the specific disease or bodily or mental disablement from which s/he suffers, "there would be a substantial risk to the mental or physical health of any person if the claimant were found not to have limited capability for work-related activity".

On "specific disease or bodily or mental disablement", see commentary to reg.19(2).

On "substantial risk to the mental or physical health of any person if the claimant were found not to have limited capability for work-related activity", see the commentary to reg.29.

Information required for determining capability for work-related activity

1A.209   **36.**—(1) Subject to paragraph (2), the information or evidence required to determine whether a claimant has limited capability for work-related activity is—

(a) any information relating to the descriptors set out in Schedule 3 as may be requested in the form of a questionnaire; and

(b) any such additional information as may be requested.

(2) Where the Secretary of State is satisfied that there is sufficient information to determine whether a claimant has limited capability for work-related activity without the information specified in paragraph (1)(a), that information will not be required for the purposes of making the determination.

DEFINITIONS

"claimant"—see WRA 2007, s.24(1).
"limited capability for work-related activity"—see WRA 2007, s.2(5).
"work-related activity"—see WRA 2007, ss.24(1), 13(7).

GENERAL NOTE

1A.210   This regulation deals with the information required for determining whether someone has limited capability for work-related activity. It is designed to give the decision-maker sufficient information to decide that matter for himself (the minority of cases), or whether to seek advice from a health care professional on the basis of the papers in respect of that decision, or to refer the claimant for a face to face WRAAt, including a medical examination (see reg.38).

Unless para.(2) operates, the claimant will have to supply (i) any information relating to the descriptors set out in Sch.3 as may be requested in the form of a questionnaire (para.(1)(a)), and (ii) such additional information relating to the relevant test as the Secretary of State asks for (para.(1)(b)). He must generally complete and return the appropriate questionnaire (para.(1)(a)), unless the Secretary of State decides that completion of the questionnaire is not necessary because without it he has sufficient information to determine whether the claimant does or does not have limited capability for work-related activity (para.(2)). Note that where the claimant is requested by the Secretary of State to complete and return the questionnaire, failure to do so can result in his being treated as not having limited capability for work-related activity (and thus not entitled to support component) (reg.37).

Failure to provide information in relation to work-related activity

37.—(1) Where a claimant fails without good cause to comply with the request referred to in regulation 36(1)(a), the claimant is, subject to paragraph (2), to be treated as not having limited capability for work-related activity.   1A.211

(2) Paragraph (1) does not apply unless—

(a) at least 6 weeks have passed since the claimant was sent the first request for the information; and

(b) the claimant was sent a further request at least 4 weeks after the date of the first request, and at least 2 weeks have passed since the further request was sent.

DEFINITIONS

"claimant"—see WRA 2007, s.24(1).
"limited capability for work-related activity"—see WRA 2007, s.2(5).
"week"—see reg.2(1).
"work-related activity"—see WRA 2007, ss.24(1), 13(7).

GENERAL NOTE

If a claimant fails without good cause (on which more, below) to comply with the requirement in reg.36(1)(a) to complete and return a limited capability for work-related activity questionnaire, he must be treated as not having limited capability for work-related activity, that is, as having no entitlement to support component. This can only happen, however, if at least six weeks have passed since the claimant was first sent the request for information, a further request for information was sent at least four weeks after the first and at least two weeks have gone by since the second request was sent.   1A.212

On applicable IB case law on calculating periods and on the matter of good cause, see further the commentary to the analogous reg.22, applicable in respect of similar processes with respect to determination of limited capability for work questions.

Claimant may be called for a medical examination to determine whether the claimant has limited capability for work-related activity

38.—(1) Where it falls to be determined whether a claimant has limited capability for work-related activity, that claimant may be called by or on behalf of a health care professional approved by the Secretary of State to attend for a medical examination.   1A.213

(2) Subject to paragraph (3), where a claimant fails without good cause to attend for or to submit to an examination listed in paragraph (1), the claimant is to be treated as not having limited capability for work-related activity.

135

(3) Paragraph (2) does not apply unless written notice of the time and place for the examination was sent to the claimant at least 7 days in advance, or unless the claimant agreed to accept a shorter period of notice whether given in writing or otherwise.

DEFINITIONS

"claimant"—see WRA 2007, s.24(1).
"health care professional"—see reg.2(1).
"limited capability for work-related activity"—see WRA 2007, s.2(5).
"work-related activity"—see WRA 2007, ss.24(1), 13(7).

GENERAL NOTE

1A.214   This regulation enables the DWP to have a claimant medically examined by a DWP Medical Service (DWPMS) health service professional (technically any health service professional approved by the Secretary of State) when a question arises as to the claimant's capability for work-related activity. Failure without good cause to attend for or submit to such an examination, of which he was given proper written notice (see para.(3)), will result in the claimant being treated as not having limited capability for work and not entitled to ESA.

This regulation is a direct analogue of reg.23 with respect to medical examination as regards the matter of limited capability for work. The points, including the application of relevant IB case law, made in the commentary to reg.23 are equally applicable here.

Matters to be taken into account in determining good cause in relation to regulations 37 or 38

1A.215   **39.** The matters to be taken into account in determining whether a claimant has good cause under regulations 37 (failure to provide information in relation to work-related activity) or 38 (failure to attend a medical examination to determine limited capability for work-related activity) include—

(a) whether the claimant was outside Great Britain at the relevant time;

(b) the claimant's state of health at the relevant time; and

(c) the nature of any disability the claimant has.

DEFINITION

"claimant"—see WRA 2007, s.24(1).

GENERAL NOTE

1A.216   This regulation, made pursuant to WRA 2007, s.9(4), stipulates that in determining whether someone had good cause for failing to provide information (under reg.37) or for failing to attend for or submit to a medical examination (under reg.38) decision-makers and appellate bodies must take into account: (i) whether the person was outside Great Britain at the relevant time; (ii) his state of health at the relevant time; and (iii) the nature of his disability. This list is not, however, exhaustive (the regulation says "shall include"). On "good cause", see further the commentary to regs 22 and 23.

136

PART 7

EFFECT OF WORK ON ENTITLEMENT TO AN EMPLOYMENT AND
SUPPORT ALLOWANCE

A claimant who works to be treated as not entitled to an employment and support allowance

40.—(1) Subject to the following paragraphs, a claimant is to be   1A.217
treated as not entitled to an employment and support allowance in any
week in which that claimant does work.

(2) Paragraph (1) does not apply to—

(a) work as a councillor;

(b) duties undertaken on either one full day or two half-days a week
    as—

    (i) a member of the Disability Living Allowance Advisory Board;
    or

    [²(ii) a member of the First-tier Tribunal where the member is
    eligible for appointment to be such a member in accordance
    with article 2(3) of the Qualifications for Appointment of
    Members to the First-tier Tribunal and Upper Tribunal
    Order 2008.]

(c) domestic tasks carried out in the claimant's own home or the care
    of a relative;

(d) duties undertaken in caring for another person who is accommo-
    dated with the claimant by virtue of arrangements made under
    any of the provisions referred to in paragraphs 28 or 29 of Sched-
    ule 8 (sums to be disregarded in the calculation of income other
    than earnings) where the claimant is in receipt of any payment
    specified in those paragraphs;

(e) any activity the claimant undertakes during an emergency to
    protect another person or to prevent serious damage to property
    or livestock; or

(f) any of the categories of work set out in regulation 45 (exempt
    work).

(3) This regulation is subject to regulation 46 (effect of work on
entitlement to contributory allowance where claimant is receiving certain regular treatment).

(4) A claimant who does work to which this regulation applies in a
week which is—

(a) the week in which the claimant first becomes entitled to a benefit,
    allowance or advantage on account of the claimant's limited capa-
    bility for work in any period; or

(b) the last week in any period in which the claimant has limited
    capability for work or is treated as having limited capability for
    work,

is to be treated as not entitled to an employment and support allowance
by virtue of paragraph (1) only on the actual day or days in that week on
which the claimant does that work.

(5) Regulation 145 (linking rules) does not apply for the purposes of calculating the beginning or end of any period of limited capability for work under paragraph (4).

(6) The day or days in a week on which a night worker works, for the purposes of [¹paragraph (4)] above, are to be calculated by reference to regulation 28 (night workers).

(7) In this regulation—

"week" means a week in respect of which a claimant is entitled to an employment and support allowance;

"work" means any work which a claimant does, whether or not that claimant undertakes it in expectation of payment;

"work as a councillor" is to be taken to include any work which a claimant undertakes as a member of any of the bodies referred to in section 177(1) of the Local Government Act 1972 or subsections 49(1) or 49(1A) of the Local Government (Scotland) Act 1973, of which the claimant is a member by reason of being a councillor.

AMENDMENTS

1. Employment and Support Allowance (Miscellaneous Amendments) Regulations 2008 (SI 2008/2428), reg.6(1) (October 27, 2008).
2. Tribunals, Courts and Enforcement Act 2007 (Transitional and Consequential Provisions) Order 2008 (SI 2008/2683), art.6(1), Sch1, para.342 (November 3, 2008).

DEFINITIONS

"claimant"—see WRA 2007, s.24(1).
"entitled"—see WRA 2007, s.24(1).
"relative"—see reg.2(1).
"week"—see para.(7) and reg.2(1).
"work"—see para.(7).
"work as a councillor"—see para.(7).

GENERAL NOTE

1A.218 This regulation needs to be read in conjunction with regs 44–46.

To find in any incapacity regime a general rule that working (whether or not for payment) negatives incapacity for work is unsurprising since, in principle, it is a strong indication of ability to work. This regulation contains just such a rule, precluding entitlement to ESA in any week in which a claimant does work. Moreover, in that period of non-entitlement, he or she will be treated as not having limited capability for work, unless the work done only negatives entitlement to IRESA (reg.44). That can happen in that work done in a week when someone, entitled to CESA, is receiving or recovering from certain regular treatments, does not negative title to CESA, but can to IRESA (regs 46 (to which para.(3) makes this regulation subject) and 44(3)). But like the incapacity benefit regime, the general preclusive rule is modified to permit engagement in a range of work without loss of benefit ("subject to the following paragraphs", one of which para.(2)(f) links this reg to reg.45 and the concept of "exempt work"). These modifications recognize that work can assist recovery or help the claimant into thinking about work and a possibility to return to work, or merely not wanting to exclude the sick and disabled from participation in civic office or a range of voluntary or charitable work.

Although, unlike its IB comparator (Incapacity for Work Regs, reg.16) the point is no longer explicit, it is submitted that the regulation can operate despite the fact that, applying the limited capability for work assessment (WCAt) , the person in fact has limited capability for work, or is someone treated as having such limited capability by virtue of other regs.

Paragraph (1) sets out the general preclusive rule: a person must be treated as capable of work on each day of any week during which he does work. "Work" for the purposes of the regulation is defined in para.(7) as any work done whether or not undertaken in expectation of payment. "Week" is a period of seven days beginning with Sunday (para.(7)).

Note, however, that this ostensibly very wide general preclusive rule is subject to the partial relief afforded by para.(4) and by reg.46 (see para.(3)) and the complete relief afforded by para.(2). Execution of some *de minimis* tasks can also be ignored as not constituting "work". Discussion is divided accordingly.

Partial relief

Paras (4), (5): Together these afford some relief from the general preclusive   **1A.219**
rule set out in para.(1). Paragraph (4) contains an obviously necessary one, it covers the worker who initially falls sick part way through his working week and/ or the period in which he is incapable of work finishes part way through a week in the course of which he returns to work. Here, the preclusive effect of the regulation is confined to ruling out only the days actually worked in that or those weeks.

Note that the linking rules in reg.145 do not apply for determining when, for the purposes of this relieving rule, a period of limited capability for work begins and ends (para.(5)). In effect, each "spell" of limited capability for work" is treated separately, thus helping those whose limited capability for work is intermittent and removing a disincentive to trying work for a while.

Para.(3): This regulation is "subject to regulation 46". That provides that those treated under reg.26 as having limited capability for work on days when receiving or recovering from certain regular treatments (e.g. chemotherapy), who work on other days of the week in which they receive or are recovering from such treatment such treatment, will not have their entitlement to CESA affected by doing that work. For the impact of such work on entitlement to IRESA, see the exclusionary "remunerative work" rules (WRA 2007, Sch.1, para.6(1)(e); reg.41) and, in terms of the IRESA "balance sheet", the impact of earnings on entitlement.

Complete relief

Para.(2) prevents the general preclusive rule in para.(1) applying to: **1A.220**
  (i) any of the categories of work in reg.45 (para.(2)(f));
  (ii) work as a councillor (see para.(7) for its breadth and see reg.88 for the abating effect on CESA of amounts of councillor's allowance over a specified weekly amount) (para.(2)(a);

  The scheme, as before, seeks to encourage sick and disabled people to participate in civic office by enabling them to receive CESA reduced or abated by the amount by which their councillor's allowance applicable to that week exceeds a specified amount.
  (iii) care of a relative or domestic tasks carried out in his own home (para. (2)(c);
  (iv) work as a foster parent or other specified carer in respect of someone accommodated in one's home in respect of which specified payments are made (para.(2)(d), Sch.8, paras 28, 29);

    (v) limited duties (one full day or two half days per week) as a member of a
the DLA Advisory Board or as First-tier Tribunal member with a disability qualification (para.(2)(b)) (i.e. someone other than a registered medical practitioner, who is experienced in dealing with the physical or mental needs of disabled persons because they work with disabled persons in a professional or voluntary capacity, or are themselves disabled (see art.2(3) of the Qualifications for Appointment of Members to the First-tier Tribunal and Upper Tribunal Order 2008 (SI 2008/2692));

    (vi) any activity undertaken during an emergency solely to protect another person or to prevent serious damage to property or livestock (para. (2)(e)).

This exemption is essential to protect the benefit position of the rescuer; of the good neighbour who looks after his/her neighbour's children when she is rushed to hospital; of the person who helps round up livestock which have strayed into a busy road; or of the good neighbour who helps fight a fire until the emergency services arrive; or the husband on ESA who is compelled to drive to rush his pregnant wife in labour to hospital because the ambulance has not arrived. These can be but speculative examples.

"Emergency" is not defined. However, note it is not qualified by terms such as "severe" or "serious" or "great", so it ought not to be construed too narrowly. By way of comparison, in the industrial injuries context, case law dealing with "in the course of employment" has brought within that phrase persons responding to emergency. There "emergency" was construed broadly to encompass a wide range of unexpected occurrences (see commentary to SSCBA 1992, s.100). A broad approach ought to be taken, similarly, to the notion of "any activity to protect another person".

Applying the de minimis principle to ignore trivial or negligible amounts of work

1A.221   It is submitted that this long-standing principle, which has applied to previous inpacity for work regimes, is equally applicable to ESA and that previous case law applies here.

CIB/5298/1997 supports the view (then found in AOG, paras 18782 and 18783) that the de minimis principle applies to enable trivial or negligible amounts of work to be ignored (paras 5–12), recognising as a practical proposition something seen as a theoretical one in *CIB/14656/96*. Deputy Commissioner Wikeley's decision in *CIB/6777/1999* contains a thorough review of the authorities on this matter. He notes that the rule here can apply irrespective of whether the work might in any event be treated as exempt under Incapacity for Work Regs, reg.17 (and thus ESA Regs, regs 40, 45). Whether work done is trivial or negligible is a matter of fact and degree. Like Commissioner Williams in *CIB/5298/1997*, who had approved guidance in the AOG, the Deputy Commissioner supported as illustrative but not exhaustive, relevant factors, those set out in DMG para.13867:

> "whether work on a day is negligible depends on its proportion to the normal working hours, the type of work and the effort required in relation to normal working duties."

Stressing the role of incapacity benefit as "an earnings replacement ... benefit for those with the appropriate contributions record who cannot work in the labour market" he (rightly in the opinion of this commentator) disagreed with Commissioner Williams in *CIB/5298/1997* who took the view that the amount of remuneration earned was always wholly irrelevant since para.(6) states that work is "work" whether or not undertaken in expectation of payment. That means, of course, that the lack of remuneration or of the expectation of it is irrelevant. The key question is really what the tasks performed tell one about the person's capacity for work. But, in contrast to the irrelevance of lack of remuneration, this author, like the Deputy Commissioner, believes that the amount of remuneration received for a relatively small degree of work-like activity, when contrasted with the weekly rate of incapacity benefit (and now ESA), surely *is* a relevant factor in deciding whether work done should be disregarded as trivial or negligible—it brings into play the "anti-abuse" element of the rules here, which arguably takes one into the realm of when the public (including other recipients of benefit) might view as inappropriate receipt of incapacity benefit or ESA by someone with what looks like a source of income from "employment", albeit only in that one week. Is that not one purpose behind the earnings limits on exempt work in Incapacity for Work Regs, reg.17 (ESA Regs, reg.45)? However, that Incapacity for Work Regs, reg.16 (ESA Regs, reg.40) stipulates particular worthy tasks as ones to be disregarded seems to cast doubt on the Deputy Commissioner's view that the identity of the person for whom the task is performed may be a material factor in applying the de minimis rule.

CIB/3507/2003 affords another illustration of work being disregarded as de minimis. The work in question was described by the Commissioner as follows:

"On 28th November 2001, DW Windows wrote a letter in which they said: 'In July of this year we approached [the claimant] to see if he would like to do a couple of hours each week at [DW Windows] doing various light duties. i.e. Making coffees, emptying bins etc and occasionally driving a vehicle to transport [Mr S. E.] the Manager who holds no driving license. There is no dispute about what DW Windows say. Nor is there any dispute about the fact that the claimant was paid £3.85 per hour and that he worked between one and three hours per week. A schedule of his weekly hours and earnings between the beginning of July and the first week of October 2001 has been produced by DW Windows. He never worked for more than three hours and consequently never earned more than £11.55, in any one week. The period covered is one of 14 weeks. During three of those weeks he worked for 1 hour only. He worked for two hours for five of those weeks and for three hours for the remaining six weeks. The average is a little above two hours per week" (paras 6, 7).

In marked contrast, in *CIB/4684/2003*, Commissioner Jacobs found the work done by the claimant was not so minimal that it could be disregarded. He did so, however, for a different reason to the tribunal which had so found on the basis that the claimant's contribution to the earnings from the post office was significant when compared to his wife's. Instead Commissioner Jacobs approached the matter thus:

"For 8 hours a week, spread over 2 mornings, the claimant manned the post office. He was not there merely to summon his wife if a customer arrived. He was there to serve any customer who wanted any of the services offered by the office. Covering the office in those circumstances amounted to work, even if there were no customers at all. He was in exactly the same position as a stallholder on a market who had no customers. Surely that stallholder would be working, even if no one bought from, or even visited, the stall? How the claimant spent his time when he was not actually serving customers is irrelevant. It would be just as irrelevant whether a market stallholder at a market spent the time trying to entice customers to the stall or merely sat reading a book" (paras 10, 11).

PART 7

EFFECT OF WORK ON ENTITLEMENT TO AN EMPLOYMENT AND
SUPPORT ALLOWANCE

Meaning of "remunerative work" for the purposes of paragraph 6(1)(e) of Schedule 1 to the Act

1A.222   **41.**—(1) For the purposes of paragraph 6(1)(e) of Schedule 1 to the Act (conditions of entitlement to an income-related allowance), "remunerative work" means any work which a claimant does for which payment is made or which is done in expectation of payment, other than work listed in paragraph (2) of regulation 40.

(2) Subject to paragraph (3), a claimant who was, or who was being treated as—

(a) engaged in remunerative work; and

(b) in respect of that work earnings to which regulation 95(1)(b) and (d) applies are paid, is to be treated as being engaged in remunerative work for the period for which those earnings are taken into account in accordance with Part 10 of these Regulations.

(3) Paragraph (2) does not apply to earnings disregarded under paragraph 1 of Schedule 7 (sums to be disregarded in the calculation of earnings).

DEFINITIONS

"claimant"—Welfare Reform Act 2007, s.24(1).
"earnings"—regs 95 and 97.

GENERAL NOTE

1A.223   Under para.6 of Sch.1 to the Welfare Reform Act, it is a condition of entitlement to income-related ESA that (among other things) the claimant is not engaged in remunerative work (para.6(1)(e)) and that, where the claimant is a member of a couple, neither is the other member of the couple (para.6(1)(f)). The meaning of the phrase "remunerative work" differs according to whether it is the claimant or her/his partner that is being considered. Regulation 41 sets out the test for the claimant and reg.42 (below), the test for the partner.

ESA is a benefit for those with limited capability for work and the general principle is that a claimant who does any work will normally not be entitled to ESA for that week (see reg.40 above). That is subject to the exceptions set out in reg.40(2). Paragraph (1) defines remunerative work as any work other than that specified in reg.40(2) with the additional requirement that it should be work "for which payment is made or which is done in expectation of payment". It is difficult to see what purpose this serves. The reg.41(1) definition is narrower than the reg.40 definition and therefore anyone falling within reg.41(1) will already have been disentitled by reg.40.

Perhaps more importantly, some claimants who are not actually working (and are not therefore disentitled by reg.40) are nevertheless *treated as* being in remunerative work (and therefore not entitled to income-related ESA) under powers conferred by para.6(3) of Sch.1 to the Act. Paragraphs (2) and (3) provide that where a claimant's employment is interrupted or comes to an end and he or she receives payment in lieu of remuneration (other than a redundancy payment) or holiday pay (unless it is payable more than four weeks after the termination or interruption of employment) then, except where those earnings are disregarded under para.1 of Sch.7, s/he is treated as engaged in remunerative work for the period during which those earnings are taken into account under Pt 10.

Meaning of "remunerative work" for the purposes of paragraph 6(1)(f) of Schedule 1 to the Act

42.—(1) For the purposes of paragraph 6(1)(f) of Schedule 1 to the Act, (conditions of entitlement to an income-related allowance where a claimant must not be a member of a couple the other member of which is engaged in remunerative work), "remunerative work" means work in which the claimant's partner is engaged or, where the partner's hours of work fluctuate, the partner is engaged on average, for not less than 24 hours a week, being work for which payment is made or which is done in expectation of payment.   1A.224

(2) In calculating the number of hours for which a claimant's partner is engaged in work so as to determine whether that partner is engaged in remunerative work, the number of hours are to be determined in accordance with paragraphs (8) and (9) of regulation 45 and those paragraphs are to be read as though they referred to the claimant's partner.

(3) The claimant's partner is to be treated as engaged in remunerative work during any period for which that partner is absent from work referred to in paragraph (1) if the absence is either without good cause or by reason of a recognised, customary or other holiday.

(4) Subject to paragraph (5), a claimant's partner who was, or who was being treated as—

(a) engaged in remunerative work; and

(b) in respect of that work earnings to which regulation 95(1)(b) and (d) applies are paid, is to be treated as being engaged in remunerative work for the period for which those earnings are taken into account in accordance with Part 10 of these Regulations.

(5) Paragraph (4) does not apply to earnings disregarded under paragraph 1 of Schedule 7 (sums to be disregarded in the calculation of earnings).

(6) For the purposes of this regulation, in determining the number of hours in which a claimant's partner is engaged or treated as engaged in remunerative work, no account is to be taken of any hours in which the claimant's partner is engaged in an employment or a scheme to which regulation 43(1) or (2) (claimants' partners not treated as engaged in remunerative work) applies.

DEFINITIONS

"claimant"—Welfare Reform Act 2007, s.24(1).
"couple"—reg.2(1).
"earnings"—regs 95 and 97.
"partner"—reg.2(1).

GENERAL NOTE

1A.225   In contrast to the position for ESA claimants, it is not a condition of entitlement that their partners should also have limited capability for work. Regulation 42 therefore defines "remunerative work" for the claimant's partner in terms that are similar to reg.5 of the IS Regulations and reg.51 of the JSA Regulations.

Circumstances under which partners of claimants entitled to an income-related allowance are not to be treated as engaged in remunerative work

1A.226   **43.**—(1) A claimant's partner is not to be treated as engaged in remunerative work in so far as—

(a) the partner is engaged in child minding in the partner's home;

(b) the partner is engaged by a charity or voluntary organisation, or is a volunteer, where the only payment received by the partner or due to be paid to the partner, is a payment which is to be disregarded under regulation 104(2) (calculation of income other than earnings) and paragraph 2 of Schedule 8 (sums to be disregarded in the calculation of income other than earnings);

(c) the partner is engaged on a scheme for which a training allowance is being paid;

(d) the partner is receiving assistance under the self-employment route;

(e) the partner is engaged in employment as any one of the following—

　(i) a part-time fireman in a fire brigade maintained in pursuance of the Fire and Rescue Services Act 2004;

　(ii) a part-time fire-fighter employed by a fire and rescue authority;

　(iii) a part-time fire-fighter employed by a fire and rescue authority (as defined in section 1 of the Fire (Scotland) Act 2005 or a joint fire and rescue board constituted by an amalgamation scheme made under section 2(1) of that Act;

　(iv) an auxiliary coastguard in respect of coast rescue activities;

　(v) a person engaged part-time in the manning or launching of a life boat;

　(vi) a member of any territorial or reserve force prescribed in Part 1 of Schedule 6 to the Social Security (Contributions) Regulations 2001; or

(f) the partner is undertaking work as a councillor;

(g) the partner is engaged in caring for a person who is accommodated with the partner by virtue of arrangements made under any of the provisions referred to in paragraphs 28 or 29 of Schedule 8 (sums to be disregarded in the calculation of income other than earnings) and the partner is in receipt of any payment specified in those paragraphs;

(h) the partner is engaged in an activity in respect of which—

　(i) a sports award has been made, or is to be made, to the partner; and

    (ii) no other payment is made or is expected to be made to the partner.

(2) A claimant's partner is not to be treated as engaged in remunerative work, where the partner is—

(a) a person who is mentally or physically disabled and by reason of that disability—

    (i) the person's earnings are reduced to 75% or less of what a person without that disability and working the same number of hours would reasonably be expected to earn in that employment or in comparable employment in the area; or

    (ii) the person's number of hours are 75% or less of what a person without that disability would reasonably be expected to undertake in that employment or in comparable employment in the area;

(b) subject to regulation 42(4) (partners treated as engaged in remunerative work), a person who would otherwise have satisfied section 126(1) of the Contributions and Benefits Act (trade disputes) or in respect of whom section 124(1) of that Act (conditions of entitlement to income support) would otherwise have had effect as modified by section 127(b) of that Act (effect of return to work);

(c) a person who would otherwise satisfy the conditions set out in paragraph 4 of Schedule 1B to the Income Support Regulations;

(d) a person who—

    (i) is in employment;

    (ii) lives in, or is temporarily absent from, a care home, an Abbeyfield Home or an independent hospital; and

    (iii) requires personal care by reason of old age, disablement, past or present dependence on alcohol or drugs, past or present mental disorder or a terminal illness.

(3) The claimant's partner is not to be treated as engaged in remunerative work on any day on which that partner is on maternity leave, paternity leave or adoption leave or is absent from work because the partner is ill.

(4) In this regulation—

"work as a councillor" has the same meaning as in regulation 40;

"volunteer" means a person who is engaged in voluntary work otherwise than for a relative, where the only payment received or due to be paid to the person by virtue of being so engaged is in respect of any expenses reasonably incurred by the person in connection with that work.

DEFINITIONS

"Abbeyfield Home"—reg.2(1).
"adoption leave"—*ibid.*
"claimant"—Welfare Reform Act 2007, s.24(1).
"Contributions and Benefits Act"—Welfare Reform Act 2007, s.65.
"councillor"—reg.2(1).
"employment"—*ibid.*

"Income Support Regulations"—*ibid.*
"independent hospital"—*ibid.*
"maternity leave" "—*ibid.*
"partner"—*ibid.*
"remunerative work"—regs 2(1), 41 and 42.
"self-employment route"—reg.2(1).
"sports award"—*ibid.*
"training allowance"—*ibid.*
"work as a councillor"—reg.40.

GENERAL NOTE

1A.227   This regulation is similar to reg.6 of the IS Regs and reg.52 of the JSA Regs.

Claimants who are treated as not entitled to any allowance at all by reason of regulation 40(1) are to be treated as not having limited capability for work

1A.228   **44.**—(1) Where a claimant is treated as not entitled to an employment and support allowance by reason of regulation 40(1), subject to paragraph (2), the claimant is to be treated as not having limited capability for work.

(2) Paragraph (1) does not apply where the claimant remains entitled to a contributory allowance, but is not entitled to an income-related allowance by reason of regulation 40(1).

(3) Paragraph (1) applies even if—

(a) it has been determined that the claimant has or is to be treated as having, under any of regulations 20 (certain claimants to be treated as having limited capability for work), 25 (hospital in-patients), 26 (claimants undergoing certain regular treatment) or 29 (exceptional circumstances), limited capability for work; or

(b) the claimant meets the conditions set out in regulation 30(2) for being treated as having limited capability for work until a determination is made in accordance with the limited capability for work assessment.

DEFINITION

"claimant"

GENERAL NOTE

1A.229   Regulation 40(1) precludes entitlement to ESA in any week in which a claimant does work. In the light of that, this regulation provides, moreover, that in that period of non-entitlement, he or she will be treated as not having limited capability for work (para.(1), unless the work done only negatives entitlement to IRESA (para.(2)). Such a situation can arise where reg.46 applies in that work done in a week when someone, entitled to CESA, is receiving or recovering from certain regular treatments, does not negative title to CESA, but can to IRESA. Paragraph (3) makes clear that the regulation can operate despite the fact that, applying the limited capability for work assessment (WCAt), the person in fact has limited capability for work incapable of work, or is someone treated as having such limited capability by virtue of certain other regs: 20 (certain claimants to be treated as having limited capability for work); 25 (hospital in-patients); 26

146

(claimants undergoing certain regular treatment); or 29 (exceptional circumstances). This suggests that this rule on treating the person as not having limited capability for work will not operate in other cases where regs treat someone (whatever the reality) as having limited capability for work: regs 30 (treated as having limited capability pending assessment) and 33(2) (certain disabled students). In those cases there will be no entitlement to ESA where the person is caught by reg.40, but the days might still rank as ones of limited capability for work.

Exempt work

45.—(1) The categories of work referred to in regulation 40(2)(f) are **1A.230** set out in the following paragraphs.

(2) Work for which the earnings in any week do not exceed £20.00.

(3) Work for which the earnings in any week do not exceed [¹£92.00] and which—

(a) is part of the claimant's treatment programme and is done under medical supervision while the claimant is an in-patient, or is regularly attending as an out-patient, of a hospital or similar institution; or

(b) is supervised by a person employed by a public or local authority or voluntary organisation engaged in the provision or procurement of work for persons who have disabilities.

(4) Work which is done for less than 16 hours a week, for which earnings in any week do not exceed [¹£92.00] and which—

(a) is done during a 52 week period beginning on the first day on which the work is done, provided that—

　(i) the claimant has not previously done specified work;

　(ii) since the beginning of the last period of specified work, the claimant has ceased to be entitled to a relevant benefit for a continuous period exceeding 12 weeks;

　(iii) not less than 52 weeks have elapsed since the claimant previously did the specified work; or

(b) done by a claimant who has or is treated as having limited capability for work-related activity.

(5) Work done in the course of receiving assistance in pursuing self-employed earner's employment whilst participating in a programme provided or other arrangements made under section 2 of the Employment and Training Act 1973(functions of the Secretary of State) or section 2 of the Enterprise and New Towns (Scotland) Act 1990(functions in relation to training for employment etc.).

(6) Work done where the claimant receives no payment of earnings and where the claimant—

(a) is engaged by a charity or voluntary organisation; or

(b) is a volunteer,

where the Secretary of State is satisfied in any of those cases that it is reasonable for the claimant to provide the service free of charge.

(7) Work done in the course of participating in a work placement approved in writing by the Secretary of State before the placement starts.

(8) The number of hours for which a claimant is engaged in work is to be determined—

(a) where no recognisable cycle has been established in respect of a claimant's work, by reference to the number of hours or, where those hours are likely to fluctuate, the average of the hours, which the claimant is expected to work in a week;

(b) where the number of hours for which the claimant is engaged fluctuate, by reference to the average of hours worked over—

    (i) if there is a recognisable cycle of work, the period of one complete cycle (including, where the cycle involves periods in which the claimant does no work, those periods but disregarding any other absences);

    (ii) in any other case, the period of five weeks immediately before the date of claim or the date on which a superseding decision is made under section 10 (decisions superseding earlier decisions) of the Social Security Act 1998, or such other length of time as may, in the particular case, enable the claimant's average hours of work to be determined more accurately.

(9) For the purposes of determining the number of hours for which a claimant is engaged in work, that number is to include any time allowed to that claimant by the claimant's employer for a meal or for refreshment, but only where that claimant is, or expects to be, paid earnings in respect of that time.

(10) In this regulation—

"relevant benefit" means—

    (a) an employment and support allowance; or

    (b) credits under regulations made under section 22(5) of the Contributions and Benefits Act,

in respect of which the question of the claimant's limited capability for work arises under the Act;

"specified work" means work done in accordance with paragraph (4);

"supervised work" means work done in accordance with paragraph (3)(a) or (b);

"volunteer" has the same meaning it has in regulation 43;

"work placement" means practical work experience with an employer, which is neither paid nor undertaken in expectation of payment.

AMENDMENTS

1. Employment and Support Allowance (Miscellaneous Amendments) Regulations 2008 (SI 2008/2428), reg.6(2) (October 27, 2008).

DEFINITIONS

"the Act"—see reg.2(1).
"claimant"—see WRA 2007, s.24(1).
"Contributions and Benefits Act"—see WRA 2007, s.65.
"employment"—see reg.2(1).
"relevant benefit"—see para.(10).
"self-employed earner"—see reg.2(1).

"specified work"—see paras (10), (4).
"supervised work"—see paras (10), (3) (a) or (b).
"voluntary organisation"—see reg.2(1).
"volunteer"—see para.(10) and reg.43(4).
"week"—see reg.2(1).
"work placement"—see para.(10).

GENERAL NOTE

This regulation needs to be read in conjunction with reg.40(1) which pre-   1A.231
cludes entitlement to ESA in any week in which a claimant does work. "Work"
for the purposes of that regulation is defined in reg.40(7) as any work done
whether or not undertaken in expectation of payment. "Week" is a period of
seven days beginning with Sunday (reg.40(7)). This regulation in contrast
defines a variety of work which ranking as "exempt work" does not pursuant to
reg.40(2)(f) preclude entitlement to ESA under the general preclusive rule in
reg.40(1).

The regulation is part of the welfare to work strategy, of encouraging people to
try out work, the better to enable a return to work.

The current categories of exempt work
Some embody an earnings limit, others both an earnings and hours limit. The
matters of determining the hours of engagement and assessing earnings are
examined further below, after considering the seven categories of exempt
work:
(1) *Work for which the earnings in any week do not exceed £20 (para.(2)):* there
    is no hours limit as such here, but it is anticipated that in practice the effect
    of the minimum wage laws will mean that DWP staff will expect a claimant
    in this category to be working less than 5 hours a week. Its prime role is the
    encouragement of social contact.
(2) *Unpaid work for a charity or voluntary organization (para.(6)(a)):* Work
    done where the claimant is engaged by a charity or voluntary organization
    is exempt where he receives no payment of earnings and the Secretary of
    State is satisfied that it is reasonable for him to provide the service free of
    charge. "Charity" is not defined in the ESA Regs, so must bear the
    meaning it does in charity law. "Voluntary organization" means a body,
    other than a public or local authority, the activities of which are carried on
    otherwise than for profit (reg.2(1)).
(3) *Work done as a volunteer (paras (6)(b), (10)):* Voluntary work other than
    that covered by para.(6)(1)(a) is thus also protected where the claimant
    receives no payment of earnings and the Secretary of State is satisfied that
    it is reasonable for him to provide the service free of charge. "Volunteer"
    is defined in para.(10) by reference to reg.43(4) to embrace a person who
    is engaged in voluntary work otherwise than for a relative, where the only
    payment received by him or due to be paid to him by virtue of being so
    engaged is in respect of any expenses reasonably incurred by him in
    connection with that work. "Relative" is widely defined: it means a close
    relative, grand-parent, grand-child, uncle, aunt, nephew or niece
    (reg.2(1)). "Close relative" covers a parent, parent-in-law, son, son-in-law,
    daughter, daughter-in-law, step-parent, step-son, step-daughter, brother,
    sister, or the spouse of any of these persons, or if that person is one of an
    unmarried couple, the other member of that couple (reg.2(1)). There are
    no hours or earnings limits.

(3) *Supervised work (paras (3, (10)):* there are two categories here. First,work done with the supervision of bodies providing or finding work for disabled people (para.(3)(a)). The bodies in question are a public or local authority or a voluntary organisation (that is, a body, other than a public or local authority, whose activities are carried on otherwise than for profit (reg.2(1)). The second category covers work while a patient of a hospital or similar institution under medical supervision as part of a treatment programme. The patient must be an in-patient or a regularly attending out-patient (para.(3)(b)). Whichever of the two categories, the earnings from the work must not exceed £92.00 a week (see further below). On "hospital or similar institution", some guidance is given in DMG, paras 18031–18033, 24018–24023. But this is not binding on tribunals or courts.

(4) *Work done in the course of receiving assistance in pursuing self-employed earner's employment whilst participating in certain programmes or arrangements (para.(5)):* this makes it easier for people receiving ESA to attempt self employment. Test Trading allows people to try out 'self employment' for a period of up to 26 weeks. Its introduction prevents participants being regarded as in work with the possibility of a loss of benefit should earnings exceed the permitted work limits.

(5) *Work done by those having, or treated as having, limited capability for work-related activity (para.(4)(b)):* those in the support group (receiving or eligible for support component) can work for an unlimited period providing it is for less than 16 hours a week (see further, below) and the earnings do not exceed £92.00 a week (see further below). This provides a new category of permitted work for people who face the greatest barriers to full-time employment.

(6) *Permitted ("specified") work for an initial period of up to 52 weeks (paras (4)(a), (10)):* this simplifies matters considerably compared to the previous reg.17(4)(A) (see 2005 edition of this book). The work done must be for less than 16 hours a week (see further, below) and the earnings in any week must not exceed £92.00 (see further, below). To qualify for this permitted work period, the person must (i) have not previously done specified work (i.e. work protected by this particular head (para.(10)); (ii) since the beginning of the last period of specified work, he must have ceased to be entitled to a "relevant" benefit (see para.(10)) for a continuous period of more than twelve weeks; and (iii) at least 52 weeks have elapsed since he last did specified work.

(7) *approved, unpaid work placements (paras (7), (10)):* "Work placement" is practical work experience with an employer, which is neither paid nor taken on in expectation of payment (para.(10)). The work placement must have been approved by the Secretary of State in writing prior to its commencement.

In determining the number of hours of engagement in work (paras (8), (9)) an averaging approach applies, varying according to whether there is or is not a recognizable cycle and whether the claimant's hours fluctuate (para.(8)). The hours of engagement include time the employer allows for meals or refreshment where the claimant is, or expects to be, paid earnings in respect of that time (para.(9)).

The earnings limit—Computation of Earnings Regs not applicable here
Unlike the position with IB, ESA is not within the sphere of the SSCBA 1992 and so the Computation of Earnings Regs cannot apply. Calculation of earnings is to be done under the rules in the ESA Regs.

150

Effect of work on entitlement to contributory allowance where claimant is receiving certain regular treatment

46. Where a claimant who is entitled to a contributory allowance and is treated as having limited capability for work by virtue of regulation 26 works on any day during a week when the claimant is, in accordance with regulation 26, receiving certain regular treatment or recovering from that treatment, that work is to have no effect on the claimant's entitlement to the contributory allowance.

1A.232

DEFINITIONS

"claimant"—see WRA 2007, s.24(1).
"contributory allowance"—see WRA 2007, s.1(7).
"entitled"—see WRA 2007, s.24(1).
"limited capability for work"—see WRA 2007, s.24(1).
"week"—see reg.2(1), WRA 2007, s.24(1).

GENERAL NOTE

This (affording an exception to the preclusive rule on work in reg.40(1)) provides that those treated under reg.26 as having limited capability for work on days when receiving or recovering from certain regular treatments (e.g. chemotherapy), who work on other days of the week in which they receive or are recovering from such treatment such treatment, will not have their entitlement to CESA affected by doing that work. For the impact of such work on entitlement to IRESA, see the exclusionary "remunerative work" rules (WRA 2007, Sch.1, para.6(1)(e); reg.41) and, in terms of the IRESA "balance sheet", the impact of earnings on entitlement.

1A.233

PART 8

CONDITIONALITY

CHAPTER 1

WORK-FOCUSED HEALTH-RELATED ASSESSMENT

Requirement to take part in a work-focused health-related assessment

47.—(1) The Secretary of State may require a claimant who satisfies the requirements in paragraph (2) to take part in one or more work-focused health-related assessments as a condition of continuing to be entitled to the full amount of employment and support allowance payable to the claimant.

(2) The requirements referred to in paragraph (1) are that the claimant—

(a) is either—

1A.234

       (i) entitled to an employment and support allowance; or

       (ii) a person who has made a claim for an employment and support allowance to which regulations under section 5(1)(c) of the Administration Act apply;

    (b) is not a member of the support group; and

    (c) has not reached the age at which a woman of the same age as the claimant would attain pensionable age.

(3) Any requirement to take part in a work-focused health-related assessment ceases to have effect if the claimant ceases to satisfy the requirements in paragraph (2).

DEFINITIONS

"Administration Act"—see WRA 2007, s.65.
"claimant"—see WRA 2007, s.24(1).
"member of the support group"—see WRA 2007, s.24(4).
"pensionable age"—see reg.2(1).
"work-focused health-related assessments"—see WRA 2007, s.11(7).

GENERAL NOTE

1A.235   This regulation, read with WRA 2007, s.11 and regs 48–53, deals with the first aspect of "conditionality", the requirements imposed on most of those who fall outside the support group as not having limited capability for work-related activity. These will constitute some 90% of ESA claimants. The policy is that ESA brings rights, responsibilities and opportunities to people with health conditions and disabilities by asking them to engage with Jobcentre Plus (and contracted providers in the private and voluntary sectors [PVS]) to work towards fulfilling their ambitions. The key to this is seen in the incorporation in entitlement to the work-related activity component of ESA of an element of conditionality modelled on those applied in the Pathways to Work programme. This has a number of elements: (i) participation in a work-focused health related assessment (WFHRAt); (ii) participation in a work-focused interview; and (iii) as resources permit (and not before 2011), undertaking work-related activity that increases the likelihood of getting a job (e.g. work trials). This regulation stipulates that as a condition of receiving in full the support component of ESA, a claimant may be required to participate in the third element of the new work capability assessment (WCA): a work-focused health related assessment (WFHRAt) (see WRA 2007, s.11 and reg.48), the first element of taking part in work-related activity (para.(1)). This requirement may, however, only be imposed on a claimant not in the support group, entitled to ESA or who makes a claim for it, who, whether male or female, has not reached the female pensionable age by reference to his/her date of birth (para.(2), reg.2(1) and link to Pensions Act 1995, Sch.4, para.1). Should such a requirement have been imposed when those conditions were met, it will cease to have effect when the claimant no longer satisfies one or more of them (e.g. ceases claiming, becomes a member of the support group because the health condition and its limiting effects have worsened, or has reached the exempting age).

    The exception for those in the support group (para.(2)(b)) may cause some practical problems, since it is envisaged that, despite its different outlook (looking to what people can do, rather than what they cannot), the WFHRAt will usually be conducted by the relevant health care professional immediately after the combined WCAt (governing eligibility for basic allowance ESA) and WRAAt (governing eligibility for support component), that is before it has been determined whether or not the claimant falls into the support group The review group which helped revise the PCA thought that conducting this assessment at the same time as the others had advantages, not least the convenience for the claimant of only having to attend a single appointment. Others expressed concerns that combining the two assessments risked confusing assessor and claimant, and creating a cause of anxiety to the latter. As is apparent from the wording of the regulations, the two assessments look at rather different things; both claimant and assessor at the same time have to consider what the claimant can and cannot do. A claimant might be fearful that elements from the WRHFAt might feed back and impact negatively on those other aspects of the WCA which determine title to benefit.

Note that failure, without good cause, to participate in a WRHFAt (regs 51, 53) is sanctioned initially by halving the amount of work-related activity component and eventually by reducing it to nil (reg.63), the reduction to cease after compliance has been induced or the requirement to participate has ceased to have effect under para.(3) (reg.64).

Work-focused health-related assessment

48. For the purposes of section 11(7)(c) of the Act, matters to be assessed in the work-focused health-related assessment include—   1A.236

    (a) difficulties which are likely to be experienced as a result of the claimant's physical or mental condition in relation to obtaining or remaining in work and how these might be managed or alleviated; and

    (b) the claimant's views on the impact of the claimant's physical or mental condition in relation to obtaining or remaining in work and any aspirations in relation to work in the light of that condition.

DEFINITIONS

    "the Act"—see reg.2(1).
    "claimant"—see WRA 2007, s.24(1).
    "work-focused health-related assessment"—see WRA 2007, s.11(7).

GENERAL NOTE

    "Work-focused health-related assessment" is defined in WRA 2007, s.11(7) as   1A.237
an assessment by an approved health care professional for the purpose of assessing the extent to which a person still has capability for work; the extent to that may be improved by the taking of steps in relation to his physical or mental condition; and such other matters relating to his physical or mental condition and the likelihood of his obtaining or remaining in work or being able to do so, as may be prescribed. This regulation prescribes those matters so as to include (the list is thus not exhaustive) the matters set out in paras (a) and (b).

Notification of assessment

49.—(1) The health care professional who is to carry out the work-   1A.238
focused health-related assessment, or a person acting on the health care professional's behalf, must notify the claimant of the requirement to attend the work-focused health-related assessment including details of the date, time and place of the assessment.

(2) Notification under paragraph (1) must be given in writing at least 7 days before the claimant is required to attend the work-focused health-

related assessment unless the claimant agrees to accept a shorter period of notice whether given in writing or otherwise.

DEFINITIONS

"claimant"—see WRA 2007, s.24(1).
"health care professional"—see reg.2(1).
"work-focused health-related assessment"—see WRA 2007, s.11(7).

GENERAL NOTE

1A.239   This requires proper notification to the claimant of the requirement to attend the work-focused health-related assessment. It must include details of that assessment's date, time and place (para.(1)). Notification must be given by, or on behalf of, the health care professional who is to carry it out (para.(1)). It must be in writing and be given at least seven days before the claimant is being required to attend, unless the claimant agrees to accept a shorter period of notice whether that shorter period be notified in writing or otherwise (para.(2)). On calculating periods of notice, see the commentary to reg.23 (requirement to attend medical examination for the limited capability for work assessment).

Determination of the place of the work-focused health-related assessment

1A.240   **50.**—(1) Subject to paragraph (2), the work-focused health-related assessment must be carried out in a medical examination centre.
(2) A work-focused health-related assessment may take place at the claimant's home if the Secretary of State is of the opinion that requiring the claimant to attend elsewhere would cause the claimant undue inconvenience or endanger the claimant's health.

DEFINITIONS

"claimant"—see WRA 2007, s.24(1).
"medical examination centre"—see reg.2(1).
"work-focused health-related assessment"—see WRA 2007, s.11(7).

GENERAL NOTE

1A.241   This stipulates that generally the work-focused health-related assessment must be carried out in a medical examination centre (para.(1)). This means premises equipped and suitable for carrying out a medical examination (reg.2(1)). But there is a discretion to carry out the assessment in the claimant's home if the Secretary of State considers that a requirement to attend a medical examination centre would endanger the claimant's health or simply cause undue inconvenience (para.(2)).

Taking part in a work-focused health-related assessment

1A.242   **51.** A claimant is to be regarded as having taken part in a work-focused health-related assessment if the claimant—
    (a) attends for the assessment at the date, time and place notified in accordance with regulation 49;
    (b) provides all information which the Secretary of State requests as being necessary for the work-focused health-related assessment; and

(c) participates in discussions to the extent the Secretary of State considers necessary for the work-focused health-related assessment.

DEFINITIONS

"claimant"—see WRA 2007, s.24(1).
"work-focused health-related assessment"—see WRA 2007, s.11(7).

GENERAL NOTE

To receive the full amount of work-related activity component, a claimant may be required to take part in a work-focused health-related assessment (WFHRAt) (WRA 2007, s.11; reg.48). Not taking part (without showing good cause) will be sanctioned by progressive reduction of the component, first by 50% and then by 100% (reg.63). This regulation stipulates when a claimant is to be regarded as having taken part. It requires not merely attendance at the proper date, time and place (para.(a)) and the provision of the information the Secretary of State considers necessary for the WFHRAt (para.(b)), but, also crucially, participation in the discussions to the extent the Secretary of State considers necessary (para.(c)). 1A.243

Deferral of requirement to take part in a work-focused health-related assessment

52.—(1) Where—   1A.244
(a) a health care professional has conducted an assessment in relation to the claimant for the purpose of enabling the Secretary of State to determine whether the claimant has limited capability for work-related activity;
(b) it appears to the health care professional that—
  (i) at least one of the descriptors set out in Schedule 3 applies to the claimant; or
  (ii) regulation 35 applies to the claimant; and
(c) the Secretary of State has not made a determination about whether the claimant has limited capability for work-related activity,
the requirement to take part in the work-focused health-related assessment does not apply until such time after the Secretary of State has made a determination in relation to the claimant's limited capability for work-related activity as the Secretary of State may decide.

(2) Where paragraph (1) applies, the health care professional must notify the claimant that the requirement to take part in the work-focused health-related assessment has been deferred, pending determination by the Secretary of State of the claimant's capability for work-related activity.

DEFINITIONS

"claimant"—see WRA 2007, s.24(1).
"health care professional"—see reg.2(1).
"limited capability for work-related activity"—see WRA 2007, s.2(5).
"work-focused health-related assessment"—see WRA 2007, s.11(7).
"work-related activity"—see WRA 2007, ss.24(1), 13(7).

1A.245　　Those who are in the support group are exempt from the requirement to participate in a work-focused health-related assessment (WFHRAt) (reg.47(2)(b)). This may cause some practical problems, since it is envisaged that, despite its different outlook (looking to what people can do, rather than what they cannot), the WFHRAt will usually be conducted by the relevant health care professional immediately after the combined WCAt (governing eligibility for basic allowance ESA) and WRAAt (governing eligibility for support component), that is before it has been determined whether or not the claimant falls into the support group.

　　This regulation sensibly provides that the health care professional carrying out the WRAAt in relation to someone whose capability for work-related activity has not been determined, must defer the WFHRAt until after that matter has been determined if that professional considers that the claimant falls within the support group (para.(1)(b)(i)) or is otherwise treated as having limited capability for work-related activity under reg.35 as terminally ill, undergoing or recovering from chemotherapy, or pregnant where there is a serious risk of damage to the woman's health or that of her unborn child if she does not refrain from work-related activity (para.(1)(b)(ii)). The health care professional must notify the claimant of the deferral pending the decision on capability for work-related activity.

Failure to take part in a work-focused health-related assessment

1A.246　　**53.**—(1) A claimant who is required to take part in a work-focused health-related assessment but fails to do so must show good cause for that failure within 5 working days of the date on which the Secretary of State gives notification of that failure.

　　(2) The Secretary of State must determine whether a claimant who is required to take part in a work-focused health-related assessment has failed to do so and, if so, whether the claimant has shown good cause for that failure in accordance with paragraph (1).

　　(3) In determining whether a claimant has shown good cause for the failure to participate in a work-focused health-related assessment, the Secretary of State must take the following matters into account—

(a) whether the claimant was outside Great Britain at the time of the notification;

(b) the claimant's state of health at the time of the work-focused health-related assessment;

(c) the nature of any disability which the claimant has; and

(d) any other matter which the Secretary of State considers appropriate.

DEFINITIONS

　　"claimant"—see WRA 2007, s.24(1).
　　"work-focused health-related assessment"—see WRA 2007, s.11(7).

GENERAL NOTE

1A.247　　Failure, without good cause, to take part (see reg.51) in a work-focused health related assessment is sanctioned by progressive reduction of work-related activity component (initially 50%, then 100%) (reg.63). This regulation deals with showing good cause when the Secretary of State has notified the claimant of his failure to take part. It requires the claimant to show good cause for such failure within five working days of the date on which the notification was given (para.(1)). It must then be determined whether there was a failure and, if so, whether the requisite good case has been shown within the stipulated time frame (para.(2)). "Good cause" is not defined, although WRA 2007, s.11(2)(h) provides power to prescribe what ranks or does not rank as "good cause. Paragraph (3) merely provides, pursuant to subs.(2)(g) of that section, four matters which must be taken into account.

CHAPTER 2

WORK-FOCUSED INTERVIEWS

Requirement to take part in a work-focused interview

54.—(1) The Secretary of State may require a claimant who satisfies the requirements in paragraph (2) to take part in one or more work-focused interviews as a condition of continuing to be entitled to the full amount of employment and support allowance payable to the claimant. **1A.248**

(2) The requirements referred to in paragraph (1) are that the claimant—

   (a) is either—

     (i) entitled to an employment and support allowance; or

     (ii) a person in respect of whom the Secretary of State has made an award under regulation 146(1);

   (b) is not a member of the support group;

   (c) has not reached the age at which a woman of the same age as the claimant would attain pensionable age; and

   (d) is not only entitled to a contributory allowance payable at a nil rate.

(3) Any requirement to take part in a work-focused interview ceases to have effect if the claimant ceases to satisfy the requirements in paragraph (2).

DEFINITIONS

"claimant"—see WRA 2007, s.24(1).
"contributory allowance"—see WRA 2007, ss.24(1), 1(7).
"member of the support group"—see WRA 2007, s.24(4).
"pensionable age"—see reg.2(1).
"work-focused interview"—see WRA 2007, s.12(7).

GENERAL NOTE

This regulation, read with WRA 2007, s.11 and regs 48–53, deals with the second aspect of "conditionality", the requirements imposed on most of those who fall outside the support group as not having limited capability for work-related activity. These will constitute some 90% of ESA claimants. The policy is **1A.249** that ESA brings rights, responsibilities and opportunities to people with health conditions and disabilities by asking them to engage with Jobcentre Plus (and contracted providers in the private and voluntary sectors [PVS]) to work towards fulfilling their ambitions. The key to this is seen in the incorporation in entitlement to the work-related activity component of ESA of an element of conditionality modelled on those applied in the Pathways to Work programme. This has a number of elements: (i) participation in a work-focused health related assessment (WFHRAt) (WRA 2007, s.11; regs 47–53); (ii) participation in a work-focused interview; and (iii) as resources permit (and not before 2011), undertaking work-related activity that increases the likelihood of getting a job (e.g. work trials). This regulation stipulates that as a condition of receiving the full amount of ESA, a claimant may be required to participate in one or more work-focused interviews, the second element of taking part in work-related activity (para.(1)). This requirement may, however, only be imposed on a claimant not in the support group, awarded ESA or an advance award of it under reg.146, who, whether male or female, has not reached the female pensionable age by reference to his/her date of birth, and who is not merely entitled to CESA at a nil rate (e.g. because of abatement under WRA 2007, ss.2, 3) (para.(2), reg.2(1) and link to Pensions Act 1995, Sch.4, para.1). Should such a requirement have been imposed when those conditions were met, it will cease to have effect when the claimant no longer satisfies one or more of them (e.g. becomes a member of the support group because the health condition and it limiting effects have worsened, or has reached the exempting age, or whose ESA entitlement drops to CESA at a nil rate) (para.(3)).

Although WRA 2007, s.16 and reg.63 enable contracting out so as to bring expertise from the private and voluntary sectors (PVS) into the process of assisting claimants to prepare for and enhance their prospects of starting or returning to work, it is envisaged, however, that the first work-focused interview will always be with someone from Jobcentre Plus and will be held around the eighth week of the assessment period.

Note that failure, without good cause, to participate in a work-focused interview (regs 55, 57, 58, 61) is sanctioned initially by halving the amount of work-related activity component and eventually by reducing it to nil (reg.63), the reduction to cease after compliance has been induced or the requirement to participate has ceased to have effect under para.(3) (reg.64).

Work-focused interview

1A.250   **55.** The purposes of a work-focused interview are any or all of the following—

  (a) assessing the claimant's prospects for remaining in or obtaining work;

  (b) assisting or encouraging the claimant to remain in or obtain work;

  (c) identifying activities that the claimant may undertake that will make remaining in or obtaining work more likely;

  (d) identifying training, educational or rehabilitation opportunities for the claimant which may make it more likely that the claimant will remain in or obtain work or be able to do so;

  (e) identifying current or future work opportunities, including self-employment opportunities, for the claimant, that are relevant to the claimant's needs and abilities.

DEFINITIONS

"claimant"—see WRA 2007, s.24(1).
"training"—see reg.2(1).
"work-focused interview"—see WRA 2007, s.12(7).

GENERAL NOTE

Pursuant to WRA 2007, s.12(7) this regulation prescribes the purposes of a 1A.251
work-focused interview as any or all of those listed in paras (a)–(e).

Notification of interview

56.—(1) The Secretary of State must notify the claimant of the 1A.252
requirement to attend the work-focused interview including details of
the date, time and place of the interview.

(2) A work-focused interview may take place at a claimant's home if it
is determined that requiring the claimant to attend elsewhere would
cause undue inconvenience to, or endanger the health of, the claimant.

(3) The notification referred to in paragraph (1) may be in writing or
otherwise.

DEFINITIONS

"claimant"—see WRA 2007, s.24(1).
"work-focused interview"—see WRA 2007, s.12(7).

GENERAL NOTE

The Secretary of State must give proper notification to the claimant that he is 1A.253
required to attend the work-focused interview. This must include details of its
date, time and place (para.(1)). The notification need not be in writing
(para.(2)). This is in marked contrast to other provisions imposing requirements
with respect to the three elements of the work capability assessment (WCA) (see
regs 22–24, 36–38, 49). So is the absence of any stipulation as to due period of
notice. As to place, none is specified (a consequence of ability to contract-out the
interviews—reg.62). But the interview can take place at the claimant's home if it
is decided that requirement to attend elsewhere would endanger his health or
simply cause undue convenience.

Taking part in a work-focused interview

57.—(1) A claimant is regarded as having taken part in a work-focused 1A.254
interview if the claimant—
   (a) attends for the interview at the place and at the date and time
       notified in accordance with regulation 56;
   (b) provides information, if requested by the Secretary of State, about
       any or all of the matters set out in paragraph (2);
   (c) participates in discussions to the extent the Secretary of State
       considers necessary, about any or all of the matters set out in
       paragraph (3);
   (d) assists the Secretary of State in the completion of an action
       plan.
(2) The matters referred to in paragraph (1)(b) are—
   (a) the claimant's educational qualifications and vocational training;

159

> (b) the claimant's work history;
> (c) the claimant's aspirations for future work;
> (d) the claimant's skills that are relevant to work;
> (e) the claimant's work-related abilities;
> (f) the claimant's caring or childcare responsibilities; and
> (g) any paid or unpaid work that the claimant is undertaking.
>
> (3) The matters referred to in paragraph (1)(c) are—
> (a) any activity the claimant is willing to undertake which may make obtaining or remaining in work more likely;
> (b) any such activity that the claimant may have previously undertaken;
> (c) any progress the claimant may have made towards remaining in or obtaining work;
> (d) any work-focused health-related assessment the claimant may have taken part in; and
> (e) the claimant's opinion as to the extent to which the ability to remain in or obtain work is restricted by the claimant's physical or mental condition.

DEFINITIONS

> "claimant"—see WRA 2007, s.24(1).
> "work-focused health-related assessment"—see WRA 2007, s.11(7).
> "work-focused interview"—see WRA 2007, s.12(7).

GENERAL NOTE

1A.255   Failure, without good cause, to take part in a work-focused interview (regs 55, 57, 58, 61) is sanctioned initially by halving the amount of work-related activity component and eventually by reducing it to nil (reg.63), the reduction to cease after compliance has been induced or the requirement to participate has ceased to have effect under para.(3) (reg.64).

This regulation sets out when a claimant is to be regarded as having taken part: attendance at the proper place, date and time (para.(1)(a)); provision of the requisite information required by the Secretary of State (paras (1)(b), (2)); participation to such an extent as the Secretary of State considers necessary in discussion about the key matters stipulated in para.(3); and assisting the Secretary of State (in reality someone in Jobcentre Plus or a contractor or employee of a contractor) in drawing up an "action plan" as defined in reg.58.

Action plan

1A.256   **58.**—(1) An action plan is a document that is completed by the Secretary of State and contains—
> (a) a record of a work-focused interview;
> (b) a record of any activity that the claimant is willing to take which may make obtaining or remaining in work more likely or which may make it more likely that the claimant will be able to do so;
> (c) any other information that the Secretary of State considers to be appropriate.

(2) An action plan must be in writing.

(3) The Secretary of State must provide a claimant who attends a work-focused interview with an action plan.

DEFINITIONS

"action plan"—see para.(1).
"claimant"—see WRA 2007, s.24(1).
"work-focused interview"—see WRA 2007, s.12(7).

GENERAL NOTE

In order to be regarded under reg.57 as having taken part in a work-focused   1A.257
interview, the claimant must assist the Secretary of State (in reality someone in
Jobcentre Plus or a contractor or employee of a contractor) in drawing up an
"action plan". This regulation defines "action plan" (para.(1)), requires it to be
in writing (para.(2)), and that the Secretary of State provides a claimant who
attends a work-focused interview with such a plan (para.(3)).

Deferral of requirement to take part in a work-focused interview

59.—(1) A requirement to take part in a work-focused interview may   1A.258
be deferred or treated as having been deferred if at the time the work-
focused interview is to take place, or was due to take place, such an
interview would not at that time be or have been—

(a) of assistance to the claimant; or

(b) appropriate in the circumstances.

(2) A decision under paragraph (1) may be made at any time after the
requirement to take part in the work-focused interview is imposed,
including after the time that the work-focused interview was due to take
place or took place.

(3) Where a requirement to take part in a work-focused interview is
deferred, or treated as having been deferred, then the time that the work-
focused interview is to take place must be redetermined.

DEFINITIONS

"claimant"—see WRA 2007, s.24(1).
"work-focused interview"—see WRA 2007, s.12(7).

GENERAL NOTE

This regulation enables deferral of a work-focused interview (or treating it as   1A.259
deferred) if holding it would not assist the claimant or otherwise be inappropriate
(para.(1)). The decision on deferral can be made at any time after the requirement to take part was imposed on the claimant, whether before or after it was
due to take place (para.(2)). If deferred, the matter of when such an interview is
to take place has to be redetermined (para.(3)).

Requirement to take part in a work-focused interview not to apply

60. The Secretary of State may determine that a requirement on a   1A.260
claimant to take part in a work-focused interview is not to apply, or is to
be treated as not having applied, if that interview would not be, or would
not have been, of assistance because the claimant is or was likely to be
starting or returning to work.

DEFINITIONS

"claimant"—see WRA 2007, s.24(1).
"work-focused interview"—see WRA 2007, s.12(7).

GENERAL NOTE

1A.261   This enables lifting of the requirement to take part in a work-focused interview, whether before or after it was due to take place, where it would not be (or be likely to have been of assistance) because the claimant is or was likely to be starting or returning to work.

Failure to take part in a work-focused interview

1A.262   **61.**—(1) A claimant who is required to take part in a work-focused interview but fails to do so must show good cause for that failure within 5 working days of the date on which the Secretary of State gives notification of that failure.

(2) The Secretary of State must determine whether a claimant who is required to take part in a work-focused interview has failed to do so and, if so, whether the claimant has shown good cause for that failure in accordance with paragraph (1).

(3) In determining whether a claimant has shown good cause for the failure to take part in a work-focused interview, the Secretary of State may take the following matters into account—

(a) that the claimant misunderstood the requirement to take part in the work-focused interview due to learning, language or literacy difficulties or any misleading information given or sent by the Secretary of State;

(b) that the claimant had transport difficulties and that no reasonable alternative was available;

(c) that the claimant was attending an interview with an employer with a view to remaining in or obtaining work;

(d) that the claimant was pursuing employment opportunities as a self-employed earner;

(e) that the claimant was attending a medical or dental appointment and that it would have been unreasonable in the circumstances to re-arrange the appointment;

(f) that the claimant was accompanying another person for whom the claimant has caring responsibilities to a medical or dental appointment and that it would have been unreasonable for that other person to re-arrange the appointment;

(g) that the claimant, a dependant or another person for whom the claimant provides care suffered an accident, sudden illness or relapse of a physical or mental condition;

(h) that the claimant was attending the funeral of a relative or close friend on the day of the work-focused interview;

(i) that the physical or mental condition of the claimant made it impossible to attend at the time and place fixed for the interview;

(j) that the established customs and practices of the religion to which the claimant belongs prevented attendance on that day or at that time;

(k) any other matter which the Secretary of State considers appropriate.

"claimant"—see WRA 2007, s.24(1).
"relative"—see reg.2(1).
"work-focused interview"—see WRA 2007, s.12(7).

GENERAL NOTE

Failure, without good cause, to participate in a work-focused interview (regs 1A.263
55, 57, 58) is sanctioned initially by halving the amount of work-related activity
component and eventually by reducing it to nil (reg.63), the reduction to cease
after compliance has been induced or the requirement to participate has ceased
to have effect under para.(3) (reg.64).

This regulation deals with showing good cause when the Secretary of State has
notified the claimant of his failure to take part. It requires the claimant to show
good cause for such failure within five working days of the date on which the
notification was given (para.(1)). It must then be determined whether there was
a failure and, if so, whether the requisite good case has been shown within the
stipulated time frame (para.(2)) "Good cause" is not defined, although WRA
2007, s.12(2)(i) provides power to prescribe what ranks or does not rank as
"good cause. Paragraph (3) merely provides, pursuant to subs.(2)(h) of that
section, eleven matters which may be taken into account.

Contracting out certain functions relating to work-focused interviews

62.—(1) Any function of the Secretary of State specified in paragraph 1A.264
(2) may be exercised by, or by employees of, such person (if any) as may
be authorised by the Secretary of State.

(2) The functions are any function under—

(a) regulation 54(1) (requirement to take part in a work-focused
interview);

(b) regulation 56(1) and (2) (notification requirement);

(c) regulation 57(1)(b) and (c) (taking part in a work-focused interview);

(d) regulation 58(1) and (3) (action plan);

(e) regulation 59(1) and (3) (deferral of requirement to take part in a
work-focused interview);

(f) regulation 60 (requirement to take part in a work-focused interview not to apply).

GENERAL NOTE

Pursuant to WRA 2007, s.16, which enables contracting-out, this regulation 1A.265
sets out in para.(2) functions of the Secretary of State under these regulations
which can be exercise by an authorised contractor or the employees of such a
contractor. The idea is to bring expertise from the private and voluntary sectors
(PVS) into the process of assisting claimants to prepare for and enhance their
prospects of starting or returning to work. It is envisaged, however, that the first
work-focused interview will always be with someone from Jobcentre Plus and will
be held around the eighth week of the assessment period. Note that sanctioning
decisions (regs 63, 64) are not-contracted out, although clearly information
provided by contractors will inform those decisions.

163

Chapter 3

Reduction of Employment and Support Allowance

Reduction of employment and support allowance

1A.266   **63.**—(1) Where the Secretary of State has determined that a claimant who was required to take part in—

(a) a work-focused health-related assessment; or

(b) a work-focused interview,

has failed to do so and has failed to show good cause for that failure in accordance with regulation 53 or 61, as the case may be ("a failure determination"), the amount of the employment and support allowance payable to the claimant is to be reduced in accordance with this regulation.

(2) Subject to paragraph (3), the amount of the reduction in relation to each failure determination is—

(a) 50% of the amount of the work-related activity component as set out in Part 4 of Schedule 4 for the first 4 benefit weeks to which, by virtue of section 10(5) of the Social Security Act 1998 or regulations made under section 10(6) of that Act, the reduction applies; and

(b) 100% of the amount of that component for each subsequent benefit week.

(3) In any benefit week, the amount of an employment and support allowance payable to a claimant is not, by virtue of this regulation, to be reduced—

(a) below 10 pence;

(b) in relation to more than—

(i) one failure determination relating to a work-focused health-related assessment; and

(ii) one failure determination relating to a work-focused interview; and

(c) by more than 100% of the amount of the work-related activity component as set out in Part 4 of Schedule 4 in any circumstances.

(4) Where a claimant is entitled to both a contributory allowance and an income-related allowance, any reduction in the claimant's allowance must first be applied to the part of that allowance treated as attributable to the claimant's contributory allowance and only if there is any amount outstanding is it to be applied to the part of that allowance treated as attributable to the claimant's income-related allowance.

(5) For the purposes of determining the amount of any income-related allowance payable, a claimant is to be treated as receiving the amount of any contributory allowance which would have been payable but for any reduction made in accordance with this regulation.

164

DEFINITIONS

"claimant"—see WRA 2007, s.24(1).
"contributory allowance"—see WRA 2007, ss.24(1), 1(7).
"failure determination"—see para.(1).
"income-related allowance"—see WRA 2007, ss.24(1), 1(7).
"work-focused health-related assessment"—see WRA 2007, s.11(7).
"work-focused interview"—see WRA 2007, s.12(7).

GENERAL NOTE

In accordance with WRA 2007, ss.12(3), 13(3), this regulation provides the   **1A.267**
sanction for failure without god cause to take part in a work focused health-related assessment and/or a work-focused interview. The sanction, put simply, is a reduction in the amount of ESA to which the person would otherwise be entitled (para.(1)). On the face of the Act and the first para of this regulation, that could be a reduction of ESA as a whole, even to nil. The legal reality —effected by the words "in accordance with the provisions of this regulation" in para.(1) and by para.(3)(c)—is that the reduction is to be effected only against the work-related activity component and not basic allowance ESA. It would have been better to have included that "promise" in the Act itself, rather than in a regulation whose terms, legislatively speaking, are more easily changeable than a "promise" or restriction in primary legislation (see JHRC, *Second Report of Session 2006–07*, HL 34/HC 263 (2006–07), para.3.18), especially as it would seem that this limitation has always been the policy intention.

The reduction is to be 50% of the work-related activity component for the first four weeks after the decision on non-participation and increases to 100% of the amount for each benefit week thereafter (para.(2)). However, the amount cannot be reduced below 10 pence (para.(3)(a)). Nor does the amount of reduction increase because there is more than one failure determination (e.g. non-participation in both assessment and interview (para.(3)(b))).

Paragraphs (4) and (5) deal with the situation where the claimant's ESA is composed both of CESA and IRESA (a common situation). Reduction is to be effected first against the amount attributable to CESA and only if after that there is a balance of reduction still to be applied, against IRESA (para.(4)). However, even where CESA is thus reduced, for the purposes of deciding on the amount of IRESA when drawing up the IRESA "balance sheet" of "needs" and "resources", the claimant is to be treated as if he were receiving the full amount of CESA to which he would otherwise be entitled but for reduction in accordance with this regulation, and not the reduced amount of CESA left after the reduction demanded by this regulation has been effected (para.(5))

Cessation of reduction

64.—(1) Any reduction imposed as a result of a failure determination   **1A.268**
which resulted from a failure to take part in a work-focused health-related assessment ceases to have effect if—

(a) the claimant complies with a requirement to attend a work-focused health-related assessment; or

(b) the claimant subsequently ceases to meet the requirements set out in regulation 47(2).

(2) Any reduction imposed as a result of a failure determination which resulted from a failure to take part in a work-focused interview ceases to have effect if—

(a) the claimant complies with a requirement to attend a work-focused interview; or

(b) the claimant subsequently ceases to meet the requirements set out in regulation 54(2).

DEFINITIONS

"claimant"—see WRA2007, s.24(1).
"failure determination"—see reg.63(1).
"work-focused health-related assessment"—see WRA 2007, s.11(7).
"work-focused interview"—see WRA 2007, s.12(7).

GENERAL NOTE

1A.269   Reduction in the amount of work-related activity component cease when the failure to participate in respect of which the reduction was imposed has been rectified, whether by taking part in a work-focused health related assessment or a work-focused interview, as the case may be. Reductions imposed must also cease to have effect if the claimant ceases to be a proper subject of the relevant requirements to participate (one or more of the conditions set out in regs 47(2) [work-focused health related assessment] or 54(2) [work-focused interview), applies as the case may be).

CHAPTER 4

NOTIFICATION

Notification under this Part

1A.270   **65.**—(1) Where written notification is to be given in accordance with this Part, such notification may be sent by post.

(2) Any notification sent by post is to be taken to have been received on the second working day after posting.

GENERAL NOTE

1A.271   This deals with notifications in respect of the conditionality elements in Pt 8 of these regulations. It stipulates that where written notifications are thereby required or envisaged (see regs 49(2),56(3)) they may be sent by post (para.(1)). If so the rule is that such notification is to be taken to have been received on the second working day after posting. (para.(2)).

CHAPTER 5

MODIFICATION OF THE ACT IN RELATION TO CLAIMS TO WHICH
SECTION 5(1)(C) OF THE ADMINISTRATION ACT APPLIES

Modifications of the Act

1A.272   **66.**—(1) Where a person has made a claim for an employment and support allowance to which section 5(1)(c) of the Administration Act applies, the Act applies with the following modifications.

(2) Section 11(1) of the Act applies—
(a) as if for sub-paragraph (a) there were substituted—
  "(a) either—
   (i) entitled to an employment and support allowance; or
   (ii) a person who has made a claim for an employment and support allowance to which regulations under section 5(1)(c) of the Administration Act apply; and"; and
(b) as if for "continuing to be" there were substituted "being".
(3) Section 12(1) of the Act applies—
(a) as if for sub-paragraph (a) there were substituted—
  "(a) either—
   (i) entitled to an employment and support allowance; or
   (ii) a person who has made a claim to which section 5 applies; and"; and
(b) as if for "continuing to be" there were substituted "being".

DEFINITIONS

"the Act"—see reg.2(1).
"Administration Act"—see WRA 2007, s.65.

GENERAL NOTE

This regulation alters the terms of WRA 2007, ss.11(1) ("work-focused health-related assessment") and 12(1) ("work-focused interview") where a person has made a claim for ESA which falls to be governed by the AA 1992, s.5(1)(c) (a claim made, or treated as made, for a period wholly or partly after the date on which it is made). In such cases, s.11(1) is to read (modifications in square brackets):

"(1) Regulations may make provision for or in connection with imposing on a person who is—
  [(a) either—
   (i) entitled to an employment and support allowance; or
   (ii) a person who has made a claim for an employment and support allowance to which regulations under section 5(1)(c) of the Administration Act apply; and]
  (b) not a member of the support group,
a requirement to take part in one or more work-focused health-related assessments as a condition of [being] entitled to the full amount payable to him in respect of the allowance apart from the regulations."

Similarly, s.12(1) is to read (modifications in square brackets):
"(1) Regulations may make provision for or in connection with imposing on a person who is—
  [(a) either—
   (i) entitled to an employment and support allowance; or
   (ii) a person who has made a claim to which section 5 applies; and]
  (b) not a member of the support group,
a requirement to take part in one or more work-focused interviews as a condition of [being] entitled to the full amount payable to him in respect of the allowance apart from the regulations."

PART 9

AMOUNTS OF ALLOWANCE

CHAPTER 1

PRESCRIBED AMOUNTS

Prescribed amounts

1A.273   **67.**—(1) Subject to regulations 68, 69 and 163 (amounts in other cases, special cases and urgent cases), the amounts prescribed for the purposes of the calculation of the amount of an income related allowance under section 4(2)(a) of the Act in relation to a claimant are such of the following amounts as may apply in the claimant's case—

   (a) an amount in respect of the claimant or, if the claimant is a member of a couple, an amount in respect of both of them determined in accordance with paragraph 1(1), (2) or (3) of Schedule 4 (amounts) as the case may be;

   (b) the amount of any premiums which may be applicable to the claimant determined in accordance with Parts 2 and 3 of that Schedule (premiums);

   (c) any amounts determined in accordance with Schedule 6 (housing costs) which may be applicable to the claimant in respect of mortgage interest repayments or such other housing costs as are prescribed in that Schedule.

   (2) Subject to regulation 69 (special cases) the amount prescribed for the purposes of the calculation of the amount of a claimant's contributory allowance under section 2(1)(a) of the Act is the amount determined in accordance with paragraph 1(1) of Schedule 4 as may apply in the claimant's case.

   (3) Subject to regulation 69, the amount of the work-related activity component and the support component are prescribed in Part 4 of Schedule 4.

DEFINITIONS

   "claimant"—see WRA 2007, s.24(1).
   "contributory allowance"—see WRA 2007, s.1(7).
   "couple"—see reg.2(1).
   "income related allowance"—see WRA 2007, s.1(7).

GENERAL NOTE

Para. (1)

1A.274   This regulation is similar to reg.17 of the IS Regulations and reg.83 of the JSA Regulations. The applicable amounts are set out in Sch.4 below.

   In the same manner as IS and JSA, this read with Sch.4, paras 1(1) (single claimant, age related), (2) (lone parent, age-related) or (3) (couple, age related) as appropriate, specifies the amounts applicable in respect of a claimant as regards IRESA: an amount for him and any partner (para.(1)(a)); applicable premiums (para.(1)(b), Sch.4, Pts 2 and 3); and applicable housing costs (para.(1)(c), Sch.6). This is, however, subject to regs 68 (amounts in other cases [polygamous marriages]), 69 (special cases) and 163 (urgent cases).

Para. (2)

This sets the prescribed amount (basic allowance) of CESA (WRA 2007,   **1A.275** s.2(1)(a)) by reference to Sch.4, para.1(1). During the assessment phase (before entitlement to support component or work related activity component arises under WRA 2007, ss.2(2) or (3) or 4(4) or (5)), there are two rates, a lower rate for those under 25, a higher one for those 25 or over (Sch.4, para.1(1)). After the assessment phase is over and title to one or other component has been satisfied, the higher rate is applicable whatever the age of the claimant. For those terminally ill covered by reg.7(1)(a) the higher rate component is available from the start of the claim on the basis of terminal illness or the date of an application for revision or supersession on that basis. The prescription of the amount is, however, subject to reg.69 (special cases). Note also that, whatever the amount of CESA thus set, it is, under WRA 2007, ss.2(1)(c) and 3, subject to reduction in respect of a variety of payments: pension payments (including permanent health insurance payments)(s.3(1)(a), (3); regs 72, 74 and 75); PPF periodic payments (s.3(1)(b), (3); reg.74); and prescribed payments to members of prescribed bodies carrying out public or local functions (currently limited to councillor's allowance and the bodies in the definition of councillor in reg.2(1)) (s.2(1)(c); regs 73, 76). The amount of CESA is also to be reduced by the amount of statutory maternity pay (s.2(2), (3); reg.80), statutory adoption pay (s.2(4), (5); reg.81) or additional statutory paternity pay (s.2(6), (7)); reg.82) to which the claimant is entitled during his period of limited capability for work.

Para. (3)

Subject to reg.69 (special cases), read with Sch.4, para.4, this specifies the   **1A.276** amounts of the support and work-related activity components, the former being the more generous. Note further that, whatever the amount of work-related activity component thus determined, it is subject to reduction for failure to comply with the conditionality requirements set by WRA 2007, ss.11–13 and Pt 8 of these Regs.

Polygamous marriages

68.—(1) Subject to regulation 69 and 163 (special cases and urgent   **1A.277** cases), where a claimant is a husband or wife by virtue of a polygamous marriage the amounts prescribed for the purposes of the calculation of the amount of an income-related allowance under section 4(2)(a) of the Act are such of the following amounts as may apply in the claimant's case—

   (a) an amount in respect of the claimant and the other party to the marriage determined in accordance with paragraph 1(3) of Schedule 4;

   (b) an amount equal to the difference between the amounts specified in paragraph 1(3)(a) (couple where both aged 18 and over) and 1(1)(b) (single claimant aged 25 and over) of Schedule 4 in respect of each spouse additional to the marriage;

(c) the amount of any premiums which are applicable to the claimant determined in accordance with Parts 2 and 3 of that Schedule (premiums);

(d) any amounts determined in accordance with Schedule 6 (housing costs) which may be applicable to the claimant in respect of mortgage interest payments or such other housing costs as are prescribed in that Schedule.

(2) In the case of a partner who is aged less than 18, the amount which applies in respect of that partner is nil unless—

(a) that partner is treated as responsible for a child; or

(b) that partner is a person who—

    (i) had that partner not been a member of a polygamous marriage would have qualified for an income-related allowance; or

    (ii) satisfies the requirements of section 3(1)(f)(iii) of the Jobseekers Act (prescribed circumstances for persons aged 16 but less than 18); or

    (iii) is the subject of a direction under section 16 of that Act (persons under 18: severe hardship).

DEFINITIONS

"the Act"—reg.2(1).
"claimant"—Welfare Reform Act 2007, s.24(1).
"couple"—reg.2(1).
"income-related allowance"—Welfare Reform Act 2007, s.24(1) and 1(7).
"Jobseekers Act"—reg.2(1).
"partner"—*ibid.*
"polygamous marriage"—*ibid.*
"single claimant"—*ibid.*

GENERAL NOTE

1A.278   This regulation is similar to reg.18 of the IS Regulations and reg.84 of the JSA Regulations.

Special cases

1A.279   **69.**—(1) In the case of a claimant to whom any paragraph in column (1) of Schedule 5 applies (amounts in special cases), the amount in respect of the claimant is to be the amount in the corresponding paragraph in column (2) of that Schedule.

(2) In Schedule 5—

"partner of a person subject to immigration control" means a person—

    (a) who is not subject to immigration control within the meaning of section 115(9) of the Immigration and Asylum Act; or

    (b) to whom section 115 of that Act does not apply by virtue of regulation 2 of the Social Security (Immigration and Asylum) Consequential Amendments Regulations 2000; and

   (c) who is a member of a couple and the member's partner is subject to immigration control within the meaning of section 115(9) of that Act and section 115 of that Act applies to the partner for the purposes of exclusion from entitlement to an income-related allowance;

"patient" means a person (other than a prisoner) who is regarded as receiving free in-patient treatment within the meaning of regulation 2(4) and (5) of the Social Security (Hospital In- Patients) Regulations 2005;

"person from abroad" has the meaning given in regulation 70;

"person in hardship" means a person who satisfies regulation 158 but only for a period not exceeding 6 weeks;

"prisoner" means a person who—

   (a) is detained in custody pending trial or sentence on conviction or under a sentence imposed by a court; or

   (b) is on temporary release in accordance with the provisions of the Prison Act 1952 or the Prisons (Scotland) Act 1989, other than a person who is detained in hospital under the provisions of the Mental Health Act 1983 or, in Scotland, under the provisions of the Mental Health (Care and Treatment) (Scotland) Act 2003 or the Criminal Procedure (Scotland) Act 1995.

DEFINITIONS

"claimant"—Welfare Reform Act 2007, s.24(1).
"couple"—reg.2(1).
"Immigration and Asylum Act"—*ibid.*
"income-related allowance"—Welfare Reform Act 2007, s.24(1) and 1(7).
"partner"—reg.2(1).

GENERAL NOTE

This regulation is similar to reg.21 of the IS Regulations and reg.85 of the JSA Regulations. Applicable amounts in special cases are prescribed by Sch.5 below.   1A.280

Special cases: supplemental—persons from abroad

70.—(1) "Person from abroad" means, subject to the following provisions of this regulation, a claimant who is not habitually resident in the United Kingdom, the Channel Islands, the Isle of Man or the Republic of Ireland.   1A.281

(2) A claimant must not be treated as habitually resident in the United Kingdom, the Channel Islands, the Isle of Man or the Republic of Ireland unless the claimant has a right to reside in (as the case may be) the United Kingdom, the Channel Islands, the Isle of Man or the Republic of Ireland other than a right to reside which falls within paragraph (3).

(3) A right to reside falls within this paragraph if it is one which exists by virtue of, or in accordance with, one or more of the following—

   (a) regulation 13 of the Immigration (European Economic Area) Regulations 2006;

(b) regulation 14 of those Regulations, but only in a case where the right exists under that regulation because the claimant is—

  (i) a jobseeker for the purpose of the definition of "qualified person" in regulation 6(1) of those Regulations; or

  (ii) a family member (within the meaning of regulation 7 of those Regulations) of such a jobseeker;

(c) Article 6 of Council Directive No. 2004/38/EC; or

(d) Article 39 of the Treaty establishing the European Community (in a case where the claimant is a person seeking work in the United Kingdom, the Channel Islands, the Isle of Man or the Republic of Ireland).

(4) A claimant is not a person from abroad if the claimant is—

(a) a worker for the purposes of Council Directive No. 2004/38/EC;

(b) a self-employed person for the purposes of that Directive;

(c) a person who retains a status referred to in sub-paragraph (a) or (b) pursuant to Article 7(3) of that Directive;

(d) a person who is a family member of a person referred to in sub-paragraph (a), (b) or (c) within the meaning of Article 2 of that Directive;

(e) a person who has a right to reside permanently in the United Kingdom by virtue of Article 17 of that Directive;

(f) a person who is treated as a worker for the purpose of the definition of "qualified person" in regulation 6(1) of the Immigration (European Economic Area) Regulations 2006 pursuant to—

  (i) regulation 5 of the Accession (Immigration and Worker Registration) Regulations 2004 (application of the 2006 Regulations in relation to a national of the Czech Republic, Estonia, Latvia, Lithuania, Hungary, Poland, Slovenia or the Slovak Republic who is an "accession State worker requiring registration"); or

  (ii) regulation 6 of the Accession (Immigration and Worker Authorisation) Regulations 2006 (right of residence of a Bulgarian or Romanian who is an "accession State national subject to worker authorisation");

(g) a refugee within the definition in Article 1 of the Convention relating to the Status of Refugees done at Geneva on 28th July 1951, as extended by Article 1(2) of the Protocol relating to the Status of Refugees done at New York on 31st January 1967;

(h) a person who has exceptional leave to enter or remain in the United Kingdom granted outside the rules made under section 3(2) of the Immigration Act 1971;

(i) a person who has humanitarian protection granted under those rules;

(j) a person who is not a person subject to immigration control within the meaning of section 115(9) of the Immigration and Asylum Act and who is in the United Kingdom as a result of deportation, expulsion or other removal by compulsion of law from another country to the United Kingdom; or

(k) a person in Great Britain who left the territory of Montserrat after 1st November 1995 because of the effect on that territory of a volcanic eruption.

DEFINITION

"Immigration and Asylum Act"—reg.2(1).

GENERAL NOTE

See the commentary to reg.21AA of the IS Regs.   1A.282

Definition of non-dependant

71.—(1) In these Regulations, "non-dependant" means any person,   1A.283 except someone to whom paragraph (2), (3) or (4) applies, who normally resides with a claimant or with whom a claimant normally resides.

(2) This paragraph applies to—

(a) any member of the claimant's family;

(b) a child or young person who is living with the claimant but who is not a member of the claimant's household;

(c) a person who lives with the claimant in order to care for the claimant or for the claimant's partner and who is engaged for that purpose by a charitable or voluntary organisation which makes a charge to the claimant or the claimant's partner for the care provided by that person;

(d) the partner of a person to whom sub-paragraph (c) applies.

(3) This paragraph applies to a person, other than a close relative of the claimant or the claimant's partner—

(a) who is liable to make payments on a commercial basis to the claimant or the claimant's partner in respect of the person's occupation of the claimant's dwelling;

(b) to whom the claimant or the claimant's partner is liable to make payments on a commercial basis in respect of the claimant's occupation of that person's dwelling;

(c) who is a member of the household of a person to whom sub-paragraph (a) or (b) applies.

(4) Subject to paragraph (5), this paragraph applies to—

(a) a person who jointly occupies the claimant's dwelling and who is either—

(i) a co-owner of that dwelling with the claimant or the claimant's partner (whether or not there are other co-owners); or

(ii) jointly liable with the claimant or the claimant's partner to make payments to a landlord in respect of the person's occupation of that dwelling;

(b) a partner of a person to whom sub-paragraph (a) applies.

(5) Where a person is a close relative of the claimant or the claimant's partner, paragraph (4) applies to that person only if the claimant's, or the claimant's partner's, co-ownership, or joint liability to make payments to a landlord in respect of occupation of the dwelling arose either before

11th April 1988 or, if later, on or before the date on which the claimant or the claimant's partner first occupied the dwelling in question.

(6) For the purposes of this regulation a person resides with another only if they share any accommodation except a bathroom, a lavatory or a communal area but not if each person is separately liable to make payments in respect of occupation of the dwelling to the landlord.

(7) In this regulation "communal area" means any area (other than rooms) of common access (including halls and passageways) and rooms of common use in sheltered accommodation.

DEFINITIONS

"child"—reg.2(1).
"claimant"—Welfare Reform Act 2007, s.24(1).
"close relative"—*ibid.*
"family"—reg.2(1) and (3).
"partner"—reg.2(1).
"voluntary organisation"—*ibid.*
"young person"—*ibid.*

GENERAL NOTE

1A.284   See the notes to reg.3 of the IS Regs.

CHAPTER 2

DEDUCTIONS FROM THE CONTRIBUTORY ALLOWANCE

Permanent health insurance

1A.285   72.—(1) For the purposes of sections 2(1)(c) and 3 of the Act (deductions from contributory allowance) pension payment is to include a permanent health insurance payment.

(2) In this regulation "permanent health insurance payment" means any periodical payment arranged by an employer under an insurance policy providing benefits in connection with physical or mental illness or disability, in relation to a former employee on the termination of that person's employment.

DEFINITIONS

"pension payment"—see WRA 2007, s.3(3).
"permanent health insurance payment"—see para.(2).

GENERAL NOTE

1A.286   WRA 2007, ss.2(1)(c) and 3(1)(a) stipulate that deductions are to be made from CESA in respect of pension payments. "Pension payments" are defined in s.3(3) in terms enabling expansion by regulations (category (c) in the definition). This regulation does just that specifying "permanent health insurance payment", defined in para.(2), as included in the term "pension payment". Note, however, that reg.75(f) means that any such payment in respect of which the employee had

174

contributed more than 50% to the premium will be treated as not counting for reduction purposes.

[¹Financial Assistance Scheme

72A.—(1) For the purposes of sections 2(1)(c) and 3 of the Act   1A.287
(deductions from contributory allowance) pension payment is to include
a Financial Assistance Scheme payment.

(2) In this regulation "Financial Assistance Scheme payment" means
a payment made under the Financial Assistance Scheme Regulations
2005.]

AMENDMENTS

1. Employment and Support Allowance (Miscellaneous Amendments) Regulations 2008 (SI 2008/2428), reg.7(1) (October 27, 2008).

DEFINITIONS

"Financial Assistance Scheme payment"—see para.(2).
"pension payment"—see WRA 2007, s.3(3).

GENERAL NOTE

WRA 2007, ss.2(1)(c) and 3(1)(a) stipulate that deductions are to be made   1A.288
from CESA in respect of pension payments. "Pension payments" are defined in
s.3(3) in terms enabling expansion by regulations (category (c) in the definition).
This regulation does just that by specifying a "Financial Assistance Scheme
payment" (defined in para.(2)) as a pension payment.

Councillor's allowance

73. For the purposes of section 3(1)(c) of the Act—   1A.289
   (a) a councillor's allowance is a payment of a prescribed description;
       and
   (b) the prescribed bodies carrying out public or local functions are
       those councils referred to in the definition of "councillor".

DEFINITIONS

"councillor"—see reg.2(1).
"councillor's allowance"—see reg.2(1).

GENERAL NOTE

Whatever the amount of CESA set by regs 67(2) (usual cases) or 69 (special   1A.290
cases), it is, under WRA 2007, ss.2(1)(c) and 3, subject to reduction in respect
of a variety of payments: including prescribed payments to members of prescribed bodies carrying out public or local functions. This regulation defines
councillor's allowance as a prescribed payment and stipulates that "prescribed
bodies carrying out public or local functions" are those bodies in the definition
of councillor in reg.2(1). On the reductive effect of councillor's allowance see
reg.76.

Deductions for pension payment and PPF payment

74.—(1) Where—   1A.291
   (a) [¹a claimant] is entitled to a contributory allowance in respect of
       any period of a week or part of a week;

175

    (b) there is—
        (i) a pension payment;
        (ii) a PPF periodic payment; or
        (iii) any combination of the payments specified in paragraphs (i) and (ii),
    payable to that person in respect of that period (or a period which forms part of that period or includes that period or part of it); and
    (c) the amount of the payment, or payments when taken together, exceeds—
        (i) if the period in question is a week, £85.00; or
        (ii) if that period is not a week, such proportion of the amount mentioned in paragraph (i) as falls to be calculated in accordance with regulation 94(1) or (6) (calculation of weekly amount of income),
the amount of that allowance is to be reduced by an amount equal to 50% of the excess.

    (2) For the purposes of this Chapter "payment" means a payment or payments, as the case may be, referred to in paragraph (1)(b).

AMENDMENTS

1. Employment and Support Allowance (Miscellaneous Amendments) Regulations 2008 (SI 2008/2428), reg.7(2) (October 27, 2008).

DEFINITIONS

    "claimant"—see WRA 2007, s.24(1).
    "payment"—see para.(2).
    "pension payment"—see WRA 2007, s.3(3); regs 73, 73A.
    "PPF periodic payment"—see WRA 2007, s.3(3).

GENERAL NOTE

1A.292   WRA 2007, ss.2(1)(c) and 3(1)(a) stipulate that deductions are to be made from CESA in respect of "pension payments" and "PPF periodic payments". This regulation provides that where one or more of these is payable to a claimant in respect of a week in respect of which he is entitled to CESA, then where the amount (or combined amount) of that payment (those payments) exceeds £85, the amount of CESA otherwise due is to be reduced by half of the excess over £85. Where the period of CESA entitlement is less than a week, 50% of the excess over an appropriate proportion of the amount of £85 as determined under regs 94(1) or (6) (calculation of amount of income) is instead to be deducted.

Payments treated as not being payments to which section 3 applies

1A.293   75. The following payments are to be treated as not being payments to which section 3 applies—
    (a) any pension payment made to a claimant as a beneficiary on the death of a member of any pension scheme;
    (b) any PPF periodic payment made to a claimant as a beneficiary on the death of a person entitled to such a payment;

(c) where a pension scheme is in deficit or has insufficient resources to meet the full pension payment, the extent of the shortfall;

(d) any pension payment made under an instrument specified in section 639(2) of the Income Tax (Earnings and Pensions) Act 2003;

(e) any guaranteed income payment;

(f) any permanent health insurance payment in respect of which the employee had contributed to the premium to the extent of more than 50%.

DEFINITIONS

"claimant"—see WRA 2007, s.24(1).
"guaranteed income payment"—see reg.2(1).
"pension payment"—see WRA 2007, s.3(3); regs 73, 73A.
"permanent health insurance payment"—see reg.72(2).
"PPF periodic payment"—see WRA 2007, s.3(3).

GENERAL NOTE

WRA 2007, ss.2(1)(c) and 3(1)(a) stipulate that deductions are to be made   1A.294
from CESA in respect of "pension payments" and "PPF periodic payments".
This regulation provides that the payments listed in it which would otherwise so
rank are not to be treated as payments to which s.3 applies, and so are not to be
deducted from CESA.

Deductions for councillor's allowance

76.—(1) Where the net amount of councillor's allowance to which a   1A.295
claimant is entitled in respect of any week exceeds [¹£92.00], an amount
equal to the excess is to be deducted from the amount of a contributory
allowance to which that person is entitled in respect of that week, and
only the balance remaining (if any) is to be payable.

(2) In paragraph (1) "net amount", in relation to any councillor's
allowance to which a claimant is entitled, means the aggregate amount of
the councillor's allowance or allowances, or remuneration to which that
claimant is entitled for the week in question, reduced by the amount of
any payment in respect of expenses wholly, exclusively and necessarily
incurred by that claimant, in that week, in the performance of the duties
of a councillor.

AMENDMENTS

1. Employment and Support Allowance (Miscellaneous Amendments) Regulations 2008 (SI 2008/2428), reg.7(3) (October 27, 2008).

DEFINITIONS

"contributory allowance"—see WRA 2007, s.1(7).
"councillor's allowance"—see reg.2(1).
"net amount"—see para.(2).

GENERAL NOTE

This regulation provides that where the net amount of councillor's allowance   1A.296
or remuneration to which the claimant is entitled in any week exceed £92, the

amount of the excess must be deducted from the amount of CESA to which he would otherwise be entitled in respect of that week. The reduction can be to nil. Only the balance of CESA remaining (if any) is to be payable. On para.(3) (determination of net amount), compare SSCBA 1992, s.30E(3). That is in similar terms apart from not specifying as para.(3) of this regulation does that the expenses must be "*wholly, exclusively and necessarily* incurred by that claimant, in that week, in *the performance of the duties* of a councillor". The IB provision specified that the expenses must have been incurred in that week in connection with his membership of the [relevant council(s)]. Subject to that, however, existing IVB and IB case law on "net amount" is relevant.

Unlike the position with computation of earnings under the Computation of Earnings Regs, no concept of averaging across the year is to be applied. In *CS 7934/95*, Commissioner Rice decided:

> "that the expenses incurred in any week by the claimant for the performance of her duties as a local authority councillor (whether for clothes, telephone rental, telephone calls, subscriptions, travel, or whatever it might be) shall for the purposes of calculating her entitlement to invalidity benefit [pursuant to SSCBA 1992, s.58(4), the similarly worded precursor of para.(3) of this section, defining 'net amount'], be deducted from the allowance or allowances to which she is entitled in respect of that week" (para.1).

It is immaterial that the benefits of expenses incurred in that week (e.g. the purchase of a dress to be worn more than once for official functions) are enjoyed in future weeks (para.9). In *CIB 2858, 2859* and *2864/2001*, Commissioner Jacobs supported as correct the approach taken by Commissioner Rice in *CS 7934/95*. He disagreed with Commissioner Williams in *R(IB) 3/01*. He accepted that s.30E should be interpreted as a whole. The phrase "in connection with" membership of the council set a limit of reasonableness on the expenditure. An expense is incurred when the liability to discharge it arises (a matter on which he agreed with Commissioner Williams), but it is not incurred in the week in which the item is used (a matter of disagreement with Commissioner Williams). In Commissioner Jacob's view the result is that s.30E has to be applied week by week, either in each week or retrospectively over a past period. The change of wording to the stricter "in the performance of the duties of a councillor" (the stricter tax approach noted by Commissioner Williams in R(IB) 3/01, para.22) may well affirm that approach. An expense is incurred in the week in which the liability arises and can only be used to reduce the reduction in incapacity benefit for that week. Income tax and national insurance deductions do not rank as "expenses in connection with a claimant's membership of a council" and cannot be deducted from the gross councillor's allowances for purposes of incapacity benefit (*R(IB) 3/01*). It is difficult to see that the alteration to "in the performance of his duties as a councillor" alters the status of income tax and NI deductions in this respect.

Date from which payments are to be taken into account

1A.297   **77.** Where regulations 74(1) and 76(1) apply, deductions must have effect, calculated where appropriate in accordance with regulation 94(1) or (6), from the first day of the benefit week in which the payment or councillor's allowance is paid to a claimant who is entitled to a contributory allowance in that week.

DEFINITIONS

"benefit week"—see reg.2(1).
"claimant"—see WRA 2007, s.24(1).

"contributory allowance"—see WRA 2007, s.1(7).
"councillor's allowance"—see reg.2(1).
"payment—see reg.74(2).

GENERAL NOTE

Deductions for pension payments, PPF periodic payments and councillor's   1A.298
allowance, calculated where appropriate under reg.94(1) or (6) (calculation of
weekly amount of income) are to have effect from the first day of the benefit week
in which they are paid to a claimant entitled to CESA in that week.

Date from which a change in the rate of the payment takes effect

78. Where a payment or councillor's allowance is already being made   1A.299
to a claimant and the rate of that payment or that allowance changes, the
deduction at the new rate must take effect, calculated where appropriate
in accordance with regulation 94(1) or (6), from the first day of the
benefit week in which the new rate of the payment or councillor's
allowance is paid.

DEFINITIONS

"benefit week"—see reg.2(1).
"claimant"—see WRA 2007, s.24(1).
"contributory allowance"—see WRA 2007, s.1(7).
"councillor's allowance"—see reg.2(1).
"payment—see reg.74(2).

GENERAL NOTE

Changes in the rate of pension payments, PPF periodic payments and council-   1A.300
lor's allowance affect the amount to be deducted from CESA. The deduction at
the new rate, calculated where appropriate under reg.94(1) or (6) (calculation of
weekly amount of income), is to have effect from the first day of the benefit week
in which the new rate of payment or councillor's allowance is paid to a claimant
entitled to CESA in that week.

Calculation of payment made other than weekly

79.—(1) Where the period in respect of which a payment or council-   1A.301
lor's allowance is paid is otherwise than weekly, an amount calculated or
estimated in accordance with regulation 94(1) or (6) is to be regarded as
the weekly amount of that payment or allowance.

(2) In determining the weekly payment, where two or more payments
are payable to a claimant, each payment is to be calculated separately in
accordance with regulation 94(1) or (6) before aggregating the sum of
those payments for the purposes of the reduction of a contributory
allowance in accordance with regulation 74.

DEFINITIONS

"benefit week"—see reg.2(1).
"claimant"—see WRA 2007, s.24(1).
"contributory allowance"—see WRA 2007, s.1(7).
"councillor's allowance"—see reg.2(1).
"payment—see reg.74(2).

GENERAL NOTE

1A.302   This provides for the case where pension payments, PPF periodic payments and councillor's allowance are paid otherwise than weekly. The amount to be deducted is to be calculated or estimated, taking each payment or allowance separately, in accordance with reg.94(1) or (6) to ascertain an appropriate weekly equivalent for the pension payment, the PPF periodic payment and the councillor's allowance (para.(1)) For the purposes of the deduction rule in reg.74, the weekly equivalents for each pension payment or PPF payment are then to be aggregated (para.(2)).

CHAPTER 3

STATUTORY PAYMENTS

Effect of statutory maternity pay on a contributory allowance

1A.303   **80.**—(1) This regulation applies where—
  (a) a woman is entitled to statutory maternity pay and, on the day immediately preceding the first day in the maternity pay period—
      (i) is in a period of limited capability for work; and
      (ii) satisfies the conditions of entitlement to a contributory allowance in accordance with section 1(2)(a) of the Act; and
  (b) on any day during the maternity pay period—
      (i) she is in a period of limited capability for work; and
      (ii) that day is not a day where she is treated as not having limited capability for work.

(2) Where this regulation applies, notwithstanding section 20(2) of the Act, a woman who is entitled to statutory maternity pay is to be entitled to a contributory allowance in respect of any day that falls within the maternity pay period.

(3) Where by virtue of paragraph (2) a woman is entitled to a contributory allowance for any week (including part of a week), the total amount of such benefit payable to her for that week is to be reduced by an amount equivalent to any statutory maternity pay to which she is entitled in accordance with Part 12 of the Contributions and Benefits Act for the same week (or equivalent part of a week where entitlement to a contributory allowance is for part of a week) and only the balance, if any, of the contributory allowance is to be payable to her.

DEFINITIONS

  "the Act"—see reg.2(1).
  "contributory allowance"—see WRA 2007, s.1(7).
  "Contributions and Benefits Act"—see WRA 2007, s.65.
  "maternity pay period"—see WRA 2007, s.20(8); SSCBA 1992, s.165(1).
  "week"—see reg.2(1).

GENERAL NOTE

In essence this provides that, where a woman's entitlement to CESA and statutory maternity pay (SMP) overlap, then during the period they coincide, despite WRA 2007, s.20(2), entitlement to CESA is preserved, but the amount payable in respect of the week or part week, as appropriate, is to be reduced (even to nil) by the amount of SMP for that week or part week—only the balance (if any) of CESA is payable. **1A.304**

Effect of statutory adoption pay on a contributory allowance

81.—(1) This regulation applies where— **1A.305**
(a) a claimant is entitled to statutory adoption pay and, on the day immediately preceding the first day in the adoption pay period—
  (i) is in a period of limited capability for work; and
  (ii) satisfies the conditions of entitlement to a contributory allowance in accordance with section 1(2)(a) of the Act; and
(b) on any day during the adoption pay period—
  (i) that claimant is in a period of limited capability for work; and
  (ii) that day is not a day where that claimant is treated as not having limited capability for work.

(2) Where this regulation applies, notwithstanding section 20(4) of the Act, a claimant who is entitled to statutory adoption pay is to be entitled to a contributory allowance in respect of any day that falls within the adoption pay period.

(3) Where by virtue of paragraph (2) a claimant is entitled to a contributory allowance for any week (including part of a week), the total amount of such benefit payable to that claimant for that week is to be reduced by an amount equivalent to any statutory adoption pay to which that claimant is entitled in accordance with Part 12ZB of the Contributions and Benefits Act for the same week (or equivalent part of a week where entitlement to a contributory allowance is for part of a week) and only the balance, if any, of the contributory allowance is to be payable to that claimant.

DEFINITIONS

"the Act"—see reg.2(1).
"adoption pay period"—see WRA 2007, s.20(8).
"claimant"—see WRA 2007, s.24(1).
"Contributions and Benefits Act"—see WRA 2007, s.65.
"contributory allowance"—see WRA 2007, s.1(7).
"week"—see reg.2(1).

GENERAL NOTE

In essence this provides that, where a claimant's entitlement to CESA and statutory adoption pay (SAP) overlap, then during the period they coincide, despite WRA 2007, s.20(2), entitlement to CESA is preserved, but the amount payable in respect of the week or part week, as appropriate, is to be reduced (even **1A.306** to nil) by the amount of SAP for that week or part week—only the balance (if any) of CESA is payable.

Effect of additional statutory paternity pay on a contributory allowance

1A.307
82.—(1) This regulation applies where—
  (a) a claimant is entitled to additional statutory paternity pay and, on the day immediately preceding the first day in the additional paternity pay period—
     (i) is in a period of limited capability for work; and
     (ii) satisfies the conditions of entitlement to a contributory allowance in accordance with section 1(2)(a) of the Act; and
  (b) on any day during the additional statutory paternity pay period—
     (i) that claimant is in a period of limited capability for work; and
     (ii) that day is not a day where that claimant is treated as not having limited capability for work.

(2) Where this regulation applies, notwithstanding section 20(6) of the Act, a claimant who is entitled to additional statutory paternity pay is to be entitled to a contributory allowance in respect of any day that falls within the additional paternity pay period.

(3) Where by virtue of paragraph (2) a person is entitled to a contributory allowance for any week (including part of a week), the total amount of such benefit payable to that claimant for that week is to be reduced by an amount equivalent to any additional statutory paternity pay to which that claimant is entitled in accordance with Part 12ZA of the Contributions and Benefits Act for the same week (or equivalent part of a week where entitlement to a contributory allowance is for part of a week) and only the balance, if any, of the contributory allowance is to be payable to that claimant.

DEFINITIONS

  "the Act"—see reg.2(1).
  "additional paternity pay period"—see WRA 2007, s.20(8).
  "claimant"—see WRA 2007, s.24(1).
  "contributory allowance"—see WRA 2007, s.1(7).
  "Contributions and Benefits Act"—see WRA 2007, s.65.
  "week"—see reg.2(1).

GENERAL NOTE

1A.308
In essence this provides that, where a claimant's entitlement to CESA and additional statutory paternity pay (ASPP) (yet to be introduced) overlap, then during the period they coincide, despite WRA 2007, s.20(2), entitlement to CESA is preserved, but the amount payable in respect of the week or part week, as appropriate, is to be reduced (even to nil) by the amount of ASPP for that week or part week—only the balance (if any) of CESA is payable.

182

PART 10

INCOME AND CAPITAL

CHAPTER 1

GENERAL

Calculation of income and capital of members of claimant's family and of a polygamous marriage

83.—(1) Subject to paragraph (4), the income and capital of a claimant's partner which by virtue of paragraph 6(2) of Schedule 1 to the Act is to be treated as income and capital of the claimant, is to be calculated in accordance with the following provisions of this Part in like manner as for the claimant; and any reference to the "claimant" is, except where the context otherwise requires, to be construed, for the purposes of this Part, as if it were a reference to the claimant's partner.   1A.309

(2) Subject to the following provisions of this Part, the income paid to, or in respect of, and capital of, a child or young person who is a member of the claimant's family is not to be treated as the income or capital of the claimant.

(3) Subject to paragraph (5), where a claimant or the partner of a claimant is married polygamously to two or more members of the claimant's household—

(a) the claimant is to be treated as possessing capital and income belonging to each such member; and

(b) the income and capital of that member is to be calculated in accordance with the following provisions of this Part in like manner as for the claimant.

(4) Where at least one member of a couple is aged less than 18 and the applicable amount of the couple falls to be determined under paragraph 1(3)(e), (f), (g), (h) or (i) of Schedule 4 (amounts), the income of the claimant's partner is not to be treated as the income of the claimant to the extent that—

(a) in the case of a couple where both members are aged less than 18, the amount specified in paragraph 1(3)(c) of that Schedule exceeds the amount specified in paragraph 1(3)(i) of that Schedule; and

(b) in the case of a couple where only one member is aged less than 18, the amount specified in paragraph 1(3)(a) of that Schedule exceeds the amount which is specified in paragraph 1(3)(h) of that Schedule.

(5) Where a member of a polygamous marriage is a partner aged less than 18 and the amount which applies in respect of that partner under regulation 68(2) (polygamous marriages) is nil, the claimant is not to be treated as possessing the income of that partner to the extent that an

amount in respect of that partner would have been included in the applicable amount if the partner had fallen within the circumstances set out in regulation 68(2)(a) or (b).

DEFINITIONS

"child"—see reg.2(1).
"family"—*ibid.*
"partner"—*ibid.*
"polygamous marriage"—*ibid.*
"young person"—*ibid.*, s.142 SSCBA.

GENERAL NOTE

1A.310   This regulation contains the basic rule on aggregation of resources of the claimant and any partner for the purposes of income-related ESA. It is similar to reg.23 of the Income Support Regs/reg.88 of the JSA Regs.

The rules governing income and capital for the purposes of income-related ESA are very similar to those applying to income support and income-based JSA. Where there are differences between the income support and the income-based JSA provisions ESA generally follows the income support model. The reader should therefore refer to the notes to the corresponding income support provision in Vol.II for further explanation of the provisions in this Part.

Income of participants in the self-employment route

1A.311   **84.** Chapters 2, 3, 4, 6, 8 and 9 of this Part and regulations 132 to 137, 142 and 143 do not apply to any income which is to be calculated in accordance with Chapter 5 of this Part (participants in the self-employment route).

DEFINITION

"self-employment route"—see reg.2(1).

GENERAL NOTE

1A.312   This is similar to reg.23A of the Income Support Regs/reg.88A of the JSA Regs.

[¹Child maintenance or] liable relative payments

1A.313   **85.** Regulations 91 to 109, 111 to 117 and Chapter 10 of this Part do not apply to any payment which is to be calculated in accordance with Chapter 8 of this Part ([²child maintenance and liable relative payments]).

AMENDMENT

1. Employment and Support Allowance (Miscellaneous Amendments) Regulations 2008 (SI 2008/2428), reg.20(2)(a) (October 27, 2008).
2. Employment and Support Allowance (Miscellaneous Amendments) Regulations 2008 (SI 2008/2428), reg.20(3) (October 27, 2008).

DEFINITION

"child maintenance"—see reg.119.

This is similar to reg.25 of the Income Support Regs/reg.89 of the JSA **1A.314** Regs.

Child support

86. [¹ . . .]

AMENDMENTS

1. Employment and Support Allowance (Miscellaneous Amendments) Regulations 2008 (SI 2008/2428), reg.20(4)(a) (October 27, 2008).

Calculation of income and capital of students

87. The provisions of Chapters 2 to 7 of this Part (income and capital) **1A.315** are to have effect in relation to students and their partners subject to the modifications set out in Chapter 10 of this Part (students).

DEFINITION

"partner"—see reg.2(1).

GENERAL NOTE

This is similar to reg.26 of the Income Support Regs/reg.91 of the JSA **1A.316** Regs.

Calculation of income which consists of earnings of participants in exempt work

88. Notwithstanding the other provisions of this Part, regulations **1A.317** 91(2), 92 to 99 and 108(3) and (4) and Schedule 7 (sums to be disregarded in the calculation of earnings) are to apply to any income which consists of earnings which is to be calculated for the purposes of regulations 45(2) to (4) (exempt work—earnings limits).

GENERAL NOTE

This regulation is necessary because the exempt work provisions are relevant **1A.318** to both contributory and income-related ESA (for the preclusive effect of work on entitlement to ESA see reg.40 and the notes to that regulation). Its effect is that the following regulations are applied in relation to contributory as well as income-related ESA for the purposes of calculating a claimant's earnings under the exempt work provisions in reg.45(2)–(4): reg.91(2) (period over which a payment is taken into account); reg.92 (calculation of earnings of self-employed earners); reg.93 (date on which income is treated as paid); reg.94 (calculation of weekly amount of income); reg.95 (earnings of employed earners); reg.96 (calculation of net earnings of employed earners); reg.97 (earnings of self-employed earners); reg.98 (calculation of net profit of self-employed earners); reg.99 (deduction of tax and contributions for self-employed earners); reg.108(3) and (4) (notional earnings) and Sch.7 (sums to be disregarded in the calculation of earnings).

Calculation of income where pension payments, PPF periodic payments or councillor's allowance payable

1A.319   **89.** Notwithstanding the other provisions of this Part, regulation 94(1) and (6) is to apply for the purposes of calculating the amount of any pension payments, PPF periodic payments or councillor's allowance to which Chapter 2 of Part 9 (deductions from the contributory allowance) applies.

DEFINITIONS

"councillor"—see reg.2(1).
"councillor's allowance"—*ibid.*

GENERAL NOTE

1A.320   Contributory JSA may be reduced if a claimant receives certain pension payments, PPF periodic payments or councillor's allowances (see regs 72 to 79). This regulation provides that reg.94(1) and (6) (calculation of weekly amount of income) are to apply for the purposes of calculating such payments.

CHAPTER 2

INCOME

Calculation of income

1A.321   **90.**—(1) For the purposes of paragraph 6(1) of Schedule 1 to the Act (conditions of entitlement to an income-related allowance), the income of a claimant is to be calculated on a weekly basis—
(a) by determining in accordance with this Part, other than Chapter 7, the weekly amount of the claimant's income; and
(b) by adding to that amount the weekly income calculated under regulation 118 (calculation of tariff income from capital).

(2) For the purposes of paragraph (1) "income" includes capital treated as income under regulation 105 (capital treated as income) and income which a claimant is treated as possessing under regulations 106 to 109 (notional income).

(3) For the purposes of paragraph 10 of Schedule 2 to the Act (effect of work), the income which consists of earnings of a claimant is to be calculated on a weekly basis by determining the weekly amount of those earnings in accordance with regulations 91(2), 92 to 99 and 108(3) and (4) and Schedule 7.

(4) For the purposes of paragraph (3), "income which consists of earnings" includes income which a claimant is treated as possessing under regulation 108(3) and (4).

(5) For the purposes of pension payments, PPF periodic payments and a councillor's allowance to which section 3 of the Act applies, the income other than earnings of a claimant is to be calculated on a weekly basis by determining in accordance with regulation 94(1), (2), (5) and

(6) the weekly amount of the pension payments, PPF periodic payment or a councillor's allowance paid to the claimant.

DEFINITIONS

"claimant"—see reg.83(1).
"councillor"—see reg.2(1).
"councillor's allowance"—*ibid.*

GENERAL NOTE

Paragraphs (1) and (2) are similar to reg.28 of the Income Support Regs/ reg.93 of the JSA Regs. They confirm that all income resources, including resources specifically treated as earnings or income, are to be taken into account for the purposes of calculating entitlement to income-related ESA.   **1A.322**

Paras (3) to (4)
Paragraph 10 of Sch.2 to the Welfare Reform Act 2007 provides for regula-   **1A.323**
tions to treat a person as not entitled to ESA because of undertaking work. See regs 40–46 which implement this. Under reg.45 certain categories of work are exempt; in the case of work referred to in reg.45(2)–(4) this is subject to earnings limits. Paragraph (3) provides that for the purpose of calculating a claimant's weekly earnings in these circumstances the following regulations apply: reg.91(2) (period over which a payment is taken into account); reg.92 (calculation of earnings of self-employed earners); reg.93 (date on which income is treated as paid); reg.94 (calculation of weekly amount of income); reg.95 (earnings of employed earners); reg.96 (calculation of net earnings of employed earners); reg.97 (earnings of self-employed earners); reg.98 (calculation of net profit of self-employed earners); reg.99 (deduction of tax and contributions for self-employed earners); reg.108(3) and (4) (notional earnings) and Sch.7 (sums to be disregarded in the calculation of earnings). See also reg.88 which makes provision that is similar to para.(3). Paragraph (4) specifically provides that such earnings include notional earnings.

Para. (5)
Section 3 of the 2007 Act (together with s.2(1)(c)) provides for deductions to   **1A.324**
be made from a claimant's contributory JSA if he receives certain pension payments, PPF periodic payments or councillor's allowances. See regs 72 to 79. Paragraph (5) provides that reg.94(1), (2), (5) and (6) (calculation of weekly amount of income) apply for the purposes of calculating the weekly amount of such payments. See also reg.89 which makes similar, but not identical, provision since it only brings reg.94(1) and (6) into play for the purpose of calculating the amount of such payments.

Calculation of earnings derived from employed earner's employment and income other than earnings

91.—(1) Earnings derived from employment as an employed earner   **1A.325**
and income which does not consist of earnings are to be taken into account over a period determined in accordance with the following provisions of this regulation and at a weekly amount determined in accordance with regulation 94 (calculation of weekly amount of income).

(2) Subject to the following provisions of this regulation, the period over which a payment is to be taken into account is to be—

(a) where the payment is monthly, a period equal to the number of weeks from the date on which the payment is treated as paid to the date immediately before the date on which the next monthly payment would have been so treated as paid whether or not the next monthly payment is actually paid;

(b) where the payment is in respect of a period which is not monthly, a period equal to the length of the period for which payment is made;

(c) in any other case, a period equal to such number of weeks as is equal to the number obtained (and any fraction is to be treated as a corresponding fraction of a week) by dividing—

   (i) the net earnings; or

   (ii) in the case of income which does not consist of earnings, the amount of that income less any amount paid by way of tax on that income which is disregarded under paragraph 1 of Schedule 8 (income other than earnings to be disregarded),

by the amount of an income-related allowance which would be payable had the payment not been made plus an amount equal to the total of the sums which would fall to be disregarded from that payment under Schedule 7 (earnings to be disregarded) or, as the case may be, any paragraph of Schedule 8 other than paragraph 1 of that Schedule, as is appropriate in the claimant's case,

and that period is to begin on the date on which the payment is treated as paid under regulation 93 (date on which income is treated as paid).

(3) The period over which a Career Development Loan, which is paid pursuant to section 2 of the Employment and Training Act 1973, is to be taken into account is the period of education and training intended to be supported by that loan.

(4) Where grant income as defined in Chapter 10 of this Part has been paid to a claimant who ceases to be a full-time student before the end of the period in respect of which that income is payable and, as a consequence, the whole or part of that income falls to be repaid by that claimant, that income is to be taken into account over the period beginning on the date on which that income is treated as paid under regulation 93 (date on which income is treated as paid) and ending—

(a) on the date on which repayment is made in full;

(b) where the grant is paid in instalments, on the day before the next instalment would have been paid had the claimant remained a full-time student; or

(c) on the last date of the academic term or vacation during which that claimant ceased to be a full-time student,

whichever is the earlier.

(5) Where, but for this paragraph—

(a) earnings not of the same kind are derived from the same source; and

(b) the periods in respect of which those earnings would fall to be taken into account overlap, wholly or partly,

those earnings are to be taken into account over a period equal to the aggregate length of those periods and that period is to begin with the earliest date on which any part of those earnings would otherwise be treated as paid under regulation 93.

(6) In a case to which paragraph (5) applies, earnings under regulation 95 (earnings of employed earners) are to be taken into account in the following order of priority—

(a) earnings normally derived from the employment;

(b) any payment to which paragraph (1)(b) or (c) of that regulation applies;

(c) any payment to which paragraph (1)(j) of that regulation applies;

(d) any payment to which paragraph (1)(d) of that regulation applies.

(7) Where earnings to which regulation 95(1)(b) to (d) applies are paid in respect of part of a day, those earnings are to be taken into account over a period equal to a day.

(8) Any earnings to which regulation 95(1)(j) applies which are paid in respect of, or on the termination of, part-time employment, are to be taken into account over a period equal to one week.

(9) In this regulation "part-time employment" means, if the claimant were entitled to income support, employment in which the claimant is not to be treated as engaged in remunerative work under regulation 5 or 6(1) and (4) of the Income Support Regulations (persons treated, or not treated, as engaged in remunerative work);

(10) For the purposes of this regulation the claimant's earnings and income which does not consist of earnings are to be calculated in accordance with Chapters 3 and 6 respectively of this Part.

DEFINITIONS

"claimant"—see reg.83(1).
"employed earner"—see reg.2(1).
"full-time student"—*ibid.*

GENERAL NOTE

This is similar to reg.29 of the Income Support Regs/reg.94(1) to (5) and (10) **1A.326** of the JSA Regs. Paragraphs (6) to (9) of reg.94 of the JSA Regs contain different provisions defining the length of the period for which a "compensation payment" is to be taken into account.

Calculation of earnings of self-employed earners

92.—(1) Except where paragraph (2) applies, where a claimant's **1A.327** income consists of earnings from employment as a self-employed earner the weekly amount of the claimant's earnings is to be determined by reference to the claimant's average weekly earnings from that employment—

(a) over a period of one year; or

(b) where the claimant has recently become engaged in that employment or there has been a change which is likely to affect the normal pattern of business, over such other period as may, in any particular case, enable the weekly amount of the claimant's earnings to be determined more accurately.

(2) Where the claimant's earnings consist of—

(a) royalties; or

(b) sums paid periodically for or in respect of any copyright

(c) payments in respect of any book registered under the Public Lending Right Scheme 1982,

those earnings are to be taken into account over a period equal to such number of weeks as is equal to the number obtained (and any fraction is to be treated as a corresponding fraction of a week) by dividing the earnings by the amount of an income-related allowance which would be payable had the payment not been made plus an amount equal to the total of the sums which would fall to be disregarded from the payment under Schedule 7 (sums to be disregarded in the calculation of earnings) as is appropriate in the claimant's case.

(3) For the purposes of this regulation the claimant's earnings are to be calculated in accordance with Chapter 4 of this Part.

DEFINITIONS

"claimant"—see reg.83(1).
"self-employed earner"—see reg.2(1).

GENERAL NOTE

1A.328   This is similar to reg.30 of the Income Support Regs/reg.95 of the JSA Regs.

Date on which income is treated as paid

1A.329   **93.**—(1) Except where paragraph (2) or (3) applies, a payment of income to which regulation 91 (calculation of earnings derived from employed earner's employment and income other than earnings) applies is to be treated as paid—

(a) in the case of a payment which is due to be paid before the first benefit week pursuant to the claim, on the date on which it is due to be paid;

(b) in any other case, on the first day of the benefit week in which it is due to be paid or the first succeeding benefit week in which it is practicable to take it into account.

(2) Employment and support allowance, income support, jobseeker's allowance, maternity allowance, short-term or long-term incapacity benefit, or severe disablement allowance is to be treated as paid on the day of the benefit week in respect of which it is payable.

(3) Working tax credit or child tax credit is to be treated as paid—

(a) where the award of that tax credit begins on the first day of a benefit week, on that day;

(b) on the first day of the benefit week that follows the date the award begins; or

(c) on the first day of the first benefit week that follows the date an award of an income-related allowance begins, if later,

until the last day of the last benefit week that coincides with or immediately follows the last day for which the award of that tax credit is made.

DEFINITION

"benefit week"—see reg.2(1).

GENERAL NOTE

This is similar to reg.31 of the Income Support Regs/reg.96 of the JSA   **1A.329.1**
Regs.

Calculation of weekly amount of income

94.—(1) For the purposes of regulation 91 (calculation of earnings   **1A.330**
derived from employed earner's employment and income other than
earnings) and Chapter 2 of Part 9 (deductions from contributory allowance), subject to paragraphs (2) to (8), where the period in respect of
which a payment is made—

(a) does not exceed a week, the weekly amount is to be the amount of
that payment;

(b) exceeds a week, the weekly amount is to be determined—

   (i) in a case where that period is a month, by multiplying the
   amount of the payment by 12 and dividing the product by
   52;

   (ii) in a case where that period is 3 months, by multiplying the
   amount of the payment by 4 and dividing the product by
   52;

   (iii) in a case where that period is a year by dividing the amount
   of the payment by 52;

   (iv) in any other case by multiplying the amount of the payment
   by 7 and dividing the product by the number equal to the
   number of days in the period in respect of which it is
   made.

(2) Where a payment for a period not exceeding a week is treated
under regulation 93(1)(a) (date on which income is treated as paid) as
paid before the first benefit week and a part is to be taken into account
for some days only in that week (the relevant days), the amount to be
taken into account for the relevant days is to be calculated by multiplying
the amount of the payment by the number equal to the number of
relevant days and dividing the product by the number of days in the
period in respect of which it is made.

(3) Where a payment is in respect of a period equal to or in excess of
a week and a part thereof is to be taken into account for some days only
in a benefit week (the relevant days), the amount to be taken into
account for the relevant days is, except where paragraph (4) applies, to
be calculated by multiplying the amount of the payment by the number
equal to the number of relevant days and dividing the product by the
number of days in the period in respect of which it is made.

(4) In the case of a payment of—

(a) maternity allowance, short-term or long-term incapacity benefit
or severe disablement allowance, the amount to be taken into
account for the relevant days is to be the amount of benefit
payable in respect of those days;

(b) an employment and support allowance, income support or a jobseeker's allowance, the amount to be taken into account for the relevant days is to be calculated by multiplying the weekly amount of the benefit by the number of relevant days and dividing the product by 7.

(5) Except in the case of a payment which it has not been practicable to treat under regulation 93(1)(b) (date on which income is treated as paid) as paid on the first day of the benefit week in which it is due to be paid, where a payment of income from a particular source is or has been paid regularly and that payment falls to be taken into account in the same benefit week as a payment of the same kind and from the same source, the amount of that income to be taken into account in any one benefit week is not to exceed the weekly amount determined under paragraph (1)(a) or (b) of the payment which under regulation 93(1)(b) is treated as paid first.

(6) Where the amount of the claimant's income fluctuates and has changed more than once, or a claimant's regular pattern of work is such that the claimant does not work every week, the foregoing paragraphs may be modified so that the weekly amount of the claimant's income is determined by reference to the claimant's average weekly income—

(a) if there is a recognisable cycle of work, over the period of one complete cycle (including, where the cycle involves periods in which the claimant does no work, those periods but disregarding any other absences);

(b) in any other case, over a period of 5 weeks or such other period as may, in the particular case, enable the claimant's average weekly income to be determined more accurately.

(7) Where income is taken into account under paragraph (4) of regulation 91 over the period specified in that paragraph, the amount of that income to be taken into account in respect of any week in that period is to be an amount equal to the amount of that income which would have been taken into account under regulation 132 (calculation of grant income) had the person to whom that income was paid not ceased to be a full-time student.

(8) Where any payment of earnings is taken into account under ['paragraph (8)] of regulation 91 (calculation of earnings derived from employed earner's employment and income other than earnings), over the period specified in that paragraph, the amount to be taken into account is to be equal to the amount of the payment.

AMENDMENT

1. Employment and Support Allowance (Miscellaneous Amendments) Regulations 2008 (SI 2008/2428), reg.8(1) (October 27, 2008).

DEFINITIONS

"benefit week"—see reg.2(1).
"claimant"—see reg.83(1).
"full-time student"—see reg.2(1).

GENERAL NOTE

This is similar to reg.32 of the Income Support Regs/reg.97 of the JSA Regs   **1A.331**
(except that there is no equivalent of para.(8) in reg.97 as the JSA rules for the
treatment of compensation payments made on the termination of part-time
employment are different (see the note to reg.94(6)–(9) of the JSA Regs in Vol.II
of this series)).

CHAPTER 3

EMPLOYED EARNERS

Earnings of employed earners

95.—(1) Subject to [¹paragraphs (2) and (3)], "earnings" means, in   **1A.332**
the case of employment as an employed earner, any remuneration or
profit derived from that employment and includes—

(a) any bonus or commission;

(b) any payment in lieu of remuneration except any periodic sum paid
to a claimant on account of the termination of the claimant's
employment by reason of redundancy;

(c) any payment in lieu of notice;

(d) any holiday pay except any payable more than 4 weeks after the
termination or interruption of employment;

(e) any payment by way of a retainer;

(f) any payment made by the claimant's employer in respect of
expenses not wholly, exclusively and necessarily incurred in the
performance of the duties of the employment, including any payment made by the claimant's employer in respect of—

  (i) travelling expenses incurred by the claimant between the
claimant's home and place of employment;

  (ii) expenses incurred by the claimant under arrangements made
for the care of a member of the claimant's family owing to the
claimant's absence from home;

(g) any award of compensation made under section 112(4) or
117(3)(a) of the Employment Rights Act 1996 (the remedies:
orders and compensation, enforcement of order and compensation);

(h) any payment or remuneration made under sections 28, 34, 64, 68
and 70 of the Employment Rights Act 1996 (right to guarantee
payments, remuneration on suspension on medical or maternity
grounds, complaints to employment tribunals);

(i) any such sum as is referred to in section 112(3) of the Contributions and Benefits Act (certain sums to be earnings for social
security purposes);

(j) where a payment of compensation is made in respect of employment which is part-time employment, the amount of the compensation;

(k) the amount of any payment by way of a non-cash voucher which has been taken into account in the computation of a person's earnings in accordance with Part 5 of Schedule 3 to the Social Security (Contributions) Regulations 2001.

(2) "Earnings" are not to include—

(a) subject to paragraph (3), any payment in kind;

(b) any remuneration paid by or on behalf of an employer to the claimant in respect of a period throughout which the claimant is on maternity leave, paternity leave or adoption leave or is absent from work because the claimant is ill;

(c) any payment in respect of expenses wholly, exclusively and necessarily incurred in the performance of the duties of the employment;

(d) any occupational pension;

(e) any lump sum payment made under the Iron and Steel Re-adaptation Benefits Scheme.

(3) Paragraph (2)(a) is not to apply in respect of any non-cash voucher referred to in paragraph (1)(k).

(4) In this regulation—

"compensation" means any payment made in respect of, or on the termination of, employment in a case where a claimant has not received or received only part of a payment in lieu of notice due or which would have been due to the claimant had that claimant not waived the right to receive it, other than—

(a) any payment specified in paragraph (1)(a) to (i);

(b) any payment specified in paragraph (2)(a) to (e);

(c) any redundancy payment within the meaning of section 135(1) of the Employment Rights Act 1996;

(d) any refund of contributions to which that person was entitled under an occupational pension scheme; and

(e) any compensation payable by virtue of section 173 of the Education Reform Act 1988;

"part-time employment" means, if the claimant were entitled to income support, employment in which the claimant is not to be treated as engaged in remunerative work under regulation 5 or 6(1) and (4) of the Income Support Regulations (persons treated, or not treated, as engaged in remunerative work).

AMENDMENT

1. Employment and Support Allowance (Miscellaneous Amendments) Regulations 2008 (SI 2008/2428), reg.8(2) (October 27, 2008).

DEFINITIONS

"adoption leave"—see reg.2(1).
"claimant"—see reg.83(1).
"employed earner"—see reg.2(1).
"family"—*ibid.*
"occupational pension"—*ibid.*

194

The equivalent income support and JSA Regs are regs 35 and 98 respectively. **1A.333** This regulation adopts the model of reg.35 of the Income Support Regs rather than reg.98 of the JSA Regs. For the differences between reg.98 and this regulation (and reg.35 of the Income Support Regs), see the notes to reg.98 of the JSA Regs in Vol.II in this series. Note also that unlike the equivalent provisions in reg.35 and reg.98, para.(1)(d) (which relates to holiday pay) does not contain any special rule relating to trade disputes.

Calculation of net earnings of employed earners

96.—(1) For the purposes of regulation 91 (calculation of earnings **1A.334** derived from employed earner's employment and income other than earnings) the earnings of a claimant derived from employment as an employed earner to be taken into account, subject to paragraph (2), are the claimant's net earnings.

(2) There is to be disregarded from a claimant's net earnings, any sum, where applicable, specified in paragraphs 1 to 12 of Schedule 7 (sums to be disregarded in the calculation of earnings).

(3) For the purposes of paragraph (1) net earnings are to be calculated by taking into account the gross earnings of the claimant from that employment less—

(a) any amount deducted from those earnings by way of—
    (i) income tax;
    (ii) primary Class 1 contributions under section 6(1)(a) of the Contributions and Benefits Act;
(b) one-half of any sum paid by the claimant in respect of a pay period by way of a contribution towards an occupational or personal pension scheme.

DEFINITIONS

"claimant"—see reg.83(1).
"employed earner"—see reg.2(1).
"occupational pension scheme"—*ibid.*
"pay period"—*ibid.*
"personal pension scheme"—*ibid.*

GENERAL NOTE

This is similar to reg.36 of the Income Support Regs/reg.99 of the JSA **1A.335** Regs.

CHAPTER 4

SELF-EMPLOYED EARNERS

Earnings of self-employed Earners

97.—(1) Subject to paragraph (2), "earnings", in the case of employ- **1A.336** ment as a self-employed earner, means the gross receipts of the employment and include any allowance paid under section 2 of the Employment and Training Act 1973 or section 2 of the Enterprise and New Towns (Scotland) Act 1990 to the claimant for the purpose of assisting the claimant in carrying on the claimant's business.

(2) "Earnings" do not include—

(a) where a claimant is involved in providing board and lodging accommodation for which a charge is payable, any payment by way of such a charge;

(b) any payment to which paragraph 28 or 29 of Schedule 8 refers (payments in respect of a person accommodated with the claimant under an arrangement made by a local authority or voluntary organisation and payments made to the claimant by a health authority, local authority or voluntary organisation in respect of persons temporarily in the claimant's care);

(c) any sports award.

DEFINITIONS

"board and lodging"—see reg.2(1).
"claimant"—see reg.83(1).
"self-employed earner"—see reg.2(1).
"sports award"—*ibid.*
"voluntary organisation"—*ibid.*

GENERAL NOTE

1A.337   This is similar to reg.37 of the Income Support Regs/reg.100 of the JSA Regs.

Calculation of net profit of self-employed earners

1A.338   **98.**—(1) For the purposes of regulation 92 (calculation of earnings of self-employed earners), the earnings of a claimant to be taken into account are to be—

(a) in the case of a self-employed earner who is engaged in employment on that self-employed earner's own account, the net profit derived from that employment;

(b) in the case of a self-employed earner whose employment is carried on in partnership or is that of a share fisherman within the meaning of the Social Security (Mariners' Benefits) Regulations 1975, that self-employed earner's share of the net profit derived from that employment less—

(i) an amount in respect of income tax and of National Insurance contributions payable under the Contributions and Benefits Act calculated in accordance with regulation 99 (deduction of tax and contributions for self-employed earners); and

(ii) one half of any premium paid in the period that is relevant under regulation 92 (calculation of earnings of self-employed earners) in respect of a personal pension scheme.

(2) There is to be disregarded from a claimant's net profit any sum, where applicable, specified in paragraphs 1 to 11 of Schedule 7.

(3) For the purposes of paragraph (1)(a) the net profit of the employment, except where paragraph (9) applies, is to be calculated by taking

into account the earnings of the employment over the period determined under regulation 92 less—

(a) subject to paragraphs (5) to (7), any expenses wholly and exclusively defrayed in that period for the purposes of that employment;

(b) an amount in respect of—

(i) income tax; and

(ii) National Insurance contributions payable under the Contributions and Benefits Act,

calculated in accordance with regulation 99 (deduction of tax and contributions for self-employed earners); and

(c) one half of any premium paid in the period that is relevant under regulation 92 in respect of a personal pension scheme.

(4) For the purposes of paragraph (1)(b), the net profit of the employment is to be calculated by taking into account the earnings of the employment over the period determined under regulation 92 less, subject to paragraphs (5) to (7), any expenses wholly and exclusively defrayed in that period for the purpose of that employment.

(5) Subject to paragraph (6), a deduction is not to be made under paragraph (3)(a) or (4) in respect of—

(a) any capital expenditure;

(b) the depreciation of any capital asset;

(c) any sum employed or intended to be employed in the setting up or expansion of the employment;

(d) any loss incurred before the beginning of the period determined under regulation 92 (calculation of earnings of self-employed earners);

(e) the repayment of capital on any loan taken out for the purposes of the employment;

(f) any expenses incurred in providing business entertainment.

(6) A deduction is to be made under paragraph (3)(a) or (4) in respect of the repayment of capital on any loan used for—

(a) the replacement in the course of business of equipment or machinery; and

(b) the repair of an existing business asset except to the extent that any sum is payable under an insurance policy for its repair.

(7) The Secretary of State will refuse to make a deduction in respect of any expenses under paragraph (3)(a) or (4) where the Secretary of State is not satisfied that the expense has been defrayed or, having regard to the nature of the expense and its amount, that it has been reasonably incurred.

(8) For the avoidance of doubt—

(a) a deduction is not to be made under paragraph (3)(a) or (4) in respect of any sum unless it has been expended for the purposes of the business;

(b) a deduction is to be made thereunder in respect of—

(i) the excess of any VAT paid over VAT received in the period determined under regulation 92;

    (ii) any income expended in the repair of an existing asset except to the extent that any sum is payable under an insurance policy for its repair;

    (iii) any payment of interest on a loan taken out for the purposes of the employment.

(9) Where a claimant is engaged in employment as a child minder the net profit of the employment is to be one-third of the earnings of that employment, less—

    (a) an amount in respect of—

        (i) income tax; and

        (ii) National Insurance contributions payable under the Contributions and Benefits Act,

    calculated in accordance with regulation 99 (deduction of tax and contributions for self-employed earners); and

    (b) one half of any premium paid in respect of a personal pension scheme.

(10) Notwithstanding regulation 92 (calculation of earnings of self-employed earners) and the foregoing paragraphs, the Secretary of State may assess any item of a claimant's income or expenditure over a period other than that determined under regulation 92 as may, in the particular case, enable the weekly amount of that item of income or expenditure to be determined more accurately.

(11) For the avoidance of doubt where a claimant is engaged in employment as a self-employed earner and that claimant is also engaged in one or more other employments as a self-employed or employed earner any loss incurred in any one of the claimant's employments is not to be offset against the claimant's earnings in any other of the claimant's employments.

DEFINITIONS

    "claimant"—see reg.83(1).
    "employment"—see reg.2(1).
    "personal pension scheme"—*ibid*.
    "self-employed earner"—*ibid*.

GENERAL NOTE

1A.339   This is similar to reg.38 of the Income Support Regs/reg.101 of the JSA Regs (except that there is no equivalent of reg.101(3) of the JSA Regs which is concerned with calculating the amount of any earnings to be deducted from contribution-based JSA).

Deduction of tax and contributions for self-employed earners

1A.340   **99.**—(1) Subject to paragraph (2), the amount to be deducted in respect of income tax under regulation 98(1)(b)(i), (3)(b)(i) or (9)(a)(i) (calculation of net profit of self-employed earners) is to be calculated on the basis of the amount of chargeable income and as if that income were assessable to income tax at the [¹ . . .] basic rate of tax less only the personal allowance to which the claimant is entitled under sections 35 and 38 to 40 of the Income Tax Act 2007 (personal reliefs) as is appropriate to the claimant's circumstances.

(2) If the period determined under regulation 92 is less than a year the earnings to which the [¹basic rate] of tax is to be applied and the amount of the personal reliefs deductible under paragraph (1) is to be calculated on a pro rata basis.

(3) The amount to be deducted in respect of National Insurance contributions under regulation 98(1)(b)(i), (3)(b)(ii) or (9)(a)(ii) is to be the total of—

(a) the amount of Class 2 contributions payable under section 11(1) or, as the case may be, 11(3) of the Contributions and Benefits Act at the rate applicable at the date of claim except where the claimant's chargeable income is less than the amount specified in section 11(4) of that Act (small earnings exception) for the tax year in which the date of claim falls; but if the assessment period is less than a year, the amount specified for that tax year is to be reduced pro rata; and

(b) the amount of Class 4 contributions (if any) which would be payable under section 15 of that Act (Class 4 contributions recoverable under the Income Tax Acts) at the percentage rate applicable at the date of claim on so much of the chargeable income as exceeds the lower limit but does not exceed the upper limit of profits and gains applicable for the tax year in which the date of claim falls; but if the assessment period is less than a year, those limits are to be reduced pro rata.

(4) In this regulation "chargeable income" means—

(a) except where sub-paragraph (b) applies, the earnings derived from the employment less any expenses deducted under paragraph (3)(a) or, as the case may be, (4) of regulation 98;

(b) in the case of employment as a child minder, one-third of the earnings of that employment.

AMENDMENT

1. Employment and Support Allowance (Miscellaneous Amendments) Regulations 2008 (SI 2008/2428), reg.8(3) (October 27, 2008).

DEFINITION

"claimant"—see reg.83(1).

GENERAL NOTE

This is similar to reg.39 of the Income Support Regs/reg.102 of the JSA Regs.   1A.341

CHAPTER 5

PARTICIPANTS IN THE SELF-EMPLOYMENT ROUTE

Interpretation

100. In this Chapter "special account" means, where a claimant was   1A.342
carrying on a commercial activity in respect of which assistance is

received under the self-employment route, the account into which the gross receipts from that activity were payable during the period in respect of which such assistance was received.

DEFINITION

"self-employment route"—see reg.2(1).

GENERAL NOTE

1A.343   This is similar to reg.39A of the Income Support Regs/reg.102A of the JSA Regs.

Treatment of gross receipts of participants in the self-employment route

1A.344   **101.** The gross receipts of a commercial activity carried on by a claimant in respect of which assistance is received under the self-employment route, are to be taken into account in accordance with the following provisions of this Chapter.

DEFINITION

"self-employment route"—see reg.2(1).

GENERAL NOTE

1A.345   This is similar to reg.39B of the Income Support Regs/reg.102B of the JSA Regs.

Calculation of income of participants in the self-employment route

1A.346   **102.**—(1) The income of a claimant who has received assistance under the self-employment route is to be calculated by taking into account the whole of the monies in the special account at the end of the last day on which such assistance was received and deducting from those monies—

(a) an amount in respect of income tax calculated in accordance with regulation 103 (deduction in respect of tax for participants in the self-employment route); and

(b) any sum to which paragraph (4) refers.

(2) Income calculated pursuant to paragraph (1) is to be apportioned equally over a period which starts on the date the income is treated as paid under paragraph (3) and is equal in length to the period beginning with the day on which assistance was first received under the self-employment route and ending on the last day on which such assistance was received.

(3) Income calculated pursuant to paragraph (1) is to be treated as paid—

(a) in the case where it is due to be paid before the first benefit week in respect of which the participant or the participant's partner first claims an income-related allowance following the last day on which assistance was received under the self-employment route, on the day in the week in which it is due to be paid which corresponds to the first day of the benefit week;

(b) in any other case, on the first day of the benefit week in which it is due to be paid.

(4) This paragraph refers, where applicable in each benefit week in respect of which income calculated pursuant to paragraph (1) is taken into account pursuant to paragraphs (2) and (3), to the sums which would have been disregarded under paragraph 7(1) of Schedule 7 had the income been earnings.

DEFINITIONS

"benefit week"—see reg.2(1).
"self-employment route"—*ibid.*

GENERAL NOTE

This is similar to reg.39C of the Income Support Regs/reg.102C of the JSA Regs. **1A.347**

Deduction in respect of tax for participants in the self-employment route

103.—(1) The amount to be deducted in respect of income tax under **1A.348** regulation 102(1)(a) (calculation of income of participants in the self-employment route) in respect of the period determined under regulation 102(2) is to be calculated as if—

(a) the chargeable income is the only income chargeable to tax;

(b) the personal allowance applicable to the person receiving assistance under the self-employment route by virtue of sections 35 and 45 to 55 of the Income Tax Act 2007 is allowable against that income; and

(c) the rate at which the chargeable income less the personal allowance is assessable to income tax is the [¹ . . .] basic rate of tax.

(2) For the purpose of paragraph (1), the [¹basic rate] of tax to be applied and the amount of the personal allowance deductible is, where the period determined under regulation 102(2) is less than a year, to be calculated on a pro rata basis.

(3) In this regulation, "chargeable income" means the monies in the special account at the end of the last day upon which assistance was received under the self-employment route.

AMENDMENT

1. Employment and Support Allowance (Miscellaneous Amendments) Regulations 2008 (SI 2008/2428), reg.8(4) (October 27, 2008).

DEFINITION

"self-employment route"—see reg.2(1).

GENERAL NOTE

This is similar to reg.39D of the Income Support Regs/reg.102D of the JSA Regs. **1A.349**

CHAPTER 6

OTHER INCOME

Calculation of income other than earnings

1A.350   **104.**—(1) For the purposes of regulation 91 (calculation of earnings derived from employed earner's employment and income other than earnings) the income of a claimant which does not consist of earnings to be taken into account will, subject to paragraphs (2) to (7), be the claimant's gross income and any capital treated as income under regulation 105 (capital treated as income).

(2) There is to be disregarded from the calculation of a claimant's gross income under paragraph (1), any sum, where applicable, specified in Schedule 8.

(3) Where the payment of any benefit under the benefit Acts is subject to any deduction by way of recovery the amount to be taken into account under paragraph (1) is to be the gross amount payable.

(4) [¹Paragraphs (5) and (5A) apply] where—

(a) a relevant payment has been made to a claimant in an academic year; and

(b) that claimant abandons, or is dismissed from, that claimant's course of study before the payment to the claimant of the final instalment of the relevant payment.

(5) [¹Where a relevant payment is made quarterly, the] amount of a relevant payment to be taken into account for the assessment period for the purposes of paragraph (1) in respect of a claimant to whom paragraph (4) applies, is to be calculated by applying the formula—

$$\frac{A - (B \times C)}{D}$$

where—

A = the total amount of the relevant payment which that claimant would have received had that claimant remained a student until the last day of the academic term in which the person abandoned, or was dismissed from, the course, less any deduction under regulation 137(6) (treatment of student loans);

B = the number of benefit weeks from the benefit week immediately following that which includes the first day of that academic year to the benefit week immediately before that which includes the day on which the claimant abandoned, or was dismissed from, that claimant's course;

C = the weekly amount of the relevant payment, before the application of the £10 disregard, which would have been taken into account as income under regulation 137(3) had the claimant not abandoned or been dismissed from, the course and, in the case of a claimant who was not entitled to an income-related allowance immediately before that claimant abandoned or was dismissed from the course, had that claimant, at that time, been entitled to an income-related allowance;

D = the number of benefit weeks in the assessment period.

[¹(5A) Where a relevant payment is made by two or more instalments in a quarter, the amount of a relevant payment to be taken into account for the assessment period for the purposes of paragraph (1) in respect of a person to whom paragraph (4) applies, shall be calculated by applying the formula in paragraph (5) but as if—

A = the total amount of relevant payments which that person received, or would have received, from the first day of the academic year to the day the person abandoned the course, or was dismissed from it, less any deduction under regulation 137(6).]

(6) [¹In this regulation]—

"academic year" and "student loan" have the same meanings as for the purposes of Chapter 10 of this Part;

[¹"assessment period" means—

    (a) in a case where a relevant payment is made quarterly, the period beginning with the benefit week which includes the day on which the claimant abandoned, or was dismissed from, the course and ending with the benefit week which includes the last day of the last quarter for which an instalment of the relevant payment was payable to that claimant;

    (b) in a case where the relevant payment is made by two or more instalments in a quarter, the period beginning with the benefit week which includes the day on which the claimant abandoned, or was dismissed from, the course and ending with the benefit week which includes—

        (i) the day immediately before the day on which the next instalment of the relevant payment would have been due had the payments continued; or

        (ii) the last day of the last quarter for which an instalment of the relevant payment was payable to that claimant,

    whichever of those dates is earlier;]

"assessment period" means the period beginning with the benefit week which includes the day on which the claimant abandoned, or was dismissed from, the course and ending with the benefit week which includes the last day of the last quarter for which an instalment of the relevant payment was payable to that claimant;

"quarter" for the purposes of the definition of "assessment period" in relation to an academic year means a period in that year—

    (a) beginning on 1st January and ending on 31st March;

    (b) beginning on 1st April and ending on 30th June;

    (c) beginning on 1st July and ending on 31st August; or

    (d) beginning on 1st September and ending on 31st December;

"relevant payment" means either a student loan or an amount intended for the maintenance of dependants referred to in regulation 132(6) (calculation of grant income) or both.

(7) In the case of income to which regulation 91(4) (calculation of income of former students) applies, the amount of income to be taken into account for the purposes of paragraph (1) is to be the amount of that income calculated in accordance with regulation 94(7) (calculation of weekly amount of income) and on the basis that none of that income has been repaid.

(8) Subject to paragraph (9), for the avoidance of doubt there is to be included as income to be taken into account under paragraph (1)—

(a) any payment to which regulation 95(2) or 97(2) (payments not earnings) applies; or

(b) in the case of a claimant who is receiving support provided under section 95 or 98 of the Immigration and Asylum Act including support provided by virtue of regulations made under Schedule 9 to that Act, the amount of such support provided in respect of essential living needs of the claimant and the claimant's partner (if any) as is specified in regulations made under paragraph 3 of Schedule 8 to that Act.

(9) In the case of a claimant who is the partner of a person subject to immigration control and whose partner is receiving support provided under section 95 or 98 of the Immigration and Asylum Act including support provided by virtue of regulations made under Schedule 9 to that Act, there is not to be included as income to be taken into account under paragraph (1) the amount of support provided in respect of essential living needs of the partner of the claimant and the claimant's dependants (if any) as is specified in regulations made under paragraph 3 of Schedule 8 to the Immigration and Asylum Act.

AMENDMENT

1. Social Security (Students and Miscellaneous Amendments) Regulations 2008 (SI 2008/1599), reg.7(2) (October 27, 2008).

DEFINITIONS

"academic year"—see reg.131(1).
"benefit week"—see reg.2(1).
"claimant"— see reg.83(1).
"full-time student"—see reg.2(1).
"student loan"—see reg.131(1).

GENERAL NOTE

1A.351   This is similar to reg.40 of the Income Support Regs/reg.103 of the JSA Regs (except that there is no equivalent to para.(9) in reg.103 of the JSA Regs).

Capital treated as income

1A.352   **105.**—(1) Capital which is payable by instalments which are outstanding on—

(a) the first day in respect of which an income-related allowance is payable or the date of the determination of the claim, whichever is earlier; or

(b) in the case of a supersession, the date of that supersession,

is to be treated as income if the aggregate of the instalments outstanding and the amount of the claimant's capital otherwise calculated in accordance with Chapter 7 of this Part exceeds £16,000.

(2) Any payment received under an annuity is to be treated as income.

(3) Any earnings to the extent that they are not a payment of income are to be treated as income.

(4) Any Career Development Loan paid pursuant to section 2 of the Employment and Training Act 1973 is to be treated as income.

(5) Where an agreement or court order provides that payments are to be made to the claimant in consequence of any personal injury to the claimant and that such payments are to be made, wholly or in part, by way of periodical payments, any such periodical payments received by the claimant (but not a payment which is treated as capital by virtue of this Part), are to be treated as income.

DEFINITION

"claimant"—see reg.83(1).

GENERAL NOTE

This is similar to reg.104 of the JSA Regs/reg.41 of the Income Support Regs (except that there is no equivalent to reg.41(4) (repayment of PAYE tax in trade dispute cases)).   1A.353

Notional income—deprivation and income on application

106.—(1) A claimant is to be treated as possessing income of which   1A.354
the claimant has deprived himself or herself for the purpose of securing entitlement to an employment and support allowance or increasing the amount of that allowance, or for the purpose of securing entitlement to, or increasing the amount of, income support or a jobseeker's allowance.

(2) Except in the case of—

(a) a discretionary trust;

(b) a trust derived from a payment made in consequence of a personal injury;

(c) an employment and support allowance;

(d) a jobseeker's allowance;

(e) working tax credit;

(f) child tax credit;

(g) a personal pension scheme, occupational pension scheme or a payment made by the Board of the Pension Protection Fund where the claimant is aged under 60;

(h) any sum to which paragraph 43(2)(a) of Schedule 9 (capital to be disregarded) applies which is administered in the way referred to in paragraph 43(1)(a) of that Schedule;

    (i) any sum to which paragraph 44(a) of Schedule 9 refers; or

    (j) rehabilitation allowance made under section 2 of the Employment and Training Act 1973,

income which would become available to the claimant upon application being made but which has not been acquired by the claimant is to be treated as possessed by the claimant but only from the date on which it could be expected to be acquired were an application made.

(3) A claimant who has attained the age of 60 is to be treated as possessing—

    (a) the amount of any income from an occupational pension scheme, a personal pension scheme or the Board of the Pension Protection Fund—

        (i) for which no claim has been made; and

        (ii) to which the claimant might expect to be entitled if a claim for it were made;

    (b) income from an occupational pension scheme which the claimant elected to defer,

but only from the date on which it could be expected to be acquired were an application for it to be made.

(4) This paragraph applies where a claimant aged not less than 60—

    (a) is entitled to money purchase benefits under an occupational pension scheme or a personal pension scheme;

    (b) fails to purchase an annuity with the funds available in that scheme; and

    (c) either—

        (i) defers in whole or in part the payment of any income which would have been payable to the claimant by that claimant's pension fund holder; or

        (ii) fails to take any necessary action to secure that the whole of any income which would be payable to the person by that claimant's pension fund holder upon the person applying for it, is so paid; or

        (iii) income withdrawal is not available to the claimant under that scheme.

(5) Where paragraph (4) applies, the amount of any income foregone is to be treated as possessed by that claimant, but only from the date on which it could be expected to be acquired were an application for it to be made.

(6) The amount of any income foregone in a case where paragraph (4)(c)(i) or (ii) applies is to be the maximum amount of income which may be withdrawn from the fund and is to be determined by the Secretary of State who will take account of information provided by the pension fund holder in accordance with regulation 7(5) of the Social Security (Claims and Payments) Regulations 1987.

(7) The amount of any income foregone in a case where paragraph (4)(c)(iii) applies is to be the income that the claimant could have received without purchasing an annuity had the funds held under the relevant occupational or personal pension scheme been held under a

scheme where income withdrawal was available and is to be determined in the manner specified in paragraph (6).

(8) In paragraph (4), "money purchase benefits" has the meaning it has in section 181 of the Pension Schemes Act 1993.

DEFINITIONS

"claimant"—see reg.83(1).
"occupational pension scheme"—see reg.2(1).
"payment"—*ibid.*
"pension fund holder"—*ibid.*
"personal pension scheme"—*ibid.*

GENERAL NOTE

This is similar to reg.42(1)–(2CA) of the Income Support Regs/ **1A.355** reg.105(1)–(5A) of the JSA Regs.

Note that under para.(1) if a person has deprived himself of income he will be caught by this rule if the purpose of the deprivation was to secure entitlement to or increase the amount of ESA *or income support or JSA*. This avoids the question that might otherwise have arisen on a claimant transferring from income support (or JSA) to ESA whether a deprivation which had only been for the purposes of income support (or JSA) could be caught by para.(1).

Notional income—income due to be paid or income paid to or in respect of a third party

107.—(1) Except in the case of a discretionary trust, or a trust derived **1A.356** from a payment made in consequence of a personal injury, any income which is due to be paid to the claimant but—

(a) has not been paid to the claimant;
(b) is not a payment prescribed in regulation 8 or 9 of the Social Security (Payments on Account, Overpayment and Recovery) Regulations 1988 (duplication and prescribed payments or maintenance payments) and not made on or before the date prescribed in relation to it,

is, except for any amount to which paragraph (2) applies, to be treated as possessed by the claimant.

(2) This paragraph applies to—

(a) an amount which is due to be paid to the claimant under an occupational pension scheme but which is not paid because the trustees or managers of the scheme have suspended or ceased payments due to an insufficiency of resources;
(b) any amount by which a payment made to the claimant from an occupational pension scheme falls short of the payment to which the claimant was due under the scheme where the shortfall arises because the trustees or managers of the scheme have insufficient resources available to them to meet in full the scheme's liabilities; or
(c) any earnings which are due to an employed earner on the termination of that employed earner's employment by reason of redundancy but which have not been paid to that employed earner.

(3) Any payment of income, other than a payment of income specified in paragraph (5), made to a third party in respect of a single claimant or the claimant's partner (but not a member of the third party's family) is to be treated—

   (a) in a case where that payment is derived from—

       (i) a payment of any benefit under the benefit Acts;

      (ii) a payment from the Armed Forces and Reserve Forces Compensation Scheme;

     (iii) a war disablement pension, war widow's pension or war widower's pension; or

     (iv) a pension payable to a person as a widow, widower or surviving civil partner under any power of Her Majesty otherwise than under an enactment to make provision about pensions for or in respect of persons who have been disabled or have died in consequence of service as members of the armed forces of the Crown,

     as possessed by that single claimant, if it is paid to the claimant or by the claimant's partner, if it is paid to the claimant's partner;

   (b) in a case where that payment is a payment of an occupational pension, a pension or other periodical payment made under a personal pension scheme or a payment made by the Board of the Pension Protection Fund, as possessed by that single claimant or, as the case may be, by the claimant's partner;

   (c) in any other case, as possessed by that single claimant or the claimant's partner to the extent that it is used for the food, ordinary clothing or footwear, household fuel, rent for which housing benefit is payable, or any housing costs to the extent that they are met under regulations 67(1)(c) or 68(1)(d) (housing costs), of that single claimant or, as the case may be, of the claimant's partner, or is used for any council tax or water charges for which that claimant or that partner is liable,

but, except where sub-paragraph (a) applies, this paragraph does not apply to any payment in kind to the third party.

(4) Any payment of income, other than a payment of income specified in paragraph (5), made to a single claimant or the claimant's partner in respect of a third party (but not in respect of another member of the claimant's family) is to be treated as possessed by that single claimant or, as the case may be, the claimant's partner, to the extent that it is kept or used by that claimant or used by or on behalf of the claimant's partner but, except where paragraph (3)(a) applies, this paragraph does not apply to any payment in kind to the third party.

(5) Paragraphs (3) and (4) do not apply in respect of a payment of income made—

   (a) under the Macfarlane Trust, the Macfarlane (Special Payments) Trust, the Macfarlane (Special Payments) (No. 2) Trust, the Fund, the Eileen Trust or [¹the Independent Living Fund (2006)];

   (b) pursuant to section 19(1)(a) of the Coal Industry Act 1994 (concessionary coal); or

  (c) pursuant to section 2 of the Employment and Training Act 1973 in respect of a person's participation—

    (i) in an employment programme specified in regulation 75(1)(a)(ii) of the Jobseeker's Allowance Regulations;

    (ii) in a training scheme specified in regulation 75(1)(b)(ii) of those Regulations;

    (iii) in the Intensive Activity Period specified in regulation 75(1)(a)(iv) of those Regulations;

    (iv) in a qualifying course within the meaning specified in regulation 17A(7) of those Regulations; or

  (d) under an occupational pension scheme, in respect of a pension or other periodical payment made under a personal pension scheme or a payment made by the Board of the Pension Protection Fund where—

    (i) a bankruptcy order has been made in respect of the person in respect of whom the payment has been made or, in Scotland, the estate of that person is subject to sequestration or a judicial factor has been appointed on that person's estate under section 41 of the Solicitors (Scotland) Act 1980;

    (ii) the payment is made to the trustee in bankruptcy or any other person acting on behalf of the creditors; and

    (iii) the person referred to in paragraph (i) and that person's partner (if any) does not possess, or is not treated as possessing, any other income apart from that payment.

(6) Where the claimant resides in a care home, an Abbeyfield Home or an independent hospital, or is temporarily absent from such a home or hospital, any payment made by a person other than the claimant or a member of the claimant's family in respect of some or all of the cost of maintaining the claimant or the claimant's partner in that home or hospital is to be treated as possessed by the claimant or the claimant's partner.

(7) In paragraph (2)(a) and (b) "resources" has the same meaning as in section 181(1) of the Pension Schemes Act 1993.

AMENDMENT

1. Employment and Support Allowance (Miscellaneous Amendments) Regulations 2008 (SI 2008/2428), reg.8(5) (October 27, 2008).

DEFINITIONS

  "Abbeyfield Home"—see reg.2(1).
  "Armed Forces and Reserve Forces Compensation Scheme"—*ibid.*
  "benefit Acts"—*ibid.*
  "care home"—*ibid.*
  "claimant"—see reg.83(1).
  "Eileen Trust"—see reg.2(1).
  "family"—*ibid.*
  "the Fund"—*ibid.*
  "independent hospital"—*ibid.*
  "the Independent Living Fund (2006)"—*ibid.*
  "Macfarlane (Special Payments) Trust"—*ibid.*
  "Macfarlane (Special Payments) (No. 2) Trust"—*ibid.*

"Macfarlane Trust"—*ibid.*
"occupational pension"—*ibid.*
"occupational pension scheme"—*ibid.*
"ordinary clothing and footwear"—*ibid.*
"partner"—*ibid.*
"payment"—*ibid.*
"personal pension"—*ibid.*
"personal pension scheme"—*ibid.*
"single claimant"—*ibid.*
"war disablement pension"—*ibid.*
"war widow's pension"—*ibid.*
"war widower's pension"—*ibid.*
"water charges"—*ibid.*

GENERAL NOTE

1A.357   This is similar to reg.42(3)–(4A) and (8A) of the Income Support Regs/ reg.105(6)–(11), together with the definition of "resources" in reg.105(16), of the JSA Regs (except that paras (3) and (4) do not contain any special provisions relating to trade disputes).

Notional income—other income

1A.358   **108.**—(1) Where a claimant's earnings are not ascertainable at the time of the determination of the claim or of any revision or supersession the Secretary of State will treat the claimant as possessing such earnings as is reasonable in the circumstances of the case having regard to the number of hours worked and the earnings paid for comparable employment in the area.

(2) Where the amount of a subsistence allowance paid to a claimant in a benefit week is less than the amount of income-based jobseeker's allowance that claimant would have received in that benefit week had it been payable to the claimant, less 50p, the claimant is to be treated as possessing the amount which is equal to the amount of income-based jobseeker's allowance which the claimant would have received in that week, less 50p.

(3) Subject to paragraph (4), where—

(a) a claimant performs a service for another person; and

(b) that person makes no payment of earnings or pays less than that paid for a comparable employment in the area,

the Secretary of State is to treat the claimant as possessing such earnings (if any) as is reasonable for that employment unless the claimant satisfies the Secretary of State that the means of that person are insufficient for the person to pay, or to pay more, for the service.

(4) Paragraph (3) will not apply—

(a) to a claimant who is engaged by a charitable or voluntary organisation or who is a volunteer if the Secretary of State is satisfied in any of those cases that it is reasonable for the claimant to provide the service free of charge;

(b) in a case where the service is performed in connection with—

(i) the claimant's participation in an employment or training programme in accordance with regulation 19(1)(q) of the Jobseeker's Allowance Regulations, other than where the

service is performed in connection with the claimant's participation in the Intensive Activity Period specified in regulation
75(1)(a)(iv) of those Regulations; or

   (ii) the claimant's or the claimant's partner's participation in an
employment or training programme as defined in regulation
19(3) of those Regulations for which a training allowance is
not payable or, where such an allowance is payable, it is
payable for the sole purpose of reimbursement of travelling or
meal expenses to the claimant or the claimant's partner participating in that programme;

(c) to a claimant who is engaged in work experience whilst participating in—

   (i) the New Deal for Lone Parents; or

   (ii) a scheme which has been approved by the Secretary of State
as supporting the objectives of the New Deal for Lone Parents; or

(d) to a claimant who is participating in a work placement approved in
writing by the Secretary of State before the placement starts;

(e) in sub-paragraph (d) "work placement" means practical work
experience with an employer, which is neither paid nor undertaken in expectation of payment.

DEFINITIONS

"benefit week"—see reg.2(1).
"claimant"—see reg.83(1).
"partner"—see reg.2(1).
"payment"—*ibid.*
"subsistence allowance"—*ibid.*
"voluntary organisation"—*ibid.*

GENERAL NOTE

This is similar to reg.42(5)–(6AA) of the Income Support Regs/   **1A.359**
reg.105(11A)–(13A), together with the definition of "work placement" in
reg.105(16), of the JSA Regs. There are some differences in reg.105 of the JSA
Regs (e.g. there is no equivalent to para.(4)(c) which relates to lone parents).

Notional income—calculation and interpretation

109.—(1) Where a claimant is treated as possessing any income under   **1A.360**
regulation 106 or 107 the foregoing provisions of this Part are to apply
for the purposes of calculating the amount of that income as if a payment
had actually been made and as if it were actual income which the
claimant does possess.

(2) Where a claimant is treated as possessing any earnings under
regulation 108(1) or (3) the foregoing provisions of this Part are to apply
for the purposes of calculating the amount of those earnings as if a
payment had actually been made and as if they were actual earnings
which the claimant does possess except that paragraph (3) of regulation
96 (calculation of net earnings of employed earners) does not apply and
the claimant's net earnings are to be calculated by taking into account
the earnings which the claimant is treated as possessing, less—

    (a) where the period over which those earnings are to be taken into account is a year or more, an amount in respect of income tax equivalent to an amount calculated by applying to those earnings the [¹ . . .] basic rate of tax in the year of assessment less only the personal allowance to which the claimant is entitled under section 257(1) of the Income and Corporation Taxes Act 1988 (personal allowance) as is appropriate to the claimant's circumstances;

    (b) where if the period over which those earnings are to be taken into account is less than a year, the earnings to which the [¹basic rate] of tax is to be applied and the amount of the personal allowance deductible under this paragraph is to be calculated on a pro rata basis;

    (c) where the weekly amount of those earnings equals or exceeds the lower earnings limit, an amount representing primary Class 1 contributions under section 6(1)(a) of the Contributions and Benefits Act, calculated by applying to those earnings the initial and main primary percentages in accordance with section 8(1)(a) and (b) of that Act; and

    (d) one-half of any sum payable by the claimant in respect of a pay period by way of a contribution towards an occupational or personal pension scheme.

AMENDMENT

1. Employment and Support Allowance (Miscellaneous Amendments) Regulations 2008 (SI 2008/2428), reg.8(6) (October 27, 2008).

DEFINITIONS

    "claimant"—see reg.83(1).
    "employed earner"—see reg.2(1).
    "pay period"—*ibid.*
    "payment"—*ibid.*

GENERAL NOTE

1A.361   This is similar to reg.42(7)–(8) of the Income Support Regs/reg.105(14)–(15) of the JSA Regs.

CHAPTER 7

CAPITAL

Capital limit

1A.362   **110.** For the purposes of paragraph 6(1)(b) of Schedule 1 to the Act as it applies to an income-related allowance (no entitlement to benefit if capital exceeds prescribed amount), the prescribed amount is £16,000.

GENERAL NOTE

This contains a similar provision to that in reg.45 of the Income Support Regs/ reg.107 of the JSA Regs.

1A.362.1

Calculation of capital

111.—(1) For the purposes of [¹sections 1(2)] and 4 of, and Part 2 of Schedule 1 to, the Act as it applies to an income-related allowance, the capital of a claimant to be taken into account is, subject to paragraph (2), to be the whole of the claimant's capital calculated in accordance with this Part and any income treated as capital under regulation 112 (income treated as capital).

1A.363

(2) There is to be disregarded from the calculation of a claimant's capital under paragraph (1) any capital, where applicable, specified in Schedule 9.

AMENDMENT

1. Employment and Support Allowance (Miscellaneous Amendments) Regulations 2008 (SI 2008/2428), reg.8(7) (October 27, 2008).

DEFINITION

"claimant"—see reg.83(1).

GENERAL NOTE

This is similar to reg.46 of the Income Support Regs/reg.108 of the JSA Regs.

1A.364

Income treated as capital

112.—(1) Any bounty derived from employment to which regulation 43(1)(e) and paragraph 12 of Schedule 7 apply and paid at intervals of at least one year is to be treated as capital.

1A.365

(2) Any amount by way of a refund of income tax paid in respect of, or deducted from, profits or income chargeable to tax under the provisions in Part 2 of the Income Tax (Trading and Other Income) Act 2005 or Part 2 of the Income Tax (Earnings and Pensions) Act 2003 is to be treated as capital.

(3) Any holiday pay which is not earnings under regulation 95(1)(d) (earnings of employed earners) is to be treated as capital.

(4) Except any income derived from capital disregarded under paragraph 1, 2, 4 to 8, 10, 16, 43 or 44 of Schedule 9, any income derived from capital is to be treated as capital but only from the date it is normally due to be credited to the claimant's account.

(5) In the case of employment as an employed earner, any advance of earnings or any loan made by the claimant's employer is to be treated as capital.

(6) Any payment under section 30 of the Prison Act 1952 (payments for discharged prisoners) or allowance under section 17 of the Prisons (Scotland) Act 1989 (allowances to prisoners on discharge) is to be treated as capital.

(7) Any charitable or voluntary payment which is not made or not due to be made at regular intervals, other than one to which paragraph (8) applies, is to be treated as capital.

(8) This paragraph applies to a payment which is made under the Macfarlane Trust, the Macfarlane (Special Payments) Trust, the Macfarlane (Special Payments) (No. 2) Trust, the Fund, the Eileen Trust or [¹the Independent Living Fund (2006)].

(9) Any arrears of subsistence allowance which are paid to a claimant as a lump sum are to be treated as capital.

AMENDMENT

1. Employment and Support Allowance (Miscellaneous Amendments) Regulations 2008 (SI 2008/2428), reg.8(5) (October 27, 2008).

DEFINITIONS

"claimant"—see reg.83(1).
"Eileen Trust"—see reg.2(1).
"employed earner"—*ibid.*
"the Fund"—*ibid.*
"the Independent Living Fund (2006)"—*ibid.*
"Macfarlane (Special Payments) Trust"—*ibid.*
"Macfarlane (Special Payments) (No. 2) Trust"—*ibid.*
"Macfarlane Trust"—*ibid.*
"subsistence allowance"—*ibid.*

GENERAL NOTE

1A.366   This is similar to reg.48 of the Income Support Regs/reg.110 of the JSA Regs (except that it does not contain any special provisions relating to trade disputes).

Calculation of capital in the United Kingdom

1A.367   **113.** Capital which a claimant possesses in the United Kingdom is to be calculated at its current market or surrender value less—
   (a) where there would be expenses attributable to sale, 10%; and
   (b) the amount of any incumbrance secured on it.

DEFINITION

"claimant"—see reg.83(1).

GENERAL NOTE

1A.368   This is similar to reg.49 of the Income Support Regs/reg.111 of the JSA Regs.

Calculation of capital outside the United Kingdom

1A.369   **114.** Capital which a claimant possesses in a country outside the United Kingdom is to be calculated—
   (a) in a case in which there is no prohibition in that country against the transfer to the United Kingdom of an amount equal to its current market or surrender value in that country, at that value;

(b) in a case where there is such a prohibition, at the price which it would realise if sold in the United Kingdom to a willing buyer,

less, where there would be expenses attributable to sale, 10% and the amount of any incumbrance secured on it.

DEFINITION

"claimant"—see reg.83(1).

GENERAL NOTE

This is similar to reg.50 of the Income Support Regs/reg.112 of the JSA Regs.   1A.370

Notional capital

115.—(1) A claimant is to be treated as possessing capital of which the   1A.371
claimant has deprived himself or herself for the purpose of securing entitlement to an employment and support allowance or increasing the amount of that allowance, or for the purpose of securing entitlement to, or increasing the amount of, income support or a jobseeker's allowance except—
   (a) where that capital is derived from a payment made in consequence of any personal injury and is placed on trust for the benefit of the claimant;
   (b) to the extent that the capital which the claimant is treated as possessing is reduced in accordance with regulation 116 (diminishing notional capital rule);
   (c) any sum to which paragraph 43(2)(a) of Schedule 9 (capital to be disregarded) applies which is administered in the way referred to in paragraph 43(1)(a); or
   (d) any sum to which paragraph 44(a) of Schedule 9 refers.
(2) Except in the case of—
   (a) a discretionary trust;
   (b) a trust derived from a payment made in consequence of a personal injury;
   (c) any loan which would be obtainable only if secured against capital disregarded under Schedule 9;
   (d) a personal pension scheme;
   (e) an occupational pension scheme or a payment made by the Board of the Pension Protection Fund where the claimant is aged under 60; or
   (f) any sum to which paragraph 43(2)(a) of Schedule 9 (capital to be disregarded) applies which is administered in a way referred to in paragraph 43(1)(a); or
   (g) any sum to which paragraph 44(a) of Schedule 9 refers,
any capital which would become available to the claimant upon application being made but which has not been acquired by the claimant is to be treated as possessed by the claimant but only from the date on which it could be expected to be acquired were an application made.
(3) Any payment of capital, other than a payment of capital specified in paragraph (5), made to a third party in respect of a single claimant or

the claimant's partner (but not a member of the third party's family) is to be treated—

(a) in a case where that payment is derived from—

    (i) a payment of any benefit under the benefit Acts;

    (ii) a payment from the Armed Forces and Reserve Forces Compensation Scheme;

    (iii) a war disablement pension, war widow's pension or war widower's pension; or

    (iv) a pension payable to a person as a widow, widower or surviving civil partner under any power of Her Majesty otherwise than under an enactment to make provision about pensions for or in respect of persons who have been disabled or who have died in consequence of service as members of the armed forces of the Crown,

as possessed by that single claimant, if it is paid to that claimant, or by the claimant's partner, if it is paid to that partner;

(b) in a case where that payment is a payment of an occupational pension, a pension or other periodical payment made under a personal pension scheme or a payment made by the Board of the Pension Protection Fund, as possessed by that single claimant or, as the case may be, by the claimant's partner;

(c) in any other case, as possessed by that single claimant or the claimant's partner to the extent that it is used for the food, ordinary clothing or footwear, household fuel, rent for which housing benefit is payable or any housing costs to the extent that they are met under regulation 67(1)(c) and 68(1)(d) (housing costs) of that single claimant or, as the case may be, of the claimant's partner, or is used for any council tax or water charges for which that claimant or partner is liable.

(4) Any payment of capital, other than a payment of capital specified in paragraph (5) made to a single claimant or the claimant's partner in respect of a third party (but not in respect of another member of the claimant's family) is to be treated as possessed by that single claimant or, as the case may be, the claimant's partner, to the extent that it is kept or used by that claimant or used by or on behalf of the claimant's partner.

(5) Paragraphs (3) and (4) will not apply in respect of a payment of capital made—

(a) under the Macfarlane Trust, the Macfarlane (Special Payments) Trust, the Macfarlane (Special Payments) (No. 2) Trust, the Fund, the Eileen Trust [¹, the Independent Living Fund (2006)], the Skipton Fund or the London Bombings Relief Charitable Fund;

(b) pursuant to section 2 of the Employment and Training Act 1973 in respect of a claimant's participation—

    (i) in an employment programme specified in regulation 75(1)(a)(ii) of the Jobseeker's Allowance Regulations;

    (ii) in a training scheme specified in regulation 75(1)(b)(ii) of those Regulations; or

    (iii) in the Intensive Activity Period specified in regulation 75(1)(a)(iv) of those Regulations; or

    (iv) in a qualifying course within the meaning specified in regulation 17A(7) of those Regulations;

(c) under an occupational pension scheme, in respect of a pension or other periodical payment made under a personal pension scheme or a payment made by the Board of the Pension Protection Fund where—

    (i) a bankruptcy order has been made in respect of the person in respect of whom the payment has been made or, in Scotland, the estate of that person is subject to sequestration or a judicial factor has been appointed on that person's estate under section 41 of the Solicitors (Scotland) Act 1980;

    (ii) the payment is made to the trustee in bankruptcy or any other person acting on behalf of the creditors; and

    (iii) the person referred to in paragraph (i) and that person's partner (if any) does not possess, or is not treated as possessing, any other income apart from that payment.

(6) Where a claimant stands in relation to a company in a position analogous to that of a sole owner or partner in the business of that company, the claimant is to be treated as if that claimant were such sole owner or partner and in such a case—

(a) the value of the claimant's holding in that company, notwithstanding regulation 111 (calculation of capital), is to be disregarded; and

(b) the claimant will, subject to paragraph (7), be treated as possessing an amount of capital equal to the value or, as the case may be, the claimant's share of the value of the capital of that company and the foregoing provisions of this Chapter are to apply for the purposes of calculating that amount as if it were actual capital which the claimant does possess.

(7) For so long as the claimant undertakes activities in the course of the business of the company, the amount which the claimant is treated as possessing under paragraph (6) is to be disregarded.

(8) Where a claimant is treated as possessing capital under any of paragraphs (1) to (6), the foregoing provisions of this Chapter are to apply for the purposes of calculating its amount as if it were actual capital which the claimant does possess.

(9) For the avoidance of doubt a claimant is to be treated as possessing capital under paragraph (1) only if the capital of which the claimant has deprived himself or herself is actual capital.

AMENDMENT

1. Employment and Support Allowance (Miscellaneous Amendments) Regs 2008 (SI 2008/2428), reg.8(8) (October 27, 2008).

DEFINITIONS

    "Armed Forces and Reserve Forces Compensation Scheme"—see reg.2(1).
    "benefit Acts"—*ibid.*
    "claimant"—see reg.83(1).

"Eileen Trust"—see reg.2(1).
"family"—*ibid.*
"the Fund"—*ibid.*
"the Independent Living Fund (2006)"—*ibid.*
"London Bombings Relief Charitable Fund"—*ibid.*
"Macfarlane (Special Payments) Trust"—*ibid.*
"Macfarlane (Special Payments) (No. 2) Trust"—*ibid.*
"Macfarlane Trust"—*ibid.*
"occupational pension"—*ibid.*
"occupational pension scheme"—*ibid.*
"ordinary clothing and footwear"—*ibid.*
"partner"—*ibid.*
"payment"—*ibid.*
"personal pension scheme"—*ibid.*
"single claimant"—*ibid.*
"Skipton Fund"—*ibid.*
"war disablement pension"—*ibid.*
"war widow's pension"—*ibid.*
"war widower's pension"—*ibid.*
"water charges"—*ibid.*

GENERAL NOTE

1A.372   This is similar to reg.51 of the Income Support Regs/reg.113 of the JSA Regs.
Note that under para.(1) if a person has deprived himself of capital he will be caught by this rule if the purpose of the deprivation was to secure entitlement to or increase the amount of ESA *or income support or JSA*. This avoids the question that might otherwise have arisen on a claimant transferring from income support (or JSA) to ESA whether a deprivation which had only been for the purposes of income support (or JSA) could be caught by para.(1).

Diminishing notional capital rule

1A.373   **116.**—(1) Where a claimant is treated as possessing capital under regulation 115(1) (notional capital), the amount which the claimant is treated as possessing—

(a) in the case of a week that is subsequent to—
  (i) the relevant week in respect of which the conditions set out in paragraph (2) are satisfied; or
  (ii) a week which follows that relevant week and which satisfies those conditions,
  is to be reduced by an amount determined under paragraph (2);

(b) in the case of a week in respect of which paragraph (1)(a) does not apply but where—
  (i) that week is a week subsequent to the relevant week; and
  (ii) that relevant week is a week in which the condition in paragraph (3) is satisfied,
  is to be reduced by the amount determined under paragraph (3).

(2) This paragraph applies to a benefit week or part-week where the claimant satisfies the conditions that—

(a) the claimant is in receipt of an income-related allowance; and

218

(b) but for regulation 115(1), the claimant would have received an additional amount of an income-related allowance in that benefit week or, as the case may be, that part-week,

and in such a case, the amount of the reduction for the purposes of paragraph (1)(a) is to be equal to that additional amount.

(3) Subject to paragraph (4), for the purposes of paragraph (1)(b) the condition is that the claimant would have been entitled to an income-related allowance in the relevant week, but for regulation 115(1), and in such a case the amount of the reduction is to be equal to the aggregate of—

(a) the amount of an income-related allowance to which the claimant would have been entitled in the relevant week but for regulation 115(1); and for the purposes of this sub-paragraph if the relevant week is a part-week that amount is to be determined by dividing the amount of an income-related allowance to which the claimant would have been so entitled by the number equal to the number of days in the part-week and multiplying the quotient by 7;

(b) the amount of housing benefit (if any) equal to the difference between the claimant's maximum housing benefit and the amount (if any) of housing benefit which the claimant is awarded in respect of the benefit week, within the meaning of regulation 2(1) of the Housing Benefit Regulations 2006 (interpretation), which includes the last day of the relevant week;

(c) the amount of council tax benefit (if any) equal to the difference between the claimant's maximum council tax benefit and the amount (if any) of council tax benefit which the claimant is awarded in respect of the benefit week which includes the last day of the relevant week, and for this purpose "benefit week" has the same meaning as in regulation 2(1) of the Council Tax Benefit Regulations 2006 (interpretation).

(4) The amount determined under paragraph (3) is to be re-determined under that paragraph if the claimant makes a further claim for an income-related allowance and the conditions in paragraph (5) are satisfied, and in such a case—

(a) sub-paragraphs (a) to (c) of paragraph (3) will apply as if for the words "relevant week" there were substituted the words "relevant subsequent week"; and

(b) subject to paragraph (6), the amount as re-determined is to have effect from the first week following the relevant subsequent week in question.

(5) The conditions are that—

(a) a further claim is made 26 or more weeks after—

(i) the date on which the claimant made a claim for an income-related allowance in respect of which the claimant was first treated as possessing the capital in question under regulation 115(1);

(ii) in a case where there has been at least one re-determination in accordance with paragraph (4), the date on which the claimant last made a claim for an income-related allowance which resulted in the weekly amount being re-determined; or

(iii) the date on which the claimant last ceased to be in receipt of an income-related allowance;

whichever last occurred; and

(b) the claimant would have been entitled to an income-related allowance but for regulation 115(1).

(6) The amount as re-determined pursuant to paragraph (4) is not to have effect if it is less than the amount which applied in that case immediately before the re-determination and in such a case the higher amount is to continue to have effect.

(7) For the purposes of this regulation—

"part-week" means a period to which Part 14 (periods of less than a week) applies;

"relevant week" means the benefit week or part-week in which the capital in question of which the claimant has deprived himself or herself within the meaning of regulation 115(1)—

(a) was first taken into account for the purpose of determining the claimant's entitlement to an income-related allowance, a jobseeker's allowance or income support; or

(b) was taken into account on a subsequent occasion for the purpose of determining or re-determining the claimant's entitlement to an income-related allowance, a jobseeker's allowance or income support on that subsequent occasion and that determination or re-determination resulted in the claimant's beginning to receive, or ceasing to receive, an income-related allowance, a jobseeker's allowance or income support;

and where more than one benefit week or part-week is identified by reference to paragraphs (a) and (b) of this definition the later or latest such benefit week or, as the case may be, the later or latest such part-week;

"relevant subsequent week" means the benefit week or part-week which includes the day on which the further claim or, if more than one further claim has been made, the last such claim was made.

DEFINITIONS

"benefit week"—see reg.2(1).
"claimant"—see reg.83(1).
"week"—see reg.2(1).

GENERAL NOTE

1A.374   This is similar to reg.51A of the Income Support Regs/reg.114 of the JSA Regs.

Capital jointly held

1A.375   **117.** Except where a claimant possesses capital which is disregarded under regulation 115(6) (notional capital), where a claimant and one or more persons are beneficially entitled in possession to any capital asset they are to be treated as if each of them were entitled in possession to the whole beneficial interest therein in an equal share and the foregoing provisions of this Chapter are to apply for the purposes of calculating the amount of capital which the claimant is treated as possessing as if it were actual capital which the claimant does possess.

DEFINITION

"claimant"—see reg.83(1).

GENERAL NOTE

This is similar to reg.52 of the Income Support Regs/reg.115 of the JSA Regs.   1A.376

Calculation of tariff income from capital

118.—(1) Except where the circumstances prescribed in paragraph (3) apply to the claimant, where the claimant's capital calculated in accordance with this Part exceeds £6,000 it is to be treated as equivalent to a weekly income of £1 for each complete £250 in excess of £6,000 but not exceeding £16,000.   1A.377

(2) Where the circumstances prescribed in paragraph (3) apply to the claimant and that claimant's capital calculated in accordance with this Part exceeds £10,000, it is to be treated as equivalent to a weekly income of £1 for each complete £250 in excess of £10,000 but not exceeding £16,000.

(3) For the purposes of paragraph (2) the prescribed circumstances are that the claimant lives permanently in—

(a) a care home or an independent hospital;

(b) an Abbeyfield Home; or

(c) accommodation provided under section 3 of, and Part 2 of the Schedule to, the Polish Resettlement Act 1947 (provision of accommodation in camps) where the claimant requires personal care by reason of old age, disablement, past or present dependence on alcohol or drugs, past or present mental disorder or a terminal illness and the care is provided in the home.

(4) For the purposes of paragraph (3), a claimant is to be treated as living permanently in such home, hospital or accommodation where the claimant is absent—

(a) from a home, hospital or accommodation referred to in sub-paragraph (a) or (b) of paragraph (3)—

(i) in the case of a claimant over pensionable age, for a period not exceeding 52 weeks; and

(ii) in any other case, for a period not exceeding 13 weeks;

(b) from accommodation referred to in sub-paragraph (c) of paragraph (3), where the claimant, with the agreement of the manager of the accommodation, intends to return to the accommodation in due course.

(5) Notwithstanding paragraphs (1) and (2), where any part of the excess is not a complete £250 that part is to be treated as equivalent to a weekly income of £1.

(6) For the purposes of paragraphs (1) and (2), capital includes any income treated as capital under [¹regulation 112 (income treated as capital)].

AMENDMENT

1. Employment and Support Allowance (Miscellaneous Amendments) Regulations 2008 (SI 2008/2428), reg.20(6) (October 27, 2008).

DEFINITIONS

"Abbeyfield Home"—see reg.2(1).
"care home"—*ibid.*
"claimant"—see reg.83(1).
"independent hospital"—see reg.2(1).

GENERAL NOTE

1A.378   This is similar to reg.53 of the Income Support Regs/reg.116 of the JSA Regs. It is not entirely clear why para.(4)(a) contains a separate rule for a claimant over pensionable age (reg.53(1C)(a) of the Income Support Regs does the same but not reg.116 of the JSA Regs), since claimants over pensionable age are not entitled to ESA (or indeed income support).

CHAPTER 8

[¹CHILD MAINTENANCE AND LIABLE RELATIVE PAYMENTS]

AMENDMENT

1. Employment and Support Allowance (Miscellaneous Amendments) Regulations 2008 (SI 2008/2428), reg.20(5) (October 27, 2008).

Interpretation

1A.379   **119.** In this Chapter—
[¹"child maintenance" means any payment towards the maintenance of a child or young person, including any payment made voluntarily and payments made under—
(a) the Child Support Act 1991;
(b) the Child Support (Northern Ireland) Order 1991;
(c) a court order;
(d) a consent order;
(e) a maintenance agreement registered for execution in the Books of Council and Session or the sheriff court books;]
"claimant" includes a young claimant;
[¹"claimant's family" shall be construed in accordance with section 137 of the Contributions and Benefits Act (interpretation of part 7 and supplementary provisions);
"housing costs" means those costs which may be met under paragraph 1(2) of Schedule 6;]

222

"liable relative" means—

    (a) a spouse, former spouse, civil partner or former civil partner of a claimant or of a member of the claimant's family;

    (b) a parent of a child or young person who is a member of the claimant's family or of a young claimant;

    (c) a person who has not been adjudged to be the father of a child or young person who is a member of the claimant's family or of a young claimant where that person is contributing towards the maintenance of that child, young person or young claimant and by reason of that contribution the claimant may reasonably be treated as the father of that child, young person or young claimant;

    (d) a person liable to maintain another person by virtue of section 78(6)(c) of the Administration Act (liability to maintain) where the latter is the claimant or a member of the claimant's family,

and, in this definition, a reference to a child's, young person's or young claimant's parent includes any person in relation to whom the child, young person or young claimant was treated as a child or a member of the family;

[¹"ordinary clothing and footwear" means clothing and footwear for normal daily use but does not include school uniforms;]

"payment" means a periodical payment or any other payment made by or derived from a liable relative [¹ . . .] but it does not include any payment—

    (a) arising from a disposition of property made in contemplation of, or as a consequence of—

        (i) an agreement to separate;

        (ii) any proceedings for judicial separation, divorce or nullity of marriage; or

        (iii) any proceedings for separation, dissolution or nullity in relation to a civil partnership;

    (b) made after the death of the liable relative;

    (c) made by way of a gift but not in aggregate or otherwise exceeding £250 in the period of 52 weeks beginning with the date on which the payment, or if there is more than one such payment the first payment, is made; and, in the case of a claimant who continues to be in receipt of an income-related allowance at the end of the period of 52 weeks, this provision is to continue to apply thereafter with the modification that any subsequent period of 52 weeks is to begin with the first day of the benefit week in which the first payment is made after the end of the previous period of 52 weeks;

    [¹(d) made to a third party, or in respect of a third party, unless the payment is—

        (i) in relation to the claimant or the claimant's family; and

223

       (ii) the payment is in respect of food, ordinary clothing or footwear, fuel, rent, housing costs, council tax or water charges;]

(e) in kind;

(f) to, or in respect of, a child or young person who is to be treated as not being a member of the claimant's household under regulation 156 (circumstances in which a person is to be treated as being or not being a member of the same household);

(g) which is not a periodical payment, to the extent that any amount of that payment—

       (i) has already been taken into account under this Part by virtue of a previous claim or determination;

      (ii) has been recovered under section 74 of the Administration Act (income support and other payments) or is currently being recovered; or

     (iii) at the time the determination is made, has been used by the claimant except where the claimant has deprived himself or herself of that amount for the purpose of securing entitlement to an income-related allowance or increasing the amount of that allowance;

"periodical payment" means—

(a) a payment which is made or is due to be made at regular intervals [¹ . . .];

(b) in a case where the liable relative has established a pattern of making payments at regular intervals, any such payment;

(c) any payment [¹, after the appropriate disregard under paragraph 60 of Schedule 8 (sums to be disregarded in the calculation of income other than earnings) has been applied to it, that does not exceed] the amount of an income-related allowance payable had that payment not been made;

(d) any payment representing a commutation of payments to which paragraph (a) or (b) of this definition applies whether made in arrears or in advance,

but does not include a payment due to be made before the first benefit week pursuant to the claim which is not so made;

"young claimant" means a person aged 16 or over but under 20 who makes a claim for an income-related allowance.

AMENDMENT

1. Employment and Support Allowance (Miscellaneous Amendments) Regulations 2008 (SI 2008/2428), reg.20(7) (October 27, 2008).

DEFINITIONS

    "benefit week"—see reg.2(1).
    "child"—*ibid.*
    "claimant"—see reg.83(1).

"family"—see reg.2(1).
"young person"—*ibid.*

GENERAL NOTE

This is similar to reg.54 of the Income Support Regs/reg.117 of the JSA Regs, 1A.380
as amended with effect from October 27, 2008—see Part III of this Supplement
(Updating material for Vol.II)

Treatment of [¹ child maintenance or] liable relative payments

120. Subject to regulation 121 (disregard of payments treated as not 1A.381
relevant income) and [²paragraph 60 of Schedule 8 (sums to be disregarded in the calculation of income other than earnings)] a payment—

(a) to the extent that it is not a payment of income, is to be treated as
    income;
(b) is to be taken into account in accordance with the following
    provisions of this Chapter.

AMENDMENTS

1. Employment and Support Allowance (Miscellaneous Amendments) Regs
2008 (SI 2008/2428), reg.20(2)(b) (October 27, 2008).
2. Employment and Support Allowance (Miscellaneous Amendments) Regs
2008 (SI 2008/2428), reg.20(8) (October 27, 2008).

DEFINITIONS

"child maintenance"—see reg.119.
"payment"—*ibid.*

GENERAL NOTE

This is similar to reg.55 of the Income Support Regs/reg.118 of the JSA Regs, 1A.382
as amended with effect from October 27, 2008—see Part III of this Supplement
(Updating material for Vol.II)

Disregard of payments treated as not relevant income

121. Where the Secretary of State treats any payment as not being 1A.383
relevant income for the purposes of section 74A of the Administration
Act (payment of benefit where maintenance payments collected by Secretary of State), that payment is to be disregarded in calculating a
claimant's income.

DEFINITIONS

"payment"—see reg.119.
"relevant income"—see reg.2(c), Social Security Benefits (Maintenance Pay-
    ments and Consequential Amendments) Regs 1996 (SI 1996/940).

GENERAL NOTE

This is similar to reg.55A of the Income Support Regs/reg.119 of the JSA 1A.384
Regs.
    Note the amendment to reg.2(c) of the Social Security Benefits (Maintenance
Payments and Consequential Amendments) Regs 1996 in Part III of this Supple-
ment (Updating material for Vol.II).

Period over which periodical payments are to be taken into account

1A.385   **122.**—(1) The period over which a periodical payment is to be taken into account is to be—

(a) in a case where the payment is made at regular intervals, a period equal to the length of that interval;

(b) in a case where the payment is due to be made at regular intervals but is not so made, such number of weeks as is equal to the number (and any fraction is to be treated as a corresponding fraction of a week) obtained by dividing the amount of that payment by the weekly amount of that periodical payment as calculated in accordance with regulation 124(4) (calculation of the weekly amount of a liable relative payment);

(c) in any other case, a period equal to a week.

(2) The period under paragraph (1) is to begin on the date on which the payment is treated as paid under regulation 125 (date on which a liable relative payment is to be treated as paid).

DEFINITION

"periodical payment"—see reg.119.

GENERAL NOTE

1A.386   This is similar to reg.56 of the Income Support Regs/reg.120 of the JSA Regs.

[¹ Period over which payments other than periodical payments are to be taken into account

1A.387   **123.**—(1) The period over which a payment other than a periodical payment (a "non-periodical payment") is to be taken into account shall be determined as follows.

(2) Except in a case where paragraph (4) applies, the number of weeks over which a non-periodical payment is to be taken into account shall be equal to the number obtained by dividing that payment by the amount referred to in paragraph (3).

(3) The amount is the aggregate of £2 and—

(a) the amount of employment and support allowance that would be payable had no payment been made, and

(b) where applicable, the maximum amount of disregard that would apply to the payment under paragraph 60 of Schedule 8.

(4) This paragraph applies in a case where a liable relative makes a periodical payment and a non-periodical payment concurrently and the weekly amount of the periodical payment (as calculated in accordance with regulation 124) is less than B.

(5) In a case where paragraph (4) applies, the non-periodical payment shall, subject to paragraphs (6) and (7), be taken into account over a period of the number of weeks equal to the number obtained by applying the formula—

$$\frac{A}{B - C}$$

(6) If the liable relative ceases to make periodical payments, the balance (if any) of the non-periodical payment shall be taken into account over the number of weeks equal to the number obtained by dividing that balance by the amount referred to in paragraph (3).

(7) If the amount of any subsequent periodical payment varies, the balance (if any) of the non-periodical payment shall be taken into account over a period of the number of weeks equal to the number obtained by applying the formula—

$$\frac{D}{B - E}$$

(8) The period under paragraph (2) or (4) shall begin on the date on which the payment is treated as paid under regulation 125 (date on which a liable relative payment is to be treated as paid) and the period under paragraph (6) or (7) shall begin on the first day of the benefit week in which the cessation or variation of the periodical payment occurred.

(9) Any fraction which arises by applying a calculation or formula referred to in this regulation shall be treated as a corresponding fraction of a week.

(10) In paragraphs (4) to (7)—

A = the amount of the non-periodical payment;

B = the aggregate of £2 and the amount of employment and support allowance that would be payable had the periodical payment not been made and, where applicable, the maximum disregard under paragraph 60 of Schedule 8;

C = the weekly amount of the periodical payment;

D = the balance (if any) of the non-periodical payment.

E = the weekly amount of any subsequent periodical payment.]

AMENDMENT

1. Employment and Support Allowance (Miscellaneous Amendments) Regulations 2008 (SI 2008/2428), reg.20(9) (October 27, 2008).

DEFINITIONS

"liable relative"—see reg.119.
"payment"—*ibid.*
"periodical payment"—*ibid.*

GENERAL NOTE

This is similar to reg.57 of the Income Support Regs/reg.121 of the JSA Regs, **1A.388** as amended with effect from October 27, 2008—see Part III of this Supplement (Updating material for Vol.II).

Calculation of the weekly amount of a [¹child maintenance or] liable relative payment

1A.389   **124.**—(1) Where a periodical payment is made or is due to be made at intervals of one week, the weekly amount is to be the amount of that payment.

(2) Where a periodical payment is made or is due to be made at intervals greater than one week and those intervals are monthly, the weekly amount is to be determined by multiplying the amount of the payment by 12 and dividing the product by 52.

(3) Where a periodical payment is made or is due to be made at intervals and those intervals are neither weekly nor monthly, the weekly amount is to be determined by dividing that payment by the number equal to the number of weeks (including any part of a week) in that interval.

(4) Where a payment is made and that payment represents a commutation of periodical payments whether in arrears or in advance, the weekly amount is to be the weekly amount of the individual periodical payments so commuted as calculated under paragraphs (1) to (3) as is appropriate.

(5) The weekly amount of a payment to which regulation 123 (period over which payments other than periodical payments are to be taken into account) applies, is to be equal to the amount of the divisor used in calculating the period over which the payment or, as the case may be, the balance is to be taken into account.

AMENDMENT

1. Employment and Support Allowance (Miscellaneous Amendments) Regulations 2008 (SI 2008/2428), reg.20(2)(c) (October 27, 2008).

DEFINITIONS

"child maintenance"—see reg.119.
"payment"—*ibid.*
"periodical payment"—*ibid.*

GENERAL NOTE

1A.390   This is similar to reg.58 of the Income Support Regs/reg.122 of the JSA Regs, as amended with effect from October 27, 2008—see Part III of this Supplement (Updating material for Vol. II).

Date on which a [¹child maintenance or] liable relative payment is to be treated as paid

1A.391   **125.**—(1) A periodical payment is to be treated as paid—
(a) in the case of a payment which is due to be made before the first benefit week pursuant to the claim, on the day in the week in which it is due to be paid which corresponds to the first day of the benefit week;
(b) in any other case, on the first day of the benefit week in which it is due to be paid unless, having regard to the manner in which an income-related allowance is due to be paid in the particular case,

it would be more practicable to treat it as paid on the first day of a subsequent benefit week.

(2) Subject to paragraph (3), any other payment is to be treated as paid—

(a) in the case of a payment which is made before the first benefit week pursuant to the claim, on the day in the week in which it is paid which corresponds to the first day of the benefit week;

(b) in any other case, on the first day of the benefit week in which it is paid unless, having regard to the manner in which an income-related allowance is due to be paid in the particular case, it would be more practicable to treat it as paid on the first day of a subsequent benefit week.

(3) Any other payment paid on a date which falls within the period in respect of which a previous payment is taken into account, not being a periodical payment, is to be treated as paid on the first day following the end of that period.

AMENDMENT

1. Employment and Support Allowance (Miscellaneous Amendments) Regulations 2008 (SI 2008/2428), reg.20(2)(d) (October 27, 2008).

DEFINITIONS

   "benefit week"—see reg.2(1).
   "child maintenance"—see reg.119.
   "payment"—*ibid.*
   "periodical payment"—*ibid.*

GENERAL NOTE

   This is similar to reg.59 of the Income Support Regs/reg.123 of the JSA Regs, **1A.391.1** as amended with effect from October 27, 2008—see Part III of this Supplement (Updating material for Vol.II).

Liable relative payments to be treated as capital

126. [¹ . . .]   **1A.392**

AMENDMENT

1. Employment and Support Allowance (Miscellaneous Amendments) Regulations 2008 (SI 2008/2428), reg.20(4)(b) (October 27, 2008).

CHAPTER 9

CHILD SUPPORT

Treatment of child support maintenance

127. [¹ . . .]   **1A.393**

AMENDMENT

1. Employment and Support Allowance (Miscellaneous Amendments) Regulations 2008 (SI 2008/2428), reg.20(4)(c) (October 27, 2008).

Calculation of the weekly amount of payments of child support maintenance

128. [¹ . . .]

AMENDMENT

1. Employment and Support Allowance (Miscellaneous Amendments) Regulations 2008 (SI 2008/2428), reg.20(4)(c) (October 27, 2008).

Date on which child support maintenance is to be treated as paid

1A.394   129. [¹ . . .]

AMENDMENT

1. Employment and Support Allowance (Miscellaneous Amendments) Regulations 2008 (SI 2008/2428), reg.20(4)(c) (October 27, 2008).

Disregard of payments treated as not relevant income

1A.395   130. [¹ . . .]

AMENDMENT

1. Employment and Support Allowance (Miscellaneous Amendments) Regulations 2008 (SI 2008/2428), reg.20(4)(c) (October 27, 2008).

CHAPTER 10

STUDENTS

Interpretation

1A.396   131.—(1) In this Chapter—
"academic year" means the period of twelve months beginning on 1st January, 1st April, 1st July or 1st September according to whether the course in question begins in the winter, the spring, the summer or the autumn respectively but if students are required to begin attending the course during August or September and to continue attending through the autumn, the academic year of the course is to be considered to begin in the autumn rather than the summer;
"access funds" means—
(a) grants made under section 7 of the Further and Higher Education Act 1992 and described as "learner support funds" or grants made under section 68 of that Act for the

purpose of providing funds on a discretionary basis to be paid to students;

(b) grants made under sections 73(a) and (c) and 74(1) of the Education (Scotland) Act 1980;

(c) grants made under Article 30 of the Education and Libraries (Northern Ireland) Order 1993, or grants, loans or other payments made under Article 5 of the Further Education (Northern Ireland) Order 1997 in each case being grants, or grants, loans or other payments as the case may be, made for the purpose of assisting students in financial difficulties;

(d) discretionary payments, known as "learner support funds", which are made available to students in further education by institutions out of funds provided by the Learning and Skills Council for England under sections 5, 6 and 9 of the Learning and Skills Act 2000; or

(e) Financial Contingency Funds made available by the Welsh Ministers;

"college of further education" means, in Scotland, an educational establishment by which further education is provided;

"contribution" means any contribution in respect of the income of a student or of any other person which the Secretary of State, the Scottish Ministers or an education authority takes into account in ascertaining the amount of the student's grant or student loan, or any sums, which in determining the amount of a student's allowance or bursary in Scotland under the Education (Scotland) Act 1980, the Scottish Ministers or education authority take into account being sums which the Scottish Ministers or the education authority consider that the holder of the allowance or bursary, the holder's parents and the holder's spouse or civil partner can reasonably be expected to contribute towards the holder's expenses;

"course of advanced education" means—

(a) a course leading to a postgraduate degree or comparable qualification, a first degree or comparable qualification, a diploma of higher education or a higher national diploma; or

(b) any other course which is of a standard above advanced GNVQ, or equivalent, including a course which is of a standard above a general certificate of education (advanced level), a Scottish national qualification (higher or advanced higher);

"covenant income" means the income payable to a student under a Deed of Covenant by a person whose income is, or is likely to be, taken into account in assessing the student's grant or award;

"education authority" means a government department, a local education authority as defined in section 212 of the Education Act 2002 (interpretation), an education authority as defined in section 123 of the Local Government (Scotland) Act 1973, an education and library board established under Article 3 of the Education and

Libraries (Northern Ireland) Order 1986, any body which is a research council for the purposes of the Science and Technology Act 1965 or any analogous government department, authority, board or body, of the Channel Islands, Isle of Man or any other country outside Great Britain;

"full-time course of advanced education" means a course of advanced education which is—

    (a) a full-time course of study which is not funded in whole or in part by the Learning and Skills Council for England or by the Welsh Ministers or a full-time course of study which is not funded in whole or in part by the Scottish Ministers at a college of further education or a full-time course of study which is a course of higher education and is funded in whole or in part by the Scottish Ministers;

    (b) a course of study which is funded in whole or in part by the Learning and Skills Council for England or by the Welsh Ministers if it involves more than 16 guided learning hours per week for the student in question, according to the number of guided learning hours per week for that student set out—

        (i) in the case of a course funded by the Learning and Skills Council for England, in the student's learning agreement signed on behalf of the establishment which is funded by that Council for the delivery of that course; or

        (ii) in the case of a course funded by the Welsh Ministers, in a document signed on behalf of the establishment which is funded by that Council for the delivery of that course; or

    (c) a course of study (not being higher education) which is funded in whole or in part by the Scottish Ministers at a college of further education if it involves—

        (i) more than 16 hours per week of classroom-based or workshop-based programmed learning under the direct guidance of teaching staff according to the number of hours set out in a document signed on behalf of the college; or

        (ii) 16 hours or less per week of classroom-based or work-shop-based programmed learning under the direct guidance of teaching staff and it involves additional hours using structured learning packages supported by the teaching staff where the combined total of hours exceeds 21 per week, according to the number of hours set out in a document signed on behalf of the college;

"full-time course of study" means a full-time course of study which—

    (a) is not funded in whole or in part by the Learning and Skills Council for England or by the Welsh Ministers or a full-time course of study which is not funded in whole or in part by the Scottish Ministers at a college of further education or a full-time course of study which is a course of higher education and is funded in whole or in part by the Scottish Ministers;

(b) a course of study which is funded in whole or in part by the Learning and Skills Council for England or by the Welsh Ministers if it involves more than 16 guided learning hours per week for the student in question, according to the number of guided learning hours per week for that student set out—

    (i) in the case of a course funded by the Learning and Skills Council for England, in the student's learning agreement signed on behalf of the establishment which is funded by that Council for the delivery of that course; or

    (ii) in the case of a course funded by the Welsh Ministers, in a document signed on behalf of the establishment which is funded by that Council for the delivery of that course; or

(c) is not higher education and is funded in whole or in part by the Scottish Ministers at a college of further education if it involves—

    (i) more than 16 hours per week of classroom-based or workshop-based programmed learning under the direct guidance of teaching staff according to the number of hours set out in a document signed on behalf of the college; or

    (ii) 16 hours or less per week of classroom-based or workshop-based programmed learning under the direct guidance of teaching staff and it involves additional hours using structured learning packages supported by the teaching staff where the combined total of hours exceeds 21 per week, according to the number of hours set out in a document signed on behalf of the college;

"full-time student" means a person who is not a qualifying young person or child within the meaning of section 142 of the Contributions and Benefits Act (child and qualifying young person) and who is—

(a) aged less than 19 and is attending or undertaking a full-time course of advanced education;

(b) aged 19 or over but under pensionable age and is attending or undertaking a full-time course of study at an educational establishment; or

(c) on a sandwich course;

"grant" (except in the definition of "access funds") means any kind of educational grant or award and includes any scholarship, studentship, exhibition, allowance or bursary but does not include a payment from access funds or any payment to which paragraph 13 of Schedule 8 or paragraph 52 of Schedule 9 applies;

"grant income" means—
   (a) any income by way of a grant;
   (b) in the case of a student other than one to whom paragraph (c) refers, any contribution which has been assessed whether or not it has been paid;
   (c) in the case of a student who is a lone parent or is a person to whom Part 4 applies, any contribution which has been assessed and which has been paid,

and any such contribution which is paid by way of a covenant is to be treated as part of the student's grant income;

"higher education" means higher education within the meaning of Part 2 of the Further and Higher Education (Scotland) Act 1992;

"last day of the course" means the date on which the last day of the final academic term falls in respect of the course in which the student is enrolled;

"period of study" means—
   (a) in the case of a course of study for one year or less, the period beginning with the start of the course and ending with the last day of the course;
   (b) in the case of a course of study for more than one year, in the first or, as the case may be, any subsequent year of the course, other than the final year of the course, the period beginning with the start of the course or, as the case may be, that year's start and ending with either—
      (i) the day before the start of the next year of the course in a case where the student's grant or loan is assessed at a rate appropriate to the student's studying throughout the year or, if the claimant does not have a grant or loan, where a loan would have been assessed at such a rate had the claimant had one; or
      (ii) in any other case the day before the start of the normal summer vacation appropriate to the student's course;
   (c) in the final year of a course of study of more than one year, the period beginning with that year's start and ending with the last day of the course;

"periods of experience" means periods of work experience which form part of a sandwich course;

"sandwich course" has the meaning prescribed in regulation 2(9) of the Education (Student Support) Regulations 2007, regulation 4(2) of the Education (Student Loans) (Scotland) Regulations 2007 or regulation 2(8) of the Education (Student Support) Regulations (Northern Ireland) 2007;

"standard maintenance grant" means—
   (a) except where paragraph (b) or (c) applies, in the case of a student attending or undertaking a course of study at the University of London or an establishment within the area comprising the City of London and the Metropolitan Police District, the amount specified for the time being in

paragraph 2(2)(a) of Schedule 2 to the Education (Mandatory Awards) Regulations 2003 ("the 2003 Regulations") for such a student;

(b) except where paragraph (c) applies, in the case of a student residing at the student's parent's home, the amount specified in paragraph 3(2) of Schedule 2 to the 2003 Regulations;

(c) in the case of a student receiving an allowance or bursary under the Education (Scotland) Act 1980, the amount of money specified for the relevant year appropriate for the student set out in the Student Support in Scotland Guide issued by the Student Awards Agency for Scotland, or its nearest equivalent in the case of a bursary provided by a college of further education or a local education authority;

(d) in any other case, the amount specified in paragraph 2(2) of Schedule 2 to the 2003 Regulations other than in paragraph (a) or (b) of that paragraph;

"student" means a person, other than a person in receipt of a training allowance, who is attending or undertaking a course of study at an educational establishment;

"student loan" means a loan towards a student's maintenance pursuant to any regulations made under section 22 of the Teaching and Higher Education Act 1998, sections [¹73(f)], 73B and 74 of the Education (Scotland) Act 1980 or article 3 of the Education (Student Support) (Northern Ireland) Order 1998 and is to include, in Scotland, amounts paid under regulation 4(1)(c) of the Students' Allowances (Scotland) Regulations 2007.

(2) For the purposes of the definition of "full-time student" in paragraph (1), a person is to be regarded as attending or, as the case may be, undertaking a full-time course of study, a full-time course of advanced education or as being on a sandwich course—

(a) subject to paragraph (3), in the case of a person attending or undertaking a part of a modular course which would be a full-time course of study for the purposes of this Part, for the period beginning on the day on which that part of the course starts and ending—

(i) on the last day on which the claimant is registered with the educational establishment as attending or undertaking that part as a full-time course of study; or

(ii) on such earlier date (if any) as the claimant finally abandons the course or is dismissed from it;

(b) in any other case, throughout the period beginning on the date on which the claimant starts attending or undertaking the course and ending on the last day of the course or on such earlier date (if any) as the claimant finally abandons it or is dismissed from it.

(3) For the purpose of sub-paragraph (a) of paragraph (2), the period referred to in that sub-paragraph is to include—

(a) where a person has failed examinations or has failed to successfully complete a module relating to a period when the claimant was attending or undertaking a part of the course as a full-time course of study, any period in respect of which the claimant attends or undertakes the course for the purpose of retaking those examinations or that module;

(b) any period of vacation within the period specified in that paragraph or immediately following that period except where the person has registered with the educational establishment to attend or undertake the final module in the course and the vacation immediately follows the last day on which the claimant is required to attend or undertake the course.

(4) In paragraph (2), "modular course" means a course of study which consists of two or more modules, the successful completion of a specified number of which is required before a person is considered by the educational establishment to have completed the course.

AMENDMENT

1. Employment and Support Allowance (Miscellaneous Amendments) Regulations 2008 (SI 2008/2428), reg.8(9) (October 27, 2008).

DEFINITION

"training allowance"—see reg.2(1).

GENERAL NOTE

1A.397   This is similar to reg.61 of the Income Support Regs. Under JSA the definitions applying to full-time students are in a slightly different form. See reg.130 of the JSA Regs for some of the definitions but the main ones are to be found in reg.1(3) and (3A)–(3E) of those Regs (see further the note to reg.130 of the JSA Regs in Vol.II of this series).

Note that in the definition of "grant income" the cases where a contribution will only be included if it is actually paid are a lone parent or a person "to whom Part 4 applies". Since Part 4 concerns who or who is not to be treated as receiving education for the purposes of para.6(1)(g) of Sch.1 to the Welfare Reform Act 2007 it is not clear what this reference means. It is presumably intended to refer to disabled students (in order to mirror the definition of "grant income" in the Income Support Regs) but it does not appear to be so limited.

Calculation of grant income

1A.398   **132.**—(1) The amount of student's grant income to be taken into account, subject to paragraphs (2) and (3), is to be the whole of the student's grant income.

(2) There is to be disregarded from the amount of a student's grant income any payment—

(a) intended to meet tuition fees or examination fees;

(b) intended to meet additional expenditure incurred by a disabled student in respect of that student's attendance on a course;

(c) intended to meet additional expenditure connected with term time residential study away from the student's educational establishment;

(d) on account of the student maintaining a home at a place other than that at which the student resides while attending the course

236

but only to the extent that the student's rent is not met by housing benefit;

(e) on account of any other person but only if that person is residing outside of the United Kingdom and there is no applicable amount in respect of that person;

(f) intended to meet the cost of books and equipment;

(g) intended to meet travel expenses incurred as a result of the student's attendance on the course;

(h) intended for the maintenance of a child dependant;

(i) intended for the child care costs of a child dependant.

(3) Where a student does not have a student loan and is not treated as possessing such a loan, there is to be excluded from the student's grant income—

(a) the sum of [^{1}£295] per academic year in respect of travel costs; and

(b) the sum of [^{2}£380] per academic year towards the costs of books and equipment,

whether or not any such costs are incurred.

(4) Subject to paragraph (6), a student's grant income except any amount intended for the maintenance of adult dependants under Part 3 of Schedule 2 to the Education (Mandatory Awards) Regulations 2003 is to be apportioned—

(a) subject to paragraph (7), in a case where it is attributable to the period of study, equally between the weeks in the period beginning with the benefit week, the first day of which coincides with, or immediately follows, the first day of the period of study and ending with the benefit week, the last day of which coincides with, or immediately precedes, the last day of the period of study;

(b) in any other case, equally between the weeks in the period beginning with the benefit week, the first day of which coincides with, or immediately follows, the first day of the period for which it is payable and ending with the benefit week, the last day of which coincides with, or immediately precedes, the last day of the period for which it is payable.

(5) Any grant in respect of an adult dependant paid under section 63(6) of the Health Services and Public Health Act 1968 (grants in respect of the provision of instruction to officers of hospital authorities) and any amount intended for the maintenance of an adult dependant under the provisions referred to in paragraph (4) is to be apportioned equally over a period of 52 weeks or, if there are 53 benefit weeks (including part-weeks) in the year, 53 weeks.

(6) In a case where a student is in receipt of a student loan or where that student could have acquired a student loan by taking reasonable steps but had not done so, any amount intended for the maintenance of an adult dependant under provisions other than those referred to in paragraph (4) is to be apportioned over the same period as the student's loan is apportioned or, as the case may be, would have been apportioned.

(7) In the case of a student on a sandwich course, any periods of experience within the period of study is to be excluded and the student's

The Employment and Support Allowance Regulations 2008

grant income is to be apportioned equally between the weeks in the period beginning with the benefit week, the first day of which immediately follows the last day of the period of experience and ending with the benefit week, the last day of which coincides with, or immediately precedes, the last day of the period of study.

AMENDMENTS

1. Social Security (Students and Miscellaneous Amendments) Regulations 2008 (SI 2008/1599), reg.7(3)(a) (October 27, 2008).
2. Social Security (Students and Miscellaneous Amendments) Regulations 2008 (SI 2008/1599), reg.7(3)(b) (October 27, 2008).

DEFINITIONS

"benefit week"—see reg.2(1).
"grant"—reg.131(1).
"grant income"—*ibid*.
"period of study"—*ibid*.
"periods of experience"—*ibid*.
"sandwich course"—*ibid*.
"student"—*ibid*.
"student loan"—*ibid*.

GENERAL NOTE

1A.399   This is similar to reg.62 of the Income Support Regs/reg.131 of the JSA Regs.

Calculation of covenant income where a contribution is assessed

1A.400   **133.**—(1) Where a student is in receipt of income by way of a grant during a period of study and a contribution has been assessed, the amount of the student's covenant income to be taken into account for that period and any summer vacation immediately following is to be the whole amount of the student's covenant income less, subject to paragraph (3), the amount of the contribution.

(2) The weekly amount of the student's covenant income is to be determined—

(a) by dividing the amount of income which falls to be taken into account under paragraph (1) by 52 or, if there are 53 benefit weeks (including part-weeks) in the year, 53; and

(b) by disregarding from the resulting amount, £5.

(3) For the purposes of paragraph (1), the contribution is to be treated as increased by the amount, if any, by which the amount excluded under regulation 132(2)(g) (calculation of grant income) falls short of the amount for the time being specified in paragraph 7(2) of Schedule 2 to the Education (Mandatory Awards) Regulations 2003 (travel expenditure).

DEFINITIONS

"benefit week"—see reg.2(1).
"contribution"—see reg.131(1).

"covenant income"—*ibid.*
"grant"—*ibid.*
"grant income"—*ibid.*
"period of study"—*ibid.*
"student"—*ibid.*

GENERAL NOTE

This is similar to reg.63 of the Income Support Regs/reg.132 of the JSA 1A.401
Regs.

Calculation of covenant income where no grant income or no contribution is assessed

134.—(1) Where a student is not in receipt of income by way of a 1A.402
grant the amount of the student's covenant income is to be calculated as
follows—

(a) any sums intended for any expenditure specified in regulation
132(2)(a) to (e), necessary as a result of the student's attendance
on the course, are to be disregarded;

(b) any covenant income, up to the amount of the standard maintenance grant, which is not so disregarded is to be apportioned
equally between the weeks of the period of study and there is to be
disregarded from the covenant income to be so apportioned the
amount which would have been disregarded under regulation
132(2)(f) and (g) and (3) had the student been in receipt of the
standard maintenance grant;

(c) the balance, if any, is to be divided by 52 or, if there are 53 benefit
weeks (including part-weeks) in the year, 53 and treated as weekly
income of which £5 is to be disregarded.

(2) Where a student is in receipt of income by way of a grant and no
contribution has been assessed, the amount of the student's covenant
income is to be calculated in accordance with paragraph (1), except
that—

(a) the value of the standard maintenance grant is to be abated by the
amount of the student's grant income less an amount equal to the
amount of any sums disregarded under regulation 132(2)(a) to
(e); and

(b) the amount to be disregarded under paragraph (1)(b) is to be
abated by an amount equal to the amount of any sums disregarded
under regulation 132(2)(f) and (g) and (3).

DEFINITIONS

"benefit week"—see reg.2(1).
"contribution"—see reg.131(1).
"covenant income"—*ibid.*
"grant"—*ibid.*
"grant income"—*ibid.*
"period of study"—*ibid.*
"student"—*ibid.*

1A.403   This is similar to reg.64 of the Income Support Regs/reg.133 of the JSA Regs.

Relationships with amounts to be disregarded under Schedule 8

1A.404   **135.** No part of a student's covenant income or grant income is to be disregarded under paragraph 16 of Schedule 8 (charitable and voluntary payments).

DEFINITIONS

"covenant income"—see reg.131(1).
"grant income"—*ibid.*
"student"—*ibid.*

GENERAL NOTE

1A.405   This is similar to reg.65 of the Income Support Regs/reg.134 of the JSA Regs.

Other amounts to be disregarded

1A.406   **136.**—(1) For the purposes of ascertaining income other than grant income, covenant income and loans treated as income in accordance with regulation 137 (treatment of student loans), any amounts intended for any expenditure specified in regulation 132(2) (calculation of grant income) necessary as a result of the student's attendance on the course is to be disregarded but only if, and to the extent that, the necessary expenditure exceeds or is likely to exceed the amount of the sums disregarded under regulation 132(2) and (3), 133(3) (calculation of covenant income where a contribution is assessed), 134(1)(a) or (b) (calculation of covenant income where no grant income or no contribution is assessed) and 137(6) on like expenditure.

(2) Where a claim is made in respect of any period in the normal summer vacation and any income is payable under a Deed of Covenant which commences or takes effect after the first day of that vacation, that income is to be disregarded.

DEFINITIONS

"covenant income"—see reg.131(1).
"grant income"—*ibid.*

GENERAL NOTE

1A.407   This is similar to reg.66 of the Income Support Regs/reg.135 of the JSA Regs.

Treatment of student loans

1A.408   **137.**—(1) A student loan is to be treated as income unless it is a specified loan or award in which case it is to be disregarded.

240

(2) For the purposes of paragraph (1), a "specified loan or award" means—

    (a) in relation to England, a loan made by the Higher Education Funding Council for England under section 65 of the Further and Higher Education Act 1992;

    (b) in relation to Wales, a loan made by the Higher Education Funding Council for Wales under section 65 of the Further and Higher Education Act 1992;

    (c) in relation to Scotland, a loan made by an educational institution from funds it has received under the Education (Access Funds) (Scotland) Regulations 1990;

    (d) in relation to Northern Ireland, an award made by the Department for Employment and Learning under article 51 of the Education and Libraries (Northern Ireland) Order 1986.

(3) In calculating the weekly amount of the loan to be taken in account as income—

    (a) in respect of a course that is of a single academic year's duration or less, a loan which is payable in respect of that period is to be apportioned equally between the weeks in the period beginning with—

        (i) except in a case where paragraph (ii) applies, the benefit week, the first day of which coincides with, or immediately follows, the first day of the single academic year;

        (ii) where the student is required to start attending the course in August or where the course is less than an academic year's duration, the benefit week, the first day of which coincides with, or immediately follows, the first day of the course,

    and ending with the benefit week, the last day of which coincides with, or immediately precedes, the last day of the course;

    (b) in respect of an academic year of a course which starts other than on 1st September, a loan which is payable in respect of that academic year is to be apportioned equally between the weeks in the period beginning with the benefit week, the first day of which coincides with, or immediately follows, the first day of that academic year and ending with the benefit week, the last day of which coincides with, or immediately precedes, the last day of that academic year but excluding any benefit weeks falling entirely within the quarter during which, in the opinion of the Secretary of State, the longest of any vacation is taken;

    (c) for the purposes of sub-paragraph (b), "quarter" is to have the same meaning as for the purposes of regulation 104(6) (calculation of income other than earnings);

    (d) in respect of the final academic year of a course (not being a course of a single year's duration), a loan which is payable in respect of that final academic year is to be apportioned equally between the weeks in the period beginning with—

        (i) except in a case where paragraph (ii) applies, the benefit week, the first day of which coincides with, or immediately follows, the first day of that academic year;

      (ii) where the final academic year starts on 1st September, the benefit week, the first day of which coincides with, or immediately follows, the earlier of 1st September or the first day of the autumn term,

and ending with the benefit week, the last day of which coincides with, or immediately precedes, the last day of the course;

  (e) in any other case, the loan is to be apportioned equally between the weeks in the period beginning with the earlier of—

      (i) the first day of the first benefit week in September; or

      (ii) the benefit week, the first day of which coincides with, or immediately follows, the first day of the autumn term,

and ending with the benefit week, the last day of which coincides with, or immediately precedes, the last day of June,

and, in all cases, from the weekly amount so apportioned there is to be disregarded £10.

(4) A student is to be treated as possessing a student loan in respect of an academic year where—

  (a) a student loan has been made to that student in respect of that year; or

  (b) the student could acquire such a loan in respect of that year by taking reasonable steps to do so.

(5) Where a student is treated as possessing a student loan under paragraph (4), the amount of the student loan to be taken into account as income is to be, subject to paragraph (6)—

  (a) in the case of a student to whom a student loan is made in respect of an academic year, a sum equal to the maximum student loan the student is able to acquire in respect of that year by taking reasonable steps to do so and either—

      (i) in the case of a student other than one to whom paragraph (ii) refers, any contribution whether or not it has been paid to that student; or

      (ii) in the case of a student who is entitled to an income-related allowance by virtue of being a student to whom regulation 18 (circumstances in which the condition that the claimant is not receiving education does not apply) applies;

  (b) in the case of a student to whom a student loan is not made in respect of an academic year, the maximum student loan that would be made to the student if—

      (i) the student took all reasonable steps to obtain the maximum student loan that student is able to acquire in respect of that year; and

      (ii) no deduction in that loan was made by virtue of the application of a means test.

(6) There is to be deducted from the amount of income taken into account under paragraph (5)—

  (a) the sum of [¹£295] per academic year in respect of travel costs; and

  (b) the sum of [²£380] per academic year towards the costs of books and equipment,

whether or not any such costs are incurred.

242

AMENDMENTS

1. Social Security (Students and Miscellaneous Amendments) Regulations 2008 (SI 2008/1599), reg.7(4)(a) (October 27, 2008).
2. Social Security (Students and Miscellaneous Amendments) Regulations 2008 (SI 2008/1599), reg.7(4)(b) (October 27, 2008).

DEFINITIONS

"academic year"—see reg.131(1).
"benefit week"—see reg.2(1).
"last day of the course"—see reg.131(1).
"student"—*ibid.*
"student loan"—*ibid.*

GENERAL NOTE

Except in relation to the disregard of a "specified loan or award" (see paras (1) and (2)), this is similar to reg.136 of the JSA Regs/reg.66A of the Income Support Regs (although under reg.66A(4)(a)(ii) a contribution will only be included if it is actually paid in the case of a lone parent as well as a disabled student).

1A.409

Under para.(1) a "specified loan or award" (defined in para.(2)) is disregarded. Regulation 66A(1) of the Income Support Regs and reg.136(1) of the JSA Regs used to provide that a "hardship loan" (defined in para.(1A) of both sets of Regulations) was disregarded. However the words "unless it is a hardship loan in which case it shall be disregarded" are omitted from reg.66A(1)/reg.136(1), and regs 66A(1A) and 136(1A) are also omitted, with effect from November 17, 2008 by regs 2(10) and 4(9) respectively of the Social Security (Miscellaneous Amendments) (No. 6) Regs 2008 (SI 2008/2767) (past the cut-off date for this Supplement). According to the Explanatory Memorandum which accompanies these amending regulations these amendments are being made because hardship loans have not been payable since May 2004. It is not known why similar provision for a disregard of a "specified loan or award" has not been made in the Income Support/JSA Regs.

Treatment of payments from access funds

138.—(1) This regulation applies to payments from access funds that are not payments to which regulation 142(2) or (3) (income treated as capital) applies.

1A.410

(2) A payment from access funds, other than a payment to which paragraph (3) applies, is to be disregarded as income.

(3) Subject to paragraph (4) and paragraph 39 of Schedule 8, any payments from access funds which are intended and used for food, ordinary clothing or footwear, household fuel, rent for which housing benefit is payable or any housing costs to the extent that they are met under regulation 67(1)(c) or 68(1)(d) (housing costs), of a single claimant or, as the case may be, of the claimant's partner, and any payments from access funds which are used for any council tax or water charges for which that claimant or partner is liable is to be disregarded as income to the extent of £20 per week.

(4) Where a payment from access funds is made—
(a) on or after 1st September or the first day of the course, whichever first occurs, but before receipt of any student loan in respect of

that year and that payment is intended for the purpose of bridging the period until receipt of the student loan; or

(b) before the first day of the course to a person in anticipation of that person becoming a student,

that payment is to be disregarded as income.

DEFINITIONS

"access funds"—see reg.131(1).
"claimant"—see reg.83(1).
"ordinary clothing or footwear"—see reg.2(1).
"payment"—*ibid.*
"single claimant"—*ibid.*
"student"—see reg.131(1).
"student loan"—*ibid.*

GENERAL NOTE

1A.411   This is similar to reg.66B of the Income Support Regs/reg.136A of the JSA Regs.

Treatment of fee loans

1A.412   **139.** A loan for fees, known as a fee loan or a fee contribution loan, made pursuant to regulations made under Article 3 of the Education (Student Support) (Northern Ireland) Order 1998, section 22 of the Teaching and Higher Education Act 1998 or section 73(f) of the Education (Scotland) Act 1980, is to be disregarded as income.

GENERAL NOTE

1A.413   This is similar to reg.66C of the Income Support Regs/reg.136B of the JSA Regs.

Disregard of contribution

1A.414   **140.** Where the claimant or the claimant's partner is a student and, for the purposes of assessing a contribution to the student's grant or student loan, the other partner's income has been taken into account, an amount equal to that contribution is to be disregarded for the purposes of assessing that other partner's income.

DEFINITIONS

"claimant"—see reg.83(1).
"contribution"—see reg.131(1).
"grant"—*ibid.*
"partner"—see reg.2(1).
"student"—see reg.131(1).
"student loan"—*ibid.*

GENERAL NOTE

1A.415   This is similar to reg.67 of the Income Support Regs/reg.137 of the JSA Regs.

Further disregard of student's income

141. Where any part of a student's income has already been taken into   **1A.416**
account for the purposes of assessing that student's entitlement to a
grant or student loan, the amount taken into account is to be disregarded
in assessing that student's income.

DEFINITIONS

"grant"—see reg.131(1).
"student"—*ibid.*
"student loan"—*ibid.*

GENERAL NOTE

This is similar to reg.67A of the Income Support Regs/reg.137A of the JSA   **1A.417**
Regs.

Income treated as capital

142.—(1) Any amount by way of a refund of tax deducted from a   **1A.418**
student's income is to be treated as capital.

(2) An amount paid from access funds as a single lump sum is to be
treated as capital.

(3) An amount paid from access funds as a single lump sum which is
intended and used for an item other than food, ordinary clothing or
footwear, household fuel, rent for which housing benefit is payable or
any housing costs to the extent that they are met under regulation
67(1)(c) or 68(1)(d), of a single claimant or, as the case may be, of the
claimant's partner, or which is used for an item other than any council
tax or water charges for which that claimant or partner is liable is to be
disregarded as capital but only for a period of 52 weeks from the date of
the payment.

DEFINITIONS

"access funds"—see reg.131(1).
"claimant"—see reg.83(1).
"ordinary clothing or footwear"—see reg.2(1).
"payment"—*ibid.*
"single claimant"—*ibid.*
"student"—see reg.131(1).

GENERAL NOTE

This is similar to reg.68 of the Income Support Regs/reg.138 of the JSA   **1A.419**
Regs.

Disregard of changes occurring during summer vacation

143. In calculating a student's income there is to be disregarded any   **1A.420**
change in the standard maintenance grant occurring in the recognised
summer vacation appropriate to the student's course, if that vacation
does not form part of the student's period of study, from the date on
which the change occurred up to the end of that vacation.

DEFINITIONS

"period of study"—see reg.131(1).
"standard maintenance grant"—*ibid*.
"student"—*ibid*.

GENERAL NOTE

1A.421   This is similar to reg.69 of the Income Support Regs/reg.139 of the JSA Regs.

PART 11

SUPPLEMENTARY PROVISIONS

CHAPTER 1

MISCELLANEOUS

Waiting days

1A.422   **144.**—(1) A claimant is not entitled to an employment and support allowance in respect of 3 days at the beginning of a period of limited capability for work.

(2) Paragraph (1) does not apply where—

(a) the claimant's entitlement to an employment and support allowance commences within 12 weeks of the claimant's entitlement to income support, state pension credit, a jobseeker's allowance, a carer's allowance or statutory sick pay coming to an end;

(b) the claimant is terminally ill and has—

(i) made a claim expressly on the ground of being terminally ill; or

(ii) made an application for supersession or revision in accordance with the Social Security and Child Support (Decisions and Appeals) Regulations 1999 which contains an express statement of being terminally ill; or

(c) the claimant has been discharged from being a member of Her Majesty's forces and 3 or more days immediately before that discharge were days of sickness absence from duty, which are recorded by the Secretary of State for Defence.

DEFINITIONS

"claimant"—see WRA 2007, s.24(1).
"a member of Her Majesty's forces"—see reg.2(1).
"terminally ill"—see reg.2(1).

GENERAL NOTE

1A.423   WRA 2007, s.22 and Sch.2, para.2 provide that "except in prescribed circumstances" a claimant cannot be entitled to ESA for a prescribed number of days at the beginning of a period of limited capability for work. This regulation sets the number of these days of non-entitlement ("waiting days") at three (para.(1)) and provides in para.(2) for the exceptions to that general rule: terminally ill claimants (including those seeking revision or supersession on the basis of being terminally ill) (sub-para.(b)); discharge from Her Majesty's forces where three or more days of recorded sickness absence from duty preceded it (sub-para.(c); and where entitlement to ESA begins within 12 weeks of entitlement to IS, SPC, JSA, carer's allowance or SSP coming to an end (sub-para.(a)). In addition, the general rule is, of course, affected by the "linking rules" (on which see reg.145) in a case of intermittent incapacity where those rules fuse into one ostensibly separate spells of limited capability for work: the "waiting days" only have to be served once in a period of limited capability for work.

Linking rules

145.—(1) Any period of limited capability for work which is separated 1A.424 from another such period by not more than 12 weeks is to be treated as a continuation of the earlier period.

(2) Where the claimant is a work or training beneficiary in accordance with regulation 148, any period of limited capability for work which is separated from another such period by not more than 104 weeks is to be treated as a continuation of the earlier period.

(3) Where the claimant claims an employment and support allowance after ceasing to be in qualifying remunerative work and—

(a) the period of limited capability for work began on the day imme-diately after the day on which the claimant so ceased;

(b) the claimant has been entitled to an employment and support allowance within the period of 104 weeks before the beginning of that period of limited capability for work; and

(c) the claimant satisfied the relevant tax credit conditions set out in paragraph (4) on the day before so ceasing,

the claimant is to be treated for the purposes of the claim as having had limited capability for work throughout the period during which those conditions were satisfied.

(4) A claimant satisfies the relevant tax credit conditions on a day if—

(a) the claimant is entitled for the day to the disability element of working tax credit (on a claim made by the claimant or by the claimant jointly with another) or would be so entitled but for the fact that the relevant income (within the meaning of Part 1 of the Tax Credits Act) in the case of the claimant or the claimant and another is such that that person is not so entitled; and

(b) either working tax credit or any element of child tax credit other than the family element is paid in respect of the day on such a claim.

(5) Where a claim for an employment and support allowance is made after the claimant ceases to be engaged in training and—

(a) that claimant was entitled to an employment and support allow-ance within the period of 8 weeks immediately before becoming so engaged;

(b) that claimant has limited capability for work on the day after ceasing to be so engaged; and

(c) that day falls not later than the end of the period of 104 weeks beginning with the end of the last week for which the claimant was entitled to an employment and support allowance, the claimant is to be treated, for the purposes of the claim, as having had limited capability for work for the period when so engaged in training.

DEFINITIONS

"child tax credit"—see reg.2(1).
"claimant"—see WRA 2007, s.24(1).
"qualifying remunerative work"—see reg.2(1).
"relevant tax credit conditions"—see para.(4).
"training"—see reg.2(1).
"week"—see reg.2(1).
"work or training beneficiary"—see reg.148.
"working tax credit"—see reg.2(1).

GENERAL NOTE

1A.425   The linking rules are crucial for those suffering from intermittent incapacity. They impact, to the claimant's benefit, as regards "waiting days"; those days of non-entitlement (see para.(2) and ESA Regs, reg.144) only have to be served once in any period of limited capability for work. They are also relevant to determining the relevant benefit year and hence the appropriate tax years to which to have regard with respect to the application of the national insurance contribution conditions (see further the commentary to Sch.1, Pt 1, paras 1–3).

Generally, the linking rule works on the basis that two ostensibly separate spells of limited capability for work will be fused into one where the separation period between the spells is not more than 12 weeks (para.(1)). This fusing does not, however, mean that days in the separation period thereby become ones of limited capability for work (*Chief Adjudication Officer v Astle* (Court of Appeal, judgment of March 17, 1999, available on LEXIS and noted in [1999] 6 J.S.S.L. 203). See further for more detail the commentary to SSCBA 1992, s.30C(1)(c) (the "linking" rule)). A period of limited capability for work can only be formed of days of actual limited capability for work and/or ones which the legislative scheme treats as ones of limited capability for work.

However, where a claimant is a "work or training beneficiary" (see reg.148), the "linking period" is 104 weeks (para.(2)). It is also 104 weeks between spells of limited capability for work where a claimant, entitled to ESA, then went into qualifying remunerative work supported or (but for income) supportable by tax credits ("satisfies the relevant tax credit conditions"), and the period of limited capability for work in respect of which the claimant is now seeking ESA began on the day after he ceased that work (paras (3), (4)).

Advance awards

1A.426   **146.**—(1) Where section 5 of the Act (advance award of income-related allowance) applies to a claim and the claimant satisfies the conditions in paragraph (3)—

(a) the claim is to be treated as if made for a period from the relevant day; and

(b) the Secretary of State may award an employment and support allowance from the relevant day.

(2) In this regulation the "relevant day" is the day after the end of a period of 13 weeks beginning on the first day on which the claimant would be entitled to an income-related allowance if the claimant satisfied the condition in paragraph 6(1)(a) of Schedule 1 to the Act. (3) The conditions are that—

(a) the Secretary of State is of the opinion that unless there is a change of circumstances the claimant will satisfy the conditions set out in section 1(3)(b) to (f) of, and Part 2 of Schedule 1 to, the Act when an income-related allowance becomes payable under the award; and

(b) the claimant is treated as having limited capability for work under regulation 20, 25, 26, [¹ 30] or 33(2) (conditions for treating a person as having limited capability for work) for the period before an income-related allowance becomes payable under the award.

(4) Where an award is made under paragraph (1)—

(a) the award for an employment and support allowance will become payable on the date on which the claimant would have been entitled to a main phase employment and support allowance if the claimant had satisfied the condition in paragraph 6(1)(a) of Schedule 1 to the Act before the relevant day;

(b) sections 4(4)(a) and 4(5)(a) of the Act do not apply to that award.

AMENDMENT

1. Employment and Support Allowance (Miscellaneous Amendments) Regulations 2008 (SI 2008/2428), reg.9(2) (October 27, 2008).

DEFINITION

"claimant"—Welfare Reform Act 2007, s.24(1).
"income-related allowance"—Welfare Reform Act 2007, s.24(1) and 1(7).
"main phase employment and support allowance"—reg.2(1).

GENERAL NOTE

See the General Note to s.5 of the Welfare Reform Act 2007.   1A.427

Recovery orders

147.—(1) Where an award of income-related allowance has been   1A.428
made to a claimant, the Secretary of State may apply to the court for a recovery order against the claimant's partner.

(2) On making a recovery order the court may order the partner to pay such amount at such intervals as it considers appropriate, having regard to all the circumstances of the partner and, in particular, the partner's income.

(3) Except in Scotland, a recovery order is to be treated for all purposes as if it were a maintenance order within the meaning of section 150(1) of the Magistrates Courts Act 1980.

(4) Where a recovery order requires the partner to make payments to the Secretary of State, the Secretary of State may, by giving notice in writing to the court which made the order, the liable person and the claimant, transfer to the claimant the right to receive payments under the order and to exercise the relevant rights in relation to the order.

(5) In paragraph 4, "the relevant rights" means, in relation to a recovery order, the right to bring any proceedings, take any steps or do any other thing under or in relation to the order.

DEFINITIONS

"partner"—see reg.2(1).
"payment"—*ibid*.

GENERAL NOTE

1A.429   See s.23 of the Welfare Reform Act 2007 and the note to that section. This regulation is similar to reg.169 of the JSA Regs.

CHAPTER 2

WORK OR TRAINING BENEFICIARIES

Work or training beneficiaries

1A.430   **148.**—(1) Subject to paragraph (2), a claimant is a "work or training beneficiary" on any day in a linking term where the claimant—
(a) had limited capability for work for more than 13 weeks in the most recent past period of limited capability for work;
(b) ceased to be entitled to an allowance or advantage at the end of that most recent past period of limited capability for work; and
(c) became engaged in work or training within one month of so ceasing to be entitled to that benefit at the end of that most recent past period of limited capability for work.

(2) A claimant is not a work or training beneficiary if—
(a) the most recent past period of limited capability for work was ended by a determination that the claimant did not have limited capability for work; and
(b) that determination was on the basis of a limited capability for work assessment.

(3) For the purposes of this Part—
"allowance or advantage" means any allowance or advantage under the Act or the Contributions and Benefits Act for which entitlement is dependent on limited capability for work;
"linking term" means a period of 104 weeks from the first day immediately following the last day in a period of limited capability for work;
"work" means work, other than work under regulation 45 (exempt work), for which payment is made or which is done in expectation of payment.

250

DEFINITIONS

"the Act"—see reg.2(1).
"allowance or advantage"—see para.(3).
"claimant"—see WRA 2007, s.24(1).
"Contributions and Benefits Act"—see WRA 2007, s.65.
"limited capability for work assessment"—see regs 2(1), 19(2), Sch.2.
"linking term"—see para.(3).
"training"—see reg.2(1).
"week"—see reg.2(1).
"work"—see para.(3).

GENERAL NOTE

This regulation, important for understanding regs 145, 149 and 150, defines   **1A.431**
who is (para.(1)), and who is not (para.(2)), a "work or training beneficiary".

Linking rules—limited capability for work

149.—(1) Where the circumstances in paragraph (2) apply, a work or   **1A.432**
training beneficiary is to be treated as having limited capability for work
for a period of 13 weeks beginning on the day within the linking term on
which the work or training beneficiary claims an employment and support allowance.

(2) The circumstances are that—

(a) the work or training beneficiary provides evidence of limited capability for work in accordance with the Medical Evidence Regulations (which prescribe the form of the doctor's statement or other
evidence required in each case); and

(b) in the most recent past period of limited capability for work, it had
been determined that the work or training beneficiary had limited
capability for work—

  (i) the claimant having been assessed in accordance with a limited capability for work assessment; or

  (ii) as a result of the claimant being treated as having limited
capability for work in accordance with regulation 20, 25, 26,
29 or 33(2) (persons to be treated as having limited capability
for work).

DEFINITIONS

"claimant"—see WRA 2007, s.24(1).
"Medical Evidence Regulations"—see re. 2(1).
"period of limited capability for work"—see reg.2(1).
"week"—see reg.2(1).
"work or training beneficiary"—see reg.148.

GENERAL NOTE

This allows a work and training beneficiary who reclaims ESA within the   **1A.433**
104-week linking term to be treated as having limited capability for work for the
first 13 weeks of that "reclaim", so long as he had in his most recent past period
of limited capability for work either been assessed as having it or treated as having
it under the terms of the regulations specified in para.(2)(b)(ii). This seems to
mean that the assessment period will be treated as having ended and the
(re)claimant can immediately be entitled not just to basic allowance ESA but also

to the appropriate component. If reg.150 applies, entitlement will be to the support component.

Linking rules—limited capability for work-related activity

1A.434   **150.** Where a work or training beneficiary was a member of the support group when the most recent past period of limited capability for work came to an end, that work or training beneficiary is to be treated as having limited capability for work-related activity for a period of 13 weeks beginning on the day within the linking term on which a claim for an employment and support allowance is made.

DEFINITIONS

"linking term"—see reg.148(3).
"member of the support group"—see WRA 2007, s.24(4).
"period of limited capability for work"—see reg.2(1).
"work or training beneficiary"—see reg.148.

GENERAL NOTE

1A.435   This means that if a work or training beneficiary reclaims ESA within the 104-week linking term, he will be treated as having limited capability for work-related activity for 13 weeks if he was a member of the support group when his most recent past period of incapacity for work, before the linking term, came to an end. In other words, he can return on day one of his reclaim to his previous level of benefit (basic allowance plus support component).

CHAPTER 3

TEMPORARY ABSENCE FROM GREAT BRITAIN

Absence from Great Britain

1A.436   **151.**—(1) A claimant who is entitled to an employment and support allowance is to continue to be so entitled during a period of temporary absence from Great Britain only in accordance with this Chapter.

(2) A claimant who continues to be entitled to a contributory allowance during a period of temporary absence will not be disqualified for receiving that allowance during that period under section 18(4) of the Act.

DEFINITIONS

"claimant"—Welfare Reform Act 2007, s.24(1).
"contributory allowance"—Welfare Reform Act 2007, s.24(1) and 1(7).

GENERAL NOTE

1A.437   Under s.1(3) of the Welfare Reform Act, it is a condition of entitlement to ESA that the claimant should be "in Great Britain". However, para.5 of Sch.2 to that

Act empowers the Secretary of State to "make provision ... as to the circumstances in which a person is to be treated as being, or not being, in Great Britain".

In addition, those entitled to a contributory allowance are disqualified under s.18(4)(a) while they are absent form Great Britain "except where regulations otherwise provide". Paragraph 6 of Sch.2 to the Act provides that "regulations may provide that in prescribed circumstances a claimant who is not in Great Britain may nevertheless be entitled to a contributory allowance".

The regulations in this Chapter are made under those powers

Short absence

152. A claimant is to continue to be entitled to an employment and support allowance during the first 4 weeks of a temporary absence from Great Britain if—   **1A.438**

(a) the period of absence is unlikely to exceed 52 weeks; and

(b) while absent from Great Britain, the claimant continues to satisfy the other conditions of entitlement to that employment and support allowance.

GENERAL NOTE

See the commentary to reg.4(1) and (2) of the IS Regs.   **1A.439**

Absence to receive medical treatment

153.—(1) A claimant is to continue to be entitled to an employment and support allowance during the first 26 weeks of a temporary absence from Great Britain if—   **1A.440**

(a) the period of absence is unlikely to exceed 52 weeks;

(b) while absent from Great Britain, the claimant continues to satisfy the other conditions of entitlement to that employment and support allowance;

(c) the claimant is absent from Great Britain solely—

(i) in connection with arrangements made for the treatment of the claimant for a disease or bodily or mental disablement directly related to the claimant's limited capability for work which commenced before leaving Great Britain; or

(ii) because the claimant is accompanying a dependent child in connection with arrangements made for the treatment of that child for a disease or bodily or mental disablement;

(d) those arrangements relate to treatment—

(i) outside Great Britain;

(ii) during the period whilst the claimant is temporarily absent from Great Britain; and

(iii) by, or under the supervision of, a person appropriately qualified to carry out that treatment; and

(e) before leaving Great Britain the claimant sought and received the permission of the Secretary of State to do so.

(2) In paragraph (1)(d)(iii), "appropriately qualified" means qualified to provide medical treatment, physiotherapy or a form of treatment which is similar to, or related to, either of those forms of treatment.

GENERAL NOTE

1A.441   Where the temporary absence is in connection with receiving medical treatment for a condition related to the claimant's limited capacity for work, or because the claimant is accompanying a dependent child who is receiving medical treatment, ESA remains payable for the first 26 weeks of absence, as long as the total length of the absence is unlikely to exceed 52 weeks. Note the requirement to obtain the Secretary of State's permission before departure. Where the medical treatment abroad is paid for by the NHS, see reg.154 below.

Absence in order to receive NHS treatment

1A.442   **154.** A claimant is to continue to be entitled to an employment and support allowance during any period of temporary absence from Great Britain if—

(a) while absent from Great Britain, the claimant continues to satisfy the other conditions of entitlement to that employment and support allowance;

(b) that period of temporary absence is for the purpose of the claimant receiving treatment at a hospital or other institution outside Great Britain where the treatment is being provided—

(i) under section 6(2) of the Health Service Act (Performance of functions outside England) or section 6(2) of the Health Service (Wales) Act (Performance of functions outside Wales);

(ii) pursuant to arrangements made under section 12(1) of the Health Service Act (Secretary of State's arrangements with other bodies), section 10(1) of the Health Service (Wales) Act (Welsh Ministers' arrangements with other bodies), paragraph 18 of Schedule 4 to the Health Service Act (Joint exercise of functions) or paragraph 18 of Schedule 3 to the Health Service (Wales) Act (Joint exercise of functions); or

(iii) under any equivalent provision in Scotland or pursuant to arrangements made under such provision; and

(c) before leaving Great Britain the claimant sought and received the permission of the Secretary of State to do so.

GENERAL NOTE

1A.443   See the commentary to reg.4(3A) of the IS Regs.

Absence of member of family of member of Her Majesty's forces

1A.444   **155.**—(1) A claimant is to continue to be entitled to an employment and support allowance during any period of temporary absence from Great Britain if—

(a) the claimant is a member of the family of a member of Her Majesty's forces and temporarily absent from Great Britain by reason only of the fact that the claimant is living with that member; and

(b) before leaving Great Britain the claimant sought and received the permission of the Secretary of State to do so.

(2) In this regulation "member of the family of a member of Her Majesty's forces" means the spouse, civil partner, son, daughter, step-son, step-daughter, father, father-in-law, step-father, mother, mother-in-law or step-mother of such a member.

CHAPTER 4

MEMBERSHIP OF HOUSEHOLD

Circumstances in which a person is to be treated as being or not being a member of the household

156.—(1) Subject to the following provisions of this regulation— 1A.445
  (a) the claimant and the claimant's partner; and
  (b) where the claimant or the claimant's partner is responsible for a child or young person, that child or young person and any child of that child or young person,
are to be treated as being members of the same household.

(2) Paragraph (1) applies even where any of them is temporarily living away from the other members of the family.

(3) Paragraph (1) does not apply to a person who is living away from the other members of the family where—
  (a) that person does not intend to resume living with the other members of the family; or
  (b) that person's absence from the other members of the family is likely to exceed 52 weeks, unless there are exceptional circumstances (for example where the person is in hospital or otherwise has no control over the length of absence), and the absence is unlikely to be substantially more than 52 weeks.

(4) Paragraph (1) does not apply in respect of any member of a couple or of a polygamous marriage where—
  (a) one, both or all of them are patients detained in a hospital provided under section 4 of the Health Service Act (high security psychiatric services), section 4 of the Health Service (Wales) Act (high security psychiatric services) or section 102 of the National Health Service (Scotland) Act 1978 (state hospitals);
  (b) one, both or all of them are—
    (i) detained in custody pending trial or sentence upon conviction or under a sentence imposed by a court; or
    (ii) on temporary release in accordance with the provisions of the Prison Act 1952 or the Prisons (Scotland) Act 1989;
  (c) the claimant is abroad and does not satisfy the conditions of Chapter 4 of this Part (temporary absence from Great Britain); or
  (d) any one of them is permanently residing in a care home, an Abbeyfield Home or an independent hospital.

(5) A child or young person is not to be treated as a member of the claimant's household where that child or young person is—

255

    (a) placed with the claimant or the claimant's partner by a local authority under section 23(2)(a) of the Children Act 1989 or by a voluntary organisation under section 59(1)(a) of that Act;

    (b) placed with the claimant or the claimant's partner prior to adoption;

    (c) in accordance with a relevant enactment, boarded out with the claimant or the claimant's partner, whether or not with a view to adoption; or

    (d) placed for adoption with the claimant or the claimant's partner pursuant to a decision under the Adoption Agencies Regulations 1983 or the Adoption Agencies (Scotland) Regulations 1996.

(6) Subject to paragraphs (7) and (8), paragraph (1) does not apply to a child or young person who is not living with the claimant and who—

    (a) in a case which does not fall within sub-paragraph (b), has been continuously absent from Great Britain for a period of more than four weeks commencing—

        (i) where that child or young person went abroad before the date of the claim for an employment and support allowance, on the date of that claim;

        (ii) in any other case, on the day which immediately follows the day on which that child or young person went abroad;

    (b) where regulation 153 (absence to receive medical treatment) applies, has been continuously absent from Great Britain for a period of more than 26 weeks, that period commencing—

        (i) where that child or young person went abroad before the date of the claim for an employment and support allowance, on the date of that claim;

        (ii) in any other case, on the day which immediately follows the day on which that child or young person went abroad;

    (c) has been an in-patient or in accommodation for a continuous period of more than 12 weeks commencing—

        (i) where that child or young person became an in-patient or, as the case may be, entered that accommodation, before the date of the claim for an employment and support allowance, with that date; or

        (ii) in any other case, with the date on which that child or young person became an inpatient or entered that accommodation, and, in either case, has not been in regular contact with either the claimant or any member of the claimant's household;

    (d) is being looked after by, or in the care of, a local authority under a relevant enactment;

    (e) has been placed with a person other than the claimant prior to adoption;

    (f) has been boarded out under a relevant enactment with a person other than the claimant prior to adoption;

    (g) has been placed for adoption pursuant to a decision under the Adoption Agencies Regulations 1983 or the Adoption Agencies (Scotland) Regulations 1996; or

(h) is detained in custody pending trial or sentence upon conviction or under a sentence imposed by a court.

(7) Sub-paragraphs (a)(i), (b)(i) and (c)(i) of paragraph (6) do not apply in a case where immediately before the date of claim for an employment and support allowance the claimant was entitled to an income-based jobseeker's allowance or income support.

(8) A child or young person to whom any of the circumstances mentioned in sub-paragraphs (d) or (h) of paragraph (6) applies is to be treated as being a member of the claimant's household only for that part of any benefit week where that child or young person lives with the claimant.

(9) In this regulation—

"accommodation" means accommodation provided by a local authority in a home owned or managed by that local authority—

(a) under sections 21 to 24 of the National Assistance Act 1948 (provision of accommodation);

(b) in Scotland, under section 13B or 59 of the Social Work (Scotland) Act 1968 (provision of residential or other establishment); or

(c) under section 25 of the Mental Health (Care and Treatment) (Scotland) Act 2003 (care and support services etc.), where the accommodation is provided for a person whose stay in that accommodation has become other than temporary; and

"voluntary organisation" has the meaning assigned to it in the Children Act 1989, or in Scotland, by section 94 of the Social Work (Scotland) Act 1968.

(10) For the purposes of these Regulations a person is responsible for a child or young person if that child or young person usually lives with that person.

DEFINITIONS

"Abbeyfield Home"—reg.2(1).
"child"—*ibid.*
"claimant"—Welfare Reform Act 2007, s.24(1).
"family"—reg.2(1) and (3).
"income-based jobseeker's allowance"—*ibid.*
"income support"—*ibid.*
"independent hospital"—*ibid.*
"partner"—*ibid.*
"polygamous marriage"—*ibid.*
"relevant enactment"—*ibid.*
"young person"—*ibid.*

GENERAL NOTE

See the commentary to reg. 16 of the IS Regs. Note however that the ESA has 1A.446 no equivalent of reg. 15 of the IS Regs. Under para.(10) whether or not a person is responsible for a child or young person for the purpose of ESA depends upon whether the "child or young person usually lives with that person" rather than, for IS, who receives child benefit.

PART 12

DISQUALIFICATION

Disqualification for misconduct etc.

1A.447   **157.**—(1) Subject to paragraph (3), paragraph (2) applies where a claimant—

(a) has limited capability for work through the claimant's own misconduct, except in a case where the limited capability is due to pregnancy or a sexually transmitted disease; or

(b) fails without good cause to attend for or submit to medical or other treatment (excluding vaccination, inoculation or major surgery) recommended by a doctor with whom, or a hospital or similar institution with which, the claimant is undergoing medical treatment, which would be likely to remove the limitation on the claimant's capability for work;

(c) fails without good cause to refrain from behaviour calculated to retard the claimant's recovery; or

(d) is, without good cause, absent from the claimant's place of residence without leaving word with the Secretary of State where the claimant may be found.

(2) A claimant referred to in paragraph (1) is to be disqualified for receiving an employment and support allowance for such period not exceeding 6 weeks as the Secretary of State may determine.

(3) Paragraph (1) does not apply where the claimant—

(a) is disqualified for receiving an employment and support allowance by virtue of regulations made under section 7 of the Social Security Fraud Act 2001; or

(b) is a person in hardship.

DEFINITIONS

"claimant"—see WRA 2007, s.24(1).
"doctor"—see reg.2(1).
"medical treatment"—see reg.2(1).
"person in hardship"—see reg.158.
"week"—see reg.2(1).

GENERAL NOTE

1A.448   Disqualification here represents an attempt to deny ESA to those whose behaviour has in some way brought about their limited capability for work, or has worsened it, or where the claimant has behaved inappropriately in some other way.

This regulation provides that (subject to the two exceptions in para.(3)), someone who falls within one of the several "heads" of disqualification examined below must be disqualified for receiving ESA. As under the sickness and invalidity benefits regime (on which see USI Regs, reg.17, revoked from April 13, 1993—pp.737–40 of Bonner, Hooker and White, *Non-Means Tested Benefit: The Legislation* (1994)), and the incapacity benefit system, the maximum period imposable is six weeks. No minimum is specified (unlike disqualification in JSA where one week is specified—Jobseekers Act 1995, s.19(3)). Although, like JSA, ESA is in principle a weekly benefit, payment for less than a week is possible, so arguably the minimum should still be one day (the minimum unit for benefit purposes). While there have been some changes of wording from that in USI Regs, reg.17, governing sickness and invalidity benefits disqualifications and from Incapacity for Work (General) Regulations 1995, reg.18, in so far as the wording remains the same as that incapacity benefit provision, case authorities on that regime and its predecessors remain authoritative. Some of the "heads" are subject to a "good cause" saving. The rulemaking power to further define or restrict "good cause" has not been exercised in this context (WRA 2007, s.18(3)).

If one or more of the "heads" apply, there must be some disqualification: the discretion afforded by the regulation goes only to the length of the period (maximum six weeks). As with exercising the equivalent discretion for job-seeker's allowance purposes, the determining authorities must act judicially and consider each case in the light of its circumstances and give reasons for their choice of period (see *R(U) 8/74(T)*; *R(S) 1/87*; *CS/002/1990*, para.6). The same rules on considering and recording decisions on the matter would apply *(R(U) 4/87)*. Some of the factors relevant in exercising the discretion in that context may equally be relevant here. The burden lies on the decision maker to show that the claimant falls clearly and squarely within the head of disqualification *(R(S) 7/83)*. Where "good cause" is the issue, it falls to the claimant to establish that he had it *(R(S) 9/51)*. *R(S) 1/87* made it abundantly clear that in the same case the same facts could put in issue more than one of the heads of disqualification in USI Regs, reg.17(1). There the heads at issue were paras 17(1)(b) and (1)(d)(ii). The poorly completed record of the SSAT's decision did not make clear on which head they rested disqualification. This was an error of law, a breach of the duty to record reasons for the decision and the material facts on which it is based. Presumably as well as complying with this duty, a tribunal should also comply with *R(U) 2/71* where the case involves the Secretary of State relying on a head of disqualification not set out in the appeal papers or the tribunal relying on a different ground to that relied on by the Secretary of State.

Para.(1)(a)

This penalises certain behaviour by the claimant. Disqualification must be 1A.449 imposed if his incapacity is due to his own misconduct, but two instances where incapacity may have arisen in consequence of what might otherwise be treated as sexual misconduct are expressly stated not to ground disqualification: (a) where the incapacity is due to a sexually transmitted disease; and (b) the case of pregnancy.

Misconduct has not been exhaustively defined. Presumably, by analogy with its use in the unemployment benefit and jobseeker's allowance contexts, it denotes conduct which is blameworthy, reprehensible and wrong. It is unclear in this context, whether merely reckless or negligent conduct will suffice. *R(S)2/53* has been thought to import a requirement of wilfulness, but this may be to read too much into a particular example of misconduct. In that case the Commissioner considered alcoholism, and upheld disqualification. Drinking to such an extent to endanger health raises a prima facie inference of misconduct which can only be rebutted if the claimant proves that the alcoholism was involuntary, the result of disease or disablement which destroyed his willpower, so that he was *unable* to refrain from excessive drinking. The particular evidence in that case of an anxiety state was insufficient to rebut the presumption. Whether in the current medical and social climate the provision could apply to incapacity through heavy smoking remains to be seen. The paragraph could have unfortunate implications for some AIDS victims such as intravenous drug users who become infected nonsexually.

Para. (1) (b)

1A.450   This seems designed to deal with a specific aspect of behaviour which may contribute to further limited capability for work or hinder recovery. Disqualification must be imposed where the claimant fails to attend for or submit to medical or other treatment. The medical or other treatment must be recommended by a doctor with whom, or a hospital or similar institution with which, he is undergoing medical treatment and be such as would be likely to render him capable of work. This formulation may reverse *R(S) 3/57*, depending on the scope of "other treatment". There the blind claimant gave up a vocational training course when she became pregnant and refused to resume it thereafter; under USI Regs, reg.17(1)(c) she had not refused treatment for her disablement since the course could have no effect on her blindness (para.6; *cf. R2/60SB*). Failure to attend for or submit to certain medical or other treatment is explicitly exempt from the sanction, namely failure to attend for or submit to vaccination or inoculation of any kind or to major surgery.

Establishing "good cause" for non-compliance precludes disqualification. In *R(S) 9/51* the claimant did so. Her non-attendance was founded on her own firm conviction that her religious beliefs (Christian Scientist) required her not to. It would not have been enough merely to establish membership of a sect whose religious rules forbade submission to treatment or examination.

Para. (1) (c)

1A.451   Disqualification here penalises a claimant who fails to refrain from behaviour calculated to retard his recovery. "Calculated to retard his recovery" does not import an intention on his part to do so; the test is an objective one: was his behaviour likely to do so. Thus in *R(S) 21/52* the Commissioner upheld disqualification of the claimant, suffering from influenza bronchitis who was taken ill after undertaking a 60-mile drive when so suffering. However in *R(S) 3/57* (above para.(1)(b)) the course was irrelevant to recovery from blindness, so leaving and refusing to resume the course could not ground disqualification. Establishing good cause for the failure precludes disqualification. Mere ignorance of the rules is not good cause (*R(S) 21/52*).

Para. (1) (d)

1A.452   This requires the claimant not to be absent from his place of residence without leaving word as to where he can be found. It is designed to penalise those who deliberately seek to avoid the Department's visiting officers who may call as part of the Department's claims control mechanisms. It will only be invoked where visits have already proved ineffective, and as a matter of law the absence must have occurred during the currency of a claim. The rule cannot apply unless the claimant has a residence; it is not to be interpreted as imposing a requirement to have one (*R(S) 7/83*), so claimants of no fixed abode cannot be caught by it. *R(S) 1/87* requires findings be made as to place of residence, any absence in the relevant period, and on whether the claimant had failed to leave word where he could be found. If those findings showed the claimant's absence from his residence without leaving word as to his whereabouts, it would then fall to the claimant to establish good cause for so acting (see para.12). A claimant's genuine difficulty in leaving word where he might be found was held to constitute good cause in *R(S) 6/55*. There the claimant lived with relatives who were out at work on the three occasions that the visiting officer called. The claimant was out in the park or at the cinema on those occasions, and there was no one with whom he could leave a message. His doctor had advised him to get out as much as possible. Mere ignorance of the rules is not good cause *(R(S) 21/52)*.

Exceptions (para. (3))

Someone disqualified under the specified fraud provision cannot be dis-   **1A.453**
qualified under this regulation (sub-para.(b)). Nor can someone who qualifies as a "person in hardship" as defined in reg.158 (sub-para.(b)).

Meaning of "person in hardship"

158.—(1) A claimant is a "person in hardship" if the claimant—   **1A.454**
   (a) has informed the Secretary of State of the circumstances on which the claimant relies to establish that fact; and
   (b) falls within paragraph (2), (3) or (5).
   (2) A claimant falls within this paragraph if—
   (a) she is pregnant;
   (b) a member of the claimant's family is pregnant;
   (c) the claimant is a single claimant aged less than 18; or
   (d) the claimant is a member of a couple and both members are aged less than 18.
   (3) Subject to paragraph (4), the claimant falls within this paragraph if the claimant or the claimant's partner—
   (a) is responsible for a child or young person who is a member of the claimant's household;
   (b) has been awarded an attendance allowance or the care component;
   (c) has claimed either attendance allowance or disability living allowance and the claim has not been determined;
   (d) devotes a considerable portion of each week to caring for another person who—
      (i) has been awarded an attendance allowance or the care component; or
      (ii) has claimed either attendance allowance or disability living allowance and the claim has not been determined; or
   (e) is aged 60 or more.
   (4) A claimant to whom paragraph (3)(c) or (3)(d)(ii) applies is a person in hardship only for 26 weeks from the date of the claim unless the claimant is a person in hardship under another provision of this regulation.
   (5) The claimant falls within this paragraph where the Secretary of State is satisfied, having regard to all the circumstances and, in particular, the matters set out in paragraph (6), that unless an employment and support allowance is paid, the claimant, or a member of the claimant's family, will suffer hardship.
   (6) The matters referred to in paragraph (5) are—
   (a) the resources which are likely to be available to the claimant and the claimant's family and the length of time for which they might be available; and
   (b) whether there is a substantial risk that essential items, including food, clothing and heating, will cease to be available to the claimant or a member of the claimant's family, or will be available at

considerably reduced levels and the length of time for which this might be so.

(7) In this regulation "care component" means the care component of disability living allowance at the highest or middle rate prescribed under section 72(3) of the Contributions and Benefits Act.

DEFINITIONS

"attendance allowance"—see reg.2(1).
"care component"—see para.(7).
"claimant"—see WRA 2007, s.24(1).
"Contributions and Benefits Act"—see WRA 2006, s.65.
"disability living allowance"—see reg.2(1).
"family"—see reg.2(1).
"person in hardship"—see para.(1).

GENERAL NOTE

1A.455   The effect of this regulation is similar to reg.140 of the JSA Regulations.

Para. (1)
1A.456   A person in hardship cannot be disqualified from receiving ESA under reg.157 (see para.(3)(b) of that reg). This paragraph defines someone as a "person in hardship" who notifies the Secretary of State of the circumstances relied on to establish this, so long as he satisfies the conditions set in paras (2), (3) or (5).

Para. (2)
1A.457   This covers a claimant who is pregnant; a claimant where a family member is pregnant; the claimant is single and under 18; and the claimant who is a member of a couple and both the claimant and partner are under 18.

Paras (3), (4)
1A.458   This covers someone aged 60 or over; someone responsible for a child or young person who is a member of his household someone who has been awarded attendance allowance (note the wider coverage of that term in reg.2(1)) or the care component (middle or higher rate) of disability living allowance (see para.(7)); and a carer who devotes a considerable portion of a week to caring for another who has been awarded attendance allowance (again note the wider coverage of that term in reg.2(1)) or the care component of DLA at middle of higher rate (see para.(7)). The paragraph also brings in, but only for 26 weeks unless the claimant also qualifies under another head, someone who has claimed attendance allowance (again note the wider coverage of that term in reg.2(1)) or middle or higher rate care component of DLA (see para.(7)), but the claim remains undetermined, or the carer devoting a substantial portion of the week to caring for someone in that position (paras (3)(c), (d)(ii), (4)).

Paras (5), (6)
1A.459   These cover the claimant where the Secretary of State is satisfied that unless ESA is paid, the claimant or a member of his family will suffer hardship. In considering whether that is the case, he must have regard to all the circumstances, particularly those set out in para.(6).

Treating a claimant as not having limited capability for work

1A.460   **159.**—(1) Subject to paragraph (2), the claimant is to be treated as not having limited capability for work if the claimant is disqualified for receiving a contributory allowance during a period of imprisonment or detention in legal custody if that disqualification is for more than 6 weeks.

(2) Where the claimant is entitled to an amount under paragraph 3 of Schedule 5 (special cases: prisoners) during a period of imprisonment or detention in legal custody, the claimant is to be treated as not having limited capability for work from the day after the day on which entitlement ended.

DEFINITIONS

"claimant"—see WRA 2007, s.24(1).
contributory allowance—see WRA 2007, s.1(7).

GENERAL NOTE

Those disqualified for contributory ESA under s.18(4) of the Welfare Reform Act for more than six weeks because they are imprisoned or detained in custody are treated by para.(1) as not having limited capability for work.   **1A.461**

Under reg.69 and para.3(b) of Sch.5, a person may be entitled to income-related ESA at a reduced rate while detained in custody pending trial or pending sentence following conviction. In those circumstances, the person is treated by para.(2) as not having limited capability for work from the day after that entitlement ends.

Exceptions from disqualification for imprisonment

160.—(1) Notwithstanding section 18(4)(b) of the Act, a claimant is not disqualified for receiving a contributory allowance for any period during which that claimant is undergoing imprisonment or detention in legal custody—   **1A.462**
- (a) in connection with a charge brought or intended to be brought against the claimant in criminal proceedings;
- (b) pursuant to any sentence; or
- (c) pursuant to any order for detention,

made by a court in such proceedings, unless paragraph (2) applies.

(2) This paragraph applies where—
- (a) a penalty is imposed on the claimant at the conclusion of the proceedings referred to in paragraph (1); or
- (b) in the case of default of payment of a sum adjudged to be paid on conviction a penalty is imposed in respect of such default.

(3) Notwithstanding section 18(4)(b) of the Act, a claimant is not to be disqualified for receiving a contributory allowance, for any period during which the claimant is undergoing detention in legal custody after the conclusion of criminal proceedings if it is a period during which the claimant is liable to be detained in a hospital or similar institution in Great Britain as a person suffering from mental disorder unless—
- (a) the claimant is detained or liable to be detained under section 45A of the Mental Health Act 1983 (hospital and limitation directions) or section 59A of the Criminal Procedure (Scotland) Act 1995 (hospital direction); or
- (b) the claimant is detained or liable to be detained under section 47 of the Mental Health Ac(removal to hospital of persons serving

sentences of imprisonment, etc.) or section 136 of the Mental Health (Care and Treatment) (Scotland) Act 2003 (transfer of prisoners for treatment for mental disorder); or

(c) section 136 of the Mental Health (Care and Treatment) (Scotland) Act 2003 (transfer of prisoners for treatment for mental disorder).

(4) Where—

(a) paragraph (3)(a) or (b) applies, in relation to a claimant; and

(b) a certificate given by or on behalf of the Secretary of State or Scottish Ministers shows the earliest date on which that claimant would have been expected to be discharged from detention under the sentence or order if the claimant had not been transferred to a hospital or similar institution, those paragraphs are to be treated as not satisfied in relation to that claimant from the day following that date.

(5) For the purposes of this regulation—

(a) "court" means any court in the United Kingdom, the Channel Islands or the Isle of Man or in any place to which the Colonial Prisoners Removal Act 1884 applies or any naval court-martial, army court-martial or air force court-martial within the meaning of the Courts-Martial (Appeals) Act 1968 or the Courts-Martial Appeal Court;

(b) "hospital or similar institution" means any place (not being a prison, a young offender institution, a secure training centre, secure accommodation in a children's home or a remand centre, and not being at or in any such place) in which persons suffering from mental disorder are or may be received for care or treatment;

(c) "penalty" means a sentence of imprisonment or detention under section 90 or 91 of the Powers of Criminal Courts (Sentencing) Act 2000, a detention and training order under section 100 of that Act, a sentence of detention for public protection under section 226 of the Criminal Justice Act 2003 or an extended sentence under section 228 of that Act or, in Scotland, under section 205, 207 or 208 of the Criminal Procedure (Scotland) Act 1995;

(d) in relation to a person who is liable to be detained in Great Britain as a result of any order made under the Colonial Prisoners Removal Act 1884, references to a prison must be construed as including references to a prison within the meaning of that Act;

(e) criminal proceedings against any person must be deemed to be concluded upon that person being found insane in those proceedings so that the person cannot be tried or that person's trial cannot proceed.

(6) Where a claimant outside Great Britain is undergoing imprisonment or detention in legal custody and, in similar circumstances in Great Britain, the claimant would, by virtue of this regulation, not have been disqualified for receiving a contributory allowance, the claimant is not disqualified for receiving that allowance by reason only of the imprisonment or detention.

DEFINITIONS

"claimant"—see WRA 2007, s.24(1).
"court"—see para.(5)(a).
"hospital or similar institution"—see para.(5)(b).
"penalty"—see para.(5)(c).
"prison"—see para.(5)(d).

GENERAL NOTE

Under s.18(4) of the WRA 2007, a claimant is disqualified for contributory   **1A.463**
ESA while "undergoing imprisonment or detention in legal custody". This
regulation establishes exceptions to that rule. Under paras (1) and (2), there is
no disqualification while the claimant is in custody pending trial or sentence
unless a penalty is imposed. Payment of contributory ESA is suspended under
reg.161 below during the period when it is not known whether a penalty will
eventually be imposed. By para.(6), the same rules is applied to claimants
imprisoned outside Great Britain. Under para.(3), there is no disqualification
where the claimant is compulsorily detained in hospital following the conclusion
of criminal proceedings unless a prison sentence is imposed and the claimant is
subsequently transferred to hospital under the specified legislation.

Suspension of payment of a contributory allowance during imprisonment

161.—(1) Subject to the following provisions of this regulation, the   **1A.464**
payment of a contributory allowance to any claimant—
  (a) which is excepted from the operation of section 18(4)(b) of the
      Act by virtue of the provisions of regulation 160(2), (3) or (6);
      or
  (b) which is payable otherwise than in respect of a period during
      which the claimant is undergoing imprisonment or detention in
      legal custody,
is suspended while that claimant is undergoing imprisonment or detention in legal custody.

(2) A contributory allowance is not to be suspended while the claimant
is liable to be detained in a hospital or similar institution, as defined in
regulation 160(5), during a period for which in the claimant's case, the
allowance is or would be excepted from the operation of section 18(4)(b)
by virtue of the provisions of regulation 160(3).

(3) Where, by virtue of this regulation, payment of a contributory
allowance is suspended for any period, the period of suspension is not to
be taken into account in calculating any period under the provisions of
regulation 38 of the Social Security (Claims and Payments) Regulations
1987 (extinguishment of right to sums payable by way of benefit which
are not obtained within the prescribed time).

DEFINITIONS

"claimant"—see WRA 2007, s.24(1).
"contributory allowance"—see WRA 2007, s.1(7).
"hospital or similar institution"—see reg.160(5).

GENERAL NOTE

See the commentary to reg.160.   **1A.465**

PART 13

URGENT CASES

Urgent cases

1A.466   **162.**—(1) In a case to which this regulation applies a claimant's weekly applicable amount and that claimant's income and capital are to be calculated in accordance with the following provisions of this Part.

(2) Subject to paragraph (3), this regulation applies to a claimant who is treated as possessing income under regulation 107(1) (notional income).

(3) This regulation is only to apply to a claimant to whom paragraph (2) applies, where the income that claimant is treated as possessing by virtue of regulation 107(1) is not readily available to that claimant; and—

(a) the amount of an income-related allowance which would be payable but for this Part is less than the amount of an income-related allowance payable by virtue of the provisions of this Part; and

(b) the Secretary of State is satisfied that, unless the provisions of this Part are applied to the claimant, the claimant or the claimant's family will suffer hardship.

GENERAL NOTE

1A.467   This regulation is similar to reg.70 of the IS Regs and reg.147 of the JSA Regs.

Applicable amounts in urgent cases

1A.468   **163.** For the purposes of calculating any entitlement to an income-related allowance under this

Part—

(a) except in a case to which sub-paragraph (b) or (c) applies, a claimant's weekly applicable amount is to be the aggregate of—

(i) 90% of the amount applicable in respect of himself or herself or, if the claimant is a member of a couple or of a polygamous marriage, of the amount applicable in respect of both of them under paragraph 1(1), (2) or (3) of Schedule 4 or, as the case may be, the amount applicable in respect of them under regulation 68 (polygamous marriages);

(ii) the amount, if applicable, specified in Part 2 of Schedule 4 (premiums);

(iii) the amount, if applicable, specified in Part 4 of Schedule 4 (components); and

(iv) any amounts applicable under regulation 67(1)(c) or, as the case may be, 68(1)(d (housing costs);

(b) in the case of a claimant to whom any paragraph of Schedule 5 (special cases) applies, the applicable amount is to be the aggregate of—

(i) 90% of the amount applicable in column 2 of that Schedule in respect of the claimant and partner (if any);

(ii) the amount, if applicable, specified in Part 2 of Schedule 4;

(iii) the amount, if applicable, specified in Part 4 of Schedule 4; and

(iv) any amounts applicable under regulation 67(1)(c) or, as the case may be, 68(1)(d); or

(c) in the case of a claimant to whom regulation 162(2) applies, where that claimant is appealing to an appeal tribunal constituted under Chapter 1 of Part 1 of the Social Security Act 1998, against a decision which embodies a determination that the claimant does not have limited capability for work, the applicable amount is to be the aggregate of—

(i) 90% of the amount applicable in respect of himself or herself or, if the claimant is a member of a couple or of a polygamous marriage, of the amount applicable in respect of both of them under paragraph 1(1), (2) or (3) of Schedule 4 or, as the case may be, the amount applicable in respect of them under regulation 68 (polygamous marriages);

(ii) the amount, if applicable, specified in Part 2 of Schedule 4 (premiums); and

(iii) any amounts applicable under regulation 67(1)(c) or, as the case may be, 68(1)(d).

GENERAL NOTE

This regulation is similar to reg.71 of the IS Regs and reg.148 of the JSA Regs.

1A.469

Assessment of income and capital in urgent cases

164.—(1) The claimant's income is to be calculated in accordance with Part 10 subject to the following modifications—

1A.470

(a) any income other than—

(i) a payment of income or income in kind made under the Macfarlane Trust, the Macfarlane (Special Payments) Trust, the Macfarlane (Special Payments) (No. 2) Trust, the Fund, the Eileen Trust or [¹ the Independent Living Fund (2006)]; or

(ii) income to which paragraph 9 (but only to the extent that a concessionary payment would be due under that paragraph for any non-payment of an income-related allowance under regulation 162 (urgent cases) or of jobseeker's allowance under regulation 147 of the Jobseeker's Allowance Regulations (urgent cases)), 35, 41(2), (3) or (4), 42, 64 or 65 of Schedule 8 (disregard of income other than earnings) applies, possessed or treated as possessed by the claimant, is to be taken into account in full notwithstanding any provision in that Part disregarding the whole or any part of that income;

(b) any income to which regulation 118 (calculation of tariff income from capital) applies is to be disregarded;

(c) income treated as capital by virtue of regulation 112(1), (2), (3) and (7) (income treated as capital) is to be taken into account as income;

(d) in a case to which regulation 162(2) (urgent cases) applies, any income to which regulation 107(1) applies is to be disregarded.

(2) The claimant's capital calculated in accordance with Part 10, but including any capital referred to in—

(a) paragraph 3;

(b) to the extent that such assets as are referred to in paragraph 10 consist of liquid assets, paragraph 10;

(c) except to the extent that the arrears referred to in paragraph 11 consist of arrears of housing benefit payable under [1 . . .] Part 7 of the Contributions and Benefits Act or any arrears of benefit due under regulation 162, or regulation 147 of the Jobseeker's Allowance Regulations (urgent cases), paragraph 11; and

(d) paragraphs 13(b), 24 and 32, of Schedule 9 (capital to be disregarded), are to be taken into account in full and the amount of an income-related allowance which would, but for this paragraph be payable under this regulation, is to be payable only to the extent that it exceeds the amount of that capital.

AMENDMENT

1. Employment and Support Allowance (Miscellaneous Amendments) Regulations 2008 (SI 2008/2428), reg.11 (October 27, 2008).

GENERAL NOTE

1A.471   This regulation is similar to reg.72 of the IS Regs and reg.149 of the JSA Regs.

PART 14

PERIODS OF LESS THAN A WEEK

Entitlement for less than a week—amount of an employment and support allowance payable

1A.472   **165.**—(1) This regulation applies where the claimant is entitled to an employment and support allowance for a part-week and is subject to the following provisions of this Part.

(2) The amount payable by way of an income-related allowance in respect of that part-week is to be calculated by applying the formula—

(a) where the claimant has no income—

$$\frac{(N \times A)}{7}$$

or
(b) where the claimant has an income—

$$\frac{N \times (A - 1)}{7} - B$$

where—

A is the claimant's weekly applicable amount in the relevant week;

B is the amount of any employment and support allowance, job-seeker's allowance, income support, maternity allowance, incapacity benefit or severe disablement allowance payable to the claimant or the claimant's partner in respect of any day in the part-week;

I is the claimant's weekly income in the relevant week; and

N is the number of days in the part week.

(3) The amount payable by way of a contributory allowance in respect of a part-week is to be calculated by applying the formula—

$$\frac{(N \times X) - Y}{7}$$

where—

X is the amount calculated in accordance with section 2(1) of the Act;

Y is the amount of any widow's benefit, widowed parent's allowance, bereavement allowance, training allowance, carer's allowance and any increase in disablement pension payable in accordance with Part 1 of Schedule 7 to the Contributions and Benefits Act (Unemployability Supplement) payable in respect of any day in the part-week;

N is the number of days in the part-week.

(4) In this Part—

"part-week" means an entitlement to an employment and support allowance in respect of any period of less than a week;

"relevant week" means the period of 7 days determined in accordance with regulation 166.

GENERAL NOTE

This regulation is similar to reg.150 of the JSA Regs.   1A.473

Relevant week

166.—(1) Where a part-week—

(a) is the whole period for which an employment and support allowance is payable, or occurs at the beginning of an award, the relevant week is the period of 7 days ending on the last day of that part-week; or

(b) occurs at the end of an award, the relevant week is the period of 7 days beginning on the first day of the part-week.

(2) Where a claimant has an award of an employment and support allowance and that claimant's benefit week changes, for the purpose of calculating the amounts of an employment and support allowance payable for the part-week beginning on the day after the last complete benefit

269

week before the change and ending immediately before the change, the relevant week is the period of 7 days beginning on the day after the last complete benefit week.

DEFINITIONS

"benefit week"—reg.2(1).
"claimant"—Welfare Reform Act 2007, s.24(1).
"part-week"—reg.165(4).
"relevant week"—*ibid.*

GENERAL NOTE

1A.474   This regulation is similar to reg.152 of the JSA Regs.

Modification in the calculation of income

1A.475   **167.** For the purposes of regulation 165 (entitlement for less than a week—amount of an employment and support allowance payable), a claimant's income and, in determining the amount payable by way of an income-related allowance, the income of any person which the claimant is treated as possessing under regulations made under section 17(3) of the Act, regulation 68 (polygamous marriages) or regulation 83 (calculation of income and capital of members of claimant's family and of a polygamous marriage), is to be calculated in accordance with Parts 10 (income and capital) and 13 (urgent cases) subject to the following changes—

(a) any income which is due to be paid in the relevant week is to be treated as paid on the first day of that week;

(b) in determining the amount payable by way of an income-related allowance, any jobseeker's allowance, employment and support allowance, income support, maternity allowance, incapacity benefit or severe disablement allowance payable in the relevant week but not in respect of any day in the part-week is to be disregarded;

(c) the amount referred to as B in regulation 165(2) is to be disregarded;

(d) in determining the amount payable by way of a contributory allowance, any widow's benefit, training allowance, widowed parent's allowance, bereavement allowance, carer's allowance and any increase in disablement pension payable in accordance with Part 1 of Schedule 7 to the Contributions and Benefits Act (unemployability supplement) which is payable in the relevant week but not in respect of any day in the part-week is to be disregarded;

(e) where the part-week occurs at the end of the claim—
    (i) any income; or
    (ii) any change in the amount of income of the same kind, which is first payable within the relevant week but not on any day in the part-week is to be disregarded;

(f) where only part of the weekly balance of income is taken into account in the relevant week, the balance is to be disregarded.

This regulation is similar to reg.153 of the JSA Regs.   **1A.476**

Reduction in certain cases

168. The reduction to be made in accordance with regulations 157   **1A.477**
and 158 is an amount equal to one seventh of the reduction which would
be made under those regulations for a week, multiplied by the number of
days in a part-week.

GENERAL NOTE

This regulation is similar to reg.154 of the JSA Regs.   **1A.478**

SCHEDULE 1   **Regulation 2(2)**

HER MAJESTY'S FORCES

PART 1

PRESCRIBED ESTABLISHMENTS AND ORGANISATIONS

1. Any of the regular naval, military or air forces of the Crown.   **1A.479**
2. Royal Fleet Reserve.
3. Royal Navy Reserve.
4. Royal Marines Reserve.
5. Army Reserve.
6. Territorial Army.
7. Royal Air Force Reserve.
8. Royal Auxiliary Air Force.
9. The Royal Irish Regiment, to the extent that its members are not members of any
force falling within paragraph 1.

PART 2

ESTABLISHMENTS AND ORGANISATIONS OF WHICH HER MAJESTY'S FORCES DO NOT
CONSIST

10. Her Majesty's forces are not to be taken to consist of any of the establishments or   **1A.480**
organisations specified in Part 1 of this Schedule by virtue only of the employment in such
establishment or organisation of the following persons—
   (a) any person who is serving as a member of any naval force of Her Majesty's forces
and who (not having been an insured person under the National Insurance Act 1965
and not having been a contributor under the Social Security Act 1975 or not being
a contributor under the Contributions and Benefits Act) locally entered that force at
an overseas base;
   (b) any person who is serving as a member of any military force of Her Majesty's forces
and who entered that force, or was recruited for that force outside the United
Kingdom, and the depot of whose unit is situated outside the United Kingdom;
   (c) any person who is serving as a member of any air force of Her Majesty's forces and
who entered that force, or was recruited for that force, outside the United Kingdom,
and is liable under the terms of engagement to serve only in a specified part of the
world outside the United Kingdom.

GENERAL NOTE

See the commentary to the definition of "member of Her Majesty's forces "in   **1A.481**
reg.2(1).

1A.482

SCHEDULE 2

ASSESSMENT OF WHETHER A CLAIMANT HAS LIMITED CAPABILITY FOR WORK

PART 1

PHYSICAL DISABILITIES

(1) *Activity*	(2) *Descriptors*	(3) *Points*
1. Walking with a walking stick or other aid if such aid is normally used.	1 (a) Cannot walk at all.	15
	(b) Cannot walk more than 50 metres on level ground without repeatedly stopping or severe discomfort.	15
	(c) Cannot walk up or down two steps even with the support of a handrail.	15
	(d) Cannot walk more than 100 metres on level ground without stopping or severe discomfort.	9
	(e) Cannot walk more than 200 metres on level ground without stopping or severe discomfort.	6
	(f) None of the above apply.	0
2. Standing and sitting.	2 (a) Cannot stand for more than 10 minutes, unassisted by another person, even if free to move around, before needing to sit down.	15
	(b) Cannot sit in a chair with a high back and no arms for more than 10 minutes before needing to move from the chair because the degree of discomfort experienced makes it impossible to continue sitting.	15
	(c) Cannot rise to standing from sitting in an upright chair without physical assistance from another person.	15
	(d) Cannot move between one seated position and another seated position located next to one another without receiving physical assistance from another person.	15
	(e) Cannot stand for more than 30 minutes, even if free to move around, before needing to sit down.	6

272

(1) Activity			(2) Descriptors	(3) Points
		(f)	Cannot sit in a chair with a high back and no arms for more than 30 minutes without needing to move from the chair because the degree of discomfort experienced makes it impossible to continue sitting.	6
		(g)	None of the above apply.	0
3. Bending or kneeling.	3	(a)	Cannot bend to touch knees and straighten up again.	15
		(b)	Cannot bend, kneel or squat, as if to pick a light object, such as a piece of paper, situated 15cm from the floor on a low shelf, and to move it and straighten up again without the help of another person.	9
		(c)	Cannot bend, kneel or squat, as if to pick a light object off the floor and straighten up again without the help of another person.	6
		(d)	None of the above apply.	0
4. Reaching.	4	(a)	Cannot raise either arm as if to put something in the top pocket of a coat or jacket.	15
		(b)	Cannot put either arm behind back as if to put on a coat or jacket.	15
		(c)	Cannot raise either arm to top of head as if to put on a hat.	9
		(d)	Cannot raise either arm above head height as if to reach for something.	6
		(e)	None of the above apply.	0
5. Picking up and moving or transferring by the use of the upper body and arms (excluding all other activities specified in Part 1 of this Schedule).	5	(a)	Cannot pick up and move a 0.5 litre carton full of liquid with either hand.	15
		(b)	Cannot pick up and move a one litre carton full of liquid with either hand.	9
		(c)	Cannot pick up and move a light but bulky object such as an empty cardboard box, requiring the use of both hands together.	6
		(d)	None of the above apply.	0
6. Manual dexterity.	6	(a)	Cannot turn a "star-headed" sink tap with either hand.	15
		(b)	Cannot pick up a £1 coin or equivalent with either hand.	15
		(c)	Cannot turn the pages of a book with either hand.	15
		(d)	Cannot physically use a pen or pencil.	9
		(e)	Cannot physically use a conventional keyboard or mouse.	9

(1) *Activity*		(2) *Descriptors*	(3) *Points*
	(f)	Cannot do up/undo small buttons, such as shirt or blouse buttons.	9
	(g)	Cannot turn a "star-headed" sink tap with one hand but can with the other.	6
	(h)	Cannot pick up a £1 coin or equivalent with one hand but can with the other.	6
	(i)	Cannot pour from an open 0.5 litre carton full of liquid.	6
	(j)	None of the above apply.	0
7. Speech.	7 (a)	Cannot speak at all.	15
	(b)	Speech cannot be understood by strangers.	15
	(c)	Strangers have great difficulty understanding speech.	9
	(d)	Strangers have some difficulty understanding speech.	6
	(e)	None of the above apply.	0
8. Hearing with a hearing aid or other aid if normally worn.	8 (a)	Cannot hear at all.	15
	(b)	Cannot hear well enough to be able to hear someone talking in a loud voice in a quiet room, sufficiently clearly to distinguish the words being spoken.	15
	(c)	Cannot hear someone talking in a normal voice in a quiet room, sufficiently clearly to distinguish the words being spoken.	9
	(d)	Cannot hear someone talking in a loud voice in a busy street, sufficiently clearly to distinguish the words being spoken.	6
	(e)	None of the above apply.	0
9. Vision including visual acuity and visual fields, in normal daylight or bright electric light, with glasses or other aid to vision if such aid is normally worn.	9 (a)	Cannot see at all.	15
	(b)	Cannot see well enough to read 16 point print at a distance of greater than 20cm.	15
	(c)	Has 50% or greater reduction of visual fields.	15
	(d)	Cannot see well enough to recognise a friend at a distance of a least 5 metres.	9
	(e)	Has 25% or more but less than 50% reduction of visual fields.	6
	(f)	Cannot see well enough to recognise a friend at a distance of at least 15 metres.	6
	(g)	None of the above apply.	0

(1)	(2)	(3)
Activity	*Descriptors*	*Points*
10 (a) Continence other than enuresis (bed wetting) where the claimant does not have an artificial stoma or urinary collecting device.	10 (a) (i) Has no voluntary control over the evacuation of the bowel.	15
	10 (a) (ii) Has no voluntary control over the voiding of the bladder.	15
	10 (a) (iii) At least once a month loses control of bowels so that the claimant cannot control the full evacuation of the bowel.	15
	10 (a) (iv) At least once a week, loses control of bladder so that the claimant cannot control the full voiding of the bladder.	15
	10 (a) (v) Occasionally loses control of bowels so that the claimant cannot control the full evacuation of the bowel.	9
	10 (a) (vi) At least once a month loses control of bladder so that the claimant cannot control the full voiding of the bladder.	6
	10 (a) (vii) Risks losing control of bowels or bladder so that the claimant cannot control the full evacuation of the bowel or the full voiding of the bladder if not able to reach a toilet quickly.	6
	10 (a) (viii) None of the above apply.	0
10 (b) Continence where the claimant uses a urinary collecting device, worn for the majority of the time including an indwelling urethral or suprapubic catheter.	10 (b) (i) Is unable to affix, remove or empty the catheter bag or other collecting device without receiving physical assistance from another person.	15
	10 (b) (ii) Is unable to affix, remove or empty the catheter bag or other collecting device without causing leakage of contents.	15
	10 (b) (iii) Has no voluntary control over the evacuation of the bowel.	15
	10 (b) (iv) At least once a month, loses control of bowels so that the claimant cannot control the full evacuation of the bowel.	15
	10 (b) (v) Occasionally loses control of bowels so that the claimant cannot control the full evacuation of the bowel.	9

(1) Activity	(2) Descriptors		(3) Points
	10 (b) (vi)	Risks losing control of bowels so that the claimant cannot control the full evacuation of the bowel if not able to reach a toilet quickly.	6
	10 (b) (vii)	None of the above apply.	0
10 (c) Continence other than enuresis (bed wetting) where the claimant has an artificial stoma.	10 (c) (i)	Is unable to affix, remove or empty stoma appliance without receiving physical assistance from another person.	15
	10 (c) (ii)	Is unable to affix remove or empty stoma appliance without causing leakage of contents.	15
	10 (c) (iii)	Where the claimant's artificial stoma relates solely to the evacuation of the bowel, at least once a week, loses control of bladder so that the claimant cannot control the full voiding of the bladder.	15
	10 (c) (iv)	Where the claimant's artificial stoma relates solely to the evacuation of the bowel, at last once a month, loses control of bladder so that the claimant cannot control the full voiding of the bladder.	9
	10 (c) (v)	Where the claimant's artificial stoma relates solely to the evacuation of the bowel, risks losing control of the bladder so that the claimant cannot control the full voiding of the bladder if not able to reach a toilet quickly.	6
	10 (c) (vi)	None of the above apply.	0
11. Remaining conscious during waking moments.	11 (a)	At least once a week, has an involuntary episode of lost or altered consciousness, resulting in significantly disrupted awareness or concentration.	15
	(b)	At least once a month, has an involuntary episode of lost or altered consciousness, resulting in significantly disrupted awareness or concentration.	9

(1)	*(2)*	*(3)*
Activity	*Descriptors*	*Points*
	(c) At least twice in the six months immediately preceding the assessment, has had an involuntary episode of lost or altered consciousness, resulting in significantly disrupted awareness or concentration.	6
	(d) None of the above apply.	0

PART 2

MENTAL, COGNITIVE AND INTELLECTUAL FUNCTION ASSESSMENT

1A.483

(1)	*(2)*	*(3)*
Activity	*Descriptors*	*Points*
12. Learning or comprehension in the completion of tasks.	12 (a) Cannot learn or understand how to successfully complete a simple task, such as setting an alarm clock, at all.	15
	(b) Needs to witness a demonstration, given more than once on the same occasion, of how to carry out a simple task before the claimant is able to learn or understand how to complete the task successfully, but would be unable to successfully complete the task the following day without receiving a further demonstration of how to complete it.	15
	(c) Needs to witness a demonstration of how to carry out a simple task, before the claimant is able to learn or understand how to complete the task successfully, but would be unable to successfully complete the task the following day without receiving a verbal prompt from another person.	9
	(d) Needs to witness a demonstration of how to carry out a moderately complex task, such as the steps involved in operating a washing machine to correctly clean clothes, before the claimant is able to learn or understand how to complete the task successfully, but would be unable to successfully complete the task the following day without receiving a verbal prompt from another person.	9

(1)	(2)	(3)
Activity	*Descriptors*	*Points*
	(e) Needs verbal instructions as to how to carry out a simple task before the claimant is able to learn or understand how to complete the task successfully, but would be unable, within a period of less than one week, to successfully complete the task the following day without receiving a verbal prompt from another person.	6
	(f) None of the above apply.	0
13. Awareness of hazard.	13 (a) Reduced awareness of the risks of everyday hazards (such as boiling water or sharp objects) would lead to daily instances of or to near-avoidance of: (i) injury to self or others; or (ii) significant damage to property or possessions, to such an extent that overall day to day life cannot successfully be managed.	15
	(b) Reduced awareness of the risks of everyday hazards would lead for the majority of the time to instances of or to near-avoidance of: (i) injury to self or others; or (ii) significant damage to property or possessions, to such an extent that overall day to day life cannot successfully be managed without supervision from another person.	9
	(c) Reduced awareness of the risks of everyday hazards has led or would lead to frequent instances of or to near-avoidance of: (i) injury to self or others; or (ii) significant damage to property or possessions, but not to such an extent that overall day to day life cannot be managed when such incidents occur.	6
	(d) None of the above apply.	0
14. Memory and concentration.	14 (a) On a daily basis, forgets or loses concentration to such an extent that overall day to day life cannot be successfully managed without receiving verbal prompting, given by someone else in the claimant's presence.	15

(1) Activity	(2) Descriptors	(3) Points
	(b) For the majority of the time, forgets or loses concentration to such an extent that overall day to day life cannot be successfully managed without receiving verbal prompting, given by someone else in the claimant's presence.	9
	(c) Frequently forgets or loses concentration to such an extent that overall day to day life can only be successfully managed with pre-planning, such as making a daily written list of all tasks forming part of daily life that are to be completed.	6
	(d) None of the above apply.	0
15. Execution of tasks.	15 (a) Is unable to successfully complete any everyday task.	15
	(b) Takes more than twice the length of time it would take a person without any form of mental disablement, to successfully complete an everyday task with which the claimant is familiar.	15
	(c) Takes more than one and a half times but no more than twice the length of time it would take a person without any form of mental disablement to successfully complete an everyday task with which the claimant is familiar.	9
	(d) Takes one and a half times the length of time it would take a person without any form of mental disablement to successfully complete an everyday task with which the claimant is familiar.	6
	(e) None of the above apply.	0
16. Initiating and sustaining personal action.	16 (a) Cannot, due to cognitive impairment or a severe disorder of mood or behaviour, initiate or sustain any personal action (which means planning, organisation, problem solving, prioritising or switching tasks).	15
	(b) Cannot, due to cognitive impairment or a severe disorder of mood or behaviour, initiate or sustain personal action without requiring verbal prompting given by another person in the claimant's presence for the majority of the time.	15

279

(1) Activity	(2) Descriptors	(3) Points
	(c) Cannot, due to cognitive impairment or a severe disorder of mood or behaviour, initiate or sustain personal action without requiring verbal prompting given by another person in the claimant's presence for the majority of the time.	9
	(d) Cannot, due to cognitive impairment or a severe disorder of mood or behaviour, initiate or sustain personal action without requiring frequent verbal prompting given by another person in the claimant's presence.	6
	(e) None of the above apply.	0
17. Coping with change.	17 (a) Cannot cope with very minor, expected changes in routine, to the extent that overall day to day life cannot be managed.	15
	(b) Cannot cope with expected changes in routine (such as a pre-arranged permanent change to the routine time scheduled for a lunch break), to the extent that overall day to day life is made significantly more difficult.	9
	(c) Cannot cope with minor, unforeseen changes in routine (such as an unexpected change of the timing of an appointment on the day it is due to occur), to the extent that overall, day to day life is made significantly more difficult.	6
	(d) None of the above apply.	0
18. Getting about.	18 (a) Cannot get to any specified place with which the claimant is, or would be, familiar.	15
	(b) Is unable to get to a specified place with which the claimant is familiar, without being accompanied by another person on each occasion.	15
	(c) For the majority of the time is unable to get to a specified place with which the claimant is familiar without being accompanied by another person.	9
	(d) Is frequently unable to get to a specified place with which the claimant is familiar without being accompanied by another person.	6
	(e) None of the above apply.	0

(1) Activity	(2) Descriptors	(3) Points
19. Coping with social situations.	19 (a) Normal activities, for example, visiting new places or engaging in social contact, are precluded because of overwhelming fear or anxiety.	15
	(b) Normal activities, for example, visiting new places or engaging in social contact, are precluded for the majority of the time due to overwhelming fear or anxiety.	
	(c) Normal activities, for example, visiting new places or engaging in social contact, are frequently precluded, due to overwhelming fear or anxiety.	6
	(d) None of the above apply.	0
20. Propriety of behaviour with other people.	20 (a) Has unpredictable outbursts of aggressive, disinhibited, or bizarre behaviour, being either: (i) sufficient to cause disruption to others on a daily basis; or (ii) of such severity that although occurring less frequently than on a daily basis, no reasonable person would be expected to tolerate them.	15
	(b) Has a completely disproportionate reaction to minor events or to criticism to the extent that the claimant has an extreme violent outburst leading to threatening behaviour or actual physical violence.	15
	(c) Has unpredictable outbursts of aggressive, disinhibited or bizarre behaviour, sufficient in severity and frequency to cause disruption for the majority of the time.	9
	(d) Has a strongly disproportionate reaction to minor events or to criticism, to the extent that the claimant cannot manage overall day to day life when such events or criticism occur.	9
	(e) Has unpredictable outbursts of aggressive, disinhibited or bizarre behaviour, sufficient to cause frequent disruption.	6
	(f) Frequently demonstrates a moderately disproportionate reaction to minor events or to criticism but not to such an extent that the claimant cannot manage overall day to day life when such events or criticism occur.	6
	(g) None of the above apply.	0

(1)	(2)	(3)
Activity	*Descriptors*	*Points*

21. Dealing with other people.	21 (a) Is unaware of impact of own behaviour to the extent that: (i) has difficulty relating to others even for brief periods, such as a few hours; or (ii) causes distress to others on a daily basis.	15
	(b) The claimant misinterprets verbal or non-verbal communication to the extent of causing himself or herself significant distress on a daily basis.	15
	(c) Is unaware of impact of own behaviour to the extent that: (i) has difficulty relating to others for longer periods, such as a day or two; or (ii) causes distress to others for the majority of the time.	9
	(d) The claimant misinterprets verbal or non-verbal communication to the extent of causing himself or herself significant distress to himself for the majority of the time.	9
	(e) Is unaware of impact of own behaviour to the extent that: (i) has difficulty relating to others for prolonged periods, such as a week; or (ii) frequently causes distress to others.	6
	(f) The claimant misinterprets verbal or non-verbal communication to the extent of causing himself or herself significant distress on a frequent basis.	6
	(g) None of the above apply.	0

DEFINITION

"claimant"—see WRA 2007, s.24(1).

GENERAL NOTE

I A note on the Work Capability Assessment (WCA), decision-making, medical examination and process

1A.484   The new Work Capability Assessment (WCA) underpinning ESA was devised by the DWP's Health Work and Wellbeing Directorate with input from two technical working groups, one focusing on mental health and learning difficulties, the other on physical function and conditions (hereinafter "review group"). The review group consisted of medical and other relevant experts. It examined how the incapacity benefits' regime's Personal Capability Assessment (PCA) could be improved and updated so as to reflect the many changes since its inception:

> "in the prevalence of disabling conditions; in advances in medical science resulting in the availability of new and more effective medical interventions; and in the workplace environment. The Disability Discrimination Act, introduced after the PCA had been developed, has influenced the ability of employers to make reasonable adjustments to accommodate people with long term disabilities. It has also raised the expectations of disabled people that adjustments should be made to enable them to work."

The work of the review group fed into the drafting of the regulations on the WCA. After that first element had been developed work continued on the second and third elements of the WCA, although nothing has been published on this. Government anticipates that the WCA will "fail" some 60,000 claimants a year who would have "passed" the PCA (DWP, *Impact Assessment of the Employment and support Allowance Regulations 2008—Public sector Impact Only* in *Explanatory Memorandum to Employment and Support Allowance Regulations 2008 (SI 2008/794) and the Employment and Support Allowance (Transitional Provisions) Regulations 2008 (SI 2008/795)*, p.9). But the three-element WCA is not merely an incapacity-based tool for determining entitlement to ESA. That remains true of its first element, but its second element is rather a more positive assessment considering ability to benefit from work-related activity with a view to promoting capacity for work. The first element is an assessment of limited capability to work (hereinafter the WCAt) (the subject of this Schedule). The second element is an assessment of limited capacity to engage in work-related activity (hereinafter WRAAt)(the subject of Sch.3). Both assessments will generally be conducted at the same time by the same health care professional. Those found not to have limited capacity for work related activity (expected to be some 90% of new claimants) will in addition have to undergo the third element of the WCA: a work-focused health related assessment (WFHRAt). In many cases, all three elements of the new WCA will be covered in a single appointment with a health care professional working for Medical Services (MS), the company which contracts with the DWP to deliver these assessments.

This schedule deals with the WCAt (what the DWP call the LCWA) and establishing limited capability for work: the core element of entitlement to ESA. The vast majority of claimants for ESA will be subject to this first element of the new WCA through a face to face assessment with a trained healthcare professional testing the claimant against the activities and descriptors in the Schedule, in the light of the material in the claimant's questionnaire, any evidence from the GP and the professional's examination. Assessment will take place much earlier than in an equivalent claim for IB.

The Government's view is that the overwhelming majority of customers are capable of some work, given the right support. The approach is designed to treat people in line with their capabilities, instead of making assumptions based on their condition. Hence, because the ESA tests are designed to assess which claimants can benefit from the help towards work afforded by work-related activity, to "write off" from the chance of work as few people as possible, very few groups are exempt from the WCAt: the terminally ill; those receiving treatment by way of intravenous, intraperitoneal or intrathecal chemotherapy; such of those recovering from such treatment as the Secretary of State is satisfied should be treated as having limited capability for work; those excluded or prevented from working as a carrier, or having been in contact with a case of relevant disease (food poisoning, infectious or notifiable diseases covered by a variety of public health enactments); and pregnant women at a certain stage in pregnancy or where there is a serious risk of damage to their or their unborn child's health if they do not refrain from work (reg.20) Hospital in patients (reg.25) and persons undergoing or recovering from certain regular treatments (e.g. plasmapheresis, radio therapy, dialysis, parenteral nutrition) for at least two days a week, (reg.26) are also treated as having limited capability for work. All such persons are exempt from the information gathering requirements with respect to the WCAt (reg.21(3) Decision-makers have discretion in respect of all claimants on whether it is necessary in their case to complete the questionnaire or require more information than is provided by the claimant's doctor under the Medical Evidence Regs (reg.21(2)). Whether someone is required to undergo a medical examination is also a matter of decision-maker discretion (reg.23) Typically, most claimants will have both to complete the questionnaire (form ESA50) and undergo medical examination, usually at a medical examination centre, but sometimes in the claimant's home. Failure to do so, without good cause, is as usual sanctioned by treating the person as not having limited capability for work, thus denying benefit (regs 22–24) The Work Capability Assessment is a face to face meeting, lasting between 75 and 90 minutes, depending on whether just two or all three elements of the WCA are carried out. It explores how the claimant's illness or disability affects their ability to work and carry out day-to-day activity Each part of the assessment will be carried out by specially trained healthcare professionals (whether doctor or nurse) approved by the Secretary of State to assess these matters and report to the decision-maker, generally in the form of a computer-generated report.

What, then, are the terms of the new WCAt (LCWA)? And in what key respects does it differ from the PCA with which readers will be familiar? The WRA 2007 stipulates merely that whether a person's capability for work is limited by his physical or mental condition and, if so, whether the limitation is such that it is not reasonable to require him to work is to be determined in accordance with regulations. ESA Regulations, reg.19(1) elaborates that this is to be determined on the basis of a limited capability for work assessment (hereinafter WCAt), that is by:

> "an assessment of the extent to which a claimant who has some specific disease or bodily or mental disablement is capable of performing the activities pre-scribed in Schedule 2 or is incapable by reason of such disease or bodily or mental disablement of performing those activities" (reg.19(2)).

This is familiar stuff for those who have worked with the all work test or its successor, personal capability assessment. The claimant is to be matched, in the light of all the evidence, by the decision-maker or tribunal against a reformulated range of activities and descriptors, and an appropriate "score" awarded. The threshold "score" for entitlement remains 15 points, but as regards its computa-tion, there are both "old" and "new" elements".

It is stressed that incapability to perform an activity must arise from a specific bodily disease or disablement, a specific mental illness or disablement, or as a direct result of treatment provided by a registered medical practitioner, for such a disease, illness or disablement (reg.19(5)). The extent of capability to perform a physical activity has, as with IB, to be assessed as if the claimant is wearing any prosthesis with which he is fitted or wearing or using any aid or appliance which is normally worn or used. In computing the score, where more than one descrip-tor in respect of a particular activity applies, only the highest is counted towards the total "score" (reg.19(4)). Otherwise one simply adds up the total of the particular scores in respect of each activity, whether physical or mental, to see if the threshold of 15 points is reached. If it is, or is exceeded, the claimant has established limited capability for work, grounding entitlement to the basic allow-ance in ESA. The matter may be determined afresh where the Secretary of State wishes to ascertain (i) whether there has been a relevant change of circumstances

284

in relation to the claimant's physical or mental condition; (ii) whether the previous decision was made in ignorance of, or was based on a mistake as to, some material fact; or at least three months have passed since the last decision (reg.19(7), (8)).

If the threshold score is not attained, limited capability for work has not been established, there can be no entitlement to ESA and the unsuccessful claimant (subject to retention of ESA pending appeal) will have to look for income maintenance to JSA or IS.

Schedule 2 contains 21 activities. Eleven deal with physical disabilities. Some of these are familiar from the PCA. Others (vision, continence, remaining conscious during waking moments) have been elaborated or broadened (e.g. there is now no requirement as regards remaining conscious that this be "without having epileptic or similar seizures during waking moments"). Sitting (PCA activity 3), standing (PCA activity 4) and rising from sitting (PCA activity 5) have in the WCA been compressed into one activity (activity 2: standing and sitting). The review of the physical function aspect of the PCA that led to Sch.2 aimed to ensure that descriptors and scores remain relevant to today's pattern of disabling conditions and their relationship to the working environment; to ensure that "the activities assessed and the scores allocated accurately reflect the level of functional limitation at which it is unreasonable to require a person to engage in work". An aim was to refocus the physical functional areas "to better reflect the activities felt to be most relevant to capacity for work—those activities that an employer might reasonably expect of his workforce" (DWP, *Transformation of the Personal Capability Assessment: Report of the Physical Function and mental Health Technical Working Groups*). The "physical disability" activities are: walking with a walking stick or other normally used aid; standing and sitting; bending or kneeling; reaching; picking up and moving or transferring by the use of the upper body and arms (excluding all the other "physical disability" activities); manual dexterity; speech; hearing with a hearing aid or other normally worn aid; vision (including visual acuity [central vision and focus] and visual fields [peripheral vision], in normal daylight or bright electric light, with glasses or other aid to vision if such aid is normally worn); continence other than enuresis (bed wetting) where the claimant does not have an artificial stoma or urinary collecting device; continence where the claimant uses a urinary collecting device, worn for the majority of the time including an indwelling urethral or suprapubic catheter; continence other than enuresis (bed wetting) where the claimant has an artificial stoma; remaining conscious during waking moments. As regards descriptors attached to these activities, as compared to the PCA, the number is not dissimilar, but those that attracted three points have gone, six now being the lowest "score" (nought not being a score at all). This was a matter which concerned several pressure groups. The review group stated that the "three point" descriptors were removed because a person could reach the threshold of 15 by satisfying five of them. It did not consider that, even in aggregate, such minimal levels of disability really amounted to "an overall level of functional limitation at which it is unreasonable to expect a person to work" (*ibid.*, p.10). But it did not explain exactly what had changed since 1995 to warrant that judgment. Some descriptors are more restrictive. The "sometimes" descriptors have gone. A score of 15 for those who cannot walk more than 50 metres without stopping applies for the PCA, but for the WCAt requires "repeatedly stopping", greater distances and lesser scores remain tied merely to "without stopping or severe discomfort". It is now specified that the chair against which one assesses sitting is one with a "high" back. Bending or kneeling remains the activity, but several of its descriptors (reflective of IB case law) specifically permit the task (picking up a light object such as a piece of paper) to be done by squatting. On "lifting and carrying" the "paperback book", of no specified size, has gone, the descriptors instead referring variously to half or full litre cartons of liquid or "a light but bulky object such as an empty cardboard box". For manual dexterity a "star-headed" sink tap is specified and the cooker control knob is no more. Advancing technology takes the activity beyond the pen and pencil to cover "a conventional keyboard or mouse" and sensibly embodies a descriptor related very much to real life problems: "cannot do up/undo small buttons, such as shirt or blouse buttons". The coin to pick up is now specified as a £1 coin or equivalent.

As regards mental functions, the review group sought to ascertain those relevant to ability to engage in work, taking into consideration the abilities and disabilities of persons with learning difficulties or other conditions which affect cognitive and intellectual function. It recognised that the level of support or prompting someone needs is an indication of how severe is their functional limitation. It considered that the mental health provisions of the PCA were not the most relevant to activities requisite for remaining in or returning to work. The exemption from the PCA for those with severe learning difficulties or autism too readily removed them from being considered in relation to ability to work without undertaking a more detailed and reliable assessment of their mental function. There are ten activities with respect to mental, cognitive and intellectual function, as opposed to the four with the PCA. This reflects a desire to deal better with the problems of this client group making up 41% of the IB caseload: This

"extensively revised mental function assessment [aims to] address a current gap in the assessment of cognitive and intellectual function, in conditions such as learning disability, autistic spectrum disorder, and acquired brain injury. It also [embodies] a new scoring system for mental function, which addresses a bias in the current PCA against people with a mental health problem, as opposed to limitation of physical function" (*ibid*, p.3).

The ten activities are: learning or comprehension in the completion of (simple) tasks; awareness of hazard; memory and concentration; executing of (everyday) tasks; initiating and sustaining personal action (planning, organisation, problem solving, prioritising or switching tasks); coping with changes in routine; getting about; coping with social situations; propriety of behaviour with other people; and dealing with other people.

II Order of treatment in this commentary
In the nature of things, this is a lengthy annotation to a Schedule which lies at the heart of determining the key question whether a claimant for ESA has limited capability for work. It aims to identify and highlight key issues and concerns and to indicate which features of a burgeoning case law on the IB personal capability assessment and its predecessor, the all work test, remain of significance and assistance: (a) in approaching what is in essence a similar task to the IB PCA (matching a claimant's health condition to a range of activities and descriptors and assigning a score); and (b) more specifically in interpreting and applying the often similarly worded terms of the activities and descriptors in the WCAt.

The case law on the IB tests is voluminous and will continue to burgeon as IB and ESA will co-exist for several years yet. That case law is fully treated in the commentary to the Schedule to the Incapacity for Work (General) Regs 1995 in Vol.I. The commentary here does not attempt to reproduce that, but instead to draw from it the crucial principles. The commentary is sub-divided as follows:
    [A] Approaching the interpretation of the Schedule as a whole.
    [B] Case law on specific activities and descriptors: Pt I: physical disabilities
    [C] Approaching Pt II: mental, cognitive and intellectual function assessment.

[A] Approaching the interpretation of the Schedule as a whole

Evidence and attention to detail: Decision-makers must pay very close attention   **1A.485**
to the precise wording of the activities and descriptors and to the matter of
appropriate evidence to ground their findings *(CSIB/12/96)*. Cases must be
decided in the light of the totality of the evidence, medical or otherwise, including that from the claimant *(CIB/15663/1996)*. His evidence does not require
corroboration unless self-contradictory or improbable *(R (I) 2/51)*. Differing
medical opinions and reports must carefully be appraised, without rigid pre-
conceptions on whether the report of the examining health professional is always
to be preferred as more disinterested and informed than that of the claimant's
GP or consultant, or vice versa (contrast *CIB/13039/1996* and *CIB/3968/1996*
with *CIB/17257/1996)*. Both types of evidence can, from different perspectives,
prove valuable *(CIB/17257/1996; CIB/21/2002)*. A tribunal is not *bound to* decide
in the same way as any particular doctor certifies; when faced with a conflict of
medical opinion, they are at liberty to prefer, giving reasons, one view rather than
another *(R(S) 1/53; CSIB/684/1997; CSIB/848/1997; CIB/309/1997; R. v Social
Security Commissioner Ex p. Dobie* (QBD, October 26, 1999)—but *cf. CIB/
17257/1996)*. But that does not warrant underestimating a DWPMS personal
capability assessment report which is based on a more intensive and detailed
clinical examination and history-taking than the invalidity benefit system *(CIB/
15663/1996)*. To prefer a DWPMS doctor's report on the grounds that it is more
detailed is not, as such, irrational *(R. v Social Security Commissioner Ex p. Dobie*,
QBD (October 26, 1999). A tribunal should not reject a claimant's appeal on the
basis that he was "not a reliable or credible witness" without giving reasons for
that finding *(CSIB/459/1997)*. It should be made clear that the claimant's evidence has been considered, what account has been taken of it, and, if rejected,
why it has been rejected *(CIB/309/1997)*. Nor should a tribunal simply record
acceptance of the DWPMS doctor's findings; rather it should make and record
its own findings on the descriptors *(CSIB/459/1997)*. The correct approach is to
weigh all the evidence in the context of the case *(CIB/3620/1998)*. In *CIB/
3074/2003* Commissioner Bano allowed the claimant's appeal because the tribunal had dismissed the appeal "on the basis of a formulaic endorsement of the
examining medical practitioner's report", rather than looking at it in the light of
its nature and the evidence as a whole. Although a tribunal cannot conduct a
physical examination of the claimant, it can use all its senses, including ocular
observation of the claimant during the hearing when considering whether the
WCAt is satisfied *(R1/01(IB)(T); R4/99 (IB))* and a tribunal medical member
can properly look at X-Rays put in evidence *(R (IB) 2/06)*. Tribunals should also
consider carefully evidence that the medical examination was perfunctory.
Equally, where the health practitioner's report disputes the claimant's account of
his disabilities in his questionnaire, natural justice requires that tribunals hear the
claimant's oral evidence about his condition, before deciding which account to
prefer *(CIB/5586/1999)*. Tribunals should be wary of adviser/representative revision of the picture painted by the claimant's questionnaire answers and the
health professional's report, and should look for supporting evidence where such
statements differ significantly from the claimant's original own assessment of his
or her condition *(CIB/2913/2001)*.

The computerised medical examination report is the end product of the
system. In that report statements or phrases can be produced mechanically by
the software, which produces relevant phrases from its memory bank, and,
unless the examining health professional using it is very careful, the statements
in the report may not necessarily represent actual wording chosen and typed in
by him. This generates an increased risk of accidental mistakes or discrepancies
being left undetected in the final product of the process. The need for careful
appraisal of the computerised report has been stressed by Commissioners

Howell and Williams (*CIB/511/2005; CIB/476/2005; CIB/1522/2005; CIB/0664/2005; CIB/3950/2007*). Section 7 of the Electronic Communications Act 2000 has no application to the computerised report form (*R(IB) 7/05*).

To reiterate: the first task is to decide from all the evidence in the case which descriptors apply, the second to calculate the scores. Decision-makers and tribunals must in the light of all relevant evidence identify the relevant health condition and consider carefully the full range of activities which may be impaired by it (*CIB/5797/1997; CIB/3589/2004*). Scoring should proceed from top to bottom, so as properly to identify the highest ranking descriptor in the range attached to the particular activity which can properly be said to apply to the claimant (*CIB/5361/1997;* reg.19(6)).

1A.486   *The WCAt is not a snapshot—the need for an approach characterized by "reason-ableness":* The "sometimes" descriptors in the PCA have not been carried over into ESA. However, the Government emphasised that, like the PCA, the WCAt was not intended to be a simple snapshot. The review group rightly emphasised that guidance to decision-makers and to the healthcare professionals involved in the assessments of capacity would indicate the factors to be taken into account in ascertaining whether a claimant can perform a particular function: ability to do it just once is not enough (the person must reliably be able to sustain or repeat the activity); distress, pain, and fatigue involved in carrying out the activity; and the detrimental effects of medication. But these are not just matters of guidance; they are legal rules established by the extensive jurisprudence on approaching the very similar exercise in the PCA. The requirement is for ability to perform the specified activities with "reasonable regularity"; there must be an element of reasonableness in the approach to the question of what someone is or is not capable of doing, including consideration of his ability to perform the activities most of the time (*C1/95(IB)*; *CSIB/17/96*), so that the question becomes whether the claimant would normally be able to perform the stated activity if and when called upon to do so (*CIB/13161/96; CIB/13508/96*)). The working environment and the matter of employability are both irrelevant (*C1/95; CIB/13161/96; CIB/13508/96*).

Where variable, intermittent and sporadic conditions and their impact on earning capacity are involved, difficult questions of judgment in assessing inca-pacity for work arise where the claimant can sometimes do things but at other times not. Neither the PCA nor the WCAt were designed to be a simple "snapshot". The system aims to assess the claimant's condition over a particular period, taking account of pain and fatigue (*CIB/14587/1996; CIB/13161/96; CIB/13508/96*), fears for health and the medical advice received by the claimant (*CSIB/12/96*). The questionnaire asks about variability—the claimant's own doctor can include material on this in the MED 4, and examining health care professionals with Medical Services have been trained to conduct examinations with these issues in mind. The structure of the legislative scheme, however, produces a problem. It embodies a test based on an examination on a particular day designed to provide information on, and assessment of, a claimant over a period of time. The "normality" approach as part of "reasonable regularity" deals with one aspect of the problem: the reference in *C1/95(IB)* to a claimant being able to accomplish a task most of the time is to be read as meaning "as and when called upon to do so". On this basis, one looks at the position which normally prevails in the period (see *CSIB/459/1997*, para.13; *CIB/911/1997*, paras 12, 13). The more difficult situation is where it is accepted that the claimant's condition is such that for certain periods he is able to cope satisfacto-rily with normal activities; the problem of the sporadic or intermittent condition. The problem generated significant disagreement among Commissioners on approach. The authoritative Tribunal of Commissioners' decision is *R(IB)*

2/99(T), endorsed by a tribunal of Commissioners in Northern Ireland in *R1/02 (IB) (T)*. *R (IB) 2/99* concerned the situation where a claimant suffered from a condition causing greater disability on some days than on others. The key question was whether the claimant was incapable of work under the PCA on days on which, if the days were viewed in isolation, he or she might not satisfy that test (para.2). While the Tribunal decision does not prescribe any one approach as *universally* applicable, the central thrust of the decision is to see as justified for the majority of cases, the "broad approach" typified by *CIB/6244/97* rather than the stricter "daily approach" exemplified by *CIB/13161/96* and *CIB/13508/96*. The Tribunal did not, however, find helpful the distinction drawn between "variable" and "intermittent" conditions in *CIB/6244/97*. Moreover, the Tribunal recognised that in some cases at least—generally when looking backwards over a prolonged period in the course of which the claimant has only had "short episodes of disablement" (for example, in the dwindling number of cases where the First tier Tribunal has to consider matters "down to the date of the hearing", or in "review or overpayment cases")—something akin to the meticulous approach in *CIB/13161/96* and *CIB/13508/96* along the lines of Commissioner Jacobs' approach to intermittent conditions in *CIB/6244/1997* would be appropriate (para.17).

The practical reality is that most cases which fall to be decided by the decision-maker in the Department do not concern entitlement to benefit for a past period. Generally, a decision on the award of benefit is "forward looking" and usually made for an indefinite period. Although the decision-maker must of course consider the period from the medical examination up to the date of his decision, that decision will rarely be concerned with entitlement to benefit for a substantial period in the past. While both the "broad" and the "daily basis" approaches are each consistent with the wording of the legislation, the "broad approach" is "the only approach that can sensibly be applied by a decision-maker, making what is in effect a prospective determination for an extended period" (para.11). The Tribunal considered the broader-based approach adopted in *R(A) 2/74* to the attendance allowance issue—was there a period *throughout* which the claimant could be said to be so severely disabled as to require at night prolonged or repeated attention in connection with bodily functions? The Tribunal decided that such an approach applies equally to incapacity benefit despite its daily basis. It noted (without using those statements to support its construction of the legislation) that such an approach accorded with ministerial statements in Parliament on the introduction of the all work test (for example, that the "all work test" [now the "personal capability assessment"] is not a "snapshot"). Nonetheless, the Tribunal stressed that:

> "the words of the legislation cannot be ignored ... [I]n those cases where relevant descriptors are expressed in terms that the claimant 'cannot', rather than 'sometimes cannot', perform the activity, one should not stray too far from an arithmetical approach that considers what the claimant's abilities are 'most of the time'—the phrase used in *C1/95(IB)*. Nevertheless, we agree that all the factors mentioned by counsel [neither of whom argued for a 'daily basis' approach]—the frequency of 'bad' days, the lengths of periods of 'bad' days and of intervening periods, the severity of the claimant's disablement on both 'good' and 'bad' days and the unpredictability of 'bad' days—are relevant when applying the broad approach. Thus a person whose condition varies from day to day and who would easily satisfy the 'all work test' on three days a week and would nearly satisfy it on the other four days might well be considered to be incapable of work for the whole week. But a person who has long periods of illness separated by periods of remission lasting some weeks during which he or she suffers no significant disablement, might well be

289

considered to be incapable of work during the periods of illness but not to be incapable of work during the periods of remission, even if the periods of illness are longer than the periods of remission. Each case must be judged on its merits and ... there are some cases where a claimant can properly be regarded as incapable of work both on days when the 'all work test' is clearly satisfied and on other days in between those days and that there are other cases where the claimant can be regarded as incapable of work only on 'bad days' ... " (para.15).

That ESA is a weekly benefit, coupled with the demise of the "sometimes" descriptors, emphasises the continued authority and propriety of this approach to the WCAt tasks. Hence, as regards forward-looking decisions, claimants whose condition is such as only to satisfy the test on four or five days a month (albeit days of severe disablement) cannot, however unpredictable those days may be, properly be regarded as satisfying the test for the whole month. It thus may be that some claimants who are unemployable nonetheless are seen as "capable of work" under the PCA or the WCAt.

In *R1/02(IB)(T)*, a Northern Ireland tribunal of Commissioners endorsed the "broad brush" approach to variable conditions in *R(IB)2/99(T)*, but also laid emphasis on para.15 of it, set out above, with one reservation. They were unhappy with the phrase "the unpredictability of 'bad' days", commenting that those who decide cases "will simply have to try to determine the likely patterns of functional limitation. Uncertainty as to the possibility of a future recurrence would not of itself usually be enough to satisfy the test which must be satisfied on the balance of probability at the time of the decision maker's decision" (para.26). Applying para.15 of *R(IB)2/99* in *CIB/2620/2000*, Commissioner Bano held that the case before him (a sufferer from dysmenorrhoea) was one of the minority of cases in which the broad approach could not be applied, one where the claimant could only be considered incapable of work on "bad days".

1A.487   *Making and recording decisions*: Setting rigorous standards for tribunals (*cf.* his approach to activity 3 in *CSIB/12/96*), Commissioner Walker in *CSIB 324/97* stipulated the following approach to making and recording decisions under the "all work" test [the predecessor of the IB PCA]:

"the best and safest practice is for a tribunal to consider and make findings of fact about, first, the disability or disabilities, be they disease or bodily or mental problems, from which an individual has been proved on the evidence to suffer. Second, they should consider and make findings of fact about which, if any of the activities set out in the Sch., are established to be adversely affected by any of those disabilities. Thirdly, and based upon appropriate findings of fact, in the case of each and every activity the tribunal should determine which descriptor best fits the case having regard to the evidence, in their view. Finally, in the reasons, they should explain why a particular activity has been held not to be adversely affected where there was a contention that it was so affected, and why a particular descriptor has been preferred to any other contended for" (para.11).

But that best and safest practice need not necessarily always be followed. For example where the issue is whether or not the tribunal believes the claimant on a matter fundamental and relevant, if on reasonable grounds the tribunal did not believe the claimant when he alleged that his responses in the questionnaire were not accurate, then the finding that the tribunal did not believe that he had been mistaken when providing those responses covered in reality all the disputed areas raised at the hearing, and it was not necessary to record specific findings of fact on each of the activity questions brought up by the claimant (per Northern Ireland Chief Commissioner Martin in *C46/97(IB)*, drawing with approval on Deputy Commissioner Ramsay's decision in *CIB/16572/96*). In para.5 of *CIB/ 4497/1998*, Commissioner Rowland sets out useful guidance on the minimum requirements of giving reasons. He noted that:

> "a statement of reasons may be adequate even though it could be improved on and, in particular, a failure to observe the 'best and safest practice' recommended in *CSIB 324/97* ... is not necessarily an error of law ... What is required by way of reasoning depends very much on the circumstances of the case before the tribunal. Those challenging reasoning must explain its inadequacy and show the significance of the inadequacy."

When applying the principles to a particular case, it should be remembered that a First Tier Tribunal has an inquisitorial role (*CIB/14442/96*). It should be cautious about exercising that role when considering mental disablement (*CIB/ 14202/1996*, see head [C] below). Where the claimant is represented by a competent adviser (e.g. a Welfare Rights officer employed by a "responsible" local authority), a tribunal is entitled to proceed on the basis that the representative will put forward all relevant points on his client's behalf and to know the case that is being made for the client. The tribunal in such a case should not be expected to inquire further into the claimant's case; to require that would be to place an impossible administrative burden on tribunals (*CSIB/389/1998*). Overall, the tribunal's task is rendered easier now in that because of the SSA 1998, the focus is on matters as at the date of the Secretary of State's decision rather than covering matters in the often lengthy period down to the date of the hearing (see further *Vol. III: Administration, Appeals and the European Dimension*).

[B] Case law on specific activities and descriptors: Part I: physical disabilities

Activity 1 walking on level ground: Tribunals should not here have regard to the case law on the same words in the context of the statutory definition of virtually unable to walk as respects the mobility component of disability living allowance. This is not merely because of the different statutory context but because the tribunal issue is essentially one of degree (*CSIB/60/96*). A tribunal must not only consider the point in distance when a claimant stops walking because of severe discomfort but also the point of onset of that discomfort (descriptors 1(b)–(e) read "without stopping *or* severe discomfort") (*CIB/3013/97*).   **1A.488**

The activity refers to walking with a walking stick or other aid "if such aid is normally used". This means if it is normally used by people acting reasonably (by analogy with the interpretation given "if such aid is normally worn" in *CIB/ 14499/1996* with respect to PCA activity 12 (vision), now Activity 9 in this Schedule).

Activity 2: standing and sitting: this combines in one activity things which in the PCA are spread across three: sitting in an upright chair with a back but no arms (activity 3); standing without the support of another person or the use of an aid except a walking stick (activity 4); and rising from sitting in an upright chair with a back but no arms without the help of another person (activity 5). Caution must therefore be exercised in extrapolating from IB case law on those PCA activities. But there still remains a need for exactitude in comparing evidence about ability to sit (e.g at home watching Television or in the tribunal room) to ability to sit in the chair prescribed in the wording of the activity (upright, high back, no arms) (*CSIB/12/96*; *CSIB/324/97*; *CSIB/457/02*; *CIB/15663/1996*; *CIB/ 2404/2001*). "Standing" does not mean standing stock-still. The normal person (the yardstick for applying the descriptors) does not do so for any length of time. As Commissioner Lloyd-Davies stated in *R(IB) 6/04*:   **1A.489**

"The quasi-involuntary movements that most people make in standing for prolonged periods do not ... count. Instead the tribunal should concentrate on how long a claimant can stand before needing or having to move around or sit down (usually because of pain in the back or legs)" (para.5).

Descriptor (d) now looks to "without physical assistance from another person", rather than (as in the PCA) "without the help of another person", so ability to do so with encouragement from another person would preclude a score under this head. The descriptor also no longer refers to "without holding on to something", so ability to rise only by using the seat or back of the chair to deliver the force necessary to rise, or provide stability while rising, no longer scores (compare *R(IB) 2/03*). Nor does holding onto one's knees to assist rising (*CIB/ 5083/2001*). Coupled with the general provision in reg.19(4) on taking account of aids normally used, ability to rise from sitting using crutches similarly precludes scoring (compare *CIB/614/98*).

1A.490   *Activity 3: bending and kneeling:* this includes squatting, thus making explicit in descriptors (b) and (c) what *R(IB) 1/02* and *Purdy v Secretary of State for Social Services* reported with it, had read into the comparable PCA provisions. The references in descriptors (b) and (c) to "straighten up again *without help of another person*" weakens the basis the argument accepted in *CSIB/12/96* that this was implicit in descriptor (a) that was decided when the qualification was not used in PCA descriptors (b) and (c).

1A.491   *Activity 4 reaching:* the comparator IB provision is activity (9). Descriptor (c) now scores only 9, as opposed to 15 under the IB regime. It does not involve raising the upper arm above head level (*CIB 2811/1995*). In contrast, descriptor (d) ("cannot raise either arm above head height as if to reach for something") requires that more than a minimal amount of the arm must be above head level. Reaching involves a degree of stretching, and involves being able to raise the upper arm above shoulder level and to go at least some way towards straightening the arm in moving it towards a notional object" (*CIB 2811/1995*, para.7) So that a claimant with full elbow flexion could probably achieve the task in (c) but not (d).

1A.492   *Activity 5: picking up and moving or transferring by the use of the upper arms and body:* The comparator IB provision is activity 8 (lifting and carrying). The new descriptor formulations avoid previous ambiguity over the meaning of "carry", and make it clear that what is covered is picking up and moving, using the upper body and arms (compare *R(IB) 5/03*).

1A.493   *Activity 6: manual dexterity:* The comparator IB provision is Activity 7. Whether one reads into the descriptors the words "safely or in safety" remains an unresolved disagreement between Commissioners (contrast *CSIB/20/1996* and *CIB/4315/1997*). A "star headed" sink tap is now specified in descriptors (a) and (g). The sink tap contemplated is "a tap requiring an ordinary amount of force to turn it, when it is closed so as to prevent water dripping through it" (*CIB/ 2404/2001*, para.10). So a tribunal there did not err by finding that the claimant could turn a tap "if it is not too tight", since anyone can have difficulty with a tap that is jammed or overtightened (*ibid.*).

Descriptor (d) ("cannot physically use a pen or pencil") probably means physically "with either hand" so as to write in a normal manner, rather than a total inability to use a pen or pencil for any purpose at all, for example, punching a hole in a sheet of paper (*R(IB)1/98*; *CIB/13161/96*; *CIB/13508/96*). The same approach would seem applicable to the more modern technology in descriptor (e).

Activity 7: speech: The comparator IB provision is Activity 10. In *CSIB/ 413/1998*, Commissioner May appeared to cast doubt on the proposition that the factor "pain" was relevant to the activity of speaking. In contrast, in *CIB/ 4306/1999* Deputy Commissioner White thought:

> "descriptor (a) covers someone who has no power of speech, and could also cover someone whose condition was such that either they had been advised not to speak or whom speaking caused such pain that they could not reasonably be said to be able to speak. I can conceive of situations in which the act of talking causes such pain that it would be right to conclude that a claimant was unable to speak. ... What the threshold of pain is in any particular case is an issue of fact for the tribunal in the light of all the evidence." (para.17)

Whether a claimant cannot be understood or cannot easily be understood so as to satisfy descriptors (b) to (d) is similarly a matter of fact for the tribunal to resolve in the light of all the evidence in the case.

Activity 8: hearing: The comparator IB provision is Activity 10, identically worded. The phrase "if normally worn" means if the aid in question is normally worn by people in the claimant's situation acting reasonably in all the circumstances (*CIB/14499/1996*). As regards descriptor (d), the wording has changed from "normal voice" to "loud voice", making the descriptor harder to satisfy than its comparator provision. But it is submitted that it still has to be considered in the light of what is reasonable. It is not reasonable (and a score could be awarded under the descriptor) if the understanding of someone talking in a loud voice can only be gained through frequent requests for repetition of what has been said (*CIB/590/1998*). Agreeing with this in *CIB/3123/2002*, Commissioner Bano added that the descriptor should be considered by reference to a claimant's ability to understand someone with whom s/he is not familiar, so that the tribunal erred in law in considering the claimant's ability to understand his wife (who always accompanied him outdoors) when on busy streets (para.8).

Activity 9: vision: the comparator IB provision is Activity 12, but the ESA activity now includes visual fields [central vision and focus] and visual acuity [peripheral vision]. The phrase "if normally worn" means if the aid in question is normally worn by people in the claimant's situation acting reasonably in all the circumstances (*CIB/14499/1996*). So if someone would be able to see perfectly well if wearing prescription sunglasses, but unreasonably refused to wear them and could not see without them, that person cannot score points under this activity. "Bright electric light" includes fluorescent light (*CIB/2952/2004*). The rubric is "daylight *or* bright electric light". In *CIB/2584/2002* Commissioner Williams saw this as meaning that an inability to meet the visual descriptors in one of those contexts, while being able to meet them in the other, would suffice to score (para.8). Dealing with a claimant adversely affected in the proximity of intense bright light, and taking account of concepts of reasonable regularity and the relevance of pain and discomfort, he was of the view (endorsing the interpretation in *C12/00–01 (IB,* below) that the

> "claimant does not need a sustained ability to read in bright artificial light to have adequate vision for these purposes, but if the exposure to bright artificial light for any significant time causes pain and/or stops her focussing and/or makes her shut her eyes to avoid the effects of the light at some point, then from that point she presumably cannot meet that descriptor even for the

1A.494

1A.495

1A.496

shortest period. The question is whether, taking those limits into account, she does or does not have the relevant level of vision" (para.18).

Descriptor (b) ("cannot see well enough to read 16 point print at a distance of greater than 20 cm") covers the ability to distinguish 16 point characters so as to be able to decipher and distinguish individual words, rather than importing sustained reading ability (is the vision good enough to read 16-point characters at the requisite distance?) (*C12/00–01 (IB); CIB/4998/1998; CIB/333/1998; CIB/ 2354/2001; CIB/2952/2004*).

Descriptors (d) and (f) both refer to "see well enough to recognize a friend" at the specified distances, five metres and 15 metres, respectively. This test only requires the claimant to be able to identify a friend who is alone at the requisite distance. It does not stipulate ability to pick the friend out from a number of people. The time it may take to "recognise" the friend is material in that it may take so long a time that it is proper to regard that time lapse as amounting to "cannot" recognise the friend (*CIB/1323/2007*).

1A.497 *Activities 10(a)–(c): continence:* Applying the descriptors involves intrusive scrutiny of the lives of claimants, those in respect of Activities 10 (a)–(c) particularly so, embracing intimate and embarrassing areas affecting a claimant's dignity. It is necessary to appreciate the nature of the problems of sufferers, the varied nature and disabling effects of irritable bowel syndrome (IBS) (see *CIB/ 14332/96*) the role of diet (*CSIB/889/1999*), various urinary collecting devices (including an indwelling uretheral or suprapubic catheter), and the effect of medication (does it negate "voluntary control"—this remains a matter of Commissioner disagreement: contrast *CSIB/38/96* [ignore its effect] with *R2/00(IB)* [take account of its effect]. It is also necessary to define carefully the terms used in the descriptors and apply them carefully.

1A.498 *Activity 10(a): Continence other than enuresis (bed wetting): the meaning of continence:* In *R(IB) 4/04,* a Tribunal of Commissioners rejected as too broad the definition advanced on behalf of the Secretary of State that "continence" relates to whether a person is able, by his actions, simply to contain his emissions of urine and excrement (para.34). Instead it made use of the relevant definition in *Blakiston's Gould Medical Dictionary* (4th edn):

> "The proper functioning of any sphincter or other structure of the gastro intestinal tract so as to prevent regurgitation or premature emptying".

1A.499 *Activity 10(a): continence other than enuresis (bed wetting) where the claimant does not have an artificial stoma or urinary collecting device: descriptors (a)(i)–(vii):* These refer variously, in the context of "no voluntary control" or "loses control", to the "voiding of the bladder", the "full voiding of the bladder", or the "full evacuation of the bowel". This would suggest that IB case authorities bringing dribbling and leaking within the sphere of "loses control" are not applicable here (see, e.g., *CSIB/880/2003*). Thus stress incontinence sufferers will find it difficult to score. Incontinence pads were held irrelevant to the issue of "voluntary control" under the IB scheme (*CSIB/880/2003*). But it is not clear whether they constitute a "urinary collecting device"; the references in 10(b) to emptying such a device would suggest they might not, but references to affix or remove, if they are properly to be read disjunctively, might suggest that they do.

1A.500 *Activity 10(b): continence where the claimant uses a urinary collecting device, worn for the majority of the time, including an indwelling uretheral or suprapubic catheter:* This has no counterpart in the IB PCA. The descriptors cover varying types of inability to use these artificial control devices to deal with urinary (bladder) incontinence. It is not wholly clear from the wording used whether incontinence pads constitute a "urinary collecting device"; the references in 10(b) to emptying such a device would suggest they might not, but references to affix or remove, if they are properly to be read disjunctively, might suggest that they do. Insofar as they may enable ability to cope outside the home without undue embarrassment, it is arguable that they should be covered.

Activity 10(c): continence other than enuresis (bed wetting) where the claimant has an artificial stoma: This has no counterpart in the IB PCA. Activity 10(c) covers both urinary (bladder) and faecal (bowel) incontinence. The descriptors cover varying types of inability to use the artificial stoma.   **1A.501**

Activity 11 remaining conscious during waking moments: Unlike the comparator IB PCA activity 14, this activity is not limited to epileptic or similar seizures. The descriptors refer variously to "an involuntary episode of lost or altered consciousness". That episode must result in "significantly disrupted awareness or concentration". "Lost consciousness" could embrace irresistible periods of sleep due to disease or medication (*CSIB/44/1997*). Commissioner Walker considered the meaning of "altered consciousness" in *CSIB/14/96*. He saw it as different from "lost consciousness" and as not coloured by that term: **1A.502**

"The discussion satisfied me that it is not possible to lay down guidelines as to what, in law, is meant by 'altered consciousness'. It is, I am equally satisfied, essentially a practical matter for a tribunal to determine in the light of medical guidance from their assessor [now medical member] and the application of commonsense. But where, as here, episodes of pain are the disabling condition it will be necessary for the tribunal to explore, and for the claimant to present appropriate evidence to allow such exploration, in some detail how the pain affects the individual during an episode. It is not, in my view, sufficient to find as a fact that during the period 'the appellant is disabled'. Nor that 'he is unable to conduct his normal daily activities'. *It is for determination first how pain forecloses these and the way in which and the extent to which it does so. Thus . . . if an individual is so distracted by the pain that he requires to lie down and otherwise retire from what he is doing then it may be possible to conclude that his consciousness has become altered by the degree of pain and he is incapable of doing anything effective other than coping with it.* But that would be a secondary finding which would require proper primary findings to justify it. Above all, I am persuaded that the concept of 'altered consciousness', which may have some medical significance, is impossible of legal definition and is a concept of difficulty for application by lay tribunals. For these reasons I do not think that it is appropriate that I should give any further guidance to the new tribunal in this case" (para.9, emphasis supplied by commentator).

The matter of giving substance to the concept "altered consciousness" and applying it to the facts of disputed cases is thus made very directly the task of the tribunal. The Commissioner's highlighted comments about the effects and implications of severe pain in this context open up possibilities under Activity 14 for, for example, those suffering frequent disabling migraines (a point supported by *C7/96(IB)* if severe) or very severe back pain. It might cover some effects of severe pain produced by endemetriosis (*CIB/12668/1996*) or the effects of severe vertigo (*C8/96(IB)*; *C13/96(IB)*; *CIB/15231/1996*). But in each case the effects of the altered consciousness must result in "significantly disrupted awareness or concentration".

1A.503 *[C] Case law on specific activities and descriptors: Pt II: mental, cognitive and intellectual function assessment*

The terms of the activities and descriptors in Pt II are so different from those in the PCA that no specific IB case law on the PCA descriptors and activities can readily be made relevant. Not so, however, IB case law on the general approach to be taken, namely that, while a tribunal has an inquisitorial function, it should be cautious about exercising it when considering mental disablement (*CIB/ 14202/1996*), unless the matter has been raised beforehand and there is in addition some medical or other evidence on the point (*R (IB) 2/98*). It cannot be stressed too much that there must be link between inability to perform and activity or task and the specific disease or bodily or mental disablement from which the claimant suffers (reg.19(2)).

1A.504

SCHEDULE 3

ASSESSMENT OF WHETHER A CLAIMANT HAS LIMITED CAPABILITY FOR WORK-RELATED ACTIVITY

Column 1 *Activity*	Column 2 *Descriptors*
1. Walking or moving on level ground.	Cannot— (a) walk (with a walking stick or other aid if such aid is normally used); (b) move (with the aid of crutches if crutches are normally used); or (c) manually propel the claimant's wheelchair; more than 30 metres without repeatedly stopping, experiencing breathlessness or severe discomfort.
2. Rising from sitting and transferring from one seated position to another.	Cannot complete both of the following— (a) rise to standing from sitting in an upright chair without receiving physical assistance from someone else; and (b) move between one seated position and another seated position located next to one another without receiving physical assistance from someone else.
3. Picking up and moving or transferring by the use of the upper body and arms (excluding standing, sitting, bending or kneeling and all other activities specified in this Schedule).	Cannot pick up and move 0.5 litre carton full of liquid with either hand.
4. Reaching.	Cannot raise either arm as if to put something in the top pocket of a coat or jacket.
5. Manual dexterity.	Cannot— (a) turn a "star-headed" sink tap with either hand; or (b) pick up a £1 coin or equivalent with either hand.

Column 1	Column 2
Activity	*Descriptors*

6. Continence.

(a) Continence other than enuresis (bed wetting) where the claimant does not have an artificial stoma or urinary collecting device.

   (a) Has no voluntary control over the evacuation of the bowel;

   (b) Has no voluntary control over the voiding of the bladder;

   (c) At least once a week, loses control of bowels so that the claimant cannot control the full evacuation of the bowel;

   (d) At least once a week, loses control of bladder so that the claimant cannot control the full voiding of the bladder;

   (e) At least once a week, fails to control full evacuation of the bowel, owing to a severe disorder of mood or behaviour; or

   (f) At least once a week, fails to control full-voiding of the bladder, owing to a severe disorder of mood or behaviour.

(b) Continence where the claimant uses a urinary collecting device, worn for the majority of the time including an indwelling urethral or suprapubic catheter.

   (a) Is unable to affix, remove or empty the catheter bag or other collecting device without receiving physical assistance from another person;

   (b) Is unable to affix, remove or empty the catheter bag or other collecting device without causing leakage of contents;

   (c) Has no voluntary control over the evacuation of the bowel;

   (d) At least once a week loses control of bowels so that the claimant cannot control the full evacuation of the bowel; or

   (e) At least once a week, fails to control full evacuation of the bowel, owing to a severe disorder of mood or behaviour.

(c) Continence other than enuresis (bed wetting) where the claimant has an artificial stoma appliance.

   (a) Is unable to affix, remove or empty stoma appliance without receiving physical assistance from another person;

   (b) Is unable to affix, remove or empty stoma without causing leakage of contents;

   (c) Where the claimant's artificial stoma relates solely to the evacuation of the bowel, has no voluntary control over voiding of bladder;

   (d) Where the claimant's artificial stoma relates solely to the evacuation of the bowel, at least once a week, loses control of the bladder so that the claimant cannot control the full voiding of the bladder; or

   (e) Where the claimant's artificial stoma relates solely to the evacuation of the bowel, at least once a week, fails to control the full voiding of the bladder, owing to a severe disorder of mood or behaviour.

7. Maintaining personal hygiene.

   (a) Cannot clean own torso (excluding own back) without receiving physical assistance from someone else;

Column 1 Activity	Column 2 Descriptors
	(b) Cannot clean own torso (excluding back) without repeatedly stopping, experiencing breathlessness or severe discomfort;
	(c) Cannot clean own torso (excluding back) without receiving regular prompting given by someone else in the claimant's presence; or
	(d) Owing to a severe disorder of mood or behaviour, fails to clean own torso (excluding own back) without receiving— (i) physical assistance from someone else; or (ii) regular prompting given by someone else in the claimant's presence.
8. Eating and drinking. (a) Conveying food or drink to the mouth.	(a) Cannot convey food or drink to the claimant's own mouth without receiving physical assistance from someone else;
	(b) Cannot convey food or drink to the claimant's own mouth without repeatedly stopping, experiencing breathlessness or severe discomfort;
	(c) Cannot convey food or drink to the claimant's own mouth without receiving regular prompting given by someone else in the claimant's physical presence; or
	(d) Owing to a severe disorder of mood or behaviour, fails to convey food or drink to the claimant's own mouth without receiving— (i) physical assistance from someone else; or (ii) regular prompting given by someone else in the claimant's presence.
(b) Chewing or swallowing food or drink.	(a) Cannot chew or swallow food or drink;
	(b) Cannot chew or swallow food or drink without repeatedly stopping, experiencing breathlessness or severe discomfort;
	(c) Cannot chew or swallow food or drink without repeatedly receiving regular prompting given by someone else in the claimant's presence; or
	(d) Owing to a severe disorder of mood or behaviour, fails to— (i) chew or swallow food or drink; or (ii) chew or swallow food or drink without regular prompting given by someone else in the claimant's presence.
9. Learning or comprehension in the completion of tasks.	(a) Cannot learn or understand how to successfully complete a simple task, such as the preparation of a hot drink, at all;

Column 1 Activity	Column 2 Descriptors
	(b) Needs to witness a demonstration, given more than once on the same occasion of how to carry out a simple task before the claimant is able to learn or understand how to complete the task successfully, but would be unable to successfully complete the task the following day without receiving a further demonstration of how to complete it; or
	(c) Fails to do any of the matters referred to in (a) or (b) owing to a severe disorder of mood or behaviour.
10. Personal action.	(a) Cannot initiate or sustain any personal action (which means planning, organisation, problem solving, prioritising or switching tasks);
	(b) Cannot initiate or sustain personal action without requiring daily verbal prompting given by someone else in the claimant's presence; or
	(c) Fails to initiate or sustain basic personal action without requiring daily verbal prompting given by some else in the claimant's presence, owing to a severe disorder of mood or behaviour.
11. Communication.	(a) None of the following forms of communication can be achieved by the claimant—
	(i) speaking (to a standard that may be understood by strangers);
	(ii) writing (to a standard that may be understood by strangers);
	(iii) typing (to a standard that may be understood by strangers);
	(iv) sign language to a standard equivalent to Level 3 British Sign Language;
	(b) None of the forms of communication referred to in (a) are achieved by the claimant, owing to a severe disorder of mood or behaviour;
	(c) Misinterprets verbal or non-verbal communication to the extent of causing distress to himself or herself on a daily basis; or
	(d) Effectively cannot make himself or herself understood to others because of the claimant's disassociation from reality owing to a severe disorder of mood or behaviour.

DEFINITIONS

"claimant"—see WRA 2007, s.24(1).

GENERAL NOTE

Establishing limited capacity for work related activity might be said to be the **1A.505** central condition of entitlement to support component. The assumption behind

ESA is that the vast majority of claimants, if given the right support, are in fact capable of some work. Government anticipates that only some 10% of claimants (those with more severe health conditions) will be entitled to the support allowance and so not be subject to work-related activity conditionality requirements. Entry to this protected support group depends on it being established—generally through a work-related activity assessment (WRAAt) of a more stringent nature than the WCAt covered by reg.19 and Sch.2—that the claimant has limited capacity for work related activity: the WRAAt is thus the second element in the revised Work Capability Assessment.

Entry to the support group is based on someone demonstrating that they have a severe level of functional limitation. This is established when by reason of the claimant's physical or mental condition, at least one of the range of descriptors in this Schedule to the ESA Regulations applies to the claimant. It is submitted here that the key elements of IB case law which carry across into interpreting and applying the provisions in Sch.2 on the WCAt will also apply here: decide in the light of the totality of the evidence, making a careful appraisal of differing medical reports; the need for careful attention to detail; the concept of reasonable regularity (the test is not a snapshot); relevant factors of pain, discomfort and of fears for the claimants health; and the need carefully to approach conditions which vary and fluctuate. But here reg.34(2) makes clear that a:

"descriptor applies to a claimant if that descriptor applies to the claimant for the majority of the time or, as the case may be, on the majority of the occasions on which the claimant undertakes or attempts to undertake the activity described by that descriptor."

There is no scoring system and the criteria are deliberately more stringent than in the WCAt. In Committee, the Minister for Employment and Welfare Reform explained both characteristics:

"The levels of functional limitation used in the descriptors for determining limited capability for work-related activity are greater because we intend to place in the support group only the minority of customers who are so severely impaired that it would not be reasonable to require them to undertake work-related activity . . . People with less severe functional limitations across a range of descriptors might score highly and be inappropriately included in the support group when they might benefit from work-related activity . . . A number of case studies were provided in the background information, which hon. Members will find helpful. [See DWP, *Welfare Reform Bill: Draft Regulations and Supporting Material* (January 2007), pp. 13–17.] Under the revised PCA, someone with a moderate learning disability would score 50 points. They would be significantly above the 15-point threshold, but we clearly would not wish to put even someone with 50 points into the support group automatically, because we are determined to ensure that the new system does not write off people with learning disabilities. The technical groups considered all the options. A crude points-based system would have unintended consequences." (*Hansard*, Standing Committee A, October 19, 2006 (afternoon), col.120 (Mr Jim Murphy MP).

However, there is an equivalent of the "exceptional circumstances" provision applicable to the limited capacity for work question, considered above. A claimant who does not pass the WRAAt can nonetheless be treated as having the requisite limited capability for work-related activity grounding membership of the support group where, by reason of the specific disease or bodily or mental disablement from which s/he suffers, "there would be a substantial risk to the mental or physical health of any person if the claimant were found not to have limited capability for work-related activity" (reg.35(2)).

300

There are only 11 activities in Sch.3: walking or moving on level ground; rising from sitting and transferring from one seated position to another; picking up and moving or transferring by means of the upper body and arms; reaching; manual dexterity; continence; maintaining personal hygiene; eating and drinking (conveying food or drink to the mouth and chewing or swallowing it); learning or comprehension in the completion of tasks; personal action (planning, organisation, problem solving, prioritising or switching tasks); and communication. The terms of the descriptors are also more stringent than in the WCAt, to avoid removing too many people from the group which affords incentive to engage in work-related activity and thus denying them the opportunity to take steps to make real their fundamental right to work. Thus, as regards walking, the single descriptor can only be met where a claimant cannot "walk" more than 30 metres without repeatedly stopping, experiencing breathlessness or severe discomfort. "Walk" covers walking with a walking stick, other aid or crunches, each if normally used; and embraces the claimant moving by manually propelling a wheelchair. That on rising from sitting etc, requires in effect that the claimant fulfil two of the 15 point descriptors in the WCAt. Most, with counterparts in the WCAt, are couched in terms equivalent to the more difficult of their 15-point descriptors.

Those meeting the WRAAt test (or satisfying the "exceptional circumstances" provision) will be placed in the support group and receive support component without having to satisfy work-related activity conditions, although they can voluntarily participate in those programmes. Their position can be reviewed periodically or where there has been a change of circumstances in the claimant's physical or mental condition or it is thought that a previous determination was made in ignorance of or a mistake as to some material fact (reg.34(4), (5)). The threshold for membership of the support group is high; many claimants in receipt of the middle and higher rates of Disability Living Allowance (DLA) may not meet it. Those who fail to establish limited capability for work-related activity will instead receive the work-related activity component.

Regulations 67(1)(a) and (2) and 68(1)(a) and (b)

SCHEDULE 4

AMOUNTS

PART 1

PRESCRIBED AMOUNTS

1. The weekly amounts specified in column (2) in respect of each person or couple specified in column (1) are the weekly amounts specified for the purposes of regulations 67(1) and 68 (prescribed amounts and polygamous marriages).   **1A.506**

(1)	(2)
Person or Couple	*Amount*
(1) Single claimant—	(1)
(a) who satisfies the conditions set out in section 2(2) or (3) or 4(4) or (5) of the Act;	(a) £60.50;
(b) aged not less than 25;	(b) £60.50;
(c) aged less than 25.	(c) £47.95;

301

(1) Person or Couple	(2) Amount

(2)	Lone parent—	(2)	
(a)	who satisfies the conditions set out in section 4(4) or (5) of the Act;	(a)	£60.50;
(b)	aged not less than 18;	(b)	£60.50;
(c)	aged less than 18.	(c)	£47.95;

(3)	Couple—	(3)	
(a)	where both members are aged not less than 18;	(a)	£94.95;
(b)	where one member is aged not less than 18 and the other member is a person under 18 who—	(b)	£94.95;
	(i) had they not been members of a couple, would (1) (2) Person or Couple Amount satisfy the requirements for entitlement to income support other than the requirement to make a claim for it; or		
	(ii) had they not been members of a couple, would satisfy the requirements for entitlement to an income-related allowance; or		
	(iii) satisfies the requirements of section 3(1)(f)(iii) of the Jobseekers Act (prescribed circumstances for persons aged 16 but less than 18); or		
	(iv) is the subject of a direction under section 16 of that Act (persons under 18: severe hardship);		
(c)	where the claimant satisfies the conditions set out in section 4(4) or (5) of the Act and both members are aged less than 18 and—	(c)	£94.95;
	(i) at least one of them is treated as responsible for a child; or		
	(ii) had they not been members of a couple, each would have qualified for an income-related allowance; or		
	(iii) had they not been members of a couple the claimant's partner would satisfy the requirements for entitlement to income support other than the requirement to make a claim for it; or		
	(iv) the claimant's partner satisfies the requirements of section 3(1)(f)(iii) of the Jobseekers Act (prescribed circumstances for persons aged 16 but less than 18); or		
	(v) there is in force in respect of the claimant's partner a direction under section 16 of that Act (persons under 18: severe hardship);		
(d)	where both members are aged less than 18 and—	(d)	£72.35;
	(i) at least one of them is treated as responsible for a child; or		
	(ii) had they not been members of a couple, each would have qualified for an income-related allowance; or		
	(iii) had they not been members of a couple the claimant's partner satisfies the requirements for entitlement to income support other than a requirement to make a claim for it; or		

(1)	*(2)*
Person or Couple	*Amount*

      (iv) the claimant's partner satisfies the requirements of section 3(1)(f)(iii) of the Jobseekers Act (prescribed circumstances for persons aged 16 but less than 18); or

      (v) there is in force in respect of the claimant's partner a direction under section 16 of that Act (persons under 18: severe hardship);

(e) where the claimant is aged not less than 25 and the claimant's partner is a person under 18 who—   (e) £60.50;

      (i) would not qualify for an income-related allowance if the person were not a member of a couple;

      (ii) would not qualify for income support if the person were not a member of a couple;

      (iii) does not satisfy the requirements of section 3(1)(f)(iii) of the Jobseekers Act (prescribed circumstances for persons aged 16 but less than 18); and

      (iv) is not the subject of a direction under section 16 of that Act (persons under 18: severe hardship);

(f) where the claimant satisfies the conditions set out in section 4(4) or (5) of the Act and the claimant's partner is a person under 18 who—   (f) £60.50;

      (i) would not qualify for an income-related allowance if the person were not a member of a couple;

      (ii) would not qualify for income support if the person [¹ were] not a member of a couple;

      (iii) does not satisfy the requirements of section 3(1)(f)(iii) of the Jobseekers Act (prescribed circumstances for persons aged 16 but less than 18); and

      (iv) is not the subject of a direction under section 16 of that Act (persons under 18: severe hardship);

(g) where the claimant satisfies the conditions set out in section 4(4) or (5) of the Act and both members are aged less than 18 and paragraph (c) does not apply;   (g) £60.50;

[¹ (h) where the claimant is aged not less than 18 but less than 25 and the claimant's partner is a person under 18 who—   (h) £47.95;

      (i) would not qualify for an income-related allowance if the person were not a member of a couple;

      (ii) would not qualify for income support if the person were not a member of a couple;

      (iii) does not satisfy the requirements of section 3(1)(f)(iii) of the Jobseekers Act (prescribed circumstances for persons aged 16 but less than 18); and

      (iv) is not the subject of a direction under section 16 of that Act (persons under 18: severe hardship);]

(i) where both members are aged less than 18 and paragraph (d) does not apply.   (i) £47.95.

Regulations 67(1)(b) and 68(1)(c)

Part 2

Premiums

1A.507   2. Except as provided in paragraph 4, the weekly premiums specified in Part 3 of this Schedule are, for the purposes of regulation 67(1)(b) and 68(1)(c), to be applicable to a claimant who satisfies the condition specified in paragraphs 5 to 8 in respect of that premium.

1A.508   3. An enhanced disability premium in respect of a person is not applicable in addition to a pensioner premium.

1A.509   4.—(1) For the purposes of this Part of this Schedule, once a premium is applicable to a claimant under this Part, a person is to be treated as being in receipt of any benefit—

(a) in the case of a benefit to which the Social Security (Overlapping Benefits) Regulations 1979 applies, for any period during which, apart from the provisions of those Regulations, the person would be in receipt of that benefit; and

(b) for any period spent by a person in undertaking a course of training or instruction provided or approved by the Secretary of State under section 2 of the Employment and Training Act 1973, or by Scottish Enterprise or Highlands and Islands Enterprise under section 2 of the Enterprise and New Towns (Scotland) Act 1990, or for any period during which the person is in receipt of a training allowance.

(2) For the purposes of the carer premium under paragraph 8, a claimant is to be treated as being in receipt of a carer's allowance by virtue of sub-paragraph (1)(a) only if and for so long as the person in respect of whose care the allowance has been claimed remains in receipt of attendance allowance, or the care component of disability living allowance at the highest or middle rate prescribed in accordance with section 72(3) of the Contributions and Benefits Act.

Pensioner premium

1A.510   5. The condition is that the claimant or the claimant's partner has attained the qualifying age for state pension credit.

Severe disability premium

1A.511   6.—(1) The condition is that the claimant is a severely disabled person.

(2) For the purposes of sub-paragraph (1), a claimant is to be treated as being a severely disabled person if, and only if—

(a) in the case of a single claimant, a lone parent or a claimant who is treated as having no partner in consequence of sub-paragraph (3)—

(i) the claimant is in receipt of the care component;

(ii) subject to sub-paragraph (4), the claimant has no non-dependants aged 18 or over normally residing with the claimant or with whom the claimant is normally residing; and

(iii) no person is entitled to, and in receipt of, a carer's allowance under section 70 of the Contributions and Benefits Act in respect of caring for the claimant;

(b) in the case of a claimant who has a partner—

(i) the claimant is in receipt of the care component;

(ii) the claimant's partner is also in receipt of the care component or attendance allowance or, if the claimant is a member of a polygamous marriage, all the partners of that marriage are in receipt of the care component or attendance allowance; and

(iii) subject to sub-paragraph (4), the claimant has no non-dependants aged 18 or over normally residing with the claimant or with whom the claimant is normally residing, and, either a person is entitled to, and in receipt of, a carer's allowance in respect of caring for only one of the couple or, in the case of a polygamous marriage, for one or more but not all the partners of the marriage or, as the case may be, no person is entitled to, and in receipt of, such an allowance in respect of caring for either member of the couple or any partner of the polygamous marriage.

(3) Where a claimant has a partner who does not satisfy the condition in sub-paragraph (2)(b)(ii) and that partner is blind or severely sight impaired or is treated as blind or

304

severely sight impaired that partner is to be treated for the purposes of sub-paragraph (2) as if the partner were not a partner of the claimant.

(4) For the purposes of sub-paragraph (2)(a)(ii) and (b)(iii) no account is to be taken of—

(a) a person receiving attendance allowance, or the care component;

(b) subject to sub-paragraph (7), a person who joins the claimant's household for the first time in order to care for the claimant or the claimant's partner and immediately before so joining the claimant or the claimant's partner was treated as a severely disabled person; or

(c) a person who is blind or severely sight impaired or is treated as blind or severely sight impaired.

(5) For the purposes of sub-paragraph (2)(b) a person is to be treated—

(a) as being in receipt of attendance allowance or the care component if the person would, but for the person being a patient for a period exceeding 28 days, be so in receipt;

(b) as being entitled to, and in receipt of, a carer's allowance if the person would, but for the person for whom the person was caring being a patient in hospital for a period exceeding 28 days, be so entitled and in receipt.

(6) For the purposes of sub-paragraph (2)(a)(iii) and (b), no account is to be taken of an award of carer's allowance to the extent that payment of such an award is backdated for a period before the date on which the award is first paid.

(7) Sub-paragraph (4)(b) is to apply only for the first 12 weeks following the date on which the person to whom that provision applies first joins the claimant's household.

(8) In sub-paragraph (2)(a)(iii) and (b), references to a person being in receipt of a carer's allowance are to include references to a person who would have been in receipt of that allowance but for the application of a restriction under section 7 of the Social Security Fraud Act 2001 (loss of benefit provisions).

(9) In this paragraph—

"blind or severely sight impaired" means registered as blind or severely sight impaired in a register compiled by a local authority under section 29 of the National Assistance Act 1948 (welfare services) or, in Scotland, has been certified as blind and in consequence the person is registered as blind in a register maintained by or on behalf of a regional or island council and a person who has ceased to be registered as blind or severely sight impaired where that person's eyesight has been regained is, nevertheless, to be treated as blind or severely sight impaired for a period of 28 weeks following the date on which the person ceased to be so registered;

"the care component" means the care component of disability living allowance at the highest or middle rate prescribed in accordance with section 72(3) of the Contributions and Benefits Act.

Enhanced disability premium

7.—(1) Subject to sub-paragraph (2), the condition is that—

1A.512

(a) the claimant's applicable amount includes the support component; or

(b) the care component of disability living allowance is, or would, but for a suspension of benefit in accordance with regulations under section 113(2) of the Contributions and Benefits Act or, but for an abatement as a consequence of hospitalisation, be payable at the highest rate prescribed under section 72(3) of that Act in respect of—

(i) the claimant; or

(ii) the claimant's partner (if any) who is aged less than the qualifying age for state pension credit.

(2) An enhanced disability premium is not applicable in respect of—

(a) a claimant who—

(i) is not a member of a couple or a polygamous marriage; and

(ii) is a patient within the meaning of regulation 69(2) and has been for a period of more than 52 weeks; or

(b) a member of a couple or a polygamous marriage where each member is a patient within the meaning of regulation 69(2) and has been for a period of more than 52 weeks.

Carer premium

1A.513 **8.**—(1) Subject to sub-paragraphs (2) and (4), the condition is that the claimant or the claimant's partner is, or both of them are, entitled to a carer's allowance under section 70 of the Contributions and Benefits Act.

(2) Where a carer premium is awarded but—

(a) the person in respect of whose care the carer's allowance has been awarded dies; or

(b) in any other case the person in respect of whom a carer premium has been awarded ceases to be entitled to a carer's allowance, the condition for the award of the premium is to be treated as satisfied for a period of 8 weeks from the relevant date specified in sub-paragraph (3).

(3) The relevant date for the purposes of sub-paragraph (2) is—

(a) where sub-paragraph (2)(a) applies, the Sunday following the death of the person in respect of whose care a carer's allowance has been awarded or the date of death if the death occurred on a Sunday; or

(b) in any other case, the date on which the person who has been entitled to a carer's allowance ceases to be entitled to that allowance.

(4) Where a person who has been entitled to a carer's allowance ceases to be entitled to that allowance and makes a claim for an income-related allowance, the condition for the award of the carer premium is to be treated as satisfied for a period of 8 weeks from the date on which—

(a) the person in respect of whose care the carer's allowance has been awarded dies; or

(b) in any other case, the person who has been entitled to a carer's allowance ceased to be entitled to that allowance.

Persons in receipt of concessionary payments

1A.514 **9.** For the purpose of determining whether a premium is applicable to a person under paragraphs 6, 7 and 8, any concessionary payment made to compensate that person for the non-payment of any benefit mentioned in those paragraphs is to be treated as if it were a payment of that benefit.

Persons in receipt of benefit

1A.515 **10.** For the purposes of this Part of this Schedule, a person is to be regarded as being in receipt of any benefit if, and only if, it is paid in respect of the person and is to be so regarded only for any period in respect of which that benefit is paid.

PART 3

WEEKLY AMOUNT OF PREMIUMS SPECIFIED IN PART 2

1A.516 **11.**—

Premium		Amount
(1) Pensioner premium for a person to whom paragraph 5 applies who—	(1)	
(a) is a single claimant and—	(a)	
(i) is entitled to the work-related activity component;	(i)	£39.55;
(ii) is entitled to the support component; or	(ii)	£34.55;
(iii) is not entitled to either of those components;	(iii)	£63.55;
(b) is a member of a couple and—	(b)	
(i) is entitled to the work-related activity component;	(i)	£70.40
(ii) is entitled to the support component; or	(ii)	£65.40;
(iii) is not entitled to either of those components.	(iii)	£94.40.

Premium	Amount
(2) Severe disability premium—	(2)
(a) where the claimant satisfies the condition in paragraph 6(2)(a);	(a) £50.35;
(b) where the claimant satisfies the condition in paragraph 6(2)(b)—	(b)
(i) if there is someone in receipt of a carer's allowance or if the person or any partner satisfies that condition only by virtue of paragraph 6(5);	(i) £50.35;
(ii) if no-one is in receipt of such an allowance.	(ii) £100.70.
(3) Carer premium.	(3) £27.75 in respect of each person who satisfies the condition specified in [¹ paragraph 8(1)].

(4) Enhanced disability premium where the conditions in paragraph 7 are satisfied.	(4) (a) £12.60 in respect of each person who is neither—
	    (i) a child or young person; nor
	    (ii) a member of a couple or a polygamous marriage, in respect of whom the conditions specified in paragraph 7 are satisfied;
	  (b) £18.15 where the claimant is a member of a couple or a polygamous marriage and the conditions specified in [¹ paragraph 7] are satisfied in respect of a member of that couple or polygamous marriage.

Regulation 67(3)

PART 4

THE COMPONENTS

12. The amount of the work-related activity component is £24.00.   **1A.517**
13. The amount of the support component is £29.00.   **1A.518**

AMENDMENT

1. Employment and Support Allowance (Miscellaneous Amendments) Regulations 2008 (SI 2008/2428), reg.14 (October 27, 2008).

GENERAL NOTE

See the commentary to reg.67 and to Sch.2 to the IS Regs. The work-related   **1A.519**
activity component and the support component are specific to income-related ESA. The amounts of those components are prescribed in paras 12 and 13 respectively.

SCHEDULE 5

SPECIAL CASES

PART 1

AMOUNTS PRESCRIBED FOR THE PURPOSES OF SECTION 4(2) OF THE ACT

Claimants without accommodation

1A.521   1. A claimant who is without accommodation.

1. The amount applicable to the claimant under regulation 67(1)(a).

Members of religious orders

1A.521.1   2. A claimant who is a member of, and fully maintained by, a religious order.

2. Nil.

Prisoners

1A.522   3. A claimant
- (a) except where sub-paragraph (b) applies, who is a prisoner;
- (b) who is detained in custody pending trial or sentence following conviction by a court.

3.
- (a) Nil;
- (b) only such amount, if any, as may be applicable under regulation 67(1)(c) and the amount of nil under regulation 67(3).

Specified cases of temporarily separated couples

1A.523   4. A claimant who is a member of a couple and who is temporarily separated from the claimant's partner where—
- (a) one member of the couple is—
  - (i) not a patient but is residing in a care home, an Abbeyfield Home or an independent hospital; or
  - (ii) resident in premises used for the rehabilitation of alcoholics or drug addicts; or
  - (iii) resident in accommodation provided under section 3 of and Part 2 of the Schedule to, the Polish Resettlement Act 1947 (provision of accommodation in camps); or
  - (iv) participating in arrangements for training made under section 2 of the Employment and Training Act 1973 or section 2 of the Enterprise and New Towns (Scotland) Act 1990 or attending a course at an employment rehabilitation centre established under

4. Either—
- (a) the amount applicable to the claimant as a member of a couple under regulation 67(1); or

that section of the 1973 Act, where the course requires the person to live away from the dwelling occupied as the home; or

    (v) in a probation or bail hostel approved for the purpose by the Secretary of State; and

(b) the other member of the couple is—

    (i) living in the dwelling occupied as the home; or

    (ii) a patient; or

    (iii) residing in a care home, an Abbeyfield Home or an independent hospital.

(b) the aggregate of the claimant's applicable amount and that of the claimant's partner assessed under the provisions of these Regulations as if each of them were a single claimant or a lone parent, whichever is the greater.

Polygamous marriages where one or more partners are temporarily separated

5. A claimant who is a member of a polygamous marriage and who is temporarily separated from a partner, where one of them is living in the home where the other member is—

(a) not a patient but is residing in a care home, an Abbeyfield Home or an independent hospital; or

(b) resident in premises used for the rehabilitation of alcoholics or drug addicts; or

(c) attending a course of training or instruction provided or approved by the Secretary of State where the course requires the person to live away from home; or

(d) in a probation or bail hostel approved for the purpose by the Secretary of State.

5. Either—

(a) the amount applicable to the members of the polygamous marriage under regulation 68; or

(b) the aggregate of the amount applicable for the members of the polygamous marriage who remain in the home under regulation 68 and the amount applicable in respect of those members not in the home calculated as if each of them were a single claimant or a lone parent, whichever is the greater.

1A.524

Couple where one member is abroad

6. Subject to paragraph 7, a claimant who is a member of a couple where one member of the couple is temporarily absent from the United Kingdom.

6. For the first 4 weeks of that absence, the amount applicable to them as a couple under regulation 67(1) or 69, as the case may be, and thereafter, the amount applicable to the claimant in Great Britain under regulation 67(1) or 69, as the case may be, as if the claimant were a single claimant or, as the case may be, lone parent.

1A.525

Couple or member of couple taking child or young person abroad for treatment

1A.526 7.— (1) A claimant who is a member of a couple where either—

    (a) the claimant or the claimant's partner is; or

    (b) both the claimant and the claimant's partner are, absent from the United Kingdom in the circumstances specified in sub-paragraph (2).

(2) For the purposes of sub-paragraph (1) the specified circumstances are—

    (a) in respect of a claimant, those in regulation 153(1)(a), (b), (c)(ii), (d) and (e);

    (b) in respect of a claimant's partner, as if regulation 153(1)(a), (b), (c)(ii), (d) and (e) applied to that partner.

7. For the first 26 weeks of that absence, the amount applicable to the claimant under regulation 67(1) or 69, as the case may be and, thereafter, if the claimant is in Great Britain the amount applicable to the claimant under regulation 67(1) or 69, as the case may be, as if the claimant were a single claimant or, as the case may be, a lone parent.

Polygamous marriages where any member is abroad

1A.527 8. Subject to paragraph 9, a claimant who is a member of a polygamous marriage where one or more members of the marriage are temporarily absent from the United Kingdom.

8. For the first 4 weeks of that absence, the amount applicable to the claimant under regulation 68 and 69, as the case may be, and thereafter, if the claimant is in Great Britain the amount applicable to the claimant under regulations 68 and 69, as the case may be, as if any members of the polygamous marriage not in the United Kingdom were not a member of the marriage.

Polygamous marriage: taking child or young person abroad for treatment

1A.528 9.—(1) A claimant who is a member of a polygamous marriage where one or more members of the marriage is absent from the United Kingdom in the circumstances specified in sub-paragraph (2).

(2) For the purposes of sub-paragraph (1) the specified circumstances are—

    (a) in respect of a claimant, those in regulation 153(1)(a), (b), (c)(ii), (d) and (e);

    (b) in respect of a claimant's partner or partners, as the case may be, as if regulation 153(1)(a), (b), (c)(ii), (d) and (e) applied to that partner or those [¹ partners].

9. For the first 26 weeks of that absence, the amount applicable to the claimant under regulations 68 and 69, as the case may be, and thereafter, if the claimant is in Great Britain the amount applicable to the claimant under regulations 68 and 69, as the case may be, as if any member of the polygamous marriage not in the United Kingdom were not a member of the marriage.

Partner of a person subject to immigration control

1A.529 10.

    (a) A claimant who is the partner of a person subject to immigration control.

10.

    (a) The amount applicable in respect of the claimant only under regulation 67(1)(a) any amount which may be applicable to

(b) Where regulation 68 (polygamous marriages) applies and the claimant is a person—
   (i) who is not subject to immigration control within the meaning of section 115(9) of the Immigration and Asylum Act; or
   (ii) to whom section 115 of that Act does not apply by virtue of regulation 2 of the Social Security (Immigration and Asylum) Consequential Amendments Regulations 2000; and
   (iii) who is a member of a couple and one or more of the person's partners is subject to immigration control within the meaning of section 115(9) of that Act and section 115 of that Act applies to that partner or those partners for the purposes of exclusion from entitlement to income-related allowance.

the claimant under regulation 67(1)(b) plus the amount applicable to the claimant under regulation 67(1)(c) or, as the case may be, regulation 69.

(b) the amount determined in accordance with that regulation or regulation 69 in respect of the claimant and any partners of the claimant who are not subject to immigration control within the meaning of section 115(9) of the Immigration and Asylum Act and to whom section 115 of that Act does not apply for the purposes of exclusion from entitlement to an income-related allowance.

Person from abroad

11. Person from abroad.	11. Nil.	**1A.530**

PART 2

AMOUNTS PRESCRIBED FOR THE PURPOSES OF SECTIONS 2(1) AND 4(2) OF THE ACT

Patients

12. A claimant who is detained, or liable to be detained under—
   (a) section 45A of the Mental Health Act 1983 (hospital and limitation directions) or section 59A of the Criminal Procedure (Scotland) Act 1995 (hospital directions); or
   (b) section 47 of the Mental Health Act 1983 (removal to hospital of persons serving sentences of imprisonment, etc.) or section

12. The amount applicable under regulation 67(2) and the amount of nil under regulation 67(3).

1A.531

136 of the Mental Health (Care and Treatment) (Scotland) Act 2003 (transfer of prisoners for treatment for mental disorder),

but not if the detention continues after the date which the Secretary of State certifies or Scottish Ministers certify would have been the earliest date on which the claimant could have been released in respect of, or from, the prison sentence if the claimant had not been detained in hospital.

1A.532 13. Subject to paragraph 12, a single claimant who has been a patient for a continuous period of more than 52 weeks or, where the claimant is one of a couple, the other member of the couple has been a patient for a continuous period of more than 52 weeks.

13. The amounts applicable under regulation 67(1)(a), (c) and (2) and the amount of nil under regulation 67(3).

Person in hardship

1A.533 14. A claimant who is a person in hardship.

14. The amount to which the claimant is entitled under regulation 67(1)(a) and (2) or 68(1)(a) is to be reduced by 20%.

AMENDMENT

1. Employment and Support Allowance (Miscellaneous Amendments) Regulations 2008 (SI 2008/2428), reg.15 (October 27, 2008).

GENERAL NOTE

1A.534 See the commentary to reg.67 and to Sch.7 to the IS Regs.

Regulations 67(1)(c) , 68[¹(1)](d)

SCHEDULE 6

HOUSING COSTS

Housing costs

1A.535 1.—(1) Subject to the following provisions of this Schedule, the housing costs applicable to a claimant are those costs—
   (a) which the claimant or, where the claimant has a partner, that partner is, in accordance with paragraph 4, liable to meet in respect of the dwelling occupied as the home which the claimant or that claimant's partner is treated as occupying; and
   (b) which qualify under paragraphs 16 to 18.
(2) In this Schedule—
"existing housing costs" means housing costs arising under an agreement entered into before 2nd October 1995, or under an agreement entered into after 1st October 1995 ("the new agreement")—
   (a) which replaces an existing agreement, provided that the person liable to meet the housing costs—
      (i) remains the same in both agreements; or
      (ii) where in either agreement more than one person is liable to meet the housing costs, the person is liable to meet the housing costs in both the existing agreement and the new agreement;
   (b) where the existing agreement was entered into before 2nd October 1995; and

312

(c) which is for a loan of the same amount as, or less than the amount of, the loan under the agreement it replaces, and for this purpose any amount payable to arrange the new agreement and included in the loan must be disregarded;

"housing costs" means those costs to which sub-paragraph (1) refers;

"new housing costs" means housing costs arising under an agreement entered into after 1st October 1995 other than an agreement referred to in the definition of "existing housing costs";

"standard rate" means the rate for the time being determined in accordance with paragraph 13.

(3) For the purposes of this Schedule a disabled person is a person—

(a) in respect of whom the main phase employment and support allowance is payable to the claimant or to a person living with the claimant;

(b) who, had that person in fact been entitled to income support, would have satisfied the requirements of paragraph 12 of Schedule 2 to the Income Support Regulations (additional condition for the disability premium);

(c) aged 75 or over; or

(d) who is disabled or severely disabled for the purposes of section 9(6) of the Tax Credits Act (maximum rate).

(4) For the purposes of sub-paragraph (3), a person will not cease to be a disabled person on account of that person being disqualified for receiving benefit or treated as not having limited capability for work by virtue of the operation of section 18(1) to (3) of the Act.

Remunerative work

2.—(1) Subject to [¹sub-paragraphs (2) to (8)], a [¹non-dependant (referred to in this paragraph as "person")] is to be treated for the purposes of this Schedule as engaged in remunerative work if that person is engaged, or, where the person's hours of work fluctuate, is engaged on average, for not less than 16 hours a week, being work for which payment is made or which is done in expectation of payment. **1A.536**

(2) Subject to sub-paragraph (3), in determining the number of hours for which a person is engaged in work where that person's hours of work fluctuate, regard is to be had to the average of hours worked over—

(a) if there is a recognisable cycle of work, the period of one complete cycle (including, where the cycle involves periods in which the person does no work, those periods but disregarding any other absences);

(b) in any other case, the period of 5 weeks immediately prior to the date of claim, or such other length of time as may, in the particular case, enable the person's weekly average hours of work to be determined more accurately.

(3) Where no recognisable cycle has been established in respect of a person's work, regard is to be had to the number of hours or, where those hours will fluctuate, the average of the hours, which that person is expected to work in a week.

(4) A person is to be treated as engaged in remunerative work during any period for which that person is absent from work referred to in sub-paragraph (1) if the absence is either without good cause or by reason of a recognised, customary or other holiday.

(5) A person is not to be treated as engaged in remunerative work on any day on which the person is on maternity leave, paternity leave or adoption leave or is absent from work because the person is ill.

(6) For the purposes of this paragraph, in determining the number of hours in which a person is engaged or treated as engaged in remunerative work, no account is to be taken of any hours in which the person is engaged in an employment or a scheme to which regulation 43(1) (circumstances under which partners of persons entitled to an income-related allowance are not to be treated as engaged in remunerative work) applies.

(7) For the purposes of sub-paragraphs (1) and (2), in determining the number of hours for which a person is engaged in work, that number is to include any time allowed to that person by that person's employer for a meal or for refreshment, but only where that person is, or expects to be, paid earnings in respect of that time.

[¹(8) A person is to be treated as not being engaged in remunerative work on any day in which that person falls within the circumstances prescribed in regulation 43(2) (circumstances in which partners of claimants entitled to an income-related allowance are not to be treated as engaged in remunerative work).

(9) Whether a claimant or the claimant's partner is engaged in, or to be treated as being engaged in, remunerative work is to be determined in accordance with regulations 41 or 42 (meaning of "remunerative work" for the purposes of paragraph 6(1)(e) and (f) of Schedule 1 to the Act) as the case may be.]

Previous entitlement to other income-related benefits

1A.537   3.—(1) Where the claimant or the claimant's partner was in receipt of, or was treated as being in receipt of, an income-based jobseeker's allowance or income support not more than 12 weeks before one of them becomes entitled to an income-related allowance or, where the claimant or the claimant's partner is a person to whom paragraph 15(2) or (13) (linking rules) refers, not more than 26 weeks before becoming so entitled and—

    (a) the applicable amount for that income-based jobseeker's allowance or income support included an amount in respect of housing costs under paragraphs 14 to 16 of Schedule 2 to the Jobseeker's Allowance Regulations or, as the case may be, paragraphs 15 to 17 of Schedule 3 to the Income Support Regulations; and

    (b) the circumstances affecting the calculation of those housing costs remain unchanged since the last calculation of those costs,

the applicable amount in respect of housing costs for an income-related allowance is to be the applicable amount in respect of those costs current when entitlement to an income-based jobseeker's allowance or income support was last determined.

(2) Where a claimant or the claimant's partner was in receipt of state pension credit not more than 12 weeks before one of them becomes entitled to [¹an income-related allowance] or, where the claimant or the claimant's partner is a person to whom paragraph 15(2) or (13) (linking rules) refers, not more than 26 weeks before becoming so entitled, and—

    (a) the appropriate minimum guarantee included an amount in respect of housing costs under paragraphs 11 to 13 of Schedule 2 to the State Pension Credit Regulations 2002; and

    (b) the circumstances affecting the calculation of those housing costs remain unchanged since the last calculation of those costs,

the applicable amount in respect of housing costs for an income-related allowance is to be the applicable amount in respect of those costs current when entitlement to state pension credit was last determined.

(3) Where, in the period since housing costs were last calculated for an income-based jobseeker's allowance, income support or, as the case may be, state pension credit, there has been a change of circumstances, other than a reduction in the amount of an outstanding loan, which increases or reduces those costs, the amount to be met under this Schedule must, for the purposes of the claim for an income-related allowance, be recalculated so as to take account of that change.

Circumstances in which a person is liable to meet housing costs

1A.538   4. A person is liable to meet housing costs where—

    (a) the liability falls upon that person or that person's partner but not where the liability is to a member of the same household as the person on whom the liability falls;

    (b) because the person liable to meet the housing costs is not meeting them, the claimant has to meet those costs in order to continue to live in the dwelling occupied as the home and it is reasonable in all the circumstances to treat the claimant as liable to meet those costs;

    (c) in practice the claimant shares the housing costs with other members of the household none of whom are close relatives either of the claimant or the claimant's partner, and—

        (i) one or more of those members is liable to meet those costs; and

        (ii) it is reasonable in the circumstances to treat the claimant as sharing responsibility.

Circumstances in which a person is to be treated as occupying a dwelling as the home

1A.539   5.—(1) Subject to the following provisions of this paragraph, a person is to be treated as occupying as the home the dwelling normally occupied as the home by that person or, if that person is a member of a family, by that person and that person's family and that person is not to be treated as occupying any other dwelling as the home.

(2) In determining whether a dwelling is the dwelling normally occupied as the claimant's home for the purposes of sub-paragraph (1) regard must be had to any other dwelling occupied by the claimant or by the claimant and that claimant's family whether or not that other dwelling is in Great Britain.

(3) Subject to sub-paragraph (4), where a claimant who has no partner is a full-time student or is on a training course and is liable to make payments (including payments of mortgage interest or, in Scotland, payments under heritable securities or, in either case, analogous payments) in respect of either (but not both) the dwelling which that claimant occupies for the purpose of attending the course of study or the training course or, as the case may be, the dwelling which that claimant occupies when not attending that course, that claimant is to be treated as occupying as the home the dwelling in respect of which that claimant is liable to make payments.

(4) A full-time student is not to be treated as occupying a dwelling as that student's home for any week of absence from it, other than an absence occasioned by the need to enter hospital for treatment, outside the period of study, if the main purposes of that student's occupation during the period of study would be to facilitate attendance on that student's course.

(5) Where a claimant has been required to move into temporary accommodation by reason of essential repairs being carried out to the dwelling normally occupied as the home and that claimant is liable to make payments (including payments of mortgage interest or, in Scotland, payments under heritable securities or, in either case, analogous payments) in respect of either (but not both) the dwelling normally occupied or the temporary accommodation, that claimant must be treated as occupying as the home the dwelling in respect of which that claimant is liable to make those payments.

(6) Where a claimant is liable to make payments in respect of two (but not more than two) dwellings, that claimant must be treated as occupying both dwellings as the home only—

(a) where that claimant has left and remains absent from the former dwelling occupied as the home through fear of violence in that dwelling or of violence by a former member of the claimant's family and it is reasonable that housing costs should be met in respect of both that claimant's former dwelling and that claimant's present dwelling occupied as the home;

(b) in the case of a couple or a member of a polygamous marriage where a partner is a fulltime student or is on a training course and it is unavoidable that that student, or they, should occupy two separate dwellings and reasonable that housing costs should be met in respect of both dwellings; or

(c) in the case where a claimant has moved into a new dwelling occupied as the home, except where sub-paragraph (5) applies, for a period not exceeding four benefit weeks from the first day of the benefit week in which the move occurs if that claimant's liability to make payments in respect of two dwellings is unavoidable.

(7) Where—

(a) a claimant has moved into a dwelling and was liable to make payments in respect of that dwelling before moving in;

(b) that claimant had claimed an income-related allowance before moving in and either that claim has not yet been determined or it has been determined but an amount has not been included under this Schedule and if the claim has been refused a further claim has been made within four weeks of the date on which the claimant moved into the new dwelling occupied as the home; and

(c) the delay in moving into the dwelling in respect of which there was liability to make payments before moving in was reasonable and—

(i) that delay was necessary in order to adapt the dwelling to meet the disablement needs of the claimant or any member of the claimant's family;

(ii) the move was delayed pending the outcome of an application for a social fund payment under Part 8 of the Contributions and Benefits Act to meet a need arising out of the move or in connection with setting up the home in the dwelling, and—

(aa) a member of the claimant's family is aged five or under;

(bb) the claimant is a person in respect of whom the main phase employment and support allowance is payable;

(cc) the claimant's applicable amount includes a pensioner premium;

(dd) the claimant's applicable amount includes a severe disability premium; or

(ee) a child tax credit is paid for a member of the claimant's family who is disabled or severely disabled for the purposes of section 9(6) of the Tax Credits Act; or

(iii) the claimant became liable to make payments in respect of the dwelling while that claimant was a patient or was in residential accommodation,

that claimant is to be treated as occupying the dwelling as the home for any period not exceeding four weeks immediately prior to the date on which that claimant moved into the dwelling and in respect of which that claimant was liable to make payments.

(8) This sub-paragraph applies to a claimant who enters residential accommodation—

(a) for the purpose of ascertaining whether the accommodation suits that claimant's needs; and

(b) with the intention of returning to the dwelling which that claimant normally occupies as the home should, in the event, the residential accommodation prove not to suit that claimant's needs,

and while in the accommodation, the part of the dwelling which that claimant normally occupies as the home is not let or sub-let to another person.

(9) A claimant to whom sub-paragraph (8) applies is to be treated as occupying the dwelling that the claimant normally occupies as the home during any period (commencing on the day that claimant enters the accommodation) not exceeding 13 weeks in which the claimant is resident in the accommodation, but only in so far as the total absence from the dwelling does not exceed 52 weeks.

(10) A claimant, other than a claimant to whom sub-paragraph (11) applies, is to be treated as occupying a dwelling as the home throughout any period of absence not exceeding 13 weeks, if, and only if—

(a) that claimant intends to return to occupy the dwelling as the home;

(b) the part of the dwelling normally occupied by that claimant has not been let or sub-let to another person; and

(c) the period of absence is unlikely to exceed 13 weeks.

(11) This sub-paragraph applies to a claimant whose absence from the dwelling that that claimant normally occupies as the home is temporary and—

(a) that claimant intends to return to occupy the dwelling as the home;

(b) the part of the dwelling normally occupied by that claimant has not been let or sub-let; and

(c) that claimant is—

(i) detained in custody on remand pending trial or, as a condition of bail, required to reside—

(aa) in a dwelling other than the dwelling that claimant occupies as the home; or

(bb) in premises approved under section 13 of the Offender Management Act 2007,

or, detained pending sentence upon conviction;

(ii) resident in a hospital or similar institution as a patient;

(iii) undergoing or, as the case may be, that claimant's partner or dependant child is undergoing, in the United Kingdom or elsewhere, medical treatment or medically approved convalescence, in accommodation other than residential accommodation;

(iv) following, in the United Kingdom or elsewhere, a training course;

(v) undertaking medically approved care of a person residing in the United Kingdom or elsewhere;

(vi) undertaking the care of a child whose parent or guardian is temporarily absent from the dwelling normally occupied by that parent or guardian for the purpose of receiving medically approved care or medical treatment;

(vii) a claimant who is, whether in the United Kingdom or elsewhere, receiving medically approved care provided in accommodation other than residential accommodation;

(viii) a full-time student to whom sub-paragraph (3) or (6)(b) does not apply;

(ix) a claimant other than a claimant to whom sub-paragraph (8) applies, who is receiving care provided in residential accommodation; or

      (x) a claimant to whom sub-paragraph (6)(a) does not apply and who has left the dwelling that claimant occupies as the home through fear of violence in that dwelling, or by a person who was formerly a member of that claimant's family; and

  (d) the period of that claimant's absence is unlikely to exceed a period of 52 weeks, or in exceptional circumstances, is unlikely substantially to exceed that period.

(12) A claimant to whom sub-paragraph (11) applies is to be treated as occupying the dwelling that claimant normally occupies as the home during any period of absence not exceeding 52 weeks beginning with the first day of that absence.

(13) In this paragraph—

"medically approved" means certified by a medical practitioner;

"patient" means a person who is undergoing medical or other treatment as an in-patient in a hospital or similar institution;

"residential accommodation" means accommodation which is a care home, an Abbeyfield Home or an independent hospital;

"training course" means such a course of training or instruction provided wholly or partly by or on behalf of or in pursuance of arrangements made with, or approved by or on behalf of, Scottish Enterprise, Highlands and Islands Enterprise, a government department or the Secretary of State.

Housing costs not met

6.—(1) No amount may be met under the provisions of this Schedule—   **1A.540**

  (a) in respect of housing benefit expenditure; or

  (b) where the claimant is living in a care home, an Abbeyfield Home or an independent hospital except where the claimant is living in such a home or hospital during a temporary absence from the dwelling the claimant occupies as the home and in so far as they relate to temporary absences, the provisions of paragraph 5(8) to (12) apply to that claimant during that absence.

(2) Subject to the following provisions of this paragraph, loans which, apart from this paragraph, qualify under paragraph 16 (loans on residential property) must not so qualify where the loan was incurred during the relevant period and was incurred—

  (a) after 27th October 2008; or

[¹(b) after 2nd May 1994 and the housing costs applicable to that loan were not met by virtue of the former paragraph 5A of Schedule 3 to the Income Support Regulations, or paragraph 4(2)(a) of Schedule 3 to the Income Support Regulations, paragraph 4(2)(a) of Schedule 2 to the Jobseeker's Allowance Regulations or paragraph 5(2)(a) of Schedule 2 to the State Pension Credit Regulations]; or

  (c) subject to sub-paragraph (3), in the 26 weeks preceding 27th October 2008 by a person—

      (i) who was not at that time entitled to income support, income-based jobseeker's allowance or state pension credit; and

      (ii) who becomes, or whose partner becomes entitled to an income-related allowance after 27th October 2008 and that entitlement is within 26 weeks of an earlier entitlement to income support, an income-based jobseeker's allowance or state pension credit of the claimant or the claimant's partner.

(3) Sub-paragraph (2)(c) will not apply in respect of a loan where the claimant has interest payments on that loan met without restrictions under an award of income support in respect of a period commencing before 27th October 2008.

(4) The "relevant period" for the purposes of this paragraph is any period during which the person to whom the loan was made—

  (a) is entitled to an income-related allowance, an income-based jobseeker's allowance, income support or state pension credit; or

  (b) has a partner and the partner is entitled to an income-related allowance, an income-based jobseeker's allowance, income support or state pension credit,

together with any linked period, that is to say a period falling between two periods separated by not more than 26 weeks in which one of the paragraphs (a) or (b) is satisfied.

(5) For the purposes of sub-paragraph (4), a person is to be treated as entitled to an income-related allowance during any period when that person or that person's partner was not so entitled because—

(a) that person or that person's partner was participating in an employment programme specified in regulation 75(1)(a)(ii) of the Jobseeker's Allowance Regulations or in the Intensive Activity Period specified in regulation 75(1)(a)(iv) of those Regulations; and

(b) in consequence of such participation that person or that person's partner was engaged in remunerative work or had an income in excess of the claimant's applicable amount as prescribed in Part 9.

(6) A person treated by virtue of paragraph 15 as being in receipt of an income-related allowance for the purposes of this Schedule is not to be treated as entitled to an income-related allowance for the purposes of sub-paragraph (4).

(7) For the purposes of sub-paragraph (4)—

(a) any week in the period of 26 weeks ending on 1st October 1995 on which there arose an entitlement to income support such as is mentioned in that sub-paragraph must be taken into account in determining when the relevant period commences; and

(b) two or more periods of entitlement and any intervening linked periods must together form a single relevant period.

(8) Where the loan to which sub-paragraph (2) refers has been applied—

(a) for paying off an earlier loan, and that earlier loan qualified under paragraph 16 during the relevant period; or

(b) to finance the purchase of a property where an earlier loan, which qualified under paragraph 16 or 17 during the relevant period in respect of another property, is paid off (in whole or in part) with monies received from the sale of that property,

then the amount of the loan to which sub-paragraph (2) applies is the amount (if any) by which the new loan exceeds the earlier loan.

(9) Notwithstanding the preceding provisions of this paragraph, housing costs must be met in any case where a claimant satisfies any of the conditions specified in sub-paragraphs (10) to (13), but—

(a) those costs must be subject to any additional limitations imposed by the sub-paragraph; and

(b) where the claimant satisfies the conditions in more than one of these sub-paragraphs, only one of them will apply in that claimant's case and the one that applies will be the one most favourable to the claimant.

(10) The conditions specified in this sub-paragraph are that—

(a) during the relevant period the claimant or a member of the claimant's family acquires an interest ("the relevant interest") in a dwelling which that claimant then occupies or continues to occupy, as the home; and

(b) in the week preceding the week in which the relevant interest was acquired, housing benefit was payable to the claimant or a member of the claimant's family,

so however that the amount to be met by way of housing costs will initially not exceed the aggregate of—

(i) the housing benefit payable in the week mentioned at sub-paragraph (10)(b); and

(ii) any amount included in the applicable amount of the claimant or a member of the claimant's family in accordance with regulation 67(1)(c) or 68(1)(d) in that week,

and is to be increased subsequently only to the extent that it is necessary to take account of any increase, arising after the date of the acquisition, in the standard rate or in any housing costs which qualify under paragraph 18 (other housing costs).

(11) The condition specified in this sub-paragraph is that the loan was taken out, or an existing loan increased, to acquire alternative accommodation more suited to the special needs of a disabled person than the accommodation which was occupied before the acquisition by the claimant.

(12) The conditions specified in this sub-paragraph are that—

(a) the loan commitment increased in consequence of the disposal of the dwelling occupied as the home and the acquisition of an alternative such dwelling; and

(b) the change of dwelling was made solely by reason of the need to provide separate sleeping accommodation for [¹persons of different sexes aged 10 or over but aged under 20] who belong to the same family as the claimant.

(13) The conditions specified in this sub-paragraph are that—

(a) during the relevant period the claimant or a member of the claimant's family acquires an interest ("the relevant interest") in a dwelling which that claimant then occupies as the home; and

(b) in the week preceding the week in which the relevant interest was acquired, the applicable amount of the claimant or a member of the claimant's family included an amount determined by reference to paragraph 18 and did not include any amount specified in paragraph 16 or paragraph 17,

so however that the amount to be met by way of housing costs will initially not exceed the amount so determined, and will be increased subsequently only to the extent that it is necessary to take account of any increase, arising after the date of acquisition, in the standard rate or in any housing costs which qualify under paragraph 18.

(14) The following provisions of this Schedule will have effect subject to the provisions of this paragraph.

Apportionment of housing costs

7.—(1) Where the dwelling occupied as the home is a composite hereditament and—   **1A.541**

(a) before 1st April 1990 for the purposes of section 48(5) of the General Rate Act 1967 (reduction of rates on dwellings), it appeared to a rating authority or it was determined in pursuance of subsection (6) of section 48 of that Act that the hereditament, including the dwelling occupied as the home, was a mixed hereditament and that only a proportion of the rateable value of the hereditament was attributable to use for the purpose of a private dwelling; or

(b) in Scotland, before 1st April 1989 an assessor acting pursuant to section 45(1) of the Water (Scotland) Act 1980 (provision as to valuation roll) has apportioned the net annual value of the premises including the dwelling occupied as the home between the part occupied as a dwelling and the remainder,

the amounts applicable under this Schedule are to be such proportion of the amounts applicable in respect of the hereditament or premises as a whole as is equal to the proportion of the rateable value of the hereditament attributable to the part of the hereditament used for the purposes of a private tenancy or, in Scotland, the proportion of the net annual value of the premises apportioned to the part occupied as a dwelling house.

(2) Subject to sub-paragraph (1) and the following provisions of this paragraph, where the dwelling occupied as the home is a composite hereditament, the amount applicable under this Schedule is to be the relevant fraction of the amount which would otherwise be applicable under this Schedule in respect of the dwelling occupied as the home.

(3) For the purposes of sub-paragraph (2), the relevant fraction is to be obtained in accordance with the formula—

$$\frac{A}{A + B}$$

where—

A is the current market value of the claimant's interest in that part of the composite hereditament which is domestic property within the meaning of section 66 of the Act of 1988;

B is the current market value of the claimant's interest in that part of the composite hereditament which is not domestic property within that section.

(4) In this paragraph—

"composite hereditament" means—

(a) as respects England and Wales, any hereditament which is shown as a composite hereditament in a local non-domestic rating list;

(b) as respects Scotland, any lands and heritages entered in the valuation roll which are part residential subjects within the meaning of section 26(1) of the Act of 1987;

"local non-domestic rating list" means a list compiled and maintained under section 41(1) of the Act of 1988;

"the Act of 1987" means the Abolition of Domestic Rates Etc. (Scotland) Act 1987;

"the Act of 1988" means the Local Government Finance Act 1988.

(5) Where responsibility for expenditure which relates to housing costs met under this Schedule is shared, the amounts applicable are to be calculated by reference to the appropriate proportion of that expenditure for which the claimant is responsible.

Existing housing costs

1A.542   **8.**—(1) Subject to the provisions of this Schedule, the existing housing costs to be met in any particular case are—

(a) where the claimant has been entitled to an employment and support allowance for a continuous period of 26 weeks or more, the aggregate of—

(i) an amount determined in the manner set out in paragraph 11 by applying the standard rate to the eligible capital for the time being owing in connection with a loan which qualifies under paragraph 16 or 17; and

(ii) an amount equal to any payments which qualify under paragraph 18(1)(a) to (c);

(b) where the claimant has been entitled to an employment and support allowance for a continuous period of not less than 8 weeks but less than 26 weeks, an amount which is half the amount which would fall to be met by applying the provisions of sub-paragraph(a);

(c) in any other case, nil.

(2) For the purposes of sub-paragraph (1) and subject to sub-paragraph (3), the eligible capital for the time being owing is to be determined on the date the existing housing costs are first met and thereafter on each anniversary of that date.

(3) Where a claimant or that claimant's partner ceases to be in receipt of or treated as being in receipt of income support, income-based jobseeker's allowance or state pension credit and one of them becomes entitled to an income-related allowance in a case to which paragraph 3 applies, the eligible capital for the time being owing is to be recalculated on each anniversary of the date on which the housing costs were first met for whichever of the benefits concerned the claimant or the claimant's partner was first entitled.

New housing costs

1A.543   **9.**—(1) Subject to the provisions of this Schedule, the new housing costs to be met in any particular case are—

(a) where the claimant has been entitled to an employment and support allowance for a continuous period of 39 weeks or more, an amount—

(i) determined in the manner set out in paragraph 11 by applying the standard rate to the eligible capital for the time being owing in connection with a loan which qualifies under paragraph 16 or 17; and

(ii) equal to any payments which qualify under paragraph 18(1)(a) to (c);

(b) in any other case, nil.

(2) For the purposes of sub-paragraph (1) and subject to sub-paragraph (3), the eligible capital for the time being owing is to be determined on the date the new housing costs are first met and thereafter on each anniversary of that date.

(3) Where a claimant or that claimant's partner ceases to be in receipt of or treated as being in receipt of income support, income-based jobseeker's allowance or state pension credit and one of them becomes entitled to an income-related allowance in a case to which [¹paragraph 3] applies, the eligible capital for the time being owing is to be recalculated on each anniversary of the date on which the housing costs were first met for whichever of the benefits concerned the claimant or that claimant's partner was first entitled.

(4) This sub-paragraph applies to a claimant who at the time the claim is made—

(a) is a person who is described in paragraph 4 or 5 of Schedule 1B of the Income Support Regulations (person caring for another person);

(b) is detained in custody pending trial or sentence upon conviction; or

(c) has been refused payments under a policy of insurance on the ground that—

(i) the claim under the policy is the outcome of a pre-existing medical condition which, under the terms of the policy, does not give rise to any payment by the insurer; or

(ii) that claimant was infected by the Human Immunodeficiency Virus;

(iii) and the policy was taken out to insure against the risk of being unable to maintain repayments on a loan which is secured by a mortgage or a charge over land, or (in Scotland) by a heritable security.

(5) This sub-paragraph applies subject to sub-paragraph (7) where a person claims an income-related allowance because of—

(a) the death of a partner; or

(b) being abandoned by that claimant's partner,

and where that claimant's family includes a child.

(6) In the case of a claimant to whom sub-paragraph (4) or (5) applies, any new housing costs are to be met as though they were existing housing costs and paragraph 8 (existing housing costs) applied to them.

(7) Sub-paragraph (5) must cease to apply to a claimant who subsequently becomes one of a couple.

General exclusions from paragraphs 8 and 9

10.—(1) Paragraphs 8 and 9 will not apply where—

    (a) the claimant's partner has attained the qualifying age for state pension credit;

    (b) the housing costs are payments—

        (i) under a co-ownership agreement;

        (ii) under or relating to a tenancy or licence of a Crown tenant; or

        (iii) where the dwelling occupied as the home is a tent, in respect of the tent and the site on which it stands.

(2) In a case falling within sub-paragraph (1), the housing costs to be met are—

    (a) where paragraph (a) of sub-paragraph (1) applies, an amount—

        (i) determined in the manner set out in paragraph 11 by applying the standard rate for the time being owing in connection with a loan which qualifies under paragraph 16 or 17; and

        (ii) equal to the payments which qualify under paragraph 18;

    (b) where paragraph (b) of sub-paragraph (1) applies, an amount equal to the payments which qualify under paragraph 18(1)(d) to (f).

1A.544

The calculation for loans

11. The weekly amount of existing housing costs or, as the case may be, new housing costs to be met under this Schedule in respect of a loan which qualifies under paragraph 16 or 17 are to be calculated by applying the formula—

$$\frac{A \times B}{52}$$

where—

    A = the amount of the loan which qualifies under paragraph 16 or 17; and

    B = the standard rate for the time being applicable in respect of that loan.

1A.545

General provisions applying to new and existing housing costs

12.—(1) Where on or after 2nd October 1995 a person enters into a new agreement in respect of a dwelling and an agreement entered into before 2nd October 1995 ("the earlier agreement") continues in force independently of the new agreement, then—

    (a) the housing costs applicable to the new agreement are to be calculated by reference to the provisions of paragraph 9 (new housing costs);

    (b) the housing costs applicable to the earlier agreement are to be calculated by reference to the provisions of paragraph 8 (existing housing costs);

and the resulting amounts are to be aggregated.

(2) Sub-paragraph (1) does not apply in the case of a claimant to whom paragraph 10 applies.

(3) Where for the time being a loan exceeds, or in a case where more than one loan is to be taken into account, the aggregate of those loans exceeds the appropriate amount specified in sub-paragraph (4), then the amount of the loan or, as the case may be, the aggregate amount of those loans, will for the purposes of this Schedule, be the appropriate amount.

(4) Subject to the following provisions of this paragraph, the appropriate amount is £100,000.

(5) Where a claimant is treated under paragraph 5(6) (payments in respect of two dwellings) as occupying two dwellings as the home, then the restrictions imposed by sub-paragraph (3) are to be applied separately to the loans for each dwelling.

(6) In a case to which paragraph 7 (apportionment of housing costs) applies, the appropriate amount for the purposes of sub-paragraph (3) is to be the lower of—

    (a) a sum determined by applying the formula—

$$P \times Q$$

    where—

    P = the relevant fraction for the purposes of paragraph 7; and

1A.546

Q = the amount or, as the case may be, the aggregate amount for the time being of any loan or loans which qualify under this Schedule; or

(b) the sum for the time being specified in sub-paragraph (4).

(7) In a case to which paragraph 16(3) or 17(3) (loans which qualify in part only) applies, the appropriate amount for the purposes of sub-paragraph (3) is to be the lower of—

(a) a sum representing for the time being the part of the loan applied for the purposes specified in paragraph 16(1) or (as the case may be) paragraph 17(1); or

(b) the sum for the time being specified in sub-paragraph (4).

(8) In the case of any loan to which paragraph 17(2)(k) (loan taken out and used for the purpose of adapting a dwelling for the special needs of a disabled person) applies the whole of the loan, to the extent that it remains unpaid, is to be disregarded in determining whether the amount for the time being specified in sub-paragraph (4) is exceeded.

(9) Where in any case the amount for the time being specified for the purposes of sub-paragraph (4) is exceeded and there are two or more loans to be taken into account under either or both paragraphs 16 and 17, then the amount of eligible interest in respect of each of those loans to the extent that the loans remain outstanding is to be determined as if each loan had been reduced to a sum equal to the qualifying portion of that loan.

(10) For the purposes of sub-paragraph (9), the qualifying portion of a loan is to be determined by applying the following formula—

$$R \times \frac{S}{T}$$

where—

R = the amount for the time being specified for the purposes of sub-paragraph (3)

S = the amount of the outstanding loan to be taken into account; and

T = the aggregate of all outstanding loans to be taken into account under paragraphs 16 and 17.

[¹ (11) Sub-paragraph (12) applies to a person who, had the person been entitled to income support and not an employment and support allowance, would have been a person to whom any of the following transitional or savings provisions would have applied—

(a) regulation 4 of the Income Support (General) Amendment No. 3 Regulations 1993 ("the 1993 Regulations");

(b) regulation 28 of the Income-related Benefits Schemes (Miscellaneous Amendments) Regulations 1995 ("the 1995 Regulations").

(12) Where this sub-paragraph applies, the amount of housing costs applicable in the particular case shall be determined as if—

(a) in a case to which regulation 4(1) of the 1993 Regulations would have applied, sub-paragraphs 12(4) to (9) do not apply;

(b) in a case to which regulation 4(4) of the 1993 Regulation would have applied, the appropriate amount is £150,000; and

(c) in a case to which the 1995 Regulations would have applied, the appropriate amount is £125,000.]

The standard rate

1A.547   **13.**—(1) The standard rate is the rate of interest applicable per annum to a loan which qualifies under this Schedule.

(2) Subject to sub-paragraph (3), the standard rate is to be 1.58% plus—

(a) the rate announced from time to time by the Monetary Policy Committee of the Bank of England as the official dealing rate, being the rate at which the Bank is willing to enter into transactions for providing short term liquidity in the money markets; or

(b) where an order under section 19 of the Bank of England Act 1998 (reserve powers) is in force, any equivalent rate determined by the Treasury under that section.

(3) The Secretary of State will determine the date from which the standard rate calculated in accordance with sub-paragraph (2) takes effect.

Excessive Housing Costs

14.—(1) Housing costs which, apart from this paragraph, fall to be met under this Schedule are to be met only to the extent specified in sub-paragraph (3) where—

(a) the dwelling occupied as the home, excluding any part which is let, is larger than is required by the claimant, that claimant's partner (if the claimant has a partner), any person under the age of 20 and any other non-dependants having regard, in particular, to suitable alternative accommodation occupied by a household of the same size; or

(b) the immediate area in which the dwelling occupied as the home is located is more expensive than other areas in which suitable alternative accommodation exists; or

(c) the outgoings of the dwelling occupied as the home which are met under paragraphs 16 to 18 are higher than the outgoings of suitable alternative accommodation in the area.

(2) For the purposes of paragraphs (a) to (c) of sub-paragraph (1), no regard is to be had to the capital value of the dwelling occupied as the home.

(3) Subject to the following provisions of this paragraph, the amount of the loan which falls to be met is to be restricted and the excess over the amounts which the claimant would need to obtain suitable alternative accommodation will not be allowed.

(4) Where, having regard to the relevant factors, it is not reasonable to expect the claimant and the claimant's partner to seek alternative cheaper accommodation, no restriction is to be made under sub-paragraph (3).

(5) In sub-paragraph (4) "the relevant factors" are—

(a) the availability of suitable accommodation and the level of housing costs in the area; and

(b) the circumstances of the claimant and those who live with the claimant, including, in particular, the age and state of health of any of those persons, the employment prospects of the claimant and, where a change in accommodation is likely to result in a change of school, the effect on the education of any person below the age of 20 who lives with the claimant.

(6) Where sub-paragraph (4) does not apply and the claimant or the claimant's partner was able to meet the financial commitments for the dwelling occupied as the home when these were entered into, no restriction is to be made under this paragraph during the 26 weeks immediately following the date on which—

(a) the claimant became entitled to an income-related allowance where the claimant's housing costs fell within one of the cases in sub-paragraph (1) on that date; or

(b) a decision took effect which was made under section 10 of the Social Security Act 1998 on the ground that the claimant's housing costs fell within one of the cases in sub-paragraph (1),

nor during the next 26 weeks if and so long as the best endeavours of the claimant are used to obtain cheaper accommodation.

(7) For the purposes of calculating any period of 26 weeks referred to in sub-paragraph (6), and for those purposes only, a person is to be treated as entitled to an income-related allowance for any period of 12 weeks or less in respect of which that person was not in receipt of an income-related allowance and which fell immediately between periods in respect of which that person was in receipt of that allowance.

(8) Any period in respect of which—

(a) an income-related allowance was paid to a claimant; and

(b) it was subsequently determined that such a claimant was not entitled to an income-related allowance for that period,

will be treated for the purposes of sub-paragraph (7) as a period in respect of which that claimant was not in receipt of an income-related allowance.

(9) Paragraphs (c) to (f) of sub-paragraph (1) of paragraph 15 will apply to sub-paragraph (7) as they apply to paragraphs 8 and 9 but with the modification that the words "Subject to sub-paragraph (2)" were omitted and references to "the claimant" were references to the person mentioned in sub-paragraph (7).

(10) References to an income-related allowance in sub-paragraphs (6) and (7) must be treated as including references to income support, income-based jobseeker's allowance and state pension credit in respect of any period which falls immediately before the appointed day.

Linking rule

15.—(1) Subject to sub-paragraph (2), for the purposes of this Schedule—

(a) a claimant is to be treated as being in receipt of an income-related allowance during the following periods—

(i) any period in respect of which it was subsequently determined that that claimant was entitled to an income-related allowance; and

1A.548

323

(ii) any period of 12 weeks or less or, as the case may be, 52 weeks or less, in respect of which that claimant was not in receipt of an income-related allowance and which fell immediately between periods in respect of which—

    (aa) that claimant was, or was treated as being, in receipt of an income-related allowance;

    (bb) that claimant was treated as entitled to an income-related allowance for the purpose of sub-paragraph (9) or (10); or

    (cc) (i) above applies;

(b) a claimant is to be treated as not being in receipt of an income-related allowance during any period other than a period to which (a)(ii) above applies in respect of which it is subsequently determined that that claimant was not so entitled;

(c) where—

    (i) the claimant was a member of a couple or a polygamous marriage; and

    (ii) the claimant's partner was, in respect of a past period, in receipt of an income-related allowance for that claimant's partner and the claimant; and

    (iii) the claimant is no longer a member of that couple or polygamous marriage; and

    (iv) the claimant made a claim for an income-related allowance within 12 weeks or, as the case may be, 52 weeks, of ceasing to be a member of that couple or polygamous marriage,

the claimant must be treated as having been in receipt of an income-related allowance for the same period as the claimant's former partner had been or had been treated, for the purposes of this Schedule, as having been;

(d) where the claimant's partner's applicable amount was determined in accordance with paragraph 1(1) (single claimant) or paragraph 1(2) (lone parents) of Part 1 of Schedule 4 (prescribed amounts) in respect of a past period, provided that the claim was made within 12 weeks or, as the case may be, 52 weeks, of the claimant and that claimant's partner becoming one of a couple or polygamous marriage, the claimant is to be treated as having been in receipt of an income-related allowance for the same period as the claimant's partner had been or had been treated, for the purposes of this Schedule, as having been;

(e) where the claimant is a member of a couple or a polygamous marriage and the claimant's partner was, in respect of a past period, in receipt of an income-related allowance for that claimant's partner and the claimant, and the claimant has begun to receive an income-related allowance as a result of an election by the members of the couple or polygamous marriage, that claimant is to be treated as having been in receipt of an income-related allowance for the same period as that claimant's partner had been or had been treated, for the purposes of this Schedule, as having been;

(f) where the claimant—

    (i) is a member of a couple or a polygamous marriage and the claimant's partner was, immediately before the participation by any member of that couple or polygamous marriage in an employment programme specified in regulation 75(1)(a)(ii) of the Jobseeker's Allowance Regulations, in the Intensive Activity Period specified in regulation 75(1)(a)(iv) of those Regulations, in receipt of an income-related allowance and the claimant's applicable amount included an amount for the couple or for the partners of the polygamous marriage; and

    (ii) has, immediately after that participation in that programme, begun to receive an income-related allowance as a result of an election under regulation 4(3) of the Social Security (Claims and Payments) Regulations 1987 by the members of the couple or polygamous marriage,

the claimant is to be treated as having been in receipt of an income-related allowance for the same period as that claimant's partner had been or had been treated, for the purposes of this Schedule, as having been;

(g) where—

    (i) the claimant was a member of a family of a person (not being a former partner) entitled to an income-related allowance and at least one other member of that family was a child or young person;

    (ii) the claimant becomes a member of another family which includes that child or young person; and

    (iii) the claimant made a claim for an income-related allowance within 12 weeks or, as the case may be, 52 weeks, of the date on which the person entitled to an income-related allowance mentioned in paragraph (i) above ceased to be so entitled,

the claimant is to be treated as being in receipt of an income-related allowance for the same period as that person had been or had been treated, for the purposes of this Schedule, as having been.

(2) Where a claimant, with the care of a child, has ceased to be in receipt of an income-related allowance in consequence of the payment of child support maintenance under the Child Support Act and immediately before ceasing to be so in receipt an amount determined in accordance with paragraph 8(1)(a)(i) or paragraph 9(1)(a)(i) was applicable to that claimant, then—

(a) if the child support maintenance assessment or, as the case may be, maintenance calculation concerned is terminated or replaced by a lower assessment or, as the case may be, calculation in consequence of the coming into force on or after 18th April 1995 of regulations made under the Child Support Act; or

(b) where the child support maintenance assessment or, as the case may be, maintenance calculation concerned is an interim maintenance assessment or, as the case may be, interim maintenance decision or default maintenance decision and, in circumstances other than those referred to in paragraph (a), it is terminated or replaced after termination by another interim maintenance assessment or, as the case may be, interim maintenance decision or default maintenance decision or by a maintenance assessment or, as the case may be, calculation made in accordance with Part 1 of Schedule 1 to the Child Support Act, in either case of a lower amount than the assessment or, as the case may be, calculation concerned,

sub-paragraph (1)(a)(ii) will apply to that claimant as if for the words "any period of 12 weeks or less" there were substituted the words "any period of 26 weeks or less".

(3) For the purposes of this Schedule, where a claimant has ceased to be entitled to an income-related allowance because that claimant or that claimant's partner is—

(a) participating in arrangements for training made under section 2 of the Employment and Training Act 1973 or section 2 of the Enterprise and New Towns (Scotland) Act 1990; or

(b) attending a course at an employment rehabilitation centre established under that section,

the claimant is to be treated as if that claimant had been in receipt of an income-related allowance for the period during which that claimant or that claimant's partner was participating in such arrangements or attending such a course.

(4) For the purposes of this Schedule, a claimant who has ceased to be entitled to an income-related allowance because—

(a) that claimant or that claimant's partner was participating in an employment programme specified in regulation 75(1)(a)(ii) of the Jobseeker's Allowance Regulations, in the Intensive Activity Period specified in regulation 75(1)(a)(iv) of those Regulations or in an employment zone scheme; and

(b) in consequence of such participation the claimant or the claimant's partner was engaged in remunerative work or had an income in excess of the claimant's applicable amount as prescribed in Part 9,

will be treated as if the claimant had been in receipt of an income-related allowance for the period during which that claimant or that claimant's partner was participating in that programme or activity.

(5) Where, for the purposes of sub-paragraphs (1), (3) and (4), a claimant is treated as being in receipt of an income-related allowance, for a certain period, that claimant will, subject to sub-paragraph (6), be treated as being entitled to an income-related allowance for the same period.

(6) Where the appropriate amount of a loan exceeds the amount specified in paragraph 12(4), sub-paragraph (5) will not apply except—

(a) for the purposes of paragraph 8(1) or 9(1); or

(b) where a claimant has ceased to be in receipt of an income-related allowance for a period of 104 weeks or less because that claimant or that claimant's partner is a work or training beneficiary within the meaning of regulation 148 (work or training beneficiaries).

(7) For the purposes of this Schedule, in determining whether a claimant is entitled to or to be treated as entitled to an income-related allowance, entitlement to a contribution-based jobseeker's allowance immediately before a period during which that claimant or

that claimant's partner is participating in an employment programme specified in regulation 75(1)(a)(ii) of the Jobseeker's Allowance Regulations, in the Intensive Activity Period specified in regulation 75(1)(a)(iv) of those Regulations is to be treated as entitlement to an income-related allowance for the purposes of any requirement that a claimant is, or has been, entitled to an income-related allowance for any period of time.

(8) For the purposes of this Schedule, sub-paragraph (9) applies where a claimant is not entitled to an income-related allowance by reason only that the claimant has—

(a) capital exceeding £16,000; or

(b) income exceeding the applicable amount which applies in that claimant's case; or

(c) both capital exceeding £16,000 and income exceeding the applicable amount which applies in that claimant's case.

(9) A claimant to whom sub-paragraph (8) applies is to be treated as entitled to an income-related allowance throughout any period of not more than 39 weeks which comprises only days—

(a) on which that claimant is entitled to a contributory allowance, a contribution-based jobseeker's allowance, statutory sick pay or incapacity benefit; or

(b) on which that claimant is, although not entitled to any of the benefits mentioned in paragraph (a) above, entitled to be credited with earnings equal to the lower earnings limit for the time being in force in accordance with regulation 8A or 8B of the Social Security (Credits) Regulations 1975.

(10) Subject to sub-paragraph (11), a claimant to whom sub-paragraph (8) applies and who is either a lone parent or a person who is described in paragraph 4 or 5 of Schedule 1B of the Income Support Regulations (persons caring for another person) is, for the purposes of this Schedule, to be treated as entitled to an income-related allowance throughout any period of not more than 39 weeks following the refusal of a claim for an income-related allowance made by or on behalf of that claimant.

(11) Sub-paragraph (10) will not apply in relation to a claimant mentioned in that sub-paragraph who, during the period referred to in that sub-paragraph—

(a) is engaged in, or is treated as engaged in, remunerative work or whose partner is engaged in, or is treated as engaged in, remunerative work;

[¹(b) is in full-time education and in receipt of disability living allowance;]

(c) is temporarily absent from Great Britain, other than in the circumstances specified in regulation 152 or 153(1)(c)(ii) (temporary absence from Great Britain).

(12) In a case where—

(a) sub-paragraphs (9) and (10) apply solely by virtue of sub-paragraph (8)(b); and

(b) the claimant's income includes payments under a policy taken out to insure against the risk that the policy holder is unable to meet any loan or payment which qualifies under paragraphs 16 to 18,

sub-paragraphs (9) and (10) will have effect as if for the words "throughout any period of not more than 39 weeks" there will be substituted the words "throughout any period that payments are made in accordance with the terms of the policy".

(13) This sub-paragraph applies—

(a) to a person who claims an income-related allowance, or in respect of whom an income-related allowance is claimed and who—

(i) received payments under a policy of insurance taken out to insure against loss of employment, and those payments are exhausted; and

(ii) had a previous award of an income-related allowance where the applicable amount included an amount by way of housing costs; and

(b) where the period in respect of which the previous award of an income-related allowance was payable ended not more than 26 weeks before the date the claim was made.

(14) Where sub-paragraph (13) applies, in determining—

(a) for the purposes of paragraph 8(1) whether a claimant has been entitled to an income-related allowance for a continuous period of 26 weeks or more; or

(b) for the purposes of paragraph 9(1) whether a claimant has been entitled to an income-related allowance for a continuous period of 39 weeks or more,

any week falling between the date of the termination of the previous award and the date of the new claim is to be ignored.

(15) In the case of a claimant who is a work or training beneficiary, the references in sub-paragraphs (1)(a)(ii), (1)(c)(iv), (1)(d) and (1)(g)(iii) to a period of 12 weeks is to be treated as references to a period of 104 weeks.

(16) For the purposes of sub-paragraph (1)(a)(ii), (1)(c)(iv), (1)(d) and (1)(g)(iii), the relevant period will be—

(a) 52 weeks in the case of a person to whom sub-paragraph (17) applies;

(b) subject to sub-paragraph (15), 12 weeks in any other case.

(17) This sub-paragraph applies, subject to sub-paragraph (18), in the case of a claimant who, on or after 27th October 2008, has ceased to be entitled to an income-related allowance because that claimant or that claimant's partner—

(a) has commenced employment as an employed earner or as a self-employed earner or has increased the hours in which that claimant or that claimant's partner is engaged in such employment;

(b) is taking active steps to establish that claimant or that claimant's partner in employment as an employed earner or as a self-employed earner under any scheme for assisting persons to become so employed which is mentioned in regulation 19(1)(r)(i) to (iii) of the Jobseeker's Allowance Regulations; or

(c) is participating in—

(i) a New Deal option;

(ii) an employment zone programme; or

(iii) the self-employment route; or

(iv) the Intensive Activity Period specified in regulation 75(1)(a)(iv) of the Jobseeker's Allowance Regulations,

and, as a consequence, that claimant or that claimant's partner was engaged in remunerative work or had income in excess of the applicable amount as prescribed in Part 9.

(18) Sub-paragraph (17) is only to apply to the extent that immediately before the day on which the claimant ceased to be entitled to an income-related allowance, that claimant's housing costs were being met in accordance with paragraph 8(1)(a), 8(1)(b) or 9(1)(a) or would have been so met but for any non-dependant deduction under paragraph 19.

(19) For the purpose of determining whether the linking rules set out in this paragraph apply in a case where a claimant's former partner was entitled to state pension credit, any reference to an income-related allowance in this Schedule is to be taken to include also a reference to state pension credit.

(20) Where a person is one to whom regulation 6(5) of the Income Support Regulations (persons not treated as engaged in remunerative work) applies, the period prescribed in paragraph (6) of that regulation is not to be included for the purposes of any linking rule or for determining whether any qualifying or other period is satisfied.

Loans on residential property

16.—(1) A loan qualifies under this paragraph where the loan was taken out to defray monies applied for any of the following purposes—   **1A.549**

(a) acquiring an interest in the dwelling occupied as the home; or

(b) paying off another loan to the extent that the other loan would have qualified under paragraph (a) above had the loan not been paid off.

(2) For the purposes of this paragraph, references to a loan include also a reference to money borrowed under a hire purchase agreement for any purpose specified in paragraphs (a) and (b) of sub-paragraph (1).

(3) Where a loan is applied only in part for the purposes specified in paragraphs (a) and (b) of sub-paragraph (1), only that portion of the loan which is applied for that purpose will qualify under this paragraph.

Loans for repairs and improvements to the dwelling occupied as the home

17.—(1) A loan qualifies under this paragraph where the loan was taken out, with or without security, for the purpose of—   **1A.550**

(a) carrying out repairs and improvements to the dwelling occupied as the home;

(b) paying any service charge imposed to meet the cost of repairs and improvements to the dwelling occupied as the home;

(c) paying off another loan to the extent that the other loan would have qualified under paragraph (a) or (b) of this sub-paragraph had the loan not been paid off,

and the loan was used for that purpose, or is used for that purpose within 6 months of the date of receipt or such further period as may be reasonable in the particular circumstances of the case.

(2) In sub-paragraph (1) "repairs and improvements" means any of the following measures undertaken with a view to maintaining the fitness of the dwelling for human

habitation or, where the dwelling forms part of a building, any part of the building containing that dwelling—

(a) provision of a fixed bath, shower, wash basin, sink or lavatory, and necessary associated plumbing, including the provision of hot water not connected to a central heating system;

(b) repairs to existing heating systems;

(c) damp proof measures;

(d) provision of ventilation and natural lighting;

(e) provision of drainage facilities;

(f) provision of facilities for preparing and cooking food;

(g) provision of insulation of the dwelling occupied as the home;

(h) provision of electric lighting and sockets;

(i) provision of storage facilities for fuel or refuse;

(j) repairs of unsafe structural defects;

(k) adapting a dwelling for the special needs of a disabled person; or

(l) provision of separate sleeping accommodation for persons of different sexes aged 10 or over but under age 20 who live with the claimant and for whom the claimant or partner is responsible.

(3) Where a loan is applied only in part for the purposes specified in sub-paragraph (1), only that portion of the loan which is applied for that purpose will qualify under this paragraph.

Other housing costs

1A.551 **18.**—(1) Subject to the deduction specified in sub-paragraph (2) and the reductions applicable in sub-paragraph (5), there are to be met under this paragraph the amounts, calculated on a weekly basis, in respect of the following housing costs—

(a) payments by way of rent or ground rent relating to a long tenancy;

(b) service charges;

(c) payments by way of rentcharge within the meaning of section 1 of the Rentcharges Act 1977;

(d) payments under a co-ownership scheme;

(e) payments under or relating to a tenancy or licence of a Crown tenant;

(f) where the dwelling occupied as the home is a tent, payments in respect of the tent and the site on which it stands.

(2) Subject to sub-paragraph (3), the deductions to be made from the weekly amounts to be met under this paragraph are—

(a) where the costs are inclusive of any of the items mentioned in paragraph 6(2) of Schedule 1 to the Housing Benefit Regulations 2006 (payment in respect of fuel charges), the deductions prescribed in that paragraph unless the claimant provides evidence on which the actual or approximate amount of the service charge for fuel may be estimated, in which case the estimated amount;

(b) where the costs are inclusive of ineligible service charges within the meaning of paragraph 1 of Schedule 1 to the Housing Benefit Regulations 2006 (ineligible service charges) the amounts attributable to those ineligible service charges or where that amount is not separated from or separately identified within the housing costs to be met under this paragraph, such part of the payments made in respect of those housing costs which are fairly attributable to the provision of those ineligible services having regard to the costs of comparable services;

(c) any amount for repairs and improvements, and for this purpose the expression "repairs and improvements" has the same meaning it has in paragraph 17(2).

(3) Where arrangements are made for the housing costs, which are met under this paragraph and which are normally paid for a period of 52 weeks, to be paid instead for a period of 53 weeks, or to be paid irregularly, or so that no such costs are payable or collected in certain periods, or so that the costs for different periods in the year are of different amounts, the weekly amount will be the amount payable for the year divided by 52.

(4) Where the claimant or a member of the claimant's family—

(a) pays for reasonable repairs or redecorations to be carried out to the dwelling they occupy; and

(b) that work was not the responsibility of the claimant or any member of the claimant's family; and

(c) in consequence of that work being done, the costs which are normally met under this paragraph are waived,

then those costs will, for a period not exceeding 8 weeks, be treated as payable.

(5) Where in England and Wales an amount calculated on a weekly basis in respect of housing costs specified in sub-paragraph (1)(e) includes water charges, that amount is to be reduced—

(a) where the amount payable in respect of water charges is known, by that amount;
(b) in any other case, by the amount which would be the likely weekly water charge had the property not been occupied by a Crown tenant.

Non-dependant deductions

19.—(1) Subject to the following provisions of this paragraph, the following deductions from the amount to be met under the preceding paragraphs of this Schedule in respect of housing costs are to be made—   **1A.552**

(a) in respect of a non-dependant aged 18 or over who is engaged in any remunerative work, £47.75;
(b) in respect of a non-dependant aged 18 or over to whom paragraph (a) does not apply, £7.40.

(2) In the case of a non-dependant aged 18 or over to whom sub-paragraph (1)(a) applies because that non-dependant is in remunerative work, where the claimant satisfies the Secretary of State that the non-dependant's gross weekly income is—

(a) less than £116.00, the deduction to be made under this paragraph will be the deduction specified in sub-paragraph (1)(b);
(b) not less than £116.00 but less than £172.00, the deduction to be made under this paragraph will be £17.00;
(c) not less than £172.00 but less than £223.00, the deduction to be made under this paragraph will be £23.35;
(d) not less than £223.00 but less than £296.00, the deduction to be made under this paragraph will be £38.20;
(e) not less than £296.00 but less than £369.00, the deduction to be made under this paragraph will be £43.50.

(3) Only one deduction is to be made under this paragraph in respect of a couple or, as the case may be, the members of a polygamous marriage, and where, but for this sub-paragraph, the amount that would fall to be deducted in respect of one member of a couple or polygamous marriage is higher than the amount (if any) that would fall to be deducted in respect of the other, or any other, member, the higher amount is to be deducted.

(4) In applying the provisions of sub-paragraph (2) in the case of a couple or, as the case may be, a polygamous marriage, regard will be had, for the purpose of sub-paragraph (2), to the couple's or, as the case may be, all the members of the polygamous marriage's, joint weekly income.

(5) Where a person is a non-dependant in respect of more than one joint occupier of a dwelling (except where the joint occupiers are a couple or members of a polygamous marriage), the deduction in respect of that non-dependant is to be apportioned between the joint occupiers (the amount so apportioned being rounded to the nearest penny) having regard to the number of joint occupiers and the proportion of the housing costs in respect of the dwelling occupied as the home payable by each of them.

(6) No deduction is to be made in respect of any non-dependants occupying the dwelling occupied as the home of the claimant, if the claimant or any partner of the claimant is—

(a) registered as blind in a register compiled under section 29 of the National Assistance Act 1948 (welfare services) or, in Scotland, has been certified as blind and in consequence he is registered as blind in a register maintained by or on behalf of a regional or islands council, or who is within 28 weeks of ceasing to be so registered;
(b) receiving in respect of that claimant or that claimant's partner either—
  (i) an attendance allowance; or
  (ii) the care component of the disability living allowance.

(7) No deduction is to be made in respect of a non-dependant—

(a) if, although the [1non-dependant] resides with the claimant, it appears to the Secretary of State that the dwelling occupied as the non-dependant's home is normally elsewhere;

   (b) if the non-dependant is in receipt of a training allowance paid in connection with youth training;

   (c) if the non-dependant is a full-time student during a period of study or, if the non-dependant is not in remunerative work, during a recognised summer vacation appropriate to the non-dependant's course;

   (d) if the non-dependant is aged under 25 and in receipt of income support, an income-based jobseeker's allowance or an income-related allowance which does not include an amount under section 4(2)(b) of the Act;

   (e) in respect of whom a deduction in the calculation of a rent rebate or allowance falls to be made under regulation 74 of the Housing Benefit Regulations 2006 (non-dependant deductions);

1A.553   [¹(f) to whom, but for paragraph (5) of regulation 71 (definition of non-dependant) paragraph (4) of that regulation would apply;]

   (g) if the non-dependant is not residing with the claimant because the non-dependant has been a patient for a period in excess of 52 weeks, or is a prisoner, and for these purposes—

      (i) "patient" has the meaning given in paragraph 5(13) and "prisoner" has the meaning given in regulation 69(2) (special cases); and

      (ii) in calculating a period of 52 weeks as a patient, any two or more distinct periods separated by one or more intervals each not exceeding 28 days is to be treated as a single period; or

   (h) if the non-dependant is in receipt of state pension credit;

   (i) in sub-paragraph (b)—

   "youth training" means—

      (i) arrangements made under section 2 of the Employment and Training Act 1973 or section 2 of the Enterprise and New Towns (Scotland) Act 1990; or

      (ii) arrangements made by the Secretary of State for persons enlisted in Her Majesty's forces for any special term of service specified in regulations made under section 2 of the Armed Forces Act 1966 (power of Defence Council to make regulations as to engagement of persons in regular forces),

   for purposes which include the training of persons who, at the beginning of their training, are under the age of 18.

   (8) In the case of a non-dependant to whom sub-paragraph (2) applies because that nondependent is in remunerative work, there is to be disregarded from that non-dependant's gross income—

   (a) any attendance allowance or disability living allowance received by that non-dependant;

   (b) any payment made under the Macfarlane Trust, the Macfarlane (Special Payments) Trust, the Macfarlane (Special Payments) (No. 2) Trust, the Fund, the Eileen Trust or [¹the Independent Living Fund (2006)] which, had that non-dependant's income fallen to be calculated under regulation 104 (calculation of income other than earnings), would have been disregarded under paragraph 22 of Schedule 8 (income in kind); and

   (c) any payment which, had that non-dependant's income fallen to be calculated under regulation 104 would have been disregarded under paragraph 41 of Schedule 8 (payments made under certain trusts and certain other payments).

Continuity with income support, an income-based jobseeker's allowance or state pension credit

1A.554   **20.**—(1) For the purpose of providing continuity between income support, an income-based jobseeker's allowance or state pension credit and an employment and support allowance—

   (a) any housing costs which would, had the claimant been entitled to income support, an income-based jobseeker's allowance or state pension credit, have been existing housing costs and not new housing costs will, despite the preceding provisions of this Schedule, be treated as existing housing costs, and any qualifications or limitations which would have applied to those costs had the award been an award of income support, an income-based jobseeker's allowance or state pension credit will likewise apply to the costs in so far as they are met in an employment and support allowance;

(b) had the award of an employment and support allowance been an award of income support or an income-based jobseeker's allowance and the housing costs which would then have been met would have included an additional amount met in accordance with paragraph 7 of Schedule 3 to the Income Support Regulations or, as the case may be, paragraph 18(1)(b) of Schedule 2 to the Jobseeker's Allowance Regulations (add back), an amount equal to that additional amount must be added to the housing costs to be met under this Schedule, but that amount must be subject to the same qualifications and limitations as it would have been had the award been of income support or an income-based jobseeker's allowance; and

(c) subject to paragraph 15(20), for the purposes of any linking rule or for determining whether any qualifying or other period is satisfied, any reference to an employment and support allowance in this Schedule must be taken also to include a reference to income support, an income-based jobseeker's allowance or state pension credit.

(2) Any loan which, had the claimant been entitled to income support and not an employment and support allowance, would have been a qualifying loan for the purposes of Schedule 3 to the Income Support Regulations by virtue of regulation 3 of the Income Support (General) Amendment and Transitional Regulations 1995 (transitional protection) must be treated also as a qualifying loan for the purposes of paragraph 16 or 17, (loans on residential property and loans for repairs and improvements to the dwelling occupied as the home) and for the purpose of determining whether a claimant would satisfy the provision of regulation 3(2) of those Regulations, a claimant in receipt of an income-related allowance must be treated as being in receipt of income support.

AMENDMENT

1. Employment and Support Allowance (Miscellaneous Amendments) Regulations 2008 (SI 2008/2428), reg.16 (October 27, 2008).

DEFINITIONS

"Abbeyfield Home"—see reg.2(1).
"attendance allowance"—*ibid.*
"care home"—*ibid.*
"child"—*ibid.*
"child support maintenance"—see reg.2(2).
"claimant"—see reg.83(1).
"couple"—see reg.2(1).
"Crown tenant"—*ibid.*
"dwelling occupied as the home"—*ibid.*
"Eileen Trust"—*ibid.*
"family"—*ibid.*
"full-time student"—*ibid.*
"the Fund"—*ibid.*
"housing benefit expenditure"—*ibid.*
"independent hospital"—*ibid.*
"the Independent Living Fund (2006)"—*ibid.*
"Macfarlane (Special Payments) Trust"—*ibid.*
"Macfarlane (Special Payments) (No. 2) Trust"—*ibid.*
"Macfarlane Trust"—*ibid.*
"maintenance assessment"—see reg.2(2).
"maintenance calculation"—*ibid.*
"non-dependant"—see reg.71.
"partner"—see reg.2(1).
"period of study"—*ibid.*
"polygamous marriage"—*ibid.*
"training allowance"—*ibid.*
"water charges"—*ibid.*

GENERAL NOTE

1A.555   This is similar to Sch.3 to the IS Regs/Sch.2 to the JSA Regs (where there are differences between those Schedules Sch.6 generally adopts the income support model).

The following are the main differences from Sch.3:

- Paragraph 2 defines when a non-dependant will be treated as in remunerative work for the purposes of Sch.6. This paragraph is necessary because the definition of remunerative work in regs 41 and 42 only applies to the claimant and the claimant's partner and does not apply for the purposes of Sch.6 (see the definition of "remunerative work" in reg.2(1)). Paragraph 2(9) specifically provides that whether a claimant or a claimant's partner is engaged in, or is to be treated as engaged in, remunerative work is to be determined in accordance with regs 41 or 42.
- There is no equivalent to para.2(2) of Sch.3 (which relates to trade disputes).
- Note also para.15(20) of this Schedule which provides that any period during which a claimant qualifies for a "housing costs run-on" under reg.6(5) of the Income Support Regs does not count for the purpose of any linking rules or determining whether any qualifying or other period is satisfied under this Schedule.
- In relation to the excessive housing costs rules, note para.14(10).
- The transitional protection provisions in Sch.3 (see para.6(2)–(4) and para.7 of Sch.3) have been omitted, although note para.12(11)-(12) which preserves the transitional protection from the ceiling on loans that is contained in reg.4 of the Income Support (General) Amendment No. 3 Regs 1993 (SI 1993/1679) and reg.28 of the Income-related Benefits Schemes (Miscellaneous Amendments) Regs 1995 (SI 1995/516) (see p.686 and p.689 respectively in Vol.II of this series for these Regulations) for a person to whom any of those provisions would have applied had he been entitled to income support.

Continuity with income support, income-based JSA and state pension credit

1A.556   In addition to the transitional protection in para.12(11)–(12), note the provisions in para.20 (which are very similar to those in para.18 of Sch.2 to the JSA Regs). Paragraph 20 is important for claimants transferring from income support or income-based JSA state pension credit where their partner has been entitled to state pension credit, to income-related ESA. For the equivalent of para.20(1)(c) where the transfer is the other way round, see para.18(1)(c) of Sch.2 to the JSA Regs for income-based JSA and reg.32 of the Income Support (General) (Jobseeker's Allowance Consequential Amendments) Regs 1996 (SI 1996/206) (p.694 in Vol.II in this series), and the new para.14(15) of Sch.3 to the Income Support Regs (see Part III of this Supplement (Updating material for Vol.II), for income support.

There are no waiting periods for housing costs for state pension credit claimants. However, note para.15(19) which provides that for the purposes of the linking rules in para.15, if a claimant's former partner was entitled to state pension credit, any reference to an income-related allowance in Sch.6 also includes a reference to state pension credit.

Regulations 96(2), 98(2)

SCHEDULE 7

SUMS TO BE DISREGARDED IN THE CALCULATION OF EARNINGS

1A.557   1.—(1) In the case of a claimant who has been engaged in remunerative work as an employed earner or, had the employment been in Great Britain, would have been so engaged—

(a) any earnings, other than items to which sub-paragraph (2) applies, paid or due to be paid from that employment which terminated before the first day of entitlement to an income-related allowance;

(b) any earnings, other than a payment of the nature described in regulation 95(1)(e) (earnings of employed earners), paid or due to be paid from that employment which has not been terminated where the claimant is not—

    (i) engaged in remunerative work; or

    (ii) suspended from employment.

(2) This sub-paragraph applies to—

(a) any payment of the nature described in regulation 95(1)(e); and

(b) any award, sum or payment of the nature described in—

    (i) regulation 95(1)(g) or (i); or

    (ii) section 34 or 70 of the Employment Rights Act 1996 (guarantee payments and suspension from work: complaints to employment tribunals),

including any payment made following the settlement of a complaint to an employment tribunal or of court proceedings.

2.—(1) In the case of a claimant to whom this paragraph applies, any earnings (other than a payment of the nature described in regulation 95(1)(e)) which relate to employment which ceased before the first day of entitlement to an income-related allowance whether or not that employment has terminated.   **1A.558**

(2) This paragraph applies to a claimant who has been engaged in part-time employment as an employed earner or, had the employment been in Great Britain, would have been so engaged; but it does not apply to a claimant who has been suspended from employment.

3. If the claimant's partner has been engaged in remunerative work as an employed earner or, had the employment been in Great Britain, would have been so engaged, any earnings paid or due to be paid on termination of that employment by way of retirement but only if—   **1A.559**

(a) on retirement the partner is entitled to a retirement pension under the Contributions and Benefits Act; or

(b) the only reason the partner is not entitled to a retirement pension under the Contribution and Benefits Act is because the contribution conditions are not satisfied.

4. In the case of a claimant who has been engaged in remunerative work or part-time employment as a self-employed earner or, had the employment been in Great Britain, would have been so engaged and who has ceased to be so employed, from the date of the cessation of the claimant's employment any earnings derived from that employment except earnings to which regulation 92(2) (royalties etc.) applies.   **1A.560**

5. In the case of a claimant who is undertaking work which falls within one of the categories in regulation 45(2) to (4) any earnings derived from that work which do not exceed the limits specified for that work of £20 in regulation 45(2) or, as the case may be, [¹£92.00] in regulation 45(3) or (4).   **1A.561**

6. Where regulation 45(2) to (4) applies to the claimant and that claimant's earnings are less than—   **1A.562**

(a) in a case to which regulation 45(2) applies, £20;

(b) in a case to which regulation 45(3) and (4) applies, [¹£92.00],

the earnings of the claimant's partner are to be disregarded to the extent that the claimant's earnings are less than £20 or, as the case may be, [¹£92.00], but only up to a maximum of £20.

7.—(1) In a case to which this paragraph applies, £20; but notwithstanding regulation 83 (calculation of income and capital of members of claimant's family and of a polygamous marriage), if this paragraph applies to a claimant it will not apply to the claimant's partner except where, and to the extent that, the earnings of the claimant which are to be disregarded under this paragraph are less than £20.   **1A.563**

(2) Subject to sub-paragraph (3), this paragraph applies in the case of a claimant to whom regulation 40(2)(a), (b) or (e), 43(1)(a), (d), (e) or (f), or (2) or 45(5) applies.

(3) Where a claimant is doing the work set out in regulation 40(2)(b) and is also undertaking any of the categories of work set out in regulation 45(2) to (4), this paragraph applies only to the extent that the claimant's earnings are less than the limit of—

    (a) £20 set out in regulation 45(2); or

    (b) [¹£92.00] set out in regulation 45(3) and (4),

as the case may be.

(4) This paragraph applies, in a case where the claimant's partner is in part-time employment and paragraph 6 does not apply.

1A.564   **8.** Notwithstanding the foregoing provisions of this Schedule, where two or more payments of earnings of the same kind and from the same source are to be taken into account in the same benefit week, because it has not been practicable to treat the payments under regulation 93(1)(b) (date on which income treated as paid) as paid on the first day of the benefit week in which they were due to be paid, there is to be disregarded from each payment the sum that would have been disregarded if the payment had been taken into account on the date on which it was due to be paid.

1A.565   **9.** Any earnings derived from employment which are payable in a country outside the United Kingdom for such period during which there is a prohibition against the transfer to the United Kingdom of those earnings.

1A.566   **10.** Where a payment of earnings is made in a currency other than sterling, any banking charge or commission payable in converting that payment into sterling.

1A.567   **11.** Any earnings which are due to be paid before the date of claim and which would otherwise fall to be taken into account in the same benefit week as a payment of the same kind and from the same source.

1A.568   **12.** In the case of a claimant who—

    (a) has been engaged in employment as a member of any territorial or reserve force prescribed in Part 1 of Schedule 6 to the Social Security (Contributions) Regulations 2001; and

    (b) by reason of that employment has failed to satisfy any of the conditions for entitlement to an income-related allowance other than paragraph 6(1)(a) of Schedule 1 to the Act (income not in excess of the applicable amount),

any earnings from that employment paid in respect of the period in which the claimant was not entitled to an income-related allowance.

1A.569   **13.** In the case of a person to whom paragraph (5) of regulation 6 of the Income Support Regulations applies, any earnings.

1A.570   **14.** In this Schedule—

"part-time employment" means, if the person were entitled to income support, employment in which the person is not to be treated as engaged in remunerative work under regulation 5 or 6(1) and (4) of the Income Support Regulations (persons treated, or not treated, as engaged in remunerative work);

"remunerative work", for the purposes of this paragraph and paragraphs 1, 3 and 4, has the meaning prescribed in regulation 5, except for paragraphs (3B) and (4) of that regulation, of the Income Support Regulations.

AMENDMENT

1. Employment and Support Allowance (Miscellaneous Amendments) Regulations 2008 (SI 2008/2428), reg.17 (October 27, 2008).

DEFINITIONS

"benefit week"—see reg.2(1).
"couple"—*ibid.*

"employed earner"—*ibid.*
"family"—*ibid.*
"partner"—*ibid.*
"polygamous marriage"—*ibid.*

GENERAL NOTE

Paras 1–4

Paragraphs 1 to 4 are similar to paras 1 to 3 of Sch.8 to the Income Support   **1A.571**
Regs/paras 1 to 4 of Sch.6 to the JSA Regs (where there are differences between
Sch.8 and Sch.6 this Schedule adopts the income support model). They contain
the earnings disregards on the termination of "remunerative work" (defined in
para.14) and on the stopping of "part-time employment" (also defined in
para.14), before the claim, as well as on the cessation of self-employment. Note
that the definitions of "remunerative work" and "part-time employment" largely
(but not entirely) import the income support tests.

Paras 5–7

The disregards in these paragraphs are different from those in Sch.8 to the   **1A.572**
Income Support Regulations/Sch.6 to the JSA Regs because of the different rules
for the effect of work on entitlement to ESA (see regs 40–46 for these rules).

The earnings limit for "exempt work" under reg.45(2) is £20 and under
reg.45(3) or (4) is £92. Paragraph 5 disregards earnings from such work up to
the relevant limit. In addition, if the claimant's earnings from such work are less
than the relevant limit, his partner's earnings are ignored to the extent of the
spare amount below the relevant limit, subject to a maximum of £20 (para.6).

Under para.7 earnings from the following attract a £20 disregard:
  (i) work undertaken by the claimant as a councillor, as a member of the
      Disability Living Allowance Advisory Board or a tribunal member with a
      disability qualification, during an emergency to protect another person,
      property or livestock, or while receiving assistance in pursuing self-
      employment under a government scheme;
 (ii) work undertaken by the claimant's partner as a childminder, as a council-
      lor, as a part-time fire-fighter, auxiliary coastguard, part-time member of
      a lifeboat crew or member of the Territorial army, or where the partner is
      receiving assistance under the "self-employment route" (defined in
      reg.2(1)), or is not to be treated as in remunerative work under one of the
      categories in reg.43(2);
(iii) part-time employment (defined in para.14) undertaken by the claimant's
      partner where the disregard under para.6 does not apply.
But note that a couple cannot have a total disregard of more than £20.

Note also that if a claimant who is working as a member of the Disability
Living Allowance Advisory Board or as a tribunal member with a disability
qualification is also doing work that counts as exempt work under reg.45(2) to
(4), the disregard under para.7 only applies to the extent that his earnings are less
than the relevant limit for that exempt work.

Paras 8–13

These paragraphs are similar to paras 10 to 13, 15A and 15C of Sch.8 to the   **1A.573**
Income Support Regs/paras 13–16 and 19 of Sch.6 to the JSA Regs (there is no
equivalent to para.13 in Sch.6 to the JSA Regs as this is concerned with the
disregard of earnings during any "housing costs run-on" under reg.6(5) of the
Income Support Regs).

SCHEDULE 8

SUMS TO BE DISREGARDED IN THE CALCULATION OF INCOME OTHER THAN EARNINGS

1A.574   **1.** Any amount paid by way of tax on income which is taken into account under regulation 104 (calculation of income other than earnings).

1A.575   **2.** Any payment in respect of any expenses incurred, or to be incurred, by a claimant who is—

(a) engaged by a charitable or voluntary organisation; or

(b) a volunteer,

if the claimant otherwise derives no remuneration or profit from the employment and is not to be treated as possessing any earnings under regulation 108(3) (notional income).

1A.576   **3.** In the case of employment as an employed earner, any payment in respect of expenses wholly, exclusively and necessarily incurred in the performance of the duties of the employment.

1A.577   **4.** In the case of a payment under Parts 11 to 12ZB of the Contributions and Benefits Act or any remuneration paid by or on behalf of an employer to the claimant who for the time being is unable to work due to illness or maternity or who is taking paternity leave or adoption leave—

(a) any amount deducted by way of primary Class 1 contributions under the Contributions and Benefits Act;

(b) one-half of any sum paid by the claimant by way of a contribution towards an occupational or personal pension scheme.

1A.578   **5.** In Northern Ireland, in the case of a payment under Parts 11 to 12ZB of the Social Security Contributions and Benefits (Northern Ireland) Act 1992, or any remuneration paid by or on behalf of an employer to the claimant who for the time being is unable to work due to illness or maternity or who is taking paternity leave or adoption leave—

(a) any amount deducted by way of primary Class 1 contributions under that Act;

(b) one-half of any sum paid by way of a contribution towards an occupational or personal pension scheme.

1A.579   **6.** Any guardian's allowance.

1A.580   **7.**—(1) Any child tax credit.

(2) Any child benefit.

1A.581   **8.** Any mobility component of disability living allowance.

1A.582   **9.** Any concessionary payment made to compensate for the non-payment of—

(a) any payment specified in paragraph 8 or 11;

(b) an [¹income-related] employment and support allowance, income support or [¹ an income-based jobseeker's allowance].

1A.583   **10.** Any mobility supplement or any payment intended to compensate for the non-payment of such a supplement.

1A.584   **11.** Any attendance allowance or the care component of disability living allowance.

1A.585   **12.** Any payment to the claimant as holder of the Victoria Cross or George Cross or any analogous payment.

1A.586   **13.**—(1) Any payment—

(a) by way of an education maintenance allowance made pursuant to—

336

    (i) regulations made under section 518 of the Education Act 1996;
    (ii) regulations made under section 49 or 73(f) of the Education (Scotland) Act 1980; or
    (iii) directions made under section 73ZA of the Education (Scotland) Act 1980 and paid under section 12(2)(c) of the Further and Higher Education (Scotland) Act 1992; or

(b) corresponding to such an education maintenance allowance, made pursuant to—
    (i) section 14 or section 181 of the Education Act 2002; or
    (ii) regulations made under section 181 of that Act.

(2) Any payment, other than a payment to which sub-paragraph (1) applies, made pursuant to—

(a) regulations made under section 518 of the Education Act 1996;

(b) regulations made under section 49 of the Education (Scotland) Act 1980; or

(c) directions made under section 73ZA of the Education (Scotland) Act 1980 and paid under section 12(2)(c) of the Further and Higher Education (Scotland) Act 1992;

in respect of a course of study attended by a child or a young person or a person who is in receipt of an education maintenance allowance made pursuant to any provision specified in sub-paragraph (1).

14. Any payment made to the claimant by way of a repayment under regulation 11(2) of the Education (Teacher Student Loans) (Repayment etc.) Regulations 2002.   **1A.587**

15.—(1) Any payment made pursuant to section 2 of the Employment and Training Act 1973 (functions of the Secretary of State) or section 2 of the Enterprise and New Towns (Scotland) Act 1990 (functions in relation to training for employment etc.) except a payment—   **1A.588**

(a) made as a substitute for an employment and support allowance;

(b) of an allowance referred to in section 2(3) of the Employment and Training Act 1973 or section 2(5) of the Enterprise and New Towns (Scotland) Act 1990;

(c) intended to meet the cost of living expenses which relate to any one or more of the items specified in sub-paragraph (2) whilst a claimant is participating in an education, training or other scheme to help the claimant enhance that claimant's employment prospects unless the payment is a Career Development Loan paid pursuant to section 2 of the Employment and Training Act 1973 and the period of education or training or the scheme, which is supported by that loan, has been completed; or

(d) made in respect of the cost of living away from home to the extent that the payment relates to rent for which housing benefit is payable in respect of accommodation which is not normally occupied by the claimant as that claimant's home.

(2) The items specified in this sub-paragraph for the purposes of sub-paragraph (1)(c) are food, ordinary clothing or footwear, household fuel, rent for which housing benefit is payable, or any housing costs to the extent that they are met under regulation 67(1)(c) or 68(1)(d) (housing costs), of the claimant or, where the claimant is a member of a family, any other member of the claimant's family, or any council tax or water charges for which that claimant or member is liable.

16.—(1) Subject to sub-paragraph (2) and paragraph 41, any relevant payment made or due to be made at regular intervals.   **1A.589**

(2) Sub-paragraph (1) is not to apply to a payment which is made by a person for the maintenance of any member of that person's family or of that person's former partner or of that person's children.

(3) In this paragraph, "relevant payment" means—

(a) a charitable payment;

(b) a voluntary payment;

(c) a payment (not falling within sub-paragraph (a) or (b) above) from a trust whose funds are derived from a payment made in consequence of any personal injury to the claimant;

(d) a payment under an annuity purchased—
    (i) pursuant to any agreement or court order to make payments to the claimant; or

       (ii) from funds derived from a payment made,

in consequence of any personal injury to the claimant; or

  (e) a payment (not falling within sub-paragraph (a) to (d) above) received by virtue of any agreement or court order to make payments to the claimant in consequence of any personal injury to the claimant.

1A.590   **17.** Subject to paragraphs 39 and 40, £10 of any of the following, namely—

  (a) a war disablement pension (except insofar as such a pension falls to be disregarded under paragraph 10 or 11);

  (b) a war widow's pension or war widower's pension;

  (c) a pension payable to a person as a widow, widower or surviving civil partner under any power of Her Majesty otherwise than under an enactment to make provision about pensions for or in respect of persons who have been disabled or have died in consequence of service as members of the armed forces of the Crown;

  (d) a guaranteed income payment;

  (e) a payment made to compensate for the non-payment of such a pension or payment as is mentioned in any of the preceding sub-paragraphs;

  (f) a pension paid by the government of a country outside Great Britain which is analogous to any of the pensions or payments mentioned in sub-paragraphs (a) to (d) above;

  (g) a pension paid to victims of National Socialist persecution under any special provision made by the law of the Federal Republic of Germany, or any part of it, or of the Republic of Austria;

  (h) any widowed mother's allowance paid pursuant to section 37 of the Contributions and Benefits Act;

  (i) any widowed parent's allowance paid pursuant to section 39A of the Contributions and Benefits Act.

1A.591   **18.** Where a claimant receives income under an annuity purchased with a loan which satisfies the following conditions—

  (a) that the loan was made as part of a scheme under which not less than 90% of the proceeds of the loan were applied to the purchase by the person to whom it was made of an annuity ending with that person's life or with the life of the survivor of two or more persons (in this paragraph referred to as "the annuitants") who include the person to whom the loan was made;

  (b) that the interest on the loan is payable by the person to whom it was made or by one of the annuitants;

  (c) that at the time the loan was made the person to whom it was made or each of the annuitants had attained the age of 65;

  (d) that the loan was secured on a dwelling in Great Britain and the person to whom the loan was made or one of the annuitants owns an estate or interest in that dwelling; and

  (e) that the person to whom the loan was made or one of the annuitants occupies the accommodation on which it was secured as that person's home at the time the interest is paid,

the amount, calculated on a weekly basis equal to—

       (i) where, or insofar as, section 369 of the Income and Corporation Taxes Act 1988 (mortgage interest payable under deduction of tax) applies to the payments of interest on the loan, the interest which is payable after deduction of a sum equal to income tax on such payments at the applicable percentage of income tax within the meaning of section 369(1A) of that Act;

      (ii) in any other case the interest which is payable on the loan without deduction of such a sum.

1A.592   **19.** Any payment made to the claimant by a person who normally resides with the claimant, which is a contribution towards that person's living and accommodation costs, except where that person is residing with the claimant in circumstances to which paragraph 20 or 21 refers.

1A.593   **20.** Where the claimant occupies a dwelling as the claimant's home and the dwelling is also occupied by another person and there is a contractual liability to make payments to the

338

claimant in respect of the occupation of the dwelling by that person or a member of that person's family—

  (a) where the aggregate of any payments made in respect of any one week in respect of the occupation of the dwelling by that person or a member of that person's family, or by that person and a member of that person's family, is less than £20, the whole of that amount; or

  (b) where the aggregate of such payments is £20 or more per week, £20.

21. Where the claimant occupies a dwelling as the claimant's home and the claimant provides in that dwelling board and lodging accommodation, an amount, in respect of each person for whom such accommodation is provided for the whole or any part of a week, equal to—   **1A.594**

  (a) where the aggregate of any payments made in respect of any one week in respect of such accommodation provided to such person does not exceed £20, 100% of such payments; or

  (b) where the aggregate of any such payments exceeds £20, £20 and 50% of the excess over £20.

22.—(1) Subject to sub-paragraphs (2) and (3), except where regulation 104(8)(b) (provision of support under section 95 or 98 of the Immigration and Asylum Act including support provided by virtue of regulations made under Schedule 9 to that Act in the calculation of income other than earnings) or regulation 107(3)(a) (notional income) applies, any income in kind;   **1A.595**

  (2) The exception under sub-paragraph (1) will not apply where the income in kind is received from the Macfarlane Trust, the Macfarlane (Special Payments) Trust, the Macfarlane (Special Payments) (No.2) Trust, the Fund, the Eileen Trust or [¹the Independent Living Fund (2006)].

  (3) The first exception under sub-paragraph (1) will not apply where the claimant is the partner of a person subject to immigration control and whose partner is receiving support provided under section 95 or 98 of the Immigration and Asylum Act including support provided by virtue of regulations made under Schedule 9 to that Act and the income in kind is support provided in respect of essential living needs of the partner of the claimant and the claimant's dependants (if any) as is specified in regulations made under paragraph 3 of Schedule 8 to the Immigration and Asylum Act.

  (4) The reference in sub-paragraph (1) to "income in kind" does not include a payment to a third party made in respect of the claimant which is used by the third party to provide benefits in kind to the claimant.

23.—(1) Any income derived from capital to which the claimant is or is treated under regulation 117 (capital jointly held) as beneficially entitled but, subject to sub-paragraph (2), not income derived from capital disregarded under paragraph 1, 2, 4 to 8, 10 or 16 of Schedule 9.   **1A.596**

  (2) Income derived from capital disregarded under paragraph 2 or 4 to 8 of Schedule 9 but only to the extent of—

  (a) any mortgage repayments made in respect of the dwelling or premises in the period during which that income accrued; or

  (b) any council tax or water charges which the claimant is liable to pay in respect of the dwelling or premises and which are paid in the period during which that income accrued.

  (3) The definition of "water charges" in regulation 2(1) is to apply to sub-paragraph (2) with the omission of the words "in so far as such charges are in respect of the dwelling which a person occupies as the home".

24. Any income which is payable in a country outside the United Kingdom for such period during which there is prohibition against the transfer to the United Kingdom of that income.   **1A.597**

25. Where a payment of income is made in a currency other than sterling, any banking charge or commission payable in converting that payment into sterling.   **1A.598**

1A.599   **26.**—(1) Any payment made to the claimant in respect of a child or young person who is a member of the claimant's family—

(a) pursuant to regulations under section 2(6)(b), 3 or 4 of the Adoption and Children Act 2002 or in accordance with a scheme approved by the Scottish Ministers under section 51A of the Adoption (Scotland) Act 1978 (schemes for payment of allowances to adopters);

(b) which is a payment made by a local authority in pursuance of section 15(1) of, and paragraph 15 of Schedule 1 to, the Children Act 1989 (local authority contribution to a child's maintenance where the child is living with a person as a result of a residence order);

(c) which is a payment made by an authority, as defined in Article 2 of the Children (Northern Ireland) Order 1995, in pursuance of Article 15 of, and paragraph 17 of Schedule 1 to, that Order (contributions by an authority to child's maintenance);

(d) in accordance with regulations made pursuant to section 14F of the Children Act 1989 (special guardianship support services).

(2) Any payment, other than a payment to which sub-paragraph (1)(a) applies, made to the claimant pursuant to regulations under section 2(6)(b), 3 or 4 of the Adoption and Children Act 2002.

1A.600   **27.** In the case of a claimant who has a child or young person—

(a) who is a member of the claimant's family; and

(b) who is residing at an educational establishment at which that child or young person is receiving relevant education,

any payment made to that educational establishment, in respect of that child or young person's maintenance by or on behalf of a person who is not a member of the family or by a member of the family out of funds contributed for that purpose by a person who is not a member of the family.

1A.601   **28.** Any payment made by a local authority to the claimant with whom a person is accommodated by virtue of arrangements made under section 23(2)(a) of the Children Act 1989 (provision of accommodation and maintenance for a child whom they are looking after) or, as the case may be, section 26 of the Children (Scotland) Act 1995 or by a voluntary organisation under section 59(1)(a) of the 1989 Act (provision of accommodation by voluntary organisations) or by a local authority under regulation 9 of the Fostering of Children (Scotland) Regulations 1996 (payment of allowances).

1A.602   **29.** Any payment made to the claimant or the claimant's partner for a person ("the person concerned"), who is not normally a member of the claimant's household but is temporarily in the claimant's care, by—

(a) a health authority;

(b) a local authority but excluding payments of housing benefit made in respect of the person concerned;

(c) a voluntary organisation;

(d) the person concerned pursuant to section 26(3A) of the National Assistance Act 1948;

(e) a Primary Care Trust established under section 16A of the National Health Service Act 1977 or by an order made under section 18(2)(c) of the Health Service Act; or

(f) a Local Health Board established under section 16BA of the National Health Service Act 1977 or by an order made under section 11 of the Health Service (Wales) Act.

1A.603   **30.**—(1) Any payment made by a local authority in accordance with—

(a) section 17, 23B, 23C or 24A of the Children Act 1989;

(b) section 12 of the Social Work (Scotland) Act 1968; or

(c) section 29 or 30 of the Children (Scotland) Act 1995 (local authorities' duty to promote welfare of children and powers to grant financial assistance to persons in, or formerly in, their care).

(2) Subject to paragraph (3), any payment (or part of a payment) made by a local authority in accordance with section 23C of the Children Act 1989 or section 29 of the Children (Scotland) Act 1995 (local authorities' duty to promote welfare of children and

powers to grant financial assistance to persons in, or formerly in, their care) to a person ("A") which A passes on to the claimant.

(3) Sub-paragraph (2) applies only where A—

(a) was formerly in the claimant's care; and

(b) is aged 18 or over; and

(c) continues to live with the claimant.

31.—(1) Subject to sub-paragraph (2) any payment received under an insurance policy, taken out to insure against the risk of being unable to maintain repayments on a loan which qualifies under paragraph 16 or 17 of Schedule 6 (housing costs—loans to acquire an interest in a dwelling, or for repairs and improvements to the dwelling, occupied as the home) and used to meet such repayments, to the extent that it does not exceed the aggregate of— **1A.604**

(a) the amount, calculated on a weekly basis, of any interest on that loan which is in excess of the amount met in accordance with Schedule 6;

(b) the amount of any payment, calculated on a weekly basis, due on the loan attributable to the repayment of capital; and

(c) any amount due by way of premiums on—

(i) that policy; or

(ii) a policy of insurance taken out to insure against loss or damage to any building or part of a building which is occupied by the claimant as the claimant's home.

(2) This paragraph does not apply to any payment which is treated as possessed by the claimant by virtue of regulation 107(3)(c) (notional income—income due to be paid or income paid to or in respect of a third party).

32.—(1) Except where paragraph 31 (or 33) applies, and subject to sub-paragraph (2), any payment made to the claimant which is intended to be used and is used as a contribution towards— **1A.605**

(a) any payment due on a loan if secured on the dwelling occupied as the home which does not qualify under Schedule 6;

(b) any interest payment or charge which qualifies in accordance with paragraphs 16 to 18 of Schedule 6 to the extent that the payment or charge is not met;

(c) any payment due on a loan which qualifies under paragraph 16 or 17 of Schedule 6 attributable to the payment of capital;

(d) any amount due by way of premiums on—

(i) an insurance policy taken out to insure against the risk of being unable to make the payments referred to in (a) to (c) above; or

(ii) a policy of insurance taken out to insure against loss or damage to any building or part of a building which is occupied by the claimant as the claimant's home;

(e) the claimant's rent in respect of the dwelling occupied by the claimant as the home but only to the extent that it is not met by housing benefit; or the claimant's accommodation charge but only to the extent that the actual charge exceeds the amount payable by a local authority in accordance with Part 3 of the National Assistance Act 1948.

(2) This paragraph does not apply to any payment which is treated as possessed by the claimant by virtue of regulation 107(3)(c).

33.—(1) Subject to sub-paragraph (2), any payment received under an insurance policy, other than an insurance policy referred to in paragraph 31, taken out to insure against the risk of being unable to maintain repayments under a regulated agreement as defined for the purposes of the Consumer Credit Act 1974 or under a hire-purchase agreement or a conditional sale agreement as defined for the purposes of Part 3 of the Hire-Purchase Act 1964. **1A.606**

(2) A payment referred to in sub-paragraph (1) is to only be disregarded to the extent that the payment received under that policy does not exceed the amounts, calculated on a weekly basis which are used to—

(a) maintain the repayments referred to in sub-paragraph (1); and

(b) meet any amount due by way of premiums on that policy.

1A.607 **34.**—(1) Subject to sub-paragraphs (2) and (3), in the case of a claimant residing in a care home, an Abbeyfield Home or an independent hospital, any payment, except a charitable or voluntary payment disregarded under paragraph 16 made to the claimant which is intended to be used and is used to meet the cost of maintaining the claimant in that home or hospital.

(2) This paragraph does not apply to a claimant for whom accommodation in a care home, an Abbeyfield Home or an independent hospital is provided by a local authority under section 26 of the National Assistance Act 1948.

(3) The amount to be disregarded under this paragraph is not to exceed the difference between—

(a) the claimant's applicable amount; and

(b) the weekly charge for the accommodation.

1A.608 **35.** Any social fund payment made pursuant to Part 8 of the Contributions and Benefits Act.

1A.609 **36.** Any payment of income which under regulation 112 (income treated as capital) is to be treated as capital.

1A.610 **37.** Any payment under Part 10 of the Contributions and Benefits Act (pensioner's Christmas bonus).

1A.611 **38.** Any payment which is due to be paid before the date of claim which would otherwise fall to be taken into account in the same benefit week as a payment of the same kind and from the same source.

1A.612 **39.** The total of a claimant's income or, if the claimant is a member of a family, the family's income and the income of any person which the claimant is treated as possessing under regulation 83(3) (calculation of income and capital of members of claimant's family and of a polygamous marriage) to be disregarded under regulation 133(2)(b) and 134(1)(c) (calculation of covenant income), regulation 137(1) and (2) (treatment of student loans), regulation 138(3) (treatment of payments from access funds) and paragraph 17 is in no case to exceed £20 per week.

1A.613 **40.** Notwithstanding paragraph 39 where two or more payments of the same kind and from the same source are to be taken into account in the same benefit week, there is to be disregarded from each payment the sum which would otherwise fall to be disregarded under this Schedule; but this paragraph is to apply only in the case of a payment which it has not been practicable to treat under regulation 93(1)(b) (date on which income is treated as paid) as paid on the first day of the benefit week in which it is due to be paid.

1A.614 **41.**—(1) Any payment made under the Macfarlane Trust, the Macfarlane (Special Payments) Trust, the Macfarlane (Special Payments) (No. 2) Trust ("the Trusts"), the Fund, the Eileen Trust or [¹the Independent Living Fund (2006)].

(2) Any payment by or on behalf of a person who is suffering or who suffered from haemophilia, or who is or was a qualifying person which derives from a payment made under any of the Trusts to which sub-paragraph (1) refers and which is made to or for the benefit of—

(a) that person's partner or former partner from whom that person is not, or where that person has died was not, estranged or divorced or with whom that person has formed a civil partnership that has not been dissolved or, where that person has died, had not been dissolved at the time of that person's death;

(b) any child who is a member of that person's family or who was such a member and who is a member of the claimant's family; or

(c) any young person who is a member of that person's family or who was such a member and who is a member of the claimant's family.

(3) Any payment by or on behalf of the partner or former partner of a person who is suffering or who suffered from haemophilia or who is or was a qualifying person provided that the partner or former partner and that person are not, or if either of them has died were not, estranged or divorced or, where the partner or former partner and that person

have formed a civil partnership, the civil partnership has not been dissolved or, if either of them has died, had not been dissolved at the time of the death, which derives from a payment made under any of the Trusts to which sub-paragraph (1) refers and which is made to or for the benefit of—

(a) the person who is suffering from haemophilia or who is a qualifying person;

(b) any child who is a member of that person's family or who was such a member and who is a member of the claimant's family; or

(c) any young person who is a member of that person's family or who was such a member and who is a member of the claimant's family.

(4) Any payment by a person who is suffering from haemophilia or who is a qualifying person, which derives from a payment under any of the Trusts to which sub-paragraph (1) refers, where—

(a) that person has no partner or former partner from whom that person is not estranged or divorced or with whom that person has formed a civil partnership that has not been dissolved, nor any child or young person who is or had been a member of that person's family; and

(b) the payment is made either—

(i) to that person's parent or step-parent; or

(ii) where that person at the date of the payment is a child, a young person or a full-time student who has not completed full-time education and had no parent or step-parent, to that person's guardian,

but only for a period from the date of the payment until the end of two years from that person's death.

(5) Any payment out of the estate of a person who suffered from haemophilia or who was a qualifying person, which derives from a payment under any of the Trusts to which sub-paragraph (1) refers, where—

(a) that person at the date of that person's death (the relevant date) had no partner or former partner from whom that person was not estranged or divorced or with whom that person had formed a civil partnership that had not been dissolved, nor any child or young person who was or had been a member of that person's family; and

(b) the payment is made either—

(i) to that person's parent or step-parent; or

(ii) where that person at the relevant date was a child, a young person or a full-time student who had not completed full-time education and had no parent or step-parent, to that person's guardian,

but only for a period of two years from the relevant date.

(6) In the case of a person to whom or for whose benefit a payment referred to in this paragraph is made, any income which derives from any payment of income or capital made under or deriving from any of the Trusts.

(7) For the purposes of sub-paragraphs (2) to (6), any reference to the Trusts is to be construed as including a reference to the Fund, the Eileen Trust, the Skipton Fund and the London Bombings Relief Charitable Fund.

42. Any payment made by the Secretary of State to compensate for the loss (in whole or in part) of entitlement to housing benefit. **1A.615**

43. Any payment made to a juror or a witness in respect of attendance at a court other than compensation for loss of earnings or for the loss of a benefit payable under the benefit Acts. **1A.616**

44. Any payment in consequence of a reduction of council tax under section 13 or section 80 of the Local Government Finance Act 1992 (reduction of liability for council tax). **1A.617**

45.—(1) Any payment or repayment made— **1A.618**

(a) as respects England, under regulation 5, 6 or 12 of the National Health Service (Travel Expenses and Remission of Charges) Regulations 2003 (travelling expenses and health service supplies);

(b) as respects Wales, under regulation 5, 6 or 11 of the National Health Service (Travelling Expenses and Remission of Charges) (Wales) Regulations 2007;

(c) as respects Scotland, under regulation 3, 5 or 11 of the National Health Service (Travelling Expenses and Remission of Charges) (Scotland) (No. 2) Regulations 2003 (travelling expenses and health service supplies).

(2) Any payment or repayment made by the Secretary of State for Health, the Scottish Ministers or the Welsh Ministers which is analogous to a payment or repayment mentioned in sub-paragraph (1).

1A.619   **46.** Any payment made to such persons entitled to receive benefits as may be determined by or under a scheme made pursuant to section 13 of the Social Security Act 1988 in lieu of vouchers or similar arrangements in connection with the provision of those benefits (including payments made in place of healthy start vouchers, milk tokens or the supply of vitamins).

1A.620   **47.** Any payment made either by the Secretary of State for Justice or by the Scottish Ministers under a scheme established to assist relatives and other persons to visit persons in custody.

1A.621   **48.** Any payment (other than a training allowance) made, whether by the Secretary of State or by any other person, under the Disabled Persons (Employment) Act 1944 to assist disabled persons to obtain or retain employment despite their disability.

1A.622   **49.** Any supplementary pension under article 23(2) of the Naval, Military and Air Forces Etc. (Disablement and Death) Service Pensions Order 2006 (pensions to widows, widowers or surviving civil partners) and any analogous payment made by the Secretary of State for Defence to any person who is not a person entitled under that Order.

1A.623   **50.** Where the claimant is in receipt of any benefit under Parts II, III or V of the Contributions and Benefits Act or pension under the Naval, Military and Air Forces Etc. (Disablement and Death) Service Pensions Order 2006, any increase in the rate of that benefit arising under Part 4 (increases for dependants) or section 106(a) (unemployability supplement) of that Act or the rate of that pension under that Order where the dependant in respect of whom the increase is paid is not a member of the claimant's family.

1A.624   **51.** In the case of a pension awarded at the supplementary rate under article 27(3) of the Personal Injuries (Civilians) Scheme 1983 (pensions to widows, widowers or surviving civil partners), the sum specified in paragraph 1(c) of Schedule 4 to that scheme.

1A.625   **52.**—(1) Any payment which is—
(a) made under any of the Dispensing Instruments to a widow, [¹widower or surviving civil partner] of a person—
    (i) whose death was attributable to service in a capacity analogous to service as a member of the armed forces of the Crown; and
    (ii) whose service in such capacity terminated before 31st March 1973; and
(b) equal to the amount specified in article 23(2) of the Naval, Military and Air Forces Etc. (Disablement and Death) Service Pensions Order 2006.

(2) In this paragraph "the Dispensing Instruments" means the Order in Council of 19th December 1881, the Royal Warrant of 27th October 1884 and the Order by His Majesty of 14th January 1922 (exceptional grants of pay, non-effective pay and allowances).

1A.626   **53.** Any payment made under the Community Care (Direct Payments) Act 1996 or under section 12B of the Social Work (Scotland) Act 1968 or under regulations made under section 57 of the Health and Social Care Act 2001 (direct payments).

1A.627   **54.**—(1) Any payment specified in sub-paragraph (2) to a claimant who was formerly a student and who has completed the course in respect of which those payments were made.

(2) The payments specified for the purposes of sub-paragraph (1) are—
(a) any grant income and covenant income as defined for the purposes of Chapter 10 of Part 10;
(b) any student loan as defined in Chapter 10 of Part 10;
(c) any contribution as defined in Chapter 10 of Part 10 which—

344

    (i) is taken into account in ascertaining the amount of a student loan referred to in paragraph (b); and

    (ii) has been paid.

55.—(1) Subject to sub-paragraph (2), in the case of a person who is receiving, or who has received, assistance under the self-employment route, any payment to the person—

    (a) to meet expenses wholly and necessarily incurred whilst carrying on the commercial activity;

    (b) which is used or intended to be used to maintain repayments on a loan taken out by that person for the purposes of establishing or carrying on the commercial activity,

in respect of which such assistance is or was received.

(2) Sub-paragraph (1) is to apply only in respect of payments which are paid to that person from the special account as defined for the purposes of Chapter 5 of Part 10.

1A.628

56. Any payment made with respect to a person on account of the provision of after-care under section 117 of the Mental Health Act 1983 or section 25 of the Mental Health (Care and Treatment) (Scotland) Act 2003 or the provision of accommodation or welfare services to which Part 3 of the National Assistance Act 1948 refers or to which the Social Work (Scotland) Act 1968 refers, which falls to be treated as notional income under paragraph (6) of regulation 107 (payments made in respect of a person living in a care home, an Abbeyfield Home or an independent hospital).

1A.629

57.—(1) Any payment of a sports award except to the extent that it has been made in respect of any one or more of the items specified in sub-paragraph (2).

(2) The items specified for the purposes of sub-paragraph (1) are food, ordinary clothing or footwear, household fuel, rent for which housing benefit is payable or any housing costs to the extent that they are met under regulation 67(1)(c) or 68(1)(d) (housing costs), of the claimant or, where the claimant is a member of a family, any other member of the claimant's family, or any council tax or water charges for which that claimant or member is liable.

(3) For the purposes of sub-paragraph (2) "food" does not include vitamins, minerals or other special dietary supplements intended to enhance the performance of the person in the sport in respect of which the award was made;

1A.630

58. Where the amount of a subsistence allowance paid to a person in a benefit week exceeds the amount of income-based jobseeker's allowance that person would have received in that benefit week had it been payable to that person, less 50p, that excess amount.

1A.631

59. In the case of a claimant participating in an employment zone programme, any discretionary payment made by an employment zone contractor to the claimant, being a fee, grant, loan or otherwise.

1A.632

60.—(1) Subject to sub-paragraph (3), any payment of child maintenance where the child or young person in respect of whom the payment is made is a member of the claimant's family except where the person making the payment is the claimant or the claimant's partner.

(2) For the purposes of sub-paragraph (1), where more than one payment of child maintenance—

    (a) in respect of more than one child or young person; or

    (b) made by more than one person in respect of a child or young person,

falls to be taken into account in any week, all such payments are to be aggregated and treated as if they were a single payment.

[² (3) No more than £20 shall be disregarded in respect of each week to which any payment of child maintenance is attributed in accordance with regulations 120 to 125 (child maintenance and liable relatives).

(4) In this paragraph, "child maintenance" shall have the same meaning as in regulation 119.]

1A.633

1A.634   **61.** In the case of a person to whom paragraph (5) of regulation 6 of the Income Support Regulations (persons not treated as in remunerative work) applies, the whole of that person's income.

1A.635   **62.** Any discretionary housing payment paid pursuant to regulation 2(1) of the Discretionary Financial Assistance Regulations 2001.

1A.636   **63.**—(1) Any payment made by a local authority or by the Welsh Ministers, to or on behalf of the claimant or the claimant's partner relating to a service which is provided to develop or sustain the capacity of the claimant or the claimant's partner to live independently in the claimant's or the claimant's partner's accommodation.

(2) For the purposes of sub-paragraph (1) "local authority" includes, in England, a county council.

1A.637   **64.** Any housing benefit to which the claimant is entitled.

1A.638   **65.** Any council tax benefit to which the claimant is entitled.

AMENDMENTS

1. Employment and Support Allowance (Miscellaneous Amendments) Regulations 2008 (SI 2008/2428), reg.18 (October 27, 2008).
2. Employment and Support Allowance (Miscellaneous Amendments) Regulations 2008 (SI 2008/2428), reg.20(10) (October 27, 2008).

DEFINITIONS

"Abbeyfield Home"—see reg.2(1).
"adoption leave"—*ibid.*
"benefit week"—*ibid.*
"board and lodging"—*ibid.*
"care home"—*ibid.*
"child"—*ibid.*
"claimant"—see reg.83(1).
"dwelling occupied as the home"—see reg.2(1).
"Eileen Trust"—*ibid.*
"employed earner"—*ibid.*
"employment zone"—*ibid.*
"family"—*ibid.*
"the Fund"—*ibid.*
"guaranteed income payment"—*ibid.*
"Immigration and Asylum Act"—*ibid.*
"independent hospital"—*ibid.*
"the Independent Living Fund (2006)"—*ibid.*
"the London Bombings Relief Charitable Fund"—*ibid.*
"Macfarlane (Special Payments) Trust"—*ibid.*
"Macfarlane (Special Payments) (No. 2) Trust"—*ibid.*
"Macfarlane Trust"—*ibid.*
"occupational pension scheme"—*ibid.*
"ordinary clothing or footwear"—*ibid.*
"partner"—*ibid.*
"payment"—*ibid.*
"personal pension scheme"—*ibid.*
"qualifying person"—*ibid.*
"self-employment route"—*ibid.*
"Skipton Fund"—*ibid.*
"sports award"—*ibid.*

"subsistence allowance"—*ibid.*
"training allowance"—*ibid.*
"voluntary organisation"—*ibid.*
"week"—*ibid.*
"young person"—*ibid.*

GENERAL NOTE

This is similar to Sch.9 to the Income Support Regs/Sch.7 to the JSA Regs (subject to some reordering and minor adjustments in the wording).   1A.639

Regulation 111(2)

SCHEDULE 9

CAPITAL TO BE DISREGARDED

1. The dwelling occupied as the home but, notwithstanding regulation 83 (calculation of income and capital of members of claimant's family and of a polygamous marriage), only one dwelling is to be disregarded under this paragraph.   1A.640

2. Any premises acquired for occupation by the claimant which that claimant intends to occupy as the home within 26 weeks of the date of acquisition or such longer period as is reasonable in the circumstances to enable the claimant to obtain possession and commence occupation of the premises.   1A.641

3. Any sum directly attributable to the proceeds of sale of any premises formerly occupied by the claimant as the home which is to be used for the purchase of other premises intended for such occupation within 26 weeks of the date of sale or such longer period as is reasonable in the circumstances to enable the claimant to complete the purchase.   1A.642

4. Any premises occupied in whole or in part by—   1A.643
(a) a partner or relative of a single claimant or any member of the family as the home where that person is aged 60 or over or is incapacitated;
(b) the former partner of a claimant as the home; but this provision is not to apply where the former partner is a person from whom the claimant is estranged or divorced or with whom the person formed a civil partnership that has been dissolved.

5. Where a claimant has ceased to occupy what was formerly the dwelling occupied as the home following the claimant's estrangement or divorce from, or dissolution of the claimant's civil partnership with, the claimant's former partner, that dwelling for a period of 26 weeks from the date on which the claimant ceased to occupy that dwelling or, where that dwelling is occupied as the home by the former partner who is a lone parent, for as long as it is so occupied.   1A.644

6. Any premises where the claimant is taking reasonable steps to dispose of those premises, for a period of 26 weeks from the date on which the claimant first took such steps, or such longer period as is reasonable in the circumstances to enable the claimant to dispose of those premises.   1A.645

7. Any premises which the claimant intends to occupy as the home, and in respect of which that claimant is taking steps to obtain possession and has sought legal advice or has commenced legal proceedings, with a view to obtaining possession, for a period of 26 weeks from the date on which the claimant first sought such advice or first commenced such proceedings whichever is earlier, or such longer period as is reasonable in the circumstances to enable the claimant to obtain possession and commence occupation of those premises.   1A.646

8. Any premises which the claimant intends to occupy as the home to which essential repairs or alterations are required in order to render them fit for such occupation, for a   1A.647

period of 26 weeks from the date on which the claimant first takes steps to effect those repairs or alterations, or such longer period as is reasonable in the circumstances to enable those repairs or alterations to be carried out and the claimant to commence occupation of the premises.

1A.648 **9.** Any future interest in property of any kind, other than land or premises in respect of which the claimant has granted a subsisting lease or tenancy, including sub-leases or sub-tenancies.

1A.649 **10.**—(1) The assets of any business owned in whole or in part by the claimant and for the purposes of which that claimant is engaged as a self-employed earner or, if the claimant has ceased to be so engaged, for such period as may be reasonable in the circumstances to allow for disposal of any such asset.

(2) The assets of any business owned in whole or in part by the claimant where that claimant—

(a) is not engaged as self-employed earner in that business by reason of some disease or bodily or mental disablement; but

(b) intends to become engaged (or, as the case may be, re-engaged) as a self-employed earner in that business as soon as the claimant recovers or is able to become engaged, or reengaged, in that business,

for a period of 26 weeks from the date on which the claim for an income-related allowance is made, or is treated as made, or, if it is unreasonable to expect the claimant to become engaged or re-engaged in that business within that period, for such longer period as is reasonable in the circumstances to enable the claimant to become so engaged or re-engaged.

(3) In the case of a person who is receiving assistance under the self-employment route, the assets acquired by that person for the purpose of establishing or carrying on the commercial activity in respect of which such assistance is being received.

(4) In the case of a person who has ceased carrying on the commercial activity in respect of which assistance was received as specified in sub-paragraph (3), the assets relating to that activity for such period as may be reasonable in the circumstances to allow for disposal of any such asset.

1A.650 **11.**—(1) Subject to sub-paragraph (2), any arrears of, or any concessionary payment made to compensate for arrears due to the non-payment of—

(a) any payment specified in paragraph 8, 10 or 11 of Schedule 8 (other income to be disregarded);

(b) an income-related allowance, an income-related benefit or an income-based job-seeker's allowance, child tax credit or working tax credit;

(c) any discretionary housing payment paid pursuant to regulation 2(1) of the Discretionary Financial Assistance Regulations 2001,

but only for a period of 52 weeks from the date of the receipt of the arrears or of the concessionary payment.

(2) In a case where the total of any arrears and, if appropriate, any concessionary payment referred to in sub-paragraph (1) relating to any one of the specified payments, benefits or allowances, amounts to £5,000 or more (referred to in this sub-paragraph and in sub-paragraph (3) as the "relevant sum") and is—

(a) paid in order to rectify, or to compensate for, an official error as defined in regulation 1(3) of the Social Security and Child Support (Decisions and Appeals) Regulations 1999; and

(b) received by the claimant in full on or after 14th October 2001,

sub-paragraph (1) is to have effect in relation to such arrears or concessionary payment either for a period of 52 weeks from the date of receipt, or, if the relevant sum is received in its entirety during the award of an income-related allowance, for the remainder of that award if that is a longer period.

(3) For the purposes of sub-paragraph (2), "the award of an income-related allowance" means—

(a) the award either of an income-related allowance, income support or of an income-based jobseeker's allowance in which the relevant sum (or first part thereof where it is paid in more than one instalment) is received; and

(b) where that award is followed by one or more further awards which in each case may be either of an income-related allowance, income support or of an income-based jobseeker's allowance and which, or each of which, begins immediately after the end of the previous award, such further awards until the end of the last such award, provided that for any such further awards the claimant—
   (i) is the person who received the relevant sum;
   (ii) is the partner of the person who received the relevant sum, or was that person's partner at the date of that person's death; or
   (iii) in the case of a joint-claim jobseeker's allowance, is a joint-claim couple either member or both members of which received the relevant sum.

12. Any sum—   **1A.651**
(a) paid to the claimant in consequence of damage to, or loss of, the home or any personal possession and intended for its repair or replacement; or
(b) acquired by the claimant (whether as a loan or otherwise) on the express condition that it is to be used for effecting essential repairs or improvements to the home,
and which is to be used for the intended purpose, for a period of 26 weeks from the date on which it was so paid or acquired or such longer period as is reasonable in the circumstances to enable the claimant to effect the repairs, replacement or improvements.

13. Any sum—   **1A.652**
(a) deposited with a housing association as defined in section 1(1) of the Housing Associations Act 1985 or section 338(1) of the Housing (Scotland) Act 1987 as a condition of occupying the home;
(b) which was so deposited and which is to be used for the purchase of another home, for the period of 26 weeks or such longer period as is reasonable in the circumstances to complete the purchase.

14. Any personal possessions except those which had or have been acquired by the claimant with the intention of reducing that claimant's capital in order to secure entitlement to an employment and support allowance, a jobseeker's allowance or to income support or to increase the amount of those benefits.   **1A.653**

15. The value of the right to receive any income under an annuity and the surrender value (if any) of such an annuity.   **1A.654**

16. Where the funds of a trust are derived from a payment made in consequence of any personal injury to the claimant or the claimant's partner, the value of the trust fund and the value of the right to receive any payment under that trust.   **1A.655**

17.—(1) Any payment made to the claimant or the claimant's partner in consequence of any personal injury to the claimant or, as the case may be, the claimant's partner.   **1A.656**
(2) But sub-paragraph (1)—
(a) applies only for the period of 52 weeks beginning with the day on which the claimant first receives any payment [²in consequence of that personal injury];
(b) does not apply to any subsequent payment made to the claimant in consequence of that injury (whether it is made by the same person or another);
(c) ceases to apply to the payment or any part of the payment from the day on which the claimant no longer possesses it;
(d) does not apply to any payment from a trust where the funds of the trust are derived from a payment made in consequence of any personal injury to the claimant.
(3) For the purpose of sub-paragraph (2)(c), the circumstances in which a claimant no longer possesses a payment or a part of it include where the claimant has used a payment or part of it to purchase an asset.

18. The value of the right to receive any income under a life interest or from a life rent.   **1A.657**

1A.658   **19.** The value of the right to receive any income which is disregarded under paragraph 9 of Schedule 7 or paragraph 24 of Schedule 8 (earnings or other income to be disregarded).

1A.659   **20.** The surrender value of any policy of life insurance.

1A.660   **21.** Where any payment of capital falls to be made by instalments, the value of the right to receive any outstanding instalments.

1A.661   **22.**—(1) Any payment made by a local authority in accordance with—
    (a) section 17, 23B, 23C or 24A of the Children Act 1989;
    (b) section 12 of the Social Work (Scotland) Act 1968; or
    (c) section 29 or 30 of the Children (Scotland) Act 1995 (local authorities' duty to promote welfare of children and powers to grant financial assistance to persons in, or formerly in, their care).
    (2) Subject to paragraph (3), any payment (or part of a payment) made by a local authority in accordance with section 23C of the Children Act 1989 or section 29 of the Children (Scotland) Act 1995 (local authorities' duty to promote welfare of children and powers to grant financial assistance to persons in, or formerly in, their care) to a person ("A") which A passes on to the claimant.
    (3) Sub-paragraph (2) applies only where A—
    (a) was formerly in the claimant's care; and
    (b) is aged 18 or over; and
    (c) continues to live with the claimant.

1A.662   **23.** Any social fund payment made pursuant to Part 8 of the Contributions and Benefits Act.

1A.663   **24.** Any refund of tax which falls to be deducted under section 369 of the Income and Corporation Taxes Act 1988 (mortgage interest payable under deduction of tax) on a payment of relevant loan interest for the purpose of acquiring an interest in the home or carrying out repairs or improvements in the home.

1A.664   **25.** Any capital which under regulation 105 or 137 (capital treated as income or treatment of student loans) is to be treated as income.

1A.665   **26.** Where a payment of capital is made in a currency other than sterling, any banking charge or commission payable in converting that payment into sterling.

1A.666   **27.**—(1) Any payment made under the Macfarlane Trust, the Macfarlane (Special Payments) Trust, the Macfarlane (Special Payments) (No. 2) Trust ("the Trusts"), the Fund, the Eileen Trust [¹, the Independent Living Fund (2006)], the Skipton Fund or the London Bombings Relief Charitable Fund.
    (2) Any payment by or on behalf of a person who is suffering or who suffered from haemophilia or who is or was a qualifying person, which derives from a payment made under any of the Trusts to which sub-paragraph (1) refers and which is made to or for the benefit of—
    (a) that person's partner or former partner from whom the person is not, or where that person has died was not, estranged or divorced or with whom the person has formed a civil partnership that has not been dissolved or, where that person has died, had not been dissolved at the time of that person's death;
    (b) any child who is a member of that person's family or who was such a member and who is a member of the claimant's family; or
    (c) any young person who is a member of that person's family or who was such a member and who is a member of the claimant's family.
    (3) Any payment by or on behalf of the partner or former partner of a person who is suffering or who suffered from haemophilia or who is or was a qualifying person provided that the partner or former partner and that person are not, or if either of them has died were not, estranged or divorced or, where the partner or former partner and that person have formed a civil partnership, the civil partnership has not been dissolved or, if either of them has died, had not been dissolved at the time of the death, which derives from a

payment made under any of the Trusts to which sub-paragraph (1) refers and which is made to or for the benefit of—

(a) the person who is suffering from haemophilia or who is a qualifying person;

(b) any child who is a member of that person's family or who was such a member and who is a member of the claimant's family; or

(c) any young person who is a member of that person's family or who was such a member and who is a member of the claimant's family.

(4) Any payment by a person who is suffering from haemophilia or who is a qualifying person, which derives from a payment under any of the Trusts to which sub-paragraph (1) refers, where—

(a) that person has no partner or former partner from whom the person is not estranged or divorced or with whom the person has formed a civil partnership that has not been dissolved, nor any child or young person who is or had been a member of that person's family; and

(b) the payment is made either—

(i) to that person's parent or step-parent; or

(ii) where that person at the date of the payment is a child, a young person or a full-time student who has not completed full-time education and had no parent or step-parent, to that person's guardian,

but only for a period from the date of the payment until the end of two years from that person's death.

(5) Any payment out of the estate of a person who suffered from haemophilia or who was a qualifying person, which derives from a payment under any of the Trusts to which sub-paragraph (1) refers, where—

(a) that person at the date of that person's death (the relevant date) had no partner or former partner from whom the person was not estranged or divorced or with whom the person had formed a civil partnership that had not been dissolved, nor any child or young person who was or had been a member of that person's family; and

(b) the payment is made either—

(i) to that person's parent or step-parent; or

(ii) where that person at the relevant date was a child, a young person or a full-time student who had not completed full-time education and had no parent or step-parent, to that person's guardian,

but only for a period of two years from the relevant date.

(6) In the case of a person to whom or for whose benefit a payment referred to in this paragraph is made, any capital resource which derives from any payment of income or capital made under or deriving from any of the Trusts.

(7) For the purposes of sub-paragraphs (2) to (6), any reference to the Trusts is to be construed as including a reference to the Fund, the Eileen Trust, the Skipton Fund or the London Bombings Relief Charitable Fund.

28. The value of the right to receive an occupational or personal pension. **1A.667**

29. The value of any funds held under a personal pension scheme. **1A.668**

30. The value of the right to receive any rent except where the claimant has a reversionary interest in the property in respect of which rent is due. **1A.669**

31. Any payment in kind made by a charity or under the Macfarlane Trust, Macfarlane (Special Payments) Trust, the Macfarlane (Special Payments) (No. 2) Trust, the Fund, the Eileen Trust or [²the Independent Living Fund (2006)]. **1A.670**

32. Any payment made pursuant to section 2 of the Employment and Training Act 1973 or section 2 of the Enterprise and New Towns (Scotland) Act 1990, but only for the period of 52 weeks beginning on the date of receipt of the payment. **1A.671**

33. Any payment made by the Secretary of State to compensate for the loss (in whole or in part) of entitlement to housing benefit. **1A.672**

1A.673   34. Any payment made to a juror or a witness in respect of attendance at a court other than compensation for loss of earnings or for the loss of a benefit payable under the benefit Acts.

1A.674   35. Any payment [²in consequence of a reduction] of council tax under section 13 or, as the case may be, section 80 of the Local Government Finance Act 1992 (reduction of liability for council tax), but only for a period of 52 weeks from the date of the receipt of the payment.

1A.675   36. Any grant made to the claimant in accordance with a scheme under section 129 of the Housing Act 1988 or section 66 of the Housing (Scotland) Act 1988 (schemes for payments to assist local housing authorities and local authority tenants to obtain other accommodation) which is to be used—
    (a) to purchase premises intended for occupation as the claimant's home; or
    (b) to carry out repairs or alterations which are required to render premises fit for occupation as the claimant's home,
for a period of 26 weeks from the date on which the claimant received such a grant or such longer period as is reasonable in the circumstances to enable the purchase, repairs or alterations to be completed and the claimant to commence occupation of those premises as the claimant's home.

1A.676   37.—(1) Any payment or repayment made—
    (a) as respects England, under regulation 5, 6 or 12 of the National Health Service (Travel Expenses and Remission of Charges) Regulations 2003 (travelling expenses and health service supplies);
    (b) as respects Wales, under regulation 5, 6 or 11 of the National Health Service (Travelling Expenses and Remission of Charges) (Wales) Regulations 2007;
    (c) as respects Scotland, under regulation 3, 5 or 11 of the National Health Service (Travelling Expenses and Remission of Charges) (Scotland) (No. 2) Regulations 2003 (travelling expenses and health service supplies);
but only for a period of 52 weeks from the date of receipt of the payment or repayment.
(2) Any payment or repayment made by the Secretary of State for Health, the Scottish Ministers or the Welsh Ministers which is analogous to a payment or repayment mentioned in sub-paragraph (1); but only for a period of 52 weeks from the date of receipt of the payment or repayment.

1A.677   38. Any payment made to such persons entitled to receive benefits as may be determined by or under a scheme made pursuant to section 13 of the Social Security Act 1988 in lieu of vouchers or similar arrangements in connection with the provision of those benefits (including payments made in place of healthy start vouchers, milk tokens or the supply of vitamins) but only for a period of 52 weeks from the date of receipt of the payment.

1A.678   39. Any payment made either by the Secretary of State for Justice or by the Scottish Ministers under a scheme established to assist relatives and other persons to visit persons in custody, but only for a period of 52 weeks from the date of receipt of the payment.

1A.679   40. Any arrears of supplementary pension which is disregarded under paragraph 49 of Schedule 8 (sums to be disregarded in the calculation of income other than earnings) or of any amount which is disregarded under paragraphs 51 or 52 of that Schedule, but only for a period of 52 weeks from the date of receipt of the arrears.

1A.680   41. Any payment (other than a training allowance) made, whether by the Secretary of State or by any other person, under the Disabled Persons (Employment) Act 1944 to assist disabled persons to obtain or retain employment despite their disability.

1A.681   42. Any payment made by a local authority under section 3 of the Disabled Persons (Employment) Act 1958 to homeworkers assisted under the Blind Homeworkers' Scheme.

43.—(1) Any sum to which sub-paragraph (2) applies and—

    (a) which is administered on behalf of a person by the High Court or the County Court under Rule 21.11(1) of the Civil Procedure Rules 1998 or by the Court of Protection;

    (b) which can only be disposed of by order or direction of any such court; or

    (c) where the person concerned is under the age of 18, which can only be disposed of by order or direction prior to that person attaining age 18.

    (2) This sub-paragraph applies to a sum which is derived from—

    (a) an award of damages for a personal injury to that person; or

    (b) compensation for the death of one or both parents where the person concerned is under the age of 18.

1A.682

44. Any sum administered on behalf of a person in accordance with an order made under section 13 of the Children (Scotland) Act 1995, or under Rule 36.14 of the Ordinary Cause Rules 1993 or under Rule 128 of the Ordinary Cause Rules, where such sum derives from—

    (a) an award of damages for a personal injury to that person; or

    (b) compensation for the death of one or both parents where the person concerned is under the age of 18.

1A.683

45. Any payment to the claimant as holder of the Victoria Cross or George Cross.

1A.684

46. In the case of a person who is receiving, or who has received, assistance under the self-employment route, any sum which is acquired by that person for the purpose of establishing or carrying on the commercial activity in respect of which such assistance is or was received but only for a period of 52 weeks from the date on which that sum was acquired.

1A.685

47.—(1) [²Any payment of a sports award] for a period of 26 weeks from the date of receipt of that payment except to the extent that it has been made in respect of any one or more of the items specified in sub-paragraph (2).

    (2) The items specified for the purposes of sub-paragraph (1) are food, ordinary clothing or footwear, household fuel, rent for which housing benefit is payable or any housing costs to the extent that they are met under regulation 67(1)(c) or 68(1)(d) (housing costs), of the claimant or, where the claimant is a member of a family, any other member of the claimant's family, or any council tax or water charges for which that claimant or member is liable.

    (3) For the purposes of sub-paragraph (2) "food" does not include vitamins, minerals or other special dietary supplements intended to enhance the performance of the person in the sport in respect of which the award was made.

1A.686

48. In the case of a claimant participating in an employment zone programme, any discretionary payment made by an employment zone contractor to the claimant, being a fee, grant, loan or otherwise, but only for the period of 52 weeks from the date of receipt of the payment.

1A.687

49. Any arrears of subsistence allowance paid as a lump sum but only for the period of 52 weeks from the date of receipt of the payment.

1A.688

50. Where an ex-gratia payment of £10,000 has been made by the Secretary of State on or after 1st February 2001 in consequence of the imprisonment or internment of—

    (a) the claimant;

    (b) the claimant's partner;

    (c) the claimant's deceased spouse or deceased civil partner; or

    (d) the claimant's partner's deceased spouse or deceased civil partner,

by the Japanese during the Second World War, £10,000.

1A.689

51. In the case of a person to whom paragraph (5) of regulation 6 of the Income Support Regulations (persons not treated as in remunerative work) applies, the whole of the claimant's capital.

1A.690

1A.691   **52.**—(1) Any payment—
(a) by way of an education maintenance allowance made pursuant to—
   (i) regulations made under section 518 of the Education Act 1996;
   (ii) regulations made under section 49 or 73(f) of the Education (Scotland) Act 1980;
   (iii) directions made under section 73ZA of the Education (Scotland) Act 1980 and paid under section 12(2)(c) of the Further and Higher Education (Scotland) Act 1992; or
(b) corresponding to such an education maintenance allowance, made pursuant to—
   (i) section 14 or section 181 of the Education Act 2002; or
   (ii) regulations made under section 181 of that Act.

(2) Any payment, other than a payment to which sub-paragraph (1) applies, made pursuant to—
(a) regulations made under section 518 of the Education Act 1996;
(b) regulations made under section 49 of the Education (Scotland) Act 1980; or
(c) directions made under section 73ZA of the Education (Scotland) Act 1980 and paid under section 12(2)(c) of the Further and Higher Education (Scotland) Act 1992,

in respect of a course of study attended by a child or a young person or a person who is in receipt of an education maintenance allowance made pursuant to any provision specified in sub-paragraph (1).

1A.692   **53.**—(1) Subject to sub-paragraph (2), the amount of any trust payment made to a claimant or a member of a claimant's family who is—
(a) a diagnosed person;
(b) the diagnosed person's partner or the person who was the diagnosed person's partner at the date of the diagnosed person's death;
(c) a parent of a diagnosed person, a person acting in the place of the diagnosed person's parents or a person who was so acting at the date of the diagnosed person's death; or
(d) a member of the diagnosed person's family (other than that person's partner) or a person who was a member of the diagnosed person's family (other than that person's partner) at the date of the diagnosed person's death.

(2) Where a trust payment is made to—
(a) a person referred to in sub-paragraph (1)(a) or (b), that sub-paragraph will apply for the period beginning on the date on which the trust payment is made and ending on the date on which that person dies;
(b) a person referred to in sub-paragraph (1)(c), that sub-paragraph will apply for the period beginning on the date on which the trust payment is made and ending two years after that date;
(c) a person referred to in sub-paragraph (1)(d), that sub-paragraph will apply for the period beginning on the date on which the trust payment is made and ending—
   (i) two years after that date; or
   (ii) on the day before the day on which that person—
     (aa)   ceases receiving full-time education; or
     (bb)   attains the age of 20,
whichever is the latest.

(3) Subject to sub-paragraph (4), the amount of any payment by a person to whom a trust payment has been made, or of any payment out of the estate of a person to whom a trust payment has been made, which is made to a claimant or a member of a claimant's family who is—
(a) the diagnosed person's partner or the person who was the diagnosed person's partner at the date of the diagnosed person's death;
(b) a parent of a diagnosed person, a person acting in the place of the diagnosed person's parents or a person who was so acting at the date of the diagnosed person's death; or
(c) a member of the diagnosed person's family (other than that person's partner) or a person who was a member of the diagnosed person's family (other than that person's partner) at the date of the diagnosed person's death,
but only to the extent that such payments do not exceed the total amount of any trust payments made to that person.

(4) Where a payment as referred to in sub-paragraph (3) is made to—

(a) a person referred to in sub-paragraph (3)(a), that sub-paragraph will apply for the period beginning on the date on which that payment is made and ending on the date on which that person dies;

(b) a person referred to in sub-paragraph (3)(b), that sub-paragraph will apply for the period beginning on the date on which that payment is made and ending two years after that date;

(c) a person referred to in sub-paragraph (3)(c), that sub-paragraph will apply for the period beginning on the date on which that payment is made and ending—

    (i) two years after that date; or

    (ii) on the day before the day on which that person—

        (aa)   ceases receiving full-time education; or

        (bb)   attains the age of 20,

whichever is the latest.

(5) In this paragraph, a reference to a person—

(a) being the diagnosed person's partner;

(b) being a member of the diagnosed person's family; or

(c) acting in the place of the diagnosed person's parents,

at the date of the diagnosed person's death will include a person who would have been such a person or a person who would have been so acting, but for the diagnosed person residing in a care home, an Abbeyfield Home or an independent hospital on that date.

(6) In this paragraph—

"diagnosed person" means a person who has been diagnosed as suffering from, or who, after that person's death, has been diagnosed as having suffered from, variant Creutzfeldt-Jakob disease;

"relevant trust" means a trust established out of funds provided by the Secretary of State in respect of persons who suffered, or who are suffering, from variant Creutzfeldt-Jakob disease for the benefit of persons eligible for payments in accordance with its provisions;

"trust payment" means a payment under a relevant trust.

54. The amount of a payment, other than a war pension within the meaning in section 25 of the Social Security Act 1989, to compensate for the fact that the claimant, the claimant's partner, the claimant's deceased spouse or deceased civil partner or the claimant's partner's deceased spouse or deceased civil partner— **1A.693**

(a) was a slave labourer or a forced labourer;

(b) had suffered property loss or had suffered personal injury; or

(c) was a parent of a child who had died,

during the Second World War.

55.—(1) Any payment made by a local authority or by the Welsh Ministers, to or on behalf of the claimant or the claimant's partner relating to a service which is provided to develop or sustain the capacity of the claimant or the claimant's partner to live independently in the claimant's or the claimant's partner's accommodation. **1A.694**

(2) For the purposes of sub-paragraph (1) "local authority" includes, in England, a county council.

56. Any payment made under the Community Care (Direct Payments) Act 1996, regulations made under section 57 of the Health and Social Care Act 2001 or under section 12B of the Social Work (Scotland) Act 1968. **1A.695**

57. Any payment made to the claimant pursuant to regulations under section 2(6)(b), 3 or 4 of the Adoption and Children Act 2002. **1A.696**

58. Any payment made to the claimant in accordance with regulations made pursuant to section 14F of the Children Act 1989 (special guardianship support services). **1A.697**

AMENDMENTS

1. Employment and Support Allowance (Miscellaneous Amendments) Regulations 2008 (SI 2008/2428), reg.8(8) (October 27, 2008).

2. Employment and Support Allowance (Miscellaneous Amendments) Regulations 2008 (SI 2008/2428), reg.19 (October 27, 2008).

DEFINITIONS

"Abbeyfield Home"—see reg.2(1).
"care home"—*ibid.*
"child"—*ibid.*
"claimant"—see reg.83(1).
"dwelling occupied as the home"—see reg.2(1).
"Eileen Trust"—*ibid.*
"employment zone"—*ibid.*
"family"—*ibid.*
"the Fund"—*ibid.*
"independent hospital"—*ibid.*
"the Independent Living Fund (2006)"—*ibid.*
"the London Bombings Relief Charitable Fund"—*ibid.*
"lone parent"—*ibid.*
"Macfarlane (Special Payments) Trust"—*ibid.*
"Macfarlane (Special Payments) (No. 2) Trust"—*ibid.*
"Macfarlane Trust"—*ibid.*
"occupational pension"—*ibid.*
"ordinary clothing or footwear"—*ibid.*
"partner"—*ibid.*
"payment"—*ibid.*
"personal pension scheme"—*ibid.*
"policy of life insurance"—*ibid.*
"qualifying person"—*ibid.*
"relative"—*ibid.*
"self-employed earner"—*ibid.*
"self-employment route"—*ibid.*
"single claimant"—*ibid.*
"Skipton Fund"—*ibid.*
"sports award"—*ibid.*
"subsistence allowance"—*ibid.*
"training allowance"—*ibid.*
"young person"—*ibid.*

GENERAL NOTE

1A.698   This is similar to Sch.10 to the Income Support Regs/Sch.8 to the JSA Regs (subject to some reordering and minor adjustments in the wording).

Paragraphs 47 to 49 of Sch.10 to the Income Support Regs have not been reproduced as they are no longer relevant.

Note that in para.14 the disregard of the value of personal possessions does not apply if they have been acquired in order to reduce capital so as to gain entitlement to, or increase the amount of, ESA, *JSA or income support*. This avoids the question that might otherwise have arisen on a claimant transferring from income support (or JSA) to ESA whether, if the acquisition had only been for the purposes of income support (or JSA), the disregard in para.14 applies.

The Employment and Support Allowance (Transitional Provisions) Regulations 2008

(SI 2008/795) *(as amended)*

ARRANGEMENT OF REGULATIONS

1. Citation, commencement and interpretation.
2. Claim for existing award.
3. Claim by person entitled or potentially entitled to existing award.
4. Claim for period before appointed day.
5. Transitional protection in relation to the Jobseekers Act 1995.

The Secretary of State for Work and Pensions in exercise of the powers   **1A.699**
conferred by section 25(2)(b) and (c) and 29 of, and paragraphs 1(1), 2
and 3(b), (c) and (d) of Schedule 4 to, the Welfare Reform Act 2007,
makes the following Regulations which are made by virtue of, or consequential on, the provisions of the Welfare Reform Act 2007 and which
are made before the end of a period of 6 months beginning with the
coming into force of those provisions.

Citation, commencement and interpretation

1.—(1) These Regulations may be cited as the Employment and   **1A.700**
Support Allowance (Transitional Provisions) Regulations 2008.

(2) This regulation and regulations 2, 3 and 4 shall come into force on
27th July 2008.

(3) Regulation 5 shall come into force on 27th October 2008.

(4) In these Regulations "income support on the grounds of disability" means income support awarded to a person to whom regulation
[¹ . . .] 13(2)(b) or (bb) of, or paragraph 7(a) or (b), 10, 12 or 13 of
Schedule 1B to, the Income Support (General) Regulations 1987 (prescribed categories of person) applies.

AMENDMENT

1. Employment and Support Allowance (Miscellaneous Amendments) Regulations 2008 (SI 2008/2428), reg.42 (October 27, 2008).

DEFINITION

"income support on the grounds of disability"—see para.(4).

GENERAL NOTE

This regulation entered into force on July 27, 2008, three months before the   **1A.701**
main ESA scheme became operative.

Claim for existing award

1A.702   **2.**—(1) A claim for incapacity benefit, severe disablement allowance or income support on the grounds of disability, whenever made, in respect of a period which begins on or after the appointed day, is to be treated as a claim for an employment and support allowance.

(2) Paragraph (1) does not apply to—

(a) a claim for incapacity benefit or severe disablement allowance relating to a period of incapacity for work which is one of two periods treated as one period of incapacity for work under section 30C(1)(c) of the Contributions and Benefits Act (linking rules);

(b) a claim made by a welfare to work beneficiary in accordance with regulation 13A of the Social Security (Incapacity for Work) (General) Regulations 1995 (welfare to work beneficiary); [¹ . . .]

(c) a claim for income support on the grounds of disability where—

(i) the claimant was previously entitled to income support on the grounds of disability, for a period of 4 or more consecutive days, and

(ii) the claimant ceased to be entitled to income support on the grounds of disability not more than 8 weeks before the commencement of the period in respect of which the current claim is made;

[¹(d) a claim for income support on the grounds of disability made by a claimant who is entitled to incapacity benefit or severe disablement allowance; or

(e) a claim for incapacity benefit made by a claimant who is entitled to income support on the grounds of disability.]

(3) Paragraph (1) does not apply insofar as a claim is treated as a claim for severe disablement allowance, maternity allowance or carer's allowance under regulation 9(1) of and Part 1 of Schedule 1 to, the Social Security (Claims and Payments) Regulations 1987 (claims treated as claimed in addition or in the alternative).

AMENDMENT

1. Employment and Support Allowance (Transitional Provisions) (Amendment) Regulations 2008 (SI 2008/2783), reg.2 (October 26, 2008).

DEFINITIONS

"appointed day"—see WRA 2007, s.29, Sch.4, para.11.
"claimant"—see WRA 2007, s.24(1).
"incapacity benefit"—see WRA 2007, s.29, Sch.4, para.11.
"income support on the grounds of disability"—see reg.1(4).
"severe disablement allowance"—see WRA 2007, s.29, Sch.4, para.11.

GENERAL NOTE

1A.703   This regulation entered into force on July 27, 2008, three months before October 27, 2008, the "appointed day" when WRA 2007, s.1 and the main ESA provisions became operative (see WRA 2007, s.29, Sch.4, para.11, and the Welfare Reform Act 2007 (Commencement No.6 and Consequential Provisions) Order 2008 (SI 2008/787), art.2(4).

It deals with claims for one or more of the benefits in the already existing incapacity benefits' regime: incapacity benefit; severe disablement allowance (limited, of course, only to those entitled to it immediately before April 6, 2001) and "income support on the grounds of disability". This last covers claims for income support by someone to whom regulation 13(2)(b) or (bb) of, or para.7(a) or (b), 10, 12 or 13 of Sch.1B to, the Income Support (General) Regs 1987 (prescribed categories of person) applies (that is someone claiming IS as a person incapable of work; as a disabled or deaf student; or as a blind person).

Paragraph (1) provides that a claim for any such benefit made on or after October 27, 2008 (the "appointed day") is to be treated as one for ESA. To this there are within reg.2 three classes of exception:

(1) Where a claim for one of those benefits which is "linked" to a previous entitlement (para.(2)(a)–(c)).

This covers claims for IB or SDA linked to a previous period of incapacity for work by the standard eight week "linking rule" in SSCCBA 1992, s.30C(1)(c) (a period extendible by regs under s.30C(3)) (sub-para.(a)). It also embraces an IB claim by a "welfare to work beneficiary" under the Incapacity for Work Regs, reg.13A (the "104 week" rule) (sub-para.(b). It also covers an incapacity/disability-based claim for IS satisfying the four consecutive days "continuity rule" which ended not more than eight weeks prior to the claim now at issue (sub-para.(c)).   **1A.704**

(2) where a person entitled to incapacity benefit or severe disablement allowance claims income support on the grounds of disability and a person who is entitled to income support on the grounds of disability claims incapacity benefit (para.(2)(d), (e)).

Memo DMG 40/08 gives an example (IB entitlement enabling IS claim):   **1A.705**

"Sue has been in receipt of IB for several years. She is not entitled to IS because her partner Mark is in remunerative work. Mark is made redundant in November 2008, and Sue claims IS on the grounds of disability. The DM makes a determination that Sue's claim is not treated as a claim for ESA, and decides the claim for IS accordingly."

(3) where a claim is treated as a claim for severe disablement allowance, maternity allowance or carer's allowance under reg.9(1) of and Pt 1 of Sch.1 to, the Social Security (Claims and Payments) Regs 1987 (claims treated as claimed in addition or in the alternative).

See further the commentary to that regulation in Vol.III.   **1A.706**

Claim by person entitled or potentially entitled to existing award

3.—(1) A person who is entitled to an existing award is excluded from making a claim for an employment and support allowance.   **1A.707**

(2) A claim for an employment and support allowance made by a person who would be entitled to an existing award if that person made a claim described in regulation 2(2), is to be treated as a claim for that award.

DEFINITION

"existing award"—see WRA 2007, s.29, Sch.4, para.11.

GENERAL NOTE

1A.708   This regulation entered into force on July 27, 2008, three months before October 27, 2008, the "appointed day" when WRA 2007, s.1 and the main ESA provisions became operative (see WRA 2007, s.29, Sch.4, para.11, and the Welfare Reform Act 2007 (Commencement No.6 and Consequential Provisions) Order 2008 (SI 2008/787), art.2(4).

Paragraph (1) deals with claims for ESA by someone entitled to an "existing award", that is, one or more of the benefits in the already existing incapacity benefits' regime: incapacity benefit; severe disablement allowance (limited, of course, only to those entitled to it immediately before April 6, 2001) and "income support on the grounds of disability" (2007, s.29, Sch.4, para.11). This last covers claims for income support under by someone to whom 13(2)(b) or (bb) of, or para.7(a) or (b), 10, 12 or 13 of Sch.1B to, the Income Support (General) Regs 1987 (prescribed categories of person) applies (that is someone claiming IS as a person incapable of work; as a disabled or deaf student; or as a blind person).

Paragraph (1) provides that someone so entitled cannot be entitled to ESA. That and an existing award are mutually exclusive.

Paragraph (2) extends that preclusion to those who claim ESA but would be entitled to an "existing award" (IB, SDA or incapacity/disability-based IS, as the case may be) if they made a "linked" claim for it as envisaged by reg.2(2).

Claim for period before appointed day

1A.709   4. Where—

(a)   (i) before the appointed day a person purports to make a claim, or

(ii) on or after the appointed day a person makes a claim,

for an employment and support allowance for a period beginning before the appointed day; and

(b) it appears to the Secretary of State that the person would be entitled to incapacity benefit or income support on the grounds of disability if that person made a claim for it in accordance wit section 1(1)(a) of the Administration Act, the purported claim or claim may be treated by the Secretary of State as a claim in the alternative for incapacity benefit or income support on the grounds of disability.

DEFINITIONS

"appointed day"—see WRA 2007, s.29, Sch.4, para.11.
"incapacity benefit"—see WRA 2007, s.29, Sch.4, para.11.
"income support on the grounds of disability"—see reg.1(4).

GENERAL NOTE

1A.710   This regulation entered into force on July 27, 2008, three months before October 27, 2008, the "appointed day" when WRA 2007, s.1 and the main ESA provisions became operative (see WRA 2007, s.29, Sch.4, para.11, and the Welfare Reform Act 2007 (Commencement No. 6 and Consequential Provisions) Order 2008 (SI 2008/787), art.2(4).

It deals with a claim for ESA made before October 27, 2008 (the "appointed day) or after that but for a period prior to the appointed day. No entitlement to ESA can arise until October 27, 2008. So such a claim can either be rejected or, under this regulation, instead treated by the Secretary of State as a claim in the alternative for incapacity benefit or income support on the grounds of disability (IS as a person incapable of work; as a disabled or deaf student; or as a blind person). But it can only be so treated if the Secretary of State is satisfied that he would have been entitled to one of those benefits has a claim been made for it.

Transitional protection in relation to the Jobseekers Act 1995

5. In relation to a person who—
(a) is entitled to an existing award; or
(b) would be entitled to an existing award if that person made a claim described in regulation 2(2),
the Jobseekers Act 1995 shall continue to have effect as if paragraphs 12(2), (5)(b) and (6) of Schedule 3 to the Welfare Reform Act 2007 had not come into effect.

1A.711

DEFINITIONS

"existing award"—see WRA 2007, s.29, Sch.4, para.11.

GENERAL NOTE

An "existing award" is an award of one or more of the benefits in the already existing incapacity benefits' regime: incapacity benefit; severe disablement allowance (limited, of course, only to those entitled to it immediately before April 6, 2001) and "income support on the grounds of disability" (2007, s.29, Sch.4, para.11). This last covers claims for income support under by someone to whom reg.6(4)(a) or 13(2)(b) or (bb) of, or para.7(a) or (b), 10, 12 or 13 of Sch.1B to, the Income Support (General) Regs 1987 (prescribed categories of person) applies (that is someone claiming IS as a person incapable of work; as a disabled worker; as a disabled or deaf student; or as a blind person). This regulation deals with those entitled to an existing award or who would be if they claimed it in respect of a "linked" period under reg.2(2). It provides that in respect of them the Jobseekers Act 1995 continues to have effect as if the changes effected by the specified provisions in WRA 2007, Sch.3 had never taken effect. In short, read the relevant Jobseekers Act provisions as laid out in the 2008/09 edition of Vol.II.

1A.712

PART I

SECTION B

TRIBUNAL REFORM

Commentary by

Mark Rowland

The Tribunal Procedure (First-tier Tribunal) (Social Entitlement Chamber) Rules 2008

The Tribunal Procedure (Upper Tribunal) Rules 2008

The Tribunal Procedure (First-tier Tribunal) (Social Entitlement Chamber) Rules 2008

(SI 2008/2685)

In force November 3, 2008

CONTENTS

PART 1

INTRODUCTION

PART 2

GENERAL POWERS AND PROVISIONS

37. Setting aside a decision which disposes of proceedings
38. Application for permission to appeal
39. Tribunal's consideration of application for permission to appeal
40. Review of a decision
41. Power to treat an application as a different type of application

SCHEDULE 1

TIME LIMITS FOR PROVIDING NOTICES OF APPEAL TO THE DECISION MAKER

SCHEDULE 2

ISSUES IN RELATION TO WHICH THE TRIBUNAL MAY REFER A PERSON FOR MEDICAL
EXAMINATION UNDER SECTION 20(2) OF THE SOCIAL SECURITY ACT 1998

After consulting in accordance with paragraph 28(1) of Schedule 5 to, the
Tribunals, Courts and Enforcement Act 2007, the Tribunal Procedure Committee has made the following Rules in exercise of the powers conferred by sections
20(2) and (3) of the Social Security Act 1998 and sections 9(3), 22 and 29(3) of,
and Schedule 5 to, the Tribunals, Courts and Enforcement Act 2007. The Lord
Chancellor has allowed the Rules in accordance with paragraph 28(3) of Schedule 5 to the Tribunals, Courts and Enforcement Act 2007.

PART 1

INTRODUCTION

Citation, commencement, application and interpretation

1.—(1) These Rules may be cited as the Tribunal Procedure (First-   **1B.2**
tier Tribunal) (Social Entitlement Chamber) Rules 2008 and come into
force on 3rd November 2008.

(2) These Rules apply to proceedings before the Tribunal which have
been assigned to the Social Entitlement Chamber by the First-tier Tribunal and Upper Tribunal (Chambers) Order 2008.

(3) In these Rules—

"the 2007 Act" means the Tribunals, Courts and Enforcement Act
2007;

"appeal" includes an application under section 19(9) of the Tax Credits Act 2002;

"appellant" means a person who makes an appeal to the Tribunal, or
a person substituted as an appellant under rule 9(1) (substitution
of parties);

"asylum support case" means proceedings concerning the provision of
support for an asylum seeker or his or her dependants;

"criminal injuries compensation case" means proceedings concerning
the payment of compensation under a scheme made under the
Criminal Injuries Compensation Act 1995;

"decision maker" means the maker of a decision against which an appeal has been brought;

"dispose of proceedings" includes, unless indicated otherwise, disposing of a part of the proceedings;

"document" means anything in which information is recorded in any form, and an obligation under these Rules to provide or allow access to a document or a copy of a document for any purpose means, unless the Tribunal directs otherwise, an obligation to provide or allow access to such document or copy in a legible form or in a form which can be readily made into a legible form;

"hearing" means an oral hearing and includes a hearing conducted in whole or in part by video link, telephone or other means of instantaneous two-way electronic communication;

"legal representative" means an authorised advocate or authorised litigator as defined by section 119(1) of the Courts and Legal Services Act 1990, an advocate or solicitor in Scotland or a barrister or solicitor in Northern Ireland;

"party" means—

    (a) a person who is an appellant or respondent in proceedings before the Tribunal;

    (b) a person who makes a reference to the Tribunal under section 28D of the Child Support Act 1991;

    (c) a person who starts proceedings before the Tribunal under paragraph 3 of Schedule 2 to the Tax Credits Act 2002; or

    (d) if the proceedings have been concluded, a person who was a party under paragraph (a), (b) or (c) when the Tribunal finally disposed of all issues in the proceedings;

"practice direction" means a direction given under section 23 of the 2007 Act;

"respondent" means—

    (a) in an appeal against a decision, the decision maker and any person other than the appellant who had a right of appeal against the decision;

    (b) in a reference under section 28D of the Child Support Act 1991—

        (i) the absent parent or non-resident parent;

        (ii) the person with care; and

        (iii) in Scotland, the child if the child made the application for a departure direction or a variation;

    (c) in proceedings under paragraph 3 of Schedule 2 to the Tax Credits Act 2002, a person on whom it is proposed that a penalty be imposed; or

    (d) a person substituted or added as a respondent under rule 9 (substitution and addition of parties);

"Social Entitlement Chamber" means the Social Entitlement Chamber of the First-tier Tribunal established by the First-tier Tribunal and Upper Tribunal (Chambers) Order 2008;

"social security and child support case" means any case allocated to
the Social Entitlement Chamber except an asylum support case
or a criminal injuries compensation case;
"Tribunal" means the First-tier Tribunal.

DEFINITIONS

"the 2007 Act"—see para.(3).
"appellant"—*ibid.*
"asylum support case"—*ibid.*
"criminal injuries compensation case"—*ibid.*
"party"—*ibid.*
"respondent"—*ibid.*
"Social Entitlement Chamber"—*ibid.*
"Tribunal"—*ibid.*

GENERAL NOTE

By para.(2), these Rules apply to all cases within the Social Entitlement
Chamber of the First-tier Tribunal which are those cases formerly dealt with by
the appeal tribunals constituted under the Social Security Act 1998, by asylum
support adjudicators (known collectively as the "asylum support tribunal")
acting under ss.103 and 103A of the Immigration and Asylum Act 1999 and by
the adjudicators of the Criminal Injuries Compensation Appeal Panel dealing
with cases under schemes made under the Criminal Injuries Compensation Act
1995.

Although the appeal tribunals dealt with a wide variety of cases outside the
scope of this work and some that could not properly be called either social
security or child support cases, these Rules treat any case within the jurisdiction
of the Chamber that is not an asylum support or criminal injuries compensation
case as a "social security and child support case".

Note that a "hearing" means an "oral hearing" so that the term "paper
hearing" is no longer appropriate for the consideration of a case on the papers.
Perhaps "paper determination" will become the commonly used term.

Overriding objective and parties' obligation to co-operate with the Tribunal

2.—(1) The overriding objective of these Rules is to enable the Tribunal to deal with cases fairly and justly.

(2) Dealing with a case fairly and justly includes—

(a) dealing with the case in ways which are proportionate to the
importance of the case, the complexity of the issues, the anticipated costs and the resources of the parties;

(b) avoiding unnecessary formality and seeking flexibility in the
proceedings;

(c) ensuring, so far as practicable, that the parties are able to participate fully in the proceedings;

(d) using any special expertise of the Tribunal effectively; and

(e) avoiding delay, so far as compatible with proper consideration of
the issues.

(3) The Tribunal must seek to give effect to the overriding objective
when it—

(a) exercises any power under these Rules; or

1B.3

369

(b) interprets any rule or practice direction.

(4) Parties must—

(a) help the Tribunal to further the overriding objective; and

(b) co-operate with the Tribunal generally.

DEFINITIONS

"party"—see r.1(3).
"practice direction"—*ibid.*
"Tribunal"—*ibid.*

GENERAL NOTE

It is nowadays conventional for procedural rules in England and Wales to set out clearly their overriding objective in this manner. The overriding objective of these Rules is rather different from that of the Civil Procedure Rules. There, one object is to ensure, so far as practical, that the parties are on an equal footing. It may be thought that that is not achievable in Citizen v State litigation before tribunals and these Rules do not require it. Instead, they emphasise the need to avoid "unnecessary formality" (see para.(2)(b)) and to promote the "enabling role" of tribunals (see para.(2)(c)) and they do not expressly refer to the resources of the tribunal in the way that the Civil Procedure Rules refer to the resources of the court as a matter to be taken into account when making procedural decisions. Perhaps, the key concept is "proportionality" (see para.(2)(a)) which is likely to be relevant in most cases where procedural decisions are being made.

By para.(3), the tribunal is required to "seek to give effect to" the overriding objective when exercising any power under the Rules or interpreting the Rules or a Practice Direction. Note that this does not extend to the exercise of powers under the Tribunal, Courts and Enforcement Act 2007 or other legislation but the principles of the overriding objective might anyway be relevant to the exercise of such powers. By para.(4), parties must help the tribunal to further the overriding objective and co-operate with the tribunal generally and a failure to do so may, in an extreme case, lead to proceedings being struck out under r.8(3)(b).

Alternative dispute resolution and arbitration

1B.4   **3.**—(1) The Tribunal should seek, where appropriate—

(a) to bring to the attention of the parties the availability of any appropriate alternative procedure for the resolution of the dispute; and

(b) if the parties wish and provided that it is compatible with the overriding objective, to facilitate the use of the procedure.

(2) Part 1 of the Arbitration Act 1996 does not apply to proceedings before the Tribunal.

DEFINITIONS

"party"—see r.1(3).
"Tribunal"—*ibid.*

GENERAL NOTE

Rule 3(1) applies only if there is an alternative procedure available. Apart from a pilot scheme in relation to disability living allowance and attendance allowance claims, there are currently no schemes available in relation to social security cases. The scope for such schemes is limited by the facts that tribunal proceedings in social security cases are relatively cheap, quick and informal and that the conditions of entitlement often allow for little compromise, which means that alternative methods of dispute resolution normally offer little advantage over tribunal proceedings. However, that is not to say that there are no cases that could be better dealt with outside the tribunal process.

PART 2

GENERAL POWERS AND PROVISIONS

Delegation to staff

4.—(1) Staff appointed under section 40(1) of the 2007 Act (tribunal **1B.5** staff and services) may, with the approval of the Senior President of Tribunals, carry out functions of a judicial nature permitted or required to be done by the Tribunal.

(2) The approval referred to at paragraph (1) may apply generally to the carrying out of specified functions by members of staff of a specified description in specified circumstances.

(3) Within 14 days after the date on which the Tribunal sends notice of a decision made by a member of staff under paragraph (1) to a party, that party may apply in writing to the Tribunal for that decision to be considered afresh by a judge.

DEFINITIONS

"the 2007 Act"—see r.1(3).
"party"—*ibid.*
"Tribunal"—*ibid.*

GENERAL NOTE

There is no need to make provision for the delegation of functions of a purely administrative nature and so this rule refers only to functions of a judicial nature. The Senior President of Tribunals has issued a Practice Statement (available at: http://www.tribunals.gov.uk/Tribunals/Rules/statements.htm) recording his approval of the delegation of functions in relation to asylum support cases and criminal injuries compensation cases but not in relation to any other type of case in the Social Entitlement Chamber. Thus, clerks lose the judicial functions they had before November 3, 2008 to strike out and reinstate cases under regs 46 and 47 of the Social Security and Child Support (Decisions and Appeals) Regs 1999, to correct decisions under reg.56 of those Regulations and to issue directions under reg.38(3). The loss of the last power may be of particular significance because it has the effect that a clerk cannot issue a warning that a failure to comply with an instruction will, or may, result in a case being struck out; such a warning must be in a direction (see r.8(1) and (3)).

Case management powers

5.—(1) Subject to the provisions of the 2007 Act and any other **1B.6** enactment, the Tribunal may regulate its own procedure.

(2) The Tribunal may give a direction in relation to the conduct or disposal of proceedings at any time, including a direction amending, suspending or setting aside an earlier direction.

(3) In particular, and without restricting the general powers in paragraphs (1) and (2), the Tribunal may—

(a) extend or shorten the time for complying with any rule, practice direction or direction;

(b) consolidate or hear together two or more sets of proceedings or parts of proceedings raising common issues, or treat a case as a lead case (whether in accordance with rule 18 (lead cases) or otherwise);

(c) permit or require a party to amend a document;

(d) permit or require a party or another person to provide documents, information, evidence or submissions to the Tribunal or a party;

(e) deal with an issue in the proceedings as a preliminary issue;

(f) hold a hearing to consider any matter, including a case management issue;

(g) decide the form of any hearing;

(h) adjourn or postpone a hearing;

(i) require a party to produce a bundle for a hearing;

(j) stay (or, in Scotland, sist) proceedings;

(k) transfer proceedings to another court or tribunal if that other court or tribunal has jurisdiction in relation to the proceedings and—

(i) because of a change of circumstances since the proceedings were started, the Tribunal no longer has jurisdiction in relation to the proceedings; or

(ii) the Tribunal considers that the other court or tribunal is a more appropriate forum for the determination of the case; or

(l) suspend the effect of its own decision pending the determination by the Tribunal or the Upper Tribunal of an application for permission to appeal against, and any appeal or review of, that decision.

DEFINITIONS

"the 2007 Act"—see r.1(3).
"dispose of proceedings"—*ibid.*
"document"—*ibid.*
"hearing"—*ibid.*
"party"—*ibid.*
"practice direction"—*ibid.*
"Tribunal"—*ibid.*

GENERAL NOTE

Para. (1)

This replaces reg.38(1) of the Social Security and Child Support (Decisions and Appeals) Regs 1999.

Para. (2)

This replaces reg.38(2) of the Social Security and Child Support (Decisions and Appeals) Regs 1999. It is in very broad terms and, although para.(3) and r.15(1) set out examples of directions the tribunal may give, they do not restrict the width of the power in this paragraph. The power must, however, be exercised so as to give effect to the overriding objective in r.2 (see r.2(3)). The procedure for applying for and giving directions is to be found in r.6. Note that, where a direction requires something to be done by a particular day, it must be done by 5pm on that day (r.12(1)) but, if that day is not a working day, the act is done in time if it is done on the next working day (r.12(2)).

Para. (3)

Sub-paragraph (c) presumably refers to grounds of appeal and other submissions, rather than to evidence, despite the statutory definition.

Sub-paragraphs (f), (g) and (h) must be read with rr.27 to 30. Sub-paragraph (h) replaces reg.51 of the Social Security and Child Support (Decisions and Appeals) Regs 1999. See the note to that provision on pp.640–643 of Vol.III of the main work for comments that will still generally be relevant. However, the overriding objective in r.2(2) may be particularly important where a power to postpone or adjourn a hearing is being considered. It requires a case to be dealt with "in ways that are proportionate to the importance of the case, the complexity of the issues, the anticipated costs and the resources of the parties" and also to the avoidance of delay but only "so far as compatible with proper consideration of the issues".

Sub-paragraph (k) applies only where the First-tier Tribunal had jurisdiction at the time the proceedings were begun. Otherwise, the Tribunal is required to strike the proceedings out under r.8(2). Rule 5(3)(k)(i) applies where the First-tier Tribunal loses jurisdiction and r.5(3)(k)(ii) applies only where the First-tier Tribunal and another tribunal have concurrent jurisdiction (which may be the case in some circumstances where a person moves to or from Northern Ireland).

Sub-paragraph (l) permits the effect of a decision to be suspended pending an appeal to the Upper Tribunal. It is usually unnecessary for the Tribunal to suspend a decision in a social security case concerned with entitlement, due to the Secretary of State's power to suspend payments under reg.16 of the Social Security and Child Support (Decisions and Appeals) Regs 1999 (see, in particular, reg.16(3)(b)(i) and (4)). In the past, the Secretary of State has generally not taken action to recover an overpayment while an appeal against a decision that the overpayment is recoverable is pending but he could now take the view that an appeal does not require him to stay his hand unless the Tribunal so directs under this provision, which would not necessarily be appropriate as a matter of course and could in any event presumably be limited to part of its decision. The power to suspend the effect of a decision may also be useful in appeals under the Social Security (Recovery of Benefits) Act 1997, because s.14 of that Act and the regulations made under it completely fail to deal with the consequences of a successful appeal to the Upper Tribunal.

Procedure for applying for and giving directions

6.—(1) The Tribunal may give a direction on the application of one or more of the parties or on its own initiative.   **1B.7**

(2) An application for a direction may be made—

(a) by sending or delivering a written application to the Tribunal; or

(b) orally during the course of a hearing.

(3) An application for a direction must include the reason for making that application.

(4) Unless the Tribunal considers that there is good reason not to do so, the Tribunal must send written notice of any direction to every party and to any other person affected by the direction.

(5) If a party or any other person sent notice of the direction under paragraph (4) wishes to challenge a direction which the Tribunal has given, they may do so by applying for another direction which amends, suspends or sets aside the first direction.

DEFINITIONS

"hearing"—see r.1(3).
"party"—*ibid.*
"Tribunal"—*ibid.*

GENERAL NOTE

There is no requirement that a person be given the opportunity to make representations before a direction is given. Plainly it is to be expected that such an opportunity would be given where a direction is to be given at a hearing but in other cases, where an application is made in writing or the tribunal proposes to issue a direction on its own initiative, it is often simpler and more proportionate to make the direction and then see whether anyone objects. If a direction is given and a party or other person affected objects to it, the remedy is to apply for another direction amending, suspending or setting aside the first direction (see para.(5)).

It is uncertain to what extent, if at all, there is any right of appeal against a direction or a refusal to give a direction. In *Dorset Healthcare NHS Foundation Trust v MH* [2009] UKUT 4 (AAC), the Upper Tribunal accepted that an appeal lay against a direction issued under r.5(3)(d) of the Tribunal Procedure (First-tier Tribunal) (Health, Education and Social Care Chamber) Rules 2008 (SI 2008/2699) (similar to r.5(3)(d) of these Rules), requiring one party to disclose documents to another. It was unnecessary for the Upper Tribunal to decide whether to accept a broad argument advanced by counsel for the Appellant, to the effect that the power to exclude a decision from the scope of the right of appeal under s.11(1) of the Tribunals, Courts and Enforcement Act 2007 means that the word "decision" in that provision must apply to *any* decision of a tribunal. The consequence of accepting that argument would be that a right of appeal under that Act lies against any decision of the First-tier Tribunal (including any decision to issue a direction) unless a decision is expressly "excluded" under s.11(8). However, it would remain open to the Upper Tribunal to refuse permission to appeal against interlocutory decisions where it would be more appropriate for the dissatisfied party to await the conclusion of proceedings in the First-tier Tribunal. The giving or refusal of a direction may provide a ground of appeal against a final decision in a case (see the beginning of the note to s.14(1) of the Social Security Act 2008 on pp.236–237 of Vol.III of the main work). In any event, in the *Dorset Healthcare* case, the Upper Tribunal emphasised the desirability of the Tribunal considering whether to vary a direction, either on its own initiative under r.5(3) or on an application under r.6(5), before contemplating granting permission to appeal, at least in a case where the original direction was made without the benefit of full argument.

Failure to comply with rules etc.

7.—(1) An irregularity resulting from a failure to comply with any   **1B.8**
requirement in these Rules, a practice direction or a direction, does not
of itself render void the proceedings or any step taken in the proceedings.

(2) If a party has failed to comply with a requirement in these Rules,
a practice direction or a direction, the Tribunal may take such action as
it considers just, which may include—

(a) waiving the requirement;
(b) requiring the failure to be remedied;
(c) exercising its power under rule 8 (striking out a party's case); or
(d) exercising its power under paragraph (3).

(3) The Tribunal may refer to the Upper Tribunal, and ask the Upper
Tribunal to exercise its power under section 25 of the 2007 Act in
relation to, any failure by a person to comply with a requirement
imposed by the Tribunal—

(a) to attend at any place for the purpose of giving evidence;
(b) otherwise to make themselves available to give evidence;
(c) to swear an oath in connection with the giving of evidence;
(d) to give evidence as a witness;
(e) to produce a document; or
(f) to facilitate the inspection of a document or any other thing
(including any premises).

DEFINITIONS

"the 2007 Act"—see r.1(3).
"document"—*ibid.*
"party"—*ibid.*
"practice direction"—*ibid.*
"Tribunal"—*ibid.*

GENERAL NOTE

Paragraphs (1) and (2)(a) enable a tribunal to overlook a breach of a rule,
practice direction or direction. On the other hand, under para.2(c), such a
breach can lead to a case being struck out under r.8, provided an appropriate
warning has been given. Alternatively, para.(3) enables a breach of a requirement
to give evidence or produce or make available a document to be referred to the
Upper Tribunal with a view to the Upper Tribunal punishing the person for
contempt of court (with a term of imprisonment of up to two years and an
unlimited fine) under s.25 of the Tribunals' Courts and Enforcement Act 2007,
as applied by r.7(4) of the Tribunal Procedure (Upper Tribunal) Rules 2008,
although that should be a last resort. Paragraph (3)(c) must be read subject to s.5
of the Oaths Act 1978, which permits a person who objects to being sworn to
make a solemn affirmation instead.

Striking out a party's case

8.—(1) The proceedings, or the appropriate part of them, will auto-   **1B.9**
matically be struck out if the appellant has failed to comply with a

direction that stated that failure by a party to comply with the direction would lead to the striking out of the proceedings or that part of them.

(2) The Tribunal must strike out the whole or a part of the proceedings if the Tribunal—

(a) does not have jurisdiction in relation to the proceedings or that part of them; and

(b) does not exercise its power under rule 5(3)(k)(i) (transfer to another court or tribunal) in relation to the proceedings or that part of them.

(3) The Tribunal may strike out the whole or a part of the proceedings if—

(a) the appellant has failed to comply with a direction which stated that failure by the appellant to comply with the direction could lead to the striking out of the proceedings or part of them;

(b) the appellant has failed to co-operate with the Tribunal to such an extent that the Tribunal cannot deal with the proceedings fairly and justly; or

(c) the Tribunal considers there is no reasonable prospect of the appellant's case, or part of it, succeeding.

(4) The Tribunal may not strike out the whole or a part of the proceedings under paragraph (2) or (3)(b) or (c) without first giving the appellant an opportunity to make representations in relation to the proposed striking out.

(5) If the proceedings, or part of them, have been struck out under paragraph (1) or (3)(a), the appellant may apply for the proceedings, or part of them, to be reinstated.

(6) An application under paragraph (5) must be made in writing and received by the Tribunal within 1 month after the date on which the Tribunal sent notification of the striking out to the appellant.

(7) This rule applies to a respondent as it applies to an appellant except that—

(a) a reference to the striking out of the proceedings is to be read as a reference to the barring of the respondent from taking further part in the proceedings; and

(b) a reference to an application for the reinstatement of proceedings which have been struck out is to be read as a reference to an application for the lifting of the bar on the respondent from taking further part in the proceedings.

(8) If a respondent has been barred from taking further part in proceedings under this rule and that bar has not been lifted, the Tribunal need not consider any response or other submission made by that respondent.

DEFINITIONS

"appellant"—see r.1(3).
"party"—*ibid.*
"respondent"—*ibid.*
"Tribunal"—*ibid.*

GENERAL NOTE

Note that, although paras (1) to (6) are expressed in terms of striking out proceedings brought by the appellant, by virtue of paras (7) and (8) they also provide for barring a respondent from taking further part in the proceedings.

Para. (1)

This provides for an automatic strike out where a person has failed to comply with a direction that carried a warning that, unless there was compliance, the case "will" be struck out. In theory, no further judicial act is required for the strike-out to take effect provided that it is clear that there has not been compliance. It is important to distinguish this paragraph from para.(3)(a), which provides for a case to be struck out for failure to comply with a direction that carried a warning that if there was no compliance the case "may" be struck out. In such a case, there needs to be a judicial decision exercising the power to strike out. However, proceedings struck out under this paragraph may be reinstated on an application under paras (5) and (6).

Para. (2)

This replaces reg.46(1)(a) of the Social Security and Child Support (Decisions and Appeals) Regs 1999. However, it is not limited to cases excluded from the scope of s.12 of the Social Security Act 1998 by virtue of Sch.2 to that Act or Sch.2 to the 1999 Regs. Moreover, unlike reg.46, its terms are mandatory, so that a final decision to the effect that the tribunal lacks jurisdiction must always be in the form of a decision to strike out the appeal. These differences suggest that the decision in *Morina v Secretary of State for Work and Pensions* [2007] EWCA Civ 749; [2007] 1 W.L.R. 3033 (also reported as *R(IS) 6/07*), in which the Court of Appeal held that that there was no right of appeal under s.14 of the Social Security Act 1998 against a decision under reg.46(1)(a), is distinguishable so that it is arguable that there is a right of appeal under s.11 of the Tribunals, Courts and Enforcement Act 2007 against a decision under this rule, even if the broader argument advanced mentioned in the annotation to r.6 above is not accepted.

By virtue of para.(4), a party must be given an opportunity to make representations before his or her case is struck out and there will be some cases where justice requires there to be a hearing, notwithstanding r.27(3).

Para. (3)

Sub-paragraphs (a) and (b) replace reg.46(1)(b) and (c) of the Social Security and Child Support (Decisions and Appeals) Regs 1999, although the concept of "want of prosecution" is replaced by the concept of a "failure to co-operate", which may apply equally to any party. Striking out is discretionary and must presumably be proportionate (see r.2(2)(a) and (3)), having regard to the culpability of the party whose case is being struck out and the amount at stake on the appeal.

Sub-paragraph (c) reintroduces a power to strike a case out where it has no reasonable prospect of success. An equivalent power in reg.48 of the 1999 Regs was revoked in 2004.

Rule 27(3) permits the Tribunal to strike out a case without a hearing but, by virtue of para.(4), a party must be given an opportunity to make representations before his or her case is struck out under sub-para.(b) or (c). Where an effective opportunity to make representations would require a hearing, it is likely to be simpler and fairer to determine the appeal in the ordinary way instead of striking it out. Thus sub-paras (b) and (c) should probably be used only in clear and obvious cases.

There is no right to make representations before a case is struck out under subparagraph (a); instead there is a right to apply for reinstatement after the event, by virtue of paras (5) and (6).

Paras (7) and (8)

This rule does not work in an entirely even-handed manner. An appellant (which may in a few cases be the Secretary of State or HMRC) may find that the whole or part of the proceedings he or she has brought are struck out. The equivalent sanction in respect of a respondent is merely being barred from taking further part in proceedings, which has the effect that the Tribunal "need not consider any response or other submission made by that respondent". This appears to mean that the Tribunal need not consider any written response or other submission even if it was submitted before the respondent was barred, particularly as the bar might otherwise be ineffective. However, the language of both para.(8) and r.24(4) suggests that the term "response" does not include the evidence provided with it. If that is correct, the effect is that, although being barred from taking further part in proceedings presumably includes being barred from providing further evidence, the Tribunal is not entitled to ignore evidence provided before the bar was imposed, which may reduce the effectiveness of the bar. In any event, the implications of barring a respondent from taking further part in proceedings are likely to be far more serious in cases where the primary duty to provide evidence lies on the respondent than in cases where it lies on the appellant.

Substitution and addition of parties

1B.10 **9.**—(1) The Tribunal may give a direction substituting a party if—

(a) the wrong person has been named as a party; or

(b) the substitution has become necessary because of a change in circumstances since the start of proceedings.

(2) The Tribunal may give a direction adding a person to the proceedings as a respondent.

(3) If the Tribunal gives a direction under paragraph (1) or (2) it may give such consequential directions as it considers appropriate.

DEFINITIONS

"party"—see r.1(3).
"respondent"—*ibid.*
"Tribunal"—*ibid.*

GENERAL NOTE

Para.(2)

A person joined as a respondent becomes a party and acquires all the rights of a party, including the right to require there to be a hearing, the right to obtain a statement of reasons and the right to apply for permission to appeal.

Given the wide scope of the definition of "respondent" in r.1(3), it will seldom be necessary to add a party as a respondent in a social security case because a person with an interest in a decision under appeal will usually have had a right of appeal against it and so will automatically be a respondent. In the past, there were at least two types of cases where non-parties were invited to attend hearings. The injured person would sometimes be invited to attend a hearing of an appeal under the Social Security (Recovery of Benefits) Act 1997 brought by a compensator even though there had been no deduction under s.8 of that Act so that the injured person had no right of appeal and no direct interest in the case.

A person in receipt of widow's benefit would sometimes be invited to attend a hearing of an appeal against a refusal to award another woman widow's benefit based on contributions paid by the same man where there was a possibility that there might have been polygamous marriages. In both cases, the reason for inviting the non-party was that success by the appellant might logically lead to an award of benefit to the non-party being revised or superseded. The problem was, and remains, that, in the unfortunate absence of any power in the Secretary of State to refer the question of revision or supersession to a tribunal, any decision on the first appeal is not binding in relation to the revision or supersession. It would be unfair for it to be binding without the question properly being referred and the non-party being given a clear indication of the grounds upon which there might be revision or supersession. It is suggested that, under the new legislation, it will be preferable in these circumstances for a non-party to be invited to attend as a witness rather than for him or her to be joined as a respondent and thereby to become a party.

No power to award costs

10. The Tribunal may not make any order in respect of costs (or, in Scotland, expenses). **1B.11**

DEFINITION

"Tribunal"—see r.1(3).

GENERAL NOTE

See the supplementary note to s.29 to the Tribunals, Courts and Enforcement Act 2007, in Pt IV below.

Representatives

11.—(1) A party may appoint a representative (whether a legal representative or not) to represent that party in the proceedings. **1B.12**

(2) Subject to paragraph (3), if a party appoints a representative, that party (or the representative if the representative is a legal representative) must send or deliver to the Tribunal written notice of the representative's name and address.

(3) In a case to which rule 23 (cases in which the notice of appeal is to be sent to the decision maker) applies, if the appellant (or the appellant's representative if the representative is a legal representative) provides written notification of the appellant's representative's name and address to the decision maker before the decision maker provides its response to the Tribunal, the appellant need not take any further steps in order to comply with paragraph (2).

(4) If the Tribunal receives notice that a party has appointed a representative under paragraph (2), it must send a copy of that notice to each other party.

(5) Anything permitted or required to be done by a party under these Rules, a practice direction or a direction may be done by the representative of that party, except signing a witness statement.

(6) A person who receives due notice of the appointment of a representative—

(a) must provide to the representative any document which is required to be provided to the represented party, and need not provide that document to the represented party; and

(b) may assume that the representative is and remains authorised as such until they receive written notification that this is not so from the representative or the represented party.

(7) At a hearing a party may be accompanied by another person whose name and address has not been notified under paragraph (2) or (3) but who, with the permission of the Tribunal, may act as a representative or otherwise assist in presenting the party's case at the hearing.

(8) Paragraphs (2) to (6) do not apply to a person who accompanies a party under paragraph (7).

DEFINITIONS

"appeal"—see r.1(3).
"appellant"—*ibid.*
"decision maker"—*ibid.*
"document"—*ibid.*
"hearing"—*ibid.*
"legal representative"—*ibid.*
"party"—*ibid.*
"practice direction"—*ibid.*
"Tribunal"—*ibid.*

GENERAL NOTE

This rule makes rather more comprehensive provision for representatives than was formerly made by reg.49(8) of the Social Security and Child Support (Decisions and Appeals) Regs 1999, but the note to that provision at p.638 of Vol.III of the main work remains relevant.

Paras (2) to (6)

These paragraphs provide for the formal appointment of a representative. Notice must be given to the Tribunal (para.(2)) unless an appellant has already given notice to the decision-maker before the decision-maker has sent the response to the appeal to the Tribunal (para.(3)), in which case the decision-maker must inform the Tribunal of the name and address of the appellant's representative (see r.24(4)(c)). A formally appointed representative may act on behalf of the party in all respects (except to sign a witness statement) and should be sent any documents that would otherwise be sent to the party (paras (5) and (6)(a)). However, it is presumably possible for the Tribunal to exclude a representative from a hearing under r.30(5) without excluding the party.

Paras (7) and (8)

These paragraphs enable a party who is present at a hearing to be represented or assisted at the hearing by any person, without there having been any formal notice of appointment. Although the Tribunal's permission is required, it is suggested that, unless r.30(5) applies, it will only exceptionally be appropriate for the Tribunal to refuse permission, particularly as the party need only provide a written notice under para.(2) in order to avoid the need for permission. Without a written notice of appointment, a person who acts as a representative at a hearing has no rights as a representative outside the hearing. Obviously, a written notice may be provided at the hearing so that the person becomes entitled to act as a full representative thereafter.

Calculating time

12.—(1) Except in asylum support cases, an act required by these 1B.13
Rules, a practice direction or a direction to be done on or by a particular
day must be done by 5pm on that day.

(2) If the time specified by these Rules, a practice direction or a
direction for doing any act ends on a day other than a working day, the
act is done in time if it is done on the next working day.

(3) In this rule "working day" means any day except a Saturday or
Sunday, Christmas Day, Good Friday or a bank holiday under section 1
of the Banking and Financial Dealings Act 1971.

<small>DEFINITIONS</small>

"asylum support case"—see r.1(3).
"practice direction"—*ibid.*
"working day"—see para.(3).

<small>GENERAL NOTE</small>

Para.(3)

Christmas Day and Good Friday are holidays under the common law in
England, Wales and Northern Ireland, rather than being bank holidays, which is
why they are specifically mentioned in this paragraph. The following days are
bank holidays in England, Wales and Northern Ireland, either because they are
mentioned in Schedule 1 to the 1971 Act or by virtue of Royal proclamations
under s.1(2) and (3) of that Act: New Year's Day, Easter Monday, the first
Monday in May, the last Monday in May, the last Monday in August, and
December 26. In Northern Ireland, there are additional bank holidays on March
17 (St Patrick's Day), by virtue of Sch.1 to the 1971 Act, and July 12 (the
anniversary of the Battle of the Boyne), by virtue of a proclamation by the
Secretary of State for Northern Ireland under s.1(5) of that Act. Where a bank
holiday would otherwise fall on a Saturday or Sunday, the following Monday
(and Tuesday, where December 26 is on a Sunday), is substituted.

Scotland has different bank holidays under the 1971 Act but they are not
always observed as public holidays as there is a tradition of observing various
local public holidays or institutional holidays instead of, or occasionally as well
as, bank holidays. The statutory bank holidays, including those announced by
Royal proclamation, are New Year's Day, January 2, Good Friday, the first
Monday in May, the last Monday in May, the first Monday in August, November
30 (St Andrew's Day), Christmas Day and December 26. Where a bank holiday
would otherwise fall on a Saturday or Sunday, the following Monday (or Tuesday, where January 2 or December 26 is on a Sunday), is substituted. These are
the relevant days for the purposes of this rule although Royal Mail does in fact
operate on November 30. November 30 is a comparatively recent addition to the
list and, where it is observed as a holiday, it is often in place of one of the other
bank holidays. Ironically, the clearing banks observe the English bank holidays so
that they are open on January 2, the first Monday in August and November 30
but are closed on Easter Monday and the last Monday in August.

The relevant days to be treated as bank holidays will depend on the part of the
United Kingdom in which the "act"—which will be the receipt of a document
where the Rules provide that a document must be received by the Tribunal or a
party within a specified time—must be performed. No specific provision is made
in respect of local holidays or other causes of postal delays where a party lives
outside the United Kingdom but the general power to extend time under
r.5(3)(a) may be invoked.

Sending and delivery of documents

1B.14   **13.**—(1) Any document to be provided to the Tribunal under these Rules, a practice direction or a direction must be—

    (a) sent by pre-paid post or delivered by hand to the address specified for the proceedings;

    (b) sent by fax to the number specified for the proceedings; or

    (c) sent or delivered by such other method as the Tribunal may permit or direct.

(2) Subject to paragraph (3), if a party provides a fax number, email address or other details for the electronic transmission of documents to them, that party must accept delivery of documents by that method.

(3) If a party informs the Tribunal and all other parties that a particular form of communication (other than pre-paid post or delivery by hand) should not be used to provide documents to that party, that form of communication must not be so used.

(4) If the Tribunal or a party sends a document to a party or the Tribunal by email or any other electronic means of communication, the recipient may request that the sender provide a hard copy of the document to the recipient. The recipient must make such a request as soon as reasonably practicable after receiving the document electronically.

(5) The Tribunal and each party may assume that the address provided by a party or its representative is and remains the address to which documents should be sent or delivered until receiving written notification to the contrary.

DEFINITIONS

    "document"—see r.1(3).
    "party"—*ibid.*
    "practice direction"—*ibid.*
    "Tribunal"—*ibid.*

GENERAL NOTE

  See the note to reg.2 of the Social Security and Child Support (Decisions and Appeals) Regs 1999 on pages 545–546 of Vol.III of the main work for comments on when documents are received and the effects of non-receipt. See also r.12.

Para. (1)
  When sending documents to the Tribunal, fax may always be used if available but email may be used only if the Tribunal has specifically said so.

Paras (2) and (3)
  When sending documents to a party, any available method of communication may be used unless the party has specifically said that fax or email may not be used. Any address or number given may be assumed to be still in use until notice to the contrary is given (see para.(5)).

Para. (4)
  This paragraph enables a party or the Tribunal to require a hard copy of a faxed or emailed document to be provided even though the fax or email delivery may have been sufficient for the purpose of complying with a time limit. It might be used, for instance, where a fax is poorly reproduced or where printing a large email attachment would be unduly onerous. Note that it is not necessary to

provide a hard copy of a fax or email unless requested to do so. However, where a time limit runs to the date a document is received, it might be wise to send a hard copy if there is any reason to doubt that the document will be received electronically even if sent.

Use of documents and information

14.—(1) The Tribunal may make an order prohibiting the disclosure or publication of— **1B.15**

(a) specified documents or information relating to the proceedings; or

(b) any matter likely to lead members of the public to identify any person whom the Tribunal considers should not be identified.

(2) The Tribunal may give a direction prohibiting the disclosure of a document or information to a person if—

(a) the Tribunal is satisfied that such disclosure would be likely to cause that person or some other person serious harm; and

(b) the Tribunal is satisfied, having regard to the interests of justice, that it is proportionate to give such a direction.

(3) If a party ("the first party") considers that the Tribunal should give a direction under paragraph (2) prohibiting the disclosure of a document or information to another party ("the second party"), the first party must—

(a) exclude the relevant document or information from any documents that will be provided to the second party; and

(b) provide to the Tribunal the excluded document or information, and the reason for its exclusion, so that the Tribunal may decide whether the document or information should be disclosed to the second party or should be the subject of a direction under paragraph (2).

(4) The Tribunal must conduct proceedings as appropriate in order to give effect to a direction given under paragraph (2).

(5) If the Tribunal gives a direction under paragraph (2) which prevents disclosure to a party who has appointed a representative, the Tribunal may give a direction that the documents or information be disclosed to that representative if the Tribunal is satisfied that—

(a) disclosure to the representative would be in the interests of the party; and

(b) the representative will act in accordance with paragraph (6).

(6) Documents or information disclosed to a representative in accordance with a direction under paragraph (5) must not be disclosed either directly or indirectly to any other person without the Tribunal's consent.

DEFINITIONS

"document"—see r.1(3).
"party"—*ibid.*
"Tribunal"—*ibid.*

GENERAL NOTE

Para. (1)

An order under this paragraph may be directed to an individual and be concerned only with an individual document (e.g. prohibiting an appellant from disclosing to someone else a document disclosed to the appellant by the respondent) or it may be directed to the public in general and effectively amount to a reporting restriction. Hearings of social security cases are usually attended only by those immediately interested in them but most hearings are, in principle, open to the public, including the press (see r.30). It is difficult to envisage it being appropriate to prohibit the publication of any information at all about a hearing held in public but it might often be appropriate to make an order prohibiting the publishing of information that may lead to a child or vulnerable adult being identified if there would otherwise be any serious risk of such publication. It will generally be necessary properly to balance the right of one person to respect of his or her private life under Art.8 of the European Convention on Human Rights and the right of another person to freedom of expression under Art.10. The existence of the powers conferred by this paragraph is a factor to be borne in mind when deciding under r.30(3) whether a hearing should be in private or in public, which requires consideration of the terms of Art.6(1).

A breach of an order made under this paragraph is a contempt of court. However, it can be enforced only through an application for committal made to the High Court or, in Scotland, the Court of Session.

Paras (2) to (6)

These paragraphs replace reg.42 of the Social Security and Child Support (Decisions and Appeals) Regs 1999, although they are not limited to medical advice or evidence. See the note to that regulation on pages 629 to 631 of Vol.III of the main work. It is suggested that "serious harm" merely means harm that would be sufficiently serious to justify what would otherwise be a breach of the right to a fair hearing guaranteed by Article 6 of the European Convention on Human Rights. Note the power in r.30(5)(c) to exclude a person from a hearing, and the power in r.33(2) not to provide a full statement of reasons, in order to give effect to a direction under para.(2). In *Dorset Healthcare NHS Foundation Trust v MH* [2009] UKUT 4 (AAC), it was made clear that serious harm was not the only ground upon which disclosure of documents may be withheld. In that case, documents were withheld from a patient on the ground of confidentiality but it was not suggested that the tribunal should see the withheld documents. It is doubtful that a tribunal could properly have regard to evidence that had not been disclosed to a party in any circumstances other than those contemplated in this rule unless, perhaps, a legally qualified representative acting for the party was prepared to consent to it doing so despite not being able to obtain the informed consent of the party.

Evidence and submissions

1B.16   **15.**—(1) Without restriction on the general powers in rule 5(1) and (2) (case management powers), the Tribunal may give directions as to—

    (a) issues on which it requires evidence or submissions;

    (b) the nature of the evidence or submissions it requires;

    (c) whether the parties are permitted or required to provide expert evidence;

(d) any limit on the number of witnesses whose evidence a party may put forward, whether in relation to a particular issue or generally;

(e) the manner in which any evidence or submissions are to be provided, which may include a direction for them to be given—
    (i) orally at a hearing; or
    (ii) by written submissions or witness statement; and

(f) the time at which any evidence or submissions are to be provided.

(2) The Tribunal may—

(a) admit evidence whether or not—
    (i) the evidence would be admissible in a civil trial in the United Kingdom; or
    (ii) the evidence was available to a previous decision maker; or

(b) exclude evidence that would otherwise be admissible where—
    (i) the evidence was not provided within the time allowed by a direction or a practice direction;
    (ii) the evidence was otherwise provided in a manner that did not comply with a direction or a practice direction; or
    (iii) it would otherwise be unfair to admit the evidence.

(3) The Tribunal may consent to a witness giving, or require any witness to give, evidence on oath, and may administer an oath for that purpose.

DEFINITIONS

"decision maker"—see r.1(3).
"hearing"—*ibid.*
"party"—*ibid.*
"practice direction"—*ibid.*
"Tribunal"—*ibid.*

GENERAL NOTE

Para. (1)
Rule 6 makes the necessary procedural provision.

Para. (2)
Paragraph (2)(a) makes explicit powers to admit evidence that were formerly implicit. Note that the Tribunal merely has a power to admit evidence that would be inadmissible in a civil trial and it cannot override any privilege of a witness not to give evidence (see the note to s.12 of the Social Security Act 1998 at p.217 of Vol.III of the main work). Beyond that, the main consideration will simply be whether the evidence is relevant.

Paragraph (2)(b) enables evidence to be excluded. This power, like all other powers under the Rules, must be exercised so as to give effect to the overriding objective in r.2 and it is suggested that it will rarely be proportionate to exclude relevant evidence simply because it is provided late, unless some prejudice would be suffered by another party or the delay makes it more difficult for the tribunal to consider the evidence.

Para. (3)
This replaces reg.43(5) of the Social Security and Child Support (Decisions and Appeals) Regs 1999 but it also makes explicit that a Tribunal may consent

to evidence being given on oath where it is the witness or a party who wishes that to be done. In practice, it is fairly rare for evidence to be given on oath in social security cases.

By virtue of s.5 of the Oaths Act 1978, any person who objects to being sworn shall be permitted to make his or her solemn affirmation instead of taking an oath. In England, Wales and Northern Ireland, a Christian or Jew usually swears an oath with the New Testament, or, in the case of a Jew, the Old Testament, in his or her uplifted hand (*Ibid.*, s.1(1)) but if the person desires to swear without holding the Bible but "with uplifted hand in the form and manner in which an oath is usually administered in Scotland", he or she must be permitted to do so (s.3). In the case of a person who is neither a Christian not a Jew, the oath shall be administered in any lawful manner (*Ibid.*, s.1(3)), but such a person may prefer to affirm.

Summoning or citation of witnesses and orders to answer questions or produce documents

1B.17   **16.**—(1) On the application of a party or on its own initiative, the Tribunal may—

(a) by summons (or, in Scotland, citation) require any person to attend as a witness at a hearing at the time and place specified in the summons or citation; or

(b) order any person to answer any questions or produce any documents in that person's possession or control which relate to any issue in the proceedings.

(2) A summons or citation under paragraph (1)(a) must—

(a) give the person required to attend 14 days' notice of the hearing or such shorter period as the Tribunal may direct; and

(b) where the person is not a party, make provision for the person's necessary expenses of attendance to be paid, and state who is to pay them.

(3) No person may be compelled to give any evidence or produce any document that the person could not be compelled to give or produce on a trial of an action in a court of law in the part of the United Kingdom where the proceedings are due to be determined.

(4) A summons, citation or order under this rule must—

(a) state that the person on whom the requirement is imposed may apply to the Tribunal to vary or set aside the summons, citation or order, if they have not had an opportunity to object to it; and

(b) state the consequences of failure to comply with the summons, citation or order.

DEFINITIONS

"document"—see r.1(3).
"hearing"—*ibid.*
"party"—*ibid.*
"Tribunal"—*ibid.*

GENERAL NOTE

This rule replaces reg.43(1)–(4) of the Social Security and Child Support (Decisions and Appeals) Regs 1999 but also includes a power to order the production of documents without requiring attendance at a hearing. A failure to comply with a summons, citation or order under this rule is a contempt of court that may be referred to the Upper Tribunal under r.7(3). The Upper Tribunal has the power to impose a term of imprisonment not exceeding two years and an unlimited fine.

Withdrawal

17.—(1) Subject to paragraph (2), a party may give notice of the   1B.18
withdrawal of its case, or any part of it—

   (a) at any time before a hearing to consider the disposal of the proceedings (or, if the Tribunal disposes of the proceedings without a hearing, before that disposal), by sending or delivering to the Tribunal a written notice of withdrawal; or

   (b) orally at a hearing.

(2) In the circumstances described in paragraph (3), a notice of withdrawal will not take effect unless the Tribunal consents to the withdrawal.

(3) The circumstances referred to in paragraph (2) are where a party gives notice of withdrawal—

   (a) under paragraph (1)(a) in a criminal injuries compensation case; or

   (b) under paragraph (1)(b).

(4) A party who has withdrawn their case may apply to the Tribunal for the case to be reinstated.

(5) An application under paragraph (4) must be made in writing and be received by the Tribunal within 1 month after—

   (a) the date on which the Tribunal received the notice under paragraph (1)(a); or

   (b) the date of the hearing at which the case was withdrawn orally under paragraph (1)(b).

(6) The Tribunal must notify each party in writing of an withdrawal under this rule.

DEFINITIONS

"criminal injuries compensation case"—see r.1(3).
"dispose of proceedings"—*ibid.*
"hearing"—*ibid.*
"party"—*ibid.*
"Tribunal"—*ibid.*

GENERAL NOTE

Paragraphs (1) and (6) replace reg.40 of the Social Security and Child Support (Decisions and Appeals) Regs 1999. However, there are differences. First, this applies to the withdrawal of a respondent's case as well as to an appeal or reference. Secondly, paras (2) and (3)(b) have the effect that a case cannot be withdrawn at a hearing without the consent of the tribunal (although it apparently can be withdrawn during an adjournment). Thirdly, paras (4) and (5) allow a party who has withdrawn a case to apply for it to be reinstated, avoiding the difficulty that arose in *Rydqvist v Secretary of State for Work and Pensions* [2002] EWCA Civ 947; [2002] 1 W.L.R. 3343. Clearly any possible prejudice to the respondent will be highly relevant when the Tribunal is considering whether to permit the case to be reinstated. The existence of the one-month time limit for an application for reinstatement may suggest that an application should be granted if made within that period unless there is a clear reason for not doing so, such as the previous conduct of the party, obvious lack of merit in the case or prejudice to another party.

Lead cases

1B.19 **18.**—(1) This rule applies if—

(a) two or more cases have been started before the Tribunal;

(b) in each such case the Tribunal has not made a decision disposing of the proceedings; and

(c) the cases give rise to common or related issues of fact or law.

(2) The Tribunal may give a direction—

(a) specifying one or more cases falling under paragraph (1) as a lead case or lead cases; and

(b) staying (or, in Scotland, sisting) the other cases falling under paragraph (1) ("the related cases").

(3) When the Tribunal makes a decision in respect of the common or related issues—

(a) the Tribunal must send a copy of that decision to each party in each of the related cases; and

(b) subject to paragraph (4), that decision shall be binding on each of those parties.

(4) Within 1 month after the date on which the Tribunal sent a copy of the decision to a party under paragraph (3)(a), that party may apply in writing for a direction that the decision does not apply to, and is not binding on the parties to, a particular related case.

(5) The Tribunal must give directions in respect of cases which are stayed or sisted under paragraph (2)(b), providing for the disposal of or further directions in those cases.

(6) If the lead case or cases lapse or are withdrawn before the Tribunal makes a decision in respect of the common or related issues, the Tribunal must give directions as to—

(a) whether another case or other cases are to be specified as a lead case or lead cases; and

(b) whether any direction affecting the related cases should be set aside or amended.

DEFINITIONS

"dispose of proceedings"—see r.1(3).
"party"—*ibid.*
"Tribunal"—*ibid.*

GENERAL NOTE

The effect of this rule could be achieved through case management directions under r.5 but the rule provides an off-the-peg process for dealing with cases raising common or related issues of fact or law. It need not be used if a different process appears more appropriate. If it is used, one or more lead cases are selected and are then treated as binding on the other cases unless, within one month of being sent a copy of the decision in the lead cases, a party in another case objects. Presumably "decision" in para.(3) must include the reasons for the decision. Paragraph (4) appears to allow an objection either on the ground that the lead case is distinguishable and does not apply for that reason or on the ground that the party simply wishes to challenge the decision in the lead case and have his or her case dealt with separately, possibly with a view to appealing. The likelihood of objections on that latter ground may be a reason for not applying this rule in the first place but it would be unfair if parties who were separately represented could not elect to have their own cases decided individually.

Where common issues of law arise in social security cases, s.26 of the Social Security Act 1998 may provide an alternative procedure.

Confidentiality in child support or child trust fund cases

19.—(1) Paragraph (3) applies to proceedings under the Child Support Act 1991 in the circumstances described in paragraph (2), other than an appeal against a reduced benefit decision (as defined in section 46(10)(b) of the Child Support Act 1991, as that section had effect prior to the commencement of section 15(b) of the Child Maintenance and Other Payments Act 2008).

1B.20

(2) The circumstances referred to in paragraph (1) are that the absent parent, non-resident parent or person with care would like their address or the address of the child to be kept confidential and has given notice to that effect—

(a) to the Secretary of State or the Child Maintenance and Enforcement Commission in the notice of appeal or when notifying any subsequent change of address;

(b) to the Secretary of State or the Child Maintenance and Enforcement Commission, whichever has made the enquiry, within 14 days after an enquiry is made; or

(c) to the Tribunal when notifying any change of address.

(3) Where this paragraph applies, the Secretary of State, the Child Maintenance and Enforcement Commission and the Tribunal must take appropriate steps to secure the confidentiality of the address, and of any information which could reasonably be expected to enable a person to identify the address, to the extent that the address or that information is not already known to each other party.

(4) Paragraph (6) applies to proceedings under the Child Trust Funds Act 2004 in the circumstances described in paragraph (5).

(5) The circumstances referred to in paragraph (4) are that a relevant person would like their address or the address of the eligible child to be kept confidential and has given notice to that effect, or a local authority with parental responsibility in relation to the eligible child would like the address of the eligible child to be kept confidential and has given notice to that effect—

(a) to HMRC in the notice of appeal or when notifying any subsequent change of address;

(b) to HMRC within 14 days after an enquiry by HMRC; or

(c) to the Tribunal when notifying any change of address.

(6) Where this paragraph applies, HMRC and the Tribunal must take appropriate steps to secure the confidentiality of the address, and of any information which could reasonably be expected to enable a person to

identify the address, to the extent that the address or that information is not already known to each other party.

(7) In this rule—

"eligible child" has the meaning set out in section 2 of the Child Trust Funds Act 2004;

"HMRC" means Her Majesty's Revenue and Customs;

"non-resident parent" and "parent with care" have the meanings set out in section 54 of the Child Support Act 1991;

"parental responsibility" has the meaning set out in section 3(9) of the Child Trust Funds Act 2004; and

"relevant person" has the meaning set out in section 22(3) of the Child Trust Funds Act 2004.

DEFINITIONS

"appeal"—see r.1(3).
"eligible child"—see para.(7).
"HMRC"—*ibid.*
"non-resident parent"—*ibid.*
"parent with care"—*ibid.*
"parental responsibility"—*ibid.*
"party"—see r.1(3).
"relevant person"—see para.(7).
"Tribunal"—see r.1(3).

1B.21   **20.**—*Omitted.*

Expenses in social security and child support cases

1B.21.1   **21.**—(1) This rule applies only to social security and child support cases.

(2) The Secretary of State may pay such travelling and other allowances (including compensation for loss of remunerative time) as the Secretary of State may determine to any person required to attend a hearing in proceedings under section 20 of the Child Support Act 1991, section 12 of the Social Security Act 1998 or paragraph 6 of Schedule 7 to the Child Support, Pensions and Social Security Act 2000.

DEFINITIONS

"hearing"—see r.1(3).
"social security and child support case"—*ibid.*

GENERAL NOTE

1B.21.2   This rule reproduces the effect of para.4(1)(a) of Sch.1 to the Social Security Act 1998. (Paragraph 4(1)(b) is replaced by a new s.20A.) It suffers from the same defect as the old provision, which is that it does not apply to all social security cases in which claimants might be required to attend hearings, although in practice the Tribunals Service seems never to have refused to pay expenses to those not within the scope of the old provision (e.g. an injured person appealing under s.11 of the Social Security (Recovery of Benefits) Act 1997).

The rule is in also unsatisfactory because it seems unlikely that para.10(4) of Sch.5 to the Tribunals, Courts and Enforcement Act 2007 envisages Rules that give the Secretary of State the power to determine what expenses are to be paid, although it is perhaps more appropriate that the power should lie with the Secretary of State rather than the Tribunal Procedure Committee.

PART 3

PROCEEDINGS BEFORE THE TRIBUNAL

CHAPTER 1

BEFORE THE HEARING

22.—*Omitted.*   1B.22

Cases in which the notice of appeal is to be sent to the decision maker

23.—(1) This rule applies to social security and child support cases   1B.23
(except references under the Child Support Act 1991 and proceedings under paragraph 3 of Schedule 2 to the Tax Credits Act 2002).

(2) An appellant must start proceedings by sending or delivering a notice of appeal to the decision maker so that it is received within the time specified in Schedule 1 to these Rules (time limits for providing notices of appeal to the decision maker).

(3) If the appellant provides the notice of appeal to the decision maker later than the time required by paragraph (2) the notice of appeal must include the reason why the notice of appeal was not provided in time.

(4) Subject to paragraph (5), where an appeal is not made within the time specified in Schedule 1, it will be treated as having been made in time if the decision maker does not object.

(5) No appeal may be made more than 12 months after the time specified in Schedule 1.

(6) The notice of appeal must be in English or Welsh, must be signed by the appellant and must state—

(a) the name and address of the appellant;

(b) the name and address of the appellant's representative (if any);

(c) an address where documents for the appellant may be sent or delivered;

(d) details of the decision being appealed; and

(e) the grounds on which the appellant relies.

(7) The decision maker must refer the case to the Tribunal immediately if—

(a) the appeal has been made after the time specified in Schedule 1 and the decision maker objects to it being treated as having been made in time; or

(b) the decision maker considers that the appeal has been made more than 12 months after the time specified in Schedule 1.

DEFINITIONS

"appeal"—see r.1(3).
"appellant"—*ibid.*
"decision maker"—*ibid.*
"social security and child support case"—*ibid.*
"Tribunal"—*ibid.*

GENERAL NOTE

This rule replaces regs 31, 32(3) and 33(1) of the Social Security and Child Support (Decisions and Appeals) Regs 1999, the rest of regs 32 and 33 being substantially amended in consequence (see Pt IV below).

Para.(1)
The social security and child support cases not within the scope of this rule fall within the scope of r.26 instead.

Para.(3)
Giving the reason for delay assists the decision-maker in deciding whether or not to object to a late appeal being treated as made in time under para.(4). It seems unlikely that a failure to comply with this paragraph would be held to render a late appeal invalid; rather it merely increases the likelihood of the Secretary of State objecting so that the case must be sent to the tribunal under para.(7)(a).

Para.(4)
The revised reg.32 of the 1999 Regs (see Pt IV, below) sits uneasily with the broad discretion conferred on the decision-maker by this paragraph.

Para.(5)
The absolute time limit of 12 months, formerly found in reg.32(1) of the 1999 Regs, is retained. The fact that the Tribunal has erroneously admitted an appeal that ought not to have been admitted because it was too late does not oblige the tribunal to determine the appeal. Instead, it must decline jurisdiction (*CAF/1913/2008*), which, under these Rules, would require the Tribunal to strike the appeal out under r.8(2).

Para.(6)
The reference to the language is included for consistency with r.22 where a similar provision thought necessary in the former Asylum Support Rules has been reproduced (with the addition of a reference to Welsh).

Para.(7)
Presumably the requirement imposed by para.(5) (that an appeal be brought not more than 12 months after the times specified in Sch.1) cannot be waived under r.7(2)(a), because to do so would entirely undermine the point of para.(5). Subject to para.(5), an appeal that is late will be admitted if the time for bringing the appeal is extended by the Tribunal under r.5(3)(a).
Where the notice of appeal fails to comply with the rules in some other respect, the decision-maker must first give the appellant the opportunity of making good the defect and, if the defect is not remedied, must send the form to the Tribunal for a decision whether or not the form complies with the rules (see reg.33 of the 1999 Regs, as amended as described in Pt IV below). There seems no reason why defects other than a failure to comply with para.(5) should not be waived under r.7(2)(a), provided that they do not in practice make it impossible to process the appeal.

Responses and replies

24.—(1) When a decision maker receives the notice of appeal or a   1B.24
copy of it, the decision maker must send or deliver a response to the
Tribunal—

(a) in asylum support cases, so that it is received within 3 days after
the date on which the Tribunal received the notice of appeal;
and

(b) in other cases, as soon as reasonably practicable after the decision
maker received the notice of appeal.

(2) The response must state—

(a) the name and address of the decision maker;

(b) the name and address of the decision maker's representative (if
any);

(c) an address where documents for the decision maker may be sent
or delivered;

(d) the names and addresses of any other respondents and their
representatives (if any);

(e) whether the decision maker opposes the appellant's case and, if so,
any grounds for such opposition which are not set out in any
documents which are before the Tribunal; and

(f) any further information or documents required by a practice
direction or direction.

(3) The response may include a submission as to whether it would be
appropriate for the case to be disposed of without a hearing.

(4) The decision maker must provide with the response—

(a) a copy of any written record of the decision under challenge, and
any statement of reasons for that decision, if they were not sent
with the notice of appeal;

(b) copies of all documents relevant to the case in the decision maker's possession, unless a practice direction or direction states
otherwise; and

(c) in cases to which rule 23 (cases in which the notice of appeal is to
be sent to the decision maker) applies, a copy of the notice of
appeal, any documents provided by the appellant with the notice
of appeal and (if they have not otherwise been provided to the
Tribunal) the name and address of the appellant's representative
(if any).

(5) The decision maker must provide a copy of the response and any
accompanying documents to each other party at the same time as it
provides the response to the Tribunal.

(6) The appellant and any other respondent may make a written
submission and supply further documents in reply to the decision maker's response.

(7) Any submission or further documents under paragraph (6) must
be provided to the Tribunal within 1 month after the date on which the
decision maker sent the response to the party providing the reply, and
the Tribunal must send a copy to each other party.

DEFINITIONS

"appeal"—see r.1(3).
"appellant"—*ibid.*
"asylum support case"—*ibid.*
"decision maker"—*ibid.*
"document"—*ibid.*
"hearing"—*ibid.*
"party"—*ibid.*
"practice direction"—*ibid.*
"respondent"—*ibid.*
"Tribunal"—*ibid.*

GENERAL NOTE

Paras (1) to (5)

These paragraphs make express provision for the decision-maker's response to an appeal, as to which the Social Security and Child Support (Decisions and Appeals) Regs 1999 were curiously silent. They largely reproduce previous practice and make no provision for any precise time limit. In part this is because some time may be taken investigating points raised in the grounds of appeal and deciding whether to revise the decision being challenged under reg.3(4A) of the 1999 Regs, which would cause the appeal to lapse under s.9(6) of the Social Security Act 1998.

Paras (6) and (7)

These paragraphs make express provision for other parties to reply to the decision-makers response. Again, the 1999 Regs made no such provision but in practice parties were given the opportunity when asked whether they wanted a hearing. A one-month time limit is now provided, but that may be regarded as a minimum period that must be given to the parties before a case is determined and it will seldom be proportionate to refuse to accept a late submission or evidence unless another party would be unduly affected by the delay, particularly where there is to be an oral hearing at which submissions and new evidence can be expected whether or not written notice has been given.

Medical and physical examination in appeals under section 12 of the Social Security Act 1998

1B.25   **25.**—(1) This rule applies only to appeals under section 12 of the Social Security Act 1998.

(2) At a hearing an appropriate member of the Tribunal may carry out a physical examination of a person if the case relates to—

(a) the extent of that person's disablement and its assessment in accordance with section 68(6) of and Schedule 6 to, or section 103 of, the Social Security Contributions and Benefits Act 1992(**13**); or

(b) diseases or injuries prescribed for the purpose of section 108 of that Act.

(3) If an issue which falls within Schedule 2 to these Rules (issues in relation to which the Tribunal may refer a person for medical examination) is raised in an appeal, the Tribunal may exercise its power under section 20 of the Social Security Act 1998 to refer a person to a health care professional approved by the Secretary of State for—

(a) the examination of that person; and

(b) the production of a report on the condition of that person.

(4) Neither paragraph (2) nor paragraph (3) entitles the Tribunal to require a person to undergo a physical test for the purpose of determining whether that person is unable to walk or virtually unable to do so.

DEFINITIONS

"hearing"—see r.1(3).
"Tribunal"—*ibid.*

GENERAL NOTE

Paragraphs (2) and (4) replace reg.52 of the Social Security and Child Support (Decisions and Appeals) Regs 1999 and para.(3) replaces reg.41. Note, however, that para.(4) applies to examinations within para.(3) as well as those within para.(2). It must do so by prescribing a "condition" under s.20(2) of the Social Security Act 1998 and thereby extending the limitation imposed by s.20(3)(b), which is otherwise confined to what may be done "at a hearing".

Social security and child support cases started by reference or information in writing

26.—(1) This rule applies to proceedings under section 28D of the Child Support Act 1991 and paragraph 3 of Schedule 2 to the Tax Credits Act 2002.

1B.26

(2) A person starting proceedings under section 28D of the Child Support Act 1991 must send or deliver a written reference to the Tribunal.

(3) A person starting proceedings under paragraph 3 of Schedule 2 to the Tax Credits Act 2002 must send or deliver an information in writing to the Tribunal.

(4) The reference or the information in writing must include—

(a) an address where documents for the person starting proceedings may be sent or delivered;

(b) the names and addresses of the respondents and their representatives (if any); and

(c) a submission on the issues that arise for determination by the Tribunal.

(5) Unless a practice direction or direction states otherwise, the person starting proceedings must also provide a copy of each document in their possession which is relevant to the proceedings.

(6) Subject to any obligation under rule 19(3) (confidentiality in child support cases), the person starting proceedings must provide a copy of the written reference or the information in writing and any accompanying documents to each respondent at the same time as they provide the written reference or the information in writing to the Tribunal.

(7) Each respondent may send or deliver to the Tribunal a written submission and any further relevant documents within one month of the date on which the person starting proceedings sent a copy of the written reference or the information in writing to that respondent.

DEFINITIONS

"document"—see r.1(3).
"practice direction"—*ibid.*
"respondent"—*ibid.*
"social security and child support case"—*ibid.*
"Tribunal"—*ibid.*

GENERAL NOTE

This rule makes specific provision for certain child support cases initiated by the Secretary of State and tax credit penalty cases initiated by HMRC. Paragraph (7) provides for responses by respondents. A one-month time limit is provided, but that may be regarded as a minimum period that must be given to the respondents before a case is determined and it will seldom be proportionate to refuse to accept a late submission or evidence unless another party would be unduly affected by the delay, particularly where there is to be an oral hearing at which submissions and new evidence can be expected whether or not written notice has been given.

CHAPTER 2

HEARINGS

Decision with or without a hearing

1B.27   27.—(1) Subject to the following paragraphs, the Tribunal must hold a hearing before making a decision which disposes of proceedings unless—

(a) each party has consented to, or has not objected to, the matter being decided without a hearing; and

(b) the Tribunal considers that it is able to decide the matter without a hearing.

(2) This rule does not apply to decisions under Part 4.

(3) The Tribunal may in any event dispose of proceedings without a hearing under rule 8 (striking out a party's case).

(4) In a criminal injuries compensation case—

(a) the Tribunal may make a decision which disposes of proceedings without a hearing; and

(b) subject to paragraph (5), if the Tribunal makes a decision which disposes of proceedings without a hearing, any party may make a written application to the Tribunal for the decision to be reconsidered at a hearing.

(5) An application under paragraph (4)(b) may not be made in relation to a decision—

(a) not to extend a time limit;

(b) not to set aside a previous decision;

(c) not to allow an appeal against a decision not to extend a time limit; or

(d) not to allow an appeal against a decision not to reopen a case.

(6) An application under paragraph (4)(b) must be received within 1 month after the date on which the Tribunal sent notice of the decision to the party making the application.

DEFINITIONS

"criminal injuries compensation case"—see r.1(3).
"dispose of proceedings"—*ibid.*
"hearing"—*ibid.*
"party"—*ibid.*
"Tribunal"—*ibid.*

GENERAL NOTE

Paras (1) to (3)

Paragraph (1) applies where the decision to be made will be one "which disposes of proceedings". It is primarily concerned with the final substantive decision on an appeal or reference but, were it not for para.(3), it would also apply to decisions to strike out proceedings. Para.(2) makes it clear that it does not apply to decisions relating to reviews and permission to appeal to the Upper Tribunal. It is less clear whether it applies to a decision whether or not to extend the time for appealing to the First-tier Tribunal. On one view, a decision not to extend time disposes of proceedings but the better argument may be that it merely prevents the proceedings from being started. However, even where this rule does not require there to be a hearing, it may be appropriate for the Tribunal to direct one under r.5(3)(f).

The paragraph has the effect that, where it applies, there must be a hearing if any party wants one. The Secretary of State or HMRC will say whether or not they want a hearing when submitting a response (see r.24(3)), reference or information. The Tribunal asks the other parties whether or not they want a hearing by sending them a form to return. If there is no reply, the party may be taken to have "not objected to the matter being decided without a hearing." In effect, therefore, these paragraphs replace reg.39 of the Social Security and Child Support (Decisions and Appeals) Regs 1999. As was the case under reg.39(5), the Tribunal must hold a hearing if not properly able to decide the matter without a hearing. Most of the comments in the note to reg.39 on pp 626–7 of the main work therefore remain relevant. However, note that the legislation no longer refers to an approved form on which a party was required to indicate whether or not he wished to have a hearing, so that the basis for the decision in *R3/04(IB)* has been removed, and that the provision in reg.46(1)(d) for simply striking proceedings out if the approved form was not returned by a party has not been re-enacted. Now, a case cannot be struck out for failure to return a form unless the Tribunal (which currently means a judge, see the note to r.4) has directed the form be returned and has warned the party that being struck out will, or may, be the consequence of not complying with the direction (see r.8(1) and (3)(a)). In *R3/04(IB)*, the requirement to issue an approved form to a party was held to be the reason why a clerk to a tribunal could not rely on an indication in the appellant's letter of appeal that a hearing was not wanted. There may still be reasons why reliance should not be placed on such an indication, not the least of which is that the appellant is unlikely to have been aware of the precise case against him or her before receiving the response to the appeal.

Entitlement to attend a hearing

28. Subject to rule 30(5) (exclusion of a person from a hearing), each party to proceedings is entitled to attend a hearing. 1B.28

"hearing"—see r.1(3).
"party"—*ibid*.

GENERAL NOTE

This makes it plain that, except where r.30(5) applies, a party may always attend a hearing even when the hearing is in private. By virtue of r.11(5) a properly appointed representative also has a right to attend a hearing, whether or not the party does so. By virtue of r.11(7), a party who attends hearing may be accompanied by a person acting as a representative or assistant.

Notice of hearings

1B.29   **29.**—(1) The Tribunal must give each party entitled to attend a hearing reasonable notice of the time and place of the hearing (including any adjourned or postponed hearing) and any changes to the time and place of the hearing.

(2) The period of notice under paragraph (1) must be at least 14 days except that—

    (a) in an asylum support case the Tribunal must give at least 1 day's and not more than 5 days' notice; and

    (b) the Tribunal may give shorter notice—

        (i) with the parties' consent; or

        (ii) in urgent or exceptional circumstances.

DEFINITIONS

"asylum support case"—see r.1(3).
"hearing"—*ibid*.
"party"—*ibid*.
"Tribunal"—*ibid*.

Public and private hearings

1B.30   **30.**—(1) Subject to the following paragraphs, all hearings must be held in public.

(2) A hearing in a criminal injuries compensation case must be held in private unless—

    (a) the appellant has consented to the hearing being held in public; and

    (b) the Tribunal considers that it is in the interests of justice for the hearing to be held in public.

(3) The Tribunal may give a direction that a hearing, or part of it, is to be held in private.

(4) Where a hearing, or part of it, is to be held in private, the Tribunal may determine who is permitted to attend the hearing or part of it.

(5) The Tribunal may give a direction excluding from any hearing, or part of it—

    (a) any person whose conduct the Tribunal considers is disrupting or is likely to disrupt the hearing;

    (b) any person whose presence the Tribunal considers is likely to prevent another person from giving evidence or making submissions freely;

(c) any person who the Tribunal considers should be excluded in order to give effect to a direction under rule 14(2) (withholding information likely to cause harm); or

(d) any person where the purpose of the hearing would be defeated by the attendance of that person.

(6) The Tribunal may give a direction excluding a witness from a hearing until that witness gives evidence.

DEFINITIONS

"appellant"—see r.1(3).
"criminal injuries compensation case"—*ibid.*
"hearing"—*ibid.*
"Tribunal"—*ibid.*

GENERAL NOTE

Paras (1) and (2)

Paragraph (1) expresses the general rule, which is that hearings should usually be in public. Paragraph (2), which applies only to criminal injuries compensation cases, is anomalous but continues the previous practice in such cases.

Para. (3)

Paragraph (3) enables the Tribunal to direct that a particular case be heard in private, either in whole or in part. In practice, this does not arise as a live issue very often because it is very rare for members of the general public to attend hearings. The issue perhaps arises primarily where one party is accompanied by a large number of people and there arises the question whether it is appropriate for them all to attend the hearing. Directing that a hearing be in private enables the numbers to be regulated under para.(4).

The Rules give no guidance as to how it is to be decided whether or not a hearing is to be in private. Regulation 49(6) of the Social Security and Child Support (Decisions and Appeals) Regs 1999 provided that a hearing could be in private only—

"(a) in the interests of national security, morals, public order or children;

(b) for the protection of the private or family life of one or more parties to the proceedings; or

(c) in special circumstances, because publicity would prejudice the interests of justice."

The language was based on Art.6(1) of the European Convention on Human Rights, but Art.6 is concerned with the right of *a party* to a public hearing. Consequently, as far as Art.6 is concerned, a party may waive that right (*Schuler-Zgraggen v Switzerland*, judgment of June 24, 1993, Series A, No.263; (1993) 16 E.H.R.R. 405, at para.58) and consent to a hearing being in private even if those grounds are not made out. Regulation 49(6) did not permit such a waiver. The reason for that may have been that there are other interests in there being a public hearing, not the least of which is the right of the public to see how justice is administered, which includes the right of the press to comment on the administration of justice. That right, too, may require the approach formerly taken in reg.49(6), although the need to protect the private or family life of people other than the parties (e.g. witnesses and people who might be mentioned in evidence) may need to be taken into account so reg.49(6)(b) may have been too narrowly drawn.

However, where the press are not present and where the parties wish a hearing to be in private so that the number of people present may be limited to avoid a timid claimant from being overwhelmed and unable properly to present his or her case, it may be open to a Tribunal to direct that the hearing be in private even if the conditions of the former reg.49(6) are not met, simply on the ground that the interests of justice require that the claimant should be enabled to put his or her case effectively (see r.2(2)(c)).

In all of this, it should not be forgotten that concerns about publicity can be met by the imposition of appropriate reporting restrictions under r.14(1). Generally, it will be preferable for the Tribunal to impose reporting restrictions rather than holding a hearing in private if the reporting restrictions will achieve all that is necessary.

Para. (4)

If a case is to be heard in private, the tribunal has a broad power to determine who may attend it. However, certain people have a right to attend a hearing even if it is in private. By r.28, a party always has a right to be present (subject to r.30(5)) and, the consequence is that, by virtue of r.11(5), so does a properly appointed representative whether the party attends or not. Where a party does attend, he or she may be accompanied by a person acting either as a representative or merely as an assistant (see r.11(7)). Plainly relevant witnesses must be allowed to attend for the purpose of giving evidence. By virtue of para.22 of Sch.7 to the Tribunals, Courts and Enforcement Act 2007, a member of the Administrative Justice and Tribunals Council, or its Scottish Committee or Welsh Committee, also has a right to attend any hearing.

Beyond that, it is all a matter of discretion, there being no equivalent to reg.49(9) of the 1999 Regs. It is likely to be desirable for the clerk or usher to be present and also a judge or Chamber President or the Senior President of Tribunals monitoring the tribunal. It is also likely to be appropriate to allow a claimant to be accompanied by a friend or relative even if he or she is there only for moral support and is not providing any actual assistance. As to others, it is suggested that, where a person has a reason for attending other than mere curiosity, the views of the parties should be ascertained and taken into account. In practice, parties seldom object to a person being present if they are made aware of a good reason for his or her presence. It will therefore generally be appropriate to allow people undergoing training to attend, whether the person is a member of the decision-maker's staff, a new judge or member of the Tribunal or a trainee lawyer shadowing the judge.

Para. (5)

This paragraph allows any person who would otherwise be entitled to attend a hearing to be excluded, where that is necessary on one of the specified grounds. Plainly the power to exclude a party or representative should be exercised only where there is absolutely no practical alternative. In relation to sub-para.(b), it would be desirable to consider whether alternative methods of giving evidence (e.g. by videolink or from behind a screen) would achieve the necessary effect and be practical.

Para. (6)

Whether witnesses should be excluded from a hearing until they give evidence depends very much on the circumstances of the case. There is often a fear that dishonest witnesses will tailor their evidence so that it fits with other evidence in the case if they hear that evidence before giving their own. Evidence can often be stronger if it is consistent without the witnesses having had the opportunity of hearing each other's answers to questions. On the other hand, witnesses can often usefully comment on other evidence and can pick up points not mentioned by other witnesses, which is important in social security cases, where parties are seldom represented by lawyers and there is rarely any proper examination-in-chief or cross-examination. Indeed, a representative may often be a witness (see the note to reg.49(8) of the 1999 Regs at p.638 of Vol.III of the main work). The Tribunal is given a broad discretion as to how to approach a case. If it intends to exclude witnesses from a hearing, it is suggested it should take the same approach to the witnesses of all parties lest it give the impression of having formed a view that the witnesses of one party only are suspected of dishonesty.

Hearings in a party's absence

31. If a party fails to attend a hearing the Tribunal may proceed with the hearing if the Tribunal—   **1B.31**
- (a) is satisfied that the party has been notified of the hearing or that reasonable steps have been taken to notify the party of the hearing; and
- (b) considers that it is in the interests of justice to proceed with the hearing.

DEFINITIONS

"hearing"—see r.1(3).
"party"—*ibid.*
"Tribunal"—*ibid.*

GENERAL NOTE

This rule replaces reg.49(4) of the Social Security and Child Support (Decisions and Appeals) Regs 1999.

CHAPTER 3

DECISIONS

Consent orders

32.—(1) The Tribunal may, at the request of the parties but only if it considers it appropriate, make a consent order disposing of the proceedings and making such other appropriate provision as the parties have agreed.   **1B.32**

(2) Notwithstanding any other provision of these Rules, the Tribunal need not hold a hearing before making an order under paragraph (1), or provide reasons for the order.

DEFINITIONS

"hearing"—see r.1(3).
"party"—*ibid.*
"Tribunal"—*ibid.*

GENERAL NOTE

Consent orders have little place in social security cases before the First-tier Tribunal because decision-makers generally have the power to revise the decision under appeal, which causes the appeal to lapse (see, for instance, s.9(1) and (6) of the Social Security Act 1998 and reg.3(4A) of the Social Security and Child Support (Decisions and Appeals) Regs 1999).

Notice of decisions

1B.33   **33.**—(1) The Tribunal may give a decision orally at a hearing.

(2) Subject to rule 14(2) (withholding information likely to cause harm), the Tribunal must provide to each party as soon as reasonably practicable after making a decision which finally disposes of all issues in the proceedings (except a decision under Part 4)—

(a) a decision notice stating the Tribunal's decision;

(b) where appropriate, notification of the right to apply for a written statement of reasons under rule 34(3); and

(c) notification of any right of appeal against the decision and the time within which, and the manner in which, such right of appeal may be exercised.

(3) In asylum support cases the notice and notifications required by paragraph (2) must be provided at the hearing or sent on the day that the decision is made.

DEFINITIONS

"asylum support case"—see r.1(3).
"hearing"—*ibid.*
"party"—*ibid.*
"Tribunal"—*ibid.*

GENERAL NOTE

Paragraph (2) replaces reg.53(1) and (3) of the Social Security and Child Support (Decisions and Appeals) Regs 1999 but para.(1) makes explicit the power to give a decision orally as well as in writing. See the notes to reg.53(1) and (2) at p.645 of the main work. It is not entirely clear whether "finally disposes of all issues in the proceedings" means something different from "disposes of proceedings" (see the note to r.27 above).

By virtue of art.8 of the First-tier Tribunal and Upper Tribunal (Composition of Tribunal) Order 2008 (SI 2008/2835) (see p.1361 of Vol.III of the main work), a decision may be made by a majority where a Tribunal is composed of more than one member. However, there is no longer an express requirement to state whether or not a decision has been made by a majority (compare reg.53(5) of the 1999 Regs).

Reasons for decisions

1B.34   **34.**—(1) In asylum support cases the Tribunal must send a written statement of reasons for a decision which disposes of proceedings (except a decision under Part 4) to each party—

(a) if the case is decided at a hearing, within 3 days after the hearing; or

(b) if the case is decided without a hearing, on the day that the decision is made.

(2) In all other cases the Tribunal may give reasons for a decision which disposes of proceedings (except a decision under Part 4)—

(a) orally at a hearing; or

(b) in a written statement of reasons to each party.

(3) Unless the Tribunal has already provided a written statement of reasons under paragraph (2)(b), a party may make a written application to the Tribunal for such statement following a decision which finally disposes of all issues in the proceedings.

(4) An application under paragraph (3) must be received within 1 month of the date on which the Tribunal sent or otherwise provided to the party a decision notice relating to the decision which finally disposes of all issues in the proceedings.

(5) If a party makes an application in accordance with paragraphs (3) and (4) the Tribunal must, subject to rule 14(2) (withholding information likely to cause harm), send a written statement of reasons to each party within 1 month of the date on which it received the application or as soon as reasonably practicable after the end of that period.

DEFINITIONS

"asylum support case"—see r.1(3).
"dispose of proceedings"—*ibid.*
"hearing"—*ibid.*
"party"—*ibid.*
"Tribunal"—*ibid.*

GENERAL NOTE

Paras (2) to (5)

These paragraphs replace reg.53(4) of the Social Security and Child Support (Decisions and Appeals) Regs 1999 but add two refinements. The first is to make it clear that reasons may be given orally but that a written statement (which could simply be a transcript) may subsequently be requested. The second is to impose a time limit, albeit not absolute, within which a tribunal must provide a statement of reasons. Whether a tribunal would be found to have erred in law because reasons were not provided "as soon as reasonably practicable" after the standard one month in circumstances where delay would not previously have been sufficient to vitiate the decision (see p.652 of Vol.III of the main work) remains to be seen. Note also that reg.53(5) has not been re-enacted, so that there is no longer any express duty to record the reasons of the dissenting member of the Tribunal where a decision is made by a majority, or even to record that the decision was reached only by a majority.

PART 4

CORRECTING, SETTING ASIDE, REVIEWING AND APPEALING TRIBUNAL DECISIONS

Interpretation

35. In this Part—   1B.35
"appeal" means the exercise of a right of appeal—

(a) under paragraph 2(2) or 4(1) of Schedule 2 to the Tax Credits Act 2002(**14**);

(b) under section 21(10) of the Child Trust Funds Act 2004(**15**); or

(c) on a point of law under section 11 of the 2007 Act; and "review" means the review of a decision by the Tribunal under section 9 of the 2007 Act.

DEFINITIONS

"the 2007 Act"—see r.1(3).
"'Tribunal"—*ibid.*

GENERAL NOTE

The references to the Tax Credits Act 2002 and the Child Trust Funds Act 2004 are to appeals against decisions in penalty cases, where the previous rights of appeal, which are not confined to points of law, remain in force (with the modification that the appeals now lie to the Upper Tribunal) in lieu of any right of appeal under s.11 of the Tribunals, Courts and Enforcement Act 2007 (see the Appeals (Excluded Decisions) Order 2008 (SI 2008/2707)). The implication of this rule is that r.38 imposes a requirement to obtain permission to appeal that did not previously exist but it is arguable that r.38 merely assumes the existence of such a requirement and so would not in fact apply to penalty appeals. Certainly, there can be no question of a review under s.9 if there is no right of appeal under s.11. From April 1, 2009, the 2002 Act and the 2004 Act will be amended so that the right of appeal on issues other than points of law in a penalty case will exist alongside a right of appeal under s.11 and it will be made clear that there is a permission requirement in respect of both rights of appeal (see paras 318, 320 and 415 of Sch.1 to the Transfer of Tribunal Functions and Revenue and Customs Appeals Order 2009 (SI 2009/56)).

Clerical mistakes and accidental slips or omissions

1B.36   **36.** The Tribunal may at any time correct any clerical mistake or other accidental slip or omission in a decision, direction or any document produced by it, by—

(a) sending notification of the amended decision or direction, or a copy of the amended document, to all parties; and

(b) making any necessary amendment to any information published in relation to the decision, direction or document.

DEFINITIONS

"document"—see r.1(3).
"party"—*ibid.*
"Tribunal"—*ibid.*

GENERAL NOTE

This rule replaces reg.56 of the Social Security and Child Support (Decisions and Appeals) Regs 1999 (see the note to that provision at p.657 of Vol.III of the main work). Note that a separate power to correct a decision arises on review (see s.9(4)(a) of the Tribunals, Courts and Enforcement Act 2007 (p.1289 of Vol.III of the main work).

Setting aside a decision which disposes of proceedings

37.—(1) The Tribunal may set aside a decision which disposes of   **1B.37** proceedings, or part of such a decision, and re-make the decision, or the relevant part of it, if—

  (a) the Tribunal considers that it is in the interests of justice to do so; and

  (b) one or more of the conditions in paragraph (2) are satisfied.

(2) The conditions are—

  (a) a document relating to the proceedings was not sent to, or was not received at an appropriate time by, a party or a party's representative;

  (b) a document relating to the proceedings was not sent to the Tribunal at an appropriate time;

  (c) a party, or a party's representative, was not present at a hearing related to the proceedings; or

  (d) there has been some other procedural irregularity in the proceedings.

(3) A party applying for a decision, or part of a decision, to be set aside under paragraph (1) must make a written application to the Tribunal so that it is received no later than 1 month after the date on which the Tribunal sent notice of the decision to the party.

DEFINITIONS

  "dispose of proceedings"—see r.1(3).
  "document"—*ibid.*
  "hearing"—*ibid.*
  "party"—*ibid.*
  "Tribunal"—*ibid.*

GENERAL NOTE

  This rule replaces reg.57(1) and (3) of the Social Security and Child Support (Decisions and Appeals) Regs 1999 (see the note to that provision at pp.659 to 661 of Vol.III of the main work). However, note that para.(2)(d) provides an additional ground for setting aside a decision so that any "procedural irregularity" giving rise to injustice may lead to a decision being set aside. The one-month time limit for making an application may be extended under r.5(3)(a). The tortuous provisions of reg.57(7) to (11) have not been re-enacted.

  Note that a separate power to set aside a decision arises on review (see s.9(4)(c) of the Tribunals, Courts and Enforcement Act 2007 at p.1289 of Vol.III of the main work).

Application for permission to appeal

38.—(1) This rule does not apply to asylum support cases or criminal   **1B.38** injuries compensation cases.

(2) A person seeking permission to appeal must make a written application to the Tribunal for permission to appeal.

(3) An application under paragraph (2) must be sent or delivered to the Tribunal so that it is received no later than 1 month after the latest of the dates that the Tribunal sends to the person making the application—

  (a) written reasons for the decision;

  (b) notification of amended reasons for, or correction of, the decision following a review; or

  (c) notification that an application for the decision to be set aside has been unsuccessful.

(4) The date in paragraph (3)(c) applies only if the application for the decision to be set aside was made within the time stipulated in rule 37 (setting aside a decision which disposes of proceedings) or any extension of that time granted by the Tribunal.

(5) If the person seeking permission to appeal sends or delivers the application to the Tribunal later than the time required by paragraph (3) or by any extension of time under rule 5(3)(a) (power to extend time)—

  (a) the application must include a request for an extension of time and the reason why the application was not provided in time; and

  (b) unless the Tribunal extends time for the application under rule 5(3)(a) (power to extend time) the Tribunal must not admit the application.

(6) An application under paragraph (2) must—

  (a) identify the decision of the Tribunal to which it relates;

  (b) identify the alleged error or errors of law in the decision; and

  (c) state the result the party making the application is seeking.

(7) If a person makes an application under paragraph (2) when the Tribunal has not given a written statement of reasons for its decision—

  (a) if no application for a written statement of reasons has been made to the Tribunal, the application for permission must be treated as such an application;

  (b) unless the Tribunal decides to give permission and directs that this sub-paragraph does not apply, the application is not to be treated as an application for permission to appeal; and

  (c) if an application for a written statement of reasons has been, or is, refused because of a delay in making the application, the Tribunal must only admit the application for permission if the Tribunal considers that it is in the interests of justice to do so.

DEFINITIONS

  "appeal"—see r.35.
  "asylum support case"—see r.1(3).
  "criminal injuries compensation case"—*ibid.*
  "dispose of proceedings"—*ibid.*
  "party"—*ibid.*
  "Tribunal"—*ibid.*

GENERAL NOTE

This rule replaces reg.58(1), (1A) and (5) of the Social Security and Child Support (Decisions and Appeals) Regs 1999 but there are three important differences. The first is that there is no absolute time limit on applications. Previously an application could not be accepted if it was more than a year late.

It is still unlikely that permission would be given where there had been such a delay but it is not inconceivable in, say, a case where an unrepresented claimant has been actively challenging some other decision and has not been told that success in that challenge depended on a successful appeal against the decision of the Tribunal. The second major change is that the test for extending the time limit is that r.5(3)(a) does not require there to be "special reasons" for extending the time limit, although this may not be of great significance because the same criteria (see the note to reg.58(5) on p.664 of Vol.III of the main work) are likely to remain relevant. The third major change is that, by virtue of para.(7) the lack of a statement of reasons does not act as an absolute bar to the Tribunal admitting an application and granting permission to appeal.

Para. (7)

Although the circumstances in which a person can demonstrate an error of law in the absence of a statement of reasons are limited, they are not negligible (see *R(IS) 11/99*). This paragraph makes provision for cases where there is no statement of reasons, either because no application has previously been made or because a statement of reasons has been refused. If there has not already been an application for a statement of reasons, the application for permission to appeal is treated as such an application either instead of, or if it so directs under sub-para.(b), as well as an application for permission to appeal. Sub-paragraph (b) applies only if the Tribunal decides to give permission to appeal either at the same time as issuing a statement of reasons or despite the refusal of such a statement. Where the Tribunal would refuse permission to appeal or would review its decision, it must give the applicant another opportunity to apply for permission to appeal in the light of its decision whether or not to issue a statement of reasons. However, it is arguable that sub-para.(b) does not prevent the Tribunal from treating the application as an application for a correction or setting aside (see r.41).

Sub-paragraph (c) (unlike sub-paras (a) and (b)) applies whether or not there has been a previous application for a statement of reasons. It has the effect of treating the delay in applying for a statement of reasons (which is the only ground upon which a statement of reasons may be refused) in the same way as delay in applying for permission to appeal. The application for permission will not be admitted unless the Tribunal is persuaded that it is in the interests of justice to admit it despite the delay, just as, under para.(5)(b), a late application for permission will not be admitted unless it is in the interests of justice to extend the time for making the application.

Tribunal's consideration of application for permission to appeal

39.—(1) On receiving an application for permission to appeal the Tribunal must first consider, taking into account the overriding objective in rule 2, whether to review the decision in accordance with rule 40 (review of a decision). **1B.39**

(2) If the Tribunal decides not to review the decision, or reviews the decision and decides to take no action in relation to the decision, or part of it, the Tribunal must consider whether to give permission to appeal in relation to the decision or that part of it.

(3) The Tribunal must send a record of its decision to the parties as soon as practicable.

(4) If the Tribunal refuses permission to appeal it must send with the record of its decision—

(a) a statement of its reasons for such refusal; and

(b) notification of the right to make an application to the Upper Tribunal for permission to appeal and the time within which, and the method by which, such application must be made.

(5) The Tribunal may give permission to appeal on limited grounds, but must comply with paragraph (4) in relation to any grounds on which it has refused permission.

DEFINITIONS

"appeal"—see r.35.
"party"—see r.1(3).
"review"—see r.35.
"Tribunal"—see r.1(3).

GENERAL NOTE

The Senior President of Tribunals has issued a Practice Statement which has the effect of replacing reg.58(6) of the Social Security and Child Support (Decisions and Appeals) Regs 1999 so that, as before, applications for permission to appeal are considered by salaried judges where the decision was made by, or by a tribunal presided over by, a fee-paid judge (see para.11 of the *Practice Statement on the composition of the tribunals in social security and child support cases in the Social Entitlement Chamber* set out in the supplementary annotation to the First-tier Tribunal and Upper Tribunal (Composition of Tribunal) Order 2008, below).

There is no requirement to obtain observations from parties other than the applicant and it is suggested that it is unnecessary to do so unless the Tribunal is contemplating reviewing the decision that is being challenged and, even then, it will not always be necessary to do so because a dissatisfied party may apply for the new decision to be set aside (see r.40(4)).

Paras (1) and (2)

Before deciding whether or not to grant permission to appeal, the Tribunal must first decide whether or not to review the decision under s.9 of the Tribunals, Courts and Enforcement Act 2007, as limited by r.40. However, it does not follow from the fact that there may be grounds for review that the decision must be reviewed. For instance, although the Tribunal may take the view that its decision is erroneous in law, it is entitled to grant permission to appeal on the basis that, if the issue is a matter of contention between the parties and there would probably be an appeal against the review decision, the issue should be resolved by the Upper Tribunal sooner rather than later.

Para. (4)

Reasons for refusing permission to appeal can usually be very brief and will often simply be that the application does not raise any point of law. Reasons can be valuable in persuading an applicant not to make an application to the Upper Tribunal in a hopeless case or in alerting the applicant of the need to rewrite the grounds. If an application raises allegations about the conduct of the Tribunal, it is likely to be desirable to make it clear whether the Tribunal disputes the accuracy of the allegations.

Para. (5)

Except where some grounds advanced are completely misconceived, it may not be helpful to grant a party without a legal representative permission to appeal on limited grounds, because doing so can make an appeal to the Upper Tribunal more complicated and the Upper Tribunal itself generally makes observations and issues directions before any response to an appeal is required, thus focussing the parties' attention on the more important issues. Moreover, the Upper Tribunal exercises an investigatory approach to appeals and so is not confined by the grounds of appeal or the grounds of permission. Where a party is represented by a lawyer used to formal pleading, other considerations may apply.

Review of a decision

40.—(1) This rule does not apply to asylum support cases or criminal injuries compensation cases. 1B.40

(2) The Tribunal may only undertake a review of a decision—

(a) pursuant to rule 39(1) (review on an application for permission to appeal); and

(b) if it is satisfied that there was an error of law in the decision.

(3) The Tribunal must notify the parties in writing of the outcome of any review, and of any right of appeal in relation to the outcome.

(4) If the Tribunal takes any action in relation to a decision following a review without first giving every party an opportunity to make representations, the notice under paragraph (3) must state that any party that did not have an opportunity to make representations may apply for such action to be set aside and for the decision to be reviewed again.

DEFINITIONS

"appeal"—see r.35.
"asylum support case"—see r.1(3).
"criminal injuries compensation case"—*ibid.*
"party"—*ibid.*
"review"—see r.35.
"Tribunal—see r.1(3).

GENERAL NOTE

Para.(2)

The power of review arises under s.9(1) of the Tribunals, Courts and Enforcement Act 2007 (see p.1288 of Vol.III of the main work). Note that it does not apply unless there is a right of appeal under s.11 and so there will be no power to review tax credit penalty decisions and child trust fund penalty decisions until April 1, 2009 (see the note to r.35).

Section 9(2) provides for the power of review to be exercised either on the tribunal's initiative or on an application, but s.9(3)(b) enables rules to provide that it is exercisable only on the Tribunal's own initiative. That is what para.(2)(a) of this rule does: a party may not make a freestanding application for a review (although if he or she does, it may be treated as an application for a correction, setting aside or permission to appeal (see r.41)) but the Tribunal may review a decision on its own initiative once there has been an application for permission to appeal. Paragraph (2)(b), made under s.9(3)(d), limits the ground of review to an error of law. Since appeals under s.11 lie only on points of law, a review therefore provides a way of avoiding an appeal where the appeal would plainly be allowed. See s.9(4), (5) and (8) for the powers of the Tribunal on review. These powers are wider than they were under s.13(2) of the Social Security Act 1998 and the similar provisions relating to housing benefit, council tax benefit and child support, which s.9, as limited by this rule, replaces. Note, however, that s.13(3) of the 1998 Act remains in place.

Para. (3)

Section 11(5)(d) has the effect that there is no right of appeal against a decision whether or not to review a decision, to take no action on a review, to set aside a decision on a review or to refer, or not refer, a matter to the Upper Tribunal on review. However, that is because there is always another decision that may be the subject of an appeal. Where the Tribunal refuses to review a decision or reviews it but takes no action, the Tribunal must consider whether to give permission to appeal against the original decision. Where the tribunal reviews a decision and either takes action itself or refers it to the Upper Tribunal to be redecided, there will be a right to apply for permission to appeal against the new decision.

Where a decision is reviewed without all the parties having had the opportunity to make representations, notice must also be given of the right to apply for the new decision to be set aside (see para.(4)).

Para. (4)

The clear implication of this paragraph is that a Tribunal may either obtain submissions from the parties other than the applicant before reviewing a case or review the case first and then wait to see whether any of the other parties objects. Plainly the second of those approaches may lead to a quicker decision and less work where there is no objection to the review. It is suggested, however, that that approach is appropriate only where the parties other than the applicant can reasonably be expected to be able to judge whether or not to object or where the ground of review and appropriate decision on review are both very clear. If submissions are obtained and all the parties assert that the decision is erroneous in point of law, the Tribunal will be obliged to set the decision aside in those cases where s.13(3) of the Social Security Act 1998 (or an equivalent provision in legislation beyond the scope of this work) applies.

Power to treat an application as a different type of application

1B.41   **41.** The Tribunal may treat an application for a decision to be corrected, set aside or reviewed, or for permission to appeal against a decision, as an application for any other one of those things.

DEFINITIONS

"appeal"—see r.35.
"review"—*ibid.*
"Tribunal"—see r.1(3).

TIME LIMITS FOR PROVIDING NOTICES OF APPEAL TO THE DECISION MAKER

Type of proceedings	*Time for providing notice of appeal*
cases other than those listed below	the latest of— (a) one month after the date on which notice of the decision being challenged was sent to the appellant; (b) if a written statement of reasons for the decision is requested, 14 days after the later of (i) the date on which the period at (a) expires; and (ii) the date on which the written statement of reasons was provided; or (c) where the appellant made an application for revision of the decision under regulation 3(1) or (3) or 3A(1) of the Social Security and Child Support (Decision & Appeals) Regulations 1999 or regulation 17(1)(a) of the Child Support (Maintenance Assessment Procedure) Regulations 1992, and that application was unsuccessful, one month of the date on which notice that the decision would not be revised was sent to the appellant
appeal against a certificate of NHS charges under section 157(1) of the Health and Social Care (Community Health and Standards) Act 2003	(a) 3 months after the latest of— (i) the date on the certificate; (ii) the date on which the compensation payment was made; (iii) if the certificate has been reviewed, the date the certificate was confirmed or a fresh certificate was issued; or (iv) the date of any agreement to treat an earlier compensation payment as having been made in final discharge of a claim made by or in respect of an injured person and arising out of the injury or death; or
	(b) if the person to whom the certificate has been issued makes an application under section 157(4) of the Health and Social Care (Community Health and Standards) Act 2003, one month after— (i) the date of the decision on that application; or (ii) if the person appeals against that decision under section 157(6) of that Act, the date on which the appeal is decided or withdrawn
appeal against a waiver decision under section 157(6) of the Health and Social Care (Community Health and Standards) Act 2003	one month after the date of the decision

Type of proceedings	Time for providing notice of appeal
appeal against a certificate of NHS charges under section 7 of the Road Traffic (NHS Charges) Act 1999	3 months after the latest of— (a) the date on which the liability under section 1(2) of the Road Traffic (NHS Charges) Act 1999 was discharged; (b) if the certificate has been reviewed, the date the certificate was confirmed or a fresh certificate was issued; or (c) the date of any agreement to treat an earlier compensation payment as having been made in final discharge of a claim made by or in respect of a traffic casualty and arising out of the injury or death
appeal against a certificate of recoverable benefits under section 11 of the Social Security (Recovery of Benefits) Act 1997	one month after the latest of— (a) the date on which any payment to the Secretary of State required under section 6 of the Social Security (Recovery of Benefits) Act 1997 was made; (b) if the certificate has been reviewed, the date the certificate was confirmed or a fresh certificate was issued; or (c) the date of any agreement to treat an earlier compensation payment as having been made in final discharge of a claim made by or in respect of an injured person and arising out of the accident, injury or disease
appeal under the Vaccine Damage Payments Act 1979	no time limit
appeal under the Tax Credits Act 2002	as set out in the Tax Credits Act 2002
appeal under the Child Trust Funds Act 2004	as set out in the Child Trust Funds Act 2004
appeal against a decision in respect of a claim for child benefit or guardian's allowance under section 12 of the Social Security Act 1998	as set out in regulation 28 of the Child Benefit and Guardian's Allowance (Decisions and Appeals) Regulations 2003

DEFINITIONS

"appeal"—see r.1(3).
"appellant"—*ibid.*
"decision maker"—*ibid.*

Rule 25(3)

1B.43

SCHEDULE 2

ISSUES IN RELATION TO WHICH THE TRIBUNAL MAY REFER A PERSON FOR MEDICAL EXAMINATION UNDER SECTION 20(2) OF THE SOCIAL SECURITY ACT 1998

An issue falls within this Schedule if the issue—
   (a) is whether the claimant satisfies the conditions for entitlement to—
      (i) an attendance allowance specified in section 64 and 65(1) of the Social Security Contributions and Benefits Act 1992;

412

    (ii) severe disablement allowance under section 68 of that Act;

    (iii) the care component of a disability living allowance specified in section 72(1) and (2) of that Act;

    (iv) the mobility component of a disability living allowance specified in section 73(1), (8) and (9) of that Act; or

    (v) a disabled person's tax credit specified in section 129(1)(b) of that Act.

(b) relates to the period throughout which the claimant is likely to satisfy the conditions for entitlement to an attendance allowance or a disability living allowance;

(c) is the rate at which an attendance allowance is payable;

(d) is the rate at which the care component or the mobility component of a disability living allowance is payable;

(e) is whether a person is incapable of work for the purposes of the Social Security Contributions and Benefits Act 1992;

(f) relates to the extent of a person's disablement and its assessment in accordance with Schedule 6 to the Social Security Contributions and Benefits Act 1992;

(g) is whether the claimant suffers a loss of physical or mental faculty as a result of the relevant accident for the purposes of section 103 of the Social Security Contributions and Benefits Act 1992;

(h) relates to any payment arising under, or by virtue of a scheme having effect under, section 111 of, and Schedule 8 to, the Social Security Contributions and Benefits Act 1992 (workmen's compensation);

(i) is whether a person has limited capability for work or work-related activity for the purposes of the Welfare Reform Act 2007.

DEFINITIONS

"Tribunal"—see r.1(3).

The Tribunal Procedure (Upper Tribunal) Rules 2008

(SI 2008/2698)

In force November 3, 2008

CONTENTS

PART 1

INTRODUCTION

PART 2

GENERAL POWERS AND PROVISIONS

PART 3

APPEALS AND REFERENCES TO THE UPPER TRIBUNAL

PART 4

JUDICIAL REVIEW PROCEEDINGS IN THE UPPER TRIBUNAL

PART 5

HEARINGS

PART 6

DECISIONS

PART 7

CORRECTING, SETTING ASIDE, REVIEWING AND APPEALING DECISIONS OF THE UPPER TRIBUNAL

41. Interpretation
42. Clerical mistakes and accidental slips or omissions
43. Setting aside a decision which disposes of proceedings
44. Application for permission to appeal
45. Upper Tribunal's consideration of application for permission to appeal
46. Review of a decision
47. Review of a decision in proceedings under the Forfeiture Act 1982

After consulting in accordance with paragraph 28(1) of Schedule 5 to, the Tribunals, Courts and Enforcement Act 2007 the Tribunal Procedure Committee has made the following Rules in exercise of the power conferred by sections 10(3), 16(9), 22 and 29(3) and (4) of, and Schedule 5 to, that Act.

The Lord Chancellor has allowed the Rules in accordance with paragraph 28(3) of Schedule 5 to the Tribunals, Courts and Enforcement Act 2007.

PART 1

INTRODUCTION

Citation, commencement, application and interpretation

1B.45   **1.**—(1) These Rules may be cited as the Tribunal Procedure (Upper Tribunal) Rules 2008 and come into force on 3rd November 2008.

(2) These Rules apply to proceedings before the Upper Tribunal.

(3) In these Rules—

"the 2007 Act" means the Tribunals, Courts and Enforcement Act 2007;

"appellant" means a person who makes an appeal, or applies for permission to appeal, to the Upper Tribunal, or a person substituted as an appellant under rule 9(1) (substitution and addition of parties);

"applicant" means a person who applies for permission to bring, or does bring, judicial review proceedings before the Upper Tribunal and, in judicial review proceedings transferred to the Upper Tribunal from a court, includes a person who was a claimant or petitioner in the proceedings immediately before they were transferred;

"disability discrimination in schools case" means proceedings before the Upper Tribunal concerning disability discrimination in the education of a child or related matters;

"dispose of proceedings" includes, unless indicated otherwise, disposing of a part of the proceedings;

"document" means anything in which information is recorded in any form, and an obligation under these Rules or any practice direction or direction to provide or allow access to a document or a copy of a document for any purpose means, unless the Upper Tribunal directs otherwise, an obligation to provide or allow access to such document or copy in a legible form or in a form which can be readily made into a legible form;

"hearing" means an oral hearing and includes a hearing conducted in whole or in part by video link, telephone or other means of instantaneous two-way electronic communication;

"interested party" means—

(a) a person who is directly affected by the outcome sought in judicial review proceedings, and has been named as an interested party under rule 28 or 29 (judicial review), or has been substituted or added as an interested party under rule 9 (substitution and addition of parties); and

(b) in judicial review proceedings transferred to the Upper Tribunal under section 25A(2) or (3) of the Judicature (Northern Ireland) Act 1978 or section 31A(2) or (3) of the Supreme Court Act 1981, a person who was an interested party in the proceedings immediately before they were transferred to the Upper Tribunal;

"judicial review proceedings" means proceedings within the jurisdiction of the Upper Tribunal pursuant to section 15 or 21 of the 2007 Act, whether such proceedings are started in the Upper Tribunal or transferred to the Upper Tribunal;

"legal representative" means an authorised advocate or authorised litigator as defined by section 119(1) of the Courts and Legal Services Act 1990, an advocate or solicitor in Scotland or a barrister or solicitor in Northern Ireland;

"mental health case" means proceedings before the Upper Tribunal on appeal against a decision in proceedings under the Mental Health Act 1983 or paragraph 5(2) of the Schedule to the Repatriation of Prisoners Act 1984;

"party" means a person who is an appellant, an applicant, a respondent or an interested party in proceedings before the Upper Tribunal, a person who has referred a question to the Upper Tribunal or, if the proceedings have been concluded, a person who was an appellant, an applicant, a respondent or an interested party when the Tribunal finally disposed of all issues in the proceedings;

"permission" includes leave in cases arising under the law of Northern Ireland;

"practice direction" means a direction given under section 23 of the 2007 Act;

"respondent" means—

(a) in an appeal, or application for permission to appeal, against a decision of another tribunal, any person other than the appellant who—

(i) was a party before that other tribunal;

        (ii) could (if they had been notified of the proceedings) have been a party before that other tribunal; or

        (iii) otherwise has a right of appeal against the decision of the other tribunal and has given notice to the Upper Tribunal that they wish to be a party to the appeal;

    (b) in an appeal against any other decision, the person who made the decision;

    (c) in judicial review proceedings—

        (i) in proceedings started in the Upper Tribunal, the person named by the applicant as the respondent;

        (ii) in proceedings transferred to the Upper Tribunal under section 25A(2) or (3) of the Judicature (Northern Ireland) Act 1978 or section 31A(2) or (3) of the Supreme Court Act 1981, a person who was a defendant in the proceedings immediately before they were transferred;

        (iii) in proceedings transferred to the Upper Tribunal under section 20(1) of the 2007 Act, a person to whom intimation of the petition was made before the proceedings were transferred, or to whom the Upper Tribunal has required intimation to be made.

    (d) in a reference under the Forfeiture Act 1982, the person whose eligibility for a benefit or advantage is in issue; or

    (e) a person substituted or added as a respondent under rule 9 (substitution and addition of parties);

"special educational needs case" means proceedings before the Upper Tribunal concerning the education of a child who has or may have special educational needs;

"working day" means any day except a Saturday or Sunday, Christmas Day, Good Friday or a bank holiday under section 1 of the Banking and Financial Dealings Act 1971.

DEFINITIONS

"the 2007 Act"—see para.(3).
"appellant"—*ibid.*
"applicant"—*ibid.*
"interested party"—*ibid.*
"judicial review proceedings"—*ibid.*
"party"—*ibid.*
"permission"—*ibid.*
"practice direction"—*ibid.*
"respondent"—*ibid.*

GENERAL NOTE

By para.(2), these Rules apply to all cases before the Upper Tribunal which not only encompasses cases formerly heard by Social Security Commissioners and Child Support Commissioners but also many other types of case. The Upper Tribunal hears appeals from all chambers of the First-tier Tribunal (and some equivalent tribunals in Wales, Scotland, and Northern Ireland) and so the definitions in para.(3) include some that are of relevance to cases entirely beyond the scope of this work, including a "disability discrimination in schools case", a "mental health case" and a "special educational needs case". There are also references in the Rules to cases under s.4 of the Safeguarding Vulnerable Groups Act 2006, which are also beyond the scope of this work.

Some amendments to the Rules will be made with effect from April 1, 2009, when the Finance and Tax Chamber of the Upper Tribunal is established. One amendment to r.1 of relevance to social security cases is likely to be the removal of head (a)(ii) of the definition of "respondent".

The Upper Tribunal also has jurisdiction in some "judicial review proceedings", by virtue of ss.15 to 21 of the Tribunals, Courts and Enforcement Act 2007. Note that the terms "applicant" and "interested party" are used only in relation to such cases. A person applying for permission to appeal *to* the Upper Tribunal is included within the term "appellant" and in all cases other than judicial review proceedings, every party other than the appellant or person making a reference is a "respondent". A person applying for a decision to be set aside or for permission to appeal *from* the Upper Tribunal is referred to in the Rules merely as "a party applying for ... " or "a person seeking ... ".

For the meaning of "bank holiday" in the definition of "working day", see the note to r.12(3) of the Tribunal Procedure (First-tier Tribunal) (Social Entitlement Chamber) Rules 2008, above.

Overriding objective and parties' obligation to co-operate with the Upper Tribunal

2.—(1) The overriding objective of these Rules is to enable the Upper **1B.46** Tribunal to deal with cases fairly and justly.

(2) Dealing with a case fairly and justly includes—

(a) dealing with the case in ways which are proportionate to the importance of the case, the complexity of the issues, the anticipated costs and the resources of the parties;

(b) avoiding unnecessary formality and seeking flexibility in the proceedings;

(c) ensuring, so far as practicable, that the parties are able to participate fully in the proceedings;

(d) using any special expertise of the Upper Tribunal effectively; and

(e) avoiding delay, so far as compatible with proper consideration of the issues.

(3) The Upper Tribunal must seek to give effect to the overriding objective when it—

(a) exercises any power under these Rules; or

(b) interprets any rule or practice direction.

(4) Parties must—

(a) help the Upper Tribunal to further the overriding objective; and

(b) co-operate with the Upper Tribunal generally.

DEFINITIONS

"party"—see r.1(3).
"practice direction"—*ibid.*

GENERAL NOTE

See the note to r.2 of the Tribunal Procedure (First-tier Tribunal) (Social Entitlement Chamber) Rules 2008, above.

Alternative dispute resolution and arbitration

1B.47   **3.**—(1) The Upper Tribunal should seek, where appropriate—

    (a) to bring to the attention of the parties the availability of any appropriate alternative procedure for the resolution of the dispute; and

    (b) if the parties wish and provided that it is compatible with the overriding objective, to facilitate the use of the procedure.

    (2) Part 1 of the Arbitration Act 1996 does not apply to proceedings before the Upper Tribunal.

DEFINITION

    "party"—see r.1(3).

GENERAL NOTE

    Rule 3(1) applies only if there is an alternative procedure available and none currently is. Such a procedure would be useful only where the Upper Tribunal was concerned with a complicated issue of fact, which is very seldom the position in a social security case.

PART 2

GENERAL POWERS AND PROVISIONS

Delegation to staff

1B.48   **4.**—(1) Staff appointed under section 40(1) of the 2007 Act (tribunal staff and services) may, with the approval of the Senior President of Tribunals, carry out functions of a judicial nature permitted or required to be done by the Upper Tribunal.

    (2) The approval referred to at paragraph (1) may apply generally to the carrying out of specified functions by members of staff of a specified description in specified circumstances.

    (3) Within 14 days after the date on which the Upper Tribunal sends notice of a decision made by a member of staff under paragraph (1) to a party, that party may apply in writing to the Upper Tribunal for that decision to be considered afresh by a judge.

DEFINITIONS

    "the 2007 Act"—see r.1(3).
    "party"—*ibid.*

GENERAL NOTE

    There is no need to make provision for the delegation of functions of a purely administrative nature and so this rule refers only to functions of a judicial nature. The Senior President of Tribunals has issued a Practice Statement (available at: http://www.tribunals.gov.uk/Tribunals/Rules/statements.htm) recording his approval of the delegation of certain functions to legally qualified members of staff of the Upper Tribunal, known as Registrars. The functions that are delegated are similar to those functions of Social Security Commissioners formerly delegated to legal officers under reg.7 of the Social Security Commissioners (Procedure) Regs 1999 and are—

    (a) exercising any case management powers under r.5 except—

        (i) extending time under r.5(3)(a) in relation to the time limits for appeals referred to in rr.21(3) and (6), 22(5), 23(2) and (5) and 44(3), (4) and (6) or in relation to the time limits for judicial review proceedings referred to in rr.28(2), (3) and (7) and 30(5);

        (ii) suspending a decision under r.5(3)(l) or (m);

        (iii) requiring a tribunal to provide reasons for its decision under r.5(3)(n);

    (b) dealing with irregularities under r.7(2) (except taking action under r.7(2)(d) or (4));

    (c) striking out under r.8(1) or (3)(a) and reinstating proceedings under r.8(5);

    (d) giving directions substituting or adding parties under r.9;

    (e) summarily assessing costs under r.10(6)(a);

    (f) making orders prohibiting disclosure or publication of documents and information under r.14;

    (g) giving directions in relation to evidence and submissions under r.15(1);

    (h) summoning (or, in Scotland, citing) witnesses and issuing orders to persons to answer questions and produce documents under r.16;

    (i) giving consent to withdraw a case and reinstating a case under r.17.

Case management powers

5.—(1) Subject to the provisions of the 2007 Act and any other enactment, the Upper Tribunal may regulate its own procedure.   **1B.49**

(2) The Upper Tribunal may give a direction in relation to the conduct or disposal of proceedings at any time, including a direction amending, suspending or setting aside an earlier direction.

(3) In particular, and without restricting the general powers in paragraphs (1) and (2), the Upper Tribunal may—

    (a) extend or shorten the time for complying with any rule, practice direction or direction;

    (b) consolidate or hear together two or more sets of proceedings or parts of proceedings raising common issues, or treat a case as a lead case;

    (c) permit or require a party to amend a document;

    (d) permit or require a party or another person to provide documents, information, evidence or submissions to the Upper Tribunal or a party;

    (e) deal with an issue in the proceedings as a preliminary issue;

    (f) hold a hearing to consider any matter, including a case management issue;

    (g) decide the form of any hearing;

    (h) adjourn or postpone a hearing;

    (i) require a party to produce a bundle for a hearing;

    (j) stay (or, in Scotland, sist) proceedings;

(k) transfer proceedings to another court or tribunal if that other court or tribunal has jurisdiction in relation to the proceedings and—

  (i) because of a change of circumstances since the proceedings were started, the Upper Tribunal no longer has jurisdiction in relation to the proceedings; or

  (ii) the Upper Tribunal considers that the other court or tribunal is a more appropriate forum for the determination of the case;

(l) suspend the effect of its own decision pending an appeal or review of that decision;

(m) in an appeal, or an application for permission to appeal, against the decision of another tribunal, suspend the effect of that decision pending the determination of the application for permission to appeal, and any appeal;

(n) require any other tribunal whose decision is the subject of proceedings before the Upper Tribunal to provide reasons for the decision, or other information or documents in relation to the decision or the proceedings in that tribunal.

DEFINITIONS

"the 2007 Act"—see r.1(3).
"dispose of proceedings"—*ibid.*
"document"—*ibid.*
"hearing" *ibid.*
"party"—*ibid.*
"permission"—*ibid.*
"practice direction"—*ibid.*

GENERAL NOTE

Para. (1)
This replaces reg.5(1) of the Social Security Commissioners (Procedure) Regs 1999.

Para. (2)
This replaces reg.20(3) of the 1999 Regs. It is in very broad terms and, although para.(3) and r.15(1) set out examples of directions the Upper Tribunal may give, they do not restrict the width of the power in this paragraph. The power must, however, be exercised so as to give effect to the overriding objective in r.2 (see r.2(3)). The procedure for applying for and giving directions is to be found in r.6. Note that, where a direction requires something to be done by a particular day, it must be done by 5pm on that day (r.12(1)) but, if that day is not a working day, the act is done in time if it is done on the next working day (r.12(2)).

Para. (3)
Sub-paragraph (a) replaces reg.5(2)(a) of the 1999 Regs.
Sub-paragraph (c) presumably refers to grounds of appeal and other submissions, rather than to evidence.

422

Sub-paragraphs (f), (g) and (h) must be read with rr.34 to 37. Sub-paragraph (h) largely replaces reg.5(2)(b) of the 1999 Regs.

Sub-paragraph (k) applies only where the Upper Tribunal had jurisdiction at the time the proceedings were begun. Otherwise, the Tribunal is required to strike the proceedings out under r.8(2). Rule 5(3)(k)(i) applies where the Upper Tribunal loses jurisdiction and r.5(3)(k)(ii) applies only where the Upper Tribunal and another tribunal have concurrent jurisdiction (which may be the case in some circumstances where a person moves to or from Northern Ireland).

Sub-paragraphs (l) and (m) permit the effect of a decision to be suspended pending an appeal from or to the Upper Tribunal. The First-tier Tribunal also has power to suspend the effect of its decision pending an appeal to the Upper Tribunal (see r.5(3)(l) of the Tribunal Procedure (First-tier Tribunal) (Social Entitlement Chamber) Rules 2008 and so the power in sub-para.(m) is most likely to be invoked where the First-tier Tribunal has refused to suspend the effect of its own decision. It is usually unnecessary to suspend a decision in a social security case concerned with entitlement, due to the Secretary of State's power to suspend payments under reg.16 of the Social Security and Child Support (Decisions and Appeals) Regs 1999 (see, in particular, reg.16(3)(b)(i) and (4)). In the past, the Secretary of State has generally not taken action to recover an overpayment while an appeal against a decision that the overpayment is recoverable is pending but he could now take the view that an appeal does not require him to stay his hand unless the tribunal so directs under this provision, which would not necessarily be appropriate as a matter of course and could in any event presumably be limited to part of its decision. The power to suspend the effect of a decision may also be useful in appeals against decisions under the Social Security (Recovery of Benefits) Act 1997, because s.14 of that Act and the regulations made under it completely fail to deal with the consequences of a successful appeal to the Upper Tribunal or an appellate court.

Sub-paragraph (n) replaces reg.20(2) of the 1999 Regs but goes further in enabling the Upper Tribunal to direct the First-tier Tribunal to provide reasons for its decision. It remains to be seen how this power will be exercised. Given the speed with which the First-tier Tribunal hears and determines cases, it may often be simpler to allow an appeal and direct a rehearing rather than to obtain reasons for a previous decision.

Procedure for applying for and giving directions

6.—(1) The Upper Tribunal may give a direction on the application of one or more of the parties or on its own initiative. **1B.50**

(2) An application for a direction may be made—

(a) by sending or delivering a written application to the Upper Tribunal; or

(b) orally during the course of a hearing.

(3) An application for a direction must include the reason for making that application.

(4) Unless the Upper Tribunal considers that there is good reason not to do so, the Upper Tribunal must send written notice of any direction to every party and to any other person affected by the direction.

(5) If a party or any other person sent notice of the direction under paragraph (4) wishes to challenge a direction which the Upper Tribunal has given, they may do so by applying for another direction which amends, suspends or sets aside the first direction.

"hearing"—see r.1(3).
"party"—*ibid.*

GENERAL NOTE

See the note to r.6 of the Tribunal Procedure (First-tier Tribunal) (Social Entitlement Chamber) Rules 2008, above.

Failure to comply with rules etc.

1B.51   **7.**—(1) An irregularity resulting from a failure to comply with any requirement in these Rules, a practice direction or a direction, does not of itself render void the proceedings or any step taken in the proceedings.

(2) If a party has failed to comply with a requirement in these Rules, a practice direction or a direction, the Upper Tribunal may take such action as it considers just, which may include—

(a) waiving the requirement;

(b) requiring the failure to be remedied;

(c) exercising its power under rule 8 (striking out a party's case); or

(d) except in mental health cases, restricting a party's participation in the proceedings.

(3) Paragraph (4) applies where the First-tier Tribunal has referred to the Upper Tribunal a failure by a person to comply with a requirement imposed by the First-tier Tribunal—

(a) to attend at any place for the purpose of giving evidence;

(b) otherwise to make themselves available to give evidence;

(c) to swear an oath in connection with the giving of evidence;

(d) to give evidence as a witness;

(e) to produce a document; or

(f) to facilitate the inspection of a document or any other thing (including any premises).

(4) The Upper Tribunal may exercise its power under section 25 of the 2007 Act (supplementary powers of the Upper Tribunal) in relation to such non-compliance as if the requirement had been imposed by the Upper Tribunal.

DEFINITIONS

"the 2007 Act"—see r.1(3).
"document"—*ibid.*
"mental health case"—*ibid.*
"party"—*ibid.*
"practice direction"—*ibid.*

GENERAL NOTE

Paragraphs (1) and (2)(a) replace reg.27 of the Social Security Commissioners (Procedure) Regs 1999 and enable the Upper Tribunal to overlook a breach of a rule, practice direction or direction. On the other hand, under para.2(c), such a breach can lead to a case being struck out under r.8, provided an appropriate warning has been given. Alternatively, the Upper Tribunal may exercise its powers under s.25 of the Tribunals, Courts and Enforcement Act 2007 to punish

the person for contempt of court (with a term of imprisonment of up to two years
and an unlimited fine). Paragraphs (3) and (4) are concerned with cases where
the First-tier Tribunal refers a case to the Upper Tribunal because there has been
non-compliance with a summons, order or direction issued by that tribunal in
connection with the attendance or examination of witnesses or the production or
inspection of documents. They are made under para.10 of Sch.5 to the 2007 Act.
A referral is necessary because the First-tier Tribunal does not have its own
power to punish for contempt. Paragraph (3)(c) must be read subject to s.5 of
the Oaths Act 1978, which permits a person who objects to being sworn to make
a solemn affirmation instead.

Striking out a party's case

8.—(1) The proceedings, or the appropriate part of them, will auto-   1B.52
matically be struck out if the appellant or applicant has failed to comply
with a direction that stated that failure by the appellant or applicant to
comply with the direction would lead to the striking out of the proceedings or that part of them.

(2) The Upper Tribunal must strike out the whole or a part of the
proceedings if the Upper Tribunal—

(a) does not have jurisdiction in relation to the proceedings or that
part of them; and

(b) does not exercise its power under rule 5(3)(k)(i) (transfer to
another court or tribunal) in relation to the proceedings or that
part of them.

(3) The Upper Tribunal may strike out the whole or a part of the
proceedings if—

(a) the appellant or applicant has failed to comply with a direction
which stated that failure by the appellant or applicant to comply
with the direction could lead to the striking out of the proceedings
or part of them;

(b) the appellant or applicant has failed to co-operate with the Upper
Tribunal to such an extent that the Upper Tribunal cannot deal
with the proceedings fairly and justly; or

(c) in proceedings which are not an appeal from the decision of
another tribunal or judicial review proceedings, the Upper Tribunal considers there is no reasonable prospect of the appellant's or
the applicant's case, or part of it, succeeding.

(4) The Upper Tribunal may not strike out the whole or a part of the
proceedings under paragraph (2) or (3)(b) or (c) without first giving the
appellant or applicant an opportunity to make representations in relation
to the proposed striking out.

(5) If the proceedings have been struck out under paragraph (1) or
(3)(a), the appellant or applicant may apply for the proceedings, or part
of them, to be reinstated.

(6) An application under paragraph (5) must be made in writing and
received by the Upper Tribunal within 1 month after the date on which
the Upper Tribunal sent notification of the striking out to the appellant
or applicant.

(7) This rule applies to a respondent as it applies to an appellant or
applicant except that—

(a) a reference to the striking out of the proceedings is to be read as a reference to the barring of the respondent from taking further part in the proceedings; and

(b) a reference to an application for the reinstatement of proceedings which have been struck out is to be read as a reference to an application for the lifting of the bar on the respondent from taking further part in the proceedings.

(8) If a respondent has been barred from taking further part in proceedings under this rule and that bar has not been lifted, the Upper Tribunal need not consider any response or other submission made by that respondent.

DEFINITIONS

"appellant"—see r.1(3).
"applicant"—*ibid*.
"party"—*ibid*.
"respondent"—*ibid*.

GENERAL NOTE

Note that, although paras (1) to (6) are expressed in terms of striking out proceedings brought by the appellant, by virtue of paras (7) and (8) they also provide for barring a respondent from taking further part in the proceedings.

Para. (1)

This provides for an automatic strike out where a person has failed to comply with a direction that carried a warning that, unless there was compliance, the case "will" be struck out. In theory, no further judicial act is required for the strike-out to take effect provided that it is clear that there has not been compliance. It is important to distinguish this paragraph from para.(3)(a), which provides for a case to be struck out for failure to comply with a direction that carried a warning that if there was no compliance the case "may" be struck out. In such a case, there needs to be a judicial decision exercising the power to strike out. It is suggested that, unless there has been a previous history of non-compliance with directions and rules, warnings should be of the "may" variety rather than the "will" variety. Note that proceedings struck out under this paragraph may be reinstated on an application under paras (5) and (6).

Para. (2)

The terms of this paragraph are mandatory, so that a final decision to the effect that the tribunal lacks jurisdiction must always be in the form of a decision to strike out the appeal.
By virtue of para.(4), a party must be given an opportunity to make representations before his or her case is struck out and there will be some cases where justice requires there to be a hearing.

Para. (3)

Sub-paragraphs (a) and (b) replace reg.5(3) of the Social Security Commissioners (Procedure) Regs 1999. By virtue of para.(4), a party must be given an opportunity to make representations before his or her case is struck out under sub-para.(b). There is no right to make representations before a case is struck out under sub-para.(a); instead there is a right to apply for reinstatement after the event, by virtue of paras (5) and (6). Striking out is discretionary and must presumably be proportionate, having regard to the culpability of the party whose case is being struck out and the amount at stake on the appeal.

Sub-paragraph (c) introduces a power to strike a case out where it has no reasonable prospect of success, but it is unlikely to have any application to social security cases because the permission requirement in respect of appeals or judicial review proceedings makes it unnecessary and it cannot apply to a reference.

Paras (7) and (8)

See the note to r.8(7) and (8) of the Tribunal Procedure (First-tier Tribunal) (Social Entitlement Chamber) Rules 2008, above. It is possible that these paragraphs will be amended with effect from April 1, 2009.

Substitution and addition of parties

9.—(1) The Upper Tribunal may give a direction substituting a party if—   **1B.53**

(a) the wrong person has been named as a party; or

(b) the substitution has become necessary because of a change in circumstances since the start of proceedings.

(2) The Upper Tribunal may give a direction adding a person to the proceedings as a respondent or, in judicial review proceedings, as an interested party.

(3) If the Upper Tribunal gives a direction under paragraph (1) or (2) it may give such consequential directions as it considers appropriate.

DEFINITIONS

"interested party"—see r.1(3).
"judicial review proceedings"—*ibid.*
"party"—*ibid.*
"respondent"—*ibid.*

GENERAL NOTE

See the note to r.9 of the Tribunal Procedure (First-tier Tribunal) (Social Entitlement Chamber) Rules 2008, above.

Orders for costs

10.—(1) The Upper Tribunal may not make an order in respect of costs (or, in Scotland, expenses) except—   **1B.54**

(a) in proceedings on appeal from another tribunal, to the extent and in the circumstances that the other tribunal had the power to make an order in respect of costs (or, in Scotland, expenses); or

(b) in proceedings other than on appeal from another tribunal or under section 4 of the Forfeiture Act 1982—

(i) under section 29(4) of the 2007 Act (wasted costs); or

(ii) if the Upper Tribunal considers that a party or its representative has acted unreasonably in bringing, defending or conducting the proceedings.

(2) The Upper Tribunal may make an order for costs (or, in Scotland, expenses) on an application or on its own initiative.

(3) A person making an application for an order under paragraph (1) must—

(a) send or deliver a written application to the Upper Tribunal and to the person against whom it is proposed that the order be made; and

(b) send or deliver a schedule of the costs or expenses claimed with the application.

(4) An application for an order under paragraph (1) may be made at any time during the proceedings but may not be made later than 14 days after the date on which the Upper Tribunal sends the decision notice recording the decision which finally disposes of all issues in the proceedings.

(5) The Upper Tribunal may not make an order under paragraph (1) against a person (the "paying person") without first—

(a) giving that person an opportunity to make representations; and

(b) if the paying person is an individual, considering that person's financial means.

(6) The amount of costs to be paid under an order under paragraph (1) may be ascertained by—

(a) summary assessment by the Upper Tribunal;

(b) agreement of a specified sum by the paying person and the person entitled to receive the costs ("the receiving person"); or

(c) assessment of the whole or a specified part of the costs (or, in Scotland, expenses) incurred by the receiving person, if not agreed.

(7) Following an order for assessment under paragraph (6)(c), the paying person or the receiving person may apply—

(a) in England and Wales, to the High Court for a detailed assessment of costs in accordance with the Civil Procedure Rules 1998 on the standard basis or, if specified in the order, on the indemnity basis;

(b) in Scotland, to the Auditor of the Court of Session for the taxation of the expenses according to the fees payable in the Court of Session; or

(c) in Northern Ireland, to the High Court for the costs to be taxed.

DEFINITIONS

"the 2007 Act"—see r.1(3).
"party"—*ibid.*

GENERAL NOTE

The effect of sub-para.(1)(a) is that there is no power to award costs in social security cases on appeal from the First-tier Tribunal, because the First-tier Tribunal has no power to award costs in such cases (see r.10 of the Tribunal Procedure (First-tier Tribunal) (Social Entitlement Chamber) Rules 2008, above, and also the supplementary note to s.29 to the Tribunals, Courts and Enforcement Act 2007, in Pt IV below). Sub-paragraph (1)(b), which may be amended from April 1, 2009, has the effect that costs may be awarded in judicial review proceedings before the Upper Tribunal only in limited circumstances, which is perhaps surprising in those cases that must be started in a court and are not automatically transferred. It also has the effect that there is no power to award costs in cases under the Forfeiture Act 1982.

Representatives

11.—(1) A party may appoint a representative (whether a legal representative or not) to represent that party in the proceedings.

(2) If a party appoints a representative, that party (or the representative if the representative is a legal representative) must send or deliver to the Upper Tribunal and to each other party written notice of the representative's name and address.

(3) Anything permitted or required to be done by a party under these Rules, a practice direction or a direction may be done by the representative of that party, except signing a witness statement.

(4) A person who receives due notice of the appointment of a representative—

(a) must provide to the representative any document which is required to be provided to the represented party, and need not provide that document to the represented party; and

(b) may assume that the representative is and remains authorised as such until they receive written notification that this is not so from the representative or the represented party.

(5) At a hearing a party may be accompanied by another person whose name and address has not been notified under paragraph (2) but who, subject to paragraph (8) and with the permission of the Upper Tribunal, may act as a representative or otherwise assist in presenting the party's case at the hearing.

(6) Paragraphs (2) to (4) do not apply to a person who accompanies a party under paragraph (5).

(7) In a mental health case if the patient has not appointed a representative the Upper Tribunal may appoint a legal representative for the patient where—

(a) the patient has stated that they do not wish to conduct their own case or that they wish to be represented; or

(b) the patient lacks the capacity to appoint a representative but the Upper Tribunal believes that it is in the patient's best interests for the patient to be represented.

(8) In a mental health case a party may not appoint as a representative, or be represented or assisted at a hearing by—

(a) a person liable to be detained or subject to guardianship or after-care under supervision, or who is a community patient, under the Mental Health Act 1983; or

(b) a person receiving treatment for mental disorder at the same hospital home as the patient.

DEFINITIONS

"document"—see r.1(3).
"hearing"—*ibid.*
"legal representative"—*ibid.*
"mental health case"—*ibid.*
"party"—*ibid.*
"permission"—*ibid.*
"practice direction"—*ibid.*

GENERAL NOTE

This rule makes rather more comprehensive provision for representatives than was formerly made by reg.17 of the Social Security Commissioners (Procedure) Regs 1999 but the note to that provision at pp.521–522 of Vol.III of the main work remains relevant.

Paras (2) to (4)

These paragraphs provide for the formal appointment of a representative who may then act on behalf of the party in all respects (except to sign a witness statement) and should be sent any documents that would otherwise be sent to the party. However, it is presumably possible for the Upper Tribunal to exclude a representative from a hearing under r.37(4) without excluding the party. Paragraph (2) may be amended from April 1, 2009 to remove the need to give notice to other parties, which is unnecessary in social security cases.

Paras (5) and (6)

These paragraphs enable a party who is present at a hearing to be represented or assisted at the hearing by any person, without there having been any formal notice of appointment. Although the Tribunal's permission is required, it is suggested that, unless r.37(4) applies, it will only exceptionally be appropriate for the Upper Tribunal to refuse permission, particularly as the party need only provide a written notice under para.(2) in order to avoid the need for permission. Without a written notice of appointment, a person who acts as a representative at a hearing has no rights as a representative outside the hearing. Obviously, a written notice may be provided at the hearing so that the person becomes entitled to act as a full representative thereafter.

Paras (7) and (8)

These paragraphs do not apply to social security cases.

Calculating time

1B.56   **12.**—(1) An act required by these Rules, a practice direction or a direction to be done on or by a particular day must be done by 5pm on that day.

(2) If the time specified by these Rules, a practice direction or a direction for doing any act ends on a day other than a working day, the act is done in time if it is done on the next working day.

(3) In a special educational needs case or a disability discrimination in schools case, the following days must not be counted when calculating the time by which an act must be done—

(a) 25th December to 1st January inclusive; and

(b) any day in August.

(4) Paragraph (3) does not apply where the Upper Tribunal directs that an act must be done by or on a specified date.

DEFINITIONS

"disability discrimination in schools case"—see r.1(3).
"practice direction"—*ibid.*
"special educational needs case"—*ibid.*
"working day"—*ibid.*

Sending and delivery of documents

13.—(1) Any document to be provided to the Upper Tribunal under   **1B.57**
these Rules, a practice direction or a direction must be—
  (a) sent by pre-paid post or delivered by hand to the address specified
       for the proceedings;
  (b) sent by fax to the number specified for the proceedings; or
  (c) sent or delivered by such other method as the Upper Tribunal may
       permit or direct.
  (2) Subject to paragraph (3), if a party provides a fax number, email
address or other details for the electronic transmission of documents to
them, that party must accept delivery of documents by that method.
  (3) If a party informs the Upper Tribunal and all other parties that a
particular form of communication, other than pre-paid post or delivery
by hand, should not be used to provide documents to that party, that
form of communication must not be so used.
  (4) If the Upper Tribunal or a party sends a document to a party or the
Upper Tribunal by email or any other electronic means of communication, the recipient may request that the sender provide a hard copy of the
document to the recipient. The recipient must make such a request as
soon as reasonably practicable after receiving the document electronically.
  (5) The Upper Tribunal and each party may assume that the address
provided by a party or its representative is and remains the address to
which documents should be sent or delivered until receiving written
notification to the contrary.

DEFINITIONS

  "document"—see r.1(3).
  "party"—*ibid.*
  "practice direction"—*ibid.*

GENERAL NOTE

  See the note to r.13 of the Tribunal Procedure (First-tier Tribunal) (Social
Entitlement Chamber) Rules 2008, above.

Use of documents and information

14.—(1) The Upper Tribunal may make an order prohibiting the   **1B.58**
disclosure or publication of—
  (a) specified documents or information relating to the proceedings;
       or
  (b) any matter likely to lead members of the public to identify any
       person whom the Upper Tribunal considers should not be iden-
       tified.
  (2) The Upper Tribunal may give a direction prohibiting the disclosure of a document or information to a person if—
  (a) the Upper Tribunal is satisfied that such disclosure would be likely
       to cause that person or some other person serious harm; and
  (b) the Upper Tribunal is satisfied, having regard to the interests of
       justice, that it is proportionate to give such a direction.

(3) If a party ("the first party") considers that the Upper Tribunal should give a direction under paragraph (2) prohibiting the disclosure of a document or information to another party ("the second party"), the first party must—

(a) exclude the relevant document or information from any documents that will be provided to the second party; and

(b) provide to the Upper Tribunal the excluded document or information, and the reason for its exclusion, so that the Upper Tribunal may decide whether the document or information should be disclosed to the second party or should be the subject of a direction under paragraph (2).

(4) The Upper Tribunal must conduct proceedings as appropriate in order to give effect to a direction given under paragraph (2).

(5) If the Upper Tribunal gives a direction under paragraph (2) which prevents disclosure to a party who has appointed a representative, the Upper Tribunal may give a direction that the documents or information be disclosed to that representative if the Upper Tribunal is satisfied that—

(a) disclosure to the representative would be in the interests of the party; and

(b) the representative will act in accordance with paragraph (6).

(6) Documents or information disclosed to a representative in accordance with a direction under paragraph (5) must not be disclosed either directly or indirectly to any other person without the Upper Tribunal's consent.

(7) Unless the Upper Tribunal gives a direction to the contrary, information about mental health cases and the names of any persons concerned in such cases must not be made public.

DEFINITIONS

"document"—see r.1(3).
"mental health case"—*ibid.*
"party"—*ibid.*

GENERAL NOTE

Para. (1)

An order under this paragraph may be directed to an individual and be concerned only with an individual document (e.g. prohibiting an appellant from disclosing to someone else a document disclosed to the appellant by the respondent) or it may be directed to the public in general and effectively amount to a reporting restriction. Hearings of social security cases are usually attended only by those immediately interested with them but most hearings are, in principle, open to the public, including the press (see r.37). It is difficult to envisage it being appropriate to prohibit the publication of any information at all about a hearing held in public (despite para.(7)) but it might often be appropriate to make an order prohibiting the publishing of information that may lead to a child or vulnerable adult being identified if there would otherwise be any serious risk of such publication. It will generally be necessary properly to balance the right of one person to respect of his or her private life under Art.8 of the European Convention on Human Rights and the right of another person to freedom of

432

expression under Art.10. The existence of the powers conferred by this paragraph is a factor to be borne in mind when deciding under r.37(2) whether a hearing should be in private or in public, which requires consideration of the terms of Art.6(1).

A breach of an order made under this paragraph is a contempt of court and may be punished by the Upper Tribunal under s.25 of the Tribunals, Courts and Enforcement Act 2007 by a term of imprisonment not exceeding two years and an unlimited fine.

Paras (2) to (6)

These paragraphs replace reg.22 of the Social Security Commissioners (Procedure) Regs 1999, although they are not limited to medical advice or evidence. See the note to the equivalent regulation that applied to appeal tribunals, on pp.629–631 of Vol.III of the main work. It is suggested that "serious harm" merely means harm that would be sufficiently serious to justify what would otherwise be a breach of the right to a fair hearing guaranteed by Art.6 of the European Convention on Human Rights. Note the power in r.37(4)(c) to exclude a person from a hearing, and the power in r.40(2) not to provide a full decision, in order to give effect to a direction under para.(2).

Para. (7)

This paragraph does not apply to social security cases and, in applying to *all* information, appears anomalous.

Evidence and submissions

15.—(1) Without restriction on the general powers in rule 5(1) and **1B.59** (2) (case management powers), the Upper Tribunal may give directions as to—

  (a) issues on which it requires evidence or submissions;

  (b) the nature of the evidence or submissions it requires;

  (c) whether the parties are permitted or required to provide expert evidence, and if so whether the parties must jointly appoint a single expert to provide such evidence;

  (d) any limit on the number of witnesses whose evidence a party may put forward, whether in relation to a particular issue or generally;

  (e) the manner in which any evidence or submissions are to be provided, which may include a direction for them to be given—

    (i) orally at a hearing; or

    (ii) by written submissions or witness statement; and

  (f) the time at which any evidence or submissions are to be provided.

(2) The Upper Tribunal may—

  (a) admit evidence whether or not—

    (i) the evidence would be admissible in a civil trial in the United Kingdom; or

    (ii) the evidence was available to a previous decision maker; or

  (b) exclude evidence that would otherwise be admissible where—

    (i) the evidence was not provided within the time allowed by a direction or a practice direction;

    (ii) the evidence was otherwise provided in a manner that did not comply with a direction or a practice direction; or

    (iii) it would otherwise be unfair to admit the evidence.

(3) The Upper Tribunal may consent to a witness giving, or require any witness to give, evidence on oath, and may administer an oath for that purpose.

DEFINITIONS

"hearing"—see r.1(3).
"party"—*ibid.*
"practice direction"—*ibid.*

GENERAL NOTE

See the note to r.15 of the Tribunal Procedure (First-tier Tribunal) (Social Entitlement Chamber) Rules 2008, above. Paragraph (3) replaces reg.25(4) of the Social Security Commissioners (Procedure) Regs 1999.

Summoning or citation of witnesses and orders to answer questions or produce documents

1B.60   **16.**—(1) On the application of a party or on its own initiative, the Upper Tribunal may—

    (a) by summons (or, in Scotland, citation) require any person to attend as a witness at a hearing at the time and place specified in the summons or citation; or

    (b) order any person to answer any questions or produce any documents in that person's possession or control which relate to any issue in the proceedings.

(2) A summons or citation under paragraph (1)(a) must—

    (a) give the person required to attend 14 days' notice of the hearing or such shorter period as the Upper Tribunal may direct; and

    (b) where the person is not a party, make provision for the person's necessary expenses of attendance to be paid, and state who is to pay them.

(3) No person may be compelled to give any evidence or produce any document that the person could not be compelled to give or produce on a trial of an action in a court of law in the part of the United Kingdom where the proceedings are due to be determined.

(4) A summons, citation or order under this rule must—

    (a) state that the person on whom the requirement is imposed may apply to the Upper Tribunal to vary or set aside the summons, citation or order, if they have not had an opportunity to object to it; and

    (b) state the consequences of failure to comply with the summons, citation or order.

DEFINITIONS

"document"—see r.1(3).
"hearing"—*ibid.*
"party"—*ibid.*

GENERAL NOTE

This rule replaces reg.25(1) to (3) of the Social Security Commissioners (Procedure) Regs 1999 but also includes a power to order the production of documents without requiring attendance at a hearing. A failure to comply with a summons, citation or order under this rule is a contempt of court that may be punished by the Upper Tribunal with a term of imprisonment not exceeding two years and an unlimited fine under s.25 of the Tribunals, Courts and Enforcement Act 2007.

Withdrawal

17.—(1) Subject to paragraph (2), a party may give notice of the withdrawal of its case, or any part of it— **1B.61**

(a) at any time before a hearing to consider the disposal of the proceedings (or, if the Upper Tribunal disposes of the proceedings without a hearing, before that disposal), by sending or delivering to the Upper Tribunal a written notice of withdrawal; or

(b) orally at a hearing.

(2) Notice of withdrawal will not take effect unless the Upper Tribunal consents to the withdrawal except in relation to an application for permission to appeal.

(3) A party which has withdrawn its case may apply to the Upper Tribunal for the case to be reinstated.

(4) An application under paragraph (3) must be made in writing and be received by the Upper Tribunal within 1 month after—

(a) the date on which the Upper Tribunal received the notice under paragraph (1)(a); or

(b) the date of the hearing at which the case was withdrawn orally under paragraph (1)(b).

(5) The Upper Tribunal must notify each party in writing of a withdrawal under this rule.

DEFINITIONS

"dispose of proceedings"—see r.1(3).
"hearing"—*ibid.*
"party"—*ibid.*
"permission"—*ibid.*

GENERAL NOTE

This rule replaces reg.26 of the Social Security Commissioners (Procedure) Regs 1999 but it applies to the withdrawal of a respondent's case as well as to the case of an appellant or person making a reference. The existence of the one-month time limit for an application for reinstatement, which did not exist in the old provision, may suggest that an application should be granted if made within that period unless there is a clear reason for not doing so, such as the previous conduct of the party, obvious lack of merit in the case or prejudice to another party.

Notice of funding of legal services

18. If a party is granted funding of legal services at any time, that party must as soon as practicable— **1B.62**

(a)   (i)   if funding is granted by the Legal Services Commission or the Northern Ireland Legal Services Commission, send a copy of the funding notice to the Upper Tribunal; or

(ii)   if funding is granted by the Scottish Legal Aid Board, send a copy of the legal aid certificate to the Upper Tribunal; and

(b)   notify every other party in writing that funding has been granted.

DEFINITION

"party"—see r.1(3).

GENERAL NOTE

This rule replaces reg.8A of the Social Security Commissioners (Procedure) Regs 1999. Public funding is rare in social security cases but it is helpful for a judge to know whether a party is funded if he or she is considering directing the party to produce a submission or a bundle of documents.

Confidentiality in child support or child trust fund cases

1B.63   **19.**—(1) Paragraph (3) applies to an appeal against a decision of the First-tier Tribunal in proceedings under the Child Support Act 1991 in the circumstances described in paragraph (2), other than an appeal against a reduced benefit decision (as defined in section 46(10)(b) of the Child Support Act 1991, as that section had effect prior to the commencement of section 15(b) of the Child Maintenance and Other Payments Act 2008).

(2) The circumstances referred to in paragraph (1) are that—

(a)   in the proceedings in the First-tier Tribunal in respect of which the appeal has been brought, there was an obligation to keep a person's address confidential; or

(b)   a person whose circumstances are relevant to the proceedings would like their address (or, in the case of the person with care of the child, the child's address) to be kept confidential and has given notice to that effect—

(i)   to the Upper Tribunal in an application for permission to appeal or notice of appeal;

(ii)   to the Upper Tribunal within 1 month after an enquiry by the Upper Tribunal; or

(iii)   to the Secretary of State, the Child Maintenance and Enforcement Commission or the Upper Tribunal when notifying a change of address after proceedings have been started.

(3) Where this paragraph applies, the Secretary of State, the Child Maintenance and Enforcement Commission and the Upper Tribunal must take appropriate steps to secure the confidentiality of the address, and of any information which could reasonably be expected to enable a person to identify the address, to the extent that the address or that information is not already known to each other party.

(4) Paragraph (6) applies to an appeal against a decision of the First-tier Tribunal in proceedings under the Child Trust Funds Act 2004 in the circumstances described in paragraph (5).

(5) The circumstances referred to in paragraph (4) are that—

(a) in the proceedings in the First-tier Tribunal in respect of which the appeal has been brought, there was an obligation to keep a person's address confidential; or

(b) a person whose circumstances are relevant to the proceedings would like their address (or, in the case of the person with care of the eligible child, the child's address) to be kept confidential and has given notice to that effect—

   (i) to the Upper Tribunal in an application for permission to appeal or notice of appeal;

   (ii) to the Upper Tribunal within 1 month after an enquiry by the Upper Tribunal; or

   (iii) to HMRC or the Upper Tribunal when notifying a change of address after proceedings have been started.

(6) Where this paragraph applies, HMRC and the Upper Tribunal must take appropriate steps to secure the confidentiality of the address, and of any information which could reasonably be expected to enable a person to identify the address, to the extent that the address or that information is not already known to each other party.

(7) In this rule—

"eligible child" has the meaning set out in section 2 of the Child Trust Funds Act 2004; and

"HMRC" means Her Majesty's Revenue and Customs.

DEFINITIONS

"eligible child"—see para.(7).
"HMRC"—*ibid.*
"party"—see r.1(3).
"permission"—*ibid.*

Power to pay expenses and allowances

20.—(1) In proceedings brought under section 4 of the Safeguarding 1B.64 Vulnerable Groups Act 2006 which are not an appeal from the decision of another tribunal or judicial review proceedings, the Secretary of State may pay such allowances for the purpose of or in connection with the attendance of persons at hearings as the Secretary of State may, with the consent of the Treasury, determine.

(2) Paragraph (3) applies to proceedings on appeal from a decision of—

(a) the First-tier Tribunal in proceedings under the Child Support Act 1991, section 12 of the Social Security Act 1998 or paragraph 6 of Schedule 7 to the Child Support, Pensions and Social Security Act 2000;

(b) the First-tier Tribunal in a war pensions and armed forces case (as defined in the Tribunal Procedure (First-tier Tribunal) (War Pensions and Armed Forces Compensation Chamber) Rules 2008); or

(c) a Pensions Appeal Tribunal for Scotland or Northern Ireland.

(3) The Lord Chancellor (or, in Scotland, the Secretary of State) may pay to any person who attends any hearing such travelling and other

allowances, including compensation for loss of remunerative time, as the Lord Chancellor (or, in Scotland, the Secretary of State) may determine.

DEFINITIONS

"hearing"—see r.1(3).
"judicial review proceedings"—*ibid.*

GENERAL NOTE

Paragraph (1) does not apply to social security cases. Paragraphs (2) and (3) reproduce the effect of para.3 of Sch.4 to the Social Security Act 1998. Paragraph (2) suffers from the same defect as the old provision, which is that it does not apply to all social security cases in which claimants might be required to attend hearings, although in practice the Tribunals Service seems never to have refused to pay expenses to those not within the scope of the old provision (e.g. an injured person appealing against a decision under the Social Security (Recovery of Benefits) Act 1997).

The rule is in also unsatisfactory because it seems unlikely that para.10(4) of Sch.5 to the Tribunals, Courts and Enforcement Act 2007 envisages Rules that give the Secretary of State the power to determine what expenses are to be paid, although it is perhaps more appropriate that the power should lie with the Secretary of State than with the Tribunal Procedure Committee.

PART 3

APPEALS AND REFERENCES TO THE UPPER TRIBUNAL

Application to the Upper Tribunal for permission to appeal

1B.65   **21.**—(1) This rule applies to an application for permission to appeal to the Upper Tribunal against any decision.

(2) A person may apply to the Upper Tribunal for permission to appeal to the Upper Tribunal against a decision of another tribunal only if—

(a) they have made an application for permission to appeal to the tribunal which made the decision challenged; and

(b) that application has been refused or has not been admitted.

(3) An application for permission to appeal must be made in writing and received by the Upper Tribunal no later than—

(a) in the case of an application under section 4 of the Safeguarding Vulnerable Groups Act 2006, 3 months after the date on which written notice of the decision being challenged was sent to the appellant; or

(b) otherwise, a month after the date on which the tribunal that made the decision under challenge sent notice of its refusal of permission to appeal, or refusal to admit the application for permission to appeal, to the appellant.

(4) The application must state—

(a) the name and address of the appellant;

(b) the name and address of the representative (if any) of the appellant;

(c) an address where documents for the appellant may be sent or delivered;

(d) details (including the full reference) of the decision challenged;

(e) the grounds on which the appellant relies; and

(f) whether the appellant wants the application to be dealt with at a hearing.

(5) The appellant must provide with the application a copy of—

(a) any written record of the decision being challenged;

(b) any separate written statement of reasons for that decision; and

(c) if the application is for permission to appeal against a decision of another tribunal, the notice of refusal of permission to appeal, or notice of refusal to admit the application for permission to appeal, from that other tribunal.

(6) If the appellant provides the application to the Upper Tribunal later than the time required by paragraph (3) or by an extension of time allowed under rule 5(3)(a) (power to extend time)—

(a) the application must include a request for an extension of time and the reason why the application was not provided in time; and

(b) unless the Upper Tribunal extends time for the application under rule 5(3)(a) (power to extend time) the Upper Tribunal must not admit the application.

(7) If the appellant makes an application to the Upper Tribunal for permission to appeal against the decision of another tribunal, and that other tribunal refused to admit the appellant's application for permission to appeal because the application for permission or for a written statement of reasons was not made in time—

(a) the application to the Upper Tribunal for permission to appeal must include the reason why the application to the other tribunal for permission to appeal or for a written statement of reasons, as the case may be, was not made in time; and

(b) the Upper Tribunal must only admit the application if the Upper Tribunal considers that it is in the interests of justice for it to do so.

Definitions

"appellant"—see r.1(3).
"document"—*ibid.*
"hearing"—*ibid.*
"permission"—*ibid.*

General Note

This replaces regs 9 and 10 of the Social Security Commissioners (Procedure) Regs 1999 but without the absolute time limit of 13 months and without any express duty on a public authority to notify a claimant that it has made an application. Note, also, that the application must now be *received* by the Upper Tribunal within the time limit (see para.(3)). The power to extend time is no longer limited to cases where there are "special reasons" but that may not make much difference in practice because the same considerations are likely to be relevant (see the note to reg.58(5) of the Social Security and Child Support (Decisions and Appeals) Regs 1999 on p.664 of Vol.III of the main work). Paragraph (7) makes it clear that, where an application for permission made to the First-tier Tribunal was made late but nonetheless accepted, there is no need for the Upper Tribunal to consider that delay (giving effect to *CIB/4791/2001*). Paragraph (7) also makes specific provision for cases where there is no statement of the First-tier Tribunal's reasons due to delay in applying for one. The word "any" in para.(5)(b) has the effect that there is no longer an irregularity just because no statement of reasons is submitted in such a case. However, it remains difficult to demonstrate an error of law without a statement of reasons and, in particular, the First-tier Tribunal's decision cannot be challenged on the ground of inadequacy of reasons in the absence of such a statement or a duty to provide one (*R(IS) 11/99*).

Decision in relation to permission to appeal

1B.66   **22.**—(1) If the Upper Tribunal refuses permission to appeal, it must send written notice of the refusal and of the reasons for the refusal to the appellant.

(2) If the Upper Tribunal gives permission to appeal—

(a) the Upper Tribunal must send written notice of the permission, and of the reasons for any limitations or conditions on such permission, to each party;

(b) subject to any direction by the Upper Tribunal, the application for permission to appeal stands as the notice of appeal and the Upper Tribunal must send to each respondent a copy of the application for permission to appeal and any documents provided with it by the appellant; and

(c) the Upper Tribunal may, with the consent of the appellant and each respondent, determine the appeal without obtaining any further response.

(3) Paragraph (4) applies where the Upper Tribunal, without a hearing, determines—

(a) an application for permission to appeal against a decision of the Health, Education and Social Care Chamber of the First-tier Tribunal, the Mental Health Review Tribunal for Wales or the Special Educational Needs Tribunal for Wales; or

(b) an application for permission to appeal under section 4 of the Safeguarding Vulnerable Groups Act 2006.

(4) In the circumstances set out at paragraph (3) the appellant may apply for the decision to be reconsidered at a hearing if the Upper Tribunal—

(a) refuses permission to appeal; or

(b) gives permission to appeal on limited grounds or subject to conditions.

(5) An application under paragraph (4) must be made in writing and received by the Upper Tribunal within 14 days after the date on which the Upper Tribunal sent written notice of its decision regarding the application to the appellant.

DEFINITIONS

"appellant"—see r.1(3).
"document"—*ibid.*
"hearing"—*ibid.*
"party"—*ibid.*
"permission"—*ibid.*
"respondent"—*ibid.*

GENERAL NOTE

Paragraphs (1) and (2) reproduce the effect of reg.11 of the Social Security Commissioners (Procedure) Regs 1999. Paragraphs (3) to (5) do not apply to social security cases.

Notice of appeal

23.—(1) This rule applies—   **1B.67**
(a) if another tribunal has given permission for a party to appeal to the Upper Tribunal; or
(b) subject to any other direction by the Upper Tribunal, if the Upper Tribunal has given permission to appeal and has given a direction that the application for permission to appeal does not stand as the notice of appeal.

(2) The appellant must provide a notice of appeal to the Upper Tribunal so that it is received within 1 month after the tribunal that gave permission to appeal sent notice of such permission to the appellant.

(3) The notice of appeal must include the information listed in rule 21(4)(a) to (e) (content of the application for permission to appeal) and, where the Upper Tribunal has given permission to appeal, the Upper Tribunal's case reference.

(4) If another tribunal has granted permission to appeal, the appellant must provide with the notice of appeal a copy of—
(a) any written record of the decision being challenged;
(b) any separate written statement of reasons for that decision; and
(c) the notice of permission to appeal.

(5) If the appellant provides the notice of appeal to the Upper Tribunal later than the time required by paragraph (2) or by an extension of time allowed under rule 5(3)(a) (power to extend time)—
(a) the notice of appeal must include a request for an extension of time and the reason why the notice was not provided in time; and
(b) unless the Upper Tribunal extends time for the notice of appeal under rule 5(3)(a) (power to extend time) the Upper Tribunal must not admit the notice of appeal.

(6) When the Upper Tribunal receives the notice of appeal it must send a copy of the notice and any accompanying documents to each respondent.

DEFINITIONS

"appellant"—see r.1(3).
"document"—*ibid.*

"party"—*ibid.*
"permission"—*ibid.*
"respondent"—*ibid.*

GENERAL NOTE

This rule largely reproduces the effects of regs 12, 13 and 16 of the Social Security Commissioners (Procedure) Regs 1999 but note that the appeal must now be *received* by the Upper Tribunal within the time limit and the power to extend time is no longer limited to cases where there are "special reasons", although that may not make much difference in practice because the same considerations are likely to be relevant (see the note to reg.58(5) of the Social Security and Child Support (Decisions and Appeals) Regs 1999 on p.664 of Vol.III of the main work).

Response to the notice of appeal

1B.68   **24.**—(1) Subject to any direction given by the Upper Tribunal, a respondent may provide a response to the notice of appeal.

(2) Any response provided under paragraph (1) must be in writing and must be sent or delivered to the Upper Tribunal so that it is received—

(a) if the application for permission stands as the notice of appeal, no later than 1 month after the date on which the Upper Tribunal sent notice that it had granted permission to appeal to the respondent; or

(b) in any other case, no later than 1 month after the date on which the Upper Tribunal sent a copy of the notice of appeal to the respondent.

(3) The response must state—

(a) the name and address of the respondent;

(b) the name and address of the representative (if any) of the respondent;

(c) an address where documents for the respondent may be sent or delivered;

(d) whether the respondent opposes the appeal;

(e) the grounds on which the respondent relies, including any grounds on which the respondent was unsuccessful in the proceedings which are the subject of the appeal, but intends to rely in the appeal; and

(f) whether the respondent wants the case to be dealt with at a hearing.

(4) If the respondent provides the response to the Upper Tribunal later than the time required by paragraph (2) or by an extension of time allowed under rule 5(3)(a) (power to extend time), the response must include a request for an extension of time and the reason why the notice was not provided in time.

(5) When the Upper Tribunal receives the response it must send a copy of the response and any accompanying documents to the appellant and each other party.

"appellant"—see r.1(3).
"document"—*ibid.*
"hearing"—*ibid.*
"party"—*ibid.*
"permission"—*ibid.*
"respondent"—*ibid.*

GENERAL NOTE

This rule replaces reg.18 of the Social Security Commissioners (Procedure) Regs 1999 but is expressly made subject to a direction by the Upper Tribunal, which makes it unnecessary to have any specific provision for a case where there is more than one respondent. In practice, the Upper Tribunal usually directs sequential responses in such a case.

Appellant's reply

25.—(1) Subject to any direction given by the Upper Tribunal, the appellant may provide a reply to any response provided under rule 24 (response to the notice of appeal).

(2) Any reply provided under paragraph (1) must be in writing and must be sent or delivered to the Upper Tribunal so that it is received within one month after the date on which the Upper Tribunal sent a copy of the response to the appellant.

(3) When the Upper Tribunal receives the reply it must send a copy of the reply and any accompanying documents to each respondent.

1B.69

DEFINITIONS

"appellant"—see r.1(3).
"document"—*ibid.*
"respondent"—*ibid.*

GENERAL NOTE

This rule replaces reg.19 of the Social Security Commissioners (Procedure) Regs 1999 but is expressly made subject to a direction by the Upper Tribunal. Where it appears to a judge granting permission to appeal that there is an obvious error in a decision of the First-tier Tribunal, it is common for the judge to direct simultaneous observations from all parties in order to speed up the process.

References under the Forfeiture Act 1982

26.—(1) If a question arises which is required to be determined by the Upper Tribunal under section 4 of the Forfeiture Act 1982, the person to whom the application for the relevant benefit or advantage has been made must refer the question to the Upper Tribunal.

(2) The reference must be in writing and must include—

(a) a statement of the question for determination;
(b) a statement of the relevant facts;
(c) the grounds upon which the reference is made; and

1B.70

(d) an address for sending documents to the person making the reference and each respondent.

(3) When the Upper Tribunal receives the reference it must send a copy of the reference and any accompanying documents to each respondent.

(4) Rules 24 (response to the notice of appeal) and 25 (appellant's reply) apply to a reference made under this rule as if it were a notice of appeal.

DEFINITIONS

"document"—see r.1(3).
"respondent"—*ibid.*

GENERAL NOTE

This rule replaces reg.14 of the Social Security Commissioners (Procedure) Regs 1999 (together with regs 16, 18 and 19 insofar as they applied to forfeiture cases).

PART 4

JUDICIAL REVIEW PROCEEDINGS IN THE UPPER TRIBUNAL

Application of this Part to judicial review proceedings transferred to the Upper Tribunal

1B.71   **27.**—(1) When a court transfers judicial review proceedings to the Upper Tribunal, the Upper Tribunal—
(a) must notify each party in writing that the proceedings have been transferred to the Upper Tribunal; and
(b) must give directions as to the future conduct of the proceedings.

(2) The directions given under paragraph (1)(b) may modify or disapply for the purposes of the proceedings any of the provisions of the following rules in this Part.

(3) In proceedings transferred from the Court of Session under section 20(1) of the 2007 Act, the directions given under paragraph (1)(b) must—
(a) if the Court of Session did not make a first order specifying the required intimation, service and advertisement of the petition, state the Upper Tribunal's requirements in relation to those matters;
(b) state whether the Upper Tribunal will consider summary dismissal of the proceedings; and
(c) where necessary, modify or disapply provisions relating to permission in the following rules in this Part.

DEFINITIONS

"the 2007 Act"—see r.1(3).
"judicial review proceedings"—*ibid.*

"party"—*ibid.*
"permission"—*ibid.*

GENERAL NOTE

This rule applies to judicial review proceedings transferred from a court, as opposed to proceedings started in the Upper Tribunal. Because cases may be transferred at any stage of the proceedings, the Upper Tribunal is given a broad power to give directions as to how the case will proceed and how much of rr.28 to 33 need apply to the case. Rules 28 and 29 cannot apply to cases transferred by the Court of Session, because there is no requirement to obtain permission to apply for judicial review in Scotland. Instead, the Upper Tribunal may hold a preliminary hearing to consider whether summary dismissal of the proceedings is appropriate, which would be equivalent to a first hearing in the Court of Session and has much the same effect as considering whether to refuse permission to apply for judicial review. Hence para.(3)(b) and r.30(2) and (3)(b).

Applications for permission to bring judicial review proceedings

28.—(1) A person seeking permission to bring judicial review proceedings before the Upper Tribunal under section 16 of the 2007 Act must make a written application to the Upper Tribunal for such permission.

(2) Subject to paragraph (3), an application under paragraph (1) must be made promptly and, unless any other enactment specifies a shorter time limit, must be sent or delivered to the Upper Tribunal so that it is received no later than 3 months after the date of the decision to which the application relates.

(3) An application for permission to bring judicial review proceedings challenging a decision of the First-tier Tribunal may be made later than the time required by paragraph (2) if it is made within 1 month after the date on which the First-tier Tribunal sent—

(a) written reasons for the decision; or
(b) notification that an application for the decision to be set aside has been unsuccessful, provided that that application was made in time.

(4) The application must state—

(a) the name and address of the applicant, the respondent and any other person whom the applicant considers to be an interested party;
(b) the name and address of the applicant's representative (if any);
(c) an address where documents for the applicant may be sent or delivered;
(d) details of the decision challenged (including the date, the full reference and the identity of the decision maker);
(e) that the application is for permission to bring judicial review proceedings;
(f) the outcome that the applicant is seeking; and
(g) the facts and grounds on which the applicant relies.

1B.72

(5) If the application relates to proceedings in a court or tribunal, the application must name as an interested party each party to those proceedings who is not the applicant or a respondent.

(6) The applicant must send with the application—

(a) a copy of any written record of the decision in the applicant's possession or control; and

(b) copies of any other documents in the applicant's possession or control on which the applicant intends to rely.

(7) If the applicant provides the application to the Upper Tribunal later than the time required by paragraph (2) or (3) or by an extension of time allowed under rule 5(3)(a) (power to extend time)—

(a) the application must include a request for an extension of time and the reason why the application was not provided in time; and

(b) unless the Upper Tribunal extends time for the application under rule 5(3)(a) (power to extend time) the Upper Tribunal must not admit the application.

(8) When the Upper Tribunal receives the application it must send a copy of the application and any accompanying documents to each person named in the application as a respondent or interested party.

DEFINITIONS

"the 2007 Act"—see r.1(3).
"applicant"—*ibid.*
"document"—*ibid.*
"interested party"—*ibid.*
"judicial review proceedings"—*ibid.*
"party"—*ibid.*
"permission"—*ibid.*
"respondent"—*ibid.*

GENERAL NOTE

This rule applies to judicial review proceedings started in the Upper Tribunal (see the note to s.15 of the Tribunals, Courts and Enforcement Act 2007 at p.1298 of Vol.III of the main work and the supplementary note to s.18 in Pt IV below, which sets out the classes of case that may be started in the Upper Tribunal in England and Wales). Rule 9 gives the Upper Tribunal wide power to substitute the correct parties and add additional parties where the applicant fails to identify the correct respondent and interested party. Where, as will currently always be the case, the decision being challenged is a decision of the First-tier Tribunal, the respondent will be the First-tier Tribunal and the parties to the case before the First-tier Tribunal, other than the applicant, will be interested parties.

Acknowledgment of service

1B.73   **29.**—(1) A person who is sent a copy of an application for permission under rule 28(8) (application for permission to bring judicial review proceedings) and wishes to take part in the proceedings must send or deliver to the Upper Tribunal an acknowledgment of service so that it is received no later than 21 days after the date on which the Upper Tribunal sent a copy of the application to that person.

(2) An acknowledgment of service under paragraph (1) must be in writing and state—

(a) whether the person intends to oppose the application for permission;

(b) their grounds for any opposition under sub-paragraph (a), or any other submission or information which it considers may assist the Upper Tribunal; and

(c) the name and address of any other person not named in the application as a respondent or interested party whom the person providing the acknowledgment considers to be an interested party.

(3) A person who is sent a copy of an application for permission under rule 28(8) but does not provide an acknowledgment of service may not take part in the application for permission, but may take part in the subsequent proceedings if the application is successful.

DEFINITIONS

"interested party"—see r.1(3).
"judicial review proceedings"—*ibid.*
"party"—*ibid.*
"permission"—*ibid.*
"respondent"—*ibid.*

GENERAL NOTE

This rule, including the 21-day time limit, is based on the procedure in the Administrative Court in England and Wales under C.P.R. rr.54.8 and 54.9. The respondent, i.e. the First-tier Tribunal whose decision is being challenged, will only rarely take part in proceedings, so that it will fall to the interested parties to decide whether or not to oppose the application, just as it does on an appeal.

Decision on permission or summary dismissal, and reconsideration of permission or summary dismissal at a hearing

30.—(1) The Upper Tribunal must send to the applicant, each respondent and any other person who provided an acknowledgment of service to the Upper Tribunal, and may send to any other person who may have an interest in the proceedings, written notice of—   1B.74

(a) its decision in relation to the application for permission; and

(b) the reasons for any refusal of the application, or any limitations or conditions on permission.

(2) In proceedings transferred from the Court of Session under section 20(1) of the 2007 Act, where the Upper Tribunal has considered whether summarily to dismiss of the proceedings, the Upper Tribunal must send to the applicant and each respondent, and may send to any other person who may have an interest in the proceedings, written notice of—

(a) its decision in relation to the summary dismissal of proceedings; and

(b) the reasons for any decision summarily to dismiss part or all of the proceedings, or any limitations or conditions on the continuation of such proceedings.

(3) Paragraph (4) applies where the Upper Tribunal, without a hearing—

(a) determines an application for permission to bring judicial review proceedings and either refuses permission, or gives permission on limited grounds or subject to conditions; or

(b) in proceedings transferred from the Court of Session, summarily dismisses part or all of the proceedings, or imposes any limitations or conditions on the continuation of such proceedings.

(4) In the circumstances specified in paragraph (3) the applicant may apply for the decision to be reconsidered at a hearing.

(5) An application under paragraph (4) must be made in writing and must be sent or delivered to the Upper Tribunal so that it is received within 14 days after the date on which the Upper Tribunal sent written notice of its decision regarding the application to the applicant.

DEFINITIONS

"the 2007 Act"—see r.1(3).
"applicant"—*ibid.*
"hearing"—*ibid.*
"judicial review proceedings"—*ibid.*
"permission"—*ibid.*
"respondent"—*ibid.*

GENERAL NOTE

This rule is based on the procedure in the Administrative Court in England and Wales under C.P.R. rr.54.10 to 54.12. An application for permission to apply for judicial review that is refused, or is only partially successful, on paper may be renewed at an oral hearing under paras (3)(a) and (4). Dismissal of judicial review proceedings at a first hearing under R.C. r.58.9 is the equivalent in Scotland of a refusal of permission to apply for judicial review in England and Wales or Northern Ireland and so equivalent provision for summary dismissal by the Upper Tribunal is made in paras (3)(b) and (4).

Responses

1B.75   **31.**—(1) Any person to whom the Upper Tribunal has sent notice of the grant of permission under rule 30(1) (notification of decision on permission), and who wishes to contest the application or support it on additional grounds, must provide detailed grounds for contesting or supporting the application to the Upper Tribunal.

(2) Any detailed grounds must be provided in writing and must be sent or delivered to the Upper Tribunal so that they are received not more than 35 days after the Upper Tribunal sent notice of the grant of permission under rule 30(1).

DEFINITION

"permission"—see r.1(3).

GENERAL NOTE

This rule, including the 35-day time limit, is based on the procedure in the Administrative Court in England and Wales under C.P.R. r.54.14(a).

Applicant seeking to rely on additional grounds

32. The applicant may not rely on any grounds, other than those grounds on which the applicant obtained permission for the judicial review proceedings, without the consent of the Upper Tribunal.

1B.76

DEFINITIONS

"applicant"—see r.1(3).
"judicial review proceedings"—*ibid.*
"permission"—*ibid.*

GENERAL NOTE

This rule is based on the procedure in the Administrative Court in England and Wales under C.P.R. r.54.15.

Right to make representations

33. Each party and, with the permission of the Upper Tribunal, any other person, may—

1B.77

(a) submit evidence, except at the hearing of an application for permission;
(b) make representations at any hearing which they are entitled to attend; and
(c) make written representations in relation to a decision to be made without a hearing.

DEFINITIONS

"hearing"—see r.1(3).
"party"—*ibid.*
"permission"—*ibid.*

GENERAL NOTE

This rule is based on the procedure in the Administrative Court in England and Wales under C.P.R. rr.54.14(b) and 54, 17.

PART 5

HEARINGS

Decision with or without a hearing

34.—(1) Subject to paragraph (2), the Upper Tribunal may make any decision without a hearing.

1B.78

(2) The Upper Tribunal must have regard to any view expressed by a party when deciding whether to hold a hearing to consider any matter, and the form of any such hearing.

DEFINITIONS

"hearing"—see r.1(3).
"party"—*ibid.*

GENERAL NOTE

This rule replaces reg.23 of the Social Security Commissioners (Procedure) Regs 1999. Regulation 23(2) specifically sated that, where a request for a hearing was made by a party, "the Commissioner shall grant the request unless he is satisfied that the proceedings can properly be determined without a hearing" but the absence of a similar provision in this rule may well make no difference because a refusal of a request for a hearing must be for a good reason. In practice, requests by unrepresented claimants are often refused because the judge is prepared to decide the case in favour of the claimant or because they are made specifically for the purpose of giving evidence in circumstances where the appeal lies on a point of law in respect of which it is clear the claimant will be unable to provide any assistance. It will normally be appropriate to give a written reason for refusing a request for an oral hearing (see r.40(4)). A direction as to whether there will be a hearing falls within the scope of r.5 (see r.5(3)(f)) and so the provisions of r.6 apply. A person applying for permission to appeal to the Upper Tribunal should indicate whether he or she wants the application to be determined at a hearing (see r.21(4)(f)), which is particularly important in social security cases where there is no right to renew orally an application refused on paper. A respondent should indicate whether or not he or she wishes there to be an oral hearing when submitting a response to an appeal or reference (see r.24(3)(f)) and the appellant is usually asked by the Upper Tribunal to do so when replying, although there is no specific provision to that effect in r.25.

Entitlement to attend a hearing

1B.79   **35.** Subject to rule 37(4) (exclusion of a person from a hearing), each party is entitled to attend a hearing.

DEFINITIONS

"hearing"—see r.1(3).
"party"—*ibid.*

GENERAL NOTE

This rule, which reproduces the effect of reg.4(6)(a) to (ff) of the Social Security Commissioners (Procedure) Regs 1999, makes it plain that, except where r.37(4) applies, a party may always attend a hearing even when the hearing is in private. By virtue of r.11(3) a properly appointed representative also has a right to attend a hearing, whether or not the party does so. By virtue of r.11(5), a party who attends a hearing may be accompanied by a person acting as a representative or assistant.

Notice of hearings

1B.80   **36.**—(1) The Upper Tribunal must give each party entitled to attend a hearing reasonable notice of the time and place of the hearing (including any adjourned or postponed hearing) and any change to the time and place of the hearing.

(2) The period of notice under paragraph (1) must be at least 14 days except that—

(a) in applications for permission to bring judicial review proceedings, the period of notice must be at least 2 working days; and

(b) the Upper Tribunal may give shorter notice—

(i) with the parties' consent; or

(ii) in urgent or exceptional cases.

DEFINITIONS

"hearing"—see r.1(3).
"judicial review proceedings"—*ibid.*
"party"—*ibid.*
"permission"—*ibid.*
"working day"—*ibid.*

GENERAL NOTE

This rule replaces reg.24(2) and (3) of the Social Security Commissioners (Procedure) Regs 1999, which was to similar effect.

Public and private hearings

37.—(1) Subject to the following paragraphs, all hearings must be held in public.   **1B.81**

(2) The Upper Tribunal may give a direction that a hearing, or part of it, is to be held in private.

(3) Where a hearing, or part of it, is to be held in private, the Upper Tribunal may determine who is entitled to attend the hearing or part of it.

(4) The Upper Tribunal may give a direction excluding from any hearing, or part of it—

(a) any person whose conduct the Upper Tribunal considers is disrupting or is likely to disrupt the hearing;

(b) any person whose presence the Upper Tribunal considers is likely to prevent another person from giving evidence or making submissions freely;

(c) any person who the Upper Tribunal considers should be excluded in order to give effect to a direction under rule 14(2) (withholding information likely to cause harm); or

(d) any person where the purpose of the hearing would be defeated by the attendance of that person.

(5) The Upper Tribunal may give a direction excluding a witness from a hearing until that witness gives evidence.

DEFINITION

"hearing"—see r.1(3).

GENERAL NOTE

Paras (1) and (2)

These paragraphs replace reg.24(5) of the Social Security Commissioners (Procedure) Regs 1999. Paragraph (1) expresses the general rule, which is that hearings should usually be in public. Paragraph (2) enables the Upper Tribunal to direct that a particular case be heard in private, either in whole or in part. Although it does not specifically provide that a hearing may take place in public only for "special reasons", as reg.24(5) did, the same considerations will still apply (see the note to r.30(3) of the Tribunal Procedure (First-tier Tribunal) (Social Entitlement Chamber) Rules 2008, above). As in the First-tier Tribunal, this does not arise as a live issue very often because it is very rare for members of the general public to attend hearings.

Where someone does attend, concerns raised by a party can often be met by the imposition of appropriate reporting restrictions under r.14(1).

Para. (3)

If a case is to be heard in private, the tribunal has a broad power to determine who may attend it. However, certain people have a right to attend a hearing even if it is in private. By r.35, a party always has a right to be present (subject to r.37(4)) and, the consequence is that, by virtue of r.11(3), so does a properly appointed representative whether the party attends or not. Where a party does attend, he or she may be accompanied by a person acting either as a representative or merely as an assistant (see r.11(5)). Plainly relevant witnesses must be allowed to attend for the purpose of giving evidence. By virtue of para.22 of Sch.7 to the Tribunals, Courts and Enforcement Act 2007, a member of the Administrative Justice and Tribunals Council, or its Scottish Committee or Welsh Committee, also has a right to attend any hearing.

Beyond that, it is all a matter of discretion, as it was under reg.24(6)(g) of the Social Security Commissioners (Procedure) Regs 1999. See the note to r.30(4) of the Tribunal Procedure (First-tier Tribunal) (Social Entitlement Chamber) Rules 2008, above.

Paras (4) and (5)

See the notes to r.30(5) and (6) of the Tribunal Procedure (First-tier Tribunal) (Social Entitlement Chamber) Rules 2008, above.

Hearings in a party's absence

1B.82   **38.** If a party fails to attend a hearing, the Upper Tribunal may proceed with the hearing if the Upper Tribunal—

   (a) is satisfied that the party has been notified of the hearing or that reasonable steps have been taken to notify the party of the hearing; and

   (b) considers that it is in the interests of justice to proceed with the hearing.

DEFINITIONS

   "hearing"—see r.1(3).
   "party"—*ibid.*

GENERAL NOTE

This reproduces the effect of reg.24(4) of the Social Security Commissioners (Procedure) Regs 1999.

PART 6

DECISIONS

Consent orders

39.—(1) The Upper Tribunal may, at the request of the parties but only if it considers it appropriate, make a consent order disposing of the proceedings and making such other appropriate provision as the parties have agreed.

(2) Notwithstanding any other provision of these Rules, the Tribunal need not hold a hearing before making an order under paragraph (1), or provide reasons for the order.

1B.83

DEFINITIONS

"hearing"—see r.1(3).
"party"—*ibid.*

GENERAL NOTE

This rule may not have a great deal of relevance to social security cases because it is concerned with cases where there needs to be an "order" and where "other appropriate provision" may need to be made and it applies only "at the request of the parties". Where the parties are agreed as to the outcome of a social security case before the Upper Tribunal, it is usually sufficient for the judge to give a decision to that effect under r.40, which may be given without reasons if the parties consent.

Decisions

40.—(1) The Upper Tribunal may give a decision orally at a hearing.

(2) Subject to rule 14(2) (withholding harmful information), the Upper Tribunal must provide to each party as soon as reasonably practicable after making a decision which finally disposes of all issues in the proceedings (except a decision under Part 7)—

(a) a decision notice stating the Tribunal's decision; and
(b) notification of any rights of review or appeal against the decision and the time and manner in which such rights of review or appeal may be exercised.

(3) The Upper Tribunal must provide written reasons for its decision with a decision notice provided under paragraph (2)(a) unless—

(a) the decision was made with the consent of the parties; or
(b) the parties have consented to the Upper Tribunal not giving written reasons.

(4) The Tribunal may provide written reasons for any decision to which paragraph (2) does not apply.

1B.84

DEFINITIONS

"hearing"—see r.1(3).
"party"—*ibid.*

GENERAL NOTE

This rule largely reproduces the effect of reg.28 of the Social Security Commissioners (Procedure) Regs 1999 (see the note to that provision at p.529 of Vol.III of the main work). However, note the insertion of the requirement to provide the decision provided "as soon as reasonably practicable". Presumably the clause "finally disposes of all issues in the proceedings" includes a decision to strike proceedings out under r.8 but does not include a refusal of permission to appeal, a refusal of permission to apply for judicial review or summary dismissal of judicial review proceedings, in respect of all of which specific provision is made (see rr.22(1), 30(1)(b) and 30(2)(b)). In any event, it is usually good practice to provide reasons for any decision (where they may not be obvious to the parties adversely affected by the decision) and para.(4) makes specific provision for that to be done.

PART 7

CORRECTING, SETTING ASIDE, REVIEWING AND APPEALING DECISIONS OF THE UPPER TRIBUNAL

Interpretation

1B.85   **41.** In this Part—
"appeal" means the exercise of a right of appeal under section 13 of the 2007 Act; and
"review" means the review of a decision by the Upper Tribunal under section 10 of the 2007 Act.

DEFINITION

"the 2007 Act"—see r.1(3).

GENERAL NOTE

This definition of "appeal" presumably does not apply where that word is used in r.44(2).

Clerical mistakes and accidental slips or omissions

1B.86   **42.** The Upper Tribunal may at any time correct any clerical mistake or other accidental slip or omission in a decision or record of a decision by—
   (a) sending notification of the amended decision, or a copy of the amended record, to all parties; and
   (b) making any necessary amendment to any information published in relation to the decision or record.

DEFINITION

"party"—see r.1(3).

GENERAL NOTE

This rule replaces reg.30 of the Social Security Commissioners (Procedure) Regs 1999. For comments, see the note to reg.56 of the Social Security and

Child Support (Decisions and Appeals) Regs 1999, the equivalent provision relating to appeal tribunals, at p.657 of Vol.III of the main work. Note that a separate power to correct a decision arises on review (see s.10(4)(a) of the Tribunals, Courts and Enforcement Act 2007).

Setting aside a decision which disposes of proceedings

43.—(1) The Upper Tribunal may set aside a decision which disposes   **1B.87**
of proceedings, or part of such a decision, and re-make the decision or the relevant part of it, if—

  (a) the Upper Tribunal considers that it is in the interests of justice to do so; and

  (b) one or more of the conditions in paragraph (2) are satisfied.

  (2) The conditions are—

  (a) a document relating to the proceedings was not sent to, or was not received at an appropriate time by, a party or a party's representative;

  (b) a document relating to the proceedings was not sent to the Upper Tribunal at an appropriate time;

  (c) a party, or a party's representative, was not present at a hearing related to the proceedings; or

  (d) there has been some other procedural irregularity in the proceedings.

  (3) A party applying for a decision, or part of a decision, to be set aside under paragraph (1) must make a written application to the Upper Tribunal so that it is received no later than 1 month after the date on which the Tribunal sent notice of the decision to the party.

DEFINITIONS

  "dispose of proceedings"—see r.1(3).
  "document"—*ibid.*
  "hearing"—*ibid.*
  "party"—*ibid.*

GENERAL NOTE

This rule replaces reg.31 of the Social Security Commissioners (Procedure) Regs 1999. See the note to that provision at pp.530–531 of Vol.III of the main work. However, note that para.(2)(d) provides an additional ground for setting aside a decision so that any "procedural irregularity" giving rise to injustice may lead to a decision being set aside. This reintroduces a ground formerly available in reg.31(1)(c) but removed in 2005 due to doubts about its validity. There can be no doubt about the validity of the new provision, given the terms of para.15(2)(d) of Sch.5 to the Tribunals, Courts and Enforcement Act 2007. The one-month time limit for making an application may be extended under r.5(3)(a). Note that a separate power to set aside a decision arises on review (see s.10(4)(c) of the 2007 Act).

Application for permission to appeal

44.—(1) A person seeking permission to appeal must make a written   **1B.88**
application to the Upper Tribunal for permission to appeal.

  (2) Paragraph (3) applies to an application under paragraph (1) in respect of a decision—

(a) on an appeal against a decision in a social security and child support case (as defined in the Tribunal Procedure (First-tier Tribunal) (Social Entitlement Chamber) Rules 2008(**20**));

(b) on an appeal against a decision in proceedings in the War Pensions and Armed Forces Compensation Chamber of the First-tier Tribunal(**21**); or

(c) in proceedings under the Forfeiture Act 1982.

(3) Where this paragraph applies, the application must be sent or delivered to the Upper Tribunal so that it is received within 3 months after the date on which the Upper Tribunal sent to the person making the application—

(a) written notice of the decision;

(b) notification of amended reasons for, or correction of, the decision following a review; or

(c) notification that an application for the decision to be set aside has been unsuccessful.

(4) Where paragraph (3) does not apply, an application under paragraph (1) must be sent or delivered to the Upper Tribunal so that it is received within 1 month after the latest of the dates on which the Upper Tribunal sent to the person making the application—

(a) written reasons for the decision;

(b) notification of amended reasons for, or correction of, the decision following a review; or

(c) notification that an application for the decision to be set aside has been unsuccessful.

(5) The date in paragraph (3)(c) or (4)(c) applies only if the application for the decision to be set aside was made within the time stipulated in rule 43 (setting aside a decision which disposes of proceedings) or any extension of that time granted by the Upper Tribunal.

(6) If the person seeking permission to appeal provides the application to the Upper Tribunal later than the time required by paragraph (3) or (4), or by any extension of time under rule 5(3)(a) (power to extend time)—

(a) the application must include a request for an extension of time and the reason why the application notice was not provided in time; and

(b) unless the Upper Tribunal extends time for the application under rule 5(3)(a) (power to extend time) the Upper Tribunal must refuse the application.

(7) An application under paragraph (1) must—

(a) identify the decision of the Tribunal to which it relates;

(b) identify the alleged error or errors of law in the decision; and

(c) state the result the party making the application is seeking.

DEFINITIONS

"appeal"—see r.41.
"dispose of proceedings"—see r.1(3).
"party"—*ibid*.
"permission"—*ibid*.

GENERAL NOTE

This rule replaces reg.33 of the Social Security Commissioners (Procedure) Regs 1999. Paragraph (3), which prescribes a three-month time limit, applies to social security cases, rather than para.(4). This generous time-limit existed under the earlier legislation because it is commonly only at this stage that parties, including the Secretary of State, HMRC and local authorities first seek legal advice.

However, one important difference is that para.(6)(b) uses the word "refuse", from which it follows that a decision by the Upper Tribunal not to extend the time for applying for permission to appeal does not prevent the applicant from applying to the appellate court for permission, although the appellate court will, of course, have regard to the delay in applying to the Upper Tribunal. This is because the condition in s.13(5) of the Tribunals, Courts and Enforcement Act 2007 (that permission have been "refused" by the Upper Tribunal before an application may be made to the appellate court) will have been satisfied. Thus, the effect of *White v Chief Adjudication Officer* [1986] 2 All E.R. 905 (also reported as an appendix to *R(S) 8/85*) has at last been reversed. In *White*, it had been held that a Commissioner's refusal to extend time for applying for leave to appeal to the Court of Appeal did not amount to a refusal of leave to appeal and was challengeable only by way of an application for judicial review.

Upper Tribunal's consideration of application for permission to appeal

45.—(1) On receiving an application for permission to appeal the Upper Tribunal may review the decision in accordance with rule 46 (review of a decision), but may only do so if—   **1B.89**

    (a) when making the decision the Upper Tribunal overlooked a legislative provision or binding authority which could have had a material effect on the decision; or

    (b) since the Upper Tribunal's decision, a court has made a decision which is binding on the Upper Tribunal and which, had it been made before the Upper Tribunal's decision, could have had a material effect on the decision.

(2) If the Upper Tribunal decides not to review the decision, or reviews the decision and decides to take no action in relation to the decision or part of it, the Upper Tribunal must consider whether to give permission to appeal in relation to the decision or that part of it.

(3) The Upper Tribunal must send a record of its decision to the parties as soon as practicable.

(4) If the Upper Tribunal refuses permission to appeal it must send with the record of its decision—

    (a) a statement of its reasons for such refusal; and

    (b) notification of the right to make an application to the relevant appellate court for permission to appeal and the time within which, and the method by which, such application must be made.

(5) The Upper Tribunal may give permission to appeal on limited grounds, but must comply with paragraph (4) in relation to any grounds on which it has refused permission.

DEFINITIONS

"appeal"—see r.41.
"permission"—see r.1(3).
"party"—*ibid*.
"review"—see r.41.

GENERAL NOTE

Paras (1) and (2)
Before deciding whether or not to grant permission to appeal, the Upper Tribunal must first decide whether or not to review the decision under s.10 of the Tribunals, Courts and Enforcement Act 2007, as limited by para.(1). A decision may be reviewed only if the judge overlooked an important piece of legislation or case law or superior court has since made a decision that suggests that the decision of the Upper Tribunal was wrong. The word "could" is used, which perhaps suggests that the Upper Tribunal might set aside a decision before hearing full argument rather than obtaining representations before deciding whether or not the decision should be reviewed.

Para. (4)
Reasons for refusing permission to appeal can usually be very brief and will often simply be that the application does not raise any point of law or does not raise an important point of principle and practice, as required by the Order made under s.13(6) of the 2007 Act (see the supplementary note to that provision in Pt IV below), or that a new point of law would not have persuaded the judge to reach a different conclusion. Reasons can be valuable in persuading an applicant not to make an application to the appellate court in a hopeless case. If an application raises allegations about the conduct of the Upper Tribunal, it is likely to assist the court if the Upper Tribunal makes it clear whether it disputes the accuracy of the allegations.

Review of a decision

1B.90   **46.**—(1) The Upper Tribunal may only undertake a review of a decision—

(a) pursuant to rule 45(1) (review on an application for permission to appeal); or

(b) pursuant to rule 47 (reviews of decisions in proceedings under the Forfeiture Act 1982).

(2) The Upper Tribunal must notify the parties in writing of the outcome of any review and of any rights of review or appeal in relation to the outcome.

(3) If the Upper Tribunal decides to take any action in relation to a decision following a review without first giving every party an opportunity to make representations, the notice under paragraph (2) must state that any party that did not have an opportunity to make representations may apply for such action to be set aside and for the decision to be reviewed again.

DEFINITIONS

"appeal"—see r.41.
"party"—see r.1(3).
"review"—see r.41.

GENERAL NOTE

Para. (1)

The power of review arises under s.10(1) of the Tribunals, Courts and Enforcement Act 2007. Section 10(2) provides for the power to be exercised either on the tribunal's initiative or on an application but s.10(3)(b) enables rules to provide that it is exercisable only on the Upper Tribunal's own initiative. That is what para.(1)(a) of this rule does. Except in a forfeiture case falling within r.47, a party may not make a free-standing application for a review (although if he or she does, the Upper Tribunal could presumably treat it as an application permission to appeal, despite the absence of an equivalent to r.41 of the Tribunal Procedure (First-tier Tribunal) (Social Entitlement Chamber) Rules 2008) but the Upper Tribunal may review a decision on its own initiative once there has been an application for permission to appeal. Rule 45(1), made under s.10(3)(d), limits the ground of review to cases where the Upper Tribunal overlooked a legislative provision or binding authority or there has since been a new binding authority. Since appeals under s.13 lie only on points of law, a review therefore provides a way of avoiding an appeal where the appeal would plainly be allowed or where the Upper Tribunal ought to deal with an overlooked issue before the question of permission to appeal is considered. See s.10(4), (5) and (6) for the powers of the Upper Tribunal on review.

Para. (2)

Section 13(8)(d) has the effect that there is no right of appeal against a decision whether or not to review a decision, to take no action on a review, to set aside a decision on a review or to refer, or not refer, a matter to the Upper Tribunal on review. However, that is because there is always another decision that may be the subject of an appeal. Where the Upper Tribunal refuses to review a decision or reviews it but takes no action, the Upper Tribunal must consider whether to give permission to appeal against the original decision. Where the tribunal reviews a decision and either takes action itself or refers it to the Upper Tribunal to be redecided, there will be a right to apply for permission to appeal against the new decision.

Where a decision is reviewed without all the parties having had the opportunity to make representations, notice must also be given of the right to apply for the new decision to be set aside (see para.(3)).

Para. (3)

The clear implication of this paragraph is that the Upper Tribunal may either obtain submissions from the parties other than the applicant before reviewing a case or review the case first and then wait to see whether any of the other parties objects. Plainly the second of those approaches may lead to a quicker decision and less work where there is no objection to the review. However, it is suggested that that approach is appropriate only where both the ground of review and the appropriate decision are very clear.

Review of a decision in proceedings under the Forfeiture Act 1982

47.—(1) A person who referred a question to the Upper Tribunal **1B.91** under rule 26 (references under the Forfeiture Act 1982) must refer the Upper Tribunal's previous decision in relation to the question to the Upper Tribunal if they—

(a) consider that the decision should be reviewed; or

(b) have received a written application for the decision to be reviewed from the person to whom the decision related.

(2) The Upper Tribunal may review the decision if—

(a) the decision was erroneous in point of law;

(b) the decision was made in ignorance of, or was based on a mistake as to, some material fact; or

(c) there has been a relevant change in circumstances since the decision was made.

(3) When a person makes the reference to the Upper Tribunal, they must also notify the person to whom the question relates that the reference has been made.

(4) The Upper Tribunal must notify the person who made the reference and the person who to whom the question relates of the outcome of the reference.

(5) If the Upper Tribunal decides to take any action in relation to a decision following a review under this rule without first giving the person who made the reference and the person to whom the question relates an opportunity to make representations, the notice under paragraph (4) must state that either of those persons who did not have an opportunity to make representations may apply for such action to be set aside and for the decision to be reviewed.

DEFINITION

"review"—see r.41.

GENERAL NOTE

Wide grounds of review are provided for in cases under the Forfeiture Act 1982, where the Upper Tribunal is the primary fact-finding body and there is no other mechanism for dealing with errors of fact that might have been made. This rule largely reproduces the effect of reg.15(2) and (3) of the Social Security Commissioners (Procedure) Regs 1999. The effect of paragraph (4) of reg.15 has not been reproduced and it is therefore merely left implicit that the Upper Tribunal may determine the date from which the review takes effect. Note that, by virtue of s.13(8)(d) of the Tribunals, Courts and Enforcement Act 2007, there is no right of appeal against a refusal to review an earlier decision or to take no action on a review and in some cases there may be no effective right of appeal against the original decision either, since such appeals are limited to points of law.

PART I

SECTION C

OTHER NEW LEGISLATION

Finance Act 2008, ss.114, 124

The Vaccine Damage Payments (Specified Disease) Order 2008

Finance Act 2008

(2008 c.9)

GENERAL NOTE

The Finance Act 2008 (Pt 7 and Sch.36) contains a range of measures 1C.2
bringing together and updating the previously separate powers of HMRC to deal
with its differing functions. Two new sections are included in this work because
they directly apply to record keeping for, and decision-making about, tax credits.
Changes have also been made by way of amendment to provisions in the Taxes
Management Act 1970, and those are set out below.

Computer records etc

114.—(1) This section applies to any enactment that, in connection 1C.3
with an HMRC matter—

(a) requires a person to produce a document or cause a document to
be produced,

(b) requires a person to permit the Commissioners or an officer of
Revenue and Customs—

    (i) to inspect a document, or

    (ii) to make or take copies of or extracts from or remove a
document,

(c) makes provision about penalties or offences in connection with the
production or inspection of documents, including in connection
with the falsification of or failure to produce or permit the inspection of documents, or

(d) makes any other provision in connection with a requirement mentioned in paragraph (a) or (b).

(2) An enactment to which this section applies has effect as if—

(a) any reference in the enactment to a document were a reference to
anything in which information of any description is recorded,
and

(b) any reference in the enactment to a copy of a document were a reference to anything onto which information recorded in the document has been copied, by whatever means and whether directly or indirectly.

(3) An authorised person may, at any reasonable time, obtain access to, and inspect and check the operation of, any computer and any associated apparatus or material which is or has been used in connection with a relevant document.

(4) In subsection (3) "relevant document" means a document that a person has been, or may be, required pursuant to an enactment to which this section applies—

(a) to produce or cause to be produced, or

(b) to permit the Commissioners or an officer of Revenue and Customs to inspect, to make or take copies of or extracts from or to remove.

(5) An authorised person may require—

(a) the person by whom or on whose behalf the computer is or has been so used, or

(b) any person having charge of, or otherwise concerned with the operation of, the computer, apparatus or material,

to provide the authorised person with such reasonable assistance as may be required for the purposes of subsection (3).

(6) Any person who—

(a) obstructs the exercise of a power conferred by this section, or

(b) fails to comply within a reasonable time with a requirement under subsection (5),

is liable to a penalty of £300.

(7) . . .

(8) . . .

(9) In this section—

"authorised person" means a person who is, or is a member of a class of persons who are, authorised by the Commissioners to exercise the powers under subsection (3),

"the Commissioners" means the Commissioners for Her Majesty's Revenue and Customs,

"enactment" includes an enactment contained in subordinate legislation (within the meaning of the Interpretation Act 1978),

"HMRC matter" means a matter in relation to which the Commissioners, or officers of Revenue and Customs, have a power or duty, and

"produce", in relation to a document, includes furnish, deliver and any other equivalent expression."

HMRC decisions etc: reviews and appeals

1C.4 **124.**—(1) The Treasury may by order made by statutory instrument make provision—

(a) for and in connection with reviews by the Commissioners, or by an officer of Revenue and Customs, of HMRC decisions, and

(b) in connection with appeals against HMRC decisions.

(2) An order under subsection (1) may, in particular, contain provision about—
- (a) the circumstances in which, or the time within which—
    - (i) a right to a review may be exercised, or
    - (ii) an appeal may be made, and
- (b) the circumstances in which, or the time at which, an appeal or review is, or may be treated as, concluded.

(3) An order under subsection (1) may, in particular, contain provision about the payment of sums by, or to, the Commissioners in cases where—
- (a) a right to a review is exercised, or
- (b) an appeal is made or determined.

(4) That includes provision about payment of sums where an appeal has been determined, but a further appeal may be or has been made, including provision—
- (a) requiring payments to be made,
- (b) enabling payments to be postponed, or
- (c) imposing conditions in connection with the making or postponement of payments.

(5) An order under subsection (1) may, in particular, contain provision about interest on any sum that is payable by, or to, the Commissioners in accordance with a decision made on the determination of an appeal.

(6) Provision under subsection (1) may be made by amending, repealing or revoking any provision of any Act or subordinate legislation (whenever passed or made, including this Act and any Act amended by it).

(7) An order under subsection (1) may—
- (a) provide that any provision contained in the order comes into force on a day appointed by an order of the Treasury made by statutory instrument (and may provide that different days may be appointed for different purposes),
- (b) contain incidental, supplemental, consequential, transitional, transitory and saving provision, and
- (c) make different provision for different purposes.

(8) A statutory instrument containing an order under subsection (1) may not be made unless a draft of it has been laid before and approved by resolution of the House of Commons.

(9) But if the order, or any other order under subsection (1) contained in the statutory instrument, is made in connection with a transfer of functions carried out under the Tribunals, Courts and Enforcement Act 2007, the statutory instrument may only be made if a draft of it has been laid before and approved by resolution of each House of Parliament.

(10) In this section—
- (a) references to appeals against HMRC decisions include any other kind of proceedings relating to an HMRC matter, and
- (b) references to the making, determination or conclusion of appeals are to be read accordingly.

(11) In this section—

"the Commissioners" means the Commissioners for Her Majesty's Revenue and Customs;

"HMRC decision" means—

    (a) any decision of the Commissioners relating to an HMRC matter, or

    (b) any decision of an officer of Revenue and Customs relating to an HMRC matter,

and references to an HMRC decision include references to anything done by such a person in connection with making such a decision or in consequence of such a decision;

"HMRC matter" means any matter connected with a function of the Commissioners or an officer of Revenue and Customs.

The Vaccine Damage Payments (Specified Disease) Order 2008

(SI 2008 No. 2103)

In force September 1, 2008

The Secretary of State for Work and Pensions makes the following Order in exercise of the powers conferred by sections 1(2)(i) and 2(2) of the Vaccine Damage Payments Act 1979.

Citation, commencement and interpretation

1.—(1) This Order may be cited as the Vaccine Damage Payments **1C.6** (Specified Disease) Order 2008 and shall come into force on 1st September 2008.

(2) In this Order, "the Act" means the Vaccine Damage Payments Act 1979.

Addition to the diseases to which the Act applies

2. Human papillomavirus is specified as a disease to which the Act **1C.7** applies.

Modification of conditions of entitlement

3. The condition of entitlement in section 2(1)(b) of the Act (age or **1C.8** time at which vaccination was carried out) shall be omitted in relation to vaccination against human papillomavirus.

PART II

UPDATING MATERIAL
VOLUME I

NON-MEANS TESTED BENEFITS

Commentary by

David Bonner

Ian Hooker

Robin White

p.4, *annotation to the Vaccine Damage Payments Act 1979, s.1(2)*
(payments to persons severely disabled by vaccination) (addition to list of
diseases)

With effect from September 1, 2008, human papillomavirus was 2.001
added to the list of diseases by the Vaccine Damage Payments (Specified
Disease) Order 2008 (SI 2008/2103). See Pt I for the text of the
Order.

p.8, *amendment to the Vaccine Damage Payments Act 1979, s.3A(1)*
(decisions reversing earlier decisions)

With effect from November 3, 2008, art.6 and Sch.3, para.31 of the 2.002
Transfer of Tribunal Functions Order 2008 (SI 2008/2833) amended
subs.(1) by replacing "an appeal tribunal" with "a tribunal".

p.8, *amendment to the Vaccine Damage Payments Act 1979, s.4 (appeals*
to appeal tribunals)

With effect from November 3, 2008, art.6 and Sch.3, para.32 of the 2.003
Transfer of Tribunal Functions Order 2008 (SI 2008/2833) amended
subs.(1) and (4) by substituting for the words "an appeal tribunal" the
words "the First-tier Tribunal". From the same date it deleted the whole
of para.(2)(b) and the "and" immediately before it.

p.10, *amendment to the Vaccine Damage Payments Act 1979, s.7A*
(correction of errors and setting aside of decisions)

With effect from November 3, 2008, art.6 and Sch.3, para.34 of the 2.004
Transfer of Tribunal Functions Order 2008 (SI 2008/2833) amended
subs.(1)(a) by replacing "3, 3A or 4" with "3 or 3A". From the same
date it deleted the whole of para.(1)(b) and the "and" immediately
before it. From that same date it also omitted from subs.(2) the words
"or set aside decisions".

p.11, *amendment to the Vaccine Damage Payments Act 1979*

At the foot of the page change "sections 10 and 11 omitted" to 2.005
"Sections 9A, 10 and 11 omitted".

p.12, *amendment to the Vaccine Damage Payments Act 1979, s.12(3)*
(financial provisions)

With effect from November 3, 2008, art.6 and Sch.3, para.34 of the 2.006
Transfer of Tribunal Functions Order 2008 (SI 2008/2833) amended
subs.(3) by omitting para.(b) completely and in para.(c) deleting "or
tribunal".

p.57, *annotation to Social Security Contributions and Benefits Act 1992, s.35 (correction to General Note)*

2.007   The references in para.2 of the General Note to August 2000 and to August 20, 2000 should be to April 2000 and to April 2, 2000.

p.61, *amendment to the Social Security Contributions and Benefits Act 1992, s.37 (widowed mother's allowance)*

2.008   With effect from October 7, 2008, s.37 was amended by s.50 of the Welfare Reform Act 2007, as follows:

in subs.(2) the words from "one of the conditions" to "person and" are omitted.

p.66, *amendment to the Social Security Contributions and Benefits Act 1992, s.39A (widowed parent's allowance)*

2.009   With effect from October 7, 2008, s.39A is amended by s.51 of the Welfare Reform Act 2007, as follows:

in subs.(3) the words from "one of the conditions" to "person and" are omitted.

pp.71–72, *annotation to the Social Security Contributions and Benefits Act 1992, s.39C: Scots marriage by habit and repute*

2.010   Modern social conditions do seem to be taking their toll on this form of marriage. In the case of *Vasilius* v *Vasilius* 2000 SCCR 679, the Lord Ordinary has prescribed seven requirements that must be satisfied. They are that:
(a) there must be cohabitation;
(b) the cohabitation must be as husband and wife;
(c) the cohabitation must be in Scotland;
(d) the cohabitation must be for a sufficient time;
(e) the parties must be reputed to be husband and wife;
(f) the repute must be sufficiently general;
(g) the parties must be free to marry each other.
Even if these requirements are satisfied the claim may yet fail if the presumption of tacit consent to marriage, which these requirements would supply, can be rebutted.

The difficulties that there may be in negotiating this tricky course can be illustrated by the decision of the Scottish Commissioners' in *CSG/648/2007*. There the couple had lived together in Scotland for many years. They were regarded by their families and by others (e.g. work colleagues) as living together as husband and wife (both of them wore wedding rings) and they spoke frequently of marrying at some time in the future. But after the male partner's death a claim for bereavement benefits failed for two reasons. First, although they were generally regarded as living in a stable relationship as if they were husband and wife, they were not reputed to *be* husband and wife, and therefore point

472

(e) above was not satisfied. Secondly, an expressed intention to marry in the future (the claimant had frequently said that she would "one day make an honest man of him") was inconsistent with a tacit consent to being already married and must therefore rebut the presumption. Given the modern attitude of couples to the matter of whether they are in fact married it seems unlikely that many will succeed in future to show that they are married by habit and repute, but it should be noted that this case may yet be taken to appeal.

p.72, *annotation to the Social Security Contributions and Benefits Act 1992, s.39C: proof of foreign marriage*

Proving the existence of a marriage that is claimed to have been celebrated in a foreign country may be difficult where there is, or was at the time, little formality in connection with the ceremony and no reliable records of marriages are maintained. For commentary regarding the correct approach to be adopted in such cases see the notes following s.48A.

2.011

p.90, *annotation to the Social Security Contributions and Benefits Act 1992, s.44: change of gender*

The effect of *Richards* has been considered further by a Tribunal of Commissioners in three cases, *CP/2862/2007, CP/1425/2007,* and *CSP/503/2007*. In those cases it was held that a claimant who has changed their gender (in all three cases a male to female change) could take advantage of the direct effect of the Directive only from the point at which she could have satisfied the conditions of the Gender Recognition Act had that act been in force at the time. Where that was so, the claimant was entitled to be treated in all respects equally to the way in which she would have been treated had she been, at the time, a natural woman. In the case of *CP/1425/2007* this meant, for example, that her retirement pension should have been increased by a period of deferment between the ages of 60 and 65 because she would have satisfied the conditions for gender reassignment in those years, notwithstanding Art. 10 of Sch.5 of the Gender Recognition Act 2004 which the Commissioners found to be in conflict with the Directive. In *CP/2862/2007*, on the other hand, the claim for deferment failed because the claimant had not shown compliance with the conditions necessary for a change of gender until after she had attained the age of 65, and so would not have been entitled any earlier to her retirement pension.

2.012

p.99, *annotation to the Social Security Contributions and Benefits Act 1992, s.48A: proof of foreign marriage*

In order to claim on the basis of the contribution record of a spouse (or civil partner) it will be necessary to show the existence of a marriage (or civil partnership). The difficulties associated with proof of some marriages have been demonstrated in *CP/4062/2004* and again in *CP/891/2008*. In both these cases the parties had been married in

2.013

Yemen from where no formal record of the marriage was available. Both parties to the marriage made statements about the celebration of the marriage and the wife, who had remained at all times in the Yemen, was interviewed there through an interpreter. Some of the information that was given about the marriage appeared to be contradictory. For that reason, and others, the claim for a Category B pension was refused. The interest in both of these cases lies in the approach taken by Commissioner Jacobs, and adopted in the later case by Deputy Commissioner Wikeley, to the absence of reliable documentary evidence of the marriage. In both cases the DM and the appeal tribunal had relied upon that absence, at least in part, as the reason for their decision that no marriage had been shown to exist. The commissioners find this to be a wrong approach. In the words of Commissioner Jacobs the absence of contemporary documentary evidence

> "is a neutral factor. The decision maker and the tribunal have to decide if the claimant is genuine or dishonest. It is wrong to approach that task by taking the lack of contemporaneous evidence as a factor against the claimant. To do so would be to assume what has to be decided."

p.114, *annotation to the Social Security Contributions and Benefits Act 1992, s.64: the day conditions for Attendance Allowance*

2.014   The limitations that these conditions impose are shown by the decision in *CA/2574/2007*. The claimant was a widow who was agoraphobic, anorexic and depressed and had lived as a recluse since the death of her husband. She was visited daily by her daughter who supplied all her physical needs and remained each day for a period of several hours to stimulate and encourage her mother. A report by a consultant psychiatrist suggested that the claimant was being kept alive by the services and the visits of her daughter. This much was accepted as true by the commissioner, but still could not qualify her for AA. The services such as shopping and housekeeping supplied by the daughter could not qualify as they were not sufficiently "personal" (see notes that follow s.72) and, although the commissioner was prepared to accept that the time spent stimulating her mother might qualify as attention in connection with the bodily functioning of the brain, it was neither "frequent" nor "continual" throughout the day so as to satisfy the conditions of subs.(2). Had the claimant been able to claim DLA (she could not because of her age) she might have succeeded in a claim for the lowest rate of that benefit on the basis that the attention was for a "significant portion of the day".

p.139, *annotation to the Social Security Contributions and Benefits Act 1992, s.72: activity of the brain as a bodily function.*

2.015   The activity of the brain as a bodily function was considered by Commissioner Mesher in *CA/2574/2007*. The claimant was an elderly widow who suffered from agoraphobia, anorexia and depression and had

474

lived as a recluse since the death of her husband three years earlier. She was visited daily by her daughter who, in addition to taking care of all her mother's physical needs by way of shopping housekeeping etc., also spent several hours each day providing stimulation and encouragement to her mother. The Commissioner allowed an appeal against the decision of a tribunal, who had failed to consider the latter involvement as attention in connection the bodily function of brain activity, though he then went on to reject the claim in entering his own decision on the ground that she could not satisfy the more restricted requirements for AA. A claim for DLA at lowest rate (had she been younger) might have been successful.

p.147, *annotation to the Social Security Contributions and Benefits Act 1992, s.72: the cooking test*

The time taken by the claimant over preparing a meal may also be relevant in deciding whether they are capable of cooking themselves a meal (*CDLA/4051/2007*). But this too, must now be taken to be a matter of judgment for a tribunal to say whether a claimant can fairly be described as capable, and a strategy of resting between stages of meal preparation has been adopted as a sensible and acceptable mode of preparing a meal. 2.016

p.162, *annotation to the Social Security Contributions and Benefits Act 1992, s.73(1) (inability to walk throughout the relevant period)*

Note that the inability to walk or virtual inability to walk must exist throughout the period on which the claim is based. This has been interpreted, in *CDLA/496/2008*, as having the same meaning as the same words in s.72 have been given in *Secretary of State for Work and Pensions v Moyna* [2003] UKHL 44; [2003] 1 W.L.R. 1929; and *R(DLA) 7/03*. There, it was explained as being a matter of judgment, rather than arithmetical calculation, whether a person could fairly be described as being unable to cook themselves a main meal throughout the period in question, and the same will be said of their ability to walk. In this case the claimant suffered from epilepsy and sometimes had seizures when she was out walking. Commissioner Rowland held that her walking ability needed to be considered in three phases; one when she was out walking normally (for which she was entitled to mobility component at the lower rate because she needed to be supervised in case she had a seizure); another when she was unable to walk immediately after a seizure, and when she could benefit from facilities for enhanced locomotion by being transported home in a car; and thirdly when she needed to sleep for a period of hours and sometimes days, to recover after the seizure. During this third period he felt she could not benefit from enhanced locomotion because she needed to remain resting and usually asleep (see *subs.(8)*). On this basis it was only the relatively short period during which she was travelling home that could qualify for benefit at the higher rate (unable to walk), and this, even if repeated, was insufficient to constitute an inability to walk throughout the period. 2.017

p.163, *annotation to the Social Security Contributions and Benefits Act 1992, s.73*

2.018   *CSDLA/627/2007* has been reported as *R (DLA) 2/08.*

p.164, *annotation to the Social Security Contributions and Benefits Act 1992, s.73: ability to walk without guidance or supervision*

2.019   Evidence as to whether a claimant has need of guidance or supervision can be derived in a number of ways. In *R1/07(DLA)* the commissioner in Northern Ireland held that evidence of the claimant's ability to drive a motor car, was properly accepted as showing the claimant's "clear headedness and competency" which could be relevant to that aspect of her ability to walk on an unfamiliar route without the need for guidance or supervision.

p.169, *annotation to the Social Security Contributions and Benefits Act 1992, s.73(8)*

2.020   See also, *CDLA/496/2008* discussed above in the update to p.162 (s.73(1)).

p.186, *amendment to the Social Security Contributions and Benefits Act 1992, s.88 (increase in respect of only one adult dependant)*

2.021   Section 28 and Sch.3, para.9(7) of the Welfare Reform Act 2007 amended s.88 with effect from October 27, 2008 by substituting the number "85" for the number "86A".

p.187, *amendment to the Social Security Contributions and Benefits Act 1992, s.89 (Earnings to include, etc.)*

2.022   Section 28 and Sch.3, para. 9(8) of the Welfare Reform Act 2007 amended s.89(1) and (1A) with effect from October 27, 2008 to read as follows:

> "(1) Except as may be prescribed, in sections 82 to 85 above any reference to earnings includes a reference to payments by way of occupational or personal pension.
> (1A) Except as may be prescribed, in sections 82 to 85 above, and in regulations under section 86A above, any reference to earnings includes a reference to payments by way of PPF periodic payments."

pp.205–207, *annotation to the Social Security Contributions and Benefits Act 1992, s.94(1) (accident arising out of and in the course of employment)*

2.023   In *CI/1654/2008*, Commissioner Jacobs considered the case of an employee who slipped and was injured while showering at an hotel before attending training session there. He held that the accident befell

476

her when in the course of her employment; her actions in making herself presentable were reasonably incidental to her duties and she was where she was because of her work. But it did not arise "out" of the employment:

"The risk was not created by her employment. It was inherent in the nature of a shower. It was a risk that anyone would run who took a shower. Indeed, it was not limited to the shower. There was a similar risk in the bathroom outside the shower. The claimant's employment did not expose her to any hazard that was additional to, or exceptional when compared with, the risk that anyone else would run who was taking a shower or using a hotel bathroom" (paras 36, 37).

Nor did SSCBA 1992, s.101 operate so as to treat this accident arising in the course of employment as also arising out of it; there was "no evidence that the accident was caused by someone else's misconduct, skylarking or negligence" (para.28).

pp.221–222, *annotation to the Social Security Contributions and Benefits Act 1992, s.101 (accident caused by another's misconduct, etc)*

For a rare case where this was considered, see *CI/1654/2008*, noted in 2.024
the update to pp.205–207.

pp.234–237, *annotation to the Social Security Contributions and Benefits Act 1992, s.113 (general provisions as to disqualification and suspension)*

For a decision of the Administrative Court on the legibility of post-tariff life prisoners to income support on transfer from prison to a mental health hospital, see *R (RD and PM) v Secretary of State for Work and Pensions,* [2008] EWHC 2635 (Admin), which confirmed that there was no such entitlement.

p.253, *annotation to the Social Security Contributions and Benefits Act 1992, s.147 (Interpretation of Part IX, etc.).*

CF/2871/2007 has been reported as *R(F) 1/08.*   2.025

pp.281–283, *annotation to the Social Security Contributions and Benefits Act 1992, Sch.3 Contributions matters: a division of responsibility)*

In *CIB/3542/1997*, Commissioner Williams set out the proper proce- 2.026
dure for determining issues in a dispute about the application of the Social Security (Earnings Factor) Regulations 1979 to a claim for incapacity benefit:

"(a) It is for the National Insurance Contributions Office of Her Majesty's Revenue and Customs to decide any question about the contribution record of a claimant for incapacity benefit.
(b) Any challenge to that decision on either an issue of fact or a question of law goes to a tax tribunal, not a social security tribunal. If an appeal involving a question about a claimant's

contributions comes before a social security tribunal, then the social security tribunal must apply regulation 38A of the Social Security and Child Support (Decisions and Appeals) Regulations 1999. This requires it to adjourn the appeal and refer the matter to the Secretary of State for onward reference to Her Majesty's Revenue and Customs for decision. The tribunal may decide the appeal only after a decision has been received from Her Majesty's Revenue and Customs.

(c) It is for the Secretary of State for Work and Pensions to decide any question about the interpretation and application of the Social Security (Earnings Factor) Regulations 1979 to the individual contribution record of any claimant for incapacity benefit.

(d) If a claimant disputes the decision of the Secretary of State on any issue of fact or law arising under the 1979 Regulations, then that dispute is to be decided by a social security tribunal. This includes any dispute about calculating the earnings factor attributable to a claimant under those regulations. If necessary, it is the task of the tribunal itself to check any disputed calculations" (para.7).

p.333, *annotation to the Social Security Contributions and Benefits Act 1992, Sch.10 (priority between persons entitled to child benefit).*

2.027   *CF/2871/2007* has been reported as *R(F) 1/08.*

pp.367–368, *amendment to the Social Security Act 1998, s.79 (Regulations and orders)*

2.028   With effect from November 3, 2008, art.6 and Sch.3, para.168 of the Transfer of Tribunal Functions Order 2008 (SI 2008/2833) amended subs.(1) by deleting the words from the beginning to "to this Act," and substituting for them the words "Subject to subsection (2A) below,". It also deleted subss.(2) and (9).

p.376, *annotation to the Gender Recognition Act 2004, Sch.5 Art.7 (Category A retirement Pension)*

2.029   Note that although *Art.7(1)* provides that any question of entitlement, and if so the rate of entitlement, is to be decided as if the person's acquired gender had always been their gender, this is subject to an exception in *para.(4)* that covers the payment and crediting of contributions, and the treatment of earnings that have been made before the change of gender. In *CP/98/2007* the claimant was over 65 at the time she changed her gender from male to female. The DM decided that the contributions she had made between the ages of 60 and 65, when she was a man, should not be included in calculating her additional state pension, but the commissioner allowed her appeal on the basis of the exception provided by *para.(4)*

p.385, *amendment to the Social Security (Credits) Regulations 1975, reg.2(1)(benefit)*

With effect from October 27, 2008 reg.48(2)(a) of the Employment   2.030
and Support Allowance (Consequential Provisions) (No.2) Regulations
2008 (SI 2008/1554) amended the definition of "benefit" in reg.2(1) to
read:

> ""benefit" includes a contribution-based jobseeker's allowance but
> not an income-based jobseeker's allowance [and includes a contribu-
> tory employment and support allowance but not an income-related
> employment and support allowance;]".

p.386, *Social Security (Credits) Regulations 1975, reg.2(1) (insertion of
new definitions and amendments of others)*

With effect from October 27, 2008 reg.48(2) of the Employment and   2.031
Support Allowance (Consequential Provisions) (No.2) Regulations 2008
(SI 2008/1554) inserted a number of new definitions and effected a
number of amendments:
Paragraph (2)(b) inserted after the definition of "contribution-based
jobseeker's allowance":

> ""contributory employment and support allowance" means a contrib-
> utory allowance under Part 1 of the Welfare Reform Act (employment
> and support allowance);".

Paragraph (2)(c) inserted after the definition of "income-based jobseeker's allowance":

> ""income-related employment and support allowance" means an
> income-related allowance under Part 1 of the Welfare Reform Act
> (employment and support allowance);".

Paragraph (2)(f) inserted after the definition of "relevant past year":

> ""the Welfare Reform Act" means the Welfare Reform Act 2007;".

Paragraph (2)(d) amended the definition of "reckonable year" by omitting the "or" at the end of para.(a) and inserting after para.(b) the
words

> "or
> (c) in relation to a contributory employment and support allow-
>   ance, the condition specified in paragraph 2(1) of Schedule 1 to
>   the Welfare Reform Act (conditions relating to national insur-
>   ance)."

Paragraph (2)(e) amended the definition of "reckonable year" by omitting the "and" at the end of para.(a) and inserting after para.(b) the
words:

"and
    (c) in relation to a contributory employment and support allow-
        ance, in paragraph 3(1)(f) of Schedule 1 to the Welfare Reform
        Act (conditions relating to national insurance);".

pp.387–388, *amendment to the Social Security (Credits) Regulations*
1975, reg.3(1) (general provisions relating to crediting)

2.032   With effect from October 27, 2008 reg.48(3) of the Employment and
Support Allowance (Consequential Provisions) (No.2) Regulations 2008
(SI 2008/1554) amended reg.3(1) to read:

"(1) Any contributions or earnings credited in accordance with
these Regulations shall be only for the purpose of enabling the person
concerned to satisfy—
    (a) in relation to short-term incapacity benefit, widowed mother's
        allowance, widowed parent's allowance, bereavement allow-
        ance, widow's pension or Category A or Category B retirement
        pension, the second contribution condition specified in relation
        to that benefit in Schedule 3 to the Contributions and Benefits
        Act; [. . .]
    (b) in relation to contribution-based jobseeker's allowance, the
        condition specified in section 2(1)(b) of the Jobseekers Act
        1995; [or
    (c) in relation to a contributory employment and support allow-
        ance, the condition specified in paragraph 2(1) of Schedule 1 to
        the Welfare Reform Act,]
and accordingly, where under any of the provisions of these Regulations a person would, but for this paragraph, be entitled to be credited
with any contributions or earnings for a year, or in respect of any week
in a year, he shall be so entitled for the purposes of any benefit only if
and to no greater extent than that by which his relevant earnings factor
for that year falls short of the level required to make that year a
reckonable year."

p.397, *amendment to the Social Security (Credits) Regulations 1975,*
reg.8(1) (Credits on termination of full-time education, training or
apprenticeship)

2.033   With effect from October 27, 2008 reg.48(4) of the Employment and
Support Allowance (Consequential Provisions) (No.2) Regulations 2008
(SI 2008/1554) amended reg.8(1) by deleting "or short term incapacity
benefit" and substituting ", short-term incapacity benefit or a contributory employment and support allowance".

p.399, *amendment to the Social Security (Credits) Regulations 1975,*
reg.8A(2)(c) (Credits for unemployment)

2.034   With effect from October 27, 2008 reg.48(5) of the Employment and
Support Allowance (Consequential Provisions) (No.2) Regulations 2008

(SI 2008/1554) amended reg.8A(2)(c) by inserting after "incapable of work" the words "or had limited capability for work".

pp.402–403, *amendment to the Social Security (Credits) Regulations 1975, reg.8B (Credits for incapacity for work)*

With effect from October 27, 2008 reg.48(6) of the Employment and Support Allowance (Consequential Provisions) (No.2) Regulations 2008 (SI 2008/1554) amended the heading to reg.8B by inserting after "incapacity for work" the words "or limited capability for work". It also amended reg.8B(2) by deleting the "or" at the end of sub-para.(a) and inserting: 2.035

"(aa) a week in which, in relation to the person concerned, each of the days—
   (i) was a day of limited capability for work for the purposes of Part 1 of the Welfare Reform Act (limited capability for work) or would have been such a day had that person been entitled to an employment and support allowance by virtue of section 1 of the Welfare Reform Act; or
   (ii) would have been such a day had the person concerned claimed an employment and support allowance or maternity allowance within the prescribed time; or".

p.404, *amendment to the Social Security (Credits) Regulations 1975, reg.8C(1) (Credits on termination of bereavement benefits)*

With effect from October 27, 2008 reg.48(7) of the Employment and Support Allowance (Consequential Provisions) (No.2) Regulations 2008 (SI 2008/1554) amended reg.8C(1) by deleting the "or" at the end of para (a) and inserting after para (b) the words: 2.036

"or
   (c) paragraph 2(1) of Schedule 1 to the Welfare Reform Act in relation to a contributory employment and support allowance.".

p.418, *amendments to the Social Security (Benefit) (Married Women and Widows Special Provisions) Regulations 1974, reg.3*

With effect from October 27, 2008 reg.64(3)(a) of the Employment and Support Allowance (Consequential Provisions) (No.2) Regulations 2008 (SI 2008/1554) amended the heading to reg.3 by inserting after "short-term incapacity benefit" the words ", contributory employment and support allowance". 2.037

From the same date, reg.64(3)(b) of those Regs amended reg.3(1)(a) and (b) by inserting after "the Act" in each of these sub-paragraphs the words "or, in relation to contributory employment and support allowance, she shall be deemed to have satisfied the first condition referred to in paragraph 1(1) of Schedule 1 to the Welfare Reform Act".

pp.419–420, *Social Security (Crediting and Treatment of Contributions, and National Insurance Numbers) Regulations 2001, reg.1(2) (insertion of new definitions and amendments of others)*

2.038   With effect from October 27, 2008 reg.49(2) of the Employment and Support Allowance (Consequential Provisions) (No.2) Regulations 2008 (SI 2008/1554) inserted a number of new definitions into and effected a number of amendments of reg.1(2):
Paragraph (b) inserted after the definition of "contributory benefit"

""contributory employment and support allowance" means a contributory allowance under Part 1 of the Welfare Reform Act (employment and support allowance);".

Paragraph (c) inserted after the definition of "earnings factor"

""income-related employment and support allowance" means an income-related allowance under Part 1 of the Welfare Reform Act (employment and support allowance);".

Paragraph (e) inserted after the definition of "relevant time"

""the Welfare Reform Act" means the Welfare Reform Act 2007;".

Paragraph (a) amended the definition of "contributory benefit" by inserting after "income-based jobseeker's allowance" the words "and includes a contributory employment and support allowance but not an income-related employment and support allowance".
Paragraph (d) amended the definition of "relevant benefit year" by adding after sub-para.(b)

"(c) paragraph 3(1)(f) of Schedule 1 to the Welfare Reform Act (conditions relating to national insurance), in relation to a contributory employment and support allowance."

With effect from November 3, 2008, art.6(1) and Sch.1, para.147 of the Tribunals, Courts and Enforcement Act 2007 (Transitional and Consequential Provisions) Order 2008 (SI 2008/2683) amended reg.1(3) by replacing "Commissioner" with ""the Upper Tribunal", and amended reg.1(4) by deleting the definition of "Commissioner".

p.422, *amendments to the Social Security (Crediting and Treatment of Contributions, and National Insurance Numbers) Regulations 2001), reg.4 (treatment for the purpose of any contributory benefit of late paid contributions)*

2.039   With effect from October 27, 2008 reg.49(3) of the Employment and Support Allowance (Consequential Provisions) (No.2) Regulations 2008 (SI 2008/1554) effected a number of amendments to reg.4:
Paragraph (a) substituted for "or short-term incapacity benefit" in reg. 4(8) the words ", short-term incapacity benefit or a contributory employment and support allowance".
Paragraph (b) inserted after reg.4(9)(b):

"(c) a contributory employment and support allowance is a reference to the condition specified in paragraph 2(1) of Schedule 1 to the Welfare Reform Act".

p.423, *amendments to the Social Security (Crediting and Treatment of Contributions, and National Insurance Numbers) Regulations 2001), reg.5 (treatment ... of late paid primary Class I contributions etc)*

With effect from October 27, 2008 reg.49(4) of the Employment and Support Allowance (Consequential Provisions) (No.2) Regulations 2008 (SI 2008/1554) effected a number of amendments to reg.5:
Paragraph (a) amended reg.5(1)(b) by deleting the "or" at the end of paragraph (i); and added after paragraph (ii)

"or
   (iii) a contributory employment and support allowance, is not paid before the beginning of the relevant benefit year,".

Paragraph (b) substituted for "or short-term incapacity benefit" in reg.5(2)(a) the words ", short-term incapacity benefit or a contributory employment and support allowance".
Paragraph (c) added after reg.5(3)(a)(ii)

"(iii) a contributory employment and support allowance is a reference to the condition specified in paragraph 1(1) of Schedule 1 to the Welfare Reform Act;".

p.424, *amendments to the Social Security (Crediting and Treatment of Contributions, and National Insurance Numbers) Regulations 2001), reg.5A (treatment ... of duly paid primary Class I contributions etc)*

With effect from October 27, 2008 reg.49(5) of the Employment and Support Allowance (Consequential Provisions) (No.2) Regulations 2008 (SI 2008/1554) amended reg.5A(a) by substituting for "or short-term incapacity benefit" the words ", short-term incapacity benefit or a contributory employment and support allowance".

p.440, *annotations to the Computation of Earnings Regulations 1996 reg.8 Calculation of weekly amount of earnings),*

CG/0607/2008 concerned the calculation of earnings in relation to the earnings limit for entitlement to a carer's allowance. This lengthy decision contains much useful comment and guidance on such cases, which seem to be a problematic area (perhaps because there is no taper—if a person's earnings are one penny over the limit, then entitlement to the carer's allowance ceases completely). The context was one in which an informal employment contract was intended to provided the appellant with earnings at but not above the earnings limit for entitlement to a carer's allowance. The appeal turned on the proper calculation of the appellant's weekly earnings. The Commissioner counsels care in looking at the definition provision in the regulations, and goes on to comment:

2.040

2.041

2.042

36. The Regulations have the primary purpose of identifying the weekly amount of a claimant's earnings. They provide answers to the questions necessary for the conversion of actual earnings of an employee into weekly amounts of earnings by which to test those earnings against the earnings limit. They are the same essential questions that must be asked in any exercise of assessing earnings for the application of any social security or tax rate or limit. There must be defined periods with defined start and end dates and defined rules for attributing actual earnings to those periods. The key questions are:

(1) Are earnings included when received, or when entitlement arises, or on some other basis?

(2) When are specific earnings received or earned?

(3) How are specific earnings linked to specific periods of assessment or benefit?

The use of deeming provisions in the Regulations means that the answers provided to those questions for carer's allowance purposes are not findings of fact about what happened, but are questions of law about how the deeming provisions in the Regulations are to be applied to those facts.

p.442, *annotations to the Computation of Earnings Regulations 1996, reg.9 (earnings of employed earners)*

2.043   *CG/0645/2008* raised, among other things, the question of the proper computation of a person's weekly earnings in relation to the earnings limit for entitlement to a carer's allowance. The tribunal made its decision without reference to the regulations, which are described as "a comprehensive code" (para.54). The facts were complex since the appellant argued that part of what she received was on behalf of a third party. The Deputy Commissioner says:

57. In my view there is a common thread running through the definitions in section 3 of SSCBA 1992 and the 1996 Regulations. That is, however expansively one defines "earnings", the earnings in question must still be the earnings of the individual in question. Thus "any remuneration or profit derived from employment" must mean derived from the claimant's employment, not from someone else's employment.

The Deputy Commissioner agrees that what are to be taken into account are payments actually received, not entitlement which has not resulted in payments, that is, payments actually received for service rendered under that person's own contract of employment.

p.455, *amendment to the Dependency Regulations 1977, reg.1 (citation etc)*

2.044   With effect from November 3, 2008, the Tribunals, Courts and Enforcement Act 2007 (Transitional and Consequential Provisions) Order 2008 (SI 2008/2683), reg.7 amended the definition of "the determining authority" to read as follows:

"the determining authority" means, as the case may require, the Secretary of State, [the First-tier Tribunal or the Upper Tribunal];

p.483, *amendment to the Overlapping Benefits Regulations, reg.2*

With effect from October 27, 2008, The Employment and Support Allowance (Consequential Provisions) (No.2) Regulations 2008 (SI 2008/1554) reg.51 amended reg.2(1) as follows: 2.045
  (a) in the definition of "contributory benefit" for " and a contribution-based jobseeker's allowance" substitute "a contribution-based jobseeker's allowance and a contributory employment and support allowance";
  (b) in the definition of "personal benefit" after "includes" insert "a contributory employment and support allowance but not an income-related employment and support allowance and includes"; and
  (c) after the definition of "1914–1918 War Injuries Scheme" insert: "the Welfare Reform Act" means the Welfare Reform Act 2007.

p.487, *amendment to the Overlapping Benefits Regulations 1977, reg.4*

With effect from October 27, 2008, The Employment and Support Allowance (Consequential Provisions) (No.2) Regulations 2008 (SI2008/1554) reg.51 amended reg.4(1)(a) by adding the words ", Part 1 of the Welfare Reform Act" after the words "industrial injuries benefits)".   2.046

p.494, *amendment to the Overlapping Benefits Regulations 1977, reg. 10*

With effect from October 27, 2008, The Employment and Support Allowance (Consequential Provisions) (No.2) Regulations 2008 (SI2008/1554) reg.51 amended para.(1) by adding: 2.047

"(k) a contributory employment and support allowance."

p.498, *amendment to the Overlapping Benefits Regulations 1977, reg.16*

With effect from October 27, 2008, The Employment and Support Allowance (Consequential Provisions) (No.2) Regulations 2008 (SI2008/1554) reg.51 amended reg.16 as follows: 2.048
  (a) after "the Act" the first time it occurs insert ", Part 1 of the Welfare Reform Act"; and
  (b) after "under it," the first time it occurs insert " Part 1 of the Welfare Reform Act and regulations made under it".

p.498, *amendment to the Overlapping Benefits Regulations 1977, reg.17*

With effect from October 27, 2008, The Employment and Support Allowance (Consequential Provisions) (No.2) Regulations 2008 (SI2008/1554) reg.51 amended reg.17 by substituting the words ", the   2.049

Jobseekers Act or Part 1 of the Welfare Reform Act" for the words "or under the Jobseekers Act" each time they occur.

p.498, *amendment to the Overlapping Benefits Regulations 1977, Sch.1*

Column (2) of para.3 should read:

"Unemployability supplement, industrial death benefit or war pension death benefit in either case payable to a woman as widow of the deceased and (except where the benefit in column (1) is widow's allowance) training allowance."

2.050   With effect from October 27, 2008, The Employment and Support Allowance (Consequential Provisions) (No.2) Regulations 2008 (SI2008/1554) reg.51 amended Sch.1 as follows: in col.(1) in para.4, after "severe disablement allowance" insert ", contributory employment and support allowance".

p.511, *annotations to the Persons Abroad Regulations 1975, reg.5*

2.051   *CP/3638/2006* has identified a lacuna in the provisions limiting the payment of pensions abroad to amounts which do not receive the benefit of annual up-rating. The decision will require careful examination in any cases where a similar point is taken. The claim in issue was initially by a wife, but later by a widow ("the appellant"). Her husband had become entitled to a Category A retirement pension in March 1976. When he emigrated to Canada that pension was frozen at the November 1975 rate. In September 2001 the appellant married him. She then became entitled to a Category B retirement pension from September 2001 based upon his contributions. That pension was fixed at the November 1975 rate (£7.90 per week) rather than the September 2001 rate (£45.20). The appellant took issue with that decision. The husband died in May 2002, and the appellant's claim was converted to one on widowhood, and the amount of the Category B retirement pension increased to £13.30 per week. A decision was also taken that she was entitled to half her husband's graduated retirement benefit; the appellant took issue with this award as well. The principal issue which arose in this appeal was whether the correct application of reg.5 following the death of the husband would be of benefit to the appellant.

The Commissioner concluded that the decision taken following the death of the husband was one which flowed from her change of status. Whereas prior to the husband's death, she came within reg.5(3)(aa), and this meant that she was not entitled to the additional benefit which would otherwise be paid under the annual up-rating orders, after his death she fell within reg.5(3)(c). The Commissioner says, in relation to the amount of the Category B retirement pension:

"28. What then is the effect of regulation 5(3)(c) in the present case? The words are in my judgment clear and have only one possible meaning. They prevent the lifting of the disqualification by virtue of regulation 4(1) only in respect of up-rating orders coming into force after the first day of the *claimant's* entitlement to retirement pension.

Accordingly, the claimant cannot from and including 27 May 2002 be disqualified for receiving any additional benefit payable by virtue of up-rating orders coming into force before that date (10 September 2001). In practice, from 27 May 2002 her Category B retirement pension is frozen at the rate set in section 44(4) of the Contributions and Benefits Act as from 9 April 2001, i.e. £72.50 per week."

In para.33 of the decision, the Commissioner addresses the appellant's entitlement to graduated retirement pension:

"33. I concluded in my draft decision that the claimant's entitlement to GRB from 27 May 2002 should not have been half of £1.18, the amount actually in payment to H immediately before his death, but should have been half of the amount generated by the graduated contributions he had paid and the amount specified in the preserved section 36(1) of the Social Security Act 1965 as at that date. I still consider that that is the "appropriate" rate under section 37(2). But, taking account of the Secretary of State's submission of 19 May 2008, I now think that I stopped at too early a point. Taking the rate of GRB identified above as appropriate, it is necessary to go on to look at the effect of regulation 5(3)(c) of the Persons Abroad Regulations. That is because the adoption of that appropriate rate to calculate the claimant's inherited GRB involves the identification of additional benefit that would be payable to her indirectly by virtue of the up-rating orders enacted since H became entitled to GRB. However, as I have decided above, regulation 5(3)(c) bites only on up-rating orders whose appointed date falls after *the claimant* became entitled to a retirement pension or GRB. For the reasons given in paragraph 30 above, although the context is the calculation of GRB, I am satisfied that the crucial date is that at which the claimant first became entitled to retirement pension of any kind, ie 10 September 2001. Accordingly, since no other sub-paragraph of regulation 5(3) applied to her as at 27 May 2002, she was able to take advantage of the appropriate rate for each unit of H's graduated contributions as specified in section 36(1) of the National Insurance Act 1965 down to April 2001 (9.06 pence). But she was not able to take advantage of the increase in that amount to 9.21 pence by the up-rating order whose appointed date was 6 April 2002."

The Commissioner also rules that the Persons Abroad Regulations were validly made.

p.547, *amendment to the Disability Living Allowance Regulations 1991,
reg.(1) (interpretation)*

With effect from November 3, 2008 reg.1(2) is amended by Sch.1 of 2.052 the Tribunals, Courts and Enforcement Act 2007, as follows:

in the definition of "adjudicating authority" for "an appeal tribunal " to the end substitute " the First-tier Tribunal or the Upper Tribunal."

p.572, *annotation to the Disability Living Allowance Regulations 1991, reg. 12: can't walk/won't walk*

2.053   The can't walk/won't walk distinction has been considered again by Commissioner Jacobs in *CDLA/3839/2007*. The commissioner concludes that the distinction apparently drawn in *R(M) 3/86* between a deliberate election not to walk and physical disablement; is no such thing. In his view (and that of others he cites), this was simply a disposal of the facts as presented in that particular case, and did not lay down any principal of law to be applied in others. In this case, the claimant was a child suffering from autism (a physical condition) who generally required two adults holding him firmly when taken on any public route to avoid the danger that would be caused to himself and others by his running off uncontrollably. The case was returned to a tribunal for them to consider, and give clear reasons, as to whether, on the evidence presented, the claimant should be regarded as virtually unable to walk.

p.573, *annotation to the Disability Living Allowance Regulations 1991, reg. 12 (entitlement to the mobility component)*

2.054   Note that the test to be applied is of "severe discomfort" not pain, or severe pain, and the evidence relied upon must be as to that test; or, at least explain the relationship with that test. In CDLA/3292/2007 the commissioner allowed the appeal of a claimant whose claim had been denied by a tribunal that relied, in part, on the evidence of her GP that she could walk only 50–100yds "without being in severe pain." While this might have been consistent with the rest of the evidence relied upon, it could not be said that it was necessarily so, and the tribunal had failed to advert to the difference stated between "severe pain" and "severe discomfort".

p.595, *annotation to the Invalid Care Allowance Regulations 1976, reg. 8 (earnings limit)*

2.055   Note the observations of the commissioner in *CG/607/2008*. Whereas most social security benefits (and most taxes) provide for a taper in respect of earnings that exceed an earnings limit, there is no such thing for Carer's Allowance; earnings that are a penny over the limit result in the total loss of benefit. In this case the claimant had taken part time work for a charity working with the disabled. She was employed for 10 hours per week at an hourly rate calculated so that her earnings would exactly match the earnings limit currently in force. Such a carefully constructed and informed work plan should not have resulted in difficulties, but a complication arose from the fact that although the wages had been expressed to be a weekly sum for the convenience of the employer, they were, in fact, paid monthly. Because the regulations define benefit weeks for Carer's Allowance as being each week beginning on a Monday, and because some calendar months contain five Mondays rather than four, this meant that in those months her earnings, if spread over a calendar month, exceeded the weekly earnings limit. As this was discovered only after five years it meant that the claimant was faced with a substantial claim for overpayment. The complexity of the Computation of Earnings Regulations resulted in four different decisions, and four different overpayment claims, by the DM, together with a different calculation by the appeal tribunal (which had allowed her appeal) and yet another by her representative before the commissioner. The commissioner came to the rescue of all of them. One must begin, he says, by going back to basics. This meant examining the definitions of the concepts that are used in the regulations. From this it emerged that earnings should be the sums payable under the claimant's contract of employment. Although the contract was oral, it was clear both from the parties' intentions, and from their consistent pattern of behaviour over almost all of the five years, that her wages were to be earned weekly even though they may have been paid monthly. This meant that the correct attribution of earnings was on a weekly basis, not monthly. There were a few weeks early in the arrangement when the claimant had worked extra hours and therefore had exceeded the earnings limit, but for the most part she had remained within that limit and, therefore, her overpayment was minimal.

p.619, *annotation to the Graduated Retirement Benefit (No.2) Regulations 1978*

CP/3539/2006 is now reported as R(P) 1/08. **2.056**

p.640, *amendment to the Widow's Benefit and Retirement Allowance Regulations 1979, reg.(1) (interpretation)*

With effect from November 3, 2008 reg.1(2) is amended by Sch.1 of **2.057**
the Tribunals, Courts and Enforcement Act 2007, as follows:

in the definition of "the determining authority" for the words "an appeal tribunal "to the end, substitute "the First-tier Tribunal or the Upper Tribunal;"

pp.669–670, *amendment to the Incapacity Benefit Regulations 1994, reg.4A(3) (days to be treated as days of incapacity for work)*

With effect from November 3, 2008, art.6(1) and para.65 of the **2.058**
Tribunals, Courts and Enforcement Act 2007 (Transitional and Consequential Provisions) Order 2008 (SI 2008/2683) amended reg.4A(3) by deleting the definition of "Commissioner" and replacing "Commissioner" with "Upper Tier Tribunal" in the definition of "official error".

p.675, *amendment to the Incapacity Benefit Regulations 1994, reg.8 (amount of councillor's allowance)*

With effect from October 1, 2008, reg.3(2) of the Social Security **2.059**
(Miscellaneous Amendments) (No.3) Regulations 2008 (SI 2008/2635)

amended reg.8 so as to increase the prescribed amount of councillor's allowance from £88.50 to £92.00.

p.727, *amendment to the Incapacity for Work (General) Regulations 1995, reg.17 (permitted earnings limits)*

2.060   With effect from October 1, 2008, reg.4 of the Social Security (Miscellaneous Amendments) (No.3) Regulations 2008 (SI 2008/2635) amended reg.17(3) and (4) so as to increase the permitted earnings limit from £88.50 to £92.00. Amounts in the annotation to reg.17 (pp.729–731) should be read accordingly from that date.

p.728, *amendments to the Incapacity for Work (General) Regulations 1995, reg.17(7) (exempt work)*

2.061   With effect from October 1, 2008, reg.4 of the Social Security (Miscellaneous Amendments) (No.3) Regulations 2008 (SI 2008/2635) amended reg.17(7) by replacing "Duties undertaken on not more than one day a week" with "Duties undertaken on either one full day or two half days a week". This aligns the exemption with that in the Employment and Support Allowance regime from October 27, 2008.

With effect from November 3, 2008, art.6(1) and para.66 of the Tribunals, Courts and Enforcement Act 2007 (Transitional and Consequential Provisions) Order 2008 (SI 2008/2683) amended reg.17(7) by substituting a new sub-para.(b):

"(b) a member of the First-tier Tribunal where the member is eligible for appointment to be such a member in accordance with article 2(3) of the Qualifications for Appointment of Members to the First-tier Tribunal and Upper Tribunal Order 2008."

p.730, *annotation to the Incapacity for Work (General) Regulations 1995, reg.17*

2.062   In light of the change in legislative text set out in the update to p.728, replace the current note headed "(4) *Tribunal work*" with:

"(4) *Tribunal and SLAB work (para.(7))*: So long as undertaken for no more than one full day or two half days in the week in question, duties undertaken as a member of the Disability Living Allowance Advisory Board or as a member of First-tier Tribunal with a disability qualification will not invoke the preclusive effect of reg.16 (para.(7)). Such a tribunal member is someone other than a registered medical practitioner, who is experienced in dealing with the physical or mental needs of disabled persons because they work with disabled persons in a professional or voluntary capacity, or are themselves disabled (see article 2(3) of the Qualifications for Appointment of Members to the First-tier Tribunal and Upper Tribunal Order 2008 (SI 2008/2692)."

pp.742–744, *annotation to Incapacity for Work (General) Regulations 1995, s.24 (dealing with the evidence, in particular with differing medical opinions and reports)*

In *CIB/4232/2007*, Deputy Commissioner Ovey found erroneous in 2.063 law a tribunal decision partly because of its too "mantra like" acceptance of the examining doctor's opinion and, mistakenly, treating him as an expert on the claimant's condition, when no full examination had been carried out. They also attributed to him the opinion of the previous examining doctor.

In *CIB/1006/2008*, Commissioner Williams in referring the case to another tribunal, noted the tribunal's failure, when preferring the examining doctor's opinion, to consider evidence about the quality of the medical examination undertaken and to take due account of errors in the IB85 report about the timing of the examination, suggesting that there might well be other errors in the report itself, and casting doubt on the weight to be given to the report.

In *CIB/1381/2008*, Commissioner Williams expressed concern that the wording of the IB85 report does not deal accurately with the current reg.27(2)(c) but reflects the pre-1997 wording. There is a key difference in terms of the timescale concerning the operation envisaged by that provision. The current text of reg.27 refers to "likely to be carried out within three months" of the PCA medical examination, the IB85 formulation in contrast is that it is to occur within the three month period. The tribunal had also failed to exercise its inquisitorial and enabling function by ignoring reg.27.

On the need to take into account previous assessments, see *CIB/516/2008* and *CIB/103/2001*.

p.815, *annotation to the Incapacity for Work (General) Regulations 1995, Sch: Activity 16: daily living: descriptor (e): "sleeping problems interfered with daytime activities"*

CIB/5336/2002 is wrongly referred to as *CIB/5536/2002*. 2.064

p.816, *annotation to the Incapacity for Work (General) Regulations 1995, Sch: Activity 17: coping with pressure: descriptor (a): "mental stress was factor in making him stop work"*

In *obiter* comments in *CIB/1361/2008*, Deputy Commissioner Wikeley 2.065 (as he then was) doubted that leaving a college course as a consequence of mental stress could properly be equated with "stopping work" for the purpose of this descriptor.

p.882, *amendment to the Child Benefit (General) Regulations 2006, reg.38 (exceptions to the rules preventing duplicate payments).*

With effect from November 3, 2008 reg.38 is amended by Sch.1 of the 2.066 Tribunals, Courts and Enforcement Act 2007 as follows:

(a) in para.2(b) omit the words "section 7 of the Social Security Act 1998 or";
(b) in para.2(c) omit the words "section 16(7) of the Social Security Act 1998 or";
(c) after para.2(c) insert:
  "(d) the First-tier Tribunal;
  (e) the Upper Tribunal."

pp.904–905, *amendments to the General Benefit Regulations 1982, reg.11 (further definition of the principles of assessment of disablement etc))*

2.067   With effect from November 3, 2008, art.6(1) and para.25 of the Tribunals, Courts and Enforcement Act 2007 (Transitional and Consequential Provisions) Order 2008 (SI 2008/2683) amended reg.11(7), (8) replacing "an appeal tribunal" with "the First-tier Tribunal".

p.910, *amendment to the General Benefit Regulations 1982, reg.16 (increase of earnings level)*

2.068   With effect from October 1, 2008, reg.2 of the Social Security (Miscellaneous Amendments) (No.3) Regulations 2008 (SI 2008/2635) increased the earnings level from £4,602 to £4,784.

p.968, *amendment to the Prescribed Diseases Regulations 1985, Sch 1, PD D12*

2.069   With effect from July 21, 2008, reg.2 of the Social Security (Industrial Injuries) (Prescribed Diseases) Amendment (No.2) Regulations 2008 (SI 2008/1552) amended both columns of the entry for PD D12 (chronic bronchitis and/or emphysema) to read:

Prescribed disease or injury	*Occupation* *Any occupation involving:*
D12. Except in the circumstances specified in regulation 2(d)— (a) chronic bronchitis; or (b) emphysema; or (c) both. where there is [. . .] evidence of a forced expiratory volume in one second (measured from the position of maximum inspiration with the claimant making maximum effort) which is— (i) at least one litre below the Appropriate mean value predicted, obtained from the following prediction formulae which give the mean values predicted in litres— i. For a man, where the measurement is made without back-extrapolation, $(3.62 \times$ Height in metres$) - (0.031 \times$ Age in years$) - 1.41$; or, where the measurement is made with back-extrapolation, $(3.71 \times$ Height in metres$) - (0.032 \times$ Age in years$) - 1.44$; ii. For a woman, where the measurement is made without back-extrapolation, $(3.29 \times$ Height in metres$) - (0.029 \times$ Age in years$) - 1.42$; or, where the measurement is made with back-extrapolation, $(3.37 \times$ Height in metres$) - (0.030 \times$ Age in years$) - 1.46$; or (ii) less than one litre.	[Exposure to coal dust (whether before or after 5th July 1948) by reason of working— (a) underground in a coal mine for a period or periods amounting in aggregate to at least 20 years; (b) on the surface of a coal mine as a screen worker for a period or periods amounting in aggregate to at least 40 years before 1st January 1983; or (c) both underground in a coal mine, and on the surface as a screen worker before 1st January 1983, where 2 years working as a surface screen worker is equivalent to 1 year working underground, amounting in aggregate to at least the equivalent of 20 years underground. Any such period or periods shall include a period or periods of incapacity while engaged in such an occupation.]

pp.989–991, *annotation to the Prescribed Diseases Regulations 1985, Sch.1, PD A12 (carpal tunnel syndrome)*

In *CI/961/2008*, Commissioner Williams found the Tribunal to have 2.070 erred law because it had not given clear reasons for deciding that the terms of prescription were not satisfied in the case. He directed the new tribunal to have in mind as an aid to interpretation and application paras 46–51 of the IIAC report *Work-related upper limb disorders*, CM 6868 (July 2006), as forming the background to the enactment of the newly worded prescription.

PART III

UPDATING MATERIAL
VOLUME II

INCOME SUPPORT, JOBSEEKER'S ALLOWANCE, STATE PENSION CREDIT AND THE SOCIAL FUND

Commentary by

Penny Wood

Richard Poynter

Nick Wikeley

David Bonner

p.5, *amendment of Social Security Contributions and Benefits Act 1992,*
s.124 (income support)

With effect from October 27, 2008 s.124 was amended by the Welfare   3.001
Reform Act 2007 as follows:

Schedule 8 repealed the word "and" at the end of sub-para.(f) of
para.(1)

Schedule 3, para.9 inserted the following after sub-para.(g) of
para.(1):

> "; and
> (h) he is not entitled to an employment and support allowance and, if
> he is a member of a couple, the other member of the couple is not
> entitled to an income-related employment and support allow-
> ance."

and added a new para.(7) as follows:

> "(7) In this section, "income-related employment and support
> allowance" means an income-related allowance under Pt 1 of the
> Welfare Reform Act 2007 (employment and support allowance)."

p.18, *amendment of Social Security Contributions and Benefits Act 1992,*
s.137(1) (interpretation of Part VII and supplementary provisions)

With effect from July 3, 2007 s.137(1) was amended by Sch.5,   3.002
para.1(4) of the Welfare Reform Act 2007 by the insertion of the following definition of "local authority" after the definition of "industrial
injuries scheme":

> " 'local authority' in relation to Scotland means a council constituted
> under section 2 of the Local Government etc. (Scotland) Act
> 1994;"

p.30, *amendment of Jobseekers Act 1995, s.1 (the jobseeker's allowance)*

With effect from October 27, 2008 s.1 was amended by Sch.3, para.12   3.003
of the Welfare Reform Act 2007 by the substitution of the following for
sub-para.(f) of para.(1):

> "(f) does not have limited capability for work;"

p.42, *amendment to Jobseekers Act 1995, s.3 (the income-based*
conditions)

With effect from October 27, 2008, s.28(1) and Sch.3, para.12(3)(a)   3.004
of the Welfare Reform Act 2007 substituted the words ", state pension
credit or an income-related employment and support allowance" for the
words "or state pension credit" in s.3(1)(b).

From the same date, s.28(1) and Sch.3, para.12(3)(b) of the same Act
inserted the following new paragraph after para.(dd) in s.3(1):

> "(de) is not a member of a couple the other member of which is
> entitled to an income-related employment and support allow-
> ance;".

p.44, *amendment to Jobseekers Act 1995, s.3A (the conditions for claims by joint-claim couples)*

3.005   With effect from October 27, 2008, s.28(1) and Sch.3, para.12(4) of the Welfare Reform Act 2007 inserted the following new paragraph after para.(cc) in s.3A(1):

"(cd) that neither member of the couple is entitled to an income-related employment and support allowance;".

p.114, *annotation to the Jobseekers Act 1995, s.19(9) (national minimum wage rates)*

3.006   With effect from October 1, 2008, the hourly rates become £5.73 for those 22 and over; £4.77 for those aged 18–21; and £3.53 for those workers under 18 who have ceased to be of compulsory school age. The change in rates was effected by the National Minimum Wage Regulations 1999 (Amendment) Regulations 2008 (SI 2008/1894).

pp.124–126, *amendment to Jobseekers Act 1995, s.35 (interpretation)*

3.007   With effect from October 27, 2008, s.28(1) and Sch.3, para.12(5)(a) of the Welfare Reform Act 2007 inserted the following new definition after the definition of "income-based jobseeker's allowance" in s.35(1):

" "income-related employment and support allowance" means an income-related allowance under Part 1 of the Welfare Reform Act 2007 (employment and support allowance);".

From the same date, s.28(1) and Sch.3, para.12(5)(b) of the same Act substituted the words "limited capability for work" for the words "capable of work" in s.35(2).

p.147, *amendment to State Pension Credit Act 2002, s.3 (savings credit)*

3.008   With effect from September 26, 2007, s.13(2) and Sch.1, para.44 of the Pensions Act 2007 substituted "pensionable age" for "the age of 65" in s.3(1)(a).

p.170, *amendment of Immigration and Asylum Act 1999, s.115(1) (Exclusion from benefits)*

3.009   With effect from October 27, 2008 s.1 was amended by Sch.3, para.19 of the Welfare Reform Act 2007 by the addition of the words "or to income-related allowance under Pt 1 of the Welfare Reform Act 2007 (employment and support allowance)" after the words "State Pension Credit Act 2002".

pp.178–179, *amendment to Child Support Act 1991, s.6 (applications by those claiming or receiving benefit)*

Section 6 was repealed with effect from July 14, 2008 (Child Main- 3.010
tenance and Other Payments Act 2008 (c.6), s.15(a), and s.58 and Sch.8
so far as it relates to the repeal of s.6, and the Child Maintenance and
Other Payments Act 2008 (Commencement) Order 2008 (SI
2008/1476) (c.67), art.2(3)(a) and (c)). However, art.2(4) of the Commencement Order provided that the repeal did not apply in relation to
"existing cases" (i.e., those where immediately before July 14, 2008 a
maintenance calculation was in force or an effective date had been set
(art.2(5)). Thus those claimants were still subject to the s.6 compulsion
but as s.46 (reduced benefit decisions) was also repealed with effect from
July 14, 2008 (see below) they could not be penalised for failing to apply
for child support. But with effect from October 27, 2008 art.3(a) of the
Child Maintenance and Other Payments Act 2008 (Commencement
No.3 and Transitional and Savings Provisions) Order 2008 (SI
2008/2548) (c.110) has brought s.15(a) fully into force and art.4 of that
Order provides that "existing cases" are to be treated as if the parent with
care had made an application under s.4 of the Child Support Act
1991.

pp.183–185, *amendment to Child Support Act 1991, s.46 (reduced benefit decisions)*

Section 46 was repealed with effect from July 14, 2008 (Child Main- 3.011
tenance and Other Payments Act 2008 (c.6), s.15(b) and s.58 and Sch.8
so far as it relates to the repeal of s.46 and the Child Maintenance and
Other Payments Act 2008 (Commencement) Order 2008 (SI
2008/1476) (c.67), art.2(2)(a) and (c)). The consequence is that all
reduced benefit decisions ceased to have effect on July 14, 2008.

pp.187–189, *amendment to Child Support Act 1995, s.10 (the child maintenance bonus)*

With effect from October 27, 2008, s.23 of the Child Support, Pen- 3.012
sions and Social Security Act 2000 is brought fully into force by the
Child Support, Pensions and Social Security Act 2000 (Commencement
No.14) Order 2008 (SI 2008/2545) (c.109), art.4. The effect is that s.10
of the Child Support Act 1995 (child maintenance bonus) is repealed in
all cases and it will no longer be possible for any person to accrue a child
maintenance bonus. However, the *quid pro quo* is that all income support,
income-based JSA and income-related ESA claimants who are getting
child maintenance payments (as defined in reg.54 of the Income Support Regulations/reg.117 of the JSA Regulations/reg.119 of the ESA
Regulations respectively (for the ESA Regulations see Part 1 of this
Supplement)) will be eligible for the child maintenance disregard. This
has been increased to £20 per week with effect from October 27, 2008

(see the amendments to para.73 of Sch.9 to the Income Support Regulations and para.70 of Sch.7 to the JSA Regulations below and para.60 of Sch.8 to the ESA Regulations in Part 1 of this Supplement).

p.198, *amendment of Income Support (General) Regulations 1987, reg.2(1) (interpretation: definition of "the benefit Acts")*

3.013   With effect from October 27, 2008, reg.2(1) and (2) of the Employment and Support Allowance (Consequential Provisions) (No.2) Regulations 2008 (SI 2008/1554) amended the definition of "the benefit Acts" in reg.2(1) to read as follows:

"'the benefit Acts' means the Contributions and Benefits Act [, the Jobseekers Act 1995 and Part 1 of the Welfare Reform Act];"

p.199, *amendment of Income Support (General) Regulations 1987, reg.2(1) (interpretation: definition of "contributory employment and support allowance")*

3.014   With effect from October 27, 2008, reg.2(1) and (2) of the Employment and Support Allowance (Consequential Provisions) (No.2) Regulations 2008 (SI 2008/1554) amended reg.2(1) by adding the following definition after the definition of "the Contributions and Benefits Act":

" 'contributory employment and support allowance' means a contributory allowance under Part 1 of the Welfare Reform Act (employment and support allowance);"

p.200, *amendment of Income Support (General) Regulations 1987, reg.2(1) (interpretation: definition of "the Employment And Support Allowance Regulations")*

3.015   With effect from October 27, 2008, reg.2(1) and (2) of the Employment and Support Allowance (Consequential Provisions) (No.2) Regulations 2008 (SI 2008/1554) amended reg.2(1) by adding the following definition after the definition of "employment":

" 'the Employment and Support Allowance Regulations" means the Employment and Support Allowance Regulations 2008;"

p.200, *amendment of Income Support (General) Regulations 1987, reg.2(1) (interpretation: definition of "income-related employment and support allowance")*

3.016   With effect from October 27, 2008, reg.2(1) and (2) of the Employment and Support Allowance (Consequential Provisions) (No.2) Regulations 2008 (SI 2008/1554) amended reg.2(1) by adding the following definition after the definition of "Immigration and Asylum Act":

" 'income-related employment and support allowance' means an income-related allowance under Part 1 of the Welfare Reform Act (employment and support allowance);"

p.204, *amendment of Income Support (General) Regulations 1987, reg.2(1) (interpretation: definition of "the Welfare Reform Act")*

With effect from October 27, 2008, reg.2(1) and (2) of the Employ- 3.017
ment and Support Allowance (Consequential Provisions) (No.2) Regulations 2008 (SI 2008/1554) amended reg.2(1) by adding the following
definition after the definition of "water charges":

" 'the Welfare Reform Act' means the Welfare Reform Act 2007;"

p.234, *amendment to the Income Support (General) Regulations 1987, reg.4ZA (prescribed categories of person)*

With effect from July 9, 2008, reg.2 of the Social Security (Students 3.018
Responsible for Children or Young Persons) Amendment Regulations
2008 (SI 2008/1826) substituted the following paragraph for para.(3)(c)
in reg.4ZA:

"(c) any other paragraph of Schedule 1B applies to him and—
      (i) in the case of a person with a partner, the partner is also a
           full-time student and either he or his partner is treated as
           responsible for a child or young person, or
      (ii) in any other case, he is treated as responsible for a child or
           young person,
    but this provision applies only for the period of the summer
    vacation appropriate to his course; or".

p.236, *annotation to the Income Support (General) Regulations 1987, reg.4ZA(3)*

The new form of para.3(c) has been introduced as a consequence of 3.019
the decision in *CJSA/2663/2006* (see the note to reg.15 of the JSA
Regulations in Vol.II in this series) in order to remove the previous
discrimination in reg.4ZA(3)(c) (reg.15(a) of the JSA Regulations also
contained the same discrimination and it has also been amended (see
below)). A student who is a single person with responsibility for a child
or young person is now eligible for income support (or JSA) on the same
basis as a student couple with responsibility for a child or young person
during the summer vacation.

Note that from October 27, 2008 *new* claims for income support
under paras 10 or 12 of Sch.1B (students who qualify for the disability
or severe disability premium, have been incapable of work for at least 28
weeks or who are receiving a disabled student's allowance on the
grounds of deafness) are no longer possible as they are treated as claims
for ESA (see reg.2(1) of the Employment and Support Allowance (Transitional Provisions) Regulations 2008 (SI 2008/795) in Part 1 of this
Supplement), unless they link with (i.e., are made not more than eight
weeks after) a previous income support entitlement for at least four days
on the grounds of disability: see reg.2(2)(c) of the Transitional Provisions Regulations; or the claimant is entitled to incapacity benefit or
severe disablement allowance: see reg.2(2)(d) of those Regulations, as

amended by the Employment and Support Allowance (Transitional Provisions) (Amendment) Regulations 2008 (SI 2008/2783); or they are in respect of a period before October 27, 2008.

Income support on the grounds of disability means "income support awarded to a person to whom regulation 13(2)(b) or (bb) of, or paragraph 7(a) or (b), 10, 12 or 13 of Schedule 1B to, the Income Support (General) Regulations 1987 (prescribed categories of person) applies" (reg.1(4) of the Transitional Provisions Regulations, as amended by reg.42 of the Employment and Support Allowance (Miscellaneous Amendments) Regulations 2008 (SI 2008/2428)). Note also that a claimant who has an existing award of income support on the grounds of disability cannot claim ESA (reg.3(1) of the Transitional Provisions Regulations); if a person claims ESA who would be entitled to income support under reg.2(2)(c) or (d) of the Transitional Provisions Regulations, the claim will be treated as a claim for income support (reg.3(2) of the Transitional Provisions Regulations); and a claim for ESA in respect of a period before October 27, 2008 may be treated by the Secretary of State as a claim in the alternative for incapacity benefit or income support on the grounds of disability (reg.4 of the Transitional Provisions Regulations).

p.252, *amendment of Income Support (General) Regulations 1987, reg.6(5) (Persons not treated as engaged in remunerative work)*

3.020   With effect from October 27, 2008, reg.2(1) and (3) of the Employment and Support Allowance (Consequential Provisions) (No.2) Regulations 2008 (SI 2008/1554) amended reg.6(5) to read as follows:

"(5) A person shall not be treated as engaged in remunerative work for the period specified in paragraph (6) in so far as—
   (a) he or his partner is engaged in work which—
      (i) is remunerative work; and
      (ii) he, or his partner, is expected to be engaged in remunerative work for a period of no less than five weeks;
   (b) he or his partner had, for a continuous period of 26 weeks ending on the day before the day on which he commenced the work referred to in sub-paragraph (a), been entitled to and in receipt of income support [, an income-based jobseeker's allowance or an income-related employment and support allowance];
   (c) he or his partner had, as at the day before the day on which he commenced the work referred to in sub-paragraph (a), an applicable amount which included—
      (i) an amount determined in accordance with Schedule 3 (housing costs) as applicable to him in respect of housing costs which qualify under paragraphs 15 to 17 of that Schedule; [. . .]
      (ii) an amount determined in accordance with Schedule 2 to the Jobseeker's Allowance Regulations 1996 (housing costs) as applicable to him in respect of housing costs

which qualify under paragraphs 14 to 16 of that Schedule; [or

(iii) an amount determined in accordance with Schedule 6 to the Employment and Support Allowance Regulations (housing costs) as applicable to him in respect of housing costs which qualify under paragraphs 16 to 18 of that Schedule; and]

(d) he or his partner remain liable to make payments in respect of such housing costs."

p.260, *annotation to the Income Support (General) Regulations 1987, reg.13(2)(b) and (bb)*

Note that from October 27, 2008 *new* claims for income support on **3.021** the ground that sub-para.(b) or (bb) applies are no longer possible as they are treated as claims for ESA (see reg.2(1) of the Employment and Support Allowance (Transitional Provisions) Regulations 2008 (SI 2008/795) in Pt A of this Supplement), unless they link with (i.e., are made not more than eight weeks after) a previous income support entitlement for at least four days on the grounds of disability: see reg.2(2)(c) of the Transitional Provisions Regulations, or the claimant is entitled to incapacity benefit or severe disablement allowance: see reg.2(2)(d) of those Regulations, as amended by the Employment and Support Allowance (Transitional Provisions) (Amendment) Regulations 2008 (SI 2008/2783), or they are in respect of a period before October 27, 2008.

Income support on the grounds of disability means "income support awarded to a person to whom regulation 13(2)(b) or (bb) of, or paragraph 7(a) or (b), 10, 12 or 13 of Schedule 1B to, the Income Support (General) Regulations 1987 (prescribed categories of person) applies" (reg.1(4) of the Transitional Provisions Regulations, as amended by reg.42 of the Employment and Support Allowance (Miscellaneous Amendments) Regulations 2008 (SI 2008/2428). Note also that a claimant who has an existing award of income support on the grounds of disability cannot claim ESA (reg.3(1) of the Transitional Provisions Regulations); if a person claims ESA who would be entitled to income support under reg.2(2)(c) or (d) of the Transitional Provisions Regulations the claim will be treated as a claim for income support (reg.3(2) of the Transitional Provisions Regulations); and a claim for ESA in respect of a period before October 27, 2008 may be treated by the Secretary of State as a claim for income support on the grounds of disability (reg.4 of the Transitional Provisions Regulations).

pp.261–262, *annotation to the Income Support (General) Regulations 1987, reg.13(2), head (i)*

On the meaning of "estranged", see *CH/3777/2007* in the note to **3.022** para.4 of Sch.10 to the Income Support Regulations below.

p.263, *amendment of Income Support (General) Regulations 1987, reg.14(2) (persons of a prescribed description)*

3.023   With effect from October 27, 2008, reg.2(1) and (4) of the Employ-ment and Support Allowance (Consequential Provisions) (No.2) Reg-ulations 2008 (SI 2008/1554) amended reg.14(2) to read as follows:

> "(2) Paragraph (1) shall not apply to a person who is—
> (a) ...;
> (b) entitled to income support or would, but for section 134(2) (provision against dual entitlement of members of family) of the Contributions and Benefits Act, be so entitled; [...]
> (c) a person to whom section 6 of the Children (Leaving Care) Act 2000 (exclusion from benefits) applies. [or
> (d) entitled to an employment and support allowance or would, but for paragraph 6(1)(d) of Schedule 1 to the Welfare Reform Act (conditions of entitlement to income-related employment and support allowance), be so entitled.]"

p.284, *commentary to Income Support (General) Regulations, reg.21 (special cases): claimants without accommodation*

3.024   The decision of the House of Lords in the *RJM* case is now available. (*R (RJM) v Secretary of State for Work and Pensions* [2008] UKHL 63 (Lords Hope, Rodger, Walker, Mance and Neuberger). Their Lordships upheld the decision of the CA on the basis that:

> "(a) RJM's claim that he has wrongfully been deprived of disability premium falls, in principle, within the ambit of A1P1, and there-fore of article 14;
> (b)   The discrimination of which RJM claims is based on his home-lessness, which is an "other status" for the purposes of article 14;
> (c)   However, the discrimination of which RJM complains has been justified by the Secretary of State".

The justification put forward by the Secretary of State and accepted by the House was as follows (per Lord Neuberger, with whom all their Lordships agreed)

> "50. First, the Secretary of State takes the view that he should encourage the disabled homeless, who are "in a vulnerable position" to seek shelter, and therefore help, rather than rendering it easier, at least in financial terms, for them to remain without accommodation. It appears that 90% of those without accommodation in this country have problems connected with substance abuse and around 45% have mental health problems. Those who are disabled need, or at least would benefit from, accommodation, as indeed is reflected by the fact that they are included among those who are accorded priority need for housing under the Housing Acts (the 1985 Act when disability pre-mium was introduced, and now the 1996 Act). As Mr Johnson [coun-sel for the Secretary of State] explains, "In the government's view,

helping homeless people into accommodation is a much more effective way of helping them than handing out money through the disability premium.

51. Secondly, the Secretary of State considers that the disabled are less likely to need a supplement if they are without accommodation than if they are not. This view is based on the proposition that, while the disability premium was not precisely calculated by reference to specific needs, much of it would be spent on heating and other household expenses, items which would not be required by someone without accommodation. Mr Johnson says that "claimants in accommodation have a range of expenses and financial pressures related to that accommodation that claimants without accommodation do not have"."

The House of Lords also held that, the Court of Appeal had not been bound to follow its earlier decision in *Campbell v South Northamptonshire District Council* [2004] EWCA Civ 409 that income-related benefits did not constitute "possessions" within Art.1 of the First Protocol of the Convention, given the subsequent decision to the contrary by the Grand Chamber of the European Court of Human Rights in *Stec v United Kingdom.*

p.285, *commentary to Income Support (General) Regulations, reg.21 (special cases): Prisoner*

The position of prisoners serving life sentences who are transferred **3.025** from prison to mental hospital under ss.45A or 47 of the Mental Health Act 1983 (or the equivalent Scottish provisions) was considered by the High Court in *R (RD and PM) v Secretary of State for Work and Pensions*, QBD (Burnett J.) [2004] EWHC 2635 (Admin). Paragraph 2A of Sch.7 provides that such a claimant is to have an applicable amount of nil "but not if his detention continues after the date on which the Secretary of State certifies or Scottish Ministers certify would have been the earliest date on which he could have been released in respect of, or from, the prison sentence, if he had not been detained in hospital." The claimants, who had both served their tariffs and were entitled to apply for parole. Each argued that "the earliest date on which he could have been released" was at the expiry of his tariff. The Court rejected that argument stating (at para.48):

"In Paragraph 2A the earliest date on which a prisoner 'could have been released in respect of, or from, the prison sentence if he had not been detained in hospital' is the first date on which he is entitled to be released. For determinate prisoners that will usually be when half of the sentence has been served. For those serving life sentences there is no such date. Therefore, post-tariff lifers, whether serving their sentence in a prison or on transfer to a mental hospital, are not entitled to Income Support under the current Regulations. The position is the same as applies to non-means tested benefits under the 1982 General Benefits Regulations."

p.306, *commentary to Income Support (General) Regulations, reg.21AA (special cases: supplemental—persons from abroad): Family members and extended family members*

3.026   The decision in *CIS/1545/2007* was upheld by the Court of Appeal in *Jeleniewicz v Secretary of State for Work and Pensions* [2008] EWCA Civ 1163.

p.309, *commentary to Income Support (General) Regulations, reg.21AA (special cases: supplemental-persons from abroad): continuous residence*

3.027   In *CIS/2258/2008*, the Commissioner held that time spent abroad did not count towards the period of five years continuous residence necessary to establish a permanent right of residence, even if it did not break the continuity of residence. The Commissioner stated (at para.18):

> "It may be that the tribunal considered that residence could survive a period of absence. That is true in one sense. A weekend break on the Continent would not interrupt the person's residence. The reason is that the person's status, on which the right to reside depends, is not affected by such absences. For example: a worker remains a worker while on holiday and retains the right to reside. The absences to which Article 16(3) refers are absences that do affect residence because the person no longer retains a status that confers the right to reside."

p.316, *commentary to Income Support (General) Regulations, reg.21AA (special cases: supplemental—persons from abroad): compatibility of right to reside test with EC law.*

3.028   The decision of the Court of Appeal in Northern Ireland has been upheld by a majority of the House of Lords [2008] UKHL 67 (Lords Hope, Carswell and Brown, Baroness Hale and Lord Neuberger dissenting).

p.338, *amendment to the Income Support (General) Regulations 1987, reg.25 (liable relative payments)*

3.029   With effect from October 27, 2008, reg.2(2)(a) of the Social Security (Child Maintenance Amendments) Regulations 2008 (SI 2008/2111) inserted the words "child maintenance or" before the words "liable relative" in the heading to reg.25.

From the same date, reg.2(3) of the same amending regulations substituted the words "child maintenance and liable relative payments" for the words "liable relatives" in reg.25.

p.338, *amendment to the Income Support (General) Regulations 1987, reg.25A (child support)*

3.030   With effect from October 27, 2008, reg.2(4)(a) of the Social Security (Child Maintenance Amendments) Regulations 2008 (SI 2008/2111) omitted reg.25A.

pp.347–349, *annotation to the Income Support (General) Regulations 1987, reg.30*

Specific provision for the treatment of public lending rights payments in the calculation of self-employed earnings was made with effect from April 7, 2008 (see the April 2008 amendments to reg.30 in Vol.II of this series). In *CIS/731/2008* the Commissioner confirms that before that date such payments counted as earnings from self-employment under the general rule in reg.30(1).   3.031

p.349, *amendment to the Income Support (General) Regulations 1987, reg.31 (date on which income is treated as paid)*

With effect from October 27, 2008, reg.2(5) of the Employment and Support Allowance (Consequential Provisions) (No.2) Regulations 2008 (SI 2008/1554) substituted the words "severe disablement allowance or employment and support allowance" for the words "or severe disablement allowance" in reg.31(2).   3.032

p.352, *amendment to the Income Support (General) Regulations 1987, reg.32 (calculation of weekly amount of income)*

With effect from October 27, 2008, reg.2(6) of the Employment and Support Allowance (Consequential Provisions) (No.2) Regulations 2008 (SI 2008/1554) substituted the words ", jobseeker's allowance or employment and support allowance" for the words "or jobseeker's allowance" in reg.32(4)(b).   3.033

pp.378–379, *amendment to the Income Support (General) Regulations 1987, reg.40 (calculation of income other than earnings)*

With effect from September 1, 2008 (or if the student's period of study begins between August 1 and August 31, 2008, the first day of the period), reg.2(2)(a) of the Social Security (Students and Miscellaneous Amendments) Regulations 2008 (SI 2008/1599) substituted the words "Paragraphs (3AA) and (3AAA) apply" for the words "Paragraph (3AA) applies" in reg.40(3A).   3.034

From the same date, reg.2(2)(b) of the same amending regulations substituted the words "Where a relevant payment is made quarterly, the" for the word "The" at the beginning of reg.40(3AA).

From the same date, reg.2(2)(c) of the same amending regulations inserted the following new paragraph after reg.40(3AA):

> "(3AAA) Where a relevant payment is made by two or more instalments in a quarter, the amount of a relevant payment to be taken into account for the assessment period for the purposes of paragraph (1) in respect of a person to whom paragraph (3A) applies, shall be calculated by applying the formula in paragraph (3AA) but as if—
> A = the total amount of relevant payments which that person received, or would have received, from the first day of the academic year to the

day the person abandoned the course, or was dismissed from it, less any deduction under regulation 66A(5)."

From the same date, reg.2(2)(d)(i) of the same amending regulations substituted the words "In this regulation" for the words "In paragraphs (3A) and (3AA)" in reg.40(3AB).

From the same date, reg.2(2)(d)(ii) of the same amending regulations substituted the following definition for the definition of "assessment period" in reg.40(3AB):

" 'assessment period' means—
   (a) in a case where a relevant payment is made quarterly, the period beginning with the benefit week which includes the day on which the person abandoned, or was dismissed from, his course and ending with the benefit week which includes the last day of the last quarter for which an instalment of the relevant payment was payable to that person;
   (b) in a case where the relevant payment is made by two or more instalments in a quarter, the period beginning with the benefit week which includes the day on which the person abandoned, or was dismissed from, his course and ending with the benefit week which includes—
       (i) the day immediately before the day on which the next instalment of the relevant payment would have been due had the payments continued; or
       (ii) the last day of the last quarter for which an instalment of the relevant payment was payable to that person,
       whichever of those dates is earlier;".

From the same date, reg.2(2)(d)(iii) of the same amending regulations inserted the following definition at the appropriate place in reg.40(3AB):

" "quarter" in relation to an assessment period means a period in that year beginning on—
   (a) 1st January and ending on 31st March;
   (b) 1st April and ending on 30th June;
   (c) 1st July and ending on 31st August; or
   (d) 1st September and ending on 31st December;".

With effect from October 27, 2008, reg.2(7) of the Employment and Support Allowance (Consequential Provisions) (No.2) Regulations 2008 (SI 2008/1554) added a new paragraph after para.(5) in reg.40:

"(6) Where the claimant—
   (a) is a member of a couple;
   (b) his partner is receiving a contributory employment and support allowance; and
   (c) that benefit has been reduced under regulation 63 of the Employment and Support Allowance Regulations,

the amount of that benefit to be taken into account is the amount as if it had not been so reduced.".

p.381, *annotation to the Income Support (General) Regulations 1987, reg.40(1), "Is it the claimant's or partner's income?"*

In *CH/1076/2008* the claimant paid half of his annuities from Abbey 3.035
Life to his wife, from whom he was separated. A tribunal found that there was either a constructive trust or an actual trust of this income in favour of the claimant's wife. The Commissioner points out that if the annuities were retirement annuity pensions in connection with a former employment, s.91 of the Pension Schemes Act 1995 would need to be considered. Section 91(1) provides:

"Subject to subsection (5), where a person is entitled, or has an accrued right, to a pension under an occupational pension scheme—
(a) the entitlement or right cannot be assigned, commuted or surrendered,
(b) the entitlement or right cannot be charged or a lien exercised in respect of it, and
(c) no set off can be exercised in respect of it,
and an agreement to effect any of those things is unenforceable."

Subsection (4) provides that this does not prevent an attachment of earnings order being made and subs.(5) states that this does not apply to an assignment in favour of the person's widow, widower or dependant. But there was no evidence in this case to suggest that the claimant's wife was a dependant. Nor was there any evidence to suggest that the transfer to the claimant's wife had taken place as part of the agreement with Abbey Life. On the facts available to him the Commissioner saw no basis for the finding of an actual or constructive trust. In addition his decision in *CH/1672/2007* did not assist the claimant as there was no court order or similar mandatory requirement to transfer the funds to the claimant's wife as there had been in that case.

p.382, *annotation to the Income Support (General) Regulations 1987, reg.40(3)*

CH/51/2008 confirms that if incapacity benefit is being reduced due to 3.036
receipt of an occupational pension this is not a "deduction by way of recovery" for the purposes of reg.40(3). The income to be taken into account is the net amount of the incapacity benefit that the claimant actually receives.

p.383, *annotation to the Income Support (General) Regulations 1987, reg.40(3A)–(3AB)*

The amendments to reg.40(3A) to (3AB) and the new reg.40(3AAA) 3.037
clarify how student loans paid by two or more instalments in a quarter

509

are to be taken into account when a student abandons or is dismissed from his course.

p.404, *annotation to the Income Support (General) Regulations 1987, reg.46 (calculation of capital)*

3.038   In *CIS/2287/2008* the Commissioner considers the question of whether the decision of the Court of Appeal in *Leeves v Chief Adjudication Officer*, reported as *R(IS) 5/99*, applies to capital. He concludes that it applies to the classification of an asset as capital. However in his view *Leeves* only applies if the capital never became a resource in the claimant's hands from the moment of its receipt or attribution. It does not apply thereafter. If a demand for repayment is made after something has become capital in the claimant's hands, it is outside the scope of *Leeves*.

It is suggested with respect that the decision in *Leeves* is not limited in this way and that it can apply where the "certain and immediate obligation to repay" does not crystallise until a later date (see, e.g., *CIS/ 647/2007* referred to in the notes to reg.23 of the Income Support Regulations under "*What constitutes income*" in Vol.II in this series). The Commissioner does not appear to be suggesting that there is any difference in the application of the principle in *Leeves* if the resource is capital, as opposed to income, and in the context of income it has been applied, at least in some cases, at a later point.

The Commissioner also confirmed that there is no formal diminishing rule for actual capital but that a similar result can be achieved using inferences in the fact finding process.

He further confirmed that reg.14 of the Social Security (Payments on account, Overpayments and Recovery) Regulations 1988 (SI 1998/664) reduces the amount of an overpayment that is recoverable. It does not by itself affect the amount of the capital that the claimant retains for the purpose of a later claim.

p.408, *annotation to the Income Support (General) Regulations 1987, reg.46 (calculation of capital)*

3.039   In *CIS/213/2004* and *CIS/214/2004* the Commissioner, having obtained a further opinion as to the remedies available under French law to Ms V if the claimant had decided to treat the property as his own, has issued a final decision to the effect that there is no reason under French law or otherwise why the value of the property should not be included in the claimant's capital.

p.445, *amendment to the Income Support (General) Regulations 1987, Ch.7 (liable relatives)*

3.040   With effect from October 27, 2008, reg.2(5) of the Social Security (Child Maintenance Amendments) Regulations 2008 (SI 2008/2111) substituted the words "child maintenance and liable relative payments" for the words "liable relatives" in the heading to Ch.7.

pp.445–447, *amendment to the Income Support (General) Regulations 1987, reg.54 (interpretation)*

With effect from October 27, 2008, reg.2(6)(a) of the Social Security **3.041** (Child Maintenance Amendments) Regulations 2008 (SI 2008/2111) inserted the following new definitions in the appropriate places in reg.54:

" "child maintenance" means any payment towards the maintenance of a child or young person, including any payment made voluntarily and payments made under—
  (a) the Child Support Act 1991;
  (b) the Child Support (Northern Ireland) Order 1991;
  (c) a court order;
  (d) a consent order;
  (e) a maintenance agreement registered for execution in the Books of Council and Session or the sheriff court books;

"claimant's family" shall be construed in accordance with section 137 of the Contributions and Benefits Act 1992 (interpretation of part 7 and supplementary provisions);

"housing costs" means those costs which may be met under regulation 17(1)(e) or 18(1)(f) (housing costs);

"ordinary clothing and footwear" means clothing and footwear for normal daily use but does not include school uniforms;".

From the same date, reg.2(6)(b) of the same amending regulations substituted the words "in the circumstances set out in s.78(6)(c) of the Social Security Administration Act 1992 (liability to maintain another person)" for the words "by virtue of section 26(3)(c) of the Act (liability to maintain)" in para.(d) of the definition of "liable relative" in reg.54.

From the same date, reg.2(6)(c)(i) of the same amending regulations omitted the words "including, except in the case of a discretionary trust, any payment which would be so made or derived upon application being made by the claimant but which has not been acquired by him but only from the date on which it could be expected to be acquired were an application made;" in the definition of "payment" in reg.54.

From the same date, reg.2(6)(c)(ii) of the same amending regulations substituted the following paragraph for para.(e) in the definition of "payment" in reg.54:

"(e) made to a third party, or in respect of a third party, unless the payment is—
    (i) in relation to the claimant or the claimant's family; and
    (ii) the payment is in respect of food, ordinary clothing or footwear, fuel, rent, housing costs, council tax or water charges;".

From the same date, reg.2(6)(d)(i) of the same amending regulations omitted the words "in pursuance of a court order or agreement for maintenance" in para.(a) of the definition of "periodical payment" in reg.54.

From the same date, reg.2(6)(d)(ii) of the same amending regulations substituted the words ", after the appropriate disregard under para.73 of Sch.9 (sums to be disregarded in the calculation of income other than earnings) has been applied to it, that does not exceed" for the words "not exceeding" in para.(c) of the definition of "periodical payment" in reg.54.

p.447, *annotation to the Income Support (General) Regulations 1987, reg.54 (interpretation)*

3.042   From October 27, 2008 regs 60A to 60D which contained separate rules for the treatment of child support maintenance have been omitted. All liable relative payments and child maintenance payments (see the new definition of "child maintenance" above) are now taken into account in accordance with regs 54 to 59.

p.448, *annotation to the Income Support (General) Regulations 1987, reg.54 (interpretation), definition of "payment"*

3.043   Under the new form of para.(e) in the definition of "payment", payments from liable relatives to third parties in respect of the claimant or the claimant's family only count as liable relative payments if the payment is for the items listed in sub-para.(ii). The same applies if the payment is to the claimant or a member of the claimant's family in respect of a third party. The test of reasonableness under the old form of para.(e) has gone.

p.449, *amendment to the Income Support (General) Regulations 1987, reg.55 (treatment of liable relative payments)*

3.044   With effect from October 27, 2008, reg.2(2)(b) of the Social Security (Child Maintenance Amendments) Regulations 2008 (SI 2008/2111) inserted the words "child maintenance or" before the words "liable relative" in the heading to reg.55.

From the same date, reg.2(7) of the same amending regulations substituted the words "paragraph 73 of Schedule 9 (sums to be disregarded in the calculation of income other than earnings)" for the words "except where regulation 60(1) (liable relative payments to be treated as capital) applies" in reg.55.

p.449, *annotation to the Income Support (General) Regulations 1987, reg.55 (treatment of child maintenance or liable relative payments)*

3.045   From October 27, 2008 reg.60 has been omitted. This means that all liable relative and child maintenance payments will be treated as income (subject to the £20 disregard of child maintenance payments in para.73 of Sch.9).

p.451, *amendment to the Income Support (General) Regulations 1987, reg.57 (period over which payments other than periodical payments are to be taken into account)*

With effect from October 27, 2008, reg.2(8) of the Social Security 3.046
(Child Maintenance Amendments) Regulations 2008 (SI 2008/2111) substituted a new reg.57:

"Period over which payments other than periodical payments are to be taken into account

57.—(1) The period over which a payment other than a periodical payment (a "non-periodical payment") is to be taken account shall be determined as follows.

(2) Except in a case where paragraph (4) applies, the number of weeks over which a non-periodical payment is to be taken into account shall be equal to the number obtained by dividing that payment by the amount referred to in paragraph (3).

(3) The amount is the aggregate of £2 and—

(a) the amount of income support that would be payable had no payment been made, and

(b) where applicable, the maximum amount of disregard that would apply to the payment under paragraph 73 of Schedule 9.

(4) This paragraph applies in a case where a liable relative makes a periodical payment and a non-periodical payment concurrently and the weekly amount of the periodical payment (as calculated in accordance with regulation 58) is less than B.

(5) In a case where paragraph (4) applies, the non-periodical payment shall, subject to paragraphs (6) and (7), be taken into account over a period of the number of weeks equal to the number obtained by applying the formula—

$$\frac{A}{B - C}$$

(6) If the liable relative ceases to make periodical payments, the balance (if any) of the non-periodical payment shall be taken into account over the number of weeks equal to the number obtained by dividing that balance by the amount referred to in paragraph (3).

(7) If the amount of any subsequent periodical payment varies, the balance (if any) of the non-periodical payment shall be taken into account over a period of the number of weeks equal to the number obtained by applying the formula—

$$\frac{D}{B - E}$$

(8) The period under paragraph (2) or (4) shall begin on the date on which the payment is treated as paid under regulation 59 (date on which a liable relative payment is treated as paid) and the period under paragraph (6) and (7) shall begin on the first day of the benefit week

in which the cessation or variation of the periodical payment occurred.

(9) Any fraction which arises by applying a calculation or formula referred to in this regulation shall be treated as a corresponding fraction of a week.

(10) In paragraphs (4) to (7)—

A = the amount of the non-periodical payment;

B = the aggregate of £2 and the amount of income support that would be payable had the periodical payment not been made and, where applicable, the maximum disregard under paragraph 73 of Schedule 9;

C = the weekly amount of the periodical payment;

D = the balance (if any) of the non-periodical payment;

E = the weekly amount of any subsequent periodical payment."

p.452, *annotation to the Income Support (General) Regulations 1987, reg.57 (period over which payments other than periodical payments are to be taken into account)*

3.047   Note that there is no longer any provision to treat liable relative payments as capital as reg.60 has been omitted with effect from October 27, 2008.

Note also that the pre-April 6, 2004 form of this regulation for "transitional cases" (i.e., where the claimant remains entitled to the child elements in income support and has not transferred to child tax credit) is no longer being retained.

p.452, *amendment to the Income Support (General) Regulations 1987, reg.58 (calculation of the weekly amount of a liable relative payment)*

3.048   With effect from October 27, 2008, reg.2(2)(c) of the Social Security (Child Maintenance Amendments) Regulations 2008 (SI 2008/2111) inserted the words "child maintenance or" before the words "liable relative" in the heading to reg.58.

p.453, *amendment to the Income Support (General) Regulations 1987, reg.59 (date on which a liable relative payment is to be treated as paid)*

3.049   With effect from October 27, 2008, reg.2(2)(d) of the Social Security (Child Maintenance Amendments) Regulations 2008 (SI 2008/2111) inserted the words "child maintenance or" before the words "liable relative" in the heading to reg.59.

p.454, *amendment to the Income Support (General) Regulations 1987, reg.60 (liable relative payments to be treated as capital)*

3.050   With effect from October 27, 2008, reg.2(4)(b) of the Social Security (Child Maintenance Amendments) Regulations 2008 (SI 2008/2111) omitted reg.60.

pp.455–460, *amendment to the Income Support (General) Regulations 1987, Ch.7A (child support)*

With effect from October 27, 2008, reg.2(4)(c) of the Social Security (Child Maintenance Amendments) Regulations 2008 (SI 2008/2111) omitted Chapter 7A.   3.051

p.476, *amendment to the Income Support (General) Regulations 1987, reg.62 (calculation of grant income)*

With effect from September 1, 2008 (or if the student's period of study begins between August 1 and August 31, 2008, the first day of the period), reg.2(3)(a) of the Social Security (Students and Miscellaneous Amendments) Regulations 2008 (SI 2008/1599) substituted "£295" for "£290" in reg.62(2A)(a).   3.052

From the same date, reg.2(3)(b) of the same amending regulations substituted "£380" for "£370" in reg.62(2A)(b).

p.484, *amendment to the Income Support (General) Regulations 1987, reg.66A (treatment of student loans)*

With effect from September 1, 2008 (or if the student's period of study begins between August 1 and August 31, 2008, the first day of the period), reg.2(4)(a) of the Social Security (Students and Miscellaneous Amendments) Regulations 2008 (SI 2008/1599) substituted "£295" for "£290" in reg.66A(5)(a).   3.053

From the same date, reg.2(4)(b) of the same amending regulations substituted "£380" for "£370" in reg.66A(5)(b).

p.500, *amendment of Income Support (General) Regulations 1987, reg.72(1) (Assessment of income and capital in urgent cases)*

With effect from October 27, 2008, reg.2(1) and (8) of the Employment and Support Allowance (Consequential Provisions) (No.2) Regulations 2008 (SI 2008/1554) amended reg.72(1)(a)(ii) by adding the words "or of employment and support allowance under regulation 164 of the Employment and Support Allowance Regulations" after the date "1996".   3.054

p.501, *amendment of Income Support (General) Regulations 1987, reg.72(2) (Assessment of income and capital in urgent cases)*

With effect from October 27, 2008, reg.2(1) and (8) of the Employment and Support Allowance (Consequential Provisions) (No.2) Regulations 2008 (SI 2008/1554) amended reg.72(2) by adding the words, "regulation 164 of the Employment and Support Allowance Regulations" after the words "these Regulations".   3.055

515

p.503, *amendment of Income Support (General) Regulations 1987, reg.73 (Amount of income support payable)*

3.056   With effect from October 27, 2008, reg.2(1) and (9) of the Employ-ment and Support Allowance (Consequential Provisions) (No.2) Reg-ulations 2008 (SI 2008/1554) amended the definition of "B" in reg.73(3) to read as follows:

> " 'B' means the amount of any income support, jobseeker's allowance, maternity allowance, short-term or long-term incapacity benefit, or [severe disablement allowance or employment and support allowance] payable in respect of any day in the part-week;".

pp.504–505, *amendment of Income Support (General) Regulations 1987, reg.75 (Modifications in the calculation of income)*

3.057   With effect from October 27, 2008, reg.2(1) and (10) of the Employ-ment and Support Allowance (Consequential Provisions) (No.2) Reg-ulations 2008 (SI 2008/1554) amended reg.75 by substituting the words "severe disablement allowance or employment and support allowance" for the words "or severe disablement allowance" in sub-paras (b), (e) and (f).

pp.515–517, *annotation to the Income Support (General) Regulations 1987, Sch.1B, para.7 (persons incapable of work)*

3.058   Note that from October 27, 2008 *new* claims for income support under para.7(a) or (b) on the ground of incapacity or deemed incapacity for work are no longer possible as they are treated as claims for ESA (see reg.2(1) of the Employment and Support Allowance (Transitional Provi-sions) Regulations 2008 (SI 2008/795) in Part 1 of this Supplement), unless they link with (i.e., are made not more than eight weeks after) a previous income support entitlement for at least four days on the grounds of disability: see reg.2(2)(c) of the Transitional Provisions Reg-ulations; or the claimant is entitled to incapacity benefit or severe dis-ablement allowance: see reg.2(2)(d) of those Regulations, as amended by the Employment and Support Allowance (Transitional Provisions) (Amendment) Regulations 2008 (SI 2008/2783); or they are in respect of a period before October 27, 2008.

Income support on the grounds of disability means "income support awarded to a person to whom reg.13(2)(b) or (bb) of, or para.7(a) or (b), 10, 12 or 13 of Schedule 1B to, the Income Support (General) Regulations 1987 (prescribed categories of person) applies" (reg.1(4) of the Transitional Provisions Regulations, as amended by reg.42 of the Employment and Support Allowance (Miscellaneous Amendments) Regulations 2008 (SI 2008/2428)). Note also that a claimant who has an existing award of income support on the grounds of disability cannot claim ESA (reg.3(1) of the Transitional Provisions Regulations); if a person claims ESA who would be entitled to income support under reg.2(2)(c) or (d) of the Transitional Provisions Regulations, the claim will be treated as a claim for income support (reg.3(2) of the

516

Transitional Provisions Regulations); and a claim for ESA in respect of a period before October 27, 2008 may be treated by the Secretary of State as a claim in the alternative for incapacity benefit or income support on the grounds of disability (reg.4 of the Transitional Provisions Regulations).

p.518, *annotation to the Income Support (General) Regulations 1987, Sch.1B (prescribed categories of person), paras 10–12 (disabled students/ deaf students)*

Note that from October 27, 2008 a *new* claim for income support under para.10 or para.12 is no longer possible as it is treated as a claim for ESA (see reg.2(1) of the Employment and Support Allowance (Transitional Provisions) Regulations 2008 (SI 2008/795) in Part 1 of this Supplement), unless it links with (i.e., is made not more than eight weeks after) a previous income support entitlement for at least four days on the grounds of disability: see reg.2(2)(c) of the Transitional Provisions Regulations; or the claimant is entitled to incapacity benefit or severe disablement allowance: see reg.2(2)(d) of those Regulations; as amended by the Employment and Support Allowance (Transitional Provisions) (Amendment) Regulations 2008 (SI 2008/2783); or it is in respect of a period before October 27, 2008. 3.059

Income support on the grounds of disability means "income support awarded to a person to whom reg.13(2)(b) or (bb) of, or para.7(a) or (b), 10, 12 or 13 of Sch.1B to, the Income Support (General) Regulations 1987 (prescribed categories of person) applies" (reg.1(4) of the Transitional Provisions Regulations, as amended by reg.42 of the Employment and Support Allowance (Miscellaneous Amendments) Regulations 2008 (SI 2008/2428)). Note also that a claimant who has an existing award of income support on the grounds of disability cannot claim ESA (reg.3(1) of the Transitional Provisions Regulations); if a person claims ESA who would be entitled to income support under reg.2(2)(c) or (d) of the Transitional Provisions Regulations, the claim will be treated as a claim for income support (reg.3(2) of the Transitional Provisions Regulations); and a claim for ESA in respect of a period before October 27, 2008 may be treated by the Secretary of State as a claim in the alternative for incapacity benefit or income support on the grounds of disability (reg.4 of the Transitional Provisions Regulations).

p.518, *annotation to the Income Support (General) Regulations 1987, Sch.1B (prescribed categories of person), para.13 (blind persons)*

Note that from October 27, 2008 a *new* claim for income support by a person to whom para.13 applies is no longer possible as it is treated as a claim for ESA (see reg.2(1) of the Employment and Support Allowance (Transitional Provisions) Regulations 2008 (SI 2008/795) in Part 1 of this Supplement), unless it links with (i.e., is made not more than eight weeks after) a previous income support entitlement for at least four days on the grounds of disability: see reg.2(2)(c) of the Transitional 3.060

Provisions Regulations; or the claimant is entitled to incapacity benefit or severe disablement allowance: see reg.2(2)(d) of those Regulations, as amended by the Employment and Support Allowance (Transitional Provisions) (Amendment) Regulations 2008 (SI 2008/2783); or it is in respect of a period before October 27, 2008.

Income support on the grounds of disability means "income support awarded to a person to whom reg.13(2)(b) or (bb) of, or para.7(a) or (b), 10, 12 or 13 of Sch.1B to, the Income Support (General) Regulations 1987 (prescribed categories of person) applies" (reg.1(4) of the Transitional Provisions Regulations, as amended by reg.42 of the Employment and Support Allowance (Miscellaneous Amendments) Regulations 2008 (SI 2008/2428)). Note also that a claimant who has an existing award of income support on the grounds of disability cannot claim ESA (reg.3(1) of the Transitional Provisions Regulations); if a person claims ESA who would be entitled to income support under reg.2(2)(c) or (d) of the Transitional Provisions Regulations, the claim will be treated as a claim for income support (reg.3(2) of the Transitional Provisions Regulations); and a claim for ESA in respect of a period before October 27, 2008 may be treated by the Secretary of State as a claim in the alternative for incapacity benefit or income support on the grounds of disability (reg.4 of the Transitional Provisions Regulations).

p.545, *amendment to the Income Support (General) Regulations 1987, Sch.3 (housing costs), para.1(housing costs)*

3.061 With effect from October 27, 2008, reg.2(11)(a)(i) of the Employment and Support Allowance (Consequential Provisions) (No.2) Regulations 2008 (SI 2008/1554) added the following new head after head (c) in para.1(3):

"(d) who is in receipt of an employment and support allowance which includes an amount under section 2(2) or (3) or 4(4) or (5) of the Welfare Reform Act (components)."

From the same date, reg.2(11)(a)(ii) of the same amending regulations added the following words after the words "disqualification etc)" in para.1(4):

"or disqualified for receiving employment and support allowance or treated as not having limited capability for work in accordance with regulations made under section 18 of the Welfare Reform Act (disqualification)".

p.545, *amendment to the Income Support (General) Regulations 1987, Sch.3 (housing costs), para.1A (previous entitlement to income-based jobseeker's allowance or state pension credit)*

3.062 With effect from October 27, 2008, reg.2(11)(b)(i) of the Employment and Support Allowance (Consequential Provisions) (No.2) Regulations 2008 (SI 2008/1554) inserted the words ", income-related employment and support allowance" after the word "allowance" in the heading.

From the same date, reg.2(11)(b)(ii) of the same amending regulations inserted the words "or income-related employment and support allowance" after the words "income-based jobseeker's allowance" each time they occur in para.1A.

From the same date, reg.2(11)(b)(iii) of the same amending regulations added the words "or paragraphs 16 to 18 of Schedule 6 to the Employment and Support Allowance Regulations" after "1996" in para.1A(1)(a).

p.548, *amendment to the Income Support (General) Regulations 1987, Sch.3 (housing costs), para.4 (housing costs not met)*

With effect from October 27, 2008, reg.2(11)(c) of the Employment and Support Allowance (Consequential Provisions) (No.2) Regulations 2008 (SI 2008/1554) inserted the words "or income-related employment and support allowance" after the words "income support" each time they occur in para.4(4). **3.063**

pp.550–551, *amendment to the Income Support (General) Regulations 1987, Sch.3 (housing costs), para.6 (existing housing costs)*

With effect from October 27, 2008, reg.2(11)(d) of the Employment and Support Allowance (Consequential Provisions) (No.2) Regulations 2008 (SI 2008/1554) substituted the words ", state pension credit or income-related employment and support allowance" for the words "or state pension credit" in para.6(1B). **3.064**

p.552, *amendment to the Income Support (General) Regulations 1987, Sch.3 (housing costs), para.8 (new housing costs)*

With effect from October 27, 2008, reg.2(11)(e) of the Employment and Support Allowance (Consequential Provisions) (No.2) Regulations 2008 (SI 2008/1554) substituted the words ", state pension credit or income-related employment and support allowance" for the words "or state pension credit" in para.8(1B). **3.065**

pp.555–558, *amendment to the Income Support (General) Regulations 1987, Sch.3 (housing costs), para.14 (linking rules)*

With effect from October 27, 2008, reg.2(11)(f)(i) of the Employment and Support Allowance (Consequential Provisions) (No.2) Regulations 2008 (SI 2008/1554) substituted the words ", incapacity benefit or contributory employment and support allowance" for the words "or incapacity benefit" in para.14(5)(a). **3.066**

From the same date, reg.2(11)(f)(ii) of the same amending regulations (as amended by reg.41(2)(a) of the Employment and Support Allowance

(Miscellaneous Amendments) Regulations 2008 (SI 2008/2428)) added the following new sub-paragraph after sub-para.(14):

"(15) For the purpose of determining whether the linking rules set out in this paragraph apply in a case where a claimant, a claimant's partner or a claimant's former partner was entitled to income-related employment and support allowance, any reference to income support in this Schedule shall be taken to include also a reference to income-related employment and support allowance;".

p.561, *amendment to the Income Support (General) Regulations 1987, Sch.3 (housing costs), para.18 (non-dependant deductions)*

3.067   With effect from October 27, 2008, reg.2(11)(g) of the Employment and Support Allowance (Consequential Provisions) (No.2) Regulations 2008 (SI 2008/1554), as amended by reg.41(2)(b) of the Employment and Support Allowance (Miscellaneous Amendments) Regulations 2008 (SI 2008/2428), added the following new head after head (h) in para.18(7):

"(i)   he is aged less than 25 and is in receipt of employment and support allowance which does not include an amount under section 4(4) or (5) of the Welfare Reform Act (components)."

pp.574–575, *annotation to the Income Support (General) Regulations 1987, Sch.3 (housing costs), para.4(4)*

3.068   In *CIS/492/2008* the claimant had been in receipt of income support until February 2006. In May 2006 he took out a mortgage to purchase his home and two days later he reclaimed income support. His claim was refused on the ground that he was not entitled to housing costs (in the form of mortgage interest) because the mortgage had been taken out during a "relevant period", i.e., a period falling between two periods of entitlement to income support separated by not more than 26 weeks (without the inclusion of the mortgage interest in his applicable amount his income exceeded his applicable amount).

The Commissioner dismissed the claimant's appeal. It was possible to argue that the loan was not incurred in a relevant period because if housing costs were not added to the claimant's applicable amount he was not entitled to income support when he reclaimed in May 2006 since his income was too high. However in order to apply para.4(4) sensibly it had to be read as if it began:

"The "relevant period" for the purposes of this paragraph is any period during which the person to whom the loan was made (a) is *or would but for paragraph (2) above be* entitled to income support".

The Commissioner also confirmed that in order to be entitled after the 26-week gap had elapsed it was necessary for the claimant to make a fresh claim.

pp.577–578, *annotation to the Income Support (General) Regulations 1987, Sch.3 (housing costs), para.4(10)*

In *CIS/1390/2007* the claimant, who had four children, three boys   3.069
aged 17, 13 and 12 and a girl aged 4, had moved to a four-bedroom
house (from a two-bedroom one) in October 2004. The tribunal concluded that the primary purpose of the move was to provide separate
sleeping accommodation for children of different sexes and that
para.4(10) applied so that the claimant was entitled to full housing costs
on her new loans. However, the Commissioner allowed the Secretary of
State's appeal, stating that it could not possibly be said that the need to
make provision for circumstances that might exist when the claimant's
daughter reached the age of 10 in December 2009 existed as at October
2004. Paragraph 4(10) was not satisfied simply because the claimant had
a genuine belief that a need currently existed. The need had to exist as
an objective matter. Furthermore, the need to provide separate sleeping
accommodation for children aged 10 or over of opposite sexes had to be
the sole reason for the move. In this case the need was too remote to say
that it was the sole reason for the move. The Commissioner also raised
the point (but did not reach a conclusion on it) that by the time the
claimant's daughter reached the age of 10 the claimant's youngest son
would be 17 (and so no longer a "child" as defined in s.137 of the
Contributions and Benefits Act). He stated that it may be necessary in
the context of para.4(10) for "child" to be given a broader meaning than
in s.137.

p.610, *amendment of Income Support (General) Regulations 1987, Sch.7,*
para.19A (Applicable amounts in special cases: Persons who have
commenced remunerative work)

With effect from October 27, 2008, reg.2(1) and (10) of the Employ-   3.070
ment and Support Allowance (Consequential Provisions) (No.2) Regulations 2008 (SI 2008/1554) amended the second column of
para.19A(1) by revoking the word "or" after head (i); adding the following head after head (ii):

> "or
> (iii) as the case may be, Schedule 6 to the Employment and Sup-
>   port Allowance Regulations (housing costs),"

and inserting the words ", income-related employment and support
allowance" after the words "income support" where they appear for the
first time in sub-para.(b).

p.614, *amendment to the Income Support (General) Regulations 1987,*
Sch.8 (sums to be disregarded in the calculation of earnings), para.4

With effect from October 27, 2008, reg.2(13) of the Employment and   3.071
Support Allowance (Consequential Provisions) (No.2) Regulations 2008
(SI 2008/1554) inserted the words "or employment and support allowance" after the words "income support" each time they occur in
para.4(7).

p.621, *amendment to the Income Support (General) Regulations 1987, Sch.9 (sums to be disregarded in the calculation of income other than earnings), para.7*

3.072   With effect from October 27, 2008, reg.2(14)(a) of the Employment and Support Allowance (Consequential Provisions) (No.2) Regulations 2008 (SI 2008/1554) substituted the words ", jobseeker's allowance or employment and support allowance" for the words "or jobseeker's allowance" in para.7(b).

p.622, *amendment to the Income Support (General) Regulations 1987, Sch.9 (sums to be disregarded in the calculation of income other than earnings), para.13*

3.073   With effect from October 27, 2008, reg.2(14)(b) of the Employment and Support Allowance (Consequential Provisions) (No.2) Regulations 2008 (SI 2008/1554) substituted the words ", severe disablement allowance or an employment and support allowance" for the words "or severe disablement allowance" in para.13(1)(a).

p.630, *amendment to the Income Support (General) Regulations 1987, Sch.9 (sums to be disregarded in the calculation of income other than earnings), para.73*

3.074   With effect from October 27, 2008, reg.2(9) of the Social Security (Child Maintenance Amendments) Regulations 2008 (SI 2008/2111) substituted the following sub-paragraphs for sub-paras (3) and (4) in para.73:

> "(3) No more than £20 shall be disregarded in respect of each week to which any payment of child maintenance is attributed in accordance with regulations 55 to 59 (child maintenance and liable relatives).
> (4) In this paragraph, "child maintenance" shall have the same meaning as in regulation 54."

pp.650–651, *annotation to the Income Support (General) Regulations 1987, Sch.9, para.73*

3.075   Section 23 of the Child Support, Pensions and Social Security Act 2000 was brought fully into force by the Child Support, Pensions and Social Security Act 2000 (Commencement No.14) Order 2008 (SI 2008/2545) (c.109), art.4, with effect from October 27, 2008. The effect is that s.10 of the Child Support Act 1995 (child maintenance bonus) has been repealed in all cases and it will no longer be possible for any person to accrue a child maintenance bonus. Instead, a claimant who is getting child maintenance payments (as defined in reg.54) will be eligible for the disregard under para.73. From October 27, 2008 this was increased to £20 per week.

p.653, *amendment to the Income Support (General) Regulations 1987, Sch.10 (capital to be disregarded), para.7*

With effect from October 27, 2008, reg.2(15)(a) of the Employment   3.076
and Support Allowance (Consequential Provisions) (No.2) Regulations
2008 (SI 2008/1554) inserted the words ", an income-related employment and support allowance" after the words "income-related benefit"
in para.7(1)(b).

From the same date, reg.2(15)(b)(i) of the same amending regulations
inserted the words ", an income-related employment and support allowance" after the words "income support" in para.7(3)(a).

From the same date, reg.2(15)(b)(ii) of the same amending regulations inserted the words ", an income-related employment and support
allowance" after the words "income support" in para.7(3)(b).

pp.665–667, *annotation to the Income Support (General) Regulations
1987, Sch.10 (capital to be disregarded), para.4*

In *CH/3777/2007* the Commissioner states that "estranged" in the   3.077
context of para.4(b) implies no more than that

> "the reason for the two people concerned no longer living together as
> a couple in the same household is that the relationship between them
> has broken down. It is not a necessary, or for that matter sufficient,
> requirement to come within the term that dealings and communica-
> tions between the two of them should be acrimonious."

The Commissioner did not accept that "estranged" required an element of disharmony because otherwise it added nothing to the reference
to a "former partner" in para.4(b) (and para.25). There were occasions
when a couple in a continuing relationship ceased living together and so
counted as a "former couple", e.g., when one of them had to go into a
residential care home, without there being any question of estrangement
between them.

pp.674–675, *annotation to the Income Support (General) Regulations
1987, Sch.10 (capital to be disregarded), para.25*

On the meaning of "estranged", see *CH/3777/2007* in the note to   3.078
para.4 of Sch.10 to the Income Support Regulations above.

p.738, *amendment of Community Charges (Deductions from Income
Support) Regulations 1990, reg.2 (Application for deductions from income
support, state pension credit or jobseeker's allowance)*

With effect from October 27, 2008, reg.53(1) and (2) of the Employ-   3.079
ment and Support Allowance (Consequential Provisions) (No.2) Regulations 2008 (SI 2008/1554) amended reg.2 by substituting the words
", jobseeker's allowance or employment and support allowance" for the
words "or jobseeker's allowance" in each of the heading, para.(1) and
para.(2)(e).

p.740, *amendment of Community Charges (Deductions from Income Support) Regulations 1990, reg.3 (Deductions from debtor's income support, state pension credit or jobseeker's allowance)*

3.080   With effect from October 27, 2008, reg.53(1) and (3) of the Employment and Support Allowance (Consequential Provisions) (No.2) Regulations 2008 (SI 2008/1554) amended reg.2 by substituting the words ", jobseeker's allowance or employment and support allowance" for the words "or jobseeker's allowance" in the heading, and the words, "income-based jobseeker's allowance or income-related employment and support allowance" for the words "or income-based jobseeker's allowance" in para.(1).

p.741, *amendment of Community Charges (Deductions from Income Support) Regulations 1990, reg.4 (Circumstances, time of making and termination of deductions)*

3.081   With effect from October 27, 2008, reg.53(1) and (4) of the Employment and Support Allowance (Consequential Provisions) (No.2) Regulations 2008 (SI 2008/1554) amended reg.4 by substituting the words ", jobseeker's allowance or employment and support allowance" for the words "or jobseeker's allowance".

p.743, *amendment of Fines (Deductions from Income Support) Regulations 1992, reg.1(2) (Citation, commencement and interpretation: definition of "benefit week")*

3.082   With effect from October 27, 2008, reg.54(1) and (2) of the Employment and Support Allowance (Consequential Provisions) (No.2) Regulations 2008 (SI 2008/1554) amended the definition of "benefit week" in reg.1(2) by adding the words "or regulation 2(1) of the Employment and Support Allowance Regulations" after the date "1996".

p.743, *amendment of Fines (Deductions from Income Support) Regulations 1992, reg.1(2) (Citation, commencement and interpretation: definition of "contributory employment and support allowance")*

3.083   With effect from October 27, 2008, reg.54(1) and (2) of the Employment and Support Allowance (Consequential Provisions) (No.2) Regulations 2008 (SI 2008/1554) amended reg.1(2) by adding the following definition after the definition of "contribution-based jobseeker's allowance":

" 'contributory employment and support allowance' means a contributory allowance under Part 1 of the Welfare Reform Act;"

p.743, *amendment of Fines (Deductions from Income Support) Regulations 1992, reg.1(2) (Citation, commencement and interpretation: definition of "the Employment and Support Allowance Regulations 2008")*

3.084   With effect from October 27, 2008, reg.54(1) and (2) of the Employment and Support Allowance (Consequential Provisions) (No.2) Regulations 2008 (SI 2008/1554) amended reg.1(2) by adding the following definition after the definition of "court":

" 'the Employment and Support Allowance Regulations' means the Employment and Support Allowance Regulations 2008;"

p.744, *amendment of Fines (Deductions from Income Support) Regulations 1992, reg.1(2) (Citation, commencement and interpretation: definition of "income-related employment and support allowance")*

With effect from October 27, 2008, reg.54(1) and (2) of the Employ-   **3.085** ment and Support Allowance (Consequential Provisions) (No.2) Regulations 2008 (SI 2008/1554) amended reg.1(2) by adding the following definition after the definition of "income-based jobseeker's allowance":

" 'income-related employment and support allowance means—
   (a) an income-related allowance under Part 1 of the Welfare Reform Act; and
   (b) in a case where, if there was no entitlement to contributory employment and support allowance, there would be entitlement to income-related employment and support allowance at the same rate, contributory employment and support allowance;"

p.744, *amendment of Fines (Deductions from Income Support) Regulations 1992, reg.1(2) (Citation, commencement and interpretation: definition of "personal allowance for a single claimant aged not less than 25")*

With effect from October 27, 2008, reg.54(1) and (2) of the Employ-   **3.086** ment and Support Allowance (Consequential Provisions) (No.2) Regulations 2008 (SI 2008/1554) amended the definition of "personal allowance for a single claimant aged not less than 25" in reg.1(2) by adding the following after sub-para.(b):

"(c) in the case of a person who is entitled to an income-related employment and support allowance, the amount specified for the time being in paragraph 1(1)(b) of column 2 of schedule 4 to the Employment and Support Allowance Regulations;"

p.744, *amendment of Fines (Deductions from Income Support) Regulations 1992, reg.1(2) (Citation, commencement and interpretation: definition of "social security office")*

With effect from October 27, 2008, reg.54(1) and (2) of the Employ-   **3.087** ment and Support Allowance (Consequential Provisions) (No.2) Regulations 2008 (SI 2008/1554) amended the definition of "social security office" in reg.1(2) by substituting the words ", jobseeker's allowance or an employment and support allowance" for the words "or a jobseeker's allowance".

p.744, *amendment of Fines (Deductions from Income Support) Regulations 1992, reg.1(2) (Citation, commencement and interpretation: definition of "the Welfare Reform Act")*

3.088   With effect from October 27, 2008, reg.54(1) and (2) of the Employment and Support Allowance (Consequential Provisions) (No.2) Regulations 2008 (SI 2008/1554) amended reg.1(2) by adding the following definition after the definition of "tribunal":

" 'the Welfare Reform Act' means the Welfare Reform Act 2007;"

p.745, *amendment of Fines (Deductions from Income Support) Regulations 1992, reg.2 (Application for deductions from income support, state pension credit or jobseeker's allowance)*

3.089   With effect from October 27, 2008, reg.54(1) and (3) of the Employment and Support Allowance (Consequential Provisions) (No.2) Regulations 2008 (SI 2008/1554) amended reg.2 by substituting the words ", jobseeker's allowance or employment and support allowance" for the words "jobseeker's allowance" each time the latter words occur.

p.745, *amendment of Fines (Deductions from Income Support) Regulations 1992, reg.2A (Information that the court may require)*

3.090   With effect from October 27, 2008, reg.54(1) and (4) of the Employment and Support Allowance (Consequential Provisions) (No.2) Regulations 2008 (SI 2008/1554) amended reg.2A by substituting the words ", a jobseeker's allowance or an employment and support allowance" for the words "or a jobseeker's allowance".

p.745, *amendment of Council Tax (Deductions from Income Support) Regulations 1992, reg.4 (Contents of application)*

3.091   With effect from October 27, 2008, reg.55(1) and (5) of the Employment and Support Allowance (Consequential Provisions) (No.2) Regulations 2008 (SI 2008/1554) amended reg.4 by substituting the words ", a jobseeker's allowance or an employment and support allowance" for the words "or jobseeker's allowance".

pp.745–746, *amendment of Fines (Deductions from Income Support) Regulations 1992, reg.4 (Deductions from offender's income support, state pension credit or jobseeker's allowance)*

3.092   With effect from October 27, 2008, reg.54(1) and (5) of the Employment and Support Allowance (Consequential Provisions) (No.2) Regulations 2008 (SI 2008/1554) amended reg.4 by substituting the words ", income-based jobseeker's allowance or income-related employment and support allowance" for the words "or income-based jobseeker's allowance" in para.(1)(a) and amending para.(2) to read as follows:

"(2) Subject to paragraphs (3) and (4) and regulation 7, where—

(a) the Secretary of State receives an application from a court in respect of an offender who is entitled to contribution-based job-seeker's allowance [or contributory employment and support allowance]; and

[(b) the amount payable, before any deductions under this para-graph, of—

    (i) contribution-based jobseeker's allowance is equal to or more than one-third of the age related amount applicable to the offender under section 4 (1) (a) of the Jobseekers Act; or

    (ii) contributory employment and support allowance is equal to or more than one third of the amount applicable *to* the offender under section 2(1)(a) of the Welfare Reform Act,

as the case may be,]

the Secretary of State may deduct a sum from that benefit which is equal to one-third of the age-related amount applicable to the offender under section 4(1)(a) of the Jobseekers Act [or under section 2(1)(a) of the Welfare Reform Act] and pay that sum to the court towards satisfaction of the fine or the sum required to be paid by compensation order."

p.748, *amendment of Fines (Deductions from Income Support) Regulations 1992, reg.7 (Circumstances, time of making and termination of deductions)*

With effect from October 27, 2008, reg.54(1) and (6) of the Employ-ment and Support Allowance (Consequential Provisions) (No.2) Reg-ulations 2008 (SI 2008/1554) amended reg.7 by substituting the words ", jobseeker's allowance or employment and support allowance" for the words "or jobseeker's allowance" each time the latter words occur.   **3.093**

p.752, *amendment of Council Tax (Deductions from Income Support) Regulations 1992, reg.1(2) (Citation, commencement and interpretation: definition of "benefit week")*

With effect from October 27, 2008, reg.55(1) and (2) of the Employ-ment and Support Allowance (Consequential Provisions) (No.2) Reg-ulations 2008 (SI 2008/1554) amended the definition of "benefit week" in reg.1(2) by adding the words ", regulation 2(1) of the Employment and Support Allowance Regulations" after the words "State Pension Credit Regulations 2002".   **3.094**

p.752, *amendment of Council Tax (Deductions from Income Support) Regulations 1992, reg.1(2) (Citation, commencement and interpretation: definition of "contributory employment and support allowance")*

With effect from October 27, 2008, reg.55(1) and (2) of the Employ-ment and Support Allowance (Consequential Provisions) (No.2) Reg-ulations 2008 (SI 2008/1554) amended reg.1(2) by adding the following   **3.095** definition after the definition of "contribution-based jobseeker's allowance":

" 'contributory employment and support allowance' means a contributory allowance under Part 1 of the Welfare Reform Act (employment and support allowance);"

p.752, *amendment of Council Tax (Deductions from Income Support) Regulations 1992, reg.1(2) (Citation, commencement and interpretation: definition of "income-related employment and support allowance")*

3.096   With effect from October 27, 2008, reg.55(1) and (2) of the Employment and Support Allowance (Consequential Provisions) (No.2) Regulations 2008 (SI 2008/1554) amended reg.1(2) by adding the following definition after the definition of "income-based jobseeker's allowance":

" 'income-related employment and support allowance' means—
  (a) an income-related allowance under Part 1 of the Welfare Reform Act; and
  (b) in a case where, if there was no entitlement to contributory employment and support allowance, there would be entitlement to income-related employment and support allowance at the same rate, contributory employment and support allowance;"

p.752, *amendment of Council Tax (Deductions from Income Support) Regulations 1992, reg.1(2) (Citation, commencement and interpretation: definition of "personal allowance for a single claimant aged not less than 25")*

3.097   With effect from October 27, 2008, reg.55(1) and (2) of the Employment and Support Allowance (Consequential Provisions) (No.2) Regulations 2008 (SI 2008/1554) amended the definition of "personal allowance for a single claimant aged not less than 25" in reg.1(2) by revoking the word "or" after sub-para.(a) adding the following after sub-para.(b):

"(c) in the case of a person who is entitled to an income-related employment and support allowance, the amount specified for the time being in paragraph 1 of column 2 of Schedule 4 to the Employment and Support Allowance Regulations;"

p.753, *amendment of Council Tax (Deductions from Income Support) Regulations 1992, reg.1(2) (Citation, commencement and interpretation: definition of "social security office")*

3.098   With effect from October 27, 2008, reg.55(1) and (2) of the Employment and Support Allowance (Consequential Provisions) (No.2) Regulations 2008 (SI 2008/1554) amended the definition of "social security office" in reg.1(2) by substituting the words ", jobseeker's allowance or an employment and support allowance" for the words "or a jobseeker's allowance".

p.753, *amendment of Council Tax (Deductions from Income Support) Regulations 1992, reg.1(2) (Citation, commencement and interpretation: definition of "the Welfare Reform Act")*

With effect from October 27, 2008, reg.55(1) and (2) of the Employ-   **3.099**
ment and Support Allowance (Consequential Provisions) (No.2) Regulations 2008 (SI 2008/1554) amended reg.1(2) by adding the following
definition after the definition of "tribunal":

" 'the Welfare Reform Act' means the Welfare Reform Act 2007;"

p.753, *amendment of Council Tax (Deductions from Income Support) Regulations 1992, reg.2 (Application for deductions from income support, state pension credit or jobseeker's allowance: England and Wales)*

With effect from October 27, 2008, reg.55(1) and (3) of the Employ-   **3.100**
ment and Support Allowance (Consequential Provisions) (No.2) Regulations 2008 (SI 2008/1554) amended reg.2 by substituting the words
", jobseeker's allowance or employment and support allowance" for the
words "or jobseeker's allowance" in the heading and the words ", a
jobseeker's allowance or an employment and support allowance" for the
words "or jobseeker's allowance" each time the latter words occur in the
body of the regulation.

p.754, *amendment of Council Tax (Deductions from Income Support) Regulations 1992, reg.3 (Application for deductions from income support, state pension credit or jobseeker's allowance: Scotland)*

With effect from October 27, 2008, reg.55(1) and (4) of the Employ-   **3.101**
ment and Support Allowance (Consequential Provisions) (No.2) Regulations 2008 (SI 2008/1554) amended reg.3 by substituting the words
", jobseeker's allowance or employment and support allowance" for the
words "or jobseeker's allowance" in the heading and the words ", a
jobseeker's allowance or an employment and support allowance" for the
words "or jobseeker's allowance" each time the latter words occur in the
body of the regulation.

p.755, *amendment of Council Tax (Deductions from Income Support) Regulations 1992, reg.5 (Deductions from debtor's income support, state pension credit or jobseeker's allowance)*

With effect from October 27, 2008, reg.55(1) and (6) of the Employ-   **3.102**
ment and Support Allowance (Consequential Provisions) (No.2) Regulations 2008 (SI 2008/1554) amended reg.5 by substituting the words
", jobseeker's allowance or employment and support allowance" for the
words "jobseeker's allowance" in the heading; the words "an income-
based jobseeker's allowance or an income-related employment and support allowance" for the words "or income-based jobseeker's allowance"
in para.(1)(a) and amending para.(2) to read as follows:

"(2) Subject to paragraphs (3) and regulation 8, where—

(a) the Secretary of State receives an application from an authority in respect of a debtor who is entitled to contribution-based job-seeker's allowance [or contributory employment and support allowance]; and

[(b) the amount payable, before any deductions under this paragraph, of—

    (i) contribution-based jobseeker's allowance is equal to or more than one-third of the age-related amount applicable to the debtor under section 4 (1) (a) of the Jobseekers Act; or

    (ii) contributory employment and support allowance is equal to or more than one third of the amount applicable to the debtor under section 2(1)(a) of the Welfare Reform Act,

as the case may be,]

the Secretary of State may deduct a sum from that benefit which is equal to one-third of the age-related amount applicable to the debtor under section 4(1)(a) of the Jobseekers Act [or under section 2 (1)(a) of the Welfare Reform Act] and pay that sum to the authority towards satisfaction of any outstanding sum which is or forms part of the amount in respect of which the liability order was made or the summary warrant or the decree was granted."

p.756, *amendment of Council Tax (Deductions from Income Support) Regulations 1992, reg.8 (Circumstances, time of making and termination of deductions)*

3.103   With effect from October 27, 2008, reg.55(1) and (7) of the Employment and Support Allowance (Consequential Provisions) (No.2) Regulations 2008 (SI 2008/1554) amended reg.8 by substituting the words "regulation 5" for the words "regulation 7 or 7A" in para.(1) and the words ", jobseeker's allowance or employment and support allowance" for the words "or jobseeker's allowance" each time the latter words occur.

p.760, *amendment to the Social Security Benefits (Maintenance Payments and Consequential Amendments) Regulations 1996, reg.2 (interpretation for the purposes of section 74A of the Act)*

3.104   With effect from October 27, 2008, reg.59(3) of the Employment and Support Allowance (Consequential Provisions) (No.2) Regulations 2008 (SI 2008/1554) added the following after reg.2(c)(ii):

"or

(iii) any income which is taken into account under Part 10 of the Employment and Support Allowance Regulations for the purposes of calculating the amount of employment and support allowance to which the claimant is entitled."

p.760, *amendment to the Social Security Benefits (Maintenance Payments and Consequential Amendments) Regulations 1996, reg.3 (persons of a prescribed description)*

With effect from October 27, 2008, reg.59(4) of the Employment and   **3.105**
Support Allowance (Consequential Provisions) (No.2) Regulations 2008
(SI 2008/1554) added the following after reg.3(b):

> "or
> (c) is referred to as a "young person" in the Employment and Support Allowance Regulations by virtue of regulation 2(1) of those Regulations."

p.760, *amendment to the Social Security Benefits (Maintenance Payments and Consequential Amendments) Regulations 1996, reg.5 (circumstances in which persons are to be treated as being members of the same household)*

With effect from October 27, 2008, reg.59(5) of the Employment and   **3.106**
Support Allowance (Consequential Provisions) (No.2) Regulations 2008
(SI 2008/1554) omitted the word "either" and inserted the words "or
regulation 156 of the Employment and Support Allowance Regulations"
after the words "Jobseeker's Allowance Regulations" in reg.5.

pp.763–776, *Social Security (Child Maintenance Bonus) Regulations 1996*

With effect from October 27, 2008, s.23 of the Child Support, Pen-   **3.107**
sions and Social Security Act 2000 was brought fully into force by the
Child Support, Pensions and Social Security Act 2000 (Commencement
No.14) Order 2008 (SI 2008/2545) (c.109), art.4. The effect is that s.10
of the Child Support Act 1995 (child maintenance bonus) has been
repealed in all cases and it will no longer be possible for any person to
accrue a child maintenance bonus. However, the *quid pro quo* is that all
income support, income-based JSA and income-related ESA claimants
who are getting child maintenance payments (as defined in reg.54 of the
Income Support Regulations/reg.117 of the JSA Regulations/reg.119 of
the ESA Regulations respectively (for the ESA Regulations see Part 1 of
this Supplement)) will be eligible for the child maintenance disregard.
This has been increased to £20 per week with effect from October 27,
2008 (see the amendments to para.73 of Sch.9 to the Income Support
Regulations and para.70 of Sch.7 to the JSA Regulations below and
para.60 of Sch.8 to the ESA Regulations in Pt 1 of this Supplement).

p.782, *amendment to the Children (Leaving Care) Social Security Benefits Regulations 2001, reg.2 (entitlement to benefits)*

With effect from October 27, 2008, reg.70 of the Employment and   **3.108**
Support Allowance (Consequential Provisions) (No.2) Regulations 2008
(SI 2008/1554) substituted the words ", income-based jobseeker's
allowance or income-related employment and support allowance" for
the words "or income-based jobseeker's allowance" in reg.2(1).

p.789, *amendment to the Child Support (Maintenance Calculation Procedure) Regulations 2000, reg.1 (citation, commencement and interpretation)*

3.109　With effect from October 27, 2008, reg.9(2)(b) of the Child Support (Consequential Provisions) Regulations 2008 (SI 2008/2543) omitted "6," and "46," in reg.1(5).

pp.790–796, *amendment to the Child Support (Maintenance Calculation Procedure) Regulations 2000, regs 8–20*

3.110　With effect from October 27, 2008, reg.9(5) of the Child Support (Consequential Provisions) Regulations 2008 (SI 2008/2543) omitted regs 8 to 20.

pp.796–797, *amendment to the Child Support (Maintenance Calculation Procedure) Regulations 2000, reg.31 (transitional provision—effective dates and reduced benefit decisions)*

3.111　With effect from October 27, 2008, reg.9(10)(a) of the Child Support (Consequential Provisions) Regulations 2008 (SI 2008/2543) omitted the words "and reduced benefit decisions" in the heading to reg.31.

From the same date, reg.9(10)(d) of the same amending regulations omitted paras (3) to (7) and (8)(b) of reg.31.

p.798, *amendment to the Child Support (Maintenance Calculations and Special Cases) Regulations 2000, reg.4 (flat rate)*

3.112　With effect from October 27, 2008, reg.61(3)(a) of the Employment and Support Allowance (Consequential Provisions) (No.2) Regulations 2008 (SI 2008/1554) omitted the word "and" after reg.4(1)(f) and added the following after reg.4(1)(g):

"and
(h) contributory employment and support allowance under section 2 of the Welfare Reform Act.".

From the same date, reg.61(3)(b) of the same amending regulations added the following after reg.4(2)(c):

"and
(d) income-related employment and support allowance under section 4 of the Welfare Reform Act.".

p.814, *amendment of Jobseeker's Allowance Regulations 1995, reg.1(3) (Interpretation: definition of "the Employment And Support Allowance Regulations")*

3.113　With effect from October 27, 2008, reg.3(1) and (2) of the Employment and Support Allowance (Consequential Provisions) (No.2) Regulations 2008 (SI 2008/1554) amended reg.1(3) by adding the following definition after the definition of "the Eileen Trust":

" 'the Employment and Support Allowance Regulations' means the Employment and Support Allowance Regulations 2008;"

p.821, *amendment of Jobseeker's Allowance Regulations 1995, reg.1(3) (Interpretation: definition of "the Welfare Reform Act")*

With effect from October 27, 2008, reg.3(1) and (2) of the Employ-   3.114
ment and Support Allowance (Consequential Provisions) (No.2) Regulations 2008 (SI 2008/1554) amended reg.1(3) by adding the following definition after the definition of "week":

" 'the Welfare Reform Act' means the Welfare Reform Act 2007;"

pp.854–856, *amendments to the Jobseeker's Allowance Regulations 1995, reg.14(1) (circumstances in which a person is treated as available)*

With effect from July 9, 2008, reg.3 of the Social Security (Students   3.115
Responsible for Children or Young Persons) Amendment Regulations 2008 (SI 2008/1826) amended reg.14(1) by substituting "15(1)(a)" for "15(a)" in each place it appears.

pp.859–860, *amendment to the Jobseeker's Allowance Regulations 1995, reg.15*

With effect from July 9, 2008, reg.3 of the Social Security (Students   3.116
Responsible for Children or Young Persons) Amendment Regulations 2008 (SI 2008/1826) amended reg.15 to read:

Circumstances in which a person is not to be regarded as available

15.—[(1)] A person shall not be regarded as available for employment in the following circumstances—

   [(a) subject to paragraph (2), if he is full-time student during the period of study];

   (b) if he is a prisoner on temporary release in accordance with the provisions of the Prison Act 1952 or rules made under section 39(6) of the Prisons (Scotland) Act 1989;

   (bb)if the period beginning on the date of claim and ending on the day before the beginning of the first week after the date of claim is less than 7 days, for that period, unless he is treated as available for employment for that period in accordance with regulation 14;

   (bc)if he is on paternity leave or ordinary or additional adoption leave by virtue of section 75A 3or 75B of the Employment Rights Act 1996;

   (c) if she is in receipt of maternity allowance or maternity pay in accordance with section 35 or sections 164–171 respectively of the Benefits Act.

   [(2) Notwithstanding paragraph (1)(a), a full-time student shall be regarded as available for employment during the period of the summer vacation appropriate to his course, but only if the first and second conditions are satisfied.

(3) The first condition is satisfied if—

(a)   in the case of a student with a partner, the partner is also a full-time student and either of them is treated as responsible for a child or a young person; or

(b)   in any other case, the student is treated as responsible for a child or young person.

(4) The second condition is satisfied if the student is—

(a)   available for employment in accordance with this Chapter; or

(b)   treated as available for employment in accordance with regulation 14(1)(a) or (k).]

p.864, *amendment to the Jobseeker's Allowance Regulations 1995, reg.17A(1) (further circumstances in which a person is treated as available etc)*

3.117   With effect from July 9, 2008, reg.3 of the Social Security (Students Responsible for Children or Young Persons) Amendment Regulations 2008 (SI 2008/1826) amended reg.17A(1) by substituting "15(1)(a)" for "15(a)".

p.915, *amendment to the Jobseeker's Allowance Regulations 1996, reg.55 (short periods of sickness)*

3.118   With effect from October 27, 2008, reg.3(9)(a)(i) of the Employment and Support Allowance (Consequential Provisions) (No.2) Regulations 2008 (SI 2008/1554) inserted the words "or not having limited capability for work" after the words "capable of work" in reg.55(1)(c).

From the same date, reg.3(9)(a)(ii) of the same amending regulations inserted the words "or as not having limited capability for work" after the words "capable of work" the second time they occur in reg.55(1).

From the same date, reg.3(9)(a)(iii) of the same amending regulations inserted the words ", employment and support allowance" after the words "incapacity benefit" in reg.55(1).

From the same date, reg.3(9)(b) of the same amending regulations inserted the words "12 weeks of an entitlement of his to employment and support allowance or" after the word "within" in reg.55(4).

p.916, *amendment to the Jobseeker's Allowance Regulations 1996, reg.55A (periods of sickness and persons receiving treatment outside Great Britain)*

3.119   With effect from October 27, 2008, reg.3(10)(a) of the Employment and Support Allowance (Consequential Provisions) (No.2) Regulations 2008 (SI 2008/1554) inserted the words "or not having limited capability for work" after the words "capable of work" in reg.55A(1)(d).

From the same date, reg.3(10)(b) of the same amending regulations inserted the words "or as not having limited capability for work" after the words "capable of work" the second time they occur in reg.55A(1).

From the same date, reg.3(10)(c) of the same amending regulations inserted the words ", employment and support allowance" after the words "incapacity benefit" in reg.55A(1).

p.924, *amendment of Jobseeker's Allowance Regulations 1995, reg.61*
(Other young persons in prescribed circumstances)

With effect from October 27, 2008, reg.3(1) and (11) of the Employ-   3.120
ment and Support Allowance (Consequential Provisions) (No.2) Regulations 2008 (SI 2008/1554) amended reg.61(1) by adding a new sub-para.(g) as follows:

> "(g) who has limited capability for work for the purposes of Part 1 of the Welfare Reform Act."

and substituting the words "1(b), (c) or (g)" for the words "1(b) or (c)" each time they occur in para.2(b).

p.960, *amendment of Jobseeker's Allowance Regulations 1995, reg.76*
(Persons of a prescribed description)

With effect from October 27, 2008, reg.3(1) and (12) of the Employ-   3.121
ment and Support Allowance (Consequential Provisions) (No.2) Regulations 2008 (SI 2008/1554) amended reg.76(2) by adding a new sub-para.(e) as follows:

> "or
> (e) entitled to an income-related employment and support allowance or would, but for paragraph 6(1)(d) of Schedule 1 to the Welfare Reform Act (conditions of entitlement to income-related employment and support allowance), be so entitled."

p.965, *amendment of Jobseeker's Allowance Regulations 1995, reg.78(6)*
(Circumstances in which a person is to be treated as being of not being a member of the household)

With effect from October 27, 2008, reg.3(1) and (13) of the Employ-   3.122
ment and Support Allowance (Consequential Provisions) (No.2) Regulations 2008 (SI 2008/1554) amended reg.78(6) by adding the words "or an income-related employment and support allowance" after the words "income support".

p.985, *amendment to the Jobseeker's Allowance Regulations 1996, reg.89*
(liable relative payments)

With effect from October 27, 2008, reg.3(2)(a) of the Social Security   3.123
(Child Maintenance Amendments) Regulations 2008 (SI 2008/2111) inserted the words "child maintenance or" before the words "liable relative" in the heading to reg.89.

From the same date, reg.3(3) of the same amending regulations substituted the words "child maintenance and liable relative payments" for the words "liable relatives" in reg.89.

p.986, *amendment to the Jobseeker's Allowance Regulations 1996, reg.90 (child support)*

3.124   With effect from October 27, 2008, reg.3(4)(a) of the Social Security (Child Maintenance Amendments) Regulations 2008 (SI 2008/2111) omitted reg.90.

p.991, *amendment to the Jobseeker's Allowance Regulations 1996, reg.96 (date on which income is treated as paid)*

3.125   With effect from October 27, 2008, reg.3(14) of the Employment and Support Allowance (Consequential Provisions) (No.2) Regulations 2008 (SI 2008/1554) substituted the words ", jobseeker's allowance or employment and support allowance" for the words "or jobseeker's allowance" in reg.96(2).

p.993, *amendment to the Jobseeker's Allowance Regulations 1996, reg.97 (calculation of weekly amount of income)*

3.126   With effect from October 27, 2008, reg.3(15) of the Employment and Support Allowance (Consequential Provisions) (No.2) Regulations 2008 (SI 2008/1554) substituted the words ", income support or employment and support allowance" for the words "or income support" in reg.97(4)(b).

pp.1005–1006, *amendment to the Jobseeker's Allowance Regulations 1996, reg.103 (calculation of income other than earnings)*

3.127   With effect from September 1, 2008 (or if the student's period of study begins between August 1 and August 31, 2008, the first day of the period), reg.4(2)(a) of the Social Security (Students and Miscellaneous Amendments) Regulations 2008 (SI 2008/1599) substituted the words "Paragraphs (5ZA) and (5AZA) apply" for the words "Paragraph (5ZA) applies" in reg.103(5).

From the same date, reg.4(2)(b) of the same amending regulations substituted the words "Where a relevant payment is made quarterly, the" for the word "The" at the beginning of reg.103(5ZA).

From the same date, reg.4(2)(c) of the same amending regulations inserted the following new paragraph after reg.103(5ZA):

> "(5AZA) Where a relevant payment is made by two or more instalments in a quarter, the amount of a relevant payment to be taken into account for the assessment period for the purposes of paragraph (1) in respect of a person to whom paragraph (5) applies, shall be calculated by applying the formula in paragraph (5ZA) but as if—

A = the total amount of relevant payments which that person received, or would have received, from the first day of the academic year to the day the person abandoned the course, or was dismissed from it, less any deduction under regulation 136(5).".

From the same date, reg.4(2)(d)(i) of the same amending regulations substituted the words "In this regulation" for the words "In paragraphs (5) and (5ZA)" in reg.103(5ZB).

From the same date, reg.4(2)(d)(ii) of the same amending regulations substituted the following definition for the definition of "assessment period" in reg.103(5ZB):

" "assessment period" means—
  (a) in a case where a relevant payment is made quarterly, the period beginning with the benefit week which includes the day on which the person abandoned, or was dismissed from, his course and ending with the benefit week which includes the last day of the last quarter for which an instalment of the relevant payment was payable to that person;
  (b) in a case where the relevant payment is made by two or more instalments in a quarter, the period beginning with the benefit week which includes the day on which the person abandoned, or was dismissed from, his course and ending with the benefit week which includes—
    (i) the day immediately before the day on which the next instalment of the relevant payment would have been due had the payments continued; or
    (ii) the last day of the last quarter for which an instalment of the relevant payment was payable to that person,
  whichever of those dates is earlier;".

From the same date, reg.4(2)(d)(iii) of the same amending regulations inserted the following definition at the appropriate place in reg.103(5ZB):

" "quarter" in relation to an assessment period means a period in that year beginning on—
  (a) 1st January and ending on 31st March;
  (b) 1st April and ending on 30th June;
  (c) 1st July and ending on 31st August; or
  (d) 1st September and ending on 31st December;".

With effect from October 27, 2008, reg.3(16) of the Employment and Support Allowance (Consequential Provisions) (No.2) Regulations 2008 (SI 2008/1554) inserted a new paragraph after para.(5A) in reg.103:

"(5B) Where the claimant—
  (a) is a member of a couple;
  (b) his partner is receiving a contributory employment and support allowance; and

(c) that benefit has been reduced under regulation 63 of the Employment and Support Allowance Regulations,

the amount of that benefit to be taken into account is the amount as if it had not been so reduced."

p.1007, *annotation to the Jobseeker's Allowance Regulations 1996, reg.103(5)–(5ZB)*

3.128   See the note to reg.40(3A) to (3AB) of the Income Support Regulations above.

p.1026, *amendment to the Jobseeker's Allowance Regulations 1996, Ch.7 (liable relatives)*

3.129   With effect from October 27, 2008, reg.3(5) of the Social Security (Child Maintenance Amendments) Regulations 2008 (SI 2008/2111) substituted the words "child maintenance and liable relative payments" for the words "liable relatives" in the heading to Ch.7.

pp.1026–1027, *amendment to the Jobseeker's Allowance Regulations 1996, reg.117 (interpretation)*

3.130   With effect from October 27, 2008, reg.3(6)(a) of the Social Security (Child Maintenance Amendments) Regulations 2008 (SI 2008/2111) inserted the following new definitions in the appropriate places in reg.117:

" "child maintenance" means any payment towards the maintenance of a child or young person, including any payment made voluntarily and payments made under—
   (a) the Child Support Act 1991;
   (b) the Child Support (Northern Ireland) Order 1991;
   (c) a court order;
   (d) a consent order;
   (e) a maintenance agreement registered for execution in the Books of Council and Session or the sheriff court books;

"claimant's family" shall be construed in accordance with section 35(1) of the Jobseekers Act 1995 (interpretation);

"housing costs" means those costs which may be met under regulation 83(f) or 84(1)(g) (housing costs);

"ordinary clothing and footwear" means clothing and footwear for normal daily use but does not include school uniforms;".

From the same date, reg.3(6)(b)(i) of the same amending regulations omitted the words "including, except in the case of a discretionary trust, any payment which would be so made or derived upon application being made by the claimant but which has not been acquired by him but only from the date on which it could be expected to be acquired were an application made;" in the definition of "payment" in reg.117.

From the same date, reg.3(6)(b)(ii) of the same amending regulations substituted the following paragraph for para.(e) in the definition of "payment" in reg.117:

"(e) made to a third party, or in respect of a third party, unless the payment is—
　(i) in relation to the claimant or the claimant's family; and
　(ii) the payment is in respect of food, ordinary clothing or footwear, fuel, rent, housing costs, council tax or water charges;".

From the same date, reg.3(6)(c)(i) of the same amending regulations omitted the words "in pursuance of a court order or agreement for maintenance" in para.(a) of the definition of "periodical payment" in reg.117.

From the same date, reg.3(6)(c)(ii) of the same amending regulations substituted the words ", after the appropriate disregard under para.70 of Sch.7 (sums to be disregarded in the calculation of income other than earnings) has been applied to it, that does not exceed" for the words "not exceeding" in para.(c) of the definition of "periodical payment" in reg.117.

p.1028, *annotation to the Jobseeker's Allowance Regulations 1996, reg.117 (interpretation)*

From October 27, 2008 regs 125 to 129 which contained separate　3.131
rules for the treatment of child support maintenance have been omitted.
All liable relative payments and child maintenance payments (see the
new definition of "child maintenance" above) are now taken into
account in accordance with regs 117 to 123.

p.1028, *annotation to the Jobseeker's Allowance Regulations 1996, reg.117 (interpretation), definition of "payment"*

See the note to reg.54 of the Income Support Regulations, definition　3.132
of "payment", above.

p.1028, *amendment to the Jobseeker's Allowance Regulations 1996,
reg.118 (treatment of liable relative payments)*

With effect from October 27, 2008, reg.3(2)(b) of the Social Security　3.133
(Child Maintenance Amendments) Regulations 2008 (SI 2008/2111)
inserted the words "child maintenance or" before the words "liable
relative" in the heading to reg.118.

From the same date, reg.3(7) of the same amending regulations substituted the words "paragraph 70 of Schedule 7 (sums to be disregarded
in the calculation of income other than earnings)" for the words "except
where regulation 124(1) (liable relative payments to be treated as capital)
applies" in reg.118.

p.1028, *annotation to the Jobseeker's Allowance Regulations 1996, reg.118 (treatment of child maintenance or liable relative payments)*

3.134   From October 27, 2008 reg.124 has been omitted. This means that all liable relative and child maintenance payments will be treated as income (subject to the £20 disregard of child maintenance payments in para.70 of Sch.7).

pp.1029–1030, *amendment to the Jobseeker's Allowance Regulations 1996, reg.121 (period over which payments other than periodical payments are to be taken into account)*

3.135   With effect from October 27, 2008, reg.3(8) of the Social Security (Child Maintenance Amendments) Regulations 2008 (SI 2008/2111) substituted a new reg.121:

"Period over which payments other than periodical payments are to be taken into account

121.–(1) The period over which a payment other than a periodical payment (a "non-periodical payment") is to be taken account shall be determined as follows.

(2) Except in a case where paragraph (4) applies, the number of weeks over which a non-periodical payment is to be taken into account shall be equal to the number obtained by dividing that payment by the amount referred to in paragraph (3).

(3) The amount is the aggregate of £2 and—

(a) the amount of jobseeker's allowance that would be payable had no payment been made, and

(b) where applicable, the maximum amount of disregard that would apply to the payment under paragraph 70 of Schedule 7.

(4) This paragraph applies in a case where a liable relative makes a periodical payment and a non-periodical payment concurrently and the weekly amount of the periodical payment (as calculated in accordance with regulation 122) is less than B.

(5) In a case where paragraph (4) applies, the non-periodical payment shall, subject to paragraphs (6) and (7), be taken into account over a period of the number of weeks equal to the number obtained by applying the formula—

$$\frac{A}{B - C}$$

(6) If the liable relative ceases to make periodical payments, the balance (if any) of the non-periodical payment shall be taken into account over the number of weeks equal to the number obtained by dividing that balance by the amount referred to in paragraph (3).

(7) If the amount of any subsequent periodical payment varies, the balance (if any) of the non-periodical payment shall be taken into account over a period of the number of weeks equal to the number obtained by applying the formula—

$$\frac{D}{B - E}$$

(8) The period under paragraph (2) or (4) shall begin on the date on which the payment is treated as paid under regulation 123 (date on which a liable relative payment is treated as paid) and the period under paragraph (6) and (7) shall begin on the first day of the benefit week in which the cessation or variation of the periodical payment occurred.

(9) Any fraction which arises by applying a calculation or formula referred to in this regulation shall be treated as a corresponding fraction of a week.

(10) In paragraphs (4) to (7)—

A = the amount of the non-periodical payment;

B = the aggregate of £2 and the amount of jobseeker's allowance that would be payable had the periodical payment not been made and, where applicable, the maximum disregard under paragraph 70 of Schedule 7;

C = the weekly amount of the periodical payment;

D = the balance (if any) of the non-periodical payment;

E = the weekly amount of any subsequent periodical payment."

p.1030, *annotation to the Jobseeker's Allowance Regulations 1996, reg.121 (period over which payments other than periodical payments are to be taken into account)*

Note that there is no longer any provision to treat liable relative payments as capital as reg.124 has been omitted with effect from October 27, 2008. **3.136**

Note also that the pre-April 6, 2004 form of this regulation for "transitional cases" (i.e., where the claimant remains entitled to the child elements in income-based JSA and has not transferred to child tax credit) is no longer being retained.

p.1030, *amendment to the Jobseeker's Allowance Regulations 1996, reg.122 (calculation of the weekly amount of a liable relative payment)*

With effect from October 27, 2008, reg.3(2)(c) of the Social Security **3.137** (Child Maintenance Amendments) Regulations 2008 (SI 2008/2111) inserted the words "child maintenance or" before the words "liable relative" in the heading to reg.122.

p.1031, *amendment to the Jobseeker's Allowance Regulations 1996, reg.123 (date on which a liable relative payment is to be treated as paid)*

With effect from October 27, 2008, reg.3(2)(d) of the Social Security **3.138** (Child Maintenance Amendments) Regulations 2008 (SI 2008/2111) inserted the words "child maintenance or" before the words "liable relative" in the heading to reg.123.

pp.1031–1032, *amendment to the Jobseeker's Allowance Regulations 1996, reg.124 (liable relative payments to be treated as capital)*

3.139   With effect from October 27, 2008, reg.3(4)(b) of the Social Security (Child Maintenance Amendments) Regulations 2008 (SI 2008/2111) omitted reg.124.

pp.1032–1034, *amendment to the Jobseeker's Allowance Regulations 1996, Chapter 8 (child support)*

3.140   With effect from October 27, 2008, reg.3(4)(c) of the Social Security (Child Maintenance Amendments) Regulations 2008 (SI 2008/2111) omitted Chapter 8.

p.1039, *amendment to the Jobseeker's Allowance Regulations 1996, reg.131 (calculation of grant income)*

3.141   With effect from September 1, 2008 (or if the student's period of study begins between August 1 and August 31, 2008, the first day of the period), reg.4(3)(a) of the Social Security (Students and Miscellaneous Amendments) Regulations 2008 (SI 2008/1599) substituted "£295" for "£290" in reg.131(3)(a).
          From the same date, reg.4(3)(b) of the same amending regulations substituted "£380" for "£370" in reg.131(3)(b).

p.1045, *amendment to the Jobseeker's Allowance Regulations 1996, reg.136 (treatment of student loans)*

3.142   With effect from September 1, 2008 (or if the student's period of study begins between August 1 and August 31, 2008, the first day of the period), reg.4(4)(a) of the Social Security (Students and Miscellaneous Amendments) Regulations 2008 (SI 2008/1599) substituted "£295" for "£290" in reg.136(5)(a).
          From the same date, reg.4(4)(b) of the same amending regulations substituted "£380" for "£370" in reg.136(5)(b).

p.1051, *amendment of Jobseeker's Allowance Regulations 1995, reg.140(3) (Meaning of "person in hardship")*

3.143   With effect from October 27, 2008, reg.3(1) and (17) of the Employment and Support Allowance (Consequential Provisions) (No.2) Regulations 2008 (SI 2008/1554) amended reg.140(3) by adding the words "or an income-related employment and support allowance" after the words "income support".

p.1063, *amendment of Jobseeker's Allowance Regulations 1995, reg.146A(3) (Meaning of "couple in hardship")*

3.144   With effect from October 27, 2008, reg.3(1) and (18) of the Employment and Support Allowance (Consequential Provisions) (No.2) Regulations 2008 (SI 2008/1554) amended reg.146A(3) by adding the words "or an income-related employment and support allowance" after the words "income support".

p.1073, *amendment of Jobseeker's Allowance Regulations 1995, reg.149(1)(a)(ii) (Assessment of income and capital in urgent cases)*

With effect from October 27, 2008, reg.3(1) and (19) of the Employment and Support Allowance (Consequential Provisions) (No.2) Regulations 2008 (SI 2008/1554) amended reg.149(1)(a)(ii) by adding the words "or of employment and support allowance under regulation 164 of the Employment and Support Allowance Regulations" after the words "Income Support Regulations". **3.145**

p.1074, *amendment of Jobseeker's Allowance Regulations 1995, reg.150(1) (Amount of jobseeker's allowance payable)*

With effect from October 27, 2008, reg.3(1) and (20) of the Employment and Support Allowance (Consequential Provisions) (No.2) Regulations 2008 (SI 2008/1554) amended the definition of "B" in reg.150(1) by substituting the words ", severe disablement allowance or employment and support allowance" for the words "or severe disablement allowance". **3.146**

p.1076, *amendment of Jobseeker's Allowance Regulations 1995, reg.153(b) (Modification in calculation of income)*

With effect from October 27, 2008, reg.3(1) and (21) of the Employment and Support Allowance (Consequential Provisions) (No.2) Regulations 2008 (SI 2008/1554) amended reg.153(b) by adding the words "or employment and support allowance" after the words "Benefits Act". **3.147**

p.1079, *amendment to the Jobseeker's Allowance Regulations 1996, reg.171 (trade disputes: exemptions from section 15 of the Act)*

With effect from October 27, 2008, reg.3(22) of the Employment and Support Allowance (Consequential Provisions) (No.2) Regulations 2008 (SI 2008/1554) omitted the word "or" at the end of reg.171(b)(i) and added after reg.171(b)(ii) **3.148**

"or
(iii) has limited capability for work.".

p.1081, *amendment to the Jobseeker's Allowance Regulations 1996, Sch.A1 (categories of members of a joint-claim couple who are not required to satisfy the conditions in s.1(2B)(b)), para.6A*

With effect from October 27, 2008, reg.3(23)(a) of the Employment and Support Allowance (Consequential Provisions) (No.2) Regulations 2008 (SI 2008/1554) inserted the following new paragraph after para.6 in Sch.A1: **3.149**

"Member has limited capability for work

6A. A person who—

(a) has limited capability for work under section 8 of the Welfare Reform Act; or

(b) is treated as having limited capability for work under regulations made under paragraph 1 of Schedule 2 to that Act; or

(c) is treated as not having limited capability for work under regulations made under section 18(1) of that Act (disqualification).".

p.1082, *amendment to the Jobseeker's Allowance Regulations 1996, Sch.A1 (categories of members of a joint-claim couple who are not required to satisfy the conditions in s.1(2B)(b)), para.12*

3.150   With effect from October 27, 2008, reg.3(23)(b) of the Employment and Support Allowance (Consequential Provisions) (No.2) Regulations 2008 (SI 2008/1554) inserted the words "or who has limited capability for work" after the words "incapable of work" in para.12.

p.1100, *amendment to the Jobseeker's Allowance Regulations 1996, Sch.2 (housing costs), para.1 (housing costs)*

3.151   With effect from October 27, 2008, reg.3(25)(a)(i) of the Employment and Support Allowance (Consequential Provisions) (No.2) Regulations 2008 (SI 2008/1554) omitted the word "or" at the end of head (c) and added the following new head after head (d) in para.1(3):

"(e) who is in receipt of an employment and support allowance which includes an amount under section 2(2) or (3) or 4(4) or (5) of the Welfare Reform Act (components)."

From the same date, reg.3(25)(a)(ii) of the same amending regulations added the following words after the words "disqualification etc.)" in para.1(4):

"or disqualified for receiving employment and support allowance or treated as not having limited capability for work in accordance with regulations made under section 18 of the Welfare Reform Act (disqualification)".

p.1100, *amendment to the Jobseeker's Allowance Regulations 1987, Sch.2 (housing costs), para.1A (previous entitlement to income support or state pension credit)*

3.152   With effect from October 27, 2008, reg.3(25)(b)(i) of the Employment and Support Allowance (Consequential Provisions) (No.2) Regulations 2008 (SI 2008/1554) inserted the words ", income-related employment and support allowance" after the words "income support" in the heading.

From the same date, reg.3(25)(b)(ii) of the same amending regulations inserted the words "or income-related employment and support

544

allowance" after the words "income support" each time they occur in para.1A.

From the same date, reg.3(25)(b)(iii) of the same amending regulations added the words "or paragraphs 16 to 18 of Schedule 6 to the Employment and Support Allowance Regulations" after the words "Income Support Regulations" in para.1A(1)(a).

From the same date, reg.3(25)(b)(iv) of the same amending regulations added the words "or paragraphs 16 or 17 of Schedule 6 to the Employment and Support Allowance Regulations" after the words "Income Support Regulations" in para.1A(1A)(a).

p.1106, *amendment to the Jobseeker's Allowance Regulations 1996, Sch.3 (housing costs), para.6 (existing housing costs)*

With effect from October 27, 2008, reg.3(25)(c)(i) of the Employment and Support Allowance (Consequential Provisions) (No.2) Regulations 2008 (SI 2008/1554) substituted the words ", state pension credit or income-related employment and support allowance" for the words "or state pension credit" in para.6(3).

From the same date, reg.3(25)(c)(ii) of the same amending regulations inserted the words "or income-related employment and support allowance" after the words "income support" in para.6(4).

3.153

pp.1106–1107, *amendment to the Jobseeker's Allowance Regulations 1996, Sch.2 (housing costs), para.7 (new housing costs)*

With effect from October 27, 2008, reg.3(25)(d)(i) of the Employment and Support Allowance (Consequential Provisions) (No.2) Regulations 2008 (SI 2008/1554) inserted the words "or income-related employment and support allowance" after the words "income support" in para.7(2A).

From the same date, reg.3(25)(d)(ii) of the same amending regulations inserted the words "or income-related employment and support allowance" after the words "income support" in para.7(2B).

3.154

p.1112, *amendment to the Jobseeker's Allowance Regulations 1996, Sch.2 (housing costs), para.13 (linking rules)*

With effect from October 27, 2008, reg.3(25)(e) of the Employment and Support Allowance (Consequential Provisions) (No.2) Regulations 2008 (SI 2008/1554) substituted the words ", incapacity benefit or contributory employment and support allowance" for the words "or incapacity benefit" in para.13(6)(a).

3.155

p.1112, *amendment to the Jobseeker's Allowance Regulations 1996, Sch.2 (housing costs), para.13 (linking rules)*

With effect from July 9, 2008, reg.3(5) of the Social Security (Students Responsible for Children or Young Persons) Amendment Regulations 2008 (SI 2008/1826) substituted "15(1)(a)" for "15(a)" in para.13(8)(b).

3.156

p.1115, *amendment to the Jobseeker's Allowance Regulations 1996, Sch.2 (housing costs), para.17 (non-dependant deductions)*

3.157   With effect from October 27, 2008, reg.3(25)(f) of the Employment and Support Allowance (Consequential Provisions) (No.2) Regulations 2008 (SI 2008/1554), as amended by reg.41(3) of the Employment and Support Allowance (Miscellaneous Amendments) Regulations 2008 (SI 2008/2428), omitted the word "or" at the end of head (g) and added the following new head after head (h) in para.17(7):

> "(i)   he is aged less than 25 and is in receipt of employment and support allowance which does not include an amount under section 4(4) or (5) of the Welfare Reform Act (components)."

p.1115, *amendment to the Jobseeker's Allowance Regulations 1996, Sch.2 (housing costs), para.18 (continuity with income support)*

3.158   With effect from October 27, 2008, reg.3(25)(g)(i) of the Employment and Support Allowance (Consequential Provisions) (No.2) Regulations 2008 (SI 2008/1554) added the words "or income-related employment and support allowance" after the words "income support" in the heading to para.18.

From the same date, reg.3(25)(g)(ii)(aa) of the same amending regulations inserted the words "or income-related employment and support allowance" after the words "income support" the first time they occur in para.18(1).

From the same date, reg.3(25)(g)(ii)(bb) of the same amending regulations added the words "or income-related employment and support allowance" after the words "income support" in para.18(1)(c).

pp.1129–1130, *amendment to the Jobseeker's Allowance Regulations 1996, Sch.6 (sums to be disregarded in the calculation of earnings), para.5*

3.159   With effect from October 27, 2008, reg.3(26) of the Employment and Support Allowance (Consequential Provisions) (No.2) Regulations 2008 (SI 2008/1554) substituted the words ", income support or an employment and support allowance" for the words "or income support" each time they occur in para.5(7).

pp.1134–1135, *amendment to the Jobseeker's Allowance Regulations 1996, Sch.6A (sums to be disregarded in the calculation of earnings of members of joint-claim couples), para.1*

3.160   With effect from October 27, 2008, reg.3(27) of the Employment and Support Allowance (Consequential Provisions) (No.2) Regulations 2008 (SI 2008/1554) substituted the words ", income support or an employment and support allowance" for the words "income support" each time they occur in para.1(5).

p.1137, *amendment to the Jobseeker's Allowance Regulations 1996, Sch.7 (sums to be disregarded in the calculation of income other than earnings), para.8*

With effect from October 27, 2008, reg.3(28)(a) of the Employment and Support Allowance (Consequential Provisions) (No.2) Regulations 2008 (SI 2008/1554) substituted the words ", income support or employment and support allowance" for the words "or income support" in para.8(b).   3.161

p.1137, *amendment to the Jobseeker's Allowance Regulations 1996, Sch.7 (sums to be disregarded in the calculation of income other than earnings), para.14*

With effect from October 27, 2008, reg.3(28)(b) of the Employment and Support Allowance (Consequential Provisions) (No.2) Regulations 2008 (SI 2008/1554) substituted the words ", severe disablement allowance or employment and support allowance" for the words "or severe disablement allowance" in para.14(1)(a).   3.162

p.1145, *amendment to the Jobseeker's Allowance Regulations 1996, Sch.7 (sums to be disregarded in the calculation of income other than earnings), para.70*

With effect from October 27, 2008, reg.3(9) of the Social Security (Child Maintenance Amendments) Regulations 2008 (SI 2008/2111) substituted the following sub-paragraphs for sub-paras (3) and (4) in para.70:   3.163

"(3) No more than £20 shall be disregarded in respect of each week to which any payment of child maintenance is attributed in accordance with regulations 118 to 123 (child maintenance and liable relatives).

(4) In this paragraph, "child maintenance" shall have the same meaning as in regulation 117."

p.1149, *annotation to the Jobseeker's Allowance Regulations 1996, Sch.7, para.70*

See the note to para.73 of Sch.9 to the Income Support Regulations above.   3.164

pp.1150–1151, *amendment to the Jobseeker's Allowance Regulations 1996, Sch.10 (capital to be disregarded), para.12*

With effect from October 27, 2008, reg.3(29)(a) of the Employment and Support Allowance (Consequential Provisions) (No.2) Regulations 2008 (SI 2008/1554) added the words " or an income-related employment and support allowance" after the words "working tax credit" in para.12(1)(b).   3.165

From the same date, reg.3(29)(b) of the same amending regulations substituted the words ", income support or of an income-related employment and support allowance" for the words "or of income support" each time they occur in para.12(3).

pp.1165–1168, *amendment to the State Pension Credit Regulations 2002, reg.1 (citation, commencement and interpretation)*

3.166   With effect from October 27, 2008, reg.4(2) of the Employment and Support Allowance (Consequential Provisions) (No.2) Regulations 2008 (SI 2008/1554) inserted a number of new definitions in reg.1(2) in the appropriate places:

" 'contributory employment and support allowance' means a contributory allowance under Part 1 of the Welfare Reform Act (employment and support allowance);"
" 'the Employment and Support Allowance Regulations' means the Employment and Support Allowance Regulations 2008;"
" 'income-related employment and support allowance' means an income-related allowance under Part 1 of the Welfare Reform Act (employment and support allowance);"
" 'the Welfare Reform Act' means the Welfare Reform Act 2007."

p.1172, *annotation to State Pension Credit Regulations 2002, reg.2 (persons not in Great Britain)*

3.167   Commissioner Jacobs has analysed the post-April 30, 2006 version of reg.2 in *CPC/2134/2007* and *CPC/3764/2007*.

In *CPC/2134/2007* the claimant, a Lithuanian national, arrived in the UK in 2000, and unsuccessfully claimed asylum. She abandoned her asylum appeal when Lithuania joined the EU in May 2004. She claimed state pension credit in January 2006 but her claim was not decided until October 2006, when it was refused on the basis that she had no right to reside. Commissioner Jacobs acknowledged that the claimant had been in the UK for more than five years but ruled that she had no permanent right of residence. Pre-accession periods of residence could not be taken into account (following *GN (EEA Regulations: five years' residence) Hungary* [2007] UKAIT 00073). The claimant had not exercised any EU right either before or after accession.

In *CPC/3764/2007* Commissioner Jacobs likewise confirmed that a pre-accession period of residence by a Slovakian national between 1997 and 2004 could not be taken into account (see also *R(IS) 3/08*). The Commissioner also analysed in detail the argument of the claimant's representative based on proportionality, concluding that the circumstances were "not sufficiently exceptional to justify ignoring the terms of the legislation governing the right to reside ... If I were to accept the representative's argument, I would not be preventing a rule being enforced in a way that was not reasonably necessary to further its purpose. Rather, I would be undermining that purpose by rewriting the scope of the right to reside and the controls on access to a social assistance system" (para.46).

In *CPC/1433/2008* Deputy Commissioner Ramsay also considered the post-April 30, 2006 version of reg.2, explaining that reg.2 as now drafted falls into two main parts: "The first part, regulation 2(2) and (3), sets out those who *will not* be treated as habitually resident, and they will not have a right to reside. The second part, regulation 2(4), sets out those who *will* be treated as having a right to reside" (at para.6). In *CPC/ 1433/2008* the claimant, a Portuguese national, moved to the UK in 2004 to join one of her sons. She had not worked in the UK but initially received jobseeker's allowance. When she reached the age of 60 in 2007, her claim to state pension credit was refused. The Deputy Commissioner held that the claimant did not have a right to reside in the UK for the purposes of reg.2. The Deputy Commissioner also found that the tribunal had erred in law in concluding on the available facts that the claimant was her son's dependant.

p.1172, *amendment to the State Pension Credit Regulations 2002, reg.3 (persons temporarily absent from Great Britain)*

With effect from October 6, 2008, reg.3(2) of the Social Security (Miscellaneous Amendments) (No.4) Regulations 2008 (SI 2008/2424) substituted a new reg.3 as follows: **3.168**

Persons temporarily absent from Great Britain

3. A claimant's entitlement to state pension credit during periods of temporary absence from Great Britain is to continue for up to 13 weeks if—
(a) the period of the claimant's absence from Great Britain is unlikely to exceed 52 weeks; and
(b) while absent from Great Britain the claimant continues to satisfy the other conditions of entitlement to state pension credit.

p.1173, *amendment to the State Pension Credit Regulations 2002, insertion of new reg.3A (persons temporarily absent from Great Britain on 6th October 2008)*

With effect from October 6, 2008, reg.3(3) of the Social Security (Miscellaneous Amendments) (No.4) Regulations 2008 (SI 2008/2424) inserted a new reg.3A as follows: **3.169**

Persons temporarily absent from Great Britain on 6th October 2008

3A. Where a claimant—
(a) is already temporarily absent from Great Britain on 6th October 2008;
(b) had a continuing entitlement to state pension credit immediately before that day; and
(c) while absent from Great Britain, continues to satisfy the other conditions of entitlement to state pension credit,
the claimant's entitlement to state pension credit is to continue during that period of absence from Great Britain for up to 13 weeks.

p.1174, *amendment to the State Pension Credit Regulations 2002, reg.5 (persons treated as being or not being members of the same household)*

3.170   With effect from October 6, 2008, reg.3(4) of the Social Security (Miscellaneous Amendments) (No.4) Regulations 2008 (SI 2008/2424) omitted reg.5(3) and substituted a new reg.5(1)(f) as follows:

"(f) he is absent from Great Britain for more than 13 weeks;"

p.1178, *amendment to the State Pension Credit Regulations 2002, amendment of reg.9 (qualifying income for the purposes of savings credit)*

3.171   With effect from October 27, 2008, reg.4(3) of the Employment and Support Allowance (Consequential Provisions) (No.2) Regulations 2008 (SI 2008/1554) added after sub-para.(f):

"(g) contributory employment and support allowance."

p.1178, *annotation to State Pension Credit Regulations 2002, reg.9 (qualifying income for the purposes of savings credit)*

3.172   In *CPC/4173/2007* the claimant, aged 76, lived with her husband, aged 61, who received incapacity benefit. Her husband's incapacity benefit did not count as qualifying income for the purposes of savings credit by virtue of reg.9(b). The claimant argued that this was discriminatory as a woman of the same age as her husband would have received retirement pension (which does count as qualifying income). Commissioner Howell QC held that reg.9 does not contravene Art.14 of the European Convention, as there was no differential treatment by reason of status. The Commissioner also ruled that there was no breach of Council Directive 79/7/EEC on equal treatment, as the circumstances fell squarely within the exclusion in art. 7, which related to the determination of pensionable ages. Moreover, the Sex Discrimination Act 1975 had no application in this context.

p.1183, *amendment to the State Pension Credit Regulations 2002, reg.13A (part-weeks)*

3.173   With effect from October 27, 2008, reg.4(4) of the Employment and Support Allowance (Consequential Provisions) (No.2) Regulations 2008 (SI 2008/1554) inserted ", an income-related employment and support allowance" after "income support" in reg.13A(1)(a).

p.1184, *amendment to the State Pension Credit Regulations 2002, reg.13B (date on which benefits are treated as paid)*

3.174   With effect from October 27, 2008, reg.4(5) of the Employment and Support Allowance (Consequential Provisions) (No.2) Regulations 2008 (SI 2008/1554) added after sub-para.(d):

"(e) contributory employment and support allowance."

p.1186, *amendment to the State Pension Credit Regulations 2002, reg. 15 (income for the purposes of the Act)*

With effect from October 27, 2008, reg.4(6) of the Employment and   3.175
Support Allowance (Consequential Provisions) (No.2) Regulations 2008
(SI 2008/1554) added after sub-para.(4)(c):

"(d) section 3 of the Welfare Reform Act (deductions from contributory allowance)."

pp.1208–1209, *amendment to the State Pension Credit Regulations 2002, Sch.I, para.6 (amount applicable for former claimants of income support or income-related jobseeker's allowance)*

With effect from October 27, 2008, reg.4(7) of the Employment and   3.176
Support Allowance (Consequential Provisions) (No.2) Regulations 2008
(SI 2008/1554) substituted ", income-based jobseeker's allowance or
income-related employment and support allowance" in the heading for
"or income-related jobseeker's allowance" and substituted ", an income-
based jobseeker's allowance or an income-related employment and support allowance" for "or an income-based jobseeker's allowance" in
sub-para.(2). The same regulation also amended sub-para.(5), omitting
"or" after sub-para.(5)(a) and inserting "or (c) for the purposes of
determining his entitlement to income-related employment and support
allowance," after sub-para.(5)(b) and ", paragraph 7 of Schedule 4 to
the Employment and Support Allowance Regulations" after "Income
Support Regulations" in sub-para.(5)(v). Finally, the same amending
regulation inserted "or paragraph 20(2) of Schedule 6 to the Employment and Support Allowance Regulations" after "Jobseeker's Allowance
Regulations" in sub-para.(10)(a).

p.1209, *annotation to State Pension Credit Regulations 2002, Sch.I (circumstances in which persons are treated as being or not being severely disabled)*

In *CPC/1446/2008*, Deputy Commissioner Wikeley considered   3.177
whether a claimant was "residing with" a non-dependent within the
meaning of Sch.1, paras 2 and 3. The Deputy Commissioner followed
CSIS/652/2003 in preferring *CSIS/2532/2003* to *CIS/185/1995* on the
parallel income support rules. A kitchen may therefore form part of
shared accommodation even if the claimant personally does not visit the
kitchen so long as he uses it in some other way (e.g. storage or for a third
party to prepare meals).

p.1210, *amendment to the State Pension Credit Regulations 2002, Sch.II, para.1 (housing costs)*

With effect from October 27, 2008, reg.4(8)(a) of the Employment   3.178
and Support Allowance (Consequential Provisions) (No.2) Regulations
2008 (SI 2008/1554) added after sub-para.(2)(a)(iii)(cc):

"or

(dd)   is in receipt of an employment and support allowance which includes an amount under section 2(2) or (3) or 4(4) or (5) of the Welfare Reform Act (components)."

The same regulation also added after "disqualification etc)" in sub-para.(3):

"or disqualified for receiving employment and support allowance or treated as not having limited capability for work in accordance with regulations made under section 18 of the Welfare Reform Act (disqualification)".

p.1214, *amendment to the State Pension Credit Regulations 2002, Sch.II, para.1(5) (housing costs not met)*

3.179   With effect from October 27, 2008, reg.4(8)(b) of the Employment and Support Allowance (Consequential Provisions) (No.2) Regulations 2008 (SI 2008/1554)
inserted ", income-related employment and support allowance" after "income-based jobseeker's allowance" in sub-para.(4) each time it occurs and substituted ", state pension credit or income-related employment and support allowance" for "or state pension credit" in sub-para.(5).

pp.1216–1217, *amendment to the State Pension Credit Regulations 2002, Sch.II, para.1(7) (the calculation for loans)*

3.180   With effect from October 27, 2008, reg.4(8)(c) of the Employment and Support Allowance (Consequential Provisions) (No.2) Regulations 2008 (SI 2008/1554) inserted ", income-related employment and support allowance" after "income support" in sub-para.(4A)(a), omitted "or" after sub-para.(4B)(a) and substituted for "and" after sub-para.(4B)(b) the following:

"or

(c)   where the earlier entitlement was to an income-related employment and support allowance, if their applicable amount included an amount determined in accordance with Schedule 6 to the Employment and Support Allowance Regulations as applicable to them in respect of a loan which qualifies under paragraph 16 to 18 of that Schedule, and".

p.1219, *amendment to the State Pension Credit Regulations 2002, Sch.II, para.1(10) (excessive housing costs)*

3.181   With effect from October 27, 2008, reg.4(8)(c) of the Employment and Support Allowance (Consequential Provisions) (No.2) Regulations

2008 (SI 2008/1554) substituted ", income-based jobseeker's allowance and income-related employment and support allowance" for "and income-based jobseeker's allowance" in para.10(10).

p.1222, *amendment to the State Pension Credit Regulations 2002, Sch.II, para.1(14) (persons residing with the claimant)*

With effect from October 27, 2008, reg.4(8)(c) of the Employment   3.182
and Support Allowance (Consequential Provisions) (No.2) Regulations 2008 (SI 2008/1554) added after para.(14)(7(f):

"(g) if he is aged less than 25 and is in receipt of employment and support allowance which does not include an amount under section 2(2) or (3) or 4(4) or (5) of the Welfare Reform Act (components)."

p.1223, *annotation to State Pension Credit Regulations 2002, Sch.II, para.5 (housing costs not met)*

The meaning of a "relevant period" within para.5(4) was considered   3.183
further in *CPC/3992/2007*, where the Deputy Commissioner followed the reasoning in *CPC/3326/2005*. It followed that a claimant who applied for backdating of state pension credit at the Department's instigation received no help with his housing costs as the effect of the backdating was to bring the mortgage within the "relevant period". The Deputy Commissioner also considered other remedies that might be open to the claimant.

p.1225, *amendment to the State Pension Credit Regulations 2002, Sch.III (special groups)*

With effect from October 6, 2008, reg.3(5) of the Social Security   3.184
(Miscellaneous Amendments) (No.4) Regulations 2008 (SI 2008/2424) omitted the figure "3" after the word "regulations" in para.1(8).

p.1233, *amendment to the State Pension Credit Regulations 2002, Sch.V (income from capital)*

With effect from October 27, 2008, reg.4(9) of the Employment and   3.185
Support Allowance (Consequential Provisions) (No.2) Regulations 2008 (SI 2008/1554) added after para.20(2)(n): "(o) income-related employment and support allowance."

The same amending regulation omitted "or" after para.20A(2)(c) and added after para.20A(2)(d):

"or
(e) paragraph 11(2) of Schedule 9 to the Employment and Support Allowance Regulations,".

pp.1237–1238, *amendment to the State Pension Credit Regulations 2002, Sch. VI (sums disregarded from claimant's earnings)*

3.186   With effect from October 27, 2008, reg.4(10) of the Employment and Support Allowance (Consequential Provisions) (No.2) Regulations 2008 (SI 2008/1554) omitted "or" after para.4(1)(a)(v) and added after para.4(1)(a)(vi): "(vii) employment and support allowance; or". The same amending regulation substituted ", income-based jobseeker's allowance or income-related employment and support allowance" for "or income-based jobseeker's allowance" in para.4(2).

p.1247, *amendment of Social Fund Cold Weather Payments (General) Regulations, reg.1(2) (Citation, commencement and interpretation: definition of "the Welfare Reform Act")*

3.187   With effect from October 27, 2008, reg.6(1) and (2) of the Employment and Support Allowance (Consequential Provisions) (No.2) Regulations 2008 (SI 2008/1554) amended reg.1(2) by adding the following definition after the definition of "the Act":

" 'the Welfare Reform Act' means the Welfare Reform Act 2007;"

p.1248, *amendment of Social Fund Cold Weather Payments (General) Regulations, reg.1(2) (Citation, commencement and interpretation: definition of "claimant")*

3.188   With effect from October 27, 2008, reg.6(1) and (2) of the Employment and Support Allowance (Consequential Provisions) (No.2) Regulations 2008 (SI 2008/1554) amended definition of "claimant" in reg.1(2) to read as follows:

" 'claimant' means a person who is claiming or has claimed income support, state pension credit [, income-based jobseeker's allowance or income-related employment and support allowance];"

p.1248, *amendment of Social Fund Cold Weather Payments (General) Regulations, reg.1(2) (Citation, commencement and interpretation: definition of "income-related employment and support allowance")*

3.189   With effect from October 27, 2008, reg.6(1) and (2) of the Employment and Support Allowance (Consequential Provisions) (No.2) Regulations 2008 (SI 2008/1554) amended reg.1(2) by adding the following definition after the definition of "income-based jobseeker's allowance":

" 'income-related employment and support allowance" means an income-related allowance under Part 1 of the Welfare Reform Act (employment and support allowance);"

p.1248, *amendment of Social Fund Cold Weather Payments (General) Regulations 1988, reg.1(2) (Citation, commencement and interpretation: definition of "forecast")*

With effect from November 1, 2008, reg.2(1) and (2) of the Social Fund Cold Weather Payments (General) Amendment Regulations 2008 (SI 2008/2569), amended the definition of "forecast" in reg.1(2) by substituting the words "Department for Work and Pensions" for the words "Department of Social Security". **3.190**

p.1250, *amendment of Social Fund Cold Weather Payments (General) Regulations 1988, reg.1A (Prescribed description of persons)*

With effect from October 27, 2008, reg.2(1) and (3) of the Social Fund Cold Weather Payments (General) Amendment Regulations 2008 (SI 2008/2569), amended reg.1A by substituting the words "paragraphs 5 to 7" for the words "paragraphs 5 to 8" in para.(1)(id); and the words ", (ib), (id) and (ie)" for the words "and (ib)" in para.(2). **3.191**

p.1250, *amendment of Social Fund Cold Weather Payments (General) Regulations, reg.1A(1) (Prescribed description of persons)*

With effect from October 27, 2008, reg.6(1) and (3) of the Employment and Support Allowance (Consequential Provisions) (No.2) Regulations 2008 (SI 2008/1554) amended reg.1A(1) by substituting the words ", income-based jobseeker's allowance or income-related employment and support allowance" for the words "or income-based jobseeker's allowance" and adding the following sub-paras. after sub-para (ic): **3.192**

"(id)   whose applicable amount includes one or more of the premiums specified in paragraphs 5 to 8 of Schedule 4 to the Employment and Support Allowance Regulations 2008; or

(ie)   whose applicable amount includes an amount under section 4(2)(b) of the Welfare Reform Act; or"

p.1253, *modification of Social Fund Cold Weather Payments (General) Regulations 1988, reg.3 (Prescribed amount) in respect of the 2008–09 Winter*

With effect from November 1, 2008, reg.3 of the Social Fund Cold Weather Payments (General) Amendment Regulations 2008 (SI 2008/2569), modified reg.3 for any period of cold weather which begins after October 31, 2008 but before April 1, 2009. As modified, reg.3 is applied as if the reference to £8.50 were to £25. **3.193**

p.1254, *amendment of Social Fund Cold Weather Payments (General) Regulations 1988, Sch.1 (Identification of stations and postcode districts)*

With effect from November 1, 2008, reg.2(1) and (4) of the Social Fund Cold Weather Payments (General) Amendment Regulations 2008 (SI 2008/2569), substituted the following for Sch.1: **3.194**

Income Support, Jobseekers' Allowance, etc.

[SCHEDULE 1   **Regulation 2(1)(a) and (2)**

IDENTIFICATION OF STATIONS AND POSTCODE DISTRICTS

Column (1)	Column (2)
Meteorological Office Station	*Postcode Districts*
1. Aberporth	SA35–48, SA64–65.
2. Albemarle	DH1–7, DH9. DL4–5, DL14–17. NE1–13, NE15–18, NE20–21, NE23, NE25–43, NE44–46. SR1–7. TS21, TS28–29.
3. Andrewsfield	AL1–10. CB1–5, CB10–11, CB21–25. CM1–9, CM11–24, CM77. CO9. RM14–20. SG1–2, SG8–14.
4. Aultbea	IV21–22, IV26, IV40, IV52–54.
5. Aviemore	AB37. PH19–26.
6. Bedford	LU1–7. MK1–19, MK40–46. NN1–16, NN29. PE19. SG3–7, SG15–19.
7. Bingley	BB1–12, BB18. BD1–24. DE4, DE45. DL8, DL11. HD1–9. HX1–7. LS21, LS27, LS29. OL1–5, OL11–16. S32–33, S35–36. SK13, SK17, SK22–23. ST13. WF15–17.
8. Bishopton	G1–5, G11–15, G20–23, G31–34, G40–46, G51–53, G60–62, G64–69, G71–78, G81–84. KA1–18, KA20–25, KA28–30. ML1–5. PA1–27, PA30, PA32.
9. Boscombe Down	BA12. RG28. SO20–23. SP1–5, SP7, SP9–11.
10. Boulmer	NE22, NE24, NE61–70. TD15.
11. Braemar	AB33–36. PH10–11, PH18.
12. Brize Norton	CV36. GL54–56. OX1–8, OX10–18, OX20, OX25–29, OX33, OX39, OX44, OX49. SN7.
13. Cardinham (Bodmin)	PL13–17, PL22–35. TR9.
14. Carlisle	CA1–8, CA13–15. DG12, DG16.
15. Cassley	IV27–28. KW11, KW13.
16. Charlwood	BN5–6, BN44. GU5–6. ME14–20. RH1–20. TN1–20, TN22, TN27.
17. Charterhall	NE71. TD3–6, TD8, TD10–12.
18. Chivenor	EX22–23, EX31–34, EX39.
19. Coleshill	B1–21, B23–38, B40, B42–50, B60–80, B90–98. CV1–12, CV21–23, CV31–35, CV37, CV47. DY1–14. LE10. WS1–15. WV1–16.

556

Column (1)	Column (2)
Meteorological Office Station	*Postcode Districts*
20. Crosby	CH1–8, CH41–49, CH60–66. FY1–8. L1–40. LL11–14. PR1–9, PR25–26. SY14. WA1–2, WA4–12. WN1–6, WN8.
21. Culdrose	TR1–8, TR10–20, TR26–27.
22. Dundrennan	DG1–2, DG5–7.
23. Dunkeswell Aerodrome	DT6–8. EX1–15, EX24. TA21. TQ1–6, TQ9–14.
24. Dyce	AB10–16, AB21–25, AB30–32, AB39, AB41–43, AB51–54. DD8–11.
25. Edinburgh Gogarbank	EH1–42, EH47–49, EH51–55. FK1–17. G63. KY3, KY11–13. PH3–5. TD13–14.
26. Eskdalemuir	DG3–4, DG10–11, DG13–14. ML12. TD1–2, TD7, TD9.
27. Filton	BS1–11, BS13–16, BS20–24, BS29–32, BS34–37, BS39–41, BS48–49. GL11–13. NP16, NP26.
28. Heathrow	BR1–8. CR0, CR2–9. DA1–2, DA4–8, DA14–18. E1–18. E1W. EC1–4. EN1–11. HA0–9. IG1–11. KT1–24. N1–22. NW1–11. RM1–13. SE1–28. SL0, SL3. SM1–7. SW1–20. TW1–20. UB1–10. W1–14. WC1–2. WD1–7, WD17–19, WD23–25.
29. Hereford-Credenhill	GL1–6, GL10, GL14–20, GL50–53. HR1–9. NP15, NP25. SY8. WR1–15.
30. Herstmonceux, West End	BN7–8, BN20–24, BN26–27. TN21, TN31–40.
31. High Wycombe	HP1–23, HP27. OX9. RG9. SL7–9.
32. Hurn (Bournemouth Airport)	BH1–25, BH31. DT1–2, DT11. SP6.
33. Isle of Portland	DT3–5.
34. Kinloss	AB38, AB44–45, AB55–56. IV1–3, IV5, IV7–20, IV30–32, IV36.
35. Kirkwall	KW15–17.
36. Lake Vyrnwy	LL20–21, LL23–25, LL41. SY10, SY15–17, SY19, SY21–22.
37. Leconfield	DN14. HU1–20. YO11–12, YO14–17, YO25.
38. Lerwick	ZE1–3.
39. Leuchars	DD1–7. KY1–2, KY4–10, KY14–16. PH1–2, PH7, PH12–14.

Column (1)	Column (2)
Meteorological Office Station	*Postcode Districts*
40. Linton on Ouse	DL1–3, DL6–7, DL9–10. HG1–5. LS1–20, LS22–26, LS28. S62–64, S70–75. TS9, TS15–16. WF1–14. YO1, YO7–8, YO10, YO19, YO23–24, YO26, YO30–32, YO41–43, YO51, YO60–62.
41. Liscombe	EX16–21, EX35–38. TA22, TA24.
42. Loch Glascarnoch	IV4, IV6, IV23–24, IV63.
43. Loftus	SR8. TS1–8, TS10–14, TS17–20, TS22–27. YO13, Y018, Y021–22.
44. Lusa	IV41–49, IV51, IV55–56.
45. Lyneham	BA1–3, BA11, BA13–15. GL7–9. RG17. SN1–6, SN8–16, SN25–26.
46. Machrihanish	KA27. PA28–29, PA31, PA34, PA37, PA41–49, PA60–76. PH36, PH38–41.
47. Manston	CM0. CT1–21. DA3, DA9–13. ME1–13. SS0–17. TN23–26, TN28–30.
48. Marham	CB6–7. IP24–28. PE12–14, PE30–38.
49. Norwich Airport	NR1–35.
50. Nottingham	CV13. DE1–3, DE5–7, DE11–15, DE21–24, DE55–56, DE65, DE72–75. LE1–9, LE11–14, LE16–19, LE65, LE67. NG1–22, NG25, NG31–34. S1–14, S17–18, S20–21, S25–26, S40–45, S60–61, S65–66, S80–81. ST10, ST14.
51. Pembrey Sands	SA1–8, SA10–18, SA31–34, SA61–63, SA66–73.
52. Plymouth	PL1–12, PL18–21. TQ7–8.
53. Redesdale	CA9. DH8. DL12–13. NE19, NE47–49.
54. Rhyl	LL15–19, LL22, LL26–32.
55. St. Athan	CF3, CF5, CF10–11, CF14–15, CF23–24, CF31–36, CF61–64, CF71–72. NP10, NP18–20.
56. St. Catherine's Point	PO30, PO38–41.
57. Salsburgh	EH43–46. ML6–11.
58. Scilly, St. Mary's	TR21–25.
59. Sennybridge	CF37–48, CF81–83. LD1–8. NP4, NP7–8, NP11–13, NP22–24, NP44. SA9, SA19–20. SY7, SY9, SY18.
60. Shap	CA10–12, CA16–17. LA8–10, LA22–23.

Column (1)	Column (2)
Meteorological Office Station	Postcode Districts
61. Shawbury	ST1–9, ST11–12, ST15–21. SY1–6, SY11–13. TF1–13.
62. South Farnborough	GU1–4, GU7–35, GU46–47, GU51–52. RG1–2, RG4–8, RG10, RG12, RG14, RG18–27, RG29–31, RG40–42, RG45. SL1–2, SL4–6. SO24.
64. Thorney Island	BN1–3, BN9–18, BN25, BN41–43, BN45. PO1–22, PO31–37. SO14–19, SO30–32, SO40–43, SO45, SO50–53.
65. Tiree	PA77–78. PH42–44.
66. Trawsgoed	LL35–40. SY20, SY23–25.
67. Tulloch Bridge	FK18–21. PA33, PA35–36, PA38, PA40. PH6, PH8–9, PH15–17, PH30–35, PH37, PH49–50.
68. Valley	LL33–34, LL42–49, LL51–78.
69. Waddington	DN1–13, DN15–22, DN31–41. LN1–13. NG23–24. PE10–11, PE20–25.
70. Walney Island	CA18–28. LA1–7, LA11–21.
71. Wattisham	CB8–9. CO1–8, CO10–16. IP1–23, IP29–33.
72. West Freugh	DG8–9. KA19, KA26.
73. Wick Airport	IV25. KW1–3, KW5–10, KW12, KW14.
74. Wittering	LE15. NN17–18. PE1–9, PE15–17, PE26–29.
75. Woodford	BL0–9. CW1–12. M1–9, M11–35, M38, M40–41, M43–46, M50, M90. OL6–10. SK1–12, SK14–16. WA3, WA13–16. WN7.
76. Yeovilton	BA4–10, BA16, BA20–22. BS25–28. DT9–10. SP8. TA1–20, TA23.]

p.1257, *amendment of Social Fund Cold Weather Payments (General) Regulations 1988, Sch.2 (Specified alternative stations)*

With effect from November 1, 2008, reg.2(1) and (5) of the Social Fund Cold Weather Payments (General) Amendment Regulations 2008 (SI 2008/2569), substituted the following for Sch.2: **3.195**

[SCHEDULE 2   **Reg 2(1A)(a) and 2(1B)(a)**

SPECIFIED ALTERNATIVE STATIONS

Column (1)	Column (2)
Meteorological Office Station	*Specified Alternative Station*
Charlwood	Kenley Airfield
Coleshill	Pershore
Hereford-Credenhill	Pershore
Kinloss	Lossiemouth
Leconfield	Loftus
Linton on Ouse	Church Fenton
Loftus	Leconfield
St. Athan	Mumbles
Shap	Keswick.]

"

p.1258, *amendment of Social Fund Winter Fuel Payments Regulations 2000, reg.1(2) (Citation, commencement and interpretation: definition of "income-related employment and support allowance")*

3.196   With effect from October 27, 2008, reg.7(1) and (2) of the Employment and Support Allowance (Consequential Provisions) (No.2) Regulations 2008 (SI 2008/1554) amended reg.1(2) by adding the following definition after the definition of "free in-patient treatment":

" 'income-related employment and support allowance' means an income-related allowance under Part 1 of the Welfare Reform Act (employment and support allowance);"

p.1260, *modification of the Social Fund Winter Fuel Payments Regulations 2000, reg.2 (Social fund winter fuel payments)*

3.197   Regulation 2 of the Social Fund Winter Fuel Payment (Temporary Increase) Regulations 2008 (SI 2008/1778) modifies reg.2 so as temporarily to increase the amounts payable as winter fuel payments during the "the 2008–09 winter" (defined as "the winter which follows the qualifying week beginning on 15th September 2008"). The modifications require reg.2 to be applied as if:
(a) the references to £100 in regs.2(1)(b)(ii) and 2(2)(b) were to £125;
(b) the references to £200 in regs.2(1)(b)(i), (2)(a) and (3), were to £250;
(c) the reference to £200 in reg.2(2)(b), were to £275;
(d) the reference to £150 in reg.2(2)(b) were to £200; and

(e) the references to £300 in regs.2(2)(a) and 2(3) were to £400.

p.1260, *amendment of Social Fund Winter Fuel Payments Regulations 2000, reg.2(1) (Social fund winter fuel payments)*

With effect from October 27, 2008, reg.7(1) and (3) of the Employ-   3.198
ment and Support Allowance (Consequential Provisions) (No.2) Regulations 2008 (SI 2008/1554) amended reg.2(1) by substituting the
words ", an income-based jobseeker's allowance or an income-related
employment and support allowance" for the words "or an income-based
jobseeker's allowance".

p.1262, *amendment of Social Fund Winter Fuel Payments Regulations 2000, reg.3(1)(a)(i) (Persons not entitled to a social fund winter fuel payments)*

With effect from October 27, 2008, reg.7(1) and (4) of the Employ-   3.199
ment and Support Allowance (Consequential Provisions) (No.2) Regulations 2008 (SI 2008/1554) amended reg.3(1)(a)(i) by substituting the
words ", income-based jobseeker's allowance or an income-related
employment and support allowance" for the words "or an income-based
jobseeker's allowance".

p.1263, *amendment of Social Fund Winter Fuel Payments Regulations 2000, reg.4(2) (Making a winter fuel payment without a claim)*

With effect from October 27, 2008, reg.7(1) and (5) of the Employ-   3.200
ment and Support Allowance (Consequential Provisions) (No.2) Regulations 2008 (SI 2008/1554) amended reg.4(2) by substituting the
words ", state pension credit or an income-related employment and
support allowance" for the words "or an income-based jobseeker's
allowance".

p.1266, *amendment of Social Fund Maternity and Funeral Expenses Regulations 2005, reg.3(1) (Interpretation: definition of "the Employment and Support Allowance Regulations")*

With effect from October 27, 2008, reg.8(1) and (2) of the Employ-   3.201
ment and Support Allowance (Consequential Provisions) (No.2) Regulations 2008 (SI 2008/1554) amended reg.3(1) by adding the following
definition after the definition of "the Act":

" 'the Employment and Support Allowance Regulations' means the
Employment and Support Allowance Regulations 2008;"

p.1267, *amendment of Social Fund Maternity and Funeral Expenses Regulations 2005, reg.3(1) (Interpretation: definition of "income-related employment and support allowance")*

With effect from October 27, 2008, reg.8(1) and (2) of the Employ-   3.202
ment and Support Allowance (Consequential Provisions) (No.2) Regulations 2008 (SI 2008/1554) amended reg.3(1) by adding the following

definition after the definition of "income-based jobseeker's allow-ance":

" 'income-related employment and support allowance" means an income-related allowance under Part 1 of the Welfare Reform Act (employment and support allowance);"

p.1268, *amendment of Social Fund Maternity and Funeral Expenses Regulations 2005, reg.3(3) (Interpretation: definition of "care establishment")*

3.203   With effect from October 27, 2008, reg.8(1) and (2) of the Employ-ment and Support Allowance (Consequential Provisions) (No.2) Reg-ulations 2008 (SI 2008/1554) amended reg.3(3) by adding the words "or regulation 2(1) of the Employment and Support Allowance Regula-tions" after the word "Regulations".

p.1268, *amendment of Social Fund Maternity and Funeral Expenses Regulations 2005, reg.4(a) (Interpretation: circumstances in which persons are to be treated as not being members of the same household)*

3.204   With effect from October 27, 2008, reg.8(1) and (2) of the Employ-ment and Support Allowance (Consequential Provisions) (No.2) Reg-ulations 2008 (SI 2008/1554) amended reg.4(a) by adding the words ", in regulation 156 of the Employment and Support Allowance Regula-tions" after the words "Income Support Regulations".

p.1271, *amendment of Social Fund Maternity and Funeral Expenses Regulations 2005, reg.5(1)(a) (Sure Start Maternity Grants: Entitlement)*

3.205   With effect from October 27, 2008, reg.8(1) and (3) of the Employ-ment and Support Allowance (Consequential Provisions) (No.2) Reg-ulations 2008 (SI 2008/1554) amended reg.5(1)(a) by revoking the words "or" after head (iv) and "and" after head (v), and adding a new head (vi) as follows:

"or
(vi) income-related employment and support allowance; and"

p.1275, *amendment of Social Fund Maternity and Funeral Expenses Regulations 2005, reg.7(4)(a) (Funeral payments: Entitlement)*

3.206   With effect from October 27, 2008, reg.8(1) and (4) of the Employ-ment and Support Allowance (Consequential Provisions) (No.2) Reg-ulations 2008 (SI 2008/1554) amended reg.7(4)(a) by revoking the word "or" after head (vi) adding the following after head (vii):

"(viii) income-related employment and support allowance; or"

PART IV

UPDATING MATERIAL
VOLUME III

ADMINISTRATION, ADJUDICATION AND
THE EUROPEAN DIMENSION

Commentary by

Mark Rowland and Robin White

pp.4–5, *Forfeiture Act 1982, s.4*

With effect from November 3, 2008, the Transfer of Tribunal Func-　4.001
tions Order 2008 (SI 2008/2833), Sch.3, para.38 (set out on p.1350 of
the main work in the form in which it was eventually approved by
Parliament) amends s.4 to reflect the replacement of Commissioners by
the Upper Tribunal. All references to Commissioners are replaced by
references to the Upper Tribunal and the definition of "Commissioner"
is removed from subs.(5). In addition, subs.(2) is amended by substituting "Tribunal Procedure Rules may make provision" for the words from
the beginning to "expedient", "the rules" are substituted for "the regulations" and paragraph (b) is repealed (together with the "and" immediately before it). Subsections (3) and (4) are also repealed.

p.14, *amendment to the Administration Act 1992, s.1*

With effect from October 27, 2008, s.28 and Sch.3, para.10 of the　4.002
Welfare Reform Act 2007 amended s.1(4) by adding after para.(ab) the
following:

"(ac) an employment and support allowance;"

p.21, *amendment to the Administration Act 1992, s.2AA*

With effect from October 27, 2008, s.28 and Sch.3, para.10 of the　4.003
Welfare Reform Act 2007 amended subs.(2) by adding:

"(f) an employment and support allowance;"

p.23, *amendment to the Administration Act 1992, s.2B*

With effect from November 3, 2008, The Transfer of Tribunal Func-　4.004
tions Order 2008 (SI2008/2833) art.102 amended subs.(6) by substituting the words "First-tier Tribunal" for the words "appeal tribunal".

p.28, *amendment to the Administration Act 1992, s.5*

With effect from April 7, 2008, s.35 of the Welfare Reform Act 2007　4.005
adds the following subsections to s.5:

"(2A) The regulations may also require such persons as are prescribed to provide a rent officer with information or evidence of such
descriptions as is prescribed.

(2B) For the purposes of subsection (2A), the Secretary of State
may prescribe any description of information or evidence which he
thinks is necessary or expedient to enable rent officers to carry out
their functions under section 122 of the Housing Act 1996.

(2C) Information or evidence required to be provided by virtue of
subsection (2A) may relate to an individual claim or award or to any
description of claims or awards."

With effect from October 27, 2008, s.28 and Sch.3, para.10 of the Welfare Reform Act 2007 amended subs.(2) by adding:

"(ac) an employment and support allowance;"

p.39, *amendment to the Administration Act 1992, s.15A*

4.006   With effect from October 27, 2008, s.28 and Sch.3, para.10 of the Welfare Reform Act 2007 amended:

(a) subs.(1) by substituting the words "an income-based jobseeker's allowance or an income-related employment and support allowance" for the words "or an income-related jobseeker's allowance".

(b) in subs.(4) in the definition of "qualifying associate" substitute:
   (i) the words ", state pension credit or an income-related employment and support allowance" for the words "or state pension credit"; and
   (ii) the words ", the State Pension Credit Act 2002 or Part I of the Welfare Reform Act 2007" for the words "or the State Pension Credit Act 2002"; and

(c) in the definition of "relevant benefits", add:
"(d) an employment and support allowance;"

p.44, *Administration Act 1992, s.71, and annotations*

4.007   With effect from October 27, 2008, s.28 and Sch.3, para.10 of the Welfare Reform Act 2007 amended s.71(11) by adding:

"(ac) an employment and support allowance;"

With effect from November 3, 2008, The Transfer of Tribunal Functions Order 2008 (SI 2008/2833) art.103 amended subs.(62) by substituting the words "First-tier Tribunal" for the words "appeal tribunal"; and the words "the Upper Tribunal" for the words "a Commissioner".

CIS/3512/2007 addressed an important point in relation to entitlement decisions and overpayment decisions which are separated in time. In this case, a decision maker in November 2004 determined that the appellant and partner were living together as husband and wife with the consequence that the appellant ceased to be entitled to income support. That decision was upheld on appeal to a tribunal in May 2005. In February 2005 a revised overpayment decision was made that a large overpayment was recoverable from the appellant. On appeal to a tribunal against that decision, a tribunal considered that the appellant and partner were not at the material time living together as husband and wife. On the Secretary of State's appeal to the Commissioner, the question of whether the second tribunal could revisit the decision on cohabitation addressed by the first tribunal was raised. The Secretary of State's representative submitted that the second tribunal was not precluded from revisiting the factual issue because of the wording of s.17 of the Social Security Act 1998 on finality of decisions. The consequence was that "while, ... the determination of the fact [of cohabitation] was conclusive for the purposes of entitlement, it was not so in relation to the issue of disclosure of a material fact [for the purposes of the overpayment decision]" (para.8). The Commissioner accepts the correctness of this proposition with some reluctance, although he commented that it appeared "absurd that the same issue of fact should be capable of being determined by two separate tribunals in a manner which is contradictory." (para.8).

CIS/1599/2007, to be reported as *R(IS)1/09*, involved a set of circumstances with some similarity to those which arose in *CIS/3512/2007*. The issue here related to the beneficial ownership of a house. The entitlement decision was to the effect that the appellant had no entitlement to income support because he had capital in excess of the prescribed limits. The appellant appealed against this decision, but was unsuccessful. Subsequently an overpayment decision was made. The appeal against this was heard by the same chairman who had heard the appeal against the entitlement decision. In that appeal, there was a full reconsideration of the issues underlying the entitlement decision, even though the chairman considered that he was bound by his earlier decision on entitlement. He had proceeded to full consideration of the factual issue in case he was wrong on the proposition that he was bound by his earlier decision. On appeal to the Commissioner, the question of apparent bias was canvassed on the initiative of the Commissioner. The ultimate conclusion was that there was nothing in this case which would lead a fair-minded and informed observed to doubt the chairman's impartiality. There was, accordingly, nothing to taint the tribunal's decision.

p.85, *amendment to the Administration Act 1992, s.105*

With effect from October 27, 2008, s.28 and Sch.3, para.10 of the Welfare Reform Act 2007 amended:

4.008

(a) subs.(1)(b) by substituting the words ", an income-based job-seeker's allowance or an income-related employment and support allowance" for the words "or an income-related jobseeker's allowance"; and

(b) in subs.(4) by inserting the words "or an income-related employment and support allowance" after the words "an income-related jobseeker's allowance"

p.86, *amendment to the Administration Act 1992, s.73*

With effect from October 27, 2008, s.28 and Sch.3, para.10 of the Welfare Reform Act 2007 amended s.73 as follows:

4.009

(a) by adding in subs.(1) " or a contributory employment and support allowance" after the words "contribution-based jobseeker's allowance"

(b) by adding the following in subs.(4):

"(c) a contributory employment and support allowance,"

With effect from October 27, 2008, s.67 and Sch.8, of the Welfare Reform Act 2007 delete the word "or" at the end of s.73(4)(a).

p.87, *amendment to the Administration Act 1992, s.74*

4.010   With effect from October 27, 2008, s.28 and Sch.3, para.10 of the Welfare Reform Act 2007 amended

(a) subs.(1)(b) and (2)(b) by substituting the words ", state pension credit or an income-related employment and support allowance" for the words "or state pension credit"; and

(b) subs. (3)(b) by substituting the words ", an income-based job-seeker's allowance or an income-related employment and support allowance" for the words "or an income-based jobseeker's allowance".

With effect from October 27, 2008, The Employment and Support Allowance (Miscellaneous Amendments) Regulations 2008 (SI 2008/2428), reg.23 provides that in para.(c), and in the full-out words after that paragraph, for "or an income-based jobseeker's allow-ance", in each place, substitute ", an income-based jobseeker's allow-ance or an income-related employment and support allowance".

p.90, *amendment to the Administration Act 1992, s.74A*

4.011   With effect from October 27, 2008, s.28 and Sch.3, para.10 of the Welfare Reform Act 2007 amended s.74A(7) by inserting the words ", an income-related employment and support allowance" after the words "an income-based jobseeker's allowance".

p.107, *amendment to the Administration Act 1992, s.109*

4.012   With effect from October 27, 2008, s.28 and Sch.3, para.10 of the Welfare Reform Act 2007 amended subs.(1) by adding the words "or an income-related employment and support allowance" after the words "income support" in both places where these words appear.

p.107, *amendment to the Administration Act 1992, s.124*

4.013   With effect from October 27, 2008, s.28 and Sch.3, para.10 of the Welfare Reform Act 2007 amended subs.(1) by inserting:

"(ac) of the provisions of Part 1 of the Welfare Reform Act 2007;"

p.110, *amendment to the Administration Act 1992, s.125*

4.014   With effect from October 27, 2008, s.28 and Sch.3, para.10 of the Welfare Reform Act 2007 amended subs.(1) by inserting the words ", Part 1 of the Welfare Reform Act 2007" after the words "the State Pension Credit Act 2002".

p.111, *amendment to the Administration Act 1992, s.126*

4.015   With effect from October 27, 2008, s.28 and Sch.3, para.10 of the Welfare Reform Act 2007 amended subs.(1) by inserting the words ", an

568

income-related employment and support allowance" after the words "state pension credit".

p.112, *amendment to the Administration Act 1992, s.130*

With effect from October 27, 2008, s.28 and Sch.3, para.10 of the   **4.016**
Welfare Reform Act 2007 amended subs.(1) by adding:

> "(f) an employment and support allowance."

p.113, *amendment to the Administration Act 1992, s.132*

With effect from October 27, 2008, s.28 and Sch.3, para.10 of the   **4.017**
Welfare Reform Act 2007 amended subs.(1) by adding:

> "(aa) an employment and support allowance;"

p.121, *amendment to the Administration Act 1992, s.159B*

With effect from October 27, 2008, s.28 and Sch.3, para.10 of the   **4.018**
Welfare Reform Act 2007:

(a) amended subs.(1) by adding:
> "(iiia) in any component of a contributory employment and support allowance,"

(b) amended subs.(6) by adding:
> "(c) in relation to a contributory employment and support allowance, means any of the sums specified in regulations under Part 1 of the Welfare Reform Act 2007 which are relevant in calculating the amount payable by way of a contributory employment and support allowance;"

(c) add a new section 159C after s.159B as follows:

"159C Effect of alteration of rates of an employment and support allowance

(1) Subject to such exceptions and conditions as may be prescribed,   **4.019**
subsection (2) or (3) shall have effect where—

(a) an award of an employment and support allowance is in force in favour of any person ("the recipient"), and

(b) an alteration—
(i) in any component of the allowance,
(ii) in the recipient's benefit income, or
(iii) in the recipient's war disablement or war widow's or widower's pension,

affects the computation of the amount of the employment and support allowance to which he is entitled.

(2) Where, as a result of the alteration, the amount of the employment and support allowance to which the recipient is entitled is increased or reduced, then, as from the commencing date, the amount of the employment and support allowance payable in the case of the recipient under the award shall be the increased or reduced amount,

without any further decision of the Secretary of State; and the award shall have effect accordingly.

(3) Where, notwithstanding the alteration, the recipient continues on and after the commencing date to be entitled to the same amount by way of an employment and support allowance as before, the award shall continue in force accordingly.

(4) Subsection (5) applies where a statement is made in the House of Commons by or on behalf of the Secretary of State which specifies—

(a) in relation to any of the items referred to in subsection (1)(b)(i) to (iii), the amount of the alteration which he proposes to make by an order under section 150 or 152 or by or under any other enactment, and

(b) the date on which he proposes to bring the alteration into force ("the proposed commencing date").

(5) If, in a case where this subsection applies, an award of an employment and support allowance is made in favour of a person before the proposed commencing date and after the date on which the statement is made, the award—

(a) may provide for the employment and support allowance to be paid as from the proposed commencing date at a rate determined by reference to the amounts of the items referred to in subsection (1)(b)(i) to (iii) which will be in force on that date, or

(b) may be expressed in terms of the amounts of those items in force at the date of the award.

(6) In this section—

"alteration" means—

(a) in relation to any component of an employment and support allowance, its alteration by or under any enactment;

(b) in relation to a person's benefit income, the alteration of any of the sums referred to in section 150 by any enactment or by an order under section 150 or 152 to the extent that any such alteration affects the amount of his benefit income;

(c) in relation to a person's war disablement pension or war widow's or widower's pension, its alteration by or under any enactment;

"benefit income", in relation to a person, means so much of his income as consists of benefit under the Contributions and Benefits Act;

"the commencing date", in relation to an alteration, means the date on which the alteration comes into force in relation to the recipient;

"component", in relation to an employment and support allowance, means any of the sums specified in regulations under Part 1 of the Welfare Reform Act 2007 which are relevant in calculating the amount payable by way of an employment and support allowance;

"war disablement pension" and "war widow's or widower's pension" have the same meaning as in section 159B."

p.124, *new s.160B, Administration Act 1992*

With effect from October 27, 2008, s.28 and Sch.3, para.10 of the   4.020
Welfare Reform Act 2007 add a new s.160B after s.160A as follows:

"160B Implementation of increases in employment and support allowance due to attainment of particular ages

(1) This section applies where—

(a) an award of an employment and support allowance is in force in favour of a person ("the recipient"), and

(b) a component has become applicable, or applicable at a particular rate, because he or some other person has reached a particular age ("the qualifying age").

(2) If, as a result of the recipient or other person reaching the qualifying age, the recipient becomes entitled to an employment and support allowance of an increased amount, the amount payable to or for him under the award shall, as from the day on which he becomes so entitled, be that increased amount, without any further decision of the Secretary of State; and the award shall have effect accordingly.

(3) Subsection (2) does not apply where, in consequence of the recipient or other person reaching the qualifying age, a question arises in relation to the recipient's entitlement to a benefit under the Contributions and Benefits Act.

(4) Subsection (2) does not apply where, in consequence of the recipient or other person reaching the qualifying age, a question arises in relation to the recipient's entitlement to an employment and support allowance, other than—

(a) the question whether the component concerned, or any other component, becomes or ceases to be applicable, or applicable at a particular rate, in the recipient's case, and

(b) the question whether, in consequence, the amount of his employment and support allowance falls to be varied.

(5) In this section, "component", in relation to a recipient and his employment and support allowance, means any of the amounts determined in accordance with regulations made under section 2(1)(a) or 4(2)(a) of the Welfare Reform Act 2007."

p.126, *amendment to the Administration Act 1992, s.170*

The Welfare Reform Act 2007, s.33, inserts, with effect from April 1,   4.021
2008 for some purposes and from October 6, 2008 for all other purposes, in the definition of "the relevant enactments" the following after subs.(5)(a)(ai):

"(aj)   sections 32 and 33 of the Welfare Reform Act 2007;"

and in the definition of the "relevant Northern Ireland enactments" inserts the following after subs.(5)(b)(ah):

"(aj)   any provision in Northern Ireland which correspond to sections 32 and 33 of the Welfare Reform Act 2007;"

Note that there appears to be a numbering error in relation to the amendment in relation to definition of relevant Northern Ireland enactments, since there appears to be no subparagraph (ai).

With effect from October 27, 2008, s.28 and Sch.3, para.10 of the Welfare Reform Act 2007 amended:

(a) the definition of "the relevant enactments" by adding:

"(aia) the provisions of Part 1 of the Welfare Reform Act 2007;"

(b) the definition of "the relevant Northern Ireland enactments" by adding:

"(aia) any provisions in Northern Ireland which correspond to the provisions of Part 1 of the Welfare Reform Act 2007;"

p.130, *amendment to the Administration Act 1992, s.179*

4.022   With effect from October 27, 2008, s.28 and Sch.3, para.10 of the Welfare Reform Act 2007 amended:

(a) subs.(3)(a) by inserting the words ", Part 1 of the Welfare Reform Act 2007" after the words "the State Pension Credit Act 2002".

(b) subs.(4) by adding:
"(af) to part 1 of the Welfare Reform Act 2007;"

(c) subs. (5) by adding:
"(ac) employment and support allowance;"

p.133, *amendment to the Administration Act 1992, s.187*

4.023   With effect from October 27, 2008, s.28 and Sch.3, para.10 of the Welfare Reform Act 2007 amended subs.(1) by adding:

"(ac) an employment and support allowance;"

p.137, *amendment to the Administration Act 1992, s.191*

4.024   With effect from October 27, 2008, s.28 and Sch.3, para.10 of the Welfare Reform Act 2007 amended:

(a) the definition of "benefit" by substituting the words ", state pension credit and an employment and support allowance" for the words "and state pension credit";

(b) the definitions by adding at the appropriate point in the list:
"contributory employment and support allowance" means a contributory allowance under Part 1 of the Welfare Reform Act 2007 (employment and support allowance);
"income-related employment and support allowance" means an income-related allowance under Part 1 of the Welfare Reform Act 2007 (employment and support allowance);

pp.147–148, *Pension Schemes Act 1993, s.170(6)*

4.025   With effect from November 3, 2008, the Transfer of Tribunal Functions Order 2008 (SI 2008/2833), Sch.3, paras 111 and 112, amends s.170(6) by substituting "First-tier Tribunal" for "appeal tribunal".

pp.149–150, *Employment Tribunals Act 1996, s.16(5)(d)*

With effect from November 3, 2008, the Transfer of Tribunal Func- 4.026
tions Order 2008 (SI 2008/2833), Sch.3, para.137, amends s.16(5)(d)
by substituting "the First-tier Tribunal" for "an appeal tribunal constituted under Chapter 1 of Part 1 of the Social Security Act 1998".

p.157, *Social Security (Recovery of Benefits) Act 1997, s.1A*

A new s.1A is inserted by s.54 of the Child Maintenance and Other 4.027
Payments Act 2008 with effect from June 10, 2008 for the purpose only
of making regulations and from October 1, 2008 for other purposes.

"1A Lump sum payments: regulation-making power

(1) The Secretary of State may by regulations make provision about
the recovery of the amount of a payment to which subsection (2)
applies (a "lump sum payment") where—
  (a) a compensation payment in consequence of a disease is made to
      or in respect of a person ("P") to whom, or in respect of whom,
      a lump sum payment has been, or is likely to be, made, and
  (b) the compensation payment is made in consequence of the same
      disease as the lump sum payment.
(2) This subsection applies to—
  (a) a payment made in accordance with the Pneumoconiosis etc.
      (Workers' Compensation) Act 1979 ("the 1979 Act"),
  (b) a payment made in accordance with Part 4 of the Child Main-
      tenance and Other Payments Act 2008, and
  (c) an extra-statutory payment (within the meaning given by sub-
      section (5)(d) below).
(3) Regulations under this section may, in particular—
  (a) make provision about the recovery of the amount of a lump sum
      payment made to or in respect of a dependant of P;
  (b) make provision enabling the recovery of the amount of a lump
      sum payment from a compensation payment (including provi-
      sion enabling the recovery of an amount which reduces the
      compensation payment to nil);
  (c) enable the amount of a lump sum payment made before com-
      mencement to be recovered from a compensation payment
      made after commencement;
  (d) make provision about certificates in respect of lump sum pay-
      ments;
  (e) apply any provision of this Act, with or without modifications.
(4) References in subsection (1) to a payment made in consequence
of a disease—
  (a) are references to a payment made by or on behalf of a person
      who is, or is alleged to be, liable to any extent in respect of the
      disease, but
  (b) do not include references to a payment mentioned in Part 1 of
      Schedule 1.

(5) In this section—

(a) "commencement" means the date on which this section comes into force,

(b) "compensation payment" means a payment within section 1(1)(a) above,

(c) "dependant" has the meaning given by section 3 of the 1979 Act, and

(d) "extra-statutory payment" means a payment made by the Secretary of State to or in respect of a person following the rejection by the Secretary of State of a claim under the 1979 Act."

The Social Security (Recovery of Benefits) (Lump Sum Payments) Regulations 2008 (SI 2008/1596) are made under this section (and other provisions of this Act). They provide for the recovery of payments within the scope of subs.(2), which are made by the Secretary of State in respect of death or disablement due to pneumoconiosis or mesothelioma, from a person making a compensation payment in respect of the relevant disease. The Regulations create a separate scheme in place of ss.2 to 9 of the Act but apply most of ss.10 onwards with modifications. The 2008 Regulations are not included in this Supplement because the schemes for making the payments fall outside the current scope of the work. They may, however be included in the next edition.

pp.165–166, *Social Security (Recovery of Benefits) Act 1997, s.10*

4.028   This section is applied with modifications to cases under the Social Security (Recovery of Benefits) (Lump Sum Payments) Regulations 2008 (SI 2008/1596) (see Sch.1, para.3).

pp.166–169, *Social Security (Recovery of Benefits) Act 1997, s.11*

4.029   Subsection (5)(b) is omitted with effect from November 3, 2008 by virtue of the Transfer of Tribunal Functions Order 2008 (SI 2008/2833), Sch.3, para.139.

This section is applied, with modifications, to cases under the Social Security (Recovery of Benefits) (Lump Sum Payments) Regulations 2008 (SI 2008/1596) (see reg.2(2) and Sch.1, para.4).

pp.169–171, *Social Security (Recovery of Benefits) Act 1997, s.12*

4.030   In the heading, "medical appeal tribunal" is replaced by "First-tier Tribunal" and, in subss.(1) and (4), "an appeal tribunal" is replaced by "the First-tier Tribunal" with effect from November 3, 2008 by virtue of the Transfer of Tribunal Functions Order 2008 (SI 2008/2833), Sch.3, para.140.

This section is applied, with modifications, to cases under the Social Security (Recovery of Benefits) (Lump Sum Payments) Regulations 2008 (SI 2008/1596) (see reg.2(2) and Sch.1, para.5 as amended by para.344 of Sch.1 to the Tribunals, Courts and Enforcement Act 2007 (Transitional and Consequential Provisions) Order 2008 (SI 2008/2683)).

574

pp.171–172, *Social Security (Recovery of Benefits) Act 1997, s.13*

Subsections (1) and (3) are omitted and the heading and subs.(2) are   4.031
amended with effect from November 3, 2008 by virtue of the Transfer of
Tribunal Functions Order 2008 (SI 2008/2833), Sch.3, para.141. In the
heading, "Social Security Commissioner" is replaced by "Upper Tribunal" and, in subs.(2), "under this section" is replaced by "to the Upper
Tribunal under section 11 of the Tribunals, Courts and Enforcement
Act 2007 which arises from any decision of the First-Tier Tribunal made
under section 12 of this Act".

This section is applied with modifications to cases under the Social
Security (Recovery of Benefits) (Lump Sum Payments) Regulations
2008 (SI 2008/1596) (see reg.2(2) and Sch.1, para.6, as amended by the
Social Security (Miscellaneous Amendments) (No.3) Regulations 2008
(SI 2008/2365), reg.6(1) and (3) and para.344 of Sch.1 to the Tribunals,
Courts and Enforcement Act 2007 (Transitional and Consequential
Provisions) Order 2008 (SI 2008/2683)).

pp.172–180, *Social Security (Recovery of Benefits) Act 1997, ss.14 to 23*

These sections are applied with modifications to cases under the   4.032
Social Security (Recovery of Benefits) (Lump Sum Payments) Regulations 2008 (SI 2008/1596) (see reg.2(2) and Sch.1, paras 7 to 15).

p.181, *Social Security (Recovery of Benefits) Act 1997, ss.28 to 30*

The definition of "benefit" in s.29 is amended with effect from Octo-   4.033
ber 27, 2008 by inserting ", an employment and support allowance"
after "a jobseeker's allowance" (Employment and Support Allowance
(Consequential Provisions) (No.2) Regulations 2008 (SI 2008/1554),
reg.50(1) and (2)).

The definitions of "appeal tribunal" and "Commissioner" are omitted
from s.29 with effect from November 3, 2008 by virtue of the Transfer
of Tribunal Functions Order 2008 (SI 2008/2833), Sch.3, para.142.

Sections 28 to 30 are applied to cases under the Social Security
(Recovery of Benefits) (Lump Sum Payments) Regulations 2008 (SI
2008/1596), with modifications to s.29 (see reg.2(2) and Sch.1,
para.18).

p.182, *Social Security (Recovery of Benefits) Act 1997, s.34*

Subsections (1) and (3) are applied to cases under the Social Security   4.034
(Recovery of Benefits) (Lump Sum Payments) Regulations 2008 (SI
2008/1596) by reg.2(2).

p.183, *Social Security (Recovery of Benefits) Act 1997, Sch.1*

This Schedule is applied to cases under the Social Security (Recovery   4.035
of Benefits) (Lump Sum Payments) Regulations 2008 (SI 2008/1596),
with modifications (see reg.2(2) and Sch.1, paras 19 and 20).

p.184, *Social Security (Recovery of Benefits) Act 1997, Sch.2*

4.036   An additional entry for "Employment and support allowance" is inserted with effect from October 27, 2008 by reg.50(1) and (3) of the Employment and Support Allowance (Consequential Provisions) (No.2) Regulations 2008 (SI 2008/1554).

pp.189–190, *Social Security Act 1998, s.2(2)*

4.037   With effect from July 27, 2008, s.2(2) is amended by para.17(1) and (2) of Sch.3 to the Welfare Reform Act 2007 by adding—

"(j) Part 1 of the Welfare Reform Act 2007"

pp.191–196, *Social Security Act 1998, ss.4 to 7*

4.038   These sections are omitted with effect from November 3, 2008 by virtue of the Transfer of Tribunal Functions Order 2008 (SI 2008/2833), Sch.3, paras 143 to 147. This is because appeal tribunals have been replaced by the First-tier Tribunal and the chairmen and members of appeal tribunals have become judges and members of the First-tier Tribunal (see arts 3 to 5 of the Order). The Order came into effect as it appeared in draft (see pp.1344–59 of Vol.III of the main work).

Note that there is a saving in art.1(5) of the Order which has the effect that ss.5 to 7 remain in force in Scotland. This is because the function of hearing appeals in Scotland under the Health and Social Care (Community Health and Standards Act) 2003 has not been transferred and so tribunals (and Social Security Commissioners) must remain in being to hear such appeals.

pp.196–197, *Social Security Act 1998, s.8*

4.039   With effect from July 27, 2008 (March 18, 2008 for regulation-making purposes), para.17(1) and (3) of Sch.3 to the Welfare Reform Act 2007 amends subs.(3) by inserting after para.(b)—

"(ba) an employment and support allowance;"

and amends subs.(4) by substituting ", the State Pension Credit Act 2002 or Part 1 of the Welfare Reform Act 2007" for "or the State Pension Credit Act 2002".

p.200, *annotation to Social Security Act 1998, s.8(5)*

CIB/3542/2007 has been reported as *R(IB) 1/09.*

p.203, *Social Security Act 1998, s.10(1)(b)*

4.040   With effect from November 3, 2008, the Transfer of Tribunal Functions Order 2008 (SI 2008/2833), Sch.3, paras 143 and 148, amends s.10(1)(b) by substituting "of the First-tier Tribunal or any decision of the Upper Tribunal which relates to any such decision" for "of an appeal tribunal or a Commissioner".

p.207, *Social Security Act 1998, s.11(3)*

With effect from October 27, 2008, para.17(1) and (4) of Sch.3 to the Welfare Reform Act 2007 amends the definition of "the current legislation" by substituting ", the State Pension Credit Act 2002 and Part 1 of the Welfare Reform Act 2007" for "and the State Pension Credit Act 2002". 4.041

pp.208–209, *Social Security Act 1998, s.12*

With effect from November 3, 2008, the Transfer of Tribunal Functions Order 2008 (SI 2008/2833), Sch.3, paras 143 and 149, amends s.12 by substituting references to the First-tier Tribunal for references to an appeal tribunal in the heading and in subss.(2), (4), (5) and (8). 4.042

pp.209–230, *annotation to Social Security Act 1998, s.12*

A tribunal is entitled to admit written evidence and prefer it to oral evidence, particularly in the absence of a motion for adjournment (*CSIS/ 21/2008*). 4.043

CSDLA/500/2007 has been reported as *R(DLA) 3/08*.

A Commissioner has discouraged tribunals from removing awards made by the Secretary of State in borderline cases where the Secretary of State has not superseded or revised the decision himself. In *CDLA/ 2738/2007*, it was said—

> "This was a borderline case. The tribunal was entitled to take the view that the claimant was not virtually unable to walk but the Secretary of State was equally entitled to take the opposite view. Where a tribunal's findings are not materially different from the Secretary of State's and the Secretary of State's conclusion in favour of the claimant is not perverse, a tribunal should be slow to interfere and must, in accordance with *R(IB) 2/04*, give reasons for considering it necessary to do so."

In *CDLA/884/2008*, he said—

> "8. An increasing number of appeals before Commissioners seem to be cases where a tribunal has made a decision less favourable to the claimant than the one the claimant was challenging before the tribunal. It is not surprising that appeals should be brought before Commissioners in such cases, particularly as the consequence of any such decision is that there will have been an overpayment, the recoverability of which will have been left undetermined by the tribunal. Tribunals need to be aware of the dangers of being both prosecutor and judge, one of which is the risk of making errors unprompted by the parties. Such errors are too common and are contributing significantly to the caseload of Commissioners. It is particularly unfortunate that two of the several errors made by the tribunal in the present case were on

points in respect of which a Tribunal of Commissioners had relatively recently given clear guidance.

9. There are other risks in being both prosecutor and judge. The most obvious is that there can be a perception that the tribunal has prejudged the case. Of course a tribunal has an inquisitorial or investigative role but here it is noteworthy that the tribunal, having apparently formed the (not unreasonable) view on the papers that the claimant's entitlement to any disability living allowance was doubtful, started the proceedings by warning the claimant that his existing award was at risk and advising him that he could withdraw his appeal. The claimant having declined to withdraw his appeal, the tribunal then launched straight into the question of the claimant's entitlement to the mobility component, by questioning him about how he had got to the hearing, without first listening to what the claimant had to say about his needs for care which was the issue upon which he had brought his appeal. It is little wonder that the claimant says, in effect, that he formed an early view that the tribunal was more interested in its own agenda than in what he had to say."

He pointed out that it was not necessarily enough to give a claimant an opportunity to withdraw his appeal; it had been said in *R(IB) 2/04* that the claimant had to be given sufficient notice to enable him to prepare his case on the new issue, which meant being given notice of the case against him where that would not be obvious to him.

"10. . . . A tribunal is in a difficult position. If it gives the claimant too robust a warning at the beginning of a hearing, it runs the risk of giving the impression of having prejudged the case. If it does not give such a robust warning, the warning may not adequately convey to the claimant the case he or she needs to consider resisting with the consequence that a decision not to withdraw the appeal, or not to ask for an adjournment, is not fully informed. This is a powerful reason for tribunals refraining from making decisions less favourable to claimants than the decisions being challenged, except in the most obvious cases (e.g., where the evidence is overwhelming or the facts are not in dispute and no element of judgment is involved or where the law has been misapplied by the Secretary of State) or after an appropriate adjournment. In such obvious cases, a failure expressly to state why a tribunal has considered a point not in issue between the parties will not necessarily render the tribunal's decision erroneous in point of law; in less obvious cases, the absence of a reason for considering the point may suggest that the discretion to do so has not been exercised properly.

11. If a tribunal does not consider the correctness of an award that is not directly in issue before it, it does not follow that it should do nothing if it has doubts about the award. The chairman is at liberty to draw the doubts to the Secretary of State's attention in the decision notice and can arrange for the parties to be sent a copy of the record of proceedings (including his or her note of evidence) without them having to request it. That would enable the Secretary of State to consider a supersession or revision and, in disability living allowance

cases, would often avoid the possibility of there having been an over-payment, which is often a consequence of a tribunal considering the issue and which often worries claimants more than the mere cessation of entitlement."

In both cases, the Commissioner restored the Secretary of State's decision. In practice, cases often turn on the claimant's own oral evidence which, if unfavourable to the claimant, is unlikely to be in dispute and, provided the findings of fact are such as to make it clear why the claimant could not be entitled to benefit in the light of that evidence, a tribunal is unlikely then to be found to have erred in not expressly stating why it took the point on its own initiative. An adjournment is also unlikely to be necessary where a case can be determined on the basis of the claimant's own oral evidence and where it could not reasonably be argued that the claimant was entitled to benefit in the light of that evidence. Borderline cases and those cases where a claimant might be able to provide further evidence require more care.

p.230, *Social Security Act 1998, s.13*

Strangely, this section is not completely repealed with effect from November 3, 2008. Subsection (2) is repealed by the Transfer of Tribunal Functions Order 2008 (SI 2008/2833), Sch.3, paras 143 and 150, being effectively replaced by s.9 of the Tribunals, Courts and Enforcement Act 2007, but subs.(3) is retained, save for "First-tier Tribunal" being substituted for "person" and "tribunal". Subsection (1) is amended to read—   4.044

"This section applies where an application is made to the First-tier Tribunal for permission to appeal to the Upper Tribunal from any decision of the First-tier Tribunal under section 12 or this section."

Subsection (4) is not amended.

pp.233–234, *Social Security Act 1998, s.14*

With effect from November 3, 2008, this section ceases to provide a right of appeal. The Transfer of Tribunal Functions Order 2008 (SI 2008/2833) abolishes the Social Security Commissioners (save for appeals under the Health Care (Community Health and Standards) Act 2003 in Scotland (see arts 1(5)(b) and 4(b)) and, by Sch.3, paras 143 and 151, repeals subss.(1) and (7) to (12). As subs.(2) has already been repealed, that leaves only subss.(3) to (6) which are amended so that they make provision as to who may exercise the right of appeal that exists under s.11 of the Tribunals, Courts and Enforcement Act 2007 from a First-tier Tribunal decision made under this Act to the Upper Tribunal. In the heading, "First-tier Tribunal to Upper Tribunal" is substituted for "tribunal to Commissioner" and, in subss.(3) and (4), "to the Upper Tribunal under section 11 of the Tribunals, Courts and Enforcement Act 2007 from any decision of the First-Tier Tribunal under section 12 or 13 above lies" is substituted for "lies under this section".   4.045

pp.236–244, *annotation to Social Security Act 1998, s.14(1)*

4.046   On November 3, 2008, the Social Security Commissioners became judges of the Upper Tribunal. The London office of the Administrative Appeals Chamber of the Upper Tribunal has since moved to 11th Floor, Cardinal Tower, 12 Farringdon Road, London EC1M 3HS. The Edinburgh office remains at George House, 126 George Street, Edinburgh EH2 4HH.

CSDLA/500/2007 has been reported as *R(DLA) 3/08.*

It is not a breach of natural justice for a tribunal to admit written evidence and prefer it to oral evidence, particularly in the absence of a motion for adjournment (*CSIS/21/2008*).

There was a breach of the rules of natural justice where a tribunal and a Commissioner did not join as a party or, at least give an opportunity to make representations to, a third party whose entitlement to benefit would inevitably effected by the their decisions. The issue arose in circumstances where a claim for widow's benefit by one women required a finding that she was validly married to the deceased contributor, which would imply that he had not been validly married to a woman already awarded benefit as a widow (*CG/1164/2006*). The real problem is that there has not, since the coming into force of the 1998 Act, been a power in the Secretary of State to refer a case to a tribunal so that entitlement may properly be considered at the same time as a related case is being heard.

pp.247–249, *annotation to Social Security Act 1998, s.14(10)*

4.047   On the narrow approach to be taken to applications for judicial review of a refusal of leave, see also *R. (Hook) v Social Security Commissioner* [2007] EWHC 1705 (Admin) (reported as *R(IS) 7/07)* and *R. (Starling) v Child Support Commissioner* [2008] EWHC 1319 (Admin).

p.249, *Social Security Act 1998, s.15*

4.048   With effect from November 3, 2008, this section ceases to provide a right of appeal. The Transfer of Tribunal Functions Order 2008 (SI 2008/2833) Sch.3, paras 143 and 152 repeals subss.(1), (2), (4) and (5) (except in Scotland for purposes explained in the note to ss. 4 to 7). This leaves only subs.(3) which (with the heading) is amended so that it make provision as to who may exercise the right of appeal that exists under s.13 of the Tribunals, Courts and Enforcement Act 2007 from an Upper Tribunal to an appellate court in a case arising out of a decision made under s.12 or s.13 of this Act. See p.1353 of Vol.III of the main work for the precise terms of the amendments.

pp.250–252, *Social Security Act 1998, annotation to s.15*

4.049   It is open to the Court of Appeal to take, on its own initiative, a point of general importance not raised before a Commissioner or in grounds of appeal (*Bulale v Secretary of State for the Home Department* [2008] EWCA Civ 806).

p.252, *Social Security Act 1998, s.15A*

With effect from November 3, 2008, the Transfer of Tribunal Functions Order 2008 (SI 2008/2833) Sch.3, paras 143 and 153 inserts a new s.15A—

    4.050

"Functions of Senior President of Tribunals

    15A.—(1) The Senior President of Tribunals shall ensure that appropriate steps are taken by the First-tier Tribunal to secure the confidentiality, in such circumstances as may be prescribed, of any prescribed material, or any prescribed classes or categories of material.
    (2) Each year the Senior President of Tribunals shall make to the Secretary of State and the Child Maintenance and Enforcement Commission a written report, based on the cases coming before the First-tier Tribunal, on the standards achieved by the Secretary of State and the Child Maintenance and Enforcement Commission in the making of decisions against which an appeal lies to the First-tier Tribunal.
    (3) The Lord Chancellor shall publish the report."

This replaces paras 7 and 10 of Sch.1.

p.252, *Social Security Act 1998, s.16*

With effect from November 3, 2008, the Transfer of Tribunal Functions Order 2008 (SI 2008/2833) Sch.3, paras 143 and 154 repeals subss.(2), (3)(a) and (6) to (9). This is because procedural rules for the First-tier Tribunal and Upper Tribunal are made under s.22 of the Tribunals, Courts and Enforcement Act 2007. (There is a saving in Scotland for reasons explained in the supplementary note to ss.4 to 7.) The power to appoint a Tribunal of Commissioners under subs.(7) is replaced by a practice statement of the Senior President of Tribunals as to the composition of the Upper Tribunal, made under the First-tier Tribunal and Upper Tribunal (Composition of Tribunal) Order 2008 (see the supplementary annotation to that order, below).

    4.051

p.254, *Social Security Act 1998, s.17(1)*

With effect from November 3, 2008, the Transfer of Tribunal Functions Order 2008 (SI 2008/2833) Sch.3, paras 143 and 155 inserts "and to any provision made by or under Chapter 2 of Part 1 of the Tribunals, Courts and Enforcement Act 2007" after "this Chapter", in the first place where it occurs. This has the effect that a decision of the Upper Tribunal or an appellate court on appeal from a decision of the First-tier Tribunal under s.12 is final.

    4.052

pp.254–256, *Social Security Act 1998, annotation to s.17(1)*

4.053   In *CIS/3517/2007*, the Commissioner expressed some surprise that a tribunal considering a recoverability appeal was not bound by findings made by a tribunal on the relevant entitlement appeal. However, whether that is surprising or not may depend on the weight the observer places on the desirability of obtaining the "right" answer. Nonetheless, there is no breach of the rules of natural justice where the same tribunal sits to hear both appeals, provided that it approaches the second case with an open mind (*R(IS) 1/09*).

p.256, *Social Security Act 1998, s.18(1)(a)*

4.054   With effect from November 3, 2008, the Transfer of Tribunal Functions Order 2008 (SI 2008/2833) Sch.3, paras 143 and 156 substitutes "or the First-tier Tribunal, or any decision of the Upper Tribunal which relates to any decision under this Chapter of the First-Tier Tribunal," for ", an appeal tribunal or a Commissioner".

pp.258–259, *Social Security Act 1998, s.20*

4.055   With effect from November 3, 2008, the Transfer of Tribunal Functions Order 2008 (SI 2008/2833) Sch.3, paras 143 and 157 amends subss.(2) and (3) and replaces the regulation-making powers with rule-making powers. It also removes the definition of "eligible person" in subs.(2) and replaces references to the "eligible person" with references to the First-tier Tribunal. For the precise terms of the amendments, see p.1354 of Vol.III of the main work.

For rules made under this section, see r.25 of the Tribunal Procedure (First-tier Tribunal) (Social Entitlement Chamber) Rules 2008 (SI 2008/2685), set out in Pt 1 of this Supplement.

p.260, *Social Security Act 1998, s.20A*

4.056   With effect from November 3, 2008, the Transfer of Tribunal Functions Order 2008 (SI 2008/2833) Sch.3, paras 143 and 158 inserts a new s.20A—

"Travelling and other allowances

20A.—(1) The Lord Chancellor may pay to any person required under this Part (whether for the purposes of this Part or otherwise) to attend for or to submit to medical or other examination or treatment such travelling and other allowances as the Lord Chancellor may determine.

(2) In subsection (1) the reference to travelling and other allowances includes compensation for loss of remunerative time but such compensation shall not be paid to any person in respect of any time during which the person is in receipt of remuneration under section 28 of, or

paragraph 5 of Schedule 2 to, the Tribunals, Courts and Enforcement Act 2007 (assessors and judges of First-Tier Tribunal)."

This replaces para.4(1)(b) (with sub-para.(2)) of Sch.1.

pp.260–261, *Social Security Act 1998, s.21*

With effect from November 3, 2008, the Transfer of Tribunal Functions Order 2008 (SI 2008/2833) Sch.3, paras 143 and 159 substitutes references to the First-tier Tribunal and the Upper Tribunal for references to an appeal tribunal and a Commissioner, respectively, in subs.(2) and substitutes "permission" for "leave" in subs.(3)(b) and (c). **4.057**

p.263, *Social Security Act 1998, s.24A*

With effect from November 3, 2008, the Transfer of Tribunal Functions Order 2008 (SI 2008/2833) Sch.3, paras 143 and 160 substitutes references to the First-tier Tribunal and the Upper Tribunal for references to an appeal tribunal and a Commissioner, respectively. **4.058**

p.264, *Social Security Act 1998, s.25(1)(b)*

With effect from November 3, 2008, the Transfer of Tribunal Functions Order 2008 (SI 2008/2833) Sch.3, paras 143 and 161 substitutes "the Upper Tribunal" for "a Commissioner". **4.059**

pp.266–267, *Social Security Act 1998, s.26*

With effect from November 3, 2008, the Transfer of Tribunal Functions Order 2008 (SI 2008/2833) Sch.3, paras 143 and 162 substitutes references to the First-tier Tribunal and the Upper Tribunal for references to an appeal tribunal and a Commissioner, respectively. **4.060**

pp.268–270, *Social Security Act 1998, s.27*

With effect from October 27, 2008, para.17(1) and (5) of Sch.3 to the Welfare Reform Act 2007 amends the definition of "benefit" in subs.(7) by inserting after para.(dd)— **4.061**

"(de) an employment and support allowance;"

and substituting "to (de)" for "to (dd)" in para.(e).

With effect from November 3, 2008, the Transfer of Tribunal Functions Order 2008 (SI 2008/2833) Sch.3, paras 143 and 163 substitutes references to the Upper Tribunal for references to a Commissioner in subss.(1)(a), (3) and 10(a) and (b).

p.272, *Social Security Act 1998, s.28*

With effect from July 27, 2008 (March 18, 2008 for regulation-making purposes), para.17(1) and (6) of Sch.3 to the Welfare Reform Act 2007 amends subs.(3) by adding— **4.062**

"; or
(g) Part 1 of the Welfare Reform Act 2007."

With effect from November 3, 2008, the Transfer of Tribunal Functions Order 2008 (SI 2008/2833) Sch.3, paras 143 and 164 amends s.28 so that it applies only to the correction of decisions of the Secretary of State because, in relation to the correction and setting aside of decisions of tribunals, it is replaced by para.15 of Sch.5 to the Tribunals, Courts and Enforcement Act 2007. In subs.(1)(a), the words "of the Secretary of State" are inserted after "decision" in both places; subs.(1)(b) (together with the "and" immediately before it) is repealed; in subs.(1A), the words "any decision of the First-tier Tribunal or" are inserted after "not include" and, in subsection (2), "or set aside decisions" is omitted.

p.273, *Social Security Act 1998, s.29(3)*

4.063   With effect from November 3, 2008, the Transfer of Tribunal Functions Order 2008 (SI 2008/2833) Sch.3, paras 143 and 165 substitutes ", the First-tier Tribunal or the Upper Tribunal" for ", an appeal tribunal or a Commissioner".

p.276, *Social Security Act 1998, s.31*

4.064   With effect from October 27, 2008 (March 18, 2008 for regulation-making purposes), para.17(1) and (7) of Sch.3 to the Welfare Reform Act 2007 inserts a new subs.(1A)—

"(1A) Regulations may provide that a determination that a person is disqualified for any period in accordance with regulations under section 18(1) to (3) of the Welfare Reform Act 2007 shall have effect for such purposes as may be prescribed as a determination that he is to be treated as not having limited capability for work for that period, and vice versa."

p.277, *Social Security Act 1998, s.39ZA*

4.065   With effect from November 3, 2008, the Transfer of Tribunal Functions Order 2008 (SI 2008/2833) Sch.3, paras 143 and 166 inserts a new s.39ZA—

"Certificates

39ZA. A document bearing a certificate which—
(a) is signed by a person authorised in that behalf by the Secretary of State, and
(b) states that the document, apart from the certificate, is a record of a decision of an officer of the Secretary of State,
shall be conclusive evidence of the decision; and a certificate purporting to be so signed shall be deemed to be so signed unless the contrary is proved."

This replaces para.13 of Sch.1 but is limited to the certification of decisions of the Secretary of State. Formerly, the Secretary of State could anomalously certify a decision of a tribunal.

p.277, *Social Security Act 1998, s.39*

With effect from November 3, 2008, the Transfer of Tribunal Functions Order 2008 (SI 2008/2833) Sch.3, paras 143 and 167 repeals the definitions of "appeal tribunal" and "Commissioner" (except in Scotland for purposes explained in the supplementary note to ss.4 to 7). **4.066**

pp.280–281, *Social Security Act 1998, s.79*

With effect from November 3, 2008, the Transfer of Tribunal Functions Order 2008 (SI 2008/2833) Sch.3, paras 143 and 168 removes the references to subs.(2) and para.6 of Sch.4 in subs.(1) and repeals subss.(2) and (9) (except in Scotland for purposes explained in the supplementary note to ss.4 to 7). **4.067**

pp.281–282, *Social Security Act 1998, s.80*

With effect from November 3, 2008, the Transfer of Tribunal Functions Order 2008 (SI 2008/2833) Sch.3, paras 143 and 169 removes the references to s.7 in subs.(1)(a), removes the references to para.12 of Sch.1 and para.2 of Sch.5 in subs.(1)(b) and repeals subss.(3) and (4) (except in Scotland for purposes explained in the supplementary note to ss.4 to 7). **4.068**

p.282, *Social Security Act 1998, s.81*

With effect from November 3, 2008, the Transfer of Tribunal Functions Order 2008 (SI 2008/2833) Sch.3, paras 143 and 170 substitutes "the First-tier Tribunal" for "an appeal tribunal constituted under Chapter 1 of Part 1" (except in Scotland for purposes explained in the supplementary note to ss.4 to 7). **4.069**

pp.284–285, *Social Security Act 1998, Sch.1*

With effect from November 3, 2008, the Transfer of Tribunal Functions Order 2008 (SI 2008/2833) Sch.3, paras 143 and 171 repeals Sch.1 (except in Scotland for purposes explained in the supplementary note to ss.4 to 7). Paras 7 and 10 have now been replaced by s.15A. Two days earlier, para.10 had been amended by the insertion of "and the Child Maintenance and Enforcement Commission" after "Secretary of State" (Child Maintenance and Other Payments Act 2008, Sch.3, para.54). Paragraph 13 has been reproduced in part as s.39ZA but there is now no provision for proving tribunal decisions, which is probably unnecessary. Apart from para.9, the other provisions of the Schedule have been replaced by provisions in the Tribunals, Courts and Enforcement Act 2007 (see s.40, Sch.2 and para.3 of Sch.5). **4.070**

p.286, *Social Security Act 1998, Sch.2*

4.071　　With effect from October 27, 2008, para.17(1) and (8) of Sch.3 to the Welfare Reform Act 2007 amends para.6(b) by adding—

> ", or
>> (iv) section 159C(1)(b) of that Act (employment and support allowance)."

p.287, *Social Security Act 1998, Sch.3*

4.072　　With effect from October 27, 2008, para.17(1) and (9) of Sch.3 to the Welfare Reform Act 2007 amends para.3 by adding—

> "; or
>> (g) section 18 of the Welfare Reform Act 2007."

pp.289–290, *Social Security Act 1998, Sch.4*

4.073　　With effect from November 3, 2008, the Transfer of Tribunal Functions Order 2008 (SI 2008/2833) Sch.3, paras 143 and 172 repeals Sch.4 (except in Scotland for purposes explained in the supplementary note to ss.4 to 7). Apart from para.7, which has fallen into disuse, the provisions of the Schedule have been replaced by provisions in the Tribunals, Courts and Enforcement Act 2007 (see Sch.3, para.3 of Sch.5 and Pt 2 of Sch.9).

p.291, *Social Security Act 1998, Sch.5*

4.074　　With effect from November 3, 2008, the Transfer of Tribunal Functions Order 2008 (SI 2008/2833) Sch.3, paras 143 and 173 repeals the words ", an appeal tribunal or Commissioner" in para.1(a) and (b) and repeals the whole of paras 2 and 5 to 8 (except in Scotland for purposes explained in the supplementary note to ss.4 to 7). This is because the power to make procedural rules for tribunals is now to be found in s.22 of the Tribunals, Courts and Enforcement Act 2007.

p.301, *amendment to the Child Support, Pensions and Social Security Act 2000, s.62*

4.075　　With effect from October 27, 2008, s.28 and Sch.3, para.20 of the Welfare Reform Act 2007:
> (i) add the following new subsection:

> "(4A) The Secretary of State may by regulations provide that, where the relevant benefit is an employment and support allowance, any income-related allowance (within the meaning of Part 1 of the Welfare Reform Act 2007) shall be payable, during the whole or part of the prescribed period, as if one or more of the following applied—
>> (a) the rate of the allowance were such reduced rate as may be prescribed;

586

(b) the allowance were payable only if there is compliance by the offender with such obligations with respect to the provision of information as may be imposed by the regulations;

(c) the allowance were payable only if the circumstances are otherwise such as may be prescribed."

(ii) amended subs. (8) by adding:

"(ba) an employment and support allowance;"

p.307, *amendment to the Child Support, Pensions and Social Security Act 2000, s.65*

With effect from October 27, 2008, s.28 and Sch.3, para.20 of the Welfare Reform Act 2007 amended subs.(4)(c) by adding the words "or (4A)" after the words "section 62(4)".   4.076

p.308, *amendment to the Social Security Fraud Act 2001, s.7*

With effect from October 27, 2008, s.28 and Sch.3, para.23 of the Welfare Reform Act 2007:   4.077

(i) added new subs.(4B) as follows:

"(4B) The Secretary of State may by regulations provide that, where the sanctionable benefit is employment and support allowance, any income-related allowance shall be payable, during the whole or a part of any period comprised in the disqualification period, as if one or more of the following applied—

(a) the rate of the allowance were such reduced rate as may be prescribed;

(b) the allowance were payable only if there is compliance by the offender with such obligations with respect to the provision of information as may be imposed by the regulations;

(c) the allowance were payable only if the circumstances are otherwise such as may be prescribed."

(ii) added the following to subs.(8):

"(ab) any benefit under Part 1 of the Welfare Reform Act 2007 (employment and support allowance) or under any provision having effect in Northern Ireland corresponding to that Part;"

p.313, *amendment to the Social Security Fraud Act 2001, s.9*

With effect from October 27, 2008, s.28 and Sch.3, para.23 of the Welfare Reform Act 2007 amended s.9:   4.078

(a) by adding in subs.(1):

"(bc) employment and support allowance"

(b) by adding after subs. (4A) the following:

"(4B) In relation to cases in which the benefit is employment and support allowance, the provision that may be made by virtue of subsection (2) is provision that, in the case of the offender's family member, any income-related allowance shall be payable, during the whole or a part of any period comprised in the relevant period, as if one or more of the following applied—

(a) the rate of the allowance were such reduced rate as may be prescribed;
(b) the allowance were payable only if there is compliance by the offender or the offender's family member, or both of them, with such obligations with respect to the provision of information as may be imposed by the regulations;
(c) the allowance were payable only if circumstances are otherwise such as may be prescribed."

p.314, *amendment to the Social Security Fraud Act 2001, s.10(3)*

4.079   With effect from October 27, 2008, s.28 and Sch.3, para.23 of the Welfare Reform Act 2007 amended subs.(3) by adding:

"(bc) any benefit under Part 1 of the Welfare Reform Act 2007 (employment and support allowance) or under any provision having effect in Northern Ireland corresponding to that Part;"

p.315, *amendment to the Social Security Fraud Act 2001, s.11(3)*

4.080   With effect from October 27, 2008, s.28 and Sch.3, para.23 of the Welfare Reform Act 2007 amended subs.(3) by inserting the words ", (4B)" after the words "(4A)" in both places.

p.316, *amendment to the Social Security Fraud Act 2001, s.13*

4.081   With effect from October 27, 2008, s.28 and Sch.3, para.23 of the Welfare Reform Act 2007 amended the definitions by adding:

" 'income-related allowance' has the same meaning as in Part 1 of the Welfare Reform Act 2007 (employment and support allowance);"

p.363, *amendment to the, Claims and Payments Regulations 1987, reg.2*

4.082   With effect from October 27, 2008, The Employment and Support Allowance (Consequential Provisions) (No.2) Regulations 2008 (SI2008/1554) reg.10, amended reg.2:

(a) by adding the following new definitions at the relevant place:

"the Employment and Support Allowance Regulations" means the Employment and Support Allowance Regulations 2008; "limited capability for work" has the same meaning as in section 1(4) of the Welfare Reform Act";

"the Welfare Reform Act" means the Welfare Reform Act 2007;

(b) by substituting the words ", a shared additional pension or an employment and support allowance under Part 1 of the Welfare Reform Act" for the words "and a shared additional pension".

p.367, *amendment to the Claims and Payments Regulations 1987, reg.3*

With effect from October 27, 2008, The Employment and Support Allowance (Consequential Provisions) (No.2) Regulations 2008 (SI 2008/1554) reg.11 amended reg.3: 4.083

(a) by adding the words "or an income-related employment and support allowance" after the word "allowance";
(b) inserting a new para.(j) as follows:

"(j) in the case of an employment and support allowance where the beneficiary has made and is pursuing an appeal against the decision of the Secretary of State that he does not have limited capability for work."

With effect from October 30, 2008, The Social Security (Miscellaneous Amendments) (No.5) Regulations 2008 (SI 2008/2667) reg.2 substitutes new para.(da) as follows:

"(da) in the case of a bereavement payment where the beneficiary is in receipt of a retirement pension at the date of death of the beneficiary's spouse or civil partner and satisfies the conditions of entitlement under section 36(1) of the Contributions and Benefits Act;"

p.369, *amendment to the Claims and Payments Regulations 1987, reg.4*

With effect from October 30, 2007, The Social Security (Claims and Information) Regulations 2007 (SI 2007/2911), reg.6 substitutes the following for paras (6A)(c) and (d): 4.084

"(c) who makes a claim for income support; or
(d) who has not attained the qualifying age and who makes a claim for a carer's allowance, disability living allowance or incapacity benefit."

With effect from October 27, 2008, The Employment and Support Allowance (Consequential Provisions) (No.2) Regulations 2008 (SI 2008/1554) reg.12 amended reg.4 by inserting the words "or an employment and support allowance" after the words "state pension credit"

With effect from October 30, 2008, The Social Security (Miscellaneous Amendments) (No.5) Regulations 2008 (SI 2008/2667) reg.2 amended reg.4 as follows:

(a) in para.(1) for "paragraphs (10) and (11)," substitute "paragraphs (10) to (11B),";

(b) in para.(1A) for "In the case of" substitute "Subject to paragraph (11A), in the case of";

(c) after para.(11) insert:

"(11A) A claim for income support or jobseeker's allowance may be made by telephone call to the telephone number specified by the Secretary of State where such a claim falls within a category of case which the Secretary of State accepts for the purposes of making a telephone claim.

(11B) Paragraph (11A) shall apply unless in any particular case the Secretary of State directs that the claim must be made in writing."

(d) in para.(12) for "paragraph (11)" substitute "paragraph (11) or (11A)".

p.386, *new regs 4G to 4I, Claims and Payments Regulations 1987*

4.085   With effect from October 27, 2008, The Employment and Support Allowance (Consequential Provisions) (No.2) Regulations 2008 (SI2008/1554) reg.13 adds new regs 4G to 4I as follows:

"Making a claim for employment and support allowance by telephone

4G.—(1) A claim ("a telephone claim") for an employment and support allowance may be made by telephone call to the telephone number specified by the Secretary of State.

(2) Where the Secretary of State, in any particular case, directs that the person making the claim approves a written statement of his circumstances, provided for the purpose by the Secretary of State, a telephone claim is not a valid claim unless the person complies with the direction.

(3) A telephone claim is defective unless the Secretary of State is provided, during that telephone call, with all the information he requires to determine the claim.

(4) Where a telephone claim is defective, the Secretary of State is to advise the person making it of the defect and of the relevant provisions of regulation 6(1F) relating to the date of claim.

(5) If the person corrects the defect within one month, or such longer period as the Secretary of State considers reasonable, of the date the Secretary of State last drew attention to the defect, the Secretary of State must treat the claim as if it had been properly made in the first instance.

Making a claim for employment and support allowance in writing

4H.—(1) A claim ("a written claim") for employment and support allowance need only be made in writing if the Secretary of State so directs in any particular case but a written claim may be made whether or not a direction is issued.

(2) A written claim must be made on a form approved for the purpose by the Secretary of State and be made in accordance with the instructions on the form.

(3) A claim in writing may also be made at the offices of—

(a) a local authority administering housing benefit or council tax benefit;

(b) a person providing to such an authority services relating to housing benefit or council tax benefit; or

(c) a person authorised to exercise the function of a local authority relating to housing benefit or council tax benefit,

if the Secretary of State has arranged with the local authority or person specified in sub-paragraph (b) or (c) for them to receive claims in accordance with this paragraph.

(4) Where a written claim is made in accordance with paragraph (3), on receipt of that claim the local authority or other person specified in that paragraph—

(a) must forward the claim to the Secretary of State as soon as reasonably practicable;

(b) may receive information or evidence relating to the claim supplied by—

(i) the person making, or who has made, the claim; or

(ii) other persons in connection with the claim,

and shall forward it to the Secretary of State as soon as reasonably practicable;

(c) may obtain information or evidence relating to the claim from the person who has made the claim, but not any medical information or evidence except for that which the claimant must provide in accordance with instructions on the form, and must forward the information or evidence to the Secretary of State as soon as reasonably practicable;

(d) may record information or evidence relating to the claim supplied or obtained in accordance with sub-paragraph (b) or (c) and may hold the information or evidence (whether as supplied or obtained or as recorded) for the purpose of forwarding it to the Secretary of State; and

(e) may give information and advice with respect to the claim to the person who makes, or who has made, the claim.

(5) Paragraphs (4)(b) to (e) apply in respect of information, evidence and advice relating to any claim whether the claim is made in accordance with paragraph (3) or otherwise.

(6) If a written claim is defective when first received, the Secretary of State is to advise the person making it of the defect and of the provisions of regulation 6(1F) relating to the date of claim.

(7) If that person corrects the defect so that the claim then satisfies the requirements of paragraph (2) and does so within one month, or such longer period as the Secretary of State considers reasonable, of the date the Secretary of State last drew attention to the defect, the claim must be treated as having been properly made in the first instance.

Claims for employment and support allowance: supplemental

4I.—(1) Where a person who is a member of a couple may be entitled to an income-related employment and support allowance the claim for an employment and support allowance must be made by whichever member of the couple they agree should claim or, in default of agreement, by such one of them as the Secretary of State may choose.

(2) Where one member of a couple ("the former claimant") is entitled to an income-related employment and support allowance under an award but a claim for an employment and support allowance is made by the other member of the couple and the Secretary of State considers that the other member is entitled to an income-related employment and support allowance, then, if both members of the couple confirm in writing that they wish the claimant to be the other member, the former claimant's entitlement terminates on the day the partner's claim is actually made or, if earlier, is treated as made.

(3) In calculating any period of one month for the purposes of regulations 4G and 4H, any period commencing on a day on which a person is first notified of a decision in connection with his failure to take part in a work-focused interview and ending on a day on which he was notified that that decision has been revised so that the decision as revised is that he did take part is to be disregarded.

(4) Employment and support allowance is a relevant benefit for the purposes of section 7A of the 1992 Act."

p.386, *annotations to Claims and Payments Regulations 1987, reg.5,*

4.086   *R(H) 2/06* concerned the interpretation of a provision of the Housing Benefit (General) Regulations 1987 (SI 1987/1971) in identical terms to reg.5(2). The Commissioner ruled that, although in some cases it may be possible to make a fresh claim which can be backdated to cover the period of a claim which has been withdrawn, the consequence of a genuine and effective withdrawal is, in the absence of any provision permitting reinstatement, to prevent any award from being made on the claim after the withdrawal took effect. Although different considerations might apply to claimants who are not fully able to manage their affairs or to understand the consequences of their actions, claimant who are not subject to any such disability would normally have to establish that the withdrawal of the claim was induced by some factor such as threatening or overbearing behaviour, deception or similar improper conduct in order to show that the notice of withdrawal of a claim was not a genuine expression of the claimant's intention at the time when the notice was given.

p.387, *amendment to Claims and Payments Regulations 1987, reg.6*

4.087   With effect from October 27, 2008, The Employment and Support Allowance (Consequential Provisions) (No.2) Regulations 2008 (SI 2008/1554) reg.14 adds new para.(1F) as follows:

"(1F) For employment and support allowance—

(a) in the case of a telephone claim made in accordance with regulation 4G(1) the date of claim is the date of the telephone call or the first day in respect of which the claim is made, if later;

(b) subject to sub-paragraph (c) in the case of a written claim which meets the requirements of regulation 4H(2) the date of claim is the date the claim form was received in an appropriate office or office mentioned in regulation 4H(3) or the first day in respect of which the claim is made, if later;

(c) where the claimant notifies the Secretary of State (by whatever means) of his intention of making a claim and, within one month or such longer period as the Secretary of State considers reasonable of first notification, a claim mentioned in sub-paragraph (b) is received, in an office mentioned in that sub-paragraph, the date of claim is the date notification was made or the first day in respect of which the claim is made, if later."

With effect from October 30, 2008, The Social Security (Miscellaneous Amendments) (No.5) Regulations 2008 (SI 2008/2667) reg.2 amended reg.6 as follows:

(a) in para.(1)(c) for "regulation 4(11)" substitute "regulation 4(11) or (11A)";

(b) in para.(21)—

(i) after "further claim" insert "for a relevant benefit"; and

(ii) for "on which the additional circumstances apply" substitute "of the decision to award, re-award, or recommence payment of the qualifying benefit on the grounds that sub-paragraph (a), (b), (c) or (d) was satisfied";

(c) in para.(33)—

(i) after "carer's allowance" insert "or for an increase in carer's allowance in respect of an adult or child dependant"; and

(ii) for the words from "is the first day" to "is payable" substitute "shall be treated as the first day of the benefit week in which the award of the qualifying benefit became payable"; and

(d) for para.(34) substitute:

"(34) Where the decision awarding a qualifying benefit is made in respect of a renewal claim where a fixed period award of that benefit has expired, or is due to expire, the date of claim for carer's allowance shall be treated as the first day of the benefit week in which the renewal award of qualifying benefit became payable."

With effect from November 3, 2008, The Tribunals, Courts and Enforcement Act 2007 (Transitional and Consequential Provisions) Order 2008 (SI 2008/2683), reg.43 substitutes in reg.6(26) and (33)(c) the words "the First-tier Tribunal, the Upper Tribunal" for the words "an appeal tribunal, a Commissioner".

p.403, *amendment to the Claims and Payments Regulations 1987, reg.7*

4.088 With effect from October 27, 2008, The Employment and Support Allowance (Consequential Provisions) (No.2) Regulations 2008 (SI 2008/1554) reg.15 amended para.(4) by substituting the words "state pension credit or employment and support allowance" for the words "or state pension credit".

p.409, *amendment to the Claims and Payments Regulations 1987, reg.10*

4.089 With effect from October 27, 2008, The Employment and Support Allowance (Consequential Provisions) (No.2) Regulations 2008 (SI 2008/1554) reg.16 amended reg.10:
   (a) by substituting in the heading the words ", severe disablement allowance or employment and support allowance" for the words "or severe disablement allowance";
   (b) by adding new para.(1A) as follows:

> "(1A) Paragraph (2) also applies to a claim for an employment and support allowance for a period of limited capability for work in relation to which the claimant gave his employer a notice of incapacity under regulation 7 of the Statutory Sick Pay (General) Regulations 1982, and for which he has been informed in writing by his employer that there is no entitlement to statutory sick pay."

p.409, *amendment to the Claims and Payments Regulations 1987, reg.11*

4.090 With effect from October 27, 2008, The Employment and Support Allowance (Consequential Provisions) (No.2) Regulations 2008 (SI 2008/1554) reg.17 amended reg.11 by substituting, in paras (1) and (2) the words ", severe disablement allowance or an employment and support allowance" for the words "or severe disablement allowance".

p.410, *amendment to the Claims and Payments Regulations 1987, reg.13*

4.091 With effect from October 27, 2008, The Employment and Support Allowance (Consequential Provisions) (No.2) Regulations 2008 (SI 2008/1554) reg.18 amended reg.13 as follows:
   (a) by omitting the word "or" after sub-para.(a);
   (b) by adding after sub-para.(b):

> "and
> (c) a claim for an employment and support allowance made by a person from abroad as defined in regulation 70 of the Employment and Support Allowance Regulations (special cases: supplemental—persons from abroad)."

p.418, *amendment to the Claims and Payments Regulations 1987, reg.16*

4.092 With effect from October 27, 2008, The Employment and Support Allowance (Consequential Provisions) (No.2) Regulations 2008 (SI

2008/1554) reg.19 amended reg.16(4) by adding the words ", employment and support allowance" after the words "incapacity benefit".

p.419, *amendment to the Claims and Payments Regulations 1987, reg.16A*

With effect from October 27, 2008, The Employment and Support 4.093
Allowance (Consequential Provisions) (No.2) Regulations 2008 (SI
2008/1554) reg.20 amended para.(2)(a) by substituting the words ",
income-based jobseeker's allowance or income-related employment and
support allowance" for the words "or income-based jobseeker's allowance".

p.422, *reg.19, Claims and Payments Regulations, and annotations*

With effect from October 6, 2008, The Social Security (Miscellaneous 4.094
Amendments) (No.4) Regulations 2008 (SI 2008/2424), reg.2 amended
reg.19(3) by adding:

"(h) state pension credit."

In *CIS/1107/2008* the Commissioner ruled that reg.19(5)(e) was
broad enough to include advice given by officials in the visa section of the
British Embassy in Addis Ababa. The appellant had, incorrectly, been
issued with a two year visa with a restriction on recourse to public funds.
This resulted in his not claiming income support until he had received
the correct visa which was for indefinite leave to remain with no restriction in relation to recourse to public funds.

p.438, *amendment to the Claims and Payments Regulations 1987, reg.22*

With effect from October 30, 2008, The Social Security (Miscella- 4.095
neous Amendments) (No.5) Regulations 2008 (SI 2008/2667) reg.2
amended reg.22(1) by substituting the words "four weekly in arrears,
weekly in advance or, where the beneficiary agrees, at intervals not
exceeding 13 weeks in arrears" for the words "four weeks, or weekly in
advance".

p.442, *new reg.26C, Claims and Payments Regulations 1987*

With effect from October 27, 2008, The Employment and Support 4.096
Allowance (Consequential Provisions) (No.2) Regulations 2008 (SI
2008/1554) reg.21 adds new reg.26C as follows:

"Employment and support allowance

26C.—(1) Subject to paragraphs (3) to (7), employment and support allowance is to be paid fortnightly in arrears on the day of the
week determined in accordance with paragraph (2).
(2) The day specified for the purposes of paragraph (1) is the day in
column (2) which corresponds to the series of numbers in column (1)

which includes the last 2 digits of the claimant's national insurance number—

(1)	(2)
00 to 19	Monday
20 to 39	Tuesday
40 to 59	Wednesday
60 to 79	Thursday
80 to 99	Friday

(3) The Secretary of State may, in any particular case or class of case, arrange that the claimant be paid otherwise than fortnightly.

(4) The Secretary of State may, in any particular case or class of case, arrange that employment and support allowance be paid on any day of the week and where it is in payment to any person and the day on which it is payable is changed, it must be paid at a daily rate of 1/7th of the weekly rate in respect of any of the days for which payment would have been made but for that change.

(5) Where the weekly amount of employment and support allowance is less than £1.00 it may be paid in arrears at intervals of not more than 13 weeks.

(6) Where the weekly amount of an employment and support allowance is less than 10 pence that allowance is not payable.

(7) The provisions of paragraph 2A of Schedule 7 (payment of income support at time of office closure) apply for the purposes of payment of employment and support allowance as they apply for the purposes of payment of income support."

p.451, *amendment to the Claims and Payments Regulations 1987, reg.32*

4.097   With effect from August 25, 2008 The Social Security (Students and Miscellaneous Amendments) Regulations 2008 (SI 2008/1599), reg.3 amended reg.32(6) as follows:

(a) in sub-para.(a), for "at the end of an assessed income period" substitute "in connection with the setting of a new assessed income period" and for "required" substitute "which the Secretary of State may require";

(b) in sub-para.(c), for "the information" substitute "any information" and after "required" insert "to be notified".

With effect from October 27, 2008, The Employment and Support Allowance (Consequential Provisions) (No.2) Regulations 2008 (SI 2008/1554) reg.22 amended reg.32 by substituting the words ", a jobseeker's allowance or an employment and support allowance" for the words "or a jobseeker's allowance".

p.462, *amendment to the Claims and Payments Regulations 1987, reg. 36*

With effect from October 27, 2008, The Employment and Support **4.098**
Allowance (Consequential Provisions) (No.2) Regulations 2008 (SI
2008/1554) reg.23 amended reg.36 by substituting the words ", an
income-related jobseeker's allowance or an income-related employment
and support allowance" for the words "or an income-related jobseeker's
allowance".

p.473, *amendment to the Claims and Payments Regulations 1987, Sch. 1*

With effect from October 27, 2008, The Employment and Support **4.099**
Allowance (Consequential Provisions) (No.2) Regulations 2008 (SI
2008/1554) reg.24 amended Sch.1 as follows:
- (a) in column (1) (benefit claimed) after the entry "Severe disablement allowance for a woman" insert "Employment and support
  allowance for a woman" and in the corresponding place in column
  (2) (alternative benefit) insert "Maternity allowance."; and
- (b) in column (2) in the entry corresponding to "Maternity allowance" (**92**) for "or severe disablement allowance" substitute,
  ", severe disablement allowance or employment and support
  allowance".

p.475, *amendment to the Claims and Payments Regulations 1987, Sch. 4*

With effect from October 6, 2008, The Social Security (Miscellaneous **4.100**
Amendments) (No.4) Regulations 2008 (SI 2008/2424), reg.2 amended
para.12 by omitting it.
   With effect from October 27, 2008, The Employment and Support
Allowance (Consequential Provisions) (No.2) Regulations 2008 (SI
2008/1554) reg.25 amended Sch.4 as follows:
- (a) in column (1) (description of benefit) after the entry "15. Shared
  additional pension" add "**16.** Employment and support allowance"; and
- (b) in column (2) (prescribed time for claiming benefit) in the corresponding place insert "The day in respect of which the claim is
  made and the period of three months immediately following
  it.".

p.483, *amendment to the Claims and Payments Regulations 1987, Sch. 9*

With effect from October 27, 2008, The Employment and Support **4.101**
Allowance (Consequential Provisions) (No.2) Regulations 2008 (SI
2008/1554) reg.26 amended Sch.9 as follows:
   (1) In para.1 (interpretation)—
   (a) in sub-para.(1)—
      (i) after the definition of "contribution-based jobseeker's
          allowance" insert—

"contributory employment and support allowance" means any contributory employment and support allowance which does not fall within the definition of "specified benefit"

(ii) in the definition of "housing costs" after paragraph (c) add—

or

(d) Schedule 6 to the Employment and Support Allowance Regulations but—

(i) excludes costs under paragraph 18(1)(f) of that Schedule (tents and tent sites); and

(ii) includes costs under paragraph 18(1)(a) (ground rent) and 18(1)(c) (rent charges) of that Schedule but only where they are paid with costs under paragraph 18(1)(b) of that Schedule (service charges);

(iii) in the definition of "mortgage payment" after para.(b) omit "or" and after para.(c) add—

"or

(d) Schedule 6 to the Employment and Support Allowance Regulations in accordance with paragraphs 8 to 11 of that Schedule (housing costs to be met in employment and support allowance) on a loan which qualifies under paragraph 16 or 17 of that Schedule, but less any amount deducted under paragraph 19 of that Schedule (non- dependant deductions),"

(iv) in the definition of "personal allowance for a single claimant aged not less than 25 years" after "Jobseeker's Allowance Regulations" add "or, in connection with employment and support allowance, paragraph 1(1)(b) of Schedule 4 to the Employment and Support Allowance Regulations"; and

(v) in the definition of "specified benefit" after para.(d) add—

"(e) subject to sub-paragraph (3), employment and support allowance;"

(b) after sub-para.(2) add—

"(3) For the purposes of the definition of "specified benefit" in sub-paragraph (1) "employment and support allowance" means—

(a) income-related employment and support allowance; and

(b) in a case where, if there was no entitlement to a contributory employment and support allowance, there would be entitlement to income-related employment and support allowance at the same rate, contributory employment and support allowance."

(2) In para.3(2A) (housing costs)—
(a) in sub-para.(b) after "State Pension Credit Regulations" insert
" or paragraph 6(10) or (13) or paragraph 19 of Schedule 6 to
the Employment and Support Allowance Regulations"; and
(b) in the description of "C" after "State Pension Credit Regulations" add or paragraph 6(10) or (13) or paragraph 19 of
Schedule 6 to the Employment and Support Allowance Regulations
(3) In para.4 (miscellaneous accommodation costs)—
(a) in sub-para.(1)—
(i) for "or state pension credit" substitute ", state pension
credit or employment and support allowance"; and
(ii) in para.(a) after "Jobseeker's Allowance Regulations"
insert

"or in the case of employment and support allowance,
regulation 2(1) of the Employment and Support Allowance
Regulations"

(b) in sub-para.(2)—
(i) for "or state pension credit" substitute ", state pension
credit or employment and support allowance";
(ii) in para.(a)—
(aa) for "or guarantee credit" substitute ", guarantee
credit or employment and support allowance"; and
(bb) after "Jobseeker's Allowance Regulations" insert ",
regulation 90 of the Employment and Support
Allowance Regulations"; and
(iii) in para.(b) for "or guarantee credit" substitute ", guarantee credit or employment and support allowance"; and
(c) in sub-para.(3)—
(i) after para.(b) omit "or"; and
(ii) after para.(c) add—

"or
(d) employment and support allowance for a period of less
than a week calculated in accordance with Part 14 of
the Employment and Support Allowance Regulations
(periods of less than a week)."

(2) In para.4A(6) (hostel payments)—
(a) after para.(a)—
(i) omit "or"; and
(ii) after para.(b) insert—

"or
(c) an award of employment and support allowance is
calculated in accordance with regulation 165 of the
Employment and Support Allowance Regulations
(entitlement of less than a week etc.)"

and

(b) after "jobseeker's allowance" the third time it occurs insert "or employment and support allowance".

(5) In para.7B (arrears of child support maintenance)—

(a) after "jobseeker's allowance" each time it occurs insert "or contributory employment and support allowance"; and

(b) after sub-para.(3) insert—

> "(3A) Subject to sub-paragraphs (4) and (5), the amount to be deducted from the beneficiary's employment and support allowance under sub-paragraph (2) is the weekly amount requested from the beneficiary's employment and support allowance by the Secretary of State, subject to a maximum of one-third of the amount applicable to the beneficiary under regulation 67(2) of the Employment and Support Allowance Regulations (prescribed amounts)."

(6) In para.7C(2)(c) (eligible loans) after sub-para.(iii) add—

(iv) employment and support allowance.

(7) In para.8(4)(a) (maximum amount of payment to third parties)—

(a) in sub-para.(ii) omit "or"; and

(b) after sub-para.(iii) add—

> "(iv) in the case of employment and support allowance, the applicable amount for the family as is awarded under paragraphs (a) to (d) of regulation 67 (prescribed amounts) or regulation 68 (polygamous marriages) of the Employment and Support Allowance Regulations; or"

p.496, *amendment to the, Claims and Payments Regulations 1987,* Sch.9A

4.102 With effect from October 27, 2008, The Employment and Support Allowance (Consequential Provisions) (No.2) Regulations 2008 (SI 2008/1554) reg.27 amended Sch.9A as follows:

(1) In para.1 (interpretation) in the definition of "relevant benefits"—

(a) after para.(c) omit "and"; and

(b) after para.(d) add—

"and

(e) income-related employment and support allowance;"

(2) In para.2(a) (specified circumstances for the purposes of regulation 34A) after sub-para.(iii) add—

"or

(iv) Schedule 6 to the Employment and Support Allowance Regulations,"

(3) In para.3 (specified part of relevant benefit)—

(a) in sub-para.(1) after "Jobseeker's Allowance Regulations" add "or, in the case of employment and support allowance, a sum equal to the amount of mortgage interest to be met in accordance with paragraphs 8 to 11 of Schedule 6 to the Employment and Support Allowance Regulations"

(b) in sub-para.(3)—
  (i) for "or income-based jobseeker's allowance" substitute "income-based jobseeker's allowance or income-related employment and support allowance";
  (ii) in para.(b) after "Jobseeker's Allowance Regulations" insert:
  "or paragraph 6(10) or (13) or 19 of Schedule 6 to the Employment and Support Allowance Regulations"
  (iii) in the definition of "A" after "Jobseeker's Allowance Regulations" add:
  "or paragraph 1 of Schedule 6 to the Employment and Support Allowance Regulations"
  (iv) in the definition of "B" after "Jobseeker's Allowance Regulations" add:
  "or paragraphs 8 to 11 of Schedule 6 to the Employment and Support Allowance Regulations"
  (v) in the definition of "C" after "Jobseeker's Allowance Regulations" add
  "or paragraph 19 of Schedule 6 to the Employment and Support Allowance Regulations"

(4) In para.4(2)(a) (direct payment: more than one loan) after "Jobseeker's Allowance Regulations" insert "or paragraph 13 of Schedule 6 to the Employment and Support Allowance Regulations".

(5) In para.10 (provision of information)—

(a) in sub-para.(2)(a) after "income support" insert ", employment and support allowance":

(b) in sub-para.(3)(a) after "income support" insert ", employment and support allowance"; and

(c) in sub-para.(4) after "(housing costs)" the first time it occurs insert:
  paragraph 3 of Schedule 6 to the Employment and Support Allowance Regulations (housing costs).

(6) In para.11(2)(a)(i) (recovery of sums wrongly paid) after "Jobseeker's Allowance Regulations" insert:
"or paragraph 13 of Schedule 6 to the Employment and Support Allowance Regulations"

p.503, *amendment to the Claims and Payments Regulations 1987, Sch.9B*

With effect from October 27, 2008, The Employment and Support Allowance (Consequential Provisions) (No.2) Regulations 2008 (SI 2008/1554) reg.28 amended Sch.9B as follows: 4.103

(1) In para.2(1) (deductions) for "or income-based jobseeker's allowance" substitute ", income-based jobseeker's allowance or income-related employment and support allowance".

(2) In para.3(1) (arrears) for "or income-based jobseeker's allowance" substitute ", income-based jobseeker's allowance or income-related employment and support allowance".

(3) In para.5(1) (flat rate maintenance) for "or income-based job-seeker's allowance" substitute ", income-based jobseeker's allowance or income-related employment and support allowance".

(4) In para.6(1) (flat rate maintenance (polygamous marriage)) for "or income-based jobseeker's allowance" substitute ", income-based jobseeker's allowance or income-related employment and support allowance".

(5) In para.8 (general) after "1987" insert ", regulation 104(3)of the Employment and Support Allowance Regulations".

pp.508–532, *Social Security Commissioners (Procedure) Regulations 1999*

4.104   With effect from November 3, 2008, paras 130 to 136 of Sch.1 to the Tribunals, Courts and Enforcement Act 2007 (Transitional and Consequential Provisions) Order 2008 (SI 2008/2683) rename these Regulations as the Forfeiture Regulations 1999, amend regs 1 and 4(1) and delete all the rest of the regulations except reg.14(1), subject to a saving in respect of Scotland (see art.3(1) and (2)(d) and (e)). What is left in England and Wales reads:

"**1.** These Regulations may be cited as the Forfeiture Regulations 1999 and shall come into force on June 1, 1999.

4.—(1) In these Regulations, unless the context otherwise requires—

"the 1998 Act" means the Social Security Act 1998.

14.—(1) For the purposes of section 4(5) of the Forfeiture Act 1982, the 1998 Act shall be prescribed as a relevant enactment."

The rest of reg.4(1) and all of regs 5 to 13, 16 to 28 and 30 to 33 are preserved in Scotland for the purposes of appeals under s.159 of the Health and Social Care (Community Health and Standards) Act 2003, which are concerned with the recovery of NHS charges and are beyond the scope of this work.

pp.537–541, *Decisions and Appeals Regulations, reg.1(3)*

4.105   With effect from July 27, 2008, regs 29 and 30 of the Employment and Support Allowance (Consequential Provisions) (No.2) Regulations 2008 (SI 2008/1554) amend the definition of "claimant" by replacing "or section 17(1) of the State Pension Credit Act" with ", section 17(1) of the State Pension Credit Act or section 24(1) of the Welfare Reform Act" and add the following new definitions—

"contributory employment and support allowance" means a contributory allowance under Part 1 of the Welfare Reform Act;
"the Employment and Support Allowance Regulations" means the Employment and Support Allowance Regulations 2008;
"failure determination" means a determination by the Secretary of State under regulation 63(1) of the Employment and Support Allowance Regulations that a claimant has failed to satisfy the requirement of regulation 47 or 54 of those Regulations (requirement to take part

in a work-focused health related assessment or a work-focused interview);
"income-related employment and support allowance" means an income-related allowance under Part 1 of the Welfare Reform Act;
"limited capability for work" has the same meaning as in section 1(4) of the Welfare Reform Act;
"the Welfare Reform Act" means the Welfare Reform Act 2007.

With effect from October 1, 2008, para.1(a) of Sch.2 to the Social Security (Recovery of Benefits) (Lump Sum Payments) Regulations 2008 (SI 2008/1596) adds the following definition—

"the Lump Sum Payments Regulations" means the Social Security (Recovery of Benefits) (Lump Sum Payments) Regulations 2008.

With effect from October 27, 2008, the words ", or has been treated as applied for under section 6(3) of that Act" are omitted from the definition of "relevant person" (Child Support (Consequential Provisions) Regulations 2008 (SI 2008/2543), reg.4(1) and (2)).
With effect from November 1, 2008, reg.4 of the Child Support (Consequential Provisions) (No.2) Regulations 2008 (SI 2008/2656) inserts the following definition—

"the Commission" means the Child Maintenance and Enforcement Commission.

It also amends the definition of "official error" by inserting ", the Commission" after references to "the Department for Work and Pensions" and "the Department" and it amends the definition of "party to the proceedings" by inserting "or where the proceedings relate to child support, the Commission" after "the Secretary of State".
With effect from November 3, 2008, paras 95 and 96 of Sch.1 to the Tribunals, Courts and Enforcement Act 2007 (Transitional and Consequential Provisions) Order 2008 (SI 2008/2683) substitute "the First-tier Tribunal" for "an appeal tribunal" in the definitions of "appeal", "party to the proceedings" and "referral" and substitute "the Upper Tribunal" for "a Commissioner" in the definition of "official error". They also remove the definitions of "clerk to the appeal tribunal", "financially qualified panel member", "legally qualified panel member", "medically qualified panel member", "out of jurisdiction appeal", "panel", "panel member", "panel member with a disability qualification" and "President". However, some of these amendments do not extend to Scotland because appeal tribunals remain in existence for the purpose of hearing appeals brought in Scotland under s.158 of the Health and Social Care (Community Health and Standards) Act 2003, concerning the recovery of NHS charges.

pp.544–545, *Decisions and Appeals Regulations, reg.2*

With effect from November 3, 2008, the references to "the clerk to the appeal tribunal" are removed by paras 95 and 97 of Sch.1 to the   4.106

Tribunals, Courts and Enforcement Act 2007 (Transitional and Consequential Provisions) Order 2008 (SI 2008/2683). However, the Tribunal Procedure (First-tier Tribunal) (Social Entitlement Chamber) Rules 2008 (SI 2008/2685), which are expressed in different terms, have a similar effect because time is generally calculated so that it runs from the date a document is sent by the First-tier Tribunal or is received by that tribunal, as the case may be.

pp.546–552, *Decisions and Appeals Regulations, reg.3*

4.107 With effect from July 27, 2008, regs 29 and 31 of the Employment and Support Allowance (Consequential Provisions) (No.2) Regulations 2008 (SI 2008/1554) make a number of amendments.

In para.(5)(c), insert "or is an employment and support allowance decision where there has been a limited capability for work determination" after "incapacity determination" the first time it occurs and, for "or the incapacity determination", substitute ", the incapacity determination or the limited capability for work determination".

In para.(5)(d), insert "is an employment and support allowance decision," after "where the decision", insert "limited capability for work determination," after "not in relation to the" and insert "the employment and support allowance decision," after "in or necessary to".

In para.(5ZB), omit "and" after sub-para.(f) and add after sub-para.(g)—

"and
(h) contributory employment and support allowance."

Insert after para.(5B)—

"(5C) A decision of the Secretary of State under section 10 made in consequence of a failure determination may be revised at any time if it contained an error to which the claimant did not materially contribute;

(5D) A decision by the Secretary of State under section 8 or 10 awarding employment and support allowance may be revised at any time if—

(a) it incorporates a determination that the condition in regulation 30 of the Employment and Support Allowance Regulations is satisfied;

(b) the condition referred to in sub-paragraph (a) was not satisfied at the time when the claim was first determined; and

(c) there is a period before the award which falls to be decided.".

In para.(7ZA)(a), for "or state pension credit" substitute ", state pension credit or an income-related employment and support allowance".

In para.(7ZA)(b), insert "or regulation 71 of the Employment and Support Allowance Regulations" after "Income Support Regulations".

In para.(7ZA)(c)(i), insert "or regulation 67 of the Employment and Support Allowance Regulations" after "Income Support Regulations".

In para.(7ZA)(d)(ii), insert ", paragraph 6(4)(a) of Schedule 4 to the Employment and Support Allowance Regulations" after "Income Support Regulations".

In para.(9) omit "nor" after sub-para.(a) and insert after sub-para.(b)—

"nor
  (c) a decision which relates to an employment and support allowance where the claimant is terminally ill, within the meaning of regulation 2(1) of the Employment and Support Allowance Regulations unless the claimant makes an application which contains an express statement that he is terminally ill and where such an application is made, the decision may be revised."

With effect from October 30, 2008, reg.3(1) and (2) of the the Social Security (Miscellaneous Amendments) (No.5) Regulations 2008 (SI 2008/2667) inserts a new para.(8C)—

"(8C) A decision made under section 8 or 10 ("the original decision") may be revised at any time—
  (a) where, on or after the date of the original decision—
    (i) a late paid contribution is treated as paid under regulation 5 of the Social Security (Crediting and Treatment of Contributions and National Insurance Numbers) Regulations 2001 (treatment of late paid contributions where no consent, connivance or negligence by the primary contributor) on a date which falls on or before the date on which the original decision was made;
    (ii) a direction is given under regulation 6 of those Regulations (treatment of contributions paid late through ignorance or error) that a late contribution shall be treated as paid on a date which falls on or before the date on which the original decision was made; or
    (iii) an unpaid contribution is treated as paid under regulation 60 of the Social Security (Contributions) Regulations 2001 (treatment of unpaid contributions where no consent, connivance or negligence by the primary contributor) on a date which falls on or before the date on which the original decision was made; and
  (b) where any of paragraphs (i), (ii) or (iii) apply, either an award of benefit would have been made or the amount of benefit awarded would have been different."

With effect from November 3, 2008, paras 95 and 98 of Sch.1 to the Tribunals, Courts and Enforcement Act 2007 (Transitional and Consequential Provisions) Order 2008 (SI 2008/2683) substitute "by Tribunal Procedure Rules" for "in regulation 31, or in a case to which regulation 32 applies within the time prescribed by that regulation," in para.(4A) and substitute "the First-tier Tribunal" for "an appeal tribunal" in para.(5A)(b).

p.558, *Decisions and Appeals Regulations, reg. 4(6) (b)*

4.108   With effect from November 3, 2008, paras 95 and 100 of Sch.1 to the Tribunals, Courts and Enforcement Act 2007 (Transitional and Consequential Provisions) Order 2008 (SI 2008/2683) substitute "the Upper Tribunal" for "a Commissioner, a Child Support Commissioner".

pp.560–563, *Decisions and Appeals Regulations, reg. 6*

4.109   With effect from July 27, 2008, regs 29 and 32 of the Employment and Support Allowance (Consequential Provisions) (No.2) Regulations 2008 (SI 2008/1554) make a number of amendments.

In para.(2)(a)(i), insert "or regulation 146 of the Employment and Support Allowance Regulations" after "Regulations".

In para.(2)(i), for "or income support" substitute ", income support or an employment and support allowance".

After para.(2)(o), add—

"(p) is a decision awarding employment and support allowance where there has been a failure determination;

(q) is a decision made in consequence of a failure determination where the reduction ceases to have effect under of regulation 64 of the Employment and Support Allowance Regulations;

(r) is an employment and support allowance decision where, since the decision was made, the Secretary of State has received medical evidence from a health care professional approved by the Secretary of State for the purposes of regulation 23 or 38 of the Employment and Support Allowance Regulations."

In para.(6)(a), insert ", regulation 137 of the Employment and Support Allowance Regulations" after "Income Support Regulations".

With effect from October 30, 2008, reg.3(1) and (3) of the Social Security (Miscellaneous Amendments) (No.5) Regulations 2008 (SI 2008/2667) amends paragraph (2)(g) by substituting "health care professional" for "doctor" and inserts a new paragraph (2)(s)—

"(s) is a decision where on or after the date on which the decision was made, a late or unpaid contribution is treated as paid under—

(i) regulation 5 of the Social Security (Crediting and Treatment of Contributions and National Insurance Numbers) Regulations 2001 (treatment of late paid contributions where no consent, connivance or negligence by the primary contributor) on a date which falls on or before the date on which the original decision was made;

(ii) regulation 6 of those Regulations (treatment of contributions paid late through ignorance or error) on a date which falls on or before the date on which the original decision was made; or

(iii)   regulation 60 of the Social Security (Contributions) Regulations 2001 (treatment of unpaid contributions where no consent, connivance or negligence by the primary contributor) on a date which falls on or before the date on which the original decision was made."

With effect from November 3, 2008, paras 95 and 101 of Sch.1 to the Tribunals, Courts and Enforcement Act 2007 (Transitional and Consequential Provisions) Order 2008 (SI 2008/2683) substitute "the First-tier Tribunal or of the Upper Tribunal" for "an appeal tribunal or of a Commissioner" in para.(2)(c) and substitute references to the First-tier Tribunal for references to an appeal tribunal in para.(2)(n).

pp.572–581, *Decisions and Appeals Regulations, reg.7*

Poor drafting was remedied by replacing para.(2)(bd) with a new   **4.110** para.(2A) and making a consequential amendment to para.(2)(bc), with effect from May 19, 2008 (Social Security (Miscellaneous Amendments) (No.2) Regulations 2008 (SI 2008/1042), reg.2). Since then, para.(2)(bc) has been replaced and para.(2A) revoked with effect from October 30, 2008 (see below).

With effect from July 27, 2008, regs 29 and 33 of the Employment and Support Allowance (Consequential Provisions) (No.2) Regulations 2008 (SI 2008/1554) make a number of amendments.

In para.(1)(a), insert "or (be)" after "(2)(b)" and for "and 3B" substitute ", 3B and 3C".

In para.(2)(b)(i), for "or state pension credit" substitute ", state pension credit or an employment and support allowance"

After para.(2)(bc), para.(2)(bd) having been omitted (see above), insert—

"(be) in the case of a claimant who is in receipt of an employment and support allowance and the claimant makes an application which contains an express statement that he is terminally ill within the meaning of regulation 2(1) of the Employment and Support Allowance Regulations, from the date the claimant became terminally ill;".

For paragraph (3), substitute—

"(3) For the purposes of paragraphs (2) and (8) "benefit week" has the same meaning, as the case may be, as in—

(a) regulation 2(1) of the Income Support Regulations;

(b) regulation 1(3) of the Jobseeker's Allowance Regulations;

(c) regulation 1(2) of the State Pension Credit Regulations; or

(d) regulation 2(1) of the Employment and Support Allowance Regulations."

In para.(7)(b)(i), add "or paragraph 6 of Schedule 4 to the Employment and Support Allowance Regulations;" after "(guarantee credit)".

In para.(7)(b)(ii)(aa), add "or regulation 71 of the Employment and Support Allowance Regulations" after "Income Support Regulations".

In para.(13)(a)(iii), for "and" substitute "or" and after head (iii) insert—

"(iv) paragraph 16 or 17 of Schedule 6 to the Employment and Support Allowance Regulations; and".

After para.(17C), insert—

"(17D) Except in a case where paragraph (23) applies, where a claimant is in receipt of an employment and support allowance and his applicable amount includes an amount determined in accordance with Schedule 6 to the Employment and Support Allowance Regulations (housing costs), and there is a reduction in the amount of eligible capital owing in connection with a loan which qualifies under paragraph 16 or 17 of that Schedule, a decision made under section 10 shall take effect—

(a) on the first anniversary of the date on which the claimant's housing costs were first met under that Schedule; or

(b) where the reduction in eligible capital occurred after the first anniversary of the date referred to in sub-paragraph (a), on the next anniversary of that date following the date of the reduction.

(17E) Where a claimant is in receipt of an employment and support allowance and payments made to that claimant which fall within paragraph 31 or 32(1)(a) to (c) of Schedule 8 to the Employment and Support Allowance Regulations have been disregarded in relation to any decision under section 8 or 10 and there is a change in the amount of interest payable—

(a) on a loan qualifying under paragraph 16 or 17 of Schedule 6 to those Regulations to which those payments relate; or

(b) on a loan not so qualifying which is secured on the dwelling occupied as the home to which those payments relate,

a decision under section 10 which is made as a result of that change in the amount of interest payable shall take effect on whichever of the dates referred to in paragraph (17F) is appropriate in the claimant's case.

(17F) The date on which a decision under section 10 takes effect for the purposes of paragraph (17E) is—

(a) the date on which the claimant's housing costs are first met under paragraph 8(1)(a), 9(1)(a) or 10(2)(a) of Schedule 6 to the Employment and Support Allowance Regulations; or

(b) where the change in the amount of interest payable occurred after the date referred to in sub-paragraph (a), on the date of the next alteration in the standard rate following the date of that change.

(17G) In paragraph (17F) "standard rate" has the same meaning as it has in paragraph 13(2) of Schedule 6 to the Employment and Support Allowance Regulations.

(17H) Where the decision is superseded in accordance with regulation 6(2)(a)(i) and the relevant circumstances are that the claimant has a non-dependant who has become entitled to main phase employment and support allowance, the superseding decision shall take effect from the date the main phase employment and support allowance is first paid to the non-dependant."

In para.(23), insert ", (17D)"after "(17A)", insert ", an employment and support allowance" after "a jobseeker's allowance" the first time it occurs and, in sub-para.(a), for "or jobseeker's allowance" substitute ", jobseeker's allowance or employment and support allowance".

After para.(34), add—

"(35) A decision made in accordance with regulation 6(2)(p), where the failure determination was made before the 13th week of entitlement, shall take effect from the first day of the benefit week following that week.

(36) A decision made in accordance with regulation 6(2)(p) where paragraph (35) does not apply shall take effect from the first day of the benefit week in which the failure determination was made.

(37) A decision made in accordance with regulation 6(2)(q) shall take effect from the first day of the benefit week in which the reduction mentioned in that sub-paragraph ceased to have effect.

(38) A decision made in accordance with regulation 6(2)(r) that embodies a determination that the claimant has limited capability for work which is the first such determination shall take effect from the beginning of the 14th week of entitlement.

(39) A decision made in accordance with regulation 6(2)(r), following an application by the claimant, that embodies a determination that the claimant has limited capability for work-related activity shall take effect from the date of the application."

With effect from October 30, 2008, reg.3(1) and (4) of the Social Security (Miscellaneous Amendments) (No.5) Regulations 2008 (SI 2008/2667) amends para.(1)(a) by inserting ", (bb)" after "(2)(b)" and substitutes para.(2)(bb) and (bc)—

"(bb) where the decision is advantageous to the claimant and is made on the Secretary of State's own initiative—
  (i) except where paragraph (ii) applies, from the beginning of the benefit week in which the Secretary of State commenced action with a view to supersession; or
  (ii) in the case of a claimant who is in receipt of income support, jobseeker's allowance or state pension credit where benefit is paid in advance and the Secretary of State commenced action with a view to supersession on a day which was not the first day of the benefit week, from the

> beginning of the benefit week following the week in which the Secretary of State commenced such action;
>
> (bc)   where—
>
> > (i) the claimant is a disabled person or a disabled person's partner;
> >
> > (ii) the decision is advantageous to the claimant; and
> >
> > (iii) the decision is made in connection with the cessation of payment of a carer's allowance relating to that disabled person,
>
> the day after the last day for which carer's allowance was paid to a person other than the claimant or the claimant's partner;".

In consequence, para.(2A) (mentioned above) is revoked. Following the insertion of reg.6(2)(s), a new para.(8A) is inserted—

> "(8A) Where a decision is superseded in accordance with regulation 6(2)(s), the superseding decision shall take effect from the date on which the late or unpaid contribution is treated as paid."

Sub-paragraphs (9)(b) and (c) are amended by substituting "date on which" for "first pay day (as specified in Schedule 6 to the Claims and Payments Regulations) after" and para.(31) is amended by omitting "immediately following the day".

With effect from November 3, 2008, paras 95 and 104 of Sch.1 to the Tribunals, Courts and Enforcement Act 2007 (Transitional and Consequential Provisions) Order 2008 (SI 2008/2683) substitute references to the First-tier Tribunal for references to an appeal tribunal and references to the Upper Tribunal for references to a Commissioner in paras (5) and (33).

pp.586–587, *Decisions and Appeals Regulations, reg.7A*

4.111   With effect from July 27, 2008, regs 29 and 34 of the Employment and Support Allowance (Consequential Provisions) (No.2) Regulations 2008 (SI 2008/1554) make a number of amendments.

For the heading substitute, "Definitions for the purposes of Chapters I and II".

In para.(1), in the definition of "payee", insert "or "employment and support allowance decision"" after "incapacity benefit decision" and add the following new definitions—

> " 'employment and support allowance decision' means a decision to award a relevant benefit or relevant credit embodied in or necessary to which is a determination that a person has or is to be treated as having limited capability for work under Part 1 of the Welfare Reform Act;
> 'limited capability for work determination' means a determination whether a person has limited capability for work by applying the test of limited capability for work or whether a person is to be treated as having limited capability for work in accordance with regulation 20 of the Employment and Support Allowance Regulations;"

p.588, *Decisions and Appeals Regulations, reg. 8*

With effect from November 3, 2008, paras 95 and 106 of Sch.1 to the   **4.112** Tribunals, Courts and Enforcement Act 2007 (Transitional and Consequential Provisions) Order 2008 (SI 2008/2683) substitute "the Upper Tribunal" for "a Commissioner" in para.(6)(b).

p.589, *Decisions and Appeals Regulations, reg. 9ZA*

With effect from October 1, 2008, para.1(b) of Sch.2 to the Social   **4.113** Security (Recovery of Benefits) (Lump Sum Payments) Regulations 2008 (SI 2008/1596), as amended by reg.6(1) and (4) of the Social Security (Miscellaneous Amendments) (No.3) Regulations 2008 (SI 2008/2365), adds a new reg.9ZA—

"Review of certificates

9ZA.—(1) A certificate may be reviewed under section 10 of the 1997 Act where the Secretary of State is satisfied that—

- (a) a mistake (whether in the computation of the amount specified or otherwise) occurred in the preparation of the certificate;
- (b) the lump sum payment recovered from a compensator who makes a compensation payment (as defined in section 1A(5) of the 1997 Act) is in excess of the amount due to the Secretary of State;
- (c) incorrect or insufficient information was supplied to the Secretary of State by the compensator who applied for the certificate and in consequence the amount of lump sum payment specified in the certificate was less than it would have been had the information supplied been correct or sufficient;
- (d) a ground for appeal is satisfied under section 11 of the 1997 Act or an appeal has been made under that section; or
- (e) a certificate has been issued and, for any reason, a recoverable lump sum payment was not included in that certificate.

(2) In this regulation and regulations 1(3) in paragraph (b) of the definition of "party to the proceedings", [² 29 and 33], where applicable—

- (a) any reference to the 1997 Act is to be construed so as to include a reference to that Act as applied by regulation 2 of the Lump Sum Payments Regulations and, where applicable, as modified by Schedule 1 to those Regulations;
- (b) [¹ "certificate" means a certificate of recoverable lump sum payments, including where any of the amounts is nil;]
- (c) "lump sum payment" is a payment to which section 1A(2) of the 1997 Act applies;
- (d) "P" is to be construed in accordance with regulations 4(1)(a)(i) and 5 of the Lump Sum Payments Regulations."

AMENDMENTS

1. Social Security (Miscellaneous Amendments) (No.3) Regulations 2008 (SI 2008/2365), reg.6(1) and (4) (October 1, 2008).

2. Tribunals, Courts and Enforcement Act 2007 (Transitional and Consequential Provisions) Order 2008 (SI 2008/2683), Sch.1, paras 95 and 107 (November 3, 2008).

p.589, *Decisions and Appeals Regulations, reg.9A(3)*

4.113.1   With effect from November 3, 2008, paras 95 and 108 of Sch.1 to the Tribunals, Courts and Enforcement Act 2007 (Transitional and Consequential Provisions) Order 2008 (SI 2008/2683) remove the words ", or the time within which an appeal may be brought under regulation 31(1),".

p.590, *Decisions and Appeals Regulations, reg.10*

4.113.2   With effect from July 27, 2008, regs 29 and 36 of the Employment and Support Allowance (Consequential Provisions) (No.2) Regulations 2008 (SI 2008/1554) substitute a new reg.10—

"Effect of determination as to capacity or capability for work

10.—(1) This regulation applies to a determination whether a person—
    (a) is capable or incapable of work;
    (b) is to be treated as capable or incapable of work;
    (c) has or does not have limited capability for work; or
    (d) is to be treated as having or not having limited capability for work.
    (2) A determination (including a determination made following a change of circumstances) as set out in paragraph (1) which is embodied in or necessary to a decision under Chapter II of Part I of the Act or on which such a decision is based shall be conclusive for the purposes of any further decision."

p.590, *Decisions and Appeals Regulations, reg.11*

4.114   With effect from July 27, 2008, regs 29 and 37 of the Employment and Support Allowance (Consequential Provisions) (No.2) Regulations 2008 (SI 2008/1554) amend reg.11(1) by inserting "or Part 1 of the Welfare Reform Act" after "Act" and, after sub-para.(a), inserting—

"(aa) whether a person is, or is to be treated as, having or not having limited capability for work; or".

pp.593–594, *Decisions and Appeals Regulations, reg.13*

4.115   With effect from July 27, 2008, regs 29 and 38 of the Employment and Support Allowance (Consequential Provisions) (No.2) Regulations 2008 (SI 2008/1554) make a number of amendments.
    In para.(1)(a), after paragraph (i) omit "or" and, after paragraph (ii), for "and" substitute—

"or

(iii) a claimant's applicable amount under regulation 67(1)(c) or 68(1)(d) of the Employment and Support Allowance Regulations; and".

In para.(2)(a), in paragraph (ii) omit "or" and, after paragraph (iii), for "and" substitute—

"or
(iv) in relation to any claimant, the applicable amount includes the severe disability premium by virtue of regulation 67(1) or 68(1) of, and paragraph 6 of Schedule 4 to, the Employment and Support Allowance Regulations; and".

p.596, *Decisions and Appeals Regulations, reg.14A*

With effect from July 27, 2008, regs 29 and 39 of the Employment and Support Allowance (Consequential Provisions) (No.2) Regulations 2008 (SI 2008/1554) make a number of amendments. **4.116**

In the heading, for "or jobseeker's allowance" substitute ", jobseeker's allowance or employment and support allowance".

In para.(1), for "or a jobseeker's allowance" substitute ", a jobseeker's allowance or an employment and support allowance" and insert "an employment and support allowance," after "partner for".

After para.(4), add—

"(5) Where an award of an employment and support allowance is made in accordance with the provisions of this regulation, paragraph 2 of Schedule 2 to the Welfare Reform Act (waiting days) shall not apply.".

pp.597–598, *Decisions and Appeals Regulations, reg.16*

With effect from November 3, 2008, paras 95 and 109 of Sch.1 to the Tribunals, Courts and Enforcement Act 2007 (Transitional and Consequential Provisions) Order 2008 (SI 2008/2683) substitute references to the First-tier Tribunal for references to an appeal tribunal, references to the Upper Tribunal for references to a Commissioner and "permission" for "leave". **4.117**

p.599, *Decisions and Appeals Regulations, reg.17(2)*

With effect from July 27, 2008, regs 29 and 40 of the Employment and Support Allowance (Consequential Provisions) (No.2) Regulations 2008 (SI 2008/1554) add— **4.118**

"(f) a person whose entitlement to an employment and support allowance is conditional on his having, or being treated as having, limited capability for work."

p.600, *annotation to Decisions and Appeals Regulations, reg.18*

CH/3584/2006 has been reported as *R(H) 1/09.*

p.600, *Decisions and Appeals Regulations, reg.19(1)*

4.119   With effect from July 27, 2008, regs 29 and 41 of the Employment and Support Allowance (Consequential Provisions) (No.2) Regulations 2008 (SI 2008/1554) amend reg.19(1) by omitting "applies" and inserting "or regulation 23 of the Employment and Support Allowance Regulations (where a question arises whether a person has limited capability for work) applies" after "capable of work".

p.602, *Decisions and Appeals Regulations, reg.20*

4.120   With effect from November 3, 2008, paras 95 and 110 of Sch.1 to the Tribunals, Courts and Enforcement Act 2007 (Transitional and Consequential Provisions) Order 2008 (SI 2008/2683) substitute references to the First-tier Tribunal for references to an appeal tribunal, references to the Upper Tribunal for references to a Commissioner and "permission" for "leave". Also, in para.(2)(a)(ii) "specified under Tribunal Procedure Rules" is substituted for "of one month specified in regulation 53(4)".

p.603, *Decisions and Appeals Regulations, reg.21(4)*

4.121   With effect from November 3, 2008, paras 95 and 111 of Sch 1 to the Tribunals, Courts and Enforcement Act 2007 (Transitional and Consequential Provisions) Order 2008 (SI 2008/2683) substitute "permission" for "leave".

p.604, *Decisions and Appeals Regulations, reg.22*

4.122   With effect from November 3, 2008, paras 95 and 112 of Sch.1 to the Tribunals, Courts and Enforcement Act 2007 (Transitional and Consequential Provisions) Order 2008 (SI 2008/2683) substitute "permission" for "leave".

pp.604–605, *Decisions and Appeals Regulations, reg.25*

4.123   With effect from November 3, 2008, paras 95 and 115 of Sch.1 to the Tribunals, Courts and Enforcement Act 2007 (Transitional and Consequential Provisions) Order 2008 (SI 2008/2683) substitute "the First-tier Tribunal" for "an appeal tribunal".

pp.605–606, *Decisions and Appeals Regulations, reg.26*

4.124   With effect from November 3, 2008, paras 95 and 116 of Sch.1 to the Tribunals, Courts and Enforcement Act 2007 (Transitional and Consequential Provisions) Order 2008 (SI 2008/2683) substitute "the First-tier Tribunal" for "an appeal tribunal".

pp.606–607, *Decisions and Appeals Regulations, reg.27*

With effect from November 3, 2008, paras 95 and 117 of Sch.1 to the   4.125
Tribunals, Courts and Enforcement Act 2007 (Transitional and Consequential Provisions) Order 2008 (SI 2008/2683) substitute "the First-
tier Tribunal" for "an appeal tribunal" and omit paragraph (3).

pp.608–609, *Decisions and Appeals Regulations, reg.29*

With effect from October 1, 2008, para.1(c) of Sch.2 to the Social   4.126
Security (Recovery of Benefits) (Lump Sum Payments) Regulations
2008 (SI 2008/1596), as amended by reg.6(1) and (5) of the Social
Security (Miscellaneous Amendments) (No.3) Regulations 2008 (SI
2008/2365) (which erroneously refers to para.1(2)(c)(ii), rather than
para.1(c)(ii)), amended reg.29 by inserting "or, as the case may be,
recoverable lump sum payments" after "recoverable benefits" in the
heading and in paras (1), (1)(a) and (6) and inserting "or, in the case of
lump sum payments, reg.13 of the Lump Sum Payments Regulations"
after "the 1997 Act" in para.(2).
   However, with effect from November 3, 2008, paras 95 and 118 of
Sch.1 to the Tribunals, Courts and Enforcement Act 2007 (Transitional
and Consequential Provisions) Order 2008 (SI 2008/2683) remove
paras (1) and (2) altogether and substitute para.(3)—

> "(3) Where it appears to the Secretary of State that a notice of
> appeal in respect of an appeal under the 1997 Act relating to a
> certificate of recoverable benefits or, as the case may be, recoverable
> lump sum payments does not contain the particulars required, the
> Secretary of State may direct the appellant to provide such partic-
> ulars."

In addition, "or application" is omitted from para.(4) and "or a written
statement or summary" is omitted from para.(5).

p.610, *Decisions and Appeals Regulations, reg.30(5)*

With effect from November 3, 2008, paras 95 and 119 of Sch.1 to the   4.127
Tribunals, Courts and Enforcement Act 2007 (Transitional and Con-
sequential Provisions) Order 2008 (SI 2008/2683) substitute "First-tier
Tribunal" for " appeal tribunal".

pp.611–612, *Decisions and Appeals Regulations, reg.31*

With effect from November 3, 2008, paras 95 and 121 of Sch.1 to the   4.128
Tribunals, Courts and Enforcement Act 2007 (Transitional and Consequential Provisions) Order 2008 (SI 2008/2683) revoke the whole of
reg.31. It is replaced by r.23 of the Tribunal Procedure (First-tier Tribunal) (Social Entitlement Chamber) Rules 2008 (SI 2008/2685), which
are set out in Pt 1 of this Supplement. (Note that, with effect from
October 1, 2008, para.1(d) of Sch.2 to the Social Security (Recovery of

Benefits) (Lump Sum Payments) Regulations 2008 (SI 2008/1596) had made some minor amendments to reg.31(3).)

pp.613–614, *Decisions and Appeals Regulations, reg.32*

4.129   With effect from November 3, 2008, paras 95 and 122 of Sch.1 to the Tribunals, Courts and Enforcement Act 2007 (Transitional and Consequential Provisions) Order 2008 (SI 2008/2683) make substantial amendments to reg.32 because the main provisions for extending time for appealing are now to be found in the Tribunal Procedure (First-tier Tribunal) (Social Entitlement Chamber) Rules 2008 (SI 2008/2685), which are set out in Pt 1 of this Supplement. As amended, the regulation provides (the new amendments being in square brackets)—

"**32.**—[(1) Where a dispute arises as to whether an appeal was brought within the time specified under Tribunal Procedure Rules the dispute shall be referred to, and determined by, the First-tier Tribunal.

(2) The Secretary of State, the Commission or the Board, as the case may be, may treat a late appeal as made in time in accordance with Tribunal Procedure Rules if the conditions in paragraphs (4) to (8) are satisfied.]

(3) [. . .]

(4) [An appeal may be treated as made in time if the Secretary of State, the Commission or the Board, as the case may be, is satisfied that it is in the interests of justice.]

(5) For the purposes of paragraph (4), it is not in the interests of justice to [treat the appeal as made in time unless] the Secretary of State or the Board, as the case may be, is satisfied that–

(a)   the special circumstances specified in paragraph (6) are relevant [. . .]; or

(b)   some other special circumstances exist which are wholly exceptional and relevant [. . .]

and as a result of those special circumstances, it was not pracable for the application to be made within the time specified in [Tribunal Procedure Rules].

(6) For the purposes of paragraph (5)(a), the special circumstances are that—

(a)   the [appellant] or a partner or dependant of the [appellant] has died or suffered serious illness;

(b)   the [appellant] is not resident in the United Kingdom; or

(c)   normal postal services were disrupted.

(7) In determining whether it is in the interests of justice to [treat the appeal as made in time], regard shall be had to the principle that the greater the amount of time that has elapsed between the expiration of the time [limit under Tribunal Procedure Rules and the submission of the notice of appeal, the more compelling should be the special circumstances.]

(8) In determining whether it is in the interests of justice to [treat the appeal as made in time], no account shall be taken of the following—

(a) that the applicant or any person acting for him was unaware of or misunderstood the law applicant to his case (including ignorance or misunderstanding the time limits imposed by [Tribunal Procedure Rules]); or

(b) that [the Upper Tribunal] or a court has taken a different view of the law from that previously understood and applied.

(9) [. . .]

(10) [. . .]

(11) [. . .]"

Not replacing "applicant" with "appellant" in paragraph (8)(a) is probably a drafting slip.

The absolute time limit of 12 months, formerly in reg.32(1), is now to be found in r.23(5) of the Tribunal Procedure (First-tier Tribunal) (Social Entitlement Chamber) Rules 2008 (see Pt 1B, above). Rule 23(2) and Sch.1 to the Rules provide the basic time limit, generally one month in social security cases, and a broad discretion in the Tribunal to extend it, subject to that absolute time limit. Rule 23(4) provides that, subject to the absolute time limit, a late appeal will be treated as made in time if the respondent does not object. It seems very odd that the Secretary of State should restrict his own power not to object in the way he has done in paras (4) to (8) of this regulation, especially as, if he does object, he is bound by r.23(7)(a) to refer the case to the Tribunal whose discretion to admit the appeal is not limited in the same way at all.

pp.615–617, *Decisions and Appeals Regulations, reg.33*

With effect from October 1, 2008, para.1(e) of Sch.2 to the Social Security (Recovery of Benefits) (Lump Sum Payments) Regulations 2008 (SI 2008/1596) amended para.(2)(a) by inserting "or as the case may be, recoverable lump sum payments" after "recoverable benefits". (As amended by reg.6(1) and (6) of the Social Security (Miscellaneous Amendments) (No.3) Regulations 2008 (SI 2008/2365) (which erroneously refers to para.1(2)(e), rather than para.1(e)) it made a similar amendment to para.(1)(d), but that has been overtaken by the amendment recorded below.)

With effect from November 3, 2008, paras 95 and 123 of Sch.1 to the Tribunals, Courts and Enforcement Act 2007 (Transitional and Consequential Provisions) Order 2008 (SI 2008/2683) make substantial amendments to reg.32 because the main provisions for extending time for appealing are now to be found in the Tribunal Procedure (First-tier Tribunal) (Social Entitlement Chamber) Rules 2008 (SI 2008/2685), which are set out in Pt 1 of this Supplement. As amended, the heading and paras (1) to (3) now provide—

"Notice of Appeal

(1) [. . .]

(2) A notice of appeal made in accordance with Tribunal Procedure Rules and on a form approved by the Secretary of State, the Commission or the Board, as the case may be, or in such other format as the

4.130

Secretary of State, the Commission or the Board, as the case may be, accepts, is to be sent or delivered to the following appropriate office—

[*(a) to (e)*, *as set out in the main work save for the amendment noted above*]

(3) Except where paragraph (4) applies, where a form does not contain the information required under Tribunal Procedure Rules the form may be returned by the Secretary of State, the Commission or the Board to the sender for completion in accordance with the Tribunal Procedure Rules."

In addition, "or application" is omitted in paras (4), (5) and (6). "Tribunal Procedure Rules" is substituted for "paragraph (1)" in paras (4) and (5) and for all the words from "paragraph 1" to the end of para.(8)(b). In para.(5), "a notice of appeal" is substituted for "an appeal or application". References to the First-tier Tribunal are substituted for references to a legally qualified panel member in para.(8)(a) and (9) and for "clerk to an appeal tribunal or to a legally qualified panel member" in para.(10) and for "panel member" in para.(8)(b). Finally, in para.(10), "notice of" is inserted after "where the".

pp.619–623, *Decisions and Appeals Regulations, regs 35 to 38*

4.131   With effect from November 3, 2008, paras 95 and 124 of Sch.1 to the Tribunals, Courts and Enforcement Act 2007 (Transitional and Consequential Provisions) Order 2008 (SI 2008/2683) revoke these regulations (with a saving under art.3(2)(c) because appeal tribunals remain in existence for the purpose of hearing appeals brought in Scotland under s.158 of the Health and Social Care (Community Health and Standards) Act 2003, concerning the recovery of NHS charges).

Regulation 35 and Sch.3 are replaced by paras 1(2) and 2(2) of Sch.2 to the Tribunals, Courts and Enforcement Act 2007 and arts 2(2)(a) and (i) and (3) of the Qualifications for Appointment of Members to the First-tier Tribunal and Upper Tribunal Order 2008 (SI 2008/2692).

Regulation 36 is replaced by art.2 of the First-tier Tribunal and Upper Tribunal (Composition of Tribunal) Order 2008 (SI 2008/2835, see p.1360 of vol III of the main work) and a Practice Statement of the Senior President of Tribunals on the composition of tribunals in social security and child support cases, dated October 30, 2008 (set out in the supplementary annotation to the order, below).

Regulation 37 is replaced by s.40 of the 2007 Act.

Regulation 38 is replaced by rr.5 and 6 of the Tribunal Procedure (First-tier Tribunal) (Social Entitlement Chamber) Rules 2008 (SI 2008/2685), which are set out in Pt 1 of this Supplement.

p.624, *Decisions and Appeals Regulations, reg.38A*

4.132   With effect from November 3, 2008, paras 95 and 125 of Sch.1 to the Tribunals, Courts and Enforcement Act 2007 (Transitional and Consequential Provisions) Order 2008 (SI 2008/2683) substitute "the First-tier Tribunal and it appears to the First-tier Tribunal," for "an appeal tribunal and it appears to the appeal tribunal, or legally qualified panel member", omit "or legally qualified panel member, as the case may be," in para.(1) and, in para.(3)(b), substitute "First-tier Tribunal" for "appeal tribunal".

pp.625–663, *Decisions and Appeals Regulations, regs 39 to 58*

With effect from November 3, 2008, paras 95 and 126 of Sch.1 to the Tribunals, Courts and Enforcement Act 2007 (Transitional and Consequential Provisions) Order 2008 (SI 2008/2683) revoke these regulations (with a saving under art.3(2)(b) because appeal tribunals remain in existence for the purpose of hearing appeals brought in Scotland under s.158 of the Health and Social Care (Community Health and Standards) Act 2003, concerning the recovery of NHS charges).   **4.133**

The revoked regulations are largely replaced by provisions in the Tribunal Procedure (First-tier Tribunal) (Social Entitlement Chamber) Rules 2008 (SI 2008/2685), which are set out in Pt 1 of this Supplement.

Regulation 39 is replaced in part by rr.5(3)(g) and 27(1) and (3) but the procedure whereby the respondent sent a form TAS 1 to the appellant has been abolished and now the equivalent form is sent by the tribunal. Rule 8(1) or (3)(a) would permit an appeal to be struck out if the form were accompanied by a direction with an appropriate warning, but that is not the current practice.

Regulation 40 is replaced by r.17.

Regulation 41 is replaced by r.25(3) and Sch.2.

Regulation 42 is replaced by r.14(2) to (6).

Regulation 43 is replaced by rr.15(3) and 16.

Regulations 46 and 47 are replaced by r.8.

Regulation 49 is replaced by rr.28 to 31.

Regulation 50 has not been replaced. In practice, the respondent (or occasionally the appellant) was usually requested or directed to provide the evidence. On the other hand, there is now power to sit with an assessor, see s.28 of the 2007 Act.

Regulation 51 has been replaced by r.5(3)(h). Fairness is likely to require the practice provided for in reg.51(2) to continue.

Regulation 52 is replaced by r.25(2).

Regulation 53 is replaced by rr.32 to 34.

Regulation 54 is replaced by the broad discretion to extend time under r.5(3)(a).

Regulation 55 is replaced only by a Practice Statement of the Senior President of Tribunals (available at *"http://www.tribunals.gov.uk/Tribunals/Rules/statements.htm*), which is to exactly the same effect as reg.55.

Regulation 56 is replaced by r.36.

Regulation 57 is replaced by r.37, which is in broader terms and allows a decision to be set aside on the ground of "some other procedural irregularity in the proceedings".

Regulation 57A has not been replaced but it is unlikely that such decisions would have been appealable anyway (see the first paragraph of the annotation to s.14(1) of the Social Security Act 1998 in the main work). Indeed, had reg.57A had any practical effect, it would probably have been ultra vires (see *Morina v Secretary of State for Work and Pensions* [2007] EWCA Civ 749; [2007] 1 W.L.R. 3033 (also reported as *R(IS) 6/07*).

Regulation 57AA is not replaced by a specific provision but r.13(2) appears to have the same effect.

Regulation 57B is concerned only with interpretation.

Regulation 58 is replaced by rr.38 and 39. Note r.38(7) which enables the First-tier Tribunal to grant permission to appeal in a case where there is no statement of reasons in the rare case where such an appeal might succeed.

p.643, *Decisions and Appeals Regulations, annotation to reg.51*

4.134   *CSDLA/500/2007* has been reported as *R(DLA) 3/08*.

pp.645–653, *Decisions and Appeals Regulations, annotation to reg.53*

4.135   *CSDLA/500/2007* has been reported as *R(DLA) 3/08*.

The extent to which a tribunal is required to give reasons for deciding that a witness is not credible was considered at length in *CIS/4022/2007*, where the Deputy Commissioner concluded, in effect, that it all depended on the nature of the dispute and the circumstances of the case.

In *CSCS/05/2008*, no statement of reasons was obtained and the Commissioner held he had no jurisdiction to hear an appeal but it is not clear that the basis for distinguishing *R(IS) 11/99* was sound. In any event, from November 3, 2008, the position is clarified by r.21(7) of the Tribunal Procedure (Upper Tribunal) Rules 2008 (SI 2008/2698), set out in Pt 1 above. For reasons given in *R(IS) 11/99*, an appeal may be justiciable without a statement of reasons and such an appeal is, in effect, treated as a late appeal, not to be admitted unless it is in the interests of justice to do so.

pp.655–656, *Decisions and Appeals Regulations, annotation to reg.55*

4.136   *CSDLA/500/2007* has been reported as *R(DLA) 3/08*.

pp.664–665, *Decisions and Appeals Regulations, reg.58A*

4.137   With effect from November 3, 2008, paras 95 and 127 of Sch.1 to the Tribunals, Courts and Enforcement Act 2007 (Transitional and Consequential Provisions) Order 2008 (SI 2008/2683) amend reg.58A by substituting "the Upper Tribunal" for "a Commissioner", in each place, and "the First-tier Tribunal" for "an appeal tribunal".

p.667, *Decisions and Appeals Regulations, Sch.2, para.5*

4.138   With effect from July 27, 2008, regs 29 and 41 of the Employment and Support Allowance (Consequential Provisions) (No.2) Regulations 2008 (SI 2008/1554) amend para.5 as follows.

After sub-para.(a), insert—

"(aa) regulation 4I (which partner should make a claim for an employment and support allowance);".

In sub-para.(h), add "or employment and support allowance" after "benefit".

After sub-para.(mm), insert—

"(mn) regulation 26C (manner and time of payment of employment and support allowance);".

pp.672–673, *Decisions and Appeals Regulations, Sch.3*

With effect from November 3, 2008, paras 95 and 128 of Sch.1 to the   **4.139**
Tribunals, Courts and Enforcement Act 2007 (Transitional and Consequential Provisions) Order 2008 (SI 2008/2683) delete this Schedule. It is replaced by paras 1(2) and 2(2) of Sch.2 to the Tribunals, Courts and Enforcement Act 2007 and arts 2(2)(a) and (i) and (3) of the Qualifications for Appointment of Members to the First-tier Tribunal and Upper Tribunal Order 2008 (SI 2008/2692).

p.677, *Decisions and Appeals Regulations, Sch.3C*

With effect from July 27, 2008, regs 29 and 41 of the Employment and   **4.134**
Support Allowance (Consequential Provisions) (No.2) Regulations 2008 (SI 2008/1554) add a new Sch.3C.

"SCHEDULE 3C

DATE FROM WHICH CHANGE OF CIRCUMSTANCES TAKES EFFECT WHERE CLAIMANT
ENTITLED TO EMPLOYMENT AND SUPPORT ALLOWANCE

1. Subject to paragraphs 2 to 7, where the amount of an employment and support allowance payable under an award is changed by a superseding decision made on the ground of a change of circumstances, that superseding decision shall take effect from the first day of the benefit week in which the relevant change of circumstances occurs or is expected to occur.

2. In the cases set out in paragraph 3, the superseding decision shall take effect from the day on which the relevant change of circumstances occurs or is expected to occur.

3. The cases referred to in paragraph 2 are where—

(a) entitlement ends, or is expected to end, for a reason other than that the claimant no longer satisfies the provisions of paragraph 6(1)(a) of Schedule 1 to the Welfare Reform Act;

(b) a child or young person referred to in regulation 156(6)(d) or (h) of the Employment and Support Allowance Regulations (child in care of local authority or detained in custody) lives, or is expected to live, with the claimant for part only of the benefit week;

(c) a person referred to in paragraph 12 of Schedule 5 to the Employment and Support Allowance Regulations—

  (i) ceases, or is expected to cease, to be a patient; or

  (ii) a member of the person's family ceases, or is expected to cease, to be a patient,

in either case for a period of less than a week;

(d) a person referred to in paragraph 3 of Schedule 5 to the Employment and Support Allowance Regulations—

  (i) ceases to be a prisoner; or

(ii) becomes a prisoner;
(e) during the currency of the claim a claimant makes a claim for a relevant social security benefit—
    (i) the result of which is that his benefit week changes; or
    (ii) in accordance with regulation 13 of the Claims and Payments Regulations and an award of that benefit on the relevant day for the purposes of that regulation means that his benefit week is expected to change.

4. A superseding decision made in consequence of a payment of income being treated as paid on a particular day under regulation 93 of the Employment and Support Allowance Regulations (date on which income is treated as paid) shall take effect from the day on which that payment is treated as paid.

5. Where—
(a) it is decided upon supersession on the ground of a relevant change of circumstances or change specified in paragraphs 9 and 10 that the amount of an employment and support allowance is, or is to be, reduced; and
(b) the Secretary of State certifies that it is impracticable for a superseding decision to take effect from the day prescribed in paragraph 9 or the preceding paragraphs of this Schedule (other than where paragraph 3(e) or 4 applies),
that superseding decision shall take effect—
    (i) where the relevant change has occurred, from the first day of the benefit week following that in which that superseding decision is made; or
    (ii) where the relevant change is expected to occur, from the first day of the benefit week following that in which that change of circumstances is expected to occur.

6. Where—
(a) a superseding decision ("the former supersession") was made on the ground of a relevant change of circumstances in the cases set out in paragraph 3(b) to (e); and
(b) that superseding decision is itself superseded by a subsequent decision because the circumstances which gave rise to the former supersession cease to apply ("the second change"),
that subsequent decision shall take effect from the date of the second change.

7. In the case of an employment and support allowance decision where there has been a limited capability for work determination, where—
(a) the Secretary of State is satisfied that, in relation to a limited capability for work determination, the claimant or payee failed to notify an appropriate office of a change of circumstances which regulations under the Administration Act required him to notify; and
(b) the claimant or payee, as the case may be, could reasonably have been expected to know that the change of circumstances should have been notified,
the superseding decision shall take effect—
    (i) from the date on which the claimant or payee, as the case may be, ought to have notified the change of circumstances; or
    (ii) if more than one change has taken place between the date from which the decision to be superseded took effect and the date of the superseding decision, from the date on which the first change ought to have been notified.

Changes other than changes of circumstances

8. Where—
(a) the Secretary of State supersedes a decision made by an appeal tribunal or a Commissioner on the grounds specified in regulation 6(2)(c)(i) (ignorance of, or mistake as to, a material fact);
(b) the decision to be superseded was more advantageous to the claimant because of the ignorance or mistake than it would otherwise have been; and
(c) the material fact—
    (i) does not relate to the limited capability for work determination embodied in or necessary to the decision; or
    (ii) relates to a limited capability for work determination embodied in or necessary to the decision and the Secretary of State is satisfied that at the time the

decision was made the claimant or payee, as the case may be, knew or could reasonably have been expected to know of it and that it was relevant,
the superseding decision shall take effect from the first day of the benefit week in which the decision of the appeal tribunal or the Commissioner took effect or was to take effect.

9. Where an amount of an employment and support allowance payable under an award is changed by a superseding decision specified in paragraph 10 the superseding decision shall take effect from the day specified in paragraph 1 for a change of circumstances.

10. The following are superseding decisions for the purposes of paragraph 9—
(a) a decision which supersedes a decision specified in regulation 6(2)(b) and (d) to (ee); and
(b) a superseding decision which would, but for paragraph 9, take effect from a date specified in regulation 7(6), (7), (12), (13), (17D) to (17F), and (33).".

p.679, *amendment to the General Benefit Regulations 1982, reg.1*

With effect from November 3, 2008, The Tribunals, Courts and Enforcement Act 2007 (Transitional and Consequential Provisions) Order 2008 (SI2008/2683), reg.24 amended the definition of "the determining authority" to read as follows: **4.141**

"the determining authority" means, as the case may require, the Secretary of State, [the First-tier Tribunal or the Upper Tribunal];

p.695, *amendment to the Incapacity Benefit Work-focused Interviews Regulations 2003, reg.12*

With effect from November 3, 2008, The Tribunals, Courts and Enforcement Act 2007 (Transitional and Consequential Provisions) Order 2008 (SI2008/2683), reg.239 amended reg.12(3) by substituting the words "(appeal to First-tier Tribunal) to the First-tier Tribunal" for the words "(appeal to appeal tribunal) to an appeal tribunal".   **4.142**

p.708, *amendment to the Jobcentre Plus Interviews Regulations 2003, reg.11*

With effect from October 27, 2008, The Employment and Support Allowance (Consequential Provisions) (No.2) Regulations 2008 (SI2008/1554) reg.71 amended reg.11(4) by inserting: **4.143**

"(aa) an income-related employment and support allowance under Part 1 of the Welfare Reform Act 2007 (employment and support allowance);"

p.713, *amendment to the Jobcentre Plus Interviews Regulations, reg.15*

With effect from November 3, 2008, The Tribunals, Courts and Enforcement Act 2007 (Transitional and Consequential Provisions) Order 2008 (SI2008/2683), reg.178 amended reg.15(3) by substituting the words "the First-tier Tribunal" for the words "an appeal tribunal".   **4.144**

623

p.721, *amendment to the Jobcentre Plus Interviews for Partners Regulations 2003, reg.14*

4.145   With effect from November 3, 2008, The Tribunals, Courts and Enforcement Act 2007 (Transitional and Consequential Provisions) Order 2008 (SI2008/2683), reg.237 amended reg.14(3) by substituting the words "the First-tier Tribunal" for the words "an appeal tribunal".

pp.723–724, *Social Security (Loss of Benefit) Regulations 2001, reg.2*

4.146   References to "employment and support allowance" are inserted into sub-paras (a)(iii) and (b)(iii) with effect from October 27, 2008 by reg.56(1) and (2) of the Employment and Support Allowance (Consequential Provisions) (No.2) Regulations 2008 (SI 2008/1554).

pp.724–725, *Social Security (Loss of Benefit) Regulations 2001, reg.3*

4.147   References to "income-related employment and support allowance" are inserted into the heading and paras (1), (4) and (5) after the references to "income support" with effect from October 27, 2008 by reg.56(1) and (3) of the Employment and Support Allowance (Consequential Provisions) (No.2) Regulations 2008 (SI 2008/1554). The same amending provisions insert the words "or, as the case may be, regulation 2(1) of the Employment and Support Allowance Regulations 2008" into para.(6) after "Regulations".

p.736, *amendment to the, Medical Evidence Regulations 1976, reg.1*

4.148   With effect from October 27, 2008, The Employment and Support Allowance (Consequential Provisions) (No.2) Regulations 2008 (SI2008/1554) reg.68 amended reg.1 by inserting the following definitions:

> "the Employment and Support Allowance Regulations" means the Employment and Support Allowance Regulations 2008;
> "limited capability for work" has the meaning given in section 1(4) of the Welfare Reform Act 2007;
> "limited capability for work assessment" means the assessment of whether a person has limited capability for work as set out in regulation 19(2) of, and in Schedule 2 to, the Employment and Support Allowance Regulations;

p.736, *amendment to the Medical Evidence Regulations 1976, reg.2*

4.149   With effect from October 27, 2008, The Employment and Support Allowance (Consequential Provisions) (No.2) Regulations 2008 (SI2008/1554) reg.68 amended reg.2 as follows:
   (a) in the heading, after "incapacity for work" insert ", limited capability for work";
   (b) in para.(1)—

    (i) after "incapable of work" insert "or having limited capability for work";

    (ii) after "personal capability assessment" each time it occurs insert "or the limited capability for work assessment";

    (iii) after "evidence of such incapacity" insert "or limited capability for work"; and

    (iv) in sub-para.(c) after "incapable of work" insert "or whether a person has or does not have limited capability for work"; and

(c) in para.(2) after "personal capability assessment" insert "or the limited capability for work assessment".

p.738, *amendment to the Medical Evidence Regulations 1976, reg.5*

With effect from October 27, 2008, The Employment and Support Allowance (Consequential Provisions) (No.2) Regulations 2008 (SI2008/1554) reg.68 amended reg.5 as follows: **4.150**

(a) in the heading after "incapacity for work" insert "or limited capability for work";

(b) in para.(1)—

    (i) after "incapacity" insert "or limited capability for work";

    (ii) after sub-para.(a) omit "or";

    (iii) after sub-para.(b) insert:

      "(c) for a period of limited capability for work which lasts less than 8 days; or

      (d) in respect of any of the first 7 days of a longer period of limited capability for work,

(c) in para.(2) for the definition of "self-certificate" substitute:

    " 'self-certificate' means either—

    (i) a declaration made by the claimant in writing, on a form approved for the purpose by the Secretary of State; or

    (ii) where the claimant has made a claim for employment and support allowance in accordance with regulation 4G of the Social Security (Claims and Payments) Regulations 1987, an oral declaration by the claimant, that the claimant has been unfit for work from a date or for a period specified in the declaration and may include a statement that the claimant expects to continue to be unfit for work on days subsequent to the date on which it is made;".

p.750, *amendment to the Payments on Account Regulations 1988, reg.1*

With effect from October 27, 2008, The Employment and Support Allowance (Consequential Provisions) (No.2) Regulations 2008 (SI2008/1554) reg.52 amended reg.1(2) as follows: **4.151**

(a) in the definition of "benefit" after "state pension credit" insert ", an employment and support allowance";

(b) after the definition of "disabled person's tax credit" insert:

"the Employment and Support Allowance Regulations" means the Employment and Support Allowance Regulations 2008;

(c) after the definition of "tax credit" insert:

"the Welfare Reform Act" means the Welfare Reform Act 2007;

With effect from November 3, 2008, The Tribunals, Courts and Enforcement Act 2007 (Transitional and Consequential Provisions) Order 2008 (SI2008/2683), reg.7 amended reg.1(2) by substituting in the definition of "adjudicating authority" the words "the First-tier Tribunal or the Upper Tribunal" for the words "an appeal tribunal" to the end.

p.752, *amendment to the Payments on Account Regulations 1988, reg.2*

4.152   With effect from October 27, 2008, The Employment and Support Allowance (Consequential Provisions) (No.2) Regulations 2008 (SI2008/1554) reg.52 amended para.(4) by adding the words "or income-related employment and support allowance" after the words "income support".

p.755, *amendment to the Payments on Account Regulations 1988, reg.4*

4.153   With effect from October 27, 2008, The Employment and Support Allowance (Consequential Provisions) (No.2) Regulations 2008 (SI2008/1554) reg.52 amended para.(3)(c) by adding the words "or income-related employment and support allowance" after the words "income support".

p.756, *amendment to the Payments on Account Regulations 1988, reg.5*

4.154   With effect from October 27, 2008, The Employment and Support Allowance (Consequential Provisions) (No.2) Regulations 2008 (SI2008/1554) reg.52 amended reg.5 by adding the words "or an income-related employment and support allowance" after the words "income-based jobseeker's allowance".

p.758, *amendment to the Payments on Account Regulations 1988, reg.7*

4.155   With effect from October 27, 2008, The Employment and Support Allowance (Consequential Provisions) (No.2) Regulations 2008 (SI2008/1554) reg.52 amended reg.7 as follows:
(a) in para.(1)(a) after "Part III of the State Pension Credit Regulations" insert:

"or Part 10 of the Employment and Support Allowance Regulations"

(b) in para.(1)(b) after "(child support maintenance)" insert:

"or Chapter 9 of Part 10 to the Employment and Support Allowance Regulations (child support)"

With effect from October 27, 2008, The Employment and Support Allowance (Miscellaneous Amendments) Regulations 2008 (SI2008/2428), reg.22 amended reg.7 by substituting the words ", income-based jobseeker's allowance, income-related employment and support allowance" for the words "and income-based jobseeker's allowance".

p.760, *amendment to the Payments on Account Regulations 1988, reg.8*

With effect from October 27, 2008, The Employment and Support 4.156 Allowance (Consequential Provisions) (No.2) Regulations 2008 (SI2008/1554) reg.52 amended reg.8 by adding the words "or income-related employment and support allowance" after the words "income-based jobseeker's allowance".

p.763, *annotations to the Payments on Account Regulations 1988, reg.13*

In the particular circumstances of the case in *CIS/0546/2008*, a Dep- 4.157 uty Commissioner decided that the appellant was entitled to the application of the set off provisions in reg.13 in the context of a claim for income support. Benefit had been stopped when it was established that the appellant and her partner were living together as husband and wife. It appeared that the appellant had not been given the opportunity to elect to make a claim for income support for herself, her partner and the children. In this case, there was a claim for income support affecting the appellant. There was an issue which 'should have been determined'. This meant that the appellant was entitled to have reg.13 applied to offset all or part of the overpayment which was recoverable from her.

p.766, *reg.14, Payments on Account Regulations 1988, and annotations*

With effect from October 27, 2008, The Employment and Support 4.158 Allowance (Consequential Provisions) (No.2) Regulations 2008 (SI2008/1554) reg.52 amended reg.14 by inserting the words ", or income-related employment and support allowance" after the words "or an income-based jobseeker's allowance" each time they occur.

In *CIS/3611/2007*, to be reported as *R(IS) 10/08,* the Commissioner effectively holds that capital held by a child should be subject to the diminishing capital rules if an overpayment arises as a result of capital held by a child of the family unit seeking entitlement to income support. This decision was followed by another Commissioner in *CIS/0498/2008.*

p.767, *amendment to the Payments on Account Regulations 1988, reg.15*

With effect from October 27, 2008, The Employment and Support 4.159 Allowance (Consequential Provisions) (No.2) Regulations 2008 (SI 2008/1554) reg.52 amended reg.15 by adding the words "an employment and support allowance" after the words "income support".

p.768, *amendment to the Payments on Account Regulations 1988, reg.16*

4.160   With effect from October 27, 2008, The Employment and Support
Allowance (Consequential Provisions) (No.2) Regulations 2008 (SI
2008/1554) reg.52 amended reg.16 as follows
    (a) in para.(4A) after sub-para.(d) add:

> "(e) an income-related employment and support allowance;
> (f) where, if there was no entitlement to a contributory
> employment and support allowance, there would be entitle-
> ment to an income-related employment and support allow-
> ance at the same rate, a contributory employment and
> support allowance."

    (b) in para.(6) after sub-para.(c) add:

> "or
> (d) in the calculation of the income of a person to whom
> income-related employment and support allowance is paya-
> ble, the amount of earnings or other income falling to be
> taken into account is reduced by paragraph 7 of Schedule 7
> to the Employment and Support Allowance Regulations
> (sums to be disregarded in the calculation of earnings) or
> paragraphs 16 and 17 of Schedule 8 to those Regulations
> (sums to be disregarded in the calculation of income other
> than earnings),"

    (c) in para.(8)—
      (i) in the definition of "personal allowance for a single claimant
aged not less than 25" for "either" substitute "an employment and support allowance,"; and
      (ii) in the definition of "specified benefit"—
        (aa) after para.(d) omit "and"; and
        (bb) after para.(e) add:

> "and
> (f) an employment and support allowance,"

p.770, *amendment to the Payments on Account Regulations 1988, reg.17*

4.161   With effect from October 27, 2008, The Employment and Support
Allowance (Consequential Provisions) (No.2) Regulations 2008 (SI
2008/1554) reg.52 amended reg.52 amended reg.17 by adding the
words "or income-related employment and support allowance" after the
words "income-based jobseeker's allowance" each time they occur.

p.792, *EP (Recoupment of JSA and IS) Regulations 1996, reg.10(2B)*

4.162   With effect from November 3, 2008, para.73 of Sch.1 to the Tribunals, Courts and Enforcement Act 2007 (Transitional and Consequential Provisions) Order 2008 (SI 2008/2683) substitutes "the First-tier
Tribunal" for "an appeal tribunal constituted under Chapter I of Part I
of the 1998 Act".

p.816, *amendment to the Work-focused Interviews for Lone Parents Regulations 2000, reg.9*

With effect from November 3, 2008, The Tribunals, Courts and Enforcement Act 2007 (Transitional and Consequential Provisions) Order 2008 (SI 2008/2683), reg.140 amended reg.9(3) by substituting the words "(appeal to First-tier Tribunal) to the First-tier Tribunal" for the words "(appeal to appeal tribunal) to an appeal tribunal". **4.163**

p.824, *amendment to the Child Benefit and Guardian's Allowance Administration Regulations 2003, reg.2*

With effect from November 3, 2008, The Tribunals, Courts and Enforcement Act 2007 (Transitional and Consequential Provisions) Order 2008 (SI 2008/2683), reg.211 makes the following changes in the definition of adjudication authority: **4.164**
  (a) in sub-para.(b) omit "Chapter 1 of Part 1 of the Social Security Act 1998 or";
  (b) in sub-para.(c) omit "within the meaning of section 39(1) of that Act or"; and
  (c) after sub-para.(c) insert "(d) the First-tier Tribunal or the Upper Tribunal;".

pp.851–852, *CB & GA (Decisions and Appeals) Regulations 2003, reg.2*

With effect from November 3, 2008, paras 212 and 213 of Sch.1 to the Tribunals, Courts and Enforcement Act 2007 (Transitional and Consequential Provisions) Order 2008 (SI 2008/2683) amend reg.2 by deleting sub-para.(a) (and the following "(b)") in each of the definitions of "appeal tribunal", "clerk to the appeal tribunal", "Commissioner" and "legally qualified panel member" and omitting "section 6 or" in the definition of "panel". This has the effect of limiting references to appeal tribunals and Commissioners to Northern Ireland, where they have not been replaced by the First-tier Tribunal and the Upper Tribunal. Unlike most of the legislation in this work, these Regulations are UK-wide, rather than GB-wide, in their scope. **4.165**

p.855, *CB & GA (Decisions and Appeals) Regulations 2003, reg.6*

With effect from November 3, 2008, paras 212 and 214 of Sch.1 to the Tribunals, Courts and Enforcement Act 2007 (Transitional and Consequential Provisions) Order 2008 (SI 2008/2683) amend reg.6 by inserting ", the Upper Tribunal" after "a Commissioner". **4.166**

pp.856–857, *CB & GA (Decisions and Appeals) Regulations 2003, reg.8*

With effect from November 3, 2008, paras 212 and 215 of Sch.1 to the Tribunals, Courts and Enforcement Act 2007 (Transitional and Consequential Provisions) Order 2008 (SI 2008/2683) amend reg.8 by inserting "or the First-tier Tribunal" after "an appeal tribunal" in paras **4.167**

(2) and (3)(b), (c) and (d) and substituting "regulations 29 and 29A apply within the time prescribed by those regulations" for "regulation 29 applies within the time prescribed by that regulation" in para.(2).

pp.857–858, *CB & GA (Decisions and Appeals) Regulations 2003, reg. 10(3)*

4.168   With effect from November 3, 2008, paras 212 and 216 of Sch.1 to the Tribunals, Courts and Enforcement Act 2007 (Transitional and Consequential Provisions) Order 2008 (SI 2008/2683) amend reg.10(3) by inserting ", the Upper Tribunal" after "a Commissioner".

pp.859–860, *CB & GA (Decisions and Appeals) Regulations 2003, reg. 13(2)(c)*

4.169   With effect from November 3, 2008, paras 212 and 217 of Sch.1 to the Tribunals, Courts and Enforcement Act 2007 (Transitional and Consequential Provisions) Order 2008 (SI 2008/2683) amend reg.13(2)(c) by inserting "the First-tier Tribunal, the Upper Tribunal" after "an appeal tribunal".

pp.862–863, *CB & GA (Decisions and Appeals) Regulations 2003, reg. 16*

4.170   With effect from November 3, 2008, paras 212 and 218 of Sch.1 to the Tribunals, Courts and Enforcement Act 2007 (Transitional and Consequential Provisions) Order 2008 (SI 2008/2683) amend reg.16 by inserting "the First-tier Tribunal, the Upper Tribunal" after "an appeal tribunal" in paras (7) and (8), inserting "the Upper Tribunal," after "determination of" in para.(8) and inserting ", the Upper Tribunal" after "a Commissioner" in para.(9A).

p.864, *CB & GA (Decisions and Appeals) Regulations 2003, reg. 17(6)(b)*

4.171   With effect from November 3, 2008, paras 212 and 219 of Sch.1 to the Tribunals, Courts and Enforcement Act 2007 (Transitional and Consequential Provisions) Order 2008 (SI 2008/2683) amend reg.17(6)(b) by inserting ", the Upper Tribunal" after "a Commissioner".

pp.865–866, *CB & GA (Decisions and Appeals) Regulations 2003, reg. 18*

4.172   With effect from November 3, 2008, paras 212 and 220 of Sch 1 to the Tribunals, Courts and Enforcement Act 2007 (Transitional and Consequential Provisions) Order 2008 (SI 2008/2683) amend reg.18 by adding references to the First-tier Tribunal and the Upper Tribunal to references to an appeal tribunal and a Commissioner, respectively, in paras (3), (4) and (5) wherever necessary and adding "or permission" after "leave" in paras (4)(c), in both places, and (5)(b).

pp.867–868, *CB & GA (Decisions and Appeals) Regulations 2003, reg.21*

With effect from November 3, 2008, paras 212 and 221 of Sch.1 to the Tribunals, Courts and Enforcement Act 2007 (Transitional and Consequential Provisions) Order 2008 (SI 2008/2683) amend reg.21 by adding references to the First-tier Tribunal and the Upper Tribunal to references to an appeal tribunal and a Commissioner, respectively, in paras (3)(a) and (b) and (4) wherever necessary and adding "or permission" after "leave" in paras (3)(b)(c) and (d) and (4).   **4.173**

p.869, *CB & GA (Decisions and Appeals) Regulations 2003, reg.21*

With effect from November 3, 2008, paras 212 and 222 of Sch.1 to the Tribunals, Courts and Enforcement Act 2007 (Transitional and Consequential Provisions) Order 2008 (SI 2008/2683) amend reg.23 by inserting "or permission" after "leave".   **4.174**

p.870, *CB & GA (Decisions and Appeals) Regulations 2003, reg.25(1)*

With effect from November 3, 2008, paras 212 and 223 of Sch.1 to the Tribunals, Courts and Enforcement Act 2007 (Transitional and Consequential Provisions) Order 2008 (SI 2008/2683) amend reg.25(1) by inserting "or to the First-tier Tribunal" after "appeal tribunal".   **4.175**

p.872, *CB & GA (Decisions and Appeals) Regulations 2003, reg.28*

With effect from November 3, 2008, paras 212 and 224 of Sch.1 to the Tribunals, Courts and Enforcement Act 2007 (Transitional and Consequential Provisions) Order 2008 (SI 2008/2683) amend reg.28 by inserting "or the First-tier Tribunal" after "appeal tribunal" in para.(1), inserting "or, as the case may be, the First-tier Tribunal" after "member" in para.(3) and inserting "or, as the case may be, regulation 29A" after "29" in para.(4).   **4.176**

It does not seem consistent with the Tribunal Procedure (First-tier Tribunal) (Social Entitlement Chamber) Rules 2008 (see Pt 1B, above) for there to continue to be a time limit in this regulation which, in effect, duplicates the time limit in the Rules.

pp.873–874, *CB & GA (Decisions and Appeals) Regulations 2003, regs 29 and 29A*

With effect from November 3, 2008, paras 212 and 225 of Sch.1 to the Tribunals, Courts and Enforcement Act 2007 (Transitional and Consequential Provisions) Order 2008 (SI 2008/2683) amend reg.29 by inserting "to the appeal tribunal" in the heading after "appeals" and inserting "to an appeal tribunal" in para.(1) after "brought". Paragraphs 212 and 226 then add a new reg.29A—   **4.177**

"Late appeals to the First-tier Tribunal

29A. In respect of an appeal to the First-tier Tribunal, the Board may treat a late appeal as made in time in accordance with Tribunal Procedure Rules if the Board is satisfied that it is in the interests of justice, but no appeal shall in any event be brought more than one year after the expiration of the last day for appealing under regulation 28."

This regulation duplicates the provision made by r.23(5) of the Tribunal Procedure (First-tier Tribunal) (Social Entitlement Chamber) Rules 2008 (see Pt 1B, above). However, HMRC does not fetter its own power not to object to a late appeal brought within the absolute time limit (compare the amended reg.32 of the Social Security and Child Support (Decisions and Appeals) Regs 1999 which is set out in the supplementary note to pp.613–614 of Vol.III of the main work, above).

pp.874–875, *CB & GA (Decisions and Appeals) Regulations 2003, reg.30*

4.178   With effect from November 3, 2008, paras 212 and 227 of Sch.1 to the Tribunals, Courts and Enforcement Act 2007 (Transitional and Consequential Provisions) Order 2008 (SI 2008/2683) amend reg.30 so that it applies to both reg.29 and reg.29A. Paragraph (1) is amended by inserting "and regulation 29A" after "29", substituting "or, as the case may be, treat the appeal as made in time" for "under that regulation" and omitting "to the application" in sub-paras (a) and (b). Paragraph (4) is amended by inserting "or, as the case may be, treat the appeal as made in time under regulation 29A" after "29" and inserting "or, as the case may be, submission of a notice of appeal" after "making of the application". Paragraph (5) is amended by inserting "or, as the case may be, treat the appeal as made in time under regulation 29A" after "29" and inserting ", the Upper Tribunal" after "a Commissioner" in sub-para.(b).

pp.875–876, *CB & GA (Decisions and Appeals) Regulations 2003, reg.31*

4.179   With effect from November 3, 2008, paras 212 and 228 of Sch.1 to the Tribunals, Courts and Enforcement Act 2007 (Transitional and Consequential Provisions) Order 2008 (SI 2008/2683) amend reg.31. New paras (1A) and (1B) are inserted—

"(1A) A notice of appeal to the First-tier Tribunal made in accordance with Tribunal Procedure Rules must be made on a form approved by the Board, or in such other format as the Board may accept.

(1B) Except where paragraph (3) applies, in respect of an appeal to the First-tier Tribunal, where a form does not contain the information required under Tribunal Procedure Rules the form may be returned by the Board to the sender for completion in accordance with the Tribunal Procedure Rules."

In para.(2), "In respect of an appeal to the appeal tribunal an approved" is substituted for "An approved". In paras (3), (4) and (7)(a), "or, as the case may be, Tribunal Procedure Rules" is inserted after "paragraph (1)". In para.(7), ", or, as the case may be, the First-tier Tribunal which," is inserted after "panel member who" and, in para.(8) ", or, as the case may be, First-tier Tribunal which," is inserted after "panel member who".

p.877, *CB & GA (Decisions and Appeals) Regulations 2003, reg.32*

With effect from November 3, 2008, paras 212 and 229 of Sch.1 to the Tribunals, Courts and Enforcement Act 2007 (Transitional and Consequential Provisions) Order 2008 (SI 2008/2683) amend reg.32 by inserting "or to the First-tier Tribunal" after "appeal to an appeal tribunal" and inserting "or, as the case may be, the First-tier Tribunal" in sub-para.(a) after "panel member"   **4.180**

p.886, *annotations to s.2, European Communities Act 1972 (State liability for breaches of Community law)*

For guidance on the application of limitation periods to *Francovich* actions, see *Spencer v Secretary of State for Work and Pensions,* and *Moore v Secretary of State for Transport,* [2008] EWCA Civ 750.   **4.181**

p.898, *annotations to Art.18 EC*

Case C-499/06 *Nerkowska,* Judgment of May 22, 2008, decides that Art.18 must be interpreted as precluding legislation of a Member State under which it refuses, generally and in all circumstances, to pay to its nationals a benefit granted to civilian victims of war or repression solely because they are not resident in the territory of that Member State through the period of payment of the benefit, but in the territory of another Member State.   **4.182**

The Commissioner's decision in *CIS/1545/2007* has been upheld by the Court of Appeal in *Jeleniewicz v Secretary of State for Work and Pensions,* [2008] EWCA Civ 1163; *R(IS) 3/09.* The Commissioner was right to rule that a claimant, a Polish national, could not rely on a claimed right to reside by a young child (without any independent means of support) whose father (with whom the claimant was no longer living) was said to have a right to reside in the United Kingdom as a student. The case before the Commissioner was characterised by a lack of clear evidence on a number of key issues. The Court of Appeal noted that the claimed right to reside was "doubly indirect in law".

A forthcoming Tribunal of Commissioners in *CIS/1471/2007* will consider the five year qualification period for the right to permanent residence and the extent to which Directive 2004/38/EC aids in the interpretation of Art.18 in the light of the judgment in the *Baumbast* case.

The Court of Appeal has upheld the Commissioner's decision in *CIS/2358/2006* in *Kaczmarek v Secretary of State for Work and Pensions,* [2008]

EWCA Civ 1310. Two key issues arose for the Court of Appeal. Having regard to Art.12, does the reference to lawful residence "for a certain time" in the *Trojani* case give rise to an eligibility based on residence of unspecified but significant duration and of a type which evidence a degree of social integration in the host Member State? Maurice Kay L.J., giving the judgment of the Court, ruled that it did not, stating that "eligibility is primarily and more appropriately a matter for normative regulation ... ." (para.16). It is suggested that this may not be the view taken by the Luxembourg Court were the matter to be raised before them. Although there is much debate about the significance of the Luxembourg Court's decision in the *Trojani* case, it can certainly be read as indicating that lawful residence for a certain, and unspecified, time which evidence a degree of social integration does give rise to the right to be treated equally with nationals. It is also true that the old system of residence permits (abandoned in Directive 2004/38/EC) did not require lawful presence for a significant period in order to obtain it. It was obtainable through employment which might then come to an end through no fault of the permit holder after very short duration without prejudice to the rights of the permit holder under the residence permit. The permit was always regarded as merely being evidence of rights arising under the EC Treaty and not as conferring those rights.

The second question was whether, under Art.18 EC, it was disproportionate to deny a right of residence to a person in the position of the appellant. Having regard to what might be regarded as corresponding provisions in Directive 2004/38/EC, Maurice Kay L.J. concluded that he was not dealing with a lacuna in the scheme in the EC Treaty. It was accordingly not disproportionate to deny the appellant a right to reside.

The House of Lords has upheld the decision of the Northern Ireland Court of Appeal in *Zalewska v Department for Social Development*, [2008] UKHL 67, to be reported as *R1/09(IS)*. In a 3–2 decision, the House of Lords decided that the United Kingdom regulations establishing the regime for A8 nationals (requiring them to register their work and to have an uninterrupted period of 12 months in employment before becoming assimilated with workers under Article 39 EC) were not inconsistent with obligations arising under the EC Treaty. The difference of opinion related to the issue of proportionality. Baroness Hale and Lord Neuberger considered that the scheme adopted was disproportionate in that the complete disenfranchisement from the protection of social security went beyond the scope of the permissible derogation in the Treaty of Accession.

p.931, *General Note*

4.183   In *CIS/185/2008* the Commissioner considers the relationship between Art.18 EC and this Directive:

"For the purposes of this decision, I am quite content to accept the Secretary of State's submission that the claimant cannot have acquired a right of permanent residence under Article 16 before Directive 2004/38/EC came into effect. However, in CIS/2358/2006 and CIS/

408/2006, I have held that a claimant can rely instead on Article 18(1) of the EC Treaty. In short, my reasoning has been that it is clear from *Baumbast v Secretary of State for the Home Department* (Case C-413/99) [2002] E.C.R. I-7091, having particular regard to what Mr Advocate General Geelhoed said at paragraphs 19 to 36 and 120 to 122 of his Opinion about the inadequacy of existing Directives, that the Directives in force before 30 April 2006 could not be regarded as the sole source of rights of residence and that, once Council Directive 2004/38/2004 had been adopted, it provided a guide as to the scope of the rights conferred directly by Article 18(1) of the EC Treaty, although not an exhaustive guide if it was possible to show a lacuna in that Directive. Thus, in CIS/408/2006, the claimant was successful even though his case would not have fallen within Directive 2004/38/EC had it been in force. In CIS/2358/2006, the claimant was unsuccessful (and now has an appeal pending before the Court of Appeal). Although Directive 2004/38/EC was not adopted until a few days after the claimant in the present case had returned to work in 2004, in my judgment it is still capable of providing a guide as to the scope of Article 18(1) as at 18 April 2003. Moreover, it is particularly appropriate to have regard to it when considering what is in effect a transitional case arising under Article 16 of the Directive itself." (para.20).

p.935, *annotations to Art.3, Dir.2004/38/EC*

Case C-127/08 *Metock and others,* Judgment of July 25, 2008, is a very   4.184
significant case on the interpretation of Art.3 on a reference from the Irish courts. It concerns national implementation of Art.3 which has some similarities with implementation in the United Kingdom, and has important implications for the interpretation of the United Kingdom's national regulations implementing the Directive. This makes it worth setting out the circumstances of some of the individuals whose cases were the subject of this reference.

Metock is a national of Cameroon who arrived in Ireland in June 2006 and whose application for asylum failed. Ikeng, born a national of Cameroon acquired United Kingdom nationality and resided and worked in Ireland since late in 2006. Metock and Ikeng met in Cameroon in 1994 and have been in a stable relationship. There are two children. They were married in Ireland in October 2006. An application for a residence card for Metock was refused on the grounds that he did not satisfy the requirement of the Irish regulations that he had resided lawfully in another Member State prior to the application.

Mr Ikogho was also a failed asylum seeker; he was subject to a deportation order at the material time. Mrs Ikogho, a United Kingdom national, has lived and worked in Ireland since 1996. Mr and Mrs Ikogho met in Ireland in 2004 and were married in June 2006. An application for a residence card was refused on the grounds that Mr Ikogho was staying illegally in Ireland at the time of his marriage.

Chinedu, a national of Nigeria is also a failed asylum seeker. Babucke is a woman of German nationality lawfully resident in Ireland. Chinedu and Babucke married in July 2006. An application for a residence card was refused on the grounds that Chinedu did not meet the condition in the national regulations of lawful residence in another Member State prior to the application.

The applicants all argued that the Irish regulations implementing the Directive were incompatible with it. Their argument was that a national of a non-member country who becomes a family member of a Union citizen while that citizen is resident in a Member State other than that of which he is a national accompanies that citizen within the meaning of Arts 3(1) and 7(2) of the Directive. The Irish Government argued that the Directive does not preclude the imposition of a condition of prior lawful residence in another Member State in the national implementing legislation.

The Court of Justice observed that nothing in the Directive makes the application of its provisions conditional on persons having previously resided in a Member State. The Court concludes:

"... Directive 2004/38 confers on all nationals of non-member countries whoa re family members of a Union citizen within the meaning of part 2 of Article 2 of that directive, and accompany or join the Union citizen in a Member State other than that of which he is a national, rights of entry into and residence in the host Member State, regardless of whether the national of a non-member country has already been lawfully resident in another Member State" (para.70).

The Court went on to consider cases where rights arose from marriage and concluded:

"... Article 3(1) of Directive 2004/38 must be interpreted as meaning that a national of a non-member countries who is the spouse of a Union citizen residing in a Member State whose nationality he does not possess and who accompanies or joins that Union citizen benefits from the provisions of that directive, irrespective of when and where their marriage took palce and of how the national of a non-member country entered the host Member State." (para.99).

In *CIS/2100/2007* the Commissioner analyses and discusses the European authorities on the notion of dependence under a regulation and two earlier directives of the European Community. He concludes that the case law is authority for the propositions: (1) a person is only dependent who actually receives support from another; (2) there need be no right to that support and it is irrelevant that there are alternative sources of support available; and (3) that support must be material, although not necessarily financial, and must provide for, or contribute towards, the basic necessities of life. (para.44).

Art. 3(2)(b)

4.185   Article 3(2)(b) requires Member States to facilitate the entry and residence of the partner of a Union citizen, with whom that citizen has a 'durable relationship'. The provision has been implemented in the United Kingdom through reg.8(5) of the Immigration (European Economic Area) Regulation 2006, which provides:

"A person satisfies the condition in this paragraph if the person is a partner of an EEA national (other than a civil partner) and can prove to the decision-maker that he is in a durable relationship with the EEA national."

In *CIS/0612/2008* the Commissioner ruled that the concepts of a "durable relationship" must be given a Community meaning. He went on to say that the concepts in Art.3(2)(b) are expressed "in ordinary words that do not require definition and can be left to the relevant fact-finding body" (para.30). However, he considered that there was an element of ambiguity in the notion of durability in that it "may mean that it has lasted or that it is capable of lasting" (para.36), although plainly it was the relationship with the partner rather than the partnership itself that had to display this quality. The relationship may have existed prior to the persons becoming partners. Subject to these considerations the question of the durability of the relationship was one of fact.

p.942, *Art.12, Directive 2004/38/EC*

A reference to the Luxembourg Court has been made in *Teixeira v Lambeth LBC* [2008] EWCA Civ 1088 in a homelessness case in the following terms: 4.186

"In circumstances where (i) an EU citizen came to the United Kingdom (ii) the EU citizen was for certain periods a worker in the United Kingdom (iii) the EU citizen ceased to be a worker but did not depart from the United Kingdom, (iv) the EU citizen has not retained her status as a worker and has no right to reside under Article 7 and has no right of permanent residence under Article 16 of Directive 2004/38 of the Council and the European Parliament (v) the EU citizen's child entered education at a time when the EU citizen was not a worker but the child remained in education in the United Kingdom during periods when the EU citizen was in work in the United Kingdom, (vi) the EU citizen is the primary carer of her child and (vii) the EU citizen and her child are not self-sufficient:

(1)   does the EU citizen only enjoy a right of residence in the United Kingdom if she satisfies the conditions set out in Directive 2004/38 of the European Parliament and the Council of 29 April 2004?;

OR

(2)   (i) does the EU citizen enjoy a right to reside derived from Article 12 of Regulation (EEC) No 1612/68 of 15 October 1968, as interpreted by the Court of Justice, without being required to satisfy the conditions set out in Directive 2004/38 of the European Parliament and of the Council of 29 April 2004; and

(ii) if so, must she have access to sufficient resources so as not to become a burden on the social assistance system of the host Member State during their proposed period of residence and have comprehensive sickness insurance cover in the host Member State?;

(iii) if so, must the child have first entered education at a time when the EU citizen was a worker in order to enjoy a right to reside derived from Article 12 of Regulation (EEC) No 1612/68 of 15 October 1968, as interpreted by the Court of Justice, or is it sufficient that the EU citizen has been a worker at some time after the child commenced education?;

(iv) does any right that the EU citizen has to reside, as the primary carer of a child in education, cease when her child attains the age of eighteen?

(3) if the answer to question 1 is yes, is the position different in circumstances such as the present case where the child commenced education prior to the date by which Directive 2004/38 of the European Parliament and of the Council of 29 April 2004 was to be implemented by the Member States but the mother did not become the primary carer and did not claim the right to reside on the basis that she was the primary carer of the child until March 2007, i.e.after the date by which the Directive was to be implemented?"

p.945, *annotations to Art.14, Directive 2004/38/EC*

4.187 Art.14(4)(b) codifies the position established under Case C-292/89 *Antonissen* [1991] E.C.R. I-745 to the effect that work seekers have a right under Art.39 EC to be in a Member State while looking for work provided that they have a genuine prospect of securing employment. This is also reflected in the Immigration (European Economic Area) Regulations 2006 which implement the Directive: see reg.6(1)(a) referring to jobseekers. This analysis of the legal position was accepted by the Commissioner in *R(IS) 8/08.*

p.946, *annotations to Art.16, Directive 2004/38/EC*

4.188 In *CIS/4299/2007* the Commissioner ruled:

"... a claimant's period of residence as a jobseeker prior to 30 April 2006, when the 2006 [Immigration (European Economic Area] Regulations came into force, may be counted as part of legal residence for the purpose of the Directive, but not for the purpose of the 2000 [Immigration (European Economic Area] Regulations." (para.26).

In para.25 the Commissioner had noted:

"The specific reason why the nature of the EEA legislation is significant concerns the position of jobseekers. Until Directive 2004/38, they had no express right to reside in EC law and they were not mentioned in the 2000 Regulations. However, in *R v Immigration Appeal Tribunal, ex parte Antonissen* (Case C-292/89) [1991] E.C.R. 1-745, the European Court of Justice decided (at paragraphs 14 and 15 of its judgment) that the right of a jobseeker to reside in a host State was implicit both in what is now Article 39 of the EC Treaty and in Regulation 1612/68/EEC. Jobseekers are, therefore, an example of a category of person who have a right to reside that derives from EC law but is not contained in domestic legislation."

The decision is under appeal to the Court of Appeal as *Secretary of State for Work and Pensions v Lassal*. The grounds of this appeal are that the appellant in this case cannot have acquired a right of residence under Art.16(1) in February 2005 because the Directive did not come into effect until April 30, 2006, and earlier directives did not guarantee any right of permanent residence. It appears that the Secretary of State accepts that residence before Directive 2004/38/EC came into force is relevant for the purposes of acquiring permanent residence on or after April 30, 2006: see *CIS/0185/2008*, para.18.

In *CIS/2258/2008* the Commissioner was considering whether the appellant could claim to be permanently resident under Art.16 in a case in which there were periods when the appellant had been absent abroad. The Commissioner ruled that the tribunal had erred in law by including in the period of residence the time when the appellant was abroad. The Commissioner says:

"17. If Article 16(1) stood on its own, any gaps in the residence would prevent a right of permanent residence arising. However, Article 16(3) allows for periods of absence. Provided that the claimant's absences comply with the conditions in that paragraph, continuity of residence is preserved. That does not affect the period of residence that is required. Continuity and the period of five years are separate, albeit related, conditions for the right to arise. This interpretation accords with the wording of the paragraph. Any other interpretation would produce a surprising result. If periods of absence were included in the period of residence, it is conceivable that a person might acquire a right of permanent residence after being resident here for a period considerably shorter than five years. It may be an extreme and unrealistic example, but a person could spend one year studying abroad, spend the next two or three years on compulsory military service abroad and then spend half of each year abroad. A person in those circumstances would surely not 'have chosen to settle long term in the host Member State', to quote recital 17 to the Directive."

It is suggested that, were the question to be raised in Luxembourg, the Court of Justice may not view the interpretation of Art.16 in the same way as the Commissioner in separating the period of residence and its continuity. It is clearly more integrationist and more compatible with the concept of citizenship of the Union to *include* permitted periods of absence abroad as part of the period of residence required to acquire the status of permanent citizenship.

p.964, *annotations to Art.4, Regulation 1408/71*

Case C-228/07 *Petersen*, Judgment of September 11, 2008, illustrates the need for careful consideration of the classification of benefits. Petersen is a German national who was working in Austria. He claimed **4.189** an incapacity pension, which was refused. While an appeal against this decision was pending, the Austrian authorities granted Petersen an advance of pension payments under provisions of Austrian law headed 'advance pension payments.' Petersen was considering returning to Germany and asked for the advance unemployment benefit to be continued after his change of residence. That application was refused. The first question before the Court was whether the benefit was an unemployment benefit or an invalidity benefit. Though the benefit had certain characteristics of both, the Court concluded that the benefit was an unemployment benefit within Art.4(1)(g).

The second question concerned the exportability of the benefit, since Austrian law provided that the benefit was payable subject to a condition of residence in the national territory. The Court noted that the provisions of Arts 69 and 71 were not applicable to the present case. However, in exercising their discretion to regulate the scheme, the Austrian authorities were required to exercise their choices having appropriate and proportionate regard to Arts 39 to 42 EC. The Court concluded that the Austrian Government had not put forward any objective justification for the condition that recipients of the benefit to which Petersen was entitled must be resident on the national territory.

p.966, *annotations to Art.3, Regulation 1408/71*

4.190   *CPC/1072/2006* was an attempt to use Art.3 of Regulation 1408/71 as a means of challenge the requirement of a right to reside as a condition of entitlement to state pension credit. The Commissioner's decision is under appeal to the Court of Appeal as *Patmalniece v Secretary of State for Work and Pensions*.

The Commissioner ruled that the Secretary of State's concession that state pension credit fell within the material scope of the regulation was plainly right. This meant that Art.3 bit, even though the benefit was listed in Annex IIa as a special non-contributory benefit. The appellant argued that the requirement of a right to reside as a condition of entitlement constituted prohibited discrimination under Art.3 which could not be justified. The Commissioner ruled:

> "I have no doubt that a requirement that is always satisfied by citizens of the Member State but not necessarily by citizens of other Member States will rarely prove justifiable in practice, but I am not satisfied that there is any principle that forbids an attempt to justify such a requirement, particularly where the cases touches upon an issue that is beyond the European Community's sphere of competence." (para.17).

He went on to say:

> "A condition that confines entitlement only to nationals of the Member State concerned is unlawful, but a condition designed to confer entitlement on all such nationals and some nationals of other member states may be justified to the extent that it is consistent with the Community's approach to social assistance." (para.19).

The Community's approach was to require Member States to extend the protection of social assistance to nationals of other Member States with a sufficient connection with the host Member States. The condition of entitlement that a person has a right to reside "is justified because such a condition distinguishes between those guaranteed equal treatrment in relation to social assistance by Community law and those for whom Community law provides no such guarantee." (para.19). The Commissioner took the view that the first step is to determine whether a person has a right to reside under Art.18 EC. This determines the question of the right to be treated equally with nationals of the Member State. The Commissioner then says:

"In effect, the approach that satisfied the Court of Appeal in *Abdirahman* that the claimed right was outside the scope of Article 12 of the EC Treaty satisfies me that the imposition of a right of residence in respect of state pension credit is justified and is not contrary to Article 3 of Regulation (EEC) 1408/71." (para.23).

That conclusion has a superficial attraction but may be challengeable in its apparent conclusion that the claimed right was outside the scope of Art.12 of the EC Treaty, when it is plainly within the scope of Art.3 of Regulation 1408/71 for reasons made clear earlier in the Commissioner's decision. If that is so, it is difficult to see how the argument that it is outside the scope of the EC Treaty can be sustained. But that is also to present a challenge to the correctness of the Court of Appeal's decision in *Abdirahman*.

p.973, *annotations to Art.10, Reg.1408/71*

Secretary of State for Work and Pensions v Burley, [2008] EWCA Civ 376, to be reported as *R(P) 2/08*, is the appeal against the decision in *CP/633/2006 and CP/634/2006*. It concerned the reduction in the payment of pension to a couple who had moved permanently to France. However, entitlement to the pension depended upon the operation of a bilateral agreement with Australia under which contributions paid in Australia were treated as paid in the United Kingdom. The Commissioner had ruled that Reg.1408/71 applied, but the Secretary of State appealed arguing that the derogation to be found in Annex VI, Point Y, para.7 applied (see para.3.317 of the main Volume). The Court of Appeal considered that the Secretary of State was correct in that the operation of Reg.1408/71 was ousted since the respondents entitlement to the retirement pension was governed by the provisions of the reciprocal agreements whose priority was preserved by the derogation. This case indicates just how important it will be to determine whether any entitlement which appears at first sight to be governed by Reg.1408/71 is not affected by the operation of a reciprocal agreement. **4.191**

p.981, *annotations to Art.13, Reg.1408/71*

Case C-352/06 *Bosmann*, Judgment of May 20, 2008, concerns the interpretation of Art.13(2)(a) which provides that the competent State is **4.192** the State in which a person is employed even if they reside in another Member State. The main principle of Art.13 is to ensure that there is only one competent State. But does that mean that there can be no entitlement to a benefit under the law of the Member State of residence? That was the question which arose in this case. Brigitte Bosmann, a Belgian national, worked in The Netherlands, but lived in Germany. When she undertook this employment, the German authorities terminated the award of child benefits for her two children. There was no comparable entitlement under Dutch law since the legislation of that country does not provide for the payment of child benefits for children over 18.

At first sight, it would seem that Bosmann was caught by Art.13(2)(a) in that, when she became employed in Germany, that country was alone the competent State for the purpose of benefits falling within the scope of Reg.1408/71. But the Court ruled that "the application of provisions from another system of legislation is not thereby always precluded" (para.20). While Community law does not *require* the German authorities to pay child benefit in respect of the two children, it does not *exclude* that possibility. How sweeping an exception to the single State rule in Art.13 is that? That remains contentious. One view is that the possibility of dual State competence is limited to family benefit cases where there remain wide variations in both the conditions of entitlement and the level of benefits. The second is that the case establishes that a State other than the competent State *may* elect to pay benefits where a person meets the conditions of entitlement in that State through some linking factor, such as residence, on the basis of national law alone. It is worth observing that the Opinion of Advocate General Mazák came to the opposite view, namely that Bosmann was not entitled to the application of German law so as to receive child benefit.

p.1089, *annotations to Annex VI, Reg.1408/71*

4.193 Note *Secretary of State for Work and Pensions v Burley,* [2008] EWCA Civ 376 reported in relation to p.973 of Vol.III above.

p.1201, *annotations to s.2, Human Rights Act 1998*

4.194 In *R (on the application of RJM) v Secretary of State for Work and Pensions,* [2008] UKHL 63, the House of Lords addressed the questions touched on in *Kay.* Lord Neuberge said:

> "64. Where the Court of Appeal considers that an earlier decision of this House, which would otherwise be binding on it, may be, or even is clearly, inconsistent with a subsequent decision of the ECtHR, then (absent wholly exceptional circumstances) the court should faithfully follow the decision of the House, and leave it to your Lordships to decide whether to modify or reverse its earlier decision. To hold otherwise would be to go against what Lord Bingham decided. As a matter of principle, it should be for this House, not for the Court of Appeal, to determine whether one of its earlier decisions has been

overtaken by a decision of the ECtHR. As a matter of practice, as the recent decision of this House in *Animal Defenders* [2008] 2 WLR 781 shows, decisions of the ECtHR are not always followed as literally as some might expect. As to what would constitute exceptional circumstances, I cannot do better than to refer back to the exceptional features which Lord Bingham identified as justifying the Court of Appeal's approach in *East Berkshire* [2004] Q.B. 558: see *Kay* [2006] 2 A.C. 465, para.45."

But the position in relation to the Court of Appeal's respect for its own previous decisions is different:

"65. When it comes to its own previous decisions, I consider that different considerations apply. It is clear from what was said in *Young* [1944] KB 718 that the Court of Appeal is freer to depart from its earlier decisions than from those of this House: a decision of this House could not, I think, be held by the Court of Appeal to have been arrived at per incuriam. Further, more recent jurisprudence suggests that the concept of per incuriam in this context has been interpreted rather generously - see the discussion in the judgment of Lloyd LJ in *Desnousse v Newham London Borough Council* [2006] EWCA Civ 547, [2006] Q.B. 831, paras 71 to 75.

66. The principle promulgated in *Young* [1944] K.B. 718 was, of course, laid down at a time when there were no international courts whose decisions had the domestic force which decisions of the ECtHR now have, following the passing of the 1998 Act, and in particular section 2(1)(a). In my judgment, the law in areas such as that of precedent should be free to develop, albeit in a principled and cautious fashion, to take into account such changes. Accordingly, I would hold that, where it concludes that one of its previous decisions is inconsistent with a subsequent decision of the ECtHR, the Court of Appeal should be free (but not obliged) to depart from that decision."

p.1210, *annotations to s.6, Human Rights Act 1998*

The proper interpretation of s.6(2)(b) has been the subject of discussion in a number of cases in the House of Lords. In July 2008, the House of Lords again considered this aspect of the Act in *Doherty v Birmingham City Council*, [2008] UKHL 57 in a case which concerned the obtaining of a possession order against a traveller under a procedure which it was argued would breach Article 8 of the Convention (on which see *Connors v United Kingdom*, (App.66746/01) May 24 2004, (2005) 40 EHRR 9; and *McCann v United Kingdom*, (App.19009/04) May 13, 2008). In the course of their deliberations, the House gives detailed consideration to the circumstances in which a breach of the Act will be avoided because of the operation of s.6(2)(b). The position adopted in earlier cases was re-affirmed. The House confirmed that three distinct situations can arise under the provision. The first is where a decision to exercise or not to exercise a power that is given in primary legislation would inevitable give rise to a violation of Convention rights. The second is at the opposite end of the spectrum where no statutory provision concerns the exercise of

4.195

discretion by a public body which acts in violation of Convention rights; such action will be unlawful under s.6(1) because s.6(2)(b) cannot apply. The third situation is said to lie in the middle:

> "This is where the act or omission takes place within the context of a scheme which primary legislation has laid down that gives general powers, such as powers of management, to a public authority . . . The answer to the question whether or not section 6(2)(b) applies will depend on the extent to which the act or omission can be said to give effect to any of the provisions of the scheme that is to be found in the statutes." (para.39, per Lord Hope of Craighead).

The House has indicated that there are two possible gateways by which a violation of Convention rights might be addressed in such situations. The first gateway provides two possibilities. The first is that the use of the interpretative obligation in s.3 results in an interpretation which avoids the violation which is alleged. The second is that the interpretative obligation does not help, but that a court of sufficient seniority can give a declaration of incompatibility under s.4 which results in a remedial order under s.10. The second gateway involves an argument that the public authority whose decision is challenged has made an improper use of its powers; this route offers a procedural protection in that the court will consider whether the public authority acted unreasonable in the *Wednesbury* sense in taking the action that it did (paras 52–55).

p.1251, *annotations to Art.8 ECHR*

4.196   In *CIS/1481/2006* which is excoriating about the behaviour of officers of the Department in the matter before him, and critical of the tribunal's approach to the case, a Commissioner has provided very useful guidance on issues concerning the use of surveillance techniques to support decision-making in the Department. In particular, there is the most helpful guidance about the application of the Regulation of Investigatory Powers Act 2000 (RIPA) to surveillance by the Department. Such action is, of course, frequently attacked as a violation of Art.8 ECHR. The Commissioner summarises a detailed section of his decision as follows:

> "50. More generally, where there is a challenge under Article 8 of the European Convention against evidence produced by the Secretary of State, or the conduct or results of surveillance are otherwise challenged before an appeal tribunal, RIPA now provides effective answers. If the Secretary of State provides the tribunal and the claimant with a copy of the application and authorisation for the surveillance, and it is clear that the authorisation covers the surveillance, then the tribunal will usually need to take matters no further. The tribunal may properly take the view that the Secretary of State can rely fully on the evidence obtained from the surveillance without further investigation by itself. If the claimant has continuing or other concerns, then he or she may take them to the investigatory powers tribunal. With that in mind, I suggest that the Secretary of State should, in cases such as this, produce the proper documentation about surveillance to an

appellant and the tribunal together with the evidence from the surveillance on which the Secretary of State seeks to rely."

p.1255, *annotations to Art.14 ECHR*

See *Hobbs, Richard, Walsh and Geen v United Kingdom* (Apps **4.197** 63684/00, 63475/00, 63484/00 and 63468/00), November 14, 2006, for the corresponding decision to that in *Runkee and White* in relation to widow's bereavement allowance in which a violation of Art.14 taken with Art.1 of Protocol 1 was found. There have been very many decisions and judgments in respect of applications against the United Kingdom in 2008 as the Strasbourg Court clears the decks of the backlog of applications concerning alleged discrimination in the sphere of bereavement benefits. The lead judgments on these benefits are *Willis, Runkee and White,* and *Hobbs, Richard, Walsh and Geen.*

AL (Serbia) v Secretary of State for the Home Department; R. (on the application of Rudi) v Secretary of State for the Home Department [2008] UKHL 42, contains a very helpful discussion by Baroness Hale of aspects of Art.14 at paras 20–35. This stresses that Strasbourg case law does not place great emphasis on the identification of an exact comparator, rather asking whether differences in otherwise similar situations justify a different treatment. It is also hinted that too much attention has been focused on the notion of 'personal characteristic' which is not central to the Strasbourg case law, although clearly differences based on such matters as sex, race or ethnic origin will require very weighty reasons if they are not to be condemned as violations of Art.14.

The issue of what is required for Art.14 to bite is taken up in *R. (on the application of RJM) v Secretary of State for Work and Pensions,* [2008] UKHL 63 (summarised in the annotations to Art.1 of Protocol 1 below). Lord Walker says:

"5. The other point on which I would comment is the expression "personal characteristics" used by the European Court of Human Rights in *Kjeldsen, Busk, Madsen and Pedersen v Denmark* (1976) 1 EHRR 711, and repeated in some later cases. "Personal characteristics" is not a precise expression and to my mind a binary approach to its meaning is unhelpful. "Personal characteristics" are more like a series of concentric circles. The most personal characteristics are those which are innate, largely immutable, and closely connected with an individual's personality: gender, sexual orientation, pigmentation of skin, hair and eyes, congenital disabilities. Nationality, language, religion and politics may be almost innate (depending on a person's family circumstances at birth) or may be acquired (though some religions do not countenance either apostates or converts); but all are regarded as important to the development of an individual's personality (they reflect, it might be said, important values protected by articles 8, 9 and 10 of the Convention). Other acquired characteristics are further out in the concentric circles; they are more concerned with what people do, or with what happens to them, than with who they are; but they may still come within article 14 (Lord Neuberger instances military status, residence or domicile, and past employment in the KGB). Like him, I would include homelessness as falling within that range, whether or not it is regarded as a matter of choice (it is often the culmination of a series of misfortunes that overwhelm an individual so that he or she can no longer cope). The more peripheral or debateable any suggested personal characteristic is, the less likely it is to come within the most sensitive area where discrimination is particularly difficult to justify."

Lord Neuberger addresses paras 35–47 to this issue in reversing the Court of Appeal to hold that homelessness is a status within Art.14. In para.45 he says:

"45. Further, while reformulations are dangerous, I consider that the concept of *"personal* characteristic" (not surprisingly, like the concept of status) generally requires one to concentrate on what somebody is, rather than what he is doing or what is being done to him. Such a characterisation approach appears not only consistent with the natural meaning of the expression, but also with the approach of the ECtHR and of this House to the issue. Hence, in *Gerger v Turkey* (App.24919/94) (unreported) 8 July 1999, the ECtHR held there could be no breach of Art.14 where the law concerned provided that "people who commit terrorist offences . . . will be treated less favourably with regard to automatic parole than persons convicted under the ordinary law", because "the distinction is made not between different groups of people, but between different types of offence" (para.69). It appears to me that, on this approach, homelessness is an "other status".

p.1255, *annotations to Art.14 ECHR (Carson v United Kingdom)*

4.198   The Strasbourg Court has delivered judgment in *Carson v United Kingdom,* (App.42184/05), Judgment of November 4, 2008, relating to the uprating of pensions abroad. In a six to one majority decision, the Strasbourg Court, largely adopting the reasoning of the House of Lords, decided that there had been no violation of Art.14 when taken in conjunction with Art.1 of Protocol 1. Though it conceded that place of residence could constitute 'other status' under Art.14, the Chamber decided that persons subject to up-rating and persons not entitled to up-rating of their pensions were not in an analogous position. But even if Art.14 applied, the differential treatment was justifiable. The Court declined to consider the complaint of a violation of Art.14 taken in conjunctions with Art.8.

p.1270, *annotations to Art.1 of Protocol 1*

4.199   In *R. (on the application of RJM) v Secretary of State for Work and Pensions,* [2008] UKHL 63, the House of Lords ruled that a question of entitlement to a disability premium as part of income support falls within the ambit of Art.1 of Protocol 1 such that Art.14 is engaged. The House affirms the general application of the Styrasbroug Court's decision in *Steç.* Lord Neuberger says:

"31. ... I recognise that the admissibility decision in *Stec* represents a departure from the principle normally applied to claims which rely on A1P1. However, *Stec* 41 EHRR SE295 was a carefully considered decision, in which the relevant authorities and principles were fully canvassed, and where the Grand Chamber of the ECtHR came to a clear conclusion, which was expressly intended to be generally applied by national courts. Accordingly, it seems to me that it would require the most exceptional circumstances before any national court should refuse to apply the decision."

The House went on to conclude that homelessness was a status within Art.14, but that the differential treatment could be justified.

pp.1283–1286, *Tribunals, Courts and Enforcement Act 2007, annotation to ss.3 to 6*

These sections came into force on November 3, 2008 together with   **4.200** most of the other provisions of Part 1 of the Act. From that date, the only provision of the Act that is reproduced in the main work but is not in force is s.27(1) to (4), which will come into force on April 1, 2009.

pp.1287–1288, *Tribunals, Courts and Enforcement Act 2007, annotation to s.7*

Following a political campaign to prevent the abolition of the Pensions   **4.201** Appeal Tribunal in England and Wales, a compromise was reached whereby the functions of that tribunal would be transferred into a separate chamber instead of the Social Entitlement Chamber. Consequently, the First-tier Tribunal and Upper Tribunal (Chambers) Order 2008 (SI 2008/2684) created three chambers in the First-tier Tribunal with effect from November 3, 2008: the Social Entitlement Chamber, the War Pensions and Armed Forces Compensation Chamber and the Health, Education and Social Care Chamber. Dr Harcourt Concannon, the former President of the Pensions Appeal Tribunal in England and Wales, has been appointed as the Acting Chamber President of the War Pensions and Armed Forces Compensation Chamber.

The Order also created the Administrative Appeals Chamber in the Upper Tribunal, as expected. His Honour Judge Gary Hickinbottom, who was the Acting Chamber President, has been appointed a High Court Judge from January 1, 2009 and is the Chamber President from that date until April 2009.

pp.1289–1290, *Tribunals, Courts and Enforcement Act 2007, annotation to s.9*

Rule 40(2) of the Tribunal Procedure (First-tier Tribunal) (Social   **4.202** Entitlement Chamber) Rules 2008 (SI 2008/2685) (set out in Pt 1 of this Supplement) provides that, in social security cases, the First-tier Tribunal may only undertake a review of a decision where there has been an application for permission to appeal and it is satisfied that there has been an error of law in the decision. When there is an application for permission to appeal, r.39(1) requires the tribunal to consider whether to review the decision before considering whether to grant permission to appeal. Because s.13(3) of the Social Security Act 1998 remains in force, the First-tier Tribunal *must* set aside its decision if all the principal parties express the view that a decision to which s.13(3) applies is erroneous in point of law. Section 13(3) applies only to decisions made under s.12 of the 1998 Act. There are similar provisions in legislation relating to housing benefit and council tax benefit and to child support, but not, for instance, in the Social Security (Recovery of Benefits) Act 1997.

Rule 40(3) and (4) provides for notice of a review decision and for the right to make representations and apply for a review decision to be set aside where a decision has been reviewed without notice to a party.

Note that tax credit and child trust fund penalty cases are "excluded decisions" until April 1, 2009 (see the annotation to s.11) and so there is no power to review such decisions. Nor does s.13(3) of the 1998 Act apply to them.

pp.1291–1291, *Tribunals, Courts and Enforcement Act 2007, annotation to s.10*

4.203   Rule 46(1) of the Tribunal Procedure (Upper Tribunal) Rules 2008 (SI 2008/2698) (set out in Pt 1 of this Supplement) provides that the Upper Tribunal may only undertake a review of a decision if it has received an application for permission to appeal or the decision was made under the Forfeiture Act 1982. In forfeiture cases, there are wide powers of review under r.47, which replace the powers of supersession formerly found in reg.15(3) of the Social Security Commissioners (Procedure) Regulations 1999 (see p.520 of Vol.III of the main work). In other cases, a decision may be reviewed only if, when making the decision, the Upper Tribunal overlooked a legislative provision or binding decision of a court or such a binding decision has been made since the Upper Tribunal gave its decision (see r.45(1)).

p.1293, *Tribunals, Courts and Enforcement Act 2007, annotation to s.11*

Subs. (1)

In *Dorset Healthcare NHS Foundation Trust v MH* [2009] UKUT 4 (AAC), it was argued that the word "decision" subs.(1) was not to be construed as narrowly as the same word had been in s.14(1) of the Social Security Act 1998 so as to exclude most interlocutory decisions (see *Morina v Secretary of State for Work and Pensions* [2007] EWCA Civ 749; [2007] 1 W.L.R. 3033 (also reported as (*R(IS) 6/07*)), because in s.11 there is the power to exclude classes of decision by order under subs.(5)(f) and even without there being such an order disproportionate interlocutory appeals could be prevented by the expedient of refusing permission. It was unnecessary for the Upper Tribunal to rule on the argument as it accepted that the particular interlocutory decision in issue was appealable in any event.

Subs. (4)   **4.204**

See rr.38 and 39 of the Tribunal Procedure (First-tier Tribunal) (Social Entitlement Chamber) Rules 2008 and rr.21 and 22 of the Tribunal Procedure (Upper Tribunal) Rules 2008 for procedural provisions in relations to applications for permission to appeal. Rule 21(2) of the Upper Tribunal Rules requires that a person apply to the First-tier Tribunal for permission before applying to the Upper Tribunal.

Subs. (5)   **4.205**

Although no appeal lies under s.11 in criminal injuries compensation cases (see subs.(5)(a)), the Lord Chief Justice has made a practice direction under s.18(6) having the effect that an application for judicial review of a decision of the First-tier Tribunal in a criminal injuries compensation case in England and Wales must be made to the Upper Tribunal or, if made to the Administrative Court, must be transferred to the Upper Tribunal.

The Appeals (Excluded Decisions) Order 2008 (SI 2008/2707, as amended by SI 2008/2780), made under subs.(5)(f), excludes asylum support cases, as expected, and also tax credit and child trust fund penalty cases. The exclusion of the penalty cases is merely because the consequential amendments made by paras 191(4) and 202(2) of Sch.3 to the Transfer of Tribunal Functions Order 2008 (see p.1357 of vol III of the main work) have the effect that an appeal to the Upper Tribunal in such cases lies under s.63(6) of the Tax Credits Act 2002 and s.24(2) of the Child Trust Funds Act 2004, respectively. Consequently, such appeals are not confined to points of law. Note, however, that from April 1, 2009, the 2002 and 2004 Acts will be amended so that the broad right of appeal to the Upper Tribunal in penalty cases will co-exist with the right of appeal on points of law under s.11 (see paras 318, 320 and 415 of Sch.1 to the Transfer of Tribunal Functions and Revenue and Customs Appeals Order 2009). Presumably the 2008 Order will be amended accordingly. The main practical advantage will be to allow the First-tier Tribunal to review such decisions under s.9.

As expected, appeals in vaccine damage cases and appeals under the Road Traffic (NHS Charges) Act 1999 have not been excluded. Note that appeals under the 1999 Act were within the jurisdiction of appeal tribunals constituted under the Social Security Act 1998 (see s.9 of the Act and reg.12 of the Road Traffic (NHS Charges) (Reviews and Appeals) Regulations 1999) only in England and Wales and so appeals lie to the First-tier Tribunal with a right of further appeal to the Upper Tribunal only in England and Wales. Note also that, whereas an appeal to the Upper Tribunal in a vaccine damage case lies only against a decision given on or after November 3, 2008, the right of appeal to the Upper Tribunal in respect of cases under the 1999 Act is made retrospective and applies to decisions of appeal tribunals, unless an appeal was actually commenced in the High Court before that date (Tribunals, Courts and Enforcement Act 2007 (Transitional and Consequential Provisions) Order 2008 (SI 2008/2683), art.5).

p.1296, *Tribunals, Courts and Enforcement Act 2007, annotation to s.13*

4.206   For the procedure for applying to the Upper Tribunal for permission to appeal, see rr.44 and 45 of the Tribunal Procedure (Upper Tribunal) Rules 2008. Note that r.44(6)(b) provides that, where the Upper Tribunal refuses to extend the time for applying for permission to appeal, it must refuse permission to appeal, thus satisfying the condition of s.13(5) and reversing the effect of *White v Chief Adjudication Officer* [1986] 2 All E.R. 905 (also reported as an appendix to *R(S) 8/85*). In *White*, it had been held that a Commissioner's refusal to extend time for applying for leave to appeal to the Court of Appeal did not amount to a refusal of leave and was challengeable only by way of an application for judicial review. Now, if permission is refused by the Upper Tribunal on the ground of delay, it is possible simply to make an application for permission to the appellate court, although that court will of course have regard to the delay in applying to the Upper Tribunal. The Appeals from the Upper Tribunal to the Court of Appeal Order 2008 (SI 2008/2834) provides that permission to appeal from a decision of the Upper Tribunal may not be given unless one of the conditions set out in subs.(6)(a) and (b) applies. Although the Order does not say so, it can apply only to decisions made by the Upper Tribunal on appeals under s.11, because subs.(7) limits the scope of the order-making power in subs.(6) to such cases.

pp.1298–1299, *Tribunals, Courts and Enforcement Act 2007, annotations to ss.15 and 16*

4.207   For the procedure for applying to the Upper Tribunal for judicial review, see rr.27 to 33 of the Tribunal Procedure (Upper Tribunal) Rules 2008.

p.1301, *Tribunals, Courts and Enforcement Act 2007, annotation to s.18*

4.208   The classes of case specified by way of a Practice Direction of the Lord Chief Justice of England and Wales under subs.(6) are—

"(a) Any decision of the First-tier Tribunal on an appeal made in the exercise of a right conferred by the Criminal Injuries Compensation Scheme in compliance with section 5(1) of the Criminal Injuries Compensation Act 1995 (appeals against decisions on review) and

(b) Any decision of the First-tier Tribunal made under Tribunal Procedure Rules or section 9 of the 2007 Act where there is no right of appeal to the Upper Tribunal and that decision is not an excluded decision within paragraph (b), (c), or (f) of section 11(5) of the 2007 Act."

This Practice Direction does not apply where the applicant seeks a declaration of incompatibility under s.4 of the Human Rights Act 1998 (see p.1208 of vol III of the main work).

p.1303, *Tribunals, Courts and Enforcement Act 2007, annotation to s.22*

See the Tribunal Procedure (First-tier Tribunal) (Social Entitlement 4.209
Chamber) Rules 2008 and the Tribunal Procedure (Upper Tribunal)
Rules 2008, set out in Pt 1 of this Supplement.

pp.1303–1304, *Tribunals, Courts and Enforcement Act 2007, annotation
to s.23*

The Senior President of Tribunals has made two Practice Directions 4.210
relating to proceedings in both the First-tier Tribunal and the Upper
Tribunal, one relating just to the Upper Tribunal and four relating only
to the First-tier Tribunal. None of the Practice Directions relating only
to the First-tier Tribunal is relevant to social security cases. The other
Directions are set out here.

"CHILD, VULNERABLE ADULT AND SENSITIVE WITNESSES

1. In this Practice Direction:
   a. "child" means a person who has not attained the age of 18;
   b. "vulnerable adult" has the same meaning as in the Safeguarding
      Vulnerable Groups Act 2006;
   c. "sensitive witness" means an adult witness where the quality of
      evidence given by the witness is likely to be diminished by
      reason of fear or distress on the part of the witness in connec-
      tion with giving evidence in the case.

Circumstances under which a child, vulnerable adult or sensitive witness may give evidence

2. A child, vulnerable adult or sensitive witness will only be required
to attend as a witness and give evidence at a hearing where the
Tribunal determines that the evidence is necessary to enable the fair
hearing of the case and their welfare would not be prejudiced by doing
so.

3. In determining whether it is necessary for a child, vulnerable
adult or sensitive witness to give evidence to enable the fair hearing of
a case the Tribunal should have regard to all the available evidence and
any representations made by the parties.

4. In determining whether the welfare of the child, vulnerable adult
or sensitive witness would be prejudiced it may be appropriate for the
Tribunal to invite submissions from interested persons, such as a
child's parents.

5. The Tribunal may decline to issue a witness summons under the
Tribunal Procedure Rules or to permit a child, vulnerable adult or
sensitive witness to give evidence where it is satisfied that the evidence
is not necessary to enable the fair hearing of the case and must decline
to do so where the witness's welfare would be prejudiced by them
giving evidence.

Manner in which evidence is given

6. The Tribunal must consider how to facilitate the giving of any evidence by a child, vulnerable adult or sensitive witness.

7. It may be appropriate for the Tribunal to direct that the evidence should be given by telephone, video link or other means directed by the Tribunal, or to direct that a person be appointed for the purpose of the hearing who has the appropriate skills or experience in facilitating the giving of evidence by a child, vulnerable adult or sensitive witness.

8. This Practice Direction is made by the Senior President of Tribunals with the agreement of the Lord Chancellor. It is made in the exercise of powers conferred by the Tribunals, Courts and Enforcement Act 2007."

"USE OF THE WELSH LANGUAGE IN TRIBUNALS IN WALES

General

1. The purpose of this Practice Direction is to reflect the principle of the Welsh Language Act 1993 that in the administration of justice in Wales, the English and Welsh languages should be treated on a basis of equality.

2. In this Practice Direction "Welsh case" means a case which is before the Tribunal in which all "individual parties" are resident in Wales or which has been classified as a Welsh case by the Tribunal. An "individual party" is a party other than a Government Department or Agency. Where not all of the "individual parties" are resident in Wales the Tribunal will decide whether the case should be classified as a Welsh case or not.

Use of the Welsh language

3. In a Welsh case the Welsh language may be used by any party or witnesses or in any document placed before the Tribunal or (subject to the listing provisions below) at any hearing.

Listing

4. Unless it is not reasonably practicable to do so a party, or their representative, must inform the Tribunal 21 days before any hearing in a Welsh case that the Welsh language will be used by the party, their representative, any witness to be called by that party or in any document to be produced by the party.

5. Where the proceedings are on appeal to the Upper Tribunal and the Welsh language was used in the Tribunal below, the Tribunal Manager must make arrangements for the continued use of the Welsh language in the proceedings before the Upper Tribunal.

6. Where practicable, a hearing in which the Welsh language is to be used must be listed before a Welsh speaking Tribunal and, where translation facilities are needed, at a venue with simultaneous translation facilities.

Interpreters

7. Whenever an interpreter is needed to translate evidence from English into Welsh or from Welsh into English, the Tribunal Manager in whose tribunal the case is to be heard must ensure that the attendance is secured of an interpreter whose name is included in the list of approved interpreters.

Witnesses

8. When a witness in a case in which the Welsh language may be used is required to give evidence on oath or affirmation the Tribunal must inform the witness that they may be sworn or affirm in Welsh or English as they wish.

9. This Practice Direction is made by the Senior President of Tribunals with the agreement of the Lord Chancellor. It is made in the exercise of powers conferred by the Tribunals, Courts and Enforcement Act 2007."

"UPPER TRIBUNAL
TRANSCRIPTS OF PROCEEDINGS

1. At any hearing where the proceedings are recorded such recordings must be preserved by the Tribunal for six months from the date of the hearing to which the recording relates, and any party to the proceedings may, within that period, apply in writing for a transcript and a transcript must be supplied to that party.

2. If a transcript is supplied to a party under paragraph 1, that party must pay for the production and supply of the transcript unless they have applied in writing for, and the Tribunal has given, a direction that the transcript be produced and supplied at public expense.

3. The Tribunal may direct a transcript be supplied at public expense if satisfied that:

    a.   a recording of the relevant proceedings is in existence; and

    b.   the party making the application;

        i. has applied, or intends to apply, for permission to challenge the Upper Tribunal's decision in another court and has reasonable grounds for bringing or intending to challenge that decision; or

       ii. has been granted permission to challenge the Upper Tribunal's decision and has brought, or intends to bring, such proceedings; or

       iii. is a respondent to any such challenge to a decision of the
Upper Tribunal in another court; and

    c. the transcript is necessary for the purpose of challenging the
Upper Tribunal's decision; and

    d. the party's financial circumstances are such that that party
cannot afford to pay for the transcript from their own income or
funds.

4. Any transcript of proceedings directed to be supplied at public
expense must be restricted to that part of the proceedings necessary
for the purposes of any such challenge.

5. For the purposes of considering an application for a transcript at
public expense, the Tribunal may give directions, for example, requiring the party to disclose details of their financial circumstances.

6. This Practice Direction is made by the Senior President of
Tribunals with the agreement of the Lord Chancellor. It is made in the
exercise of powers conferred by the Tribunals, Courts and Enforcement Act 2007."

Practice Directions are published at—http://www.tribunals.gov.uk/
Tribunals/Rules/directions.htm.

Note that, where a Practice Direction imposes obligations on a party
to proceedings, a breach of the Practice Direction has the same effect as
a breach of Tribunal Procedure Rules or a direction made by a tribunal
and can result in a case being struck out (see r.7(2) of the Tribunal
Procedure (First-tier Tribunal) (Social Entitlement Chamber) Rules
2008 and r.7(2) of the Tribunal Procedure (Upper Tribunal) Rules
2008.

p.1304, *Tribunals, Courts and Enforcement Act 2007, annotation to s.24*

4.211   See r.3 of the Tribunal Procedure (First-tier Tribunal) (Social Entitlement Chamber) Rules 2008 and r.3 of the Tribunal Procedure (Upper
Tribunal) Rules 2008.

p.1305, *Tribunals, Courts and Enforcement Act 2007, annotation to s.25*

4.212   Where a person has failed to comply with a relevant requirement in
First-tier Tribunal proceedings, that tribunal may refer the case to the
Upper Tribunal which may exercise its powers under this section as
though the First-tier Tribunal had been the Upper Tribunal (see r.7(3)
of the Tribunal Procedure (First-tier Tribunal) (Social Entitlement
Chamber) Rules 2008 and r.7(3) and (4) of the Tribunal Procedure
(Upper Tribunal) Rules 2008). The powers of the High Court and the
Court of Session include the power to punish a person for contempt of
court. Failure to comply with a direction, order, summons or citation
issued by a tribunal is a contempt of court but is unlikely to be punish-
able unless accompanied by a warning (which is a specific requirement
in respect of orders, summonses and citations issued under r.16 of either
set of Rules). The maximum punishment that may be imposed is a

sentence of two years' imprisonment or an unlimited fine (see the Contempt of Court Act 1981 ss.14 and 15).

pp.1305–1306, *Tribunals, Courts and Enforcement Act 2007, s.27*

Subsections (1) to (4) will not be brought into force until April 1, 2009   **4.213**
(Tribunals, Courts and Enforcement Act 2007 (Commencement No.6 and Transitional Provisions) Order 2008 (SI 2008/2696), art.6(a)).

p.1307, *Tribunals, Courts and Enforcement Act 2007, annotation to s.29*

Contrary to the suggestion in the main work, it is at least arguable that   **4.214**
there is no power to make a wasted costs order in the Social Entitlement Chamber of the First-tier Tribunal or in the Upper Tribunal on appeal from that chamber. Rule 10 of the Tribunal Procedure (First-tier Tribunal) (Social Entitlement Chamber) Rules 2008 provides that the tribunal "shall not make any order in respect of costs (or, in Scotland, expenses)" and r.10(1)(a) of the Tribunal Procedure (Upper Tribunal) Rules 2008 applies the same approach to appeals from the Social Entitlement Chamber. The doubt arises because Tribunal Procedure Rules may qualify only subss.(1) and (2) of s.29. If subs.(4) confers a free-standing power, it remains available notwithstanding the Tribunal Procedure Rules. However, the better approach may be that subs.(4) merely describes the circumstances in which the broad power in subs.(2) to determine "by whom" costs are to be paid is to be exercised against representatives.

p.1313, *Tribunals, Courts and Enforcement Act 2007, annotation to s.40*

Rule 4 of the Tribunal Procedure (First-tier Tribunal) (Social Entitle-   **4.215**
ment Chamber) Rules 2008 and r.4 of the Tribunal Procedure (Upper Tribunal) Rules 2008 provide for the delegation of judicial functions of the tribunals to staff, subject to the approval of the Senior President of Tribunals. For the extent to which the Senior President of Tribunals has given his approval, see the annotations to those provisions in Pt 1 of this Supplement.

Staff appointed to tribunals whose functions have been transferred to the First-tier Tribunal or the Upper Tribunal are treated as having been appointed under this section (Tribunals, Courts and Enforcement Act 2007 (Commencement No.6 and Transitional Provisions) Order 2008 (SI 2008/2696), art.3).

p.1321, *Tribunals, Courts and Enforcement Act 2007, annotation to Sch.2*

Article 2(2)(a) and (i) and (3) of the Qualifications for Appointment   **4.216**
of Members to the First-tier Tribunal and Upper Tribunal Order 2008 (SI 2008/2692), made under para.2(2) of Sch.2, prescribes qualifications similar to those formerly required of medically qualified panel members, financially qualified panel members and disability qualified panel members of appeal tribunals.

p.1334, *Tribunals, Courts and Enforcement Act 2007, annotation to Sch.4, para.15*

4.217   The First-tier Tribunal and Upper Tribunal (Composition of Tribunal) Order 2008 (SI 2008/2835) (see pp.1359–1361 of the main work) prescribes the composition of tribunals in broad terms and the Senior President of Tribunals has issued a Practice Statement that more or less maintains the *status quo* as to the precise composition of tribunals to hear particular cases (see the supplementary annotation to the Composition of Tribunal Order, below).

p.1340, *Tribunals, Courts and Enforcement Act 2007, annotation to Sch.5*

4.218   See the Tribunal Procedure (First-tier Tribunal) (Social Entitlement Chamber) Rules 2008 and the Tribunal Procedure (Upper Tribunal) Rules 2008, set out in Pt 1 of this Supplement.

pp.1344–1359, *Transfer of Tribunal Functions Order 2008*

4.219   This Order was approved by the House of Lords on October 23, 2008 and has been numbered SI 2008/2833. As mentioned in the annotation on p.1344 of the main work, the Order had already been approved by the House of Commons but Lord Craig of Radley had put down a motion opposing the Order. He also put down a Parliamentary Question asking why the Pensions Appeal Tribunal in England and Wales was being abolished, which resulted in a debate on October 14, 2008. In the course of his answer to the question, Lord Bach, the Parliamentary Under-Secretary of State, Ministry of Justice, indicated that it had been accepted by the Government that the functions of the Pensions Appeal Tribunal in England and Wales should be transferred to a separate chamber of the First-tier Tribunal. A joint statement by the Minister and the Senior President of Tribunals, issued on October 16, 2008, gave further details and assurances. In the light of those assurances, Lord Craig withdrew his motion (or, more accurately, an amendment to the motion that the Order be approved) on October 23, 2008 and so the Order was passed, only a week and a half before it was to come into force.

pp.1359–1361, *Composition of Tribunal Order*

4.220   This Order was approved by the House of Lords on October 23, 2008 and has been numbered SI 2008/2835. The Senior President has issued a number of Practice Statements, setting out his determinations under arts 2(1), 3(2), 4(2) and 6 as to how, and in what circumstances, a tribunal should be constituted otherwise than in the default position provided in the Order. (A Practice Statement is different from a Practice Direction under s.23, which would require the approval of the Lord Chancellor and would be inappropriate in this context since it is the Senior President of Tribunals alone who is given the function of making the determinations under the Order, which has itself been made by the

Lord Chancellor.) The Practice Statements in respect of the composition of tribunals relevant to social security cases are in the following terms—

"COMPOSITION OF TRIBUNALS IN SOCIAL SECURITY AND CHILD SUPPORT CASES IN THE SOCIAL ENTITLEMENT CHAMBER ON OR AFTER 3 NOVEMBER 2008

1. In this Practice Statement;
a. "the 2008 Order" means the First-tier Tribunal and Upper Tribunal (Composition of Tribunal) Order 2008;
b. "the Qualifications Order" means the Qualifications for Appointment of Members to the First-tier Tribunal and Upper Tribunal Order 2008;
c. "the 2008 Rules" means the Tribunal Procedure (First-tier Tribunal) (Social Entitlement Chamber) Rules 2008;
d. "social security and child support case" has the meaning given in rule 1(3) of the 2008 Rules.
2. In exercise of the powers conferred by the 2008 Order the Senior President of Tribunals makes the following determinations and supplementary provision:-
3. The number of members of the Tribunal must not exceed three.
4. Where the appeal relates to an attendance allowance or a disability living allowance under Part III of the Social Security Contributions and Benefits Act 1992, the Tribunal must, subject to paragraphs 8 to 13, consist of a Tribunal Judge, a Tribunal Member who is a registered medical practitioner, and a Tribunal Member who has a disability qualification as set out in article 2(3) of the Qualifications Order.
5. Where—
a. the appeal involves the personal capability assessment, as defined in regulation 2(1) of the Social Security (Incapacity for Work)(General) Regulations 1995;
b. the appeal involves the limited capability for work assessment, as defined in regulation 2(1) of the Employment and Support Allowance Regulations 2008;
c. the appeal involves the determination of limited capability for work- related activity within the meaning of regulations 34 and 35 of the Employment and Support Allowance Regulations 2008;
d. the appeal is made under section 11(1)(b) of the Social Security (Recovery of Benefits) Act 1997;
e. the appeal raises issues relating to severe disablement allowance under section 68 of the Social Security Contributions and Benefits Act 1992 or industrial injuries benefit under Part V of that Act (except for an appeal where the only issue is whether there

657

should be a declaration of an industrial accident under section 29(2) of the Social Security Act 1998);

f.   the appeal is made under section 4 of the Vaccine Damage Payments Act 1979;

g.   the appeal is against a certificate of NHS charges under section 157(1) of the Health and Social Care (Community Health and Standards) Act 2003;

h.   the appeal arises under Part IV of the Child Maintenance and Other Payments Act 2008;

the Tribunal must, subject to paragraphs 7 to 14, consist of a Tribunal Judge and a Tribunal Member who is a registered medical practitioner.

6. In any other case the Tribunal must consist of a Tribunal Judge.

7. The Chamber President may determine that the Tribunal constituted under paragraph 5 or 6 must also include—

a.   a Tribunal Member who is an accountant within the meaning of Article 2(i) of the Qualifications Order, where the appeal may require the examination of financial accounts;

b.   an additional Member who is a registered medical practitioner, where the complexity of the medical issues in the appeal so demands;

c.   such an additional Tribunal Judge or Member as he considers appropriate for the purposes of providing further experience for that additional Judge or Member or for assisting the Chamber President in the monitoring of standards of decision-making.

8. Where the Chamber President considers, in a particular case, that a matter that would otherwise be decided in accordance with paragraphs 4 or 5 only raises questions of law and the expertise of any of the other members is not necessary to decide the matter, the Chamber President may direct that the Tribunal must consist of a Tribunal Judge, or a Tribunal Judge and any Tribunal Member whose experience and qualifications are necessary to decide the matter.

9. The powers of the Chamber President referred to in paragraphs 7, 8, 10 and 12 may be delegated to a Regional Tribunal Judge and those referred to in paragraphs 7, 8 and 12 may be delegated to a District Tribunal Judge.

10. A decision, including a decision to give a direction or make an order, made under, or in accordance with, rules 5 to 9, 11, 14 to 19, 25(3), 30, 32, 36, 37 or 41 of the 2008 Rules may be made by a Tribunal Judge, except that a decision made under, or in accordance, with rule 7(3) or rule 5(3)(b) to treat a case as a lead case (whether in accordance with rule 18 (lead cases) or otherwise) of the 2008 Rules must be made by the Chamber President.

11. The determination of an application for permission to appeal under rule 38 of the 2008 Rules and the exercise of the power of review under section 9 of the Tribunals, Courts and Enforcement Act 2007 must be carried out—

a. where the Judge who constituted or was a member of the Tribunal that made the decision was a fee-paid Judge, by a salaried Tribunal Judge; or

b. where the Judge who constituted or was a member of the Tribunal that made the decision was a salaried Judge, by that Judge or, if it would be impracticable or cause undue delay, by another salaried Tribunal Judge,

save that, where the decision is set aside under section 9(4)(c) of the Act, the matter may only be re-decided under section 9(5)(a) by a Tribunal composed in accordance with paragraph 4, 5 or 6 above.

12. Where the Tribunal consists of a Tribunal Judge and one or two Tribunal Members, the Tribunal Judge shall be the presiding member. Where the Tribunal comprises more than one Tribunal Judge, the Chamber President must select the presiding member. The presiding member may regulate the procedure of the Tribunal.

13. Under rule 34(2) of the 2008 Rules it will be for the presiding member to give any written statement of reasons.

14. In rule 25(2) (Medical and physical examination in appeals under section 12 of the Social Security Act 1998) of the 2008 Rules "an appropriate member" of the Tribunal is a Tribunal Member who is a registered medical practitioner."

"COMPOSITION OF TRIBUNALS IN RELATION TO MATTERS THAT FALL TO BE DECIDED BY THE ADMINISTRATIVE APPEALS CHAMBER OF THE UPPER TRIBUNAL ON OR AFTER 3 NOVEMBER 2008

1. In this Practice Statement;

a. "the 2007 Act" means the Tribunals, Courts and Enforcement Act 2007;

b. "the 2008 Order" means the First-tier Tribunal and Upper Tribunal (Composition of Tribunal) Order 2008;

c. "the 2008 Rules" means the Upper Tribunal Rules 2008;

2. In exercise of the powers conferred by the 2008 Order the Senior President of Tribunals makes the following determinations and supplementary provision:—

3. In accordance with articles 3 and 4 of the 2008 Order, any matter that falls to be decided by the Administrative Appeals Chamber of the Upper Tribunal is to be decided by one judge of the Upper Tribunal (or by a Registrar if the Senior President of Tribunals has approved that they may decide the matter) except that—

a. where the Senior President of Tribunals or the Chamber President considers that the matter involves a question of law of special difficulty or an important point of principle or practice, or that it is otherwise appropriate, the matter is to be decided by two or three judges of the Upper Tribunal; and

b. where the matter is the determination of an appeal brought under section 4 of the Safeguarding Vulnerable Groups Act

2006 (otherwise than by the striking out of the appeal under rule 8(2) or (3)(a) or (b) of the 2008 Rules), the matter is to be decided by—

  i. one judge and two other members of the Upper Tribunal; or

  ii. where the Senior President of Tribunals or Chamber President considers that the matter involves a question of law of special difficulty or an important point of principle or practice, or that it is otherwise appropriate, two judges and one other member of the Upper Tribunal.

4. Other members of the Upper Tribunal may be chosen under paragraph 3(b) only if they satisfy the requirements of paragraph 5 or the requirements of paragraphs 6 and 7.

5. The requirements of this paragraph are—

a. experience in the provision of services which must or may be provided by local authorities under the Adoption Act 1976 or the Children Act 1989 or which are similar to such services, and

b. experience in relevant social work.

6. The requirements of this paragraph are—

a. experience in the provision of services by a Health Authority, a Special Health Authority, a National Health Service trust, an NHS foundation trust or a Primary Care Trust;

b. experience in the provision of education in a school or in an institution within the further education sector; or

c. experience of being employed by a local education authority in connection with the exercise of its functions under Part I of the Education Act 1996.

7. The requirements of this paragraph are—

a. experience in the conduct of disciplinary investigations;

b. experience on an Area Child Protection Committee, or similar experience;

c. experience of taking part in child protection conferences or in child protection review conferences, or similar experience; or

d. experience in negotiation the conditions of service of employees.

8. Where more than one member of the Upper Tribunal is to decide a matter, the "presiding member" for the purposes of article 7 of the 2008 Order and the paragraphs below is—

a. the senior judge, as determined by the Senior President of Tribunals or Chamber President, if the tribunal is composed under paragraph 3(a) of (b)(ii); or

b. the judge if the tribunal is composed under paragraph 3(b)(i).

9. Where, under paragraph 3(a) or (b), two or three members of the Upper Tribunal have been chosen to give a decision that will, or may, dispose of proceedings, any ancillary matter that arises before that decision is given may be decided by—

a. the presiding member; or

b. by all the members so chosen; or

   c. otherwise than at a hearing, by a judge or Registrar (who the Senior President of Tribunals has approved may decide the matter) nominated by the Chamber President or presiding member.

10. Where the Upper Tribunal has given a decision that disposes of proceedings ("the substantive decision"), any matter decided under, or in accordance with, rule 5(3)(l) or Part 7 of the 2008 Rules or section 9 of the 2007 Act must be decided by the same member or members of the Upper Tribunal as gave the substantive decision.

11. Paragraph 10 does not apply where complying with it would be impractical or would cause undue delay and, in such a case, the matter decided under, or in accordance with, rule 5(3)(l) or Part 7 of the 2008 Rules or section 9 of the 2007 Act must be decided by—

   a. if the substantive decision was given by more than one member of the Upper Tribunal and the presiding member or any other judge from that constitution is available, the members of the Upper Tribunal who gave the substantive decision and are available to decide the matter;

   b. otherwise, another judge of the Upper Tribunal nominated by the Chamber President."

These Practice Statements are intended largely to continue the practice in appeal tribunals and for Commissioners. The Practice Statement for the First-tier Tribunal therefore largely replicates regs 36 and 58(6) of the Social Security and Child Support (Decisions and Appeals) Regulations 1999 but para.8 provides for rather more flexibility and makes it unnecessary for a tribunal to include expert members when only points of law arise. In the Upper Tribunal, para.3(a) of the Practice Statement for the Upper Tribunal provides for the tribunal to be composed of more than one judge in circumstances where a Tribunal of Commissioners could formerly have been constituted under s.16(7) of the Social Security Act 1998. Again there is more flexibility. Two or three judges (as opposed to three or more Commissioners, although the power to appoint more than three Commissioners that existed from 1999 was never exercised) may sit to consider a case raising an important point of principle or practice even if it does not involve a question of law of special difficulty.

All the Practice Statements are published at—*http://www.tribunals. gov.uk/Tribunals/Rules/statements.htm.*

PART V

UPDATING MATERIAL
VOLUME IV

TAX CREDITS AND EMPLOYER PAID
SOCIAL SECURITY

Commentary by

Nick Wikeley and David Williams

p.4, *arrangement of sections of Taxes Management Act 1970*

The title to s.34 should now read "Ordinary time limit of 4 years".   5.001

p.8, *amendment of the Taxes Management Act 1970, s.9ZB (correction of personal or trustee return by Revenue)*

With effect from April 6, 2008, s.119(1) of the Finance Act 2008   5.002
amended subs.(1) by inserting "(a) –" after "correct" and inserting at
the end

"and
  (b) anything else in the return that the officer has reason to believe
      is incorrect in the light of information available to the offi-
      cer."

p.10, *amendment of the Taxes Management Act 1970, s.12B (records to be kept for purposes of returns)*

With effect from April 6, 2008, s.115 of, and Sch.37, para.2 to, the   5.003
Finance Act 2008 amended s.12B in various respects. First, subs.(2) was
amended by substituting "otherwise" for "in any other case" in para.(b),
and inserting after that paragraph:

"or (in either case) such earlier day as may be specified in writing by
the Commissioners for Her Majesty's Revenue and Customs (and
different days may be specified for different cases)."

The same provisions omit para.(b) and the "and" before it in subs.(3)
and insert after it:

"(3A) The Commissioners for Her Majesty's Revenue and Customs
may by regulations—
  (a) provide that the records required to be kept and preserved
      under this section include, or do not include, records specified
      in the regulations, and
  (b) provide that those records include supporting documents so
      specified."

The Finance Act 2008 also substituted a new subs.(4) as follows:

"(4) The duty under subsection (1) or (2A) to preserve records may
be discharged—
  (a) by preserving them in any form and by any means, or
  (b) by preserving the information contained in them in any form
      and by any means, subject to subsection (4A) and any condi-
      tions or further exceptions specified in writing by the Commis-
      sioners for Her Majesty's Revenue and Customs."

Finally, the Finance Act 2008 substituted "Subsection (4)(b) does not
apply in the case of the following kinds of records" for "The records
which fall within this subsection are" in subs.(4A) and inserted after
subs.(5B) a new subs.(5C):

"(5C) Regulations under this section may—
(a) make different provision for different cases, and
(b) make provision by reference to things specified in a notice published by the Commissioners for Her Majesty's Revenue and Customs in accordance with the regulations (and not withdrawn by a subsequent notice)."

p.12, *amendment of the Taxes Management Act 1970, s.29 (assessment where loss of tax discovered)*

5.004   With effect from April 6, 2008, s.118 of, and Sch.39, para.3 to, the Finance Act 2008 amended subs.(4) by substituting "was brought about carelessly or deliberately by" for "is attributable to fraudulent or negligent conduct on the part of".

p.14, *amendment of the Taxes Management Act 1970, s.33 (error or mistake)*

5.005   With effect from April 6, 2008, s.118 of, and Sch.39 para.5 to, the Finance Act 2008 amended subs.(1) by substituting "not more than four years after the end of" for "not later than five years after the 31st January next following".

p.15, *amendment of the Taxes Management Act 1970, s.34 (ordinary time-limit of six years)*

5.006   With effect from April 6, 2008, s.118 of, and Sch.39 para.7 to, the Finance Act 2008 replaced the title of the section with "**Ordinary time limit of 4 years**" and substituted "not more than four years after the end of" for "not later than five years after the 31st January next following" in subs. (1).

p.15, *amendment of the Taxes Management Act 1970, s.35 (time-limit: income received after year for which they are assessable)*

5.007   With effect from April 6, 2008, s.118 of, and Sch.39 para.8 to, the Finance Act 2008 substituted "not more than four years after the end of" for "within six years after" in subs.(1).

p.15, *amendment of the Taxes Management Act 1970, s.36 (fraudulent or negligent conduct)*

5.008   With effect from April 6, 2008, s.118 of, and Sch.39 para.9 to, the Finance Act 2008 substituted "**Loss of tax brought about carelessly or deliberately etc**" for the heading **Fraudulent or negligent conduct**. In addition, the following further amendments were made. First, new subss.(1)–(1B) were substituted for subs.(1):

"(1) An assessment on a person in a case involving a loss of income tax or capital gains tax brought about carelessly by the person may be made at any time not more than 6 years after the end of the year of assessment to which it relates (subject to subsection (1A) and any other provision of the Taxes Acts allowing a longer period).

(1A) An assessment on a person in a case involving a loss of income tax or capital gains tax—

(a) brought about deliberately by the person,

(b) attributable to a failure by the person to comply with an obligation under section 7, or

(c) attributable to arrangements in respect of which the person has failed to comply with an obligation under section 309, 310 or 313 of the Finance Act 2004 (obligation of parties to tax avoidance schemes to provide information to Her Majesty's Revenue and Customs), may be made at any time not more than 20 years after the end of the year of assessment to which it relates (subject to any provision of the Taxes Acts allowing a longer period).

(1B) In subsections (1) and (1A) references to a loss brought about by the person who is the subject of the assessment include a loss brought about by another person acting on behalf of that person."

Secondly, in subs.(2) the amendments substituted "Where the person mentioned in subsection (1) or (1A) ("the person in default")" for "Where the person in default" and substituted "subsection (1A) or (1B)" for "subsection (1) above". Lastly, "or (1A)", was inserted after "(1)" in subs. (3) and "subsections (1) and (1A)" substituted for "subsection (1)" in subs.(4).

p.18, *amendment of the Taxes Management Act 1970, s.54(6) (settling of appeals by agreement)*

With effect from November 3, 2008, art.6(1) of, and Sch.1, para.193 to, the Tribunals, Courts and Enforcement Act 2007 (Transitional and Consequential Provisions) Order 2008 (SI 2008/2683) amended the Tax Credits (Appeals) Regulations 2002 (SI 2002/2926), reg.3, so as to remove sub-para.(a) in the modified subs.(6), along with the following "and" and "(b)".

p.21, *amendment of the Taxes Management Act 1970, s.118 (interpretation)*

With effect from April 6, 2008, s.118 of, and Sch.39 para.15 to, the 5.009 Finance Act 2008 inserted new subss.(5), (6), and (7):

"(5) For the purposes of this Act a loss of tax or a situation is brought about carelessly by a person if the person fails to take reasonable care to avoid bringing about that loss or situation.

(6) Where—

(a) information is provided to Her Majesty's Revenue and Customs,

(b) the person who provided the information, or the person on whose behalf the information was provided, discovers some time later that the information was inaccurate, and

(c) that person fails to take reasonable steps to inform Her Majesty's Revenue and Customs, any loss of tax or situation brought about by the inaccuracy shall be treated for the purposes of this Act as having been brought about carelessly by that person.

(7) In this Act references to a loss of tax or a situation brought about deliberately by a person include a loss of tax or a situation that arises as a result of a deliberate inaccuracy in a document given to Her Majesty's Revenue and Customs by or on behalf of that person."

p.69, *annotation to Social Security Contributions and Benefits Act 1992, Sch.11, para.2 (circumstances in which periods of entitlement to SSP do not arise)*

5.010   The effect of the Court of Appeal's decision in *HMRC v Thorn Baker Ltd* ([2007] EWCA Civ 626) has been reversed with effect from October 27, 2008 by reg.2 of the Fixed-term Employees (Prevention of Less Favourable Treatment) (Amendment) Regulations 2008 (SI 2008/2776). This amends reg.19(1) of the Fixed-term Employees (Prevention of Less Favourable Treatment) Regulations 2002 (SI 2002/2034). The aim of the amendment is to ensure that agency workers are treated in the same way as all other employees with regard to entitlement to SSP, regardless of the length of their contract, and whether they are directly or indirectly employed. As a result agency workers with contracts for 3 months or less are no longer excluded from access to SSP.

pp.81–82, *Social Security Act 1998, as modified, ss.5 to 7*

5.010.1   With effect from November 3, 2008, these provisions are repealed by the Transfer of Tribunal Functions Order 2008 (SI 2008/2833), Sch.3, paras 143 to 147 and therefore they are no longer applied in child trust fund cases (Tribunals, Courts and Enforcement Act 2007 (Transitional and Consequential Provisions) Order 2008 (SI 2008/2683), Sch.1, paras 260 and 264).

pp.82–83, *Social Security Act 1998, as modified, s.12*

5.010.2   The following amendments have effect from November 3, 2008. They are the consequence of the functions of appeal tribunals being transferred to the First-tier Tribunal constituted under the Tribunals, Courts and Enforcement Act 2007. For that Act, see Vol.III of the main work. The rules for the tribunal are set out in Pt 1 of this supplement.

In the heading, for "appeal tribunal", substitute "First-tier Tribunal" (Transfer of Tribunal Functions Order 2008 (SI 2008/2833), Sch.3, paras 143 and 149(a)).

In subs.(1), for "an appeal tribunal", substitute "the First-tier Tribunal" (Tribunals, Courts and Enforcement Act 2007 (Transitional and Consequential Provisions) Order 2008 (SI 2008/2683), Sch.1, paras 191 and 194(b)).

In subs.(8), for "an appeal tribunal", substitute "the First-tier Tribunal" (Transfer of Tribunal Functions Order 2008 (SI 2008/2833), Sch.3, paras 143 and 149(b)).

pp.83–84, *Social Security Act 1998, as modified, s.13*

In subs.(1), for the words "to a person" to the end, there is substituted   5.010.3
"to the First-tier Tribunal for permission to appeal to the Upper Tribunal from any decision of the First-tier Tribunal under s.12 or this
section", with effect from November 3, 2008, and subs.(2) is repealed
from the same date (Transfer of Tribunal Functions Order 2008 (SI
2008/2833), Sch.3, paras 143 and 150(a) and (b)). Given that subs.(3)
has never applied to tax credit or child trust fund cases and that the
definition in subs.(4) has therefore become redundant with the repeal of
s.14(7), it is difficult to see why what is left of this section is still thought
to have sufficient substance to be worth applying to such cases.

pp.84–85, *Social Security Act 1998, as modified, s.14*

The text should have made clear that subss.(3)(c), (5) and (6) are not   5.010.4
applied to child trust fund cases.

The following amendments have effect from November 3, 2008. They
are the consequence of the abolition of the Social Security Commissioners. An appeal from the First-tier Tribunal now lies to the Upper
Tribunal under s.11 of the Tribunals, Courts and Enforcement Act 2007
(see Vol.III of the main work). This section now merely makes provision
as to who may exercise that right of appeal.

In the heading, for "tribunal to Commissioner" substitute "First-tier
Tribunal to Upper Tribunal" (Transfer of Tribunal Functions Order
2008 (SI 2008/2833), paras 143 and 151(a)).

Subsections (1) and (7) to (12) are repealed (*ibid.*, Sch.3, paras 143
and 151(b) and (d)) and so are no longer applied to tax credit and child
trust fund cases (Tribunals, Courts and Enforcement Act 2007 (Transitional and Consequential Provisions) Order 2008 (SI 2008/2683),
Sch.1, paras 191, 196, 197, 260, 267 and 268).

In subs.(3), for "lies under this section" substitute "to the Upper
Tribunal under section 11 of the Tribunals, Courts and Enforcement
Act 2007 from any decision of the First-tier Tribunal under section 12 or
13 above lies" (Transfer of Tribunal Functions Order 2008 (SI
2008/2833), Sch.3, paras 143 and 151(c)) but, in child trust fund cases,
the words "under section 12 or 13 above" are further substituted by "on
a child trust fund appeal" (Child Trust Funds (Non-tax Appeals) Regulations 2005 (SI 2005/191), reg.8(2)(a), as amended by the Tribunals,
Courts and Enforcement Act 2007 (Transitional and Consequential
Provisions) Order 2008 (SI 2008/2683), Sch.1, paras 260 and
267(b)(i)).

p.89, *Social Security Act 1998, as modified, s.15*

By virtue of the Transfer of Tribunal Functions Order 2008 (SI   5.010.5
2008/2833) and with effect from November 3, 2008, Sch.3, paras 143
and 152, the heading of s.15 is replaced by, "Applications for Permission
to appeal against a decision of the Upper Tribunal", subss.(1), (2), (4)
and (5) are repealed and subs.(3) is amended so that it reads—

"An application for permission to appeal from a decision of the Upper Tribunal in respect of a decision of the First-tier Tribunal under section 12 or 13 may only be made by—
  (a) a person who, before the proceedings before the Upper Tribunal were begun, was entitled to appeal to the Upper Tribunal from the decision to which the Upper Tribunal's decision relates;
  (b) any other person who was a party to the proceedings in which the first decision mentioned in paragraph (a) above was given;
  (c) any other person who was authorised by regulations to apply for permission."

The right of appeal to which this section refers exists by virtue of s.13 of the Tribunals, Courts and Enforcement Act 2007 (see Vol.III of the main work).

pp.90–91, *Social Security Act 1998, as modified, s.16*

5.010.6   Subsections (2), (3)(a), and (6) to (9) are repealed by the Transfer of Tribunal Functions Order 2008 (SI 2008/2833), Sch.3, paras 143 and 154 with effect from November 3, 2008. In consequence, the whole of subs.(3) is no longer applied to tax credit and child trust fund cases (Tribunals, Courts and Enforcement Act 2007 (Transitional and Consequential Provisions) Order 2008 (SI 2008/2683), Sch.1, paras 191, 199, 260 and 270).

p.91, *Social Security Act 1998, as modified, s.17*

5.010.7   Minor amendments are made with effect from November 3, 2008. In both substituted versions of subsection (1), after paragraph (b), insert

"(c) any provision made by or under chapter 2 of Part I of the Tribunals, Courts and Enforcement Act 2007,"

and, for "an appeal tribunal or lies to a Commissioner", substitute "the First-tier Tribunal or lies to the Upper Tribunal" (Tribunals, Courts and Enforcement Act 2007 (Transitional and Consequential Provisions) Order 2008 (SI 2008/2683), Sch.1, paras 191, 200, 260 and 271). The "and" at the end of para.(a) is moved in the child trust fund version but is overlooked in the tax credit version.

pp.91–92, *Social Security Act 1998, as modified, s.28*

5.010.8   In consequence of amendments made to s.28 by the Transfer of Tribunal Functions Order 2008 (SI 2008/2833) with effect from November 3, 2008, it is no longer applied to either tax credit cases or child trust fund cases (Tribunals, Courts and Enforcement Act 2007 (Transitional and Consequential Provisions) Order 2008 (SI 2008/2683), Sch.1, paras 191, 201, 260 and 272).

pp.92–93, *Social Security Act 1998, as modified, s.39*

The definitions of "appeal tribunal" and "Commissioner" are 5.010.9
repealed by the Transfer of Tribunal Functions Order 2008 (SI
2008/2833), Sch.3, paras 143 and 167, with effect from November 3,
2008. From, April 1, 2009, the definition of "claimant" that exists for
child trust fund purposes will also be repealed (Transfer of Tribunal
Functions and Revenue and Customs Appeal Order 2009 (SI 2009/56),
Sch.2, paras 131 and 134).

pp.93–95, *Social Security Act 1998, as modified, ss.79, 80 and 84*

With effect from November 3, 2008, these sections are no longer 5.010.10
expressly applied to child trust fund cases (Tribunals, Courts and
Enforcement Act 2007 (Transitional and Consequential Provisions)
Order 2008 (SI 2008/2683), Sch.1, paras 260 and 274).

pp.95–97, *Social Security Act 1998, as modified, Sch.1 and Sch.4*

With effect from November 3, 2008, these Schedules are repealed by 5.010.11
the Transfer of Tribunal Functions Order 2008 (SI 2008/2833), Sch.3,
paras 143, 171 and 172 and therefore are no longer applied to tax credit
or child trust fund cases (Tribunals, Courts and Enforcement Act 2007
(Transitional and Consequential Provisions) Order 2008 (SI
2008/2683), Sch.1, paras 191, 197, 260, 264 and 268).

p.97, *Social Security Act 1998, as modified, Sch.5*

With effect from November 3, 2008, paras 2 and 5 to 8 are repealed, 5.010.12
as are the words ", an appeal tribunal or a Commissioner" in para.1(a)
and (b) (which makes para.1 redundant in tax credit and child trust fund
cases) (Transfer of Tribunal Functions Order 2008 (SI 2008/2833),
Sch.3, paras 143 and 173).

p.153, *amendment of the Tax Credits Act 2002, s.28 (overpayments)*

With effect from July 21, 2008, s.113 of, and Sch.36, para.90 to, the 5.011
Finance Act 2008 omitted subss.(3) and (4).

p.156, *annotation to the Tax Credits Act 2002, s.31 (incorrect statements
etc.)*

The amendments to s.36 of the Taxes Management Act 1970 (see 5.012
note to p.15 of main volume above) have now replaced the test of
"fraudulently or negligently" with "carelessly or deliberately" in connection with all penalties dealt with by HMRC other than tax credits
penalties. The test in this section is now out of line with those that apply
generally for tax penalties.

p.178, *annotation to the Tax Credits Act 2002, s.63(6) (tax credit appeals etc: temporary modifications)*

5.013 Appeals under s.63(6) to the Upper Tribunal against tax credit penalty decisions are "excluded decisions" for the purposes of s.11(1) of the Tribunals, Courts and Enforcement Act 2007 (see Appeals (Excluded Decisions) Order 2008 (SI 2008/2707), art.2(b)). The reason for this is that such appeals may include an appeal against the amount of the penalty imposed, which may be on an issue of fact (and so would not necessarily fall within the criteria for an appeal on a point of law under s.11). The designation of such appeals as excluded decisions for the purposes of s.11 is intended to preserve the broader appeal rights under s.63(6).

p.223, *amendment of the Income Tax (Earnings and Pensions) Act 2003. s.318 (childcare: exemption for employer-provided care)*

5.014 With effect from September 1, 2008, reg.2 of the Income Tax (Qualifying Child Care) Regulations 2008 (SI 2008/2170), amended subs.(5) by inserting "(za) in England, that under Part 10A of the Children Act 1989(2) or Part 3 of the Childcare Act 2006" before para.(a) and omitting "England and" in para.(a).

p.226, *amendment of the Income Tax (Earnings and Pensions) Act 2003. s.318C (childcare: meaning of "qualifying child care")*

5.015 With effect from September 1, 2008, reg.3 of the Income Tax (Qualifying Child Care) Regulations 2008 (SI 2008/2170) amended subs.(2) by omitting para.(b) and inserting after that paragraph "(ba) by a person registered under Part 3 of the Childcare Act 2006" as well as substituting for para.(c) "(c) by or under the direction of the proprietor of a school on the school premises (subject to subsection (2B)". The amending regulations also omitted para.(eb) (and the "or" after it) in subs.(2) and inserted at the end:

", or (g) by a foster parent under the Fostering Services Regulations 2002 in relation to a child other than one whom the foster parent is fostering."

The amending regulations also inserted after subs.(2) the following:

"(2A) In subsection (2)(c)—
"proprietor", in relation to a school, means
    (a) the governing body incorporated under section 19 of the Education Act 2002, or
    (b) if there is no such body, the person or body of persons responsible for the management of the school;
"school" means a school that Her Majesty's Chief Inspector of Education, Children's Services and Skills (the "Chief Inspector") is or may be required to inspect;
"school premises" means premises that may be inspected as part of an inspection of the school by the Chief Inspector.

(2B) Care provided for a child in England is not registered or approved care under subsection (2)(c) if:

(a) it is provided during school hours for a child who has reached compulsory school age, or

(b) it is provided in breach of a requirement to register under Part 3 of the Childcare Act 2006."

Finally, the amending regulations omitted the "or" after para.(e) in subs.(3) and inserted at the end:

"or

(g) by a foster parent under the Fostering Services (Wales) Regulations 2003 in relation to a child other than one whom the foster parent is fostering."

p.248, *amendment of the Income Tax (Earnings and Pensions) Act 2003. s.677 (UK social security benefits wholly exempt from tax: Table B)*

With effect from April 6, 2008, s.46 of the Finance Act 2008 amended Pt 1 of Table B (Benefits payable under primary legislation) by inserting at the appropriate places as follows: 5.016

In-work credit	ETA 1973	Section 2
	ETA(NI) 1950	Section 1
In-work emergency discretion fund payment	ETA 1973	Section 2
In-work emergency fund Payment	ETA(NI) 1950	Section 1", and

Return to work credit	ETA 1973	Section 2
	ETA(NI) 1950	Section 1

Note: the abbreviations used are:

ETA(NI) 1950	The Employment and Training Act (Northern Ireland) 1950 (c. 29 (N.I.))

and

ETA 1973	The Employment and Training Act 1973 (c. 50)

p.283, *annotation to the Child Trust Funds Act 2004, s.24(2) (temporary modifications)*

Appeals under s.24(2) to the Upper Tribunal against penalty decisions are "excluded decisions" for the purposes of s.11(1) of the Tribunals, Courts and Enforcement Act 2007 (see Appeals (Excluded Decisions) 5.017

Order 2008 (SI 2008/2707), art.2(c)). The reason for this is that such appeals may include an appeal against the amount of the penalty imposed, which may be on an issue of fact (and so would not necessarily fall within the criteria for an appeal on a point of law under s.11). The designation of such appeals as excluded decisions for the purposes of s.11 is intended to preserve the broader appeal rights under s.24(2).

p.340, *amendment of the Income Tax Act 2007, s.831 (foreign income of individuals in the United Kingdom for temporary purpose)*

5.018   With effect from April 6, 2008, s.24 of the Finance Act 2008 amended subs.(1) by substituting for para.(b): "(b) during the tax year in question the individual spends (in total) less than 183 days in the United Kingdom." Section 24 also inserted after subs.(1) the following:

"(1A) In determining whether an individual is within subsection (1)(b) treat a day as a day spent by the individual in the United Kingdom if (and only if) the individual is present in the United Kingdom at the end of the day.

(1B) But in determining that issue do not treat as a day spent by the individual in the United Kingdom any day on which the individual arrives in the United Kingdom as a passenger if—

(a) the individual departs from the United Kingdom on the next day, and

(b) during the time between arrival and departure the individual does not engage in activities that are to a substantial extent unrelated to the individual's passage through the United Kingdom."

p.341, *amendment of the Income Tax Act 2007, s.832 (employment income of individuals in the United Kingdom for temporary purpose)*

5.019   With effect from April 6, 2008, s.24 of the Finance Act 2008 amended s.832 by inserting after subs. (1):

"(1A) In determining whether an individual is within subsection (1)(b) treat a day as a day spent by the individual in the United Kingdom if (and only if) the individual is present in the United Kingdom at the end of the day.

(1B) But in determining that issue do not treat as a day spent by the individual in the United Kingdom any day on which the individual arrives in the United Kingdom as a passenger if—

(a) the individual departs from the United Kingdom on the next day, and

(b) during the time between arrival and departure the individual does not engage in activities that are to a substantial extent unrelated to the individual's passage through the United Kingdom."

p.383, *amendment of the Working Tax Credits (Entitlement and Maximum Rate) Regulations 2002, reg.14 (entitlement to childcare element of working tax credit)*

With effect from September 1, 2008, reg.2(2) of the Tax Credits   5.020
(Miscellaneous Amendments) (No.2) Regulations 2008 (SI 2008/2169)
amended para.(2) by omitting sub-para.(2)(a)(ii) and inserting after that
paragraph "(iia) by a person registered under Part 3 of the Childcare Act
2006;". In addititon, reg.2(2) substituted for sub-para.(2)(a)(iii) the
following:

> "(iii) in respect of any period on or before the last day the child is
> treated as a child for the purpose of this regulation by or under
> the direction of the proprietor of a school on the school premises
> (subject to subsection 2(B));";

Finally, reg.2(2) inserted "or" at the end of sub-para.(2)(a)(vi) and
omitted sub-para.(2)(a)(viii) and the "or" before it.

Regulation 2(3) of the same amending regulations inserted after
para.(2) the following:

> "(2A) In paragraph (2)(a)(iii)—
> "proprietor", in relation to a school, means—
>> (a) the governing body incorporated under section 19 of the
>> Education Act 2002, or
>> (b) if there is no such body, the person or body of persons
>> responsible for the management of the school;
> "school" means a school that Her Majesty's Chief Inspector of
> Education, Children's Services and Skills (the "Chief Inspector") is
> or may be required to inspect;
> "school premises" means premises that may be inspected as part of
> an inspection of the school by the Chief Inspector.
> (2B) Care provided for a child in England is not registered or
> approved care under paragraph (2)(a)(iii) if—
>> (a) it is provided during school hours for a child who has reached
>> compulsory school age, or
>> (b) it is provided in breach of a requirement to register under Part
>> 3 of the Childcare Act 2006."

p.383, *annotation to the Working Tax Credits (Entitlement and Maximum Rate) Regulations 2002, reg.14(5) (entitlement to childcare element of working tax credit)*

The scope of reg.14(5) was discussed by the Deputy Commissioner in   5.021
CTC/3646/2007, where the Deputy Commissioner upheld a tribunal's
decision to refuse to take account of apportioned fees for a "waiting
class". Regulation 15(3) could not therefore be applied on the facts. The
issue is further clarified by the addition of a definition of "full time
education" to the Child Tax Credit Regulations by SI 2008/2169,
reg.7(3) with effect from September 1, 2008 (see note to main volume
p.448 below).

p.408, *amendment of the Tax Credits (Definition and Calculation of Income) Regulations 2002, reg.4 (employment income)*

5.022　　With effect from September 1, 2008, reg.4(a) of the Tax Credits (Miscellaneous Amendments) (No.2) Regulations 2008 (SI 2008/2169) inserted in Table 1 in item 16 in para.(a) ", Better Off In-Work Credit" after "In-Work Credit" and omitted "or" at the end, and inserted after para.(b):

> "(c) under the City Strategy Pathfinder Pilots,
> (d) by way of an In-Work Emergency Discretion Fund payment pursuant to arrangements made by the Secretary of State, or
> (e) by way of an Up-front Childcare Fund payment pursuant to arrangements made by the Secretary of State."

Regulation 4(b) inserted after item 16A the following new item:

> "**16B.** Any In-Work Emergency Fund payment made to a person pursuant to arrangements made by the Department of Economic Development under section 1 of the Employment and Training Act (Northern Ireland) 1950."

Regulation 4(c) inserted after item 19 the following new item:

> "**20.** Pay As You Earn (PAYE) settlement agreements made under Part 6 of the Income Tax (PAYE) Regulations ("the PAYE Regulations") 2003.
>
> For the purposes of this item the special arrangements under regulation 141 of the PAYE Regulations also apply."

p.423, *amendment of the Tax Credits (Definition and Calculation of Income) Regulations 2002, reg.8 (student income)*

5.023　　With effect from September 1, 2008, reg.5(2) of the Tax Credits (Miscellaneous Amendments) (No.2) Regulations 2008 (SI 2008/2169) substituted for para.(a) the following:

> "(a) in England, any adult dependant's grant payable—
> > (i) under regulation 41 of the Education (Student Support) Regulations 2006 in relation to an academic year which begins on or after 1st September 2006 but before 1st September 2007;
> > (ii) under regulation 43 of the Education (Student Support) Regulations 2007 in relation to an academic year which begins on or after 1st September 2007 but before 1st September 2008;
> > (iii) under regulation 42 of the Education (Student Support) Regulations 2008 in relation to an academic year which begins on or after 1st September 2008 but before 1st September 2009; or
> > (iv) under regulation 44 of the Education (Student Support) (No. 2) Regulations 2008 in relation to an academic year which begins on or after 1st September 2009;".

Regulation 5(3) substituted for para.(d) the following:

"(d) in Wales, any adult dependant's grant payable—
    (i) under regulation 22 of the Assembly Learning Grants and Loans (Higher Education) (Wales) Regulations 2006 in relation to an academic year which begins on or after 1st September 2006 but before 1st September 2007;
    (ii) under regulation 26 of the Assembly Learning Grants and Loans (Higher Education) (Wales) Regulations 2007 in relation to an academic year which begins on or after 1st September 2007 but before 1st September 2008; or
    (iii) under regulation 26 of the Assembly Learning Grants and Loans (Higher Education) (Wales) Regulations 2008 in relation to an academic year which begins on or after 1st September 2008."

p.447, *amendment of the Child Tax Regulations 2002, reg.2(1)* *(interpretation)*

With effect from September 1, 2008, reg.7(2) of the Tax Credits (Miscellaneous Amendments) (No.2) Regulations 2008 (SI 2008/2169) omitted "or who falls within the terms of regulation 4" in the definition of "child".   5.024

p.448, *amendment of the Child Tax Regulations 2002, reg.2(1)* *(interpretation)*

With effect from September 1, 2008, reg.7(3) of the Tax Credits (Miscellaneous Amendments) (No.2) Regulations 2008 (SI 2008/2169) inserted after the definition of "the family element of child tax credit" and "the individual element of child tax credit" the following new definition: 5.025

""full-time education" means education received by a person attending a course of education where, in pursuit of that course, the time spent receiving instruction or tuition, undertaking supervised study, examination or practical work or taking part in any exercise, experiment or project for which provision is made in the curriculum of the course, exceeds or exceeds on average 12 hours a week in normal term-time, and shall include gaps between the ending of one course and the commencement of another, where the person is enrolled on and commences the latter course;".

Regulation 7(4) inserted after the definition of "placing for adoption" the following new definition:

""qualifying body" means—
    (a) the Careers Service or Connexions Service;
    (b) the Ministry of Defence;
    (c) in Northern Ireland, the Department for Employment and Learning or an Education and Library Board established under Article 3 of the Education and Libraries (Northern Ireland) Order 1986; or

(d) for the purposes of applying Council Regulation (EEC) No. 1408/71, any corresponding body in another member state;".

Finally, reg.7(5) omitted the definition of "recognised educational establishment".

pp.450–451, *amendment of the Child Tax Regulations 2002, reg.3(1) (circumstances in which a person is or is not responsible for a child or qualifying young person)*

5.026   With effect from September 1, 2008, reg.8(1) of the Tax Credits (Miscellaneous Amendments) (No.2) Regulations 2008 (SI 2008/2169) amended r.4.1 by omitting "child (having attained the age of sixteen) or" in Case D, "The child (having attained the age of sixteen) or" in Case E and "The child (having attained the age of sixteen) or" and the second paragraph in Case F. Regulation 8(1) also inserted after Case F the following new Cases:

> "Case G: The qualifying young person has a spouse, civil partner or partner with whom they are living and the spouse, civil partner or partner is not in full-time education or approved training as provided for under regulation 5(3).
>
> Case H: The responsible person is the spouse, civil partner or partner of a qualifying young person with whom they are living.
>
> This Case does not apply to persons in receipt of child tax credit for a qualifying young person who is living with a partner on the day before 1st September 2008."

p.453, *annotation to the Child Tax Credit Regulations 2002, reg.3 (circumstances in which a person is or is not responsible for a child or qualifying young person)*

5.027   In *CTC/3096/2007* the Commissioner emphasised the need to apply the "main responsibility" test. See also *CTC/1686/2007* where the Commissioner compares these rules with those for child benefit and child support.

p.455, *amendment of the Child Tax Regulations 2002, reg.4 (period for which a person who attains the age of sixteen remains a child)*

5.028   With effect from September 1, 2008, reg.9(1) of the Tax Credits (Miscellaneous Amendments) (No.2) Regulations 2008 (SI 2008/2169) substituted a new reg.4:

> **"Period for which a person who attains the age of sixteen is a qualifying young person**
>
> 4.—(1) A person who attains the age of sixteen is a qualifying young person from the date on which that person attained that age until 31st August which next follows that date.
>
> (2) Paragraph (1) is subject to regulation 5 but as if there were no requirement to satisfy the first condition specified in paragraph (3) of that regulation."

pp.455–456, *amendment of the Child Tax Regulations 2002, reg.5 (maximum age and prescribed conditions for a qualifying young person)*

With effect from September 1, 2008, reg.10(2) of the Tax Credits   5.029
(Miscellaneous Amendments) (No.2) Regulations 2008 (SI 2008/2169)
substituted "by means of a contract of employment" for "to him by
virtue of his employment or any office held by him" in para.(3)(ab) and
substituted "a qualifying body" for "the Careers Service, the Con-
nexions Service or the Department for Employment and Learning" in
para.(3)(b)(ii). Regulation 10(3) substituted for the words from the
beginning of para.(5) to the end of sub-para.(b) the following:

"(5) For the purposes of paragraphs (3) and (4) a person shall be
treated as being in full-time education if full-time education is received
by that person by undertaking a course—
(a) at a school or college, or
(b) where that person has been receiving that education prior to
attaining the age of sixteen, elsewhere, if approved by the
Board, "

p.477, *amendment of the Tax Credits (Claims and Notifications) Regulations 2002, reg.5(2) (manner in which claims to be made)*

With effect from September 1, 2008, reg.12 of the Tax Credits (Mis-   5.030
cellaneous Amendments) (No. 2) Regulations 2008 (SI 2008/2169)
substituted for sub-para.(b) the following:

"(b) in such other manner as the Board may decide having regard to
all the circumstances."

p.479, *annotation to the Tax Credits (Claims and Notifications) Regulations 2002, reg.7 (time-limit for claims (if otherwise entitled to tax credit up to three months earlier))*

A Commissioner drew attention to the practice of protective claims in   5.031
CTC/591/2008 when refusing a later claim.

p.484, *amendment of the Tax Credits (Claims and Notifications) Regulations 2002, reg.13 (circumstances in which claims made by one member of a couple to be treated as also made by the other member of the couple)*

With effect from September 1, 2008, reg.12 of the Tax Credits (Mis-   5.032
cellaneous Amendments) (No.2) Regulations 2008 (SI 2008/2169)
amended para.(1) by inserting "or (3)" after "(2)" and inserting after
para.(2) the following new paragraph:

"(3) A claim for a tax credit made by one member of a couple is to
be treated as also made by the other member of the couple in such
manner and in such circumstances as the Board may decide."

HMRC has indicated that the new provision in para.(3) initially applies
to telephone claims only. The effect is to require both partners to fill in

the forms confirming the claims while validating the initial claim as a joint claim.

p.508, *amendment of the Tax Credits (Payments by the Commissioners) Regulations 2002, reg.11 (postponement of payment)*

5.032.1   With effect from November 3, 2008, art.6(1) of, and Sch.1, para.190 to, the Tribunals, Courts and Enforcement Act 2007 (Transitional and Consequential Provisions) Order 2008 (SI 2008/2683) substituted "the appropriate tribunal, the Upper Tribunal, the Northern Ireland" for "an appeal tribunal, a" in paras (2) and (4) of reg.11. The same amendment substituted "the appropriate tribunal" for "an appeal tribunal" in para.(4)(b), "Appropriate tribunal" for "Appeal tribunal" in para.(5) and "Northern Ireland Social" for "Social" in para.(6).

pp.518–519, *amendment of the Tax Credits (Appeals) (No.2) Regulations 2002, reg.1(3) (citation, commencement, duration and interpretation)*

5.032.2   With effect from November 3, 2008, art.6(1) of, and Sch.1, para.205 to, the Tribunals, Courts and Enforcement Act 2007 (Transitional and Consequential Provisions) Order 2008 (SI 2008/2683) omitted the following definitions: "a case"; "clerk to the appeal tribunal"; "the date of notification"; "decision"; "financially qualified panel member"; "legally qualified panel member"; "medically qualified panel member"; "panel"; "panel member"; "panel member with a disability qualification"; "penalty determination"; "penalty proceedings"; and "President".

p.520, *amendment of the Tax Credits (Appeals) (No.2) Regulations 2002, reg.2 (service of notices or documents)*

5.032.3   With effect from November 3, 2008, art.6(1) of, and Sch.1, para.206 to, the Tribunals, Courts and Enforcement Act 2007 (Transitional and Consequential Provisions) Order 2008 (SI 2008/2683) omitted "to the clerk to the appeal tribunal or"; and "by the clerk of the appeal tribunal or" in sub-para.(a) and "the clerk to the appeal tribunal or" in sub-para.(b).

p.521, *amendment of the Tax Credits (Appeals) (No.2) Regulations 2002, reg.3 (other persons with a right of appeal or a right to make an application for a direction)*

5.032.4   With effect from November 3, 2008, art.6(1) of, and Sch.1, para.207 to, the Tribunals, Courts and Enforcement Act 2007 (Transitional and Consequential Provisions) Order 2008 (SI 2008/2683) substituted "the First-tier Tribunal" for "an appeal tribunal".

p.522, *amendment of the Tax Credits (Appeals) (No.2) Regulations 2002, reg.4 (time within which appeal is to be brought)*

5.032.5   With effect from November 3, 2008, art.6(1) of, and Sch.1, para.208 to, the Tribunals, Courts and Enforcement Act 2007 (Transitional and

Consequential Provisions) Order 2008 (SI 2008/2683) substituted "the First-tier Tribunal" for "a legally qualified panel member".

pp.522–523, *amendment of the Tax Credits (Appeals) (No.2) Regulations 2002, reg.4*

With effect from November 3, 2008, art.6(1) of, and Sch.1, para.209   **5.032.6**
to, the Tribunals, Courts and Enforcement Act 2007 (Transitional and Consequential Provisions) Order 2008 (SI 2008/2683) substituted "The Board may treat a late appeal as made in time" for "The time within which an appeal must be brought may be extended" and substituted "(4)" for "(2)" in para.(1). The same amendment omitted paras (2) and (3) and substituted a new para.(4) as follows: "(4) An appeal may be treated as made in time if the Board is satisfied that it is in the interests of justice." The following further amendments were made. In para.(5), "treat the appeal as made in time unless the Board are" was substituted for "grant the application unless the panel member is, or the Board are, as the case may be,". The words "to the application" were omitted in sub-paras (a) and (b) and the word "appellant" substituted for "applicant" in para.(6). The expressions "treat the appeal as made in time" was substituted for "grant an application" and "submission of the notice of appeal, the more compelling should be the special circumstances." for the words "making of the application" to the end in para.(7). Finally, "treat the appeal as made in time" was substituted for "grant an application" in para.(8) and "the Upper Tribunal" for "a Commissioner" in para.(8)(b) and paras (9) to (11) were omitted.

pp.524–525, *repeal of the Tax Credits (Appeals) (No.2) Regulations 2002, regs 6 (Making of an application for an extension of time) and 7 (Making an application for a direction)*

With effect from November 3, 2008, art.6(1) of, and Sch.1, para.210   **5.032.7**
to, the Tribunals, Courts and Enforcement Act 2007 (Transitional and Consequential Provisions) Order 2008 (SI 2008/2683) omitted regs 6 and 7.

pp.526–556, *repeal of the Tax Credits (Appeals) (No.2) Regulations 2002, regs 9–27 (procedure on appeal)*

With effect from November 3, 2008, art.6(1) of, and Sch.1, para.210   **5.032.8**
to, the Tribunals, Courts and Enforcement Act 2007 (Transitional and Consequential Provisions) Order 2008 (SI 2008/2683) omitted regs 9 to 27.

pp.557–575, *repeal of the Social Security Commissioners (Procedure) (Tax Credits Appeals) Regulations 2002*

With effect from November 3, 2008, art.6(2) of, and Sch.2 to, the   **5.032.9**
Tribunals, Courts and Enforcement Act 2007 (Transitional and Consequential Provisions) Order 2008 (SI 2008/2683) repealed the whole of

the Social Security Commissioners (Procedure) (Tax Credits Appeals) Regulations 2002.

p.607, *amendment of Tax Credits (Child Care Providers) (Miscellaneous Revocation and Transitional Provisions) (England) Scheme 2007, art.4 (revocation of the 2005 Scheme and transitional provision)*

With effect from November 3, 2008, art.6(1) of, and Sch.1, para.329 to, the Tribunals, Courts and Enforcement Act 2007 (Transitional and Consequential Provisions) Order 2008 (SI 2008/2683), inserted ", with the modifications in paragraph (3)," after "effect" in para.(2) and inserted after para.(2) the following:

"(3) For the purposes of paragraph (2) the 2005 Scheme is amended as follows—
 (a) in article 2 omit the definitions of "the Tribunal" and "the Tribunal Regulations";
 (b) in article 11—
  (i) in paragraphs (1) and (5) for "Tribunal" substitute "First-tier Tribunal";
  (ii) for paragraph (2) substitute—
"(2) Tribunal Procedure Rules shall apply to an appeal under paragraph (1) as they apply to an appeal under section 79M of the 1989 Act."; and
 (c) omit paragraphs (3) and (4)."

p.608, *annotation to the Tax Credits (Child Care Providers) (Miscellaneous Revocation and Transitional Provisions) (England) Scheme 2007*

5.033   As noted in the main volume, this Scheme applies only to England. For the Welsh equivalent, see the Tax Credits (Approval of Child Care Providers) (Wales) Scheme 2007 (SI 2007/226 (W.20)), as amended by the Tax Credits (Approval of Child Care Providers) (Wales) (Amendment) Scheme 2008 (SI 2008/2687 (W.237)).

p.616, *repeal of the Statutory Sick Pay (General) Regulations 1982, reg.3A (maximum entitlement to Statutory Sick Pay in a period of entitlement)*

5.034   With effect from October 27, 2008, reg.3 of the Statutory Sick Pay (General) (Amendment) Regulations 2008 (SI 2008/1735) revoked reg.3A.

p.622, *amendment of the Statutory Sick Pay (General) Regulations 1982, reg.9A (liability of the Commissioners of Inland Revenue for payments of statutory sick pay)*

5.035   With effect from November 3, 2008, art.6(1) of, and Sch.1, para.18 to, the Tribunals, Courts and Enforcement Act 2007 (Transitional and Consequential Provisions) Order 2008 (SI 2008/2683) substituted for the words "a Social Security Appeal Tribunal" to the end of reg.9A(3) the expression "the First-tier Tribunal or the Upper Tribunal."

p.627, *amendment of the Statutory Sick Pay (General) Regulations 1982, reg. 15 (provision of information by employers to employees)*

With effect from October 27, 2008, reg.2(2)(a) of the Statutory Sick 5.036
Pay (General) (Amendment) Regulations 2008 (SI 2008/1735) substituted a new para.(3)(a) as follows:

"(a) the information mentioned in paragraph (1) above is a statement informing the employee of—
    (i) the reason why the period of entitlement ended;
    (ii) the date of the last day in respect of which the employer is or was liable to make a payment of statutory sick pay to him."

p.628, *amendment of the Statutory Sick Pay (General) Regulations 1982, reg. 15 (provision of information by employers to employees)—*

With effect from October 27, 2008, reg.2(2)(b) of the Statutory Sick 5.037
Pay (General) (Amendment) Regulations 2008 (SI 2008/1735) substituted a new para.(4)(a) as follows:

"(a) the information mentioned in paragraph (1) above is a statement informing the employee of—
    (i) the reason why the period of entitlement is expected to end;
    (ii) the date of the last day in respect of which the employer is or was expected to be liable to make a payment of statutory sick pay to him."

p.629, *repeal of the Statutory Sick Pay (General) Regulations 1982, reg. 15A (statements relating to the payment of statutory sick pay)*

With effect from October 27, 2008, reg.3 of the Statutory Sick Pay 5.038
(General) (Amendment) Regulations 2008 (SI 2008/1735) revoked reg.15A.

p.665, *amendment of the Statutory Maternity Pay (General) Regulations 1986, reg. 7 (liability of Commissioners of Inland Revenue to pay statutory maternity pay)*

With effect from November 3, 2008, art.6(1) of, and Sch.1, para.42 5.039
to, the Tribunals, Courts and Enforcement Act 2007 (Transitional and Consequential Provisions) Order 2008 (SI 2008/2683) substituted for the words "a Social Security Appeal Tribunal" to the end of reg.7(2) the expression "the First-tier Tribunal or the Upper Tribunal."

p.678, *amendment of the Statutory Maternity Pay (General) Regulations 1986, reg. 25A (provision of information relating to claims for certain other benefits)*

With effect from October 27, 2008, reg.46 of the Employment and 5.040
Support Allowance (Consequential Provisions) (No.2) Regulations 2008

(SI 2008/1554) substituted ", incapacity benefit or an employment and support allowance" for "or incapacity benefit" in reg.25A(1).

p.829, *amendment of the Child Trust Funds (Non-tax appeals) Regulations 2005, reg.2 (interpretation)*

5.041   With effect from November 3, 2008, art.6(1) of, and Sch.1, para.261 to, the Tribunals, Courts and Enforcement Act 2007 (Transitional and Consequential Provisions) Order 2008 (SI 2008/2683) made consequential amendments to reg.2 (omitted from the main volume).

p.829, *amendment of the Child Trust Funds (Non-tax appeals) Regulations 2005, reg.3 (prescribed manner of notice of appeal)*

5.042   With effect from November 3, 2008, art.6(1) of, and Sch.1, para.262 to, the Tribunals, Courts and Enforcement Act 2007 (Transitional and Consequential Provisions) Order 2008 (SI 2008/2683) inserted ", in respect of an appeal to an appeal tribunal," in reg.3(1) after "notice of appeal".

p.829, *amendment of the Child Trust Funds (Non-tax appeals) Regulations 2005, regs 4–15 (omitted from the main volume)*

5.043   With effect from November 3, 2008, art.6(1) of, and Sch.1, paras 263–274 to, the Tribunals, Courts and Enforcement Act 2007 (Transitional and Consequential Provisions) Order 2008 (SI 2008/2683) made consequential amendments to regs 4–15 (omitted from the main volume).

p.829, *amendment of the Child Trust Funds (Appeals) Regulations 2005, reg.1 (citation, commencement, duration and interpretation)*

5.044   With effect from November 3, 2008, art.6(1) of, and Sch.1, para.291 to, the Tribunals, Courts and Enforcement Act 2007 (Transitional and Consequential Provisions) Order 2008 (SI 2008/2683) substituted "the First-tier Tribunal" for "an appeal tribunal" in the definition of "appeal" in sub-para.(3) and omitted the definitions of "clerk to the appeal tribunal", "decision notice", "financially qualified panel member", "legally qualified panel member" and "the President", as well as omitting sub-para.(4).

p.829, *amendment of the Child Trust Funds (Appeals) Regulations 2005, reg.2 (service of notice or documents)*

5.045   With effect from November 3, 2008, art.6(1) of, and Sch.1, para.292 to, the Tribunals, Courts and Enforcement Act 2007 (Transitional and Consequential Provisions) Order 2008 (SI 2008/2683) omitted "the clerk to the appeal tribunal or to" and "the clerk to the appeal tribunal or by" in sub-para.(a) and omitted "the clerk to the appeal tribunal or" in sub-para.(b).

p.830, *amendment of the Child Trust Funds (Appeals) Regulations 2005, reg.3 (disputes about notices of appeal)*

With effect from November 3, 2008, art.6(1) of, and Sch.1, para.293   **5.046** to, the Tribunals, Courts and Enforcement Act 2007 (Transitional and Consequential Provisions) Order 2008 (SI 2008/2683) substituted "the First-tier Tribunal" for "a legally qualified panel member".

p.830, *amendment of the Child Trust Funds (Appeals) Regulations 2005, reg.4 (late appeals)*

With effect from November 3, 2008, art.6(1) of, and Sch.1, para.294   **5.047** to, the Tribunals, Courts and Enforcement Act 2007 (Transitional and Consequential Provisions) Order 2008 (SI 2008/2683) substituted "(4) to (8) are satisfied, the Board may treat an appeal as made in time where an appeal is" for "(2) to (8) are satisfied, an appeal may be" in para. (1), omitted paras. (2) and (3) and substituted a new para.(4) as follows:

"(4) The Board must not treat the appeal as made in time unless the Board is satisfied that it is in the interests of justice."

The same amending regulations substituted "treat the appeal as made in time unless the Board are" for "grant an application unless the panel member is, or the Board are, as the case may be," in para.(5) and omitted "to the application" in sub-paras (5)(a) and (b). In addition, they substituted "appellant" for "applicant", in each place in para.(6), and in para.(7) substituted "treat the appeal as made in time" for "grant the application" and "submission of the notice of appeal, the more compelling should be the special circumstances." for the words "making of the application" to the end of para. (7). Finally, para.(8) has been amended by substituting "treat the appeal as made in time" for "grant an application" and "appellant" for "applicant" in sub-para.(8)(a) and "the Upper Tribunal" for "a Social Security Commissioner" in sub-para.(9), while paras (9) and (10) have been omitted.

pp.832–846, *repeal of the Child Trust Funds (Appeals) Regulations 2005, regs 6 (composition of appeal tribunals)—25 (application for leave to appeal to a Commissioner from an appeal tribunal)*

With effect from November 3, 2008, art.6(1) of, and Sch.1, para.295   **5.048** to, the Tribunals, Courts and Enforcement Act 2007 (Transitional and Consequential Provisions) Order 2008 (SI 2008/2683) omitted regs 6–25.

pp.846–862, *repeal of the Social Security Commissioners (Procedure) (Child Trust Funds) Regulations 2005*

With effect from November 3, 2008, art.6(2) of, and Sch.2 to, the   **5.049** Tribunals, Courts and Enforcement Act 2007 (Transitional and Consequential Provisions) Order 2008 (SI 2008/2683) repealed the whole of the Social Security Commissioners (Procedure).

PART VI

FORTHCOMING CHANGES AND UP-RATING OF BENEFITS

FORTHCOMING CHANGES

This section aims to give users of Social Security Legislation 2008/09 **6.001** some information on significant changes coming into force between November 5, 2008—the date to which this Supplement is up to date—and mid-April 2009, the date to which the 2009/10 edition will be up to date. The information here reflects our understanding of sources available to us as at mid-January 2009 and users should be aware that there will no doubt be further legislative amendment between then and mid-April 2009. This Part of the Supplement will at least enable users to access the relevant legislation on the OPSI website (*http://www.opsi. gov.uk/legislation*)

REGULATIONS

Social Security (Lone Parents and Miscellaneous Amendments) Regulations 2008 (SI 2008/3051)

In force November 24, 2008, October 26, 2009 and October 25, 2010

6.002   The main change effected by these regulations is that lone parents with older children will no longer be entitled to income support solely on the grounds of being a lone parent. The change is being introduced in stages and applies to lone parents:

- with an only or youngest child aged 12 or over, from 24.11.08;
- with an only or youngest child aged 10 or over, from 26.10.09;
- with an only or youngest child aged 7 or over, from 25.10.10.

The new rules apply to new or repeat claims for income support made on or after the relevant commencement date. However, the Schedule to the Regulations contains special provisions for certain existing income support claimants.

There is also some transitional protection for lone parents who are entitled to income support solely on the grounds of being a lone parent and are full-time students or on a New Deal for Lone Parents full-time training course.

Lone parents who are entitled to income support solely on the grounds of being a lone parent will be required to take part in a work-focused interview ("WFI") every 13 weeks under the lone parents WFI scheme or the Jobcentre Plus scheme during their final year of entitlement to income support.

In addition, a number of amendments are made to the labour market conditions for JSA, which are intended to introduce "additional flexibilities" for lone parents (as well as parents and others with caring responsibilities).

Tax Credits Act 2002 (Transitional Provisions) Order 2008 (SI 2008/3151)

In force December 9, 2008

6.003   These regulations extend yet again the final date on which income support and income-based JSA can include amounts for children. The final date is now December 31, 2011.

They also enable the DWP to make a claim for tax credits on behalf of a lone parent whose entitlement to income support ends as a result of her only or youngest child reaching the prescribed age (see the Social Security (Lone Parents and Miscellaneous Amendments) Regulations 2008 above) if she has not made the claim herself.

Social Security (Housing Costs Special Arrangements) (Amendment and Modification) Regulations 2008 (SI 2008/3195)

In force January 5, 2009

These regulations amend and modify the housing costs provisions in the Income Support Regulations, the JSA Regulations, the ESA Regulations and the State Pension Credit Regulations. 6.004

Standard rate of interest

The Income Support, JSA, ESA and State Pension Credit Regulations are amended so that the standard rate of interest applied to eligible loans is no longer calculated by using the Bank of England base rate plus 1.58% but instead will be a fixed figure of 6.8%. According to the Explanatory Memorandum which accompanies this SI, this figure will be reviewed within the next six months. This change is being made in recognition of the different types of mortgages that claimants have, e.g.., fixed rate mortgages which are not affected by reductions (or increases) in the Bank of England rate.

Waiting periods; capital limit for loans; and two year time limit for interest on eligible loans for JSA claimants

Broadly, the effect of these Regulations is that for certain claimants the Income Support, JSA and ESA Regulations are modified as follows:

- the waiting period for both new and existing housing costs to be met "in full" is reduced to 13 weeks;
- the capital limit for loans is increased from £100,000 to £200,000;
- in the case of JSA only, housing costs in respect of eligible loans (*i.e.*, those taken out to buy a home or for repairs/improvements) will only be payable for two years.

The Explanatory Memorandum states that these changes to the housing costs rules are being introduced in order to provide help more quickly to homeowners in the current economic climate. They are intended to be temporary measures, to be reviewed once the housing market recovers. The matter was considered to be sufficiently urgent for the proposals not to be referred to the Social Security Advisory Committee ("SSAC") before the regulations were introduced but according to the Explanatory Memorandum, they will be referred to SSAC as soon as practicable.

However, as already stated, the changes do not apply to all claimants and reference needs to be made to the detailed provisions of the Regulations to ascertain which claimants will be assisted by them

NEW BENEFIT RATES FROM APRIL 2009

NEW BENEFIT RATES FROM APRIL 2009

(Benefits covered in Volume I)

	April 2008	April 2009
	£ pw	£ pw
Disability benefits		
Attendance allowance		
higher rate	67.00	70.35
lower rate	44.85	47.10
Disability living allowance		
care component		
highest rate	67.00	70.35
middle rate	44.85	47.10
lowest rate	17.75	18.65
mobility component		
higher rate	46.75	49.10
lower rate	17.75	18.65
Carer's allowance	50.55	53.10
Severe disablement allowance		
basic rate	51.05	57.45
age related addition—higher rate	17.75	15.65
age related addition—middle rate	11.40	9.10
age related addition—lower rate	5.70	5.35
Maternity benefits		
Maternity allowance		
standard rate	117.18	123.06
Bereavement benefits and retirement pensions		
Widowed parent's allowance or widowed mother's allowance	90.70	95.25

	April 2008 £ pw	April 2009 £ pw
Bereavement allowance or widow's pension		
standard rate	90.70	95.25
Retirement pension		
Category A	90.70	95.25
Category B (higher)	90.70	95.25
Category B (lower)	54.35	57.05
Category C (higher)	54.35	57.05
Category C (lower)	32.50	34.15
Category D	54.35	57.05
Incapacity benefit		
Long-term incapacity benefit		
basic rate	84.50	89.80
increase for age—higher rate	17.75	15.65
increase for age—lower rate	8.90	6.55
invalidity allowance—higher rate	17.75	15.65
invalidity allowance—middle rate	11.40	9.10
invalidity allowance—lower rate	5.70	5.35
Short-term incapacity benefit		
under pension age—higher rate	75.40	80.15
under pension age—lower rate	63.75	67.75
over pension age—higher rate	84.50	89.80
over pension age—lower rate	81.10	86.20
Dependency increases		
Adult		
carer's allowance	30.20	31.70
severe disablement allowance	30.20	31.70
maternity allowance	39.40	41.35
retirement pension	54.35	57.05
long-term incapacity benefit	50.55	53.10
short-term incapacity benefit under pension age	39.40	41.35
short-term incapacity benefit over pension age	48.65	51.10
Child	11.35*	11.35*
Industrial injuries benefits		
Disablement benefit		
aged 18 and over or under 18 with dependants —		
100%	136.80	143.60
90%	123.12	129.24
80%	109.44	114.88
70%	95.76	100.52
60%	82.08	86.16
50%	68.40	71.80
40%	54.72	57.44
30%	41.04	43.08

New Benefit Rates from April 2009

	April 2003 £ pw	April 2004 £ pw
20%	27.36	28.72
aged under 18 with no dependants —		
100%	83.85	88.05
90%	75.47	79.25
80%	67.08	70.44
70%	58.70	61.64
60%	50.31	52.83
50%	41.93	44.03
40%	33.54	35.22
30%	25.16	26.42
20%	16.77	17.61
unemployability supplement		
basic rate	84.50	88.75
increase for adult dependant	50.55	53.10
increase for child dependant	11.35★	11.35★
increase for early incapacity—higher rate	17.75	18.65
increase for early incapacity—middle rate	11.40	12.00
increase for early incapacity—lower rate	5.70	6.00
constant attendance allowance		
exceptional rate	109.60	115.00
intermediate rate	82.20	86.25
normal maximum rate	54.80	57.50
part-time rate	27.40	28.75
exceptionally severe disablement allowance	54.80	57.50
Reduced earnings allowance		
maximum rate	54.72	57.44
Death benefit		
widow's pension		
higher rate	90.70	95.25
lower rate	27.21	28.58
widower's pension	90.70	95.25
Benefits in respect of children		
Child's special allowance	11.35★	11.35★

★ These sums payable in respect of children are reduced if payable in respect of the only, elder or eldest child for whom child benefit is being paid (see reg.8 of the social Security (Overlaping Benefits) Regulations 1979).

	April 2003 £ pw	April 2004 £ pw
Guardian's allowance	13.45	14.10

Child benefit	April 2008	January 2009
only, elder or eldest child (couple)	18.80	20.00
only, elder or eldest child (lone parent)	18.80	20.00
each subsequent child	12.55	13.20

NEW BENEFIT RATES FROM APRIL 2009

(Benefits covered in Volume II and Employment and Support Allowance (from October 2008))

	April/Oct 2008 £ pw	April 2009 £ pw
Contribution-based jobseeker's allowance		
personal rates—*aged under 18*	47.95	50.95
aged 18 to 24	47.95	50.95
aged 25 or over	60.50	64.30

	April/Oct 2008 £ pw	April 2009 £ pw
Contribution-based employment and support allowance		
Assessment phase		
Personal rate—single person aged under 25	47.95	50.95
Aged 25 or over	60.50	64.30
Main phase		
Personal rate—single claimant	60.50	64.30
Employment and support allowance components		
Work related activity component	24.00	25.50
Support component	29.00	30.85
Income support and income-based jobseeker's allowance and income-based employment and support allowance		
personal allowances		
single person—*aged under 25*	47.95	50.95
aged 25 or over	60.50	64.30

New Benefit Rates from April 2009

		April/Oct 2008 £ pw	April 2009 £ pw
lone parent	*aged under 18*	47.95	50.95
	aged 18 or over	60.50	64.30
couple	*both aged under 18*	47.95	50.95
	both aged under 18, with a child	72.35	76.90
	one aged under 18, one aged under 25	47.95	50.95
	one aged under 18, one aged 25 or over	60.50	64.30
	both aged 18 or over	94.95	100.95
	both under 18 (main phase ESA)	60.50	64.30
	both under 18 with child (main phase ESA)	94.95	100.95
	claimant main phase ESA, partner under 18	60.50	64.30
	one aged 18 or over, one aged under 18 (ESA)	94.95	100.95
child		52.59	56.11

premiums
family—*ordinary*		16.75	17.30
lone parent		16.75	17.30

breavement
pensioner—*single person (JSA only ESA))*		63.55	65.70
couple		94.40	97.50
enhanced pensioner		94.40	97.50
higher pensioner—*single person (JSA and ESA)*		63.55	65.70
couple		94.40	97.50
disability—*single person*		25.85	27.50
couple		26.85	39.15
enhanced disability—*single person*		12.60	13.40
couple		18.15	19.30
child		19.60	20.65
severe disability—*single person*		50.35	52.85
couple (one qualifies)		50.35	52.85
couple (both qualify)		100.70	105.70
disabled child		48.72	51.24
carer		27.75	29.50

	April/Oct 2008	April 2009
	£ pw	£ pw

Pension credit

Standard minimum guarantee

single person	124.05	130.00
couple	189.35	198.45

Additional amount for severe disability

single person	50.35	52.85
couple (one qualifies)	50.35	52.85
couple (both qualify)	100.70	105.70

Additional amount for carers	27.75	29.50

Savings credit threshold

single person	91.20	96.00
couple	145.80	153.40

Maximum savings credit

single person	19.71	20.40
couple	26.13	27.03

NEW TAX CREDIT AND EMPLOYER-PAID BENEFIT RATES
2009–10
(Benefits covered in Volume IV)

	2008–09	2009–10
	£ pa	£ pa

Working tax credit

Basic element	1,800	1,890
Couple and lone parent element	1,770	1,860
30 hour element	735	775
Disabled worker element	2,405	2,530
Severe disability element	1,020	1,075
50+ Return to work payment (under 30 hours)	1,235	1,300
50+ Return to work payment (30 or more hours)	1,840	1,935

Child tax credit

Family element	545	545
Family element, baby addition	545	545
Child element	2,085	2,235
Disabled child element	2,540	2,670
Severely disabled child element	1,020	1,075

Tax credit income thresholds

Income disregard	25,000	25,000
First threshold	6,420	6,420
First threshold for those entitled to child tax credit only	15,575	16,040
First withdrawal rate—39%		
Second threshold	50,000	50,000
Second withdrawal rate—6.67%		

Employer paid benefits	**2008–09**	**2009–10**
	£ pw	£ pw
Standard rates		
Statutory sick pay	75.40	79.15
Statutory maternity pay	117.18	123.06
Statutory paternity pay	11.718	123.06
Statutory adoption pay	117.18	123.06
Income threshold	90.00	95.00